The Ten Be
Ways To Sa
Estate Taxe

The I B P Seri
In Estate Planning and A

Guide to Planning the Farm Estate with (
Paul Douglass

Complete Guide to the Marital Deduction
Joseph Erdman

Complete Book of Wills and Trusts with (
Albert M. Lehrmar

Estate Planner's Kit
Jack Arthur Kirby

The Ten Best Ways To Save Estate Taxes

Gilbert M. Cantor
and
Robert L. Franklin

Institute for Business Planning

INSTITUTE for BUSINESS PLANNING, Inc.
IBP Plaza • Englewood Cliffs, N. J. 07632

About the Authors

GILBERT M. CANTOR, principal author of the book, is one of America's most knowledgeable and successful estate planning experts. A 1951 graduate of Harvard Law School, he is the founder, President, and senior attorney of Gilbert M. Cantor Associates, a Pennsylvania professional corporation.

Mr. Cantor is the author and co-author of several books, including *The Barnes Foundation, Reality vs. Myth* and *Attorney's Handbook on Charitable Giving*. He has contributed articles on private foundations and irrevocable trusts to Prentice-Hall's *Tax Exempt Organizations* and *Successful Estate Planning Ideas and Methods*. And he is the author of many other articles on estate planning and tax-oriented subjects.

Besides his law practice and legal writing, Mr. Cantor has taught political science at The Wharton School of the University of Pennsylvania, and he has served on boards of directors and boards of trustees of a number of business corporations and private foundations. He is widely sought as a lecturer.

ROBERT L. FRANKLIN, co-author, is a 1962 graduate of Temple University School of Law, and is a member of the law firm Franklin/Grodinsky/Boonin in Philadelphia. He was an associate editor of Temple Law Quarterly (1961-62). He also taught as a member on the part-time faculty of Temple University School of Law (1965-1977).

He served as a law clerk to Hon. A. L. Freedman, U. S. District Court (1962) and as a law clerk to a Philadelphia Common Pleas Court judge, Hon. Gerald A. Gleason (1964-1970).

What This Estate Planning Book Will Do for You

You will profit from this book by increasing your knowledge of estate planning—knowledge that will benefit your clients and yourself. Whether you are an attorney, accountant, trust officer or insurance adviser, this book will help you find tax-saving solutions.

This book will enable you to make a substantial planning improvement in almost every case that comes your way. You will find clear explanations of the nature, the uses, and the hazards of each technique described in these chapters. Informative checklists offer rapid assistance in identifying the right tax-saving technique for each of your clients.

You will be given persuasive reasons for using the irrevocable life insurance trust in relatively modest estates. The authors of this book take the mystery out of the private annuity and show you how easy it is to create one. You will see how helpful the private annuity can be in many situations—even though it is widely ignored by estate planners.

You will discover the use of the estate trust as a marital deduction device. You will learn its special uses—even though some estate planners have never even heard of it.

Sample documents and numerous examples of special clauses will greatly facilitate your drafting of effective estate planning instruments.

The concluding chapter tells you how to convert a $150 fee to a $1500 fee and earn it. It describes ways to eliminate undercompensated estate planning. You will read about a simple method of installment payment that will improve your cash flow and win your client's approval at the same time.

The ten best ways to save estate taxes are:
1. Marital Deduction
2. Charitable Deduction
3. Generation-Skipping Transfers
4. Termination of Joint Ownership
5. Lifetime Gift Program
6. Private Annuity
7. Irrevocable Life Insurance Trust
8. Qualified Pension and Profit-Sharing Plans
9. Close Corporation Recapitalization and Tax-Saving Alternatives
10. Postmortem Options

This book explains and clarifies each of these ten basic techniques for you with reference to the Tax Reform Act of 1976. It provides you with the up-to-date information you must have today.

Contents

Appendix C   Forms To Carry Out the Estate Plan *(cont.)*

Foreword

A Reading of This Foreword is Essential to Proper
Utilization of This Book.

1. *"The Ten Best Ways" as method.* The number "ten" in our title
is somewhat arbitrary. The contents of several chapters could have been
combined and treated as aspects of a single subject, e.g., lifetime gifts.
Other chapters, such as Nine and Ten, in a sense combine several dis-
tinct tax saving techniques which we have chosen to pull together. Other
devices which may appeal to the reader, such as the new "orphan's
exclusion," have been disregarded by the authors as relatively insignifi-
cant.

The important point, from the authors' viewpoint, is not to insist
that there are ten, rather than eight or fourteen, "best ways" to save
estate taxes. Rather, it is our hope that the book as a whole will encourage a new and more fruitful approach to estate planning than is commonly used.

The usual approach of the estate planner, as we have observed it, is
to review the available data, to seize upon the most obvious tax-saving
techniques—commonly the marital deduction, and then to see if any
other ideas emerge from the materials or otherwise "occur" to the planner. The idea of this book, in contrast, is to expose each client's situation
automatically and routinely to all of the book's techniques. The planner
then "carves down" from ten instead of "building up" from one or two.

The use of this approach to estate planning increases the planning
opportunities and reduces the chance of omitting measures that can be
significant to the client and his family. It is relatively easy to apply, as the
chapters and their subdivisions function as a tax saving checklist. The
results have been very gratifying in the authors' practice, and we are
confident that other practitioners and their clients will benefit similarly.
For suggestions on the presentation of your work product and fees, your
attention is invited to Chapter Eleven.

Consistent with our goal of amplifying the scope and effectiveness,
and hence the value, of your estate planning services, we have endeavored to introduce and to demystify some of the techniques which are not
widely known or utilized, such as the private annuity, the "estate trust"
discussed in Chapter One, and certain charitable transactions. Our hope
is to move these devices from the realm of the unusual to that of the
routine. With more familiar measures, such as the "power of appoint-

ment" marital deduction trust and the irrevocable insurance trust, we have tried to suggest certain nuances and also various hazards that might otherwise escape your attention. It was not our purpose, however, nor would a single volume suffice, to create an estate tax legal encyclopedia. It is assumed that you will follow our discussion of a particular technique with your own perusal of the applicable legal authorities and that you will take action on the basis of your own interpretations and judgment.

2. *Key to tax calculations.* Throughout the book you will find numerous examples of the estate tax savings to be attained by means of the techniques discussed. In some cases, the assumptions and the calculations are set forth in full. In others, the tax savings are more concisely summarized. Except where other assumptions are stated in the text, you should assume that:

(a) The adjusted gross estate is determined by assuming that deductible debts and expenses are equal to 5 percent of the gross estate.
(b) All deaths occur after 1980, so that the full $47,000 unified credit is available.
(c) There are no lifetime transfers which bear on the estate tax calculations.
(d) No marital deduction in excess of 50 percent of the adjusted gross estate is utilized.
(e) No credits are available for property previously taxed.
(f) The total allowable credit for State death taxes has been utilized.

For the method of calculating the unified (gift and estate) tax under the Tax Reform Act of 1976, see [¶500.3]. (Throughout the book, this Act is referred to as TRA 76, and the Tax Reform Act of 1969 is called TRA 69.)

3. *Acknowledgments.* For whatever clarity we have achieved in our exposition, a significant measure of the credit is due to the professional editorial efforts of IBP's Olivia Goldenberg. Our completion of the book prior to the Tax Reform Act of 1984 may also be attributed to Ms. Goldenberg's gentle but near-relentless encouragement.

For technical assistance in several chapters, we fondly and gratefully acknowledge the efforts of our colleague, Nancy Rothkopf, Esquire. For the really difficult parts—the calculation of the tax on "net gifts" in Chapter Five comes quickly to mind—we called on Ms. Rothkopf, and she always came through.

For typing this stuff over and over again we acknowledge our indebtedness to Secrephone, a division of Shopper Publications, Inc., and to Linda Brodie, Melanie Cohen, Maureen McCauley and Camille Ray, of our office staff.

Gilbert M. Cantor
Robert L. Franklin

1

Marital Deduction

**THE MARITAL DEDUCTION AND
HOW TO TAKE ADVANTAGE OF IT**

Assets passing to or for the benefit of a decedent's surviving spouse may qualify for an estate tax deduction. This is known as the "marital deduction" (Sec. 2056 of the Code).

The marital deduction is the most widely used and most important of the ten best ways to save estate taxes for several reasons:

☐ As the greater of $250,000 or 50 percent of the adjusted gross estate can qualify for the marital deduction, it can have a very substantial impact on the tax computation. (Rarely, for example, do the deductions available for administration expenses or for charitable gifts reach the same level as the allowable marital deduction in the estate of a married person.)

☐ The impact of the marital deduction is heightened by the fact that the estate tax (like the income tax) is imposed on a graduated scale. Where a decedent, for example, gives 50 percent of his adjusted gross estate to his surviving spouse, the 50 percent comes "off the top" of his adjusted gross estate. It removes taxable assets at the highest brackets otherwise applicable to the estate. The balance of the estate, to the extent not sheltered by tax credits, is taxable at the lower applicable brackets.

☐ As the requisite beneficiary of the marital deduction gift is the decedent's spouse, who is commonly a primary object of his bounty anyway (as compared, say, with possible charitable beneficiaries), married persons can frequently obtain the deduction with little or no distortion of their basic estate planning objectives.

1

The following figures illustrate the dramatic tax avoidance that the marital deduction yields:

Tax Avoidance Through Use of the Marital Deduction

	Federal Estate Tax	
Adjusted Gross Estate	*Without Marital Deduction*	*Using 50% Marital Deduction*
$ 300,000	$ 37,200	$ 0
500,000	98,800	21,400
1,000,000	265,600	98,800

All too often efforts to take advantage of the marital deduction exemplify the old saying, "familiarity breeds contempt." There are two aspects of this problem. One is that the practitioner may not fully appreciate the technical requirements of qualifying for the marital deduction. The other is that he may overlook the tremendous flexibility available to meet a client's objectives and still qualify for this deduction. The former can lead to a tax disaster, the latter to needless diminution of benefits potentially available to the surviving spouse and others. As the poet said: " . . . which is worse I know not, but I know that both are ill."[1]

[¶100.1]   How to Qualify for the Marital Deduction

Here is a checklist of the basic requirements:

☐ An interest in property qualifies for the marital deduction only if:

1. The property with respect to which the deduction is claimed is included in the decdent's gross estate, and
2. The interest passes to the surviving spouse.

☐ Such an interest will fail to qualify for the marital deduction if:

1. It is a "terminable interest," an interest which will fail or terminate when a period of time elapses, or when a stipulated event or contingency occurs, or when a stipulated event or contingency fails to occur (Sec. 2056(b)(1) of the Code), and

---

[1]A.E. Housman, *The Collected Poems of A.E. Housman*, Holt, Rinehart and Winston (New York, 1965), page 186.

2. Any other interest in the same property passes to a person other than the spouse or her estate and such other person may possess or enjoy his interest in the property after the failure or termination of the surviving spouse's interest.

(This is the so-called "terminable interest rule.")

☐ There are three exceptions to the terminable interest rule:

1. A trust under which the surviving spouse is given the income for life, payable to her annually or more frequently, and a general power to appoint (direct the distribution of) the principal;
2. Life insurance proceeds payable in annual or more frequent installments (or annual or more frequent payments under an interest option), with the first payment due not later than 13 months after death, where the surviving spouse has a general power to appoint to herself while living or to appoint any amount unpaid at her death; and
3. Interests which may fail or terminate (a) if the surviving spouse fails to survive for a stipulated period not exceeding six months or (b) if the decedent and his spouse die as a result of a common disaster.

(A "general power" of appointment, for purposes of exceptions to the terminable interest rule, must be a power which the surviving spouse may exercise, whether during her lifetime or by will, in favor of herself or her estate, and it must be exercisable by her alone and in all events.)

☐ The allowable marital deduction cannot exceed either of the following:

1. The value of the interest passing to the surviving spouse.
2. The greater of $250,000 or 50 percent of the decedent's adjusted gross estate. The "adjusted gross estate" is the gross estate minus funeral expenses, administration expenses, claims against the estate, and mortgage debts if the value of the mortgaged property is included in the gross estate.

[¶100.2]   How the Tax Reform Act of 1976
Enlarged the Marital Deduction

Prior to January 1, 1977, the maximum allowable marital deduction was 50 percent of the decedent's adjusted gross estate.

Under TRA 76, the maximum marital deduction has been changed to 50 percent of the adjusted gross estate or $250,000, whichever is greater.

Where the adjusted gross estate is less than $500,000, the $250,000 figure will exceed 50 percent of it. Where the adjusted gross estate is exactly $500,000, 50 percent of it will be equal to $250,000. Where the adjusted gross estate exceeds $500,000, 50 percent of it will be greater than $250,000. For example, if the decedent's adjusted gross estate is $600,000, the maximum allowable marital deduction will be $300,000.

Therefore, TRA 76 has increased the allowable marital deduction only for cases in which the adjusted gross estate is less than $500,000.

As we shall see, however, the *greater* marital deduction is not always the *optimum* marital deduction. Where the adjusted gross estate is less than $500,000, it will not always be advisable to provide for a $250,000 marital deduction. And in any size estate it will sometimes be advisable to use less than a 50 percent marital deduction. The main reason for this is that the tax impact of the marital deduction gift in the estate of the surviving spouse may more than offset the tax saving it provides in the estate of the first spouse to die. (See ¶101, below.)

[¶100.3]   How Community Property States Are Affected by TRA 76

The marital deduction was introduced for the purpose of achieving equality of tax treatment for interspousal transfers as between common law States and community property States.

There are presently eight community property States: Arizona, California, Idaho, Louisiana, Nevada, New Mexico, Texas and Washington. In these States, the laws provide generally that property acquired by spouses during marriage (other than by gift, devise or descent) belongs equally to both spouses. Where that is the law, only the decedent's share of the community property is includible in the decedent's estate for estate tax purposes; the share of the surviving spouse is excluded.

A comparable estate tax result for residents of common law States was provided by allowing a deduction up to 50 percent of the adjusted gross estate for property passing to a surviving spouse.

TRA 76, by providing the alternate $250,000 marital deduction amount, disturbed the parity in favor of decedents in common law States. Where the adjusted gross estate is less than $500,000, a $250,000 marital deduction provides a greater tax reduction than the 50 percent which is "built into" the community property situation. In order to restore the balance, TRA 76 provides a partial marital deduction for estates consisting of community property. Essentially, it makes the marital deduction available to the extent $250,000 exceeds the deceased spouse's share of the community property.

[¶101]   THE TAX IMPACT AND HOW TO COMPUTE IT

To determine the effect of the marital deduction in a particular estate, we must first deduct from the gross estate the items which are to be claimed as deductions under Sec. 2053 of the Code — funeral expenses, administration expenses, and debts.

(1) If we assume a decedent dies after 1980 (so that there will be a unified credit of $47,000), with a $530,000 gross estate; no taxable lifetime gifts; $30,000 of Sec. 2053 deductions; and a full marital deduction, the estate tax would be computed as follows:

Gross estate	$530,000
Less allowable Sec. 2053 deductions	30,000
Adjusted gross estate	500,000
Less marital deduction	250,000
Taxable estate (tentative tax base)	250,000
Estate tax on tentative tax base	$ 70,800
Less unified credit	47,000
	23,800
Less credit for State death taxes (if paid)	2,400
Estate tax payable	21,400

(2) Assuming the same figures but no marital deduction, the estate tax would be computed as follows:

Gross estate	$530,000
Less allowable Sec. 2053 deduction	30,000
Taxable estate (tentative tax base)	500,000
Estate tax on tentative tax base	$155,800
Less unified credit	47,000
	108,800
Less credit for State death taxes (if paid)	10,000
Estate tax payable	98,800

In this case the effect of the full marital deduction, as compared with no marital deduction, is to reduce the estate tax from $98,800 to $21,400, a saving of $74,400. (However, as we shall see, optimum use of the marital deduction will not necessarily mean maximum use of it. The estate planner will in certain circumstances make computations as illustrated in paragraph 1, above, using less than the allowable marital deduction.)

(3) Let us turn next to the tax impact of the marital deduction in the estate of the surviving spouse. Assets which are given outright to a surviving spouse, and other assets over which the spouse is given a general power of appointment, become part of her gross estate for estate tax purposes. This means that any assets of a decedent's estate which qualify for the marital deduction will be includible (to the extent they are not consumed or otherwise diminished) in the gross estate of the surviving spouse.

Therefore, what the marital deduction accomplishes *per se* is not necessarily the avoidance, but rather the deferral, of estate tax. The qualifying assets are not taxed in the decedent's estate but the estate tax may catch up with them in the estate of the spouse. The tax on these assets in the second estate may even be higher than the tax that was avoided in the prior one. On the other hand, its impact may be avoided or diminished in these ways:

☐ By reason of the graduated scale of estate tax rates, as well as the unified credit available to each estate, there may be a lesser tax or no tax in the second estate.

☐ The assets involved may decline in value or may be wholly or partly consumed during the lifetime of the surviving spouse.

☐ The surviving spouse (if not precluded by trust or other arrangements) may reduce the estate tax otherwise applicable by means of lifetime gifts, or by use of the marital deduction in favor of a subsequent spouse, or by utilizing the charitable deduction or other techniques discussed in this book.

☐ The amount of tax saved by the marital deduction in the first estate can be invested to produce income for the surviving spouse, and such income offsets and may even exceed the estate tax on the marital deduction assets in the second estate.

Despite these mitigating factors, the potential tax impact of the marital deduction in the estate of the surviving spouse must always be considered. This consideration affects the quantum of assets to be given to the surviving spouse in two ways:

(a) *Overqualifying the marital deduction.* If we provide a gift of a decedent's entire estate to his spouse, the estate will be entitled to a marital deduction of 50 percent of the adjusted gross estate or $250,000, whichever is greater. But such a gift adds to the surviving spouse's gross estate not only the marital deduction amount but the entire distributable estate.

Following the example in paragraph (1) above, if the testator with the $530,000 gross estate gave his entire distributable estate to his wife, she would receive his gross estate . . .

diminished by:		$530,000
Sec. 2053 deductions	$30,000	
Estate tax	21,400	
State death tax	2,400	
		53,800
Leaving a distributable estate amounting to		476,200
As the marital deduction amounted to		250,000
the excess above the marital deduction is		$226,200

The surviving spouse receives $476,200, of which only $250,000 escaped tax by reason of the marital deduction. The estate tax on this $476,000 in her estate (assuming she has no other estate) would be about $130,000.

Had the decedent's plan been so designed as to add to his wife's gross estate only the $250,000 that qualified for the marital deduction, her gross estate would have been $250,000 rather than $476,000. The estate tax on the $250,000 gross estate would be about $58,000, a difference of $72,000.

Accordingly, the objective in such situations is to give the surviving spouse, and thereby subject to tax in her estate, only the portion of the decedent's estate which is intended to qualify for the marital deduction. (A gift which goes beyond that limit is sometimes referred to as an "overqualified" marital deduction.) We normally pursue that objective by dividing the estate into two portions. We obtain the desired marital deduction by allocating one of these portions (the desired amount or percentage) to an outright gift or trust or other arrangement that qualifies for the deduction. We dispose of the other, or "nonmarital," portion in a way that will not add it to the gross estate of the surviving spouse.

The nonmarital portion will escape the surviving spouse's gross estate if it is given to the testator's children or other nonspouse beneficiaries. We can also accomplish the desired end by placing this portion in a trust for the family, with benefits to the surviving spouse limited so as not to draw the trust assets into her gross estate.[2]

(b) *Underqualifying the marital deduction.* Only by computing the effects of the marital deduction in the estates of both spouses can we determine whether, and the extent to which, the marital deduction

---

[2]Where all or a major part of the gross estate is owned by the spouses jointly, this optimum division of the estate can be accomplished only if the joint ownership is terminated as to an adequate portion of the assets involved. See Chapter 4 for discussion of the appropriate approach to such termination.

should be used. Tables 1 and 2 are designed to depict the entire impact of the marital deduction.

To illustrate the estate tax savings that can be made available by maximum use of the marital deduction, we have used a gross estate of $500,000 in Table 1 and a gross estate of $2,000,000 in Table 2. The additional assumptions for each table are:

1. Sec. 2053 deductions are equal to 5% of the gross estate
2. The second spouse to die has no gross estate other than that acquired from the first
3. Deaths occur after 1980, so that $47,000 unified credit applies
4. Maximum credit for State taxes is also available

Each table shows the figures on three assumptions:

1. "A"—that no part of the first decedent's estate is added to the gross estate of the surviving spouse and no marital deduction is obtained;
2. "B"—that the entire estate is given to the surviving spouse and that the maximum marital deduction is obtained; and
3. "C"—a maximum marital deduction gift passes to the surviving spouse and the nonmarital portion is not added to that person's gross estate.

If we examine the bottom line of Table 2, and compare column (A) with column (C), it may appear that very little has been saved through the optimum use of the marital deduction represented by column (C). But if we consider also the estate tax payable at the death of the first spouse in columns (A) and (C), it is clear that the column (C) approach makes available for enjoyment during the lifetime of the second spouse $247,500 more than the column (A) approach. This "extra" amount, invested at 6 percent would produce about $15,000 per year, which would otherwise be lost.

A similar analysis applies to columns (A) and (B) of Table 1. In each case in which the marital deduction is potentially useful, similar computations and comparisons are required. And where the testator's spouse has assets of her own (contrary to the assumption used in Tables 1 and 2), additional computations involving less than the maximum marital deduction may be required. [See ¶102(3)].

In connection with the tax computations and the potential impact of the marital deduction, two technical points to be remembered are:

(1) Achievement of the maximum marital deduction requires that inheritance and estate taxes be borne by the nonmarital portion. If any of such taxes are payable from the marital deduction portion, that payment will reduce the amount passing to the surviving spouse. Thus it will reduce the marital deduction, thereby increasing the estate tax. The

Table 1

At Death of First Spouse:	(A) No Marital Deduction	(B) Entire Estate to Spouse	(C) Marital Deduction Gift to Spouse; Balance not added to Spouse's estate
Gross estate Less Section 2053 deductions	$500,000 25,000	$500,000 25,000	$500,000 25,000
Adjusted gross estate Less marital deduction	475,000 0	475,000 237,500	475,000 237,500
Taxable estate	475,000	237,500	237,500
Tax before unified credit Unified credit	147,300 47,000	66,800 47,000	66,800 47,000
State tax credit	100,300 9,200	19,800 2,100	19,800 2,100
Estate tax payable	$ 91,100	$ 17,700	$ 17,700
At Death of Second Spouse:			
Gross estate Less Section 2053 deductions	0	$455,200* 22,700	$237,500 11,900
Taxable estate	0	432,500	225,600
Tax before unified credit Unified credit		132,800 47,000	63,000 47,000
State tax credit	0	85,800 7,800	16,000 1,800
Estate tax payable	0	78,000	14,200
TOTAL TAXES FOR BOTH ESTATES	$ 91,100	$ 95,700	$ 31,900

*It is assumed that the second spouse inherits the estate after deduction of Section 2053 expenses and taxes, and that no credit for prior taxes is available in the estate of the second spouse.

Table 2

At Death of First Spouse	(A) No Marital Deduction	(B) Entire Estate to Spouse	(C) Marital Deduction Gift to Spouse; Balance Not Added to Spouse's estate
Gross estate	$2,000,000	$2,000,000	$2,000,000
Less Section 2053 deductions	100,000	100,000	100,000
Adjusted gross estate	1,900,000	1,900,000	1,900,000
Less marital deduction	0	950,000	950,000
Taxable estate	1,900,000	950,000	950,000
Tax before unified credit	635,800	326,300	326,300
Unified credit	47,000	47,000	47,000
	588,800	279,300	279,300
State tax credit	92,400	30,400	30,400
Estate tax payable	$ 496,400	$ 248,900	$ 248,900
At Death of Second Spouse:			
Gross estate	0	$1,620,000*	$ 950,000
Less Section 2053 deductions		81,000	47,500
Taxable estate	0	1,539,000	902,500
Tax before unified credit		573,300	308,000
Unified credit		47,000	47,000
	0	526,300	261,000
State tax credit		67,000	27,700
Estate tax payable	0	459,300	233,300
TOTAL TAXES FOR BOTH ESTATES	$ 496,400	$ 708,200	$ 482,200

*It is assumed that the second spouse inherits the estate after deduction of Section 2053 expenses and taxes, and that no credit for prior taxes is available in the estate of the second spouse.

increased estate tax burden on the marital deduction share will reduce it further, again increasing the estate tax, and so on, in a circular computation. Therefore, it is both customary and important to direct the payment of all such taxes from the nonmarital portion of the estate where the maximum marital deduction is desired.

(2) As a result of TRA 76, it will generally be appropriate to direct that the marital deduction share of the estate be computed without regard to any generation-skipping trusts[3] of which the testator is a deemed transferor. Under Sec. 2602(c)(5)(A) of the Code, the assets of generation-skipping transfers will in certain circumstances by included in the deemed transferor's gross estate for purposes of computing the marital deduction. Such inclusion may result in an undesired inflation of the marital deduction share.

[¶102]   WHEN SHOULD THE MARITAL DEDUCTION BE USED?

(1) *Family relationships.* While your tax projections will frequently provide a major element of estate planning decisions, there are other ingredients which you should consider. Among these are family relationships, especially the relationship of the spouses.

Sometimes a client, having a happy marriage and confidence in his wife, and perhaps considering that "his" assets are morally if not technically hers as well as his, may wish to leave his entire estate outright to his wife and let her provide for the children as she may deem best, even though such a design will "overqualify" the marital deduction. The effect of such a plan is exemplified in column (B) of Tables 1 and 2.

Our computation of the difference in the tax result of giving his entire estate to his wife, on one hand, and providing for her by means of a marital deduction gift and a nonmarital trust (the latter to be excluded from her gross estate), on the other, will tell our client the "price" of his election. He has a right, of course, to pay the price and make that election.

The client should understand, however, that he can go rather far to provide substantial benefits, considerable control, and great flexibility for his wife without subjecting her estate to unnecessary taxation at her death:

☐ You can provide an outright gift to his wife of the marital deduction portion of his estate (which is the larger portion, since achieving

---

[3]For a discussion of generation-skipping trusts, see Chapter 3.

the maximum marital deduction means that estate and inheritance taxes should be paid out of the nonmarital portion).

□ You can provide a trust of the nonmarital portion, giving his wife the income for life, and any or all of the following:

□ The noncumulative right to withdraw the greater of $5,000 or 5 percent of the trust principal in each calendar year.

□ The right during her lifetime to direct or appoint gifts from trust principal to children and grandchildren.

□ The right to receive such portions of principal as the trustees deem necessary or advisable in order to maintain her customary standard of living and for any emergency needs.

□ The power to appoint the remaining principal by her will to anyone other than her estate or creditors of herself or her estate.

These provisions will in many cases encourage the client to elect a nonmarital trust. Through his marital gift and nonmarital trust provisions he can maximize the assets passing eventually to his children, without feeling that he has tied his wife in chains. (The trust provisions above listed are intended to be suggestive rather than exhaustive, the subject being more fully developed in Chapter 3).

Occasionally you will meet with a client who wishes to leave nothing, or as little as possible, to his wife. This may involve a marriage that is not terminal but full of hostility. Or it may involve, at least on the surface, a fear that assets given to the wife may end up in the hands of her importuning relatives or a designing second husband.

Here, too, your tax computations will tell your client the "price" of his election not to take advantage of the marital deduction. If the wife has a right under State law to elect to take against the will, this right should also be weighed in the balance. For example, if she has a right by election to take a one-third share outright, he might "offer" her by the terms of his will a 50 percent marital deduction trust, in the hope that she may prefer the income and restricted control of one-half to the income and complete control of one-third.

But even where no spouse's election is involved, the antispouse client may be able to satisfy his impulse sufficiently without sacrificing the tax benefit of the marital deduction, especially if he is more concerned to restrict her benefits during lifetime than her testamentary powers. For example, he can place 50 percent of his adjusted gross estate—or any smaller portion—in a trust which will give his wife only income during her lifetime, with a general power to appoint the principal by her will. He may even go further and deprive her of income, using the so-called "estate trust," provided the principal and accumulated income are distributed to the wife's estate at her death. And, of course, he need give her no interest at all in the nonmarital portion of his estate.

To summarize: the quality or character of the family relationship will in certain cases indicate preliminarily either an outright gift of the entire estate to the spouse, or no gift to her at all, regardless of the tax consequences. However, in many if not most of these cases it will be possible to make optimum use of the marital deduction without a wide departure from basic personal goals.

(2) *Size of testator's estate.* As the estate tax is imposed on a graduated scale, it will be obvious that the advantage of the marital deduction increases disproportionately with increases of the adjusted gross estate.

At the upper level, we reach the point of diminishing advantage only for an estate which has a tentative tax base of more than $5,000,000 and is, therefore, in the top 70 percent bracket, and where the spouse's estate is taxable at a lower rate. In such cases, any additional marital deduction will apply evenly at the top bracket, while the tax rate in the second spouse's estate, applicable to the marital deduction gift at the time of her subsequent death, will continue to rise. (All too few are the occasions on which we must invite a client's attention to this aspect.)

At the lower end of the scale, the unified credit introduced by TRA 76 becomes relevant. The estate tax exemption of $60,000, which was available to estates of decedents who died prior to January 1, 1977, and also the lifetime gift tax exemption of $30,000, were abolished by TRA 76. Those exemptions were replaced with a unified credit, which increases in stages from $30,000 in 1977, to $47,000 in 1981 and years following. If we compute the exemptions to which this increasing credit will be equivalent, we find the following:

Year	Unified Credit	Exemption Equivalent
1977	$30,000	$120,000
1978	$34,000	$134,000
1979	$38,000	$147,000
1980	$42,500	$162,000
1981 (and following)	$47,000	$175,625

Under the old law, an adjusted gross estate of $120,000 could be sheltered from estate tax by a combination of a 50 percent marital deduction ($60,000) and the estate tax exemption of $60,000. Under TRA 76, after 1980, an adjusted gross estate of $425,625 can be sheltered by a $250,000 marital deduction and the unified credit equivalent to a $175.625 exemption. (Using a 50 percent rather than a $250,000 marital deduction, approximately $351,000 would be so sheltered.)

Where the sum of the exemption equivalent and the available marital deduction exceed the adjusted gross estate, it may be advisable to limit the marital deduction gift to the excess above the exemption equivalent. The nonmarital portion, equal to the exemption equivalent, would be placed in a trust which will "skip" the surviving spouse's estate for estate tax purposes.

With an adjusted gross estate of $300,625, for example, assuming death occurs after the year 1980, such a plan would allocate $175,625[4] to the nonmarital trust. The marital deduction gift would be $125,000. In this way the decedent's estate would pass free of estate tax, while only $125,000 (rather than the maximum marital deduction of $250,000) would be added to the gross estate of the surviving spouse.

Other considerations may lead us to depart from the plan which our computations indicate. In relatively small estates (sometimes in larger ones), the division between marital and nonmarital shares which our figures suggest may be outweighed by considerations of:

(a)   the clients' desire for the greatest possible simplicity in their estate arrangements
(b)   the probability that the surviving spouse will consume principal during her or his lifetime
(c)   the differential in estate planning expense

(3) *Size of spouse's estate.* In the foregoing discussion and computations we have assumed, for the most part, that the surviving spouse will have no gross estate other than that which the marital deduction gift will provide. But this is frequently not the case. The other spouse may have a separate estate acquired through earnings, savings, inheritance, or lifetime gifts. Indeed, the reduction during lifetime of the inequality between the spouses' estates is a significant objective of estate planning, as discussed in Chapters 4 and 5.[5]

Where the beneficiary-spouse's estate is equal to or greater than that of the testator—indeed,   henever her estate is not *de minimis*—it is essential that estate tax computations be made for both estates. The marital deduction assets passing to or for the benefit of the surviving spouse, to the extent not diminished or consumed in her lifetime, are includible in her gross estate. This means that the use of the marital deduction in the first estate will increase the estate tax in the second, or it may create an estate tax in the second estate if the latter would otherwise

---

[4]It is assumed that no part of the unified credit has been exhausted by lifetime gifts.

[5]In Chapter 5 we discuss the interaction between lifetime and postmortem marital deductions, the effects of adding back taxable lifetime gifts in computing the estate tax, and the new unified credit.

have been sheltered from tax by the unified credit. The added estate tax burden which the marital deduction gift imposes in the second estate will in some cases outweigh the estate tax saving which it provides in the first.

Assume, for example, that Spouse A has an adjusted gross estate of $500,000, that Spouse B also has an adjusted gross estate of $500,000, and that their deaths will occur after 1980 (thus providing the full unified credit in each case). Use of a 50 percent marital deduction would reduce the estate tax of Spouse A from $145,800 to $68,400, a saving of $77,400. However, the addition of that 50 percent ($250,000) to Spouse B's estate would increase B's potential estate tax from $145,800 to $227,900, an increase of $82,100. In this example, the tax increase in B's estate is $4700 greater than the tax saved in A's estate ($82,100 minus $77,400 = $4700).

The computations indicated in the preceding paragraph do not end the matter, for three reasons:

First, they ignore the income consequence of tax deferral in A's estate. The amount of tax which is avoided at A's death can be invested to produce an income for B. This additional income will approach and may in time exceed the estate tax loss resulting from the increase of B's gross estate. This is, of course, affected by B's income tax level and life expectancy. The younger the parties, the greater the weight that can sensibly be given to this income factor.

Second, and similarly, our computations of a net estate tax "loss" omitted consideration of the probability of principal consumption during B's lifetime. Where (1) the parties are young and (b) it is likely that substantial principal invasion will be required for the maintenance of the surviving spouse, we may choose to save the estate tax in A's estate via the full marital deduction on the assumption that the projected estate tax in B's estate will in fact not materialize.

And third, alternate computations should be made with marital deduction gifts less than 50 percent in A's estate. A lesser marital deduction may eliminte the estate tax "loss" originally computed. Or it may reduce it to the point where it may be balanced or overcome by the additional income factor in A's estate or the principal consumption probability in B's.

There is no magic formula for all this. We must make the computations and weigh in the balance the various considerations of the parties' ages, income potentialities, and special factors that may emerge in each situation. A requirement that B survive A by six months in order to receive the marital deduction gift (see ¶105) can provide some assurance that our factual assumptions will not be nullified by a common disaster.

In some cases, the relative sizes of the spouses' estates and the estate tax consequences of *any* marital deduction gift will incontrovertibly demonstrate that no marital deduction should be used. But in many cases, the complex of factors we have mentioned will lead us to take the "bird in the hand" approach. That is, we will use a full or partial marital deduction in A's estate even though the projected estate tax increase in B's estate is greater than the projected estate tax saving in A's.

In doubtful or borderline cases, two additional considerations may lead us to take the "bird in the hand" approach:

(1) With the passage of time and changing circumstances, the marital deduction may yield a greater benefit than was indicated on the day of our computations; and

(2) If new computations at the time of A's death show that the marital deduction is of doubtful utility, B can renounce the marital deduction gift. If promptly done, the disclaimer will not be taxable as a gift by B.

Of course, the computations and analysis we have outlined should also be made with respect to a marital deduction gift from B to A.

[¶102.1]   Tax Impact When Using less Than
             the New Maximum Marital Deduction

Prior to TRA 76, the maximum marital deduction was 50 percent of the decedent's adjusted gross estate. Where 50 percent of the adjusted gross estate is less than $250,000, TRA 76 has increased the maximum marital deduction to $250,000.

In our discussion of the relevance of family relationships to use of the marital deduction, and in our discussion of the size of the surviving spouse's estate as an element in computing its tax impact, we referred to the possibility of using less than the maximum marital deduction. This possibility was significant even prior to TRA 76, and it remains so today where 50 percent of the adjusted gross estate exceeds the new maximum. But for estates to which the new maximum may apply, TRA 76 requires us to determine whether, or the extent to which, the additional deduction should be utilized.

Table 3 (at page 18) is designed to facilitate such a determination. That table assumes that a husband predeceases his wife and that she has no estate of her own. The husband's adjusted gross estate at several levels is indicated in the left-hand column. Assuming deaths after 1980 (thus providing the full unified credit) and maximum credits for State death taxes, the table shows at each level the tax in the husband's estate, the tax in the wife's estate, and the total taxes, on two assumptions: (1) use of the new $250,000 maximum marital deduction, and (2) a marital deduction gift of 50 percent of the adjusted gross estate. In each case, it is also assumed that the balance (or nonmarital portion) of the husband's estate will by-pass the wife's for estate tax purposes.

The results are as follows:

(1) For examples with adjusted gross estates up to $350,000, use of the new maximum marital deduction creates a tax in the wife's estate which the 50 percent formula avoids. This results in a net tax disadvantage.

(2) At the $400,000 level, the 50 percent formula produces a tax in the husband's estate which the new maximum avoids. But the 50 percent deduction still results in lower total taxes.

(3) For the examples ranging from $400,000 to $500,000, the total taxes are the same, regardless of the marital deduction selected. The 50 percent formula is a little more costly in the husband's estate.

The table indicates that the new maximum provides very little tax saving. The little tax saving it provides is available only for a narrow range of estates. (If we assume that the surviving spouse has some assets prior to the marital gift, this range will be even narrower.) For most clients whose adjusted gross estates are less than $500,000, our computations will not encourage use of the new maximum marital deduction.

Whenever we use less than the maximum, it is especially important to arrange for periodic reviews in order to adjust the amount or formula for significant changes in the estate. This applies whether the applicable maximum for a particular estate is $250,000 or 50 percent of the adjusted gross estate. Such reviews are also important in all borderline cases, even if the maximum (old or new) has been utilized.

[¶103] FOUR WAYS TO OBTAIN THE MARITAL DEDUCTION

The practitioner who has decided to use the marital deduction for his client must next determine how to use it. By what mode or modes of transfer to the surviving spouse shall the desired marital deduction be obtained?

Before discussing the various forms or types of marital deduction gifts, we must emphasize the need for care in meeting the technical requirements for each type of transfer selected. Strict adherence to these requirements is important for these reasons:

(1) Marital deduction provisions have been the subject of continuing scrutiny and recurrent technical attacks by the IRS.;

(2) There is ample latitude for beneficial marital deduction arrangements without indulging in hazardous departures from recognized norms; and

(3) Where the scheme of estate disposition and plans for meeting

Table 3
ALTERNATE MARITAL DEDUCTION RESULTS

Husband's Adjusted GROSS Estate		Husband's Tax	Wife's Adjusted Gross Estate	Wife's Tax	Total Tax
200,000	Maximum Marital Ded.	0	$200,000	$ 6,600	$ 6,600
	½ Marital Ded.	0	100,000	0	0
300,000	Maximum Marital Ded.	0	250,000	21,400	21,400
	½ Marital Ded.	0	150,000	0	0
350,000	Maximum Marital Ded.	0	250,000	21,400	21,400
	½ Marital Ded.	0	75,000	0	0
400,000	Maximum Marital Ded.	0	250,000	21,400	21,400
	½ Marital Ded.	6,600	200,000	6,600	13,200
450,000	Maximum Marital Ded.	6,600	250,000	21,400	28,000
	½ Marital Ded.	14,000	225,000	14,000	28,000
475,000	Maximum Marital Ded.	14,000	250,000	21,400	35,400
	½ Marital Ded.	17,700	237,500	17,7〜0	35,400

liquidity needs depend upon the effective use of the marital deduction, its loss can be disastrous.

For a specific example, one who selects the commonly used "power of appointment trust" would be expected to provide for the surviving spouse to receive all of the trust income, at least annually, and to have a general power of appointment over the trust principal. Again, one who chooses an "estate trust" would be expected to provide for the trust principal and any accumulated income to be added to the estate of the surviving spouse at the time of her death. Nevertheless, cases are from time to time reported in which the draftsman has daringly departed from these basic stipulations.

In one such case a husband left his residuary estate in trust for his wife. The terms of the trust provided for her to receive so much of the income as the trustee deemed necessary. According to the stipulated terms, at her death the principal and accumulated income "shall be distributed to the executor or administrator of her estate . . . to pay costs of administration . . . and the remaining balance shall be distributed to . . . persons designated in her will. . . ." If the power of appointment is not exercised, the remaining corpus is to be paid over to her estate.

IRS ruled that the trust did not qualify for the marital deduction. It was not an "estate trust" (see footnote below) *because the entire principal and accumlated income need not be added to the wife's estate at her death.* It would be allowable as an estate trust as to the portion allocable to administration expenses, except that there was no way to determine the amount which would eventually be distributable to the wife's estate for these expenses. And it did not qualify as a "power of appointment trust," notwithstanding her general power of appointment, *because the wife was not entitled to all the income for life.* Rev. Rul. 75-128, 1975 - 1 CB 308, 311.[6] In the marital deduction field, the creation of hybrids is a hazardous occupation.

The following are a number of alternate ways for interests passing at death to qualify for the marital deduction.

[¶103.1]   Benefits of Outright
Marital Deduction Gifts

By "outright" gifts we mean those in which the interest passing to the surviving spouse passes directly to her or him, free of any trust or

---

[6]Note, however, that Rev. Rul. 72-333, CB 1972-2, 530, states that a "combination trust" qualifies for the marital deduction where a surviving spouse is to receive all the income for life and, at her death, principal is to be distributed for payment of administration expenses, with the balance passing to persons designated in her will. In this situation, while there is no way to predict, as of the date of the decedent's death, what portion of his estate will ultimately be distributed to his spouse's estate for administration expenses, "it is obvious that no part of the trust fails to meet either the conditions of an estate trust or the requirements of Section 2056(b)-5."

limitation other than a permissible time-delay or common-disaster condition as discussed in [¶105], below. Such gifts may take a variety of forms:

☐ A gift to the surviving spouse, by will or trust instrument. This may be a gift of a specific asset, or a specified sum, or a stated portion of a larger fund, e.g., a percentage or fraction of a residuary estate or a trust corpus.

☐ An interest passing to the surviving spouse as a result of his or her election to take against the will or other conveyances.

☐ Property owned by a decedent and decedent's spouse jointly with right of survivorship or as tenants by the entireties.

☐ A bank balance passing to the surviving spouse under terms of a tentative or "Totten" trust account.[7]

In each case, the interest will qualify for the marital deduction only if or to the extent the property involved is included in the decedent's gross estate and passes to the surviving spouse. And the deduction is allowable only for the lesser of: (1) the value of the interest passing to the surviving spouse or (b) the statutory limit ($250,000 or 50 percent of the adjusted gross estate, whichever is greater).

Among the benefits of an outright marital deduction gift are these:

☐ It avoids the various technical hazards which are inherent in the use of power of appointment trusts and estate trusts. (We have touched on these, and they are more fully developed below.)

☐ It avoids the expenses of trust administration.

☐ It give the beneficiary greater freedom of action than is usually available with a trust.

Among the potential disadvantages are these:

☐ It provides no assurance of adequate property management.

☐ It provides no assurance of principal preservation.

☐ It provides no protection against the hazards of the beneficiary's improvidence, generosity, or incapacity.

☐ It may increase the expenses of administration and the State inheritance taxes in the estate of the surviving spouse.

[¶103.2]   Power of Appointment Trust

Basically, a "power of appointment trust" is one in which the spouse is entitled to receive all of the income for life, annually or more

---

[7]Such an account is one titled in the name of A "in trust for" B, where A has full rights of ownership during his lifetime but any balance remaining at his death passes to B.

frequently, and has a general power of appointment over the principal (that is, the power to appoint it to herself or her estate).

As the spouse's interest in such a trust will terminate on a certain event, namely, her death, whereupon the principal will pass to someone other than herself or her estate unless she appoints it to her estate, such an interest would fail to qualify by reason of the "terminable interest rule" but for the specific exceptions set forth in Sec. 2056 (b) (5) of the Code. Under that Section, in order for an interest passing (whether or not in trust) from a decedent to the surviving spouse to qualify for the marital deduction it must satisfy all of the following conditions:

☐ The surviving spouse must be entitled for life to either —

(a) All of the income from the entire interest or from a specific portion of the entire interest, or

(b) a specific portion of all the income from the entire interest.

☐ The income must be payable to the surviving spouse annually or at more frequent intervals.

☐ The surviving spouse must have the power to appoint the entire interest or the specific portion (from which the income is received) either to herself or to her estate.

☐ Such power of appointment must be exercisable by the surviving spouse alone and (whether by will or by lifetime instrument) must be exercisable "in all events."

☐ The entire interest or the specific portion involved must not be subject to a power in any other person to appoint any part to any person other than the surviving spouse.

In determining whether or not these five conditions are satisfied by the instrument of transfer, reference is made to the State law under which the interest passes or under which the trust is administered. For example, Reg. Sec. 20.2056(b)-(5)(e) provides that the silence of the governing instrument as to the frequency of income payment will not be regarded as a failure to satisfy the condition of annual or more frequent income payments unless the applicable law permits payment to be made less frequently than annually.

In *Com'r v. Bosch*, 337 U.S. 456 (1967), the Supreme Court held that the federal authorities, in applying local law, are not bound by a determination as to property interests by a State trial court but are bound only by the decision of the highest State court. Absent a decision by the highest court, the federal authority must apply what it finds to be the State law after giving "proper regard" to relevant rulings of other courts of the State.

Let us now consider in greater detail, as this is the most common form of marital deduction gift, the technical elements of the mandatory income and power of appointment terms, the optional principal invasion provisions, and the prohibition against principal diversion, of the power of appointment trust:

(1) *Mandatory income provisions.* The income requirement of this type of trust has essentially two aspects, which will be treated *seriatim*—the *quantum* of income and the *frequency* of payment:

(a) The surviving spouse must receive "all" of the income of whatever interest is to qualify for the marital deduction. How much income is "all" the income?

Reg. Sec. 20.2056(b)-5(f)(1) indicates that this requirement is met if the effect of the trust arrangements is to give the surviving spouse for life substantially the degree of beneficial enjoyment of the trust property which the principles of trust law accord to a person who is designated without qualification as the life beneficiary of a trust. This means, essentially, that the document and the surrounding circumstances must evidence the decedent's intent that his or her spouse will receive such amount of income (or have such use of the trust property) as (1) is a return or use which is reasonable in proportion to the value of the trust principal and (2) is consistent with the preservation of the trust principal.

Such a standard is obviously imprecise, but some security for the estate planner can be derived from the following related guidelines:

☐ The designation of the spouse as sole income beneficiary for life will be sufficient unless the terms of the trust and the surrounding circumstances considered as a whole evidence *an intent to deprive* the spouse of the requisite degree of enjoyment (income or use of the trust property) [Reg. Sec. 2056(b)-5(f)(1)].

☐ If the overall effect of a trust is to give the spouse the requisite degree of enjoyment, it is immaterial whether that result is brought about by rules set forth in the trust instrument or, in their absence, by rules supplied by State law [Reg. Sec. 2056(b)-5(f) (2)].

☐ In addition, Reg. Sec. 20.2056(b)-5(f)(6) indicates that a trust will be considered as satisfying this phase of the income requirement if the surviving spouse has the right, exercisable in all events, to have the trust principal distributed to her at any time during her life.

☐ Reg. Sec. 20.2056(b)-(5)(f)(7) provides that the trust will not be disqualified by reason of a provision that the income right of the surviving spouse shall not be subject to assignment, alienation, pledge, attachment or claims of creditors—the usual "spendthrift" clause.

☐ If it is evident from the nature of the trust assets and the applicable rules for management of the trust that the distribution of rents, ordinary cash dividends, and interest as income to the surviving spouse will give her the substantial beneficial enjoyment which is required, the trust will not be disqualified by provisions requiring stock dividends and the proceeds of sale of trust assets to be allocated to principal. Under the same principles (i.e., where substantial beneficial enjoyment is provided), it is permissible to subject income to depletion charges (on assets subject to depletion), depreciation, trustees' commissions, and other charges. [Reg. Sec. 2056(b)-5(f)(3)].

Beyond our scrutiny of the "substantivc" provisions of the governing instrument (viewed in the context of surrounding circumstances and applicable State law), special attention must be given to provisions for management or administration of the trust.

Here, again, the basic principles are the same. Provisions granting administrative powers to the trustee will not disqualify the trust if they do not evidence the intent to deprive the surviving spouse of the requisite beneficial enjoyment. And this adverse intent will not be found if the entire terms of the trust are such that the local courts will impose reasonable limitations on the person exercising the powers [Reg. Sec. 2056(b)-5(f)(4)].

More specifically, the trustee's powers to determine the allocation of receipts and disbursements as between income and principal, to apply income or principal for the benefit of the spouse, and to retain assets passing to the trust, will not necessarily disqualify the trust principal for the marital deduction. Thus, Reg. Sec. 20.2056(b)-5(f)(4) provides that the power to retain assets which consist substantially of unproductive property, i.e., which do not yield a reasonable income for the spouse, will not necessarily defeat the marital deduction. The marital deduction is available if the applicable rules for administration of the trust require, or permit the spouse to require, that the trustee either make the property productive or convert it within a reasonable time. Nor will such powers disqualify the trust if the applicable rules require the trustee to use the degree of judgment and care in exercise of the powers which a prudent man would use if he were the owner of the trust assets.

These principles and guidelines are explained further, with examples, in Rev. Rul. 69-56, 1969 — CB 224:

> *Example 1:* It is assumed that: (a) The governing instrument does not direct the trustee to favor other beneficiaries over the surviving spouse. (b) State law authorizes the exercise of the discretions (or execution of the directions) involved, or there is no State law so authorizing, or State law denies such powers or directions to the trustee except to the extent provided in the governing instrument. (c) The governing instrument gives the trustee the following powers or directions:
>
> (1) To apportion or not to apportion, between successive beneficial

interests (e.g., life tenant and remainderman) interest income and expense, rental income and expense, real estate taxes, or other items of periodic income and expense. (Under applicable State law, the fiduciary's determination must be made so as to balance fairly the interests of successive beneficiaries.)

(2) To treat ordinary cash dividends as income when received, regardless of the declaration date or record date.

(3) To treat extraordinary cash dividends as principal.

(4) To treat stock dividends as principal.

(5) To treat capital gains dividends of regulated investment companies as principal.

(6) To charge to income or principal executors' or trustees' commissions, legal and accounting fees, custodian fees, and similar administration expenses.

(7) To maintain reasonable reserves for depreciation, depletion, amortization, and obsolescence.

(8) With respect to interest-bearing bonds and like obligations, to amortize or not to amortize both premium and discounts.

The ruling states that in the circumstances assumed, such powers or directions do not evidence an intention to deprive the surviving spouse of the beneficial enjoyment required by the Code, so that inclusion of them in the governing instrument will not defeat or diminish the marital deduction.

Example 2: It is assumed that the governing instrument gives the trustee a general power to determine the allocation of receipts and expenditures between income and principal. Also, State law requires the trustee to balance fairly the interests of the income beneficiary and the remainderman. The ruling holds that the grant of such a power, under State law of the character indicated, does not in and of itself evidence an intention to deprive the surviving spouse of the requisite beneficial enjoyment and will not defeat or diminish the marital deduction.

Example 3: It is assumed that the governing instrument contains no provision pertaining to allocation of receipts and expenditures as between income and principal. The ruling holds that the fact of reliance solely upon State law for guidance of the trustee in such matters does not result in disallowance or diminution of the marital deduction.

Example 4 deals with two powers unrelated to allocations between income and principal. It is assumed that the governing instrument does not preclude the local court from imposing reasonable limitations upon such powers in order to protect the interest of the surviving spouse. In this example, the fiduciary is given the following powers:

1. To retain cash included in the trust fund without investing it for such period of time as the trustee shall deem advisable, whenever he or she shall determine that it is inadvisable to invest such cash.

2. To make distributions in cash, or in other trust assets at current values, or partly in each, allocating specific assets to particular distributees, and for this purpose to make reasonable determinations of current values.

The ruling holds that in the circumstances assumed the powers do not deprive the surviving spouse of substantially full beneficial enjoyment of the interest transferred, so that those powers will not defeat or diminish the marital deduction.

(b) The income must be paid to the surviving spouse in annual or more frequent installments.

Of the two aspects of the income requirement for the power of appointment trust, quantum and frequency—frequency is by far the easier to comprehend. Simply, the income must be paid to the surviving spouse at least once a year.

This requirement should present no conceptual or practical difficulty for the trustee as the trust continues. At the inception of the trust, however, there may be a technical or administrative problem, especially in the case of a testamentary trust. The period of administration of the decedent's estate—preceding the establishment of the trust and the inception of trust distributions—may and commonly will last for more than a year following the decedent's death. Will this delay defeat the marital deduction?

Reg. Sec. 20-2056(b)-(5)(f)(9) makes it clear that the interest will not fail merely because the spouse is not entitled to the income from estate assets during the period prior to distribution of those assets by the executor, unless the executor is, by the decedent's will, authorized or directed to delay distribution beyond the period reasonably required for administration of the decedent's estate.

Paragraphs (a) and (b), above, summarize the principles by which the adequancy of the surviving spouse's right to trust income is governed. In the light of these principles, we recommend the following:

☐ To ensure that the income provision (or, for that matter, any other trust element) will be adequate for the marital deduction, reliance should be placed primarily on the will or other trust instrument rather than State law. In the first place, we do not know which State's law will be applicable at the time of the decedent's death. And, in the second place, we do not know what the law of any particular State will be at the time of the decedent's death.

☐ In the will or other trust instrument, the intent to give the surviving spouse the requisite income or enjoyment should be made quite explicit. It should not be left to inference from the general language of the document and the surrounding circumstances.

☐ Specifically, the trustee should be directed to distribute *all* of the net income to the spouse in *annual or more frequent instalments*. And the "net income" should be defined to include all items or amounts within the meaning of the term "income" in the estate tax marital deduction provisions of the Code in effect at the time of the testator's or grantor's death.

☐ Consideration should be given to eliminating all provisions which directly or indirectly permit the accumulation of income. In many if not most cases, these powers are present for reasons of history rather than utility.

☐ The following restrictions should be used:

> In accordance with my desire and intent that the marital deduction portion shall qualify for the federal estate tax marital deduction, I direct that, notwithstanding any other provision of my Will:
>
> A. My fiduciaries, in the administration of my estate and the Marital Deduction Trust, and in the exercise of any power relating thereto, shall use the degree of judgment and care which a prudent person would exercise if he or she were the owner of the estate and trust assets.
>
> B. If any property of the Marital Deduction Portion or the Marital Deduction Trust is or becomes unproductive, my wife shall have the right, which may be exercised by instrument in writing, to require my fiduciaries within a reasonable time either to make such property productive of a reasonable income or to dispose of it and invest the proceeds in property which is productive of a reasonable income.
>
> C. My fiduciaries shall not have any rights, powers, duties, privileges or immunities which would disqualify the Marital Deduction Portion for the marital deduction. All provisions of my Will shall be construed in such manner, and the powers and discretions herein conferred shall be exercised only to the extent and in such manner, as to assure compliance with the estate tax marital deduction provisions of the Internal Revenue Code in this respect. Any provision of my Will which is incapable of being so construed or applied shall be inapplicable.

In this suggested provision, paragraphs A and B were developed from the Regulations. Paragraph C is a "saving clause" which is designed to meet possible future attacks upon the marital deduction with reference to administrative powers not presently dealt with in the Regulations or Revenue Rulings. While the utility of such a catchall provision might be considered problematical, such a saving clause was effective in Rev. Rul. 75-440, 1975-2 CB 372. That ruling involved a general trust power to invest principal in life insurance, a provision which endangered the marital deduction because life insurance is an investment which does not produce current income for the surviving spouse. The power involved was determined to be inapplicable to the marital deduction trust by virtue of a saving clause which purported to void any power which jeopardized the marital deduction. On the other hand, where the disqualifying power clearly applies to the marital deduction trust, a saving clause which seeks to revoke the power in the event of adverse I.R.S. action will not override the power for estate tax purposes (Rev. Rul. 65-144, 1965-1 CB 422.

(2) *Mandatory general power of appointment.* In addition to the income rights discussed above, the surviving spouse must be given a general power of appointment over the trust principal. A general power, for this purpose, is a power of appointment which the surviving spouse can exercise (a) in favor of herself or her estate, and which she can exercise (b) alone and (c) in all events:

(a) Under Reg. Sec. 20-2056(b)-5(g), the power is sufficiently broad if, and only if, it is one of the following:

(1) An unlimited power to appoint the trust principal to herself at any time following the decedent's death (e.g., unlimited power to withdraw or "invade" principal).

(2) An unlimited power to appoint the trust principal to her estate. (If exercisable during her lifetime, it must be exercisable at any time prior to her death. If exercisable by will, it must be exercisable irrespective of the time of her death.)

(3) A combination of (1) and (2). Any of the foregoing powers gives the surviving spouse the requisite authority to divert the trust assets to whomever she may choose. The interest which is subject to such a power will not fail to satisfy this condition merely because takers in default of its exercise are designated by the decedent.

(b) A power is not exercisable by the surviving spouse "alone" if the exercise of the power requires the joinder or consent of any other person.

(c) A power is not exercisable by the surviving spouse "in all events" if:

(1) It can be terminated during her lifetime by any event other than her complete exercise or release of it.

(2) It may be exercised only for a limited purpose.

(3) As a lifetime power to invade principal, its exercise is subject to any condition in law or in the instrument.

(4) As a testamentary power of appointment, it cannot be effectively exercised immediately following the decedent's death (e.g., if it cannot be exercised prior to distribution of the assets by the executor).

The power will not, however, be disqualified by reason of merely formal limitations, such as the requirement of a particular kind of writing, or delivery of the writing to the trustee, or reasonable notice. It is permissible to require that a testamentary power be exercised by a will executed after the decedent's death or that the exercise be by specific reference to the power.

It should be noted that if the surviving spouse has the requisite power either to appoint to herself or to her estate, it is immaterial that she also has one or more lesser powers. If she has a testamentary power to appoint to her estate, a limited power of withdrawal or appointment during her lifetime has no adverse effect. Conversely, if she has an unlimited power to withdraw principal during her lifetime, she may be given a limited testamentary power of appointment.

(3) *Optional principal invasion provisions.* Assuming that the mandatory income and power of appointment requirements of this type of marital deduction trust have been met, a broad range of supplemental provisions for lifetime principal distributions are permissible.

There are, of course, situations in which no lifetime use of principal will be considered necessary or appropriate. At the other extreme are cases in which the surviving spouse will be authorized to withdraw principal at will, so that she may even terminate the trust, if she so desires, on the day of its inception. (Such a power of invasion, as we have seen, is not "supplemental" but constitutes a general power of appointment for marital deduction purposes.)

With respect to the grant of an unlimited power of principal withdrawal, the considerations are essentially the same as those discussed in Paragraph 103.1 with respect to outright gifts. Where the trustee's spouse recognizes the potential advantages of a trust but does not wish to have her inheritance "tied up," the unlimited power of withdrawal may offer a satisfactory solution. Trust advantages are made available, but she can open the trust "door" at any time.

Between the extremes of unlimited principal invasion and no principal invasion, a variety of possibilities are available:

☐ Provide for the trustee to distribute or apply principal for the spouse's emergency needs, or to maintain her customary standard of living, or for other stated uses.

☐ Permit the spouse to withdraw principal from time to time within stipulated dollar or percentage limits (annual or total or both).

☐ Permit the spouse to make gifts of principal to whomever she may please, or to a limited class of beneficiaries. (Withdrawals to pay taxes resulting from such gifts should also be permitted. Concurrence of the trustee, or of one or more of several trustees, may be made a condition precedent to such gifts.)

Where the spouse is given broad, or even unlimited, principal invasion powers, it is normally prudent also to authorize the trustee to distribute or apply principal for her maintenance or emergency needs. The reason for this is that a physical or mental affliction may prevent the spouse from requesting distributions at the very times when they are most needed.

In estate planning situations we commonly encounter a husband who does not wish to give his wife unlimited access to the marital deduction principal and a wife who does not want to "go hat in hand" to a trustee to justify and plead for occasional principal distributions. A variant of the above-listed principal invasion provisions which will frequently meet the concerns of both spouses in that situation is the guaranteed after-tax "spendable income." To develop such a clause, the clients are asked to estimate the annual amount which they would consider sufficient, after income taxes are paid, to provide for the wife's comfortable maintenance. We then provide, in the marital deduction trust:

1. To the extent the annual after-tax income of the surviving spouse (from all sources) is less than the stipulated amount, she can require the amount of the deficiency to be distributed to her from principal.

2. The stipulated amount will be adjusted each year with changes in the consumer price index, so that the "guaranteed spendable income" will not be eroded by inflation.

3. If there are children who will be dependent on the spouse for support, we can provide a higher annual amount during the estimated period of dependency.

4. The trustee will be authorized to make discretionary distributions also, in case the amount needed by the spouse has been underestimated or for unusual needs that may arise.

Apart from their utility in meeting the needs of the surviving spouse, principal invasion provisions such as those we have mentioned above will frequently permit you to continue your tax planning after the testator's death. Thus, even where the spouse's income from all sources appears to be more than adequate to meet all anticipated needs, tax considerations may nevertheless indicate that the trustee be empowered to distribute principal for the spouse's maintenance or for other purposes.

For example, assume that the testator's adjusted gross estate of $600,000 is to be left in two trusts, a power of appointment marital deduction trust and a nonmarital or residuary trust. Assume that the marital deduction trust will have principal assets of $300,000 and that the nonmarital trust will have principal assets (after payment of estate and inheritance taxes) of about $260,000. Assume that the former trust will yield an annual income of $18,000, the latter of $15,600. And assume that all trust income is payable to the surviving spouse and that principal can be distributed by the trustee if needed for her maintenance.

If the surviving spouse in this example were to receive the income of both trusts, totaling $33,600, and if that sum were adequate to cover her taxes and living expenses, she would receive $33,600 of taxable income from the trusts each year, and the principal of both trusts would remain intact.

On the other hand, if the will were drafted to permit the trustee to accumulate the income of the nonmarital trust and add it to principal, the trustee could distribute each year to the surviving spouse, from the principal of the marital deduction trust, an amount equal to the income accumulated in the nonmarital trust. The spouse could receive $33,600 from the marital deduction trust ($18,000 of income plus $15,600 of principal[8]). She would receive nothing from the nonmarital trust.

From this pattern two advantageous results would accrue:

1. The annual trust income of $33,600 would be taxed to two taxpayers, rather than entirely to the surviving spouse, thus reducing the annual income tax bite.

2. Each year the sum of $15,600 would in effect be shifted from the marital deduction trust (via principal invasion) to the nonmarital trust (via income accumulation). Thus we reduce the trust which will be taxable in the surviving spouse's estate in favor of the trust which presumably will not.

If the surviving spouse in this example has no gross estate other than the principal of the marital deduction trust, operation of the suggested principal invasion program for a ten-year period would reduce her gross estate from $300,000 to $144,000, which would pass free of estate tax. The results are the saving of the estate tax on a $300,000 estate and the cumulative income tax savings above mentioned.

Similarly, and especially where substantial amounts are involved, estate and income tax planning may suggest that the surviving spouse be authorized to make gifts out of the marital deduction trust principal, and to direct the payment out of principal of any taxes which the gifts may involve. By making such gifts the spouse can reduce her gross estate and divert taxable income (of the transferred property) to one or more additional taxpayers. (For a complete discussion of such a gift program, see Chapter 5.) To protect the spouse against her own generosity or undue pressure from potential donees, the testator or grantor may wish to stipulate that such gifts can be made only with the approval of an independent trustee.

---

[8]This illustration is simplified in the sense that each year's principal distribution would presumably reduce the income of the trust for the following year, thus requiring a somewhat larger principal invasion each year if the total of the annual income and principal distributions are to be maintained at $33,600.

4. *Prohibition against principal diversion.* We have discussed the provisions that must be included and some that may be included in a "power of appointment trust." There is one type of provision that may not be included. *Caveat:* Inclusion of a clause which permits the trustee or any other party—except the surviving spouse—to divert or to cause the diversion of principal to or for the benefit of anyone other than the surviving spouse will result in loss of the marital deduction. Except to the extent she may appoint otherwise, the surviving spouse must be the sole beneficiary of the marital deduction trust.

Sample provisions of a "power of appointment trust" can be found in Appendix C.

Among the benefits of a power of appointment trust are these:

☐ It can provide all the protections which trusts generally can provide: against the disability or improvidence of the beneficiary, against creditors' claims, and the like.

☐ It can be used to provide professional management of property.

☐ It may, depending on applicable law, result in State inheritance tax savings.

☐ It can be adapted to relatively rigid or to extremely liberal and flexible dispositive schemes.

Among the potential disadvantages, depending on how the trust terms are drafted, are these:

☐ It may provide for the surviving spouse income in excess of need, with unfortunate income tax consequences.

☐ The beneficiary's freedom of action is reduced.

☐ Costs of administration, as with all trusts, are involved.

[¶103.3]   Estate Trust

The "estate trust" is one which provides for the income to be accumulated, or for the income to be distributed to the surviving spouse or accumulated in the trustee's discretion, and for all the principal and income remaining at the spouse's death to pass to her estate. The sole requirement for such a trust to qualify for the marital deduction is that all of the income and principal ultimately be distributable to the spouse or her estate.

While the "power of appointment trust" is a statutory exception to the terminable interest rule, the "estate trust" is not. As the interest of the surviving spouse in the estate trust cannot fail or terminate in favor of any person other than the spouse or her estate, the trust does not violate the terminable interest rule (see ¶100.1); no "exception" to the rule is needed.

Thus the estate trust is a relatively simple device. The complex criteria for a statutory exception to the terminable interest rule are not involved. Yet this form of trust is not widely known and where known is too frequently ignored.

The terms of the estate trust may preclude distribution of income or principal to the surviving spouse, so that the entire trust fund will pass to her estate. On the other hand, provisions permitting the spouse to receive income or principal during her lifetime will not disqualify the trust. Indeed, all of the pricipal invasion provisions which are discussed in connection with the power of appointment trust can be considered for use with the estate trust.

Whenever accumulated income is distributed, whether to the spouse while living or to her estate following her death, the distribution will be subject to the throwback rule for income-tax purposes. The "throwback rule" taxes the accumulated income of a trust to the beneficiary somewhat as if the amounts had been distributed each year rather than accumulated. When distribution is made to the estate of the deceased spouse on termination of the trust, the estate is a beneficiary separate from the spouse and is, therefore, entitled to allocate the accumulation distribution to the throwback years. In those years the estate was not in existence and had no other income, so that the application of the throwback rule in this context produces no tax penalty.

As there is no requirement for the income of the estate trust to be distributed, there is no requirement that the trust property be made to produce a fair return or to yield any income at all. Accordingly, such a trust can be used to obtain the marital deduction while holding in trust such nonproductive assets as antique collections, undeveloped land, or closely held stock on which dividends are not likely to be paid.

The estate trust will sometimes be the appropriate marital deduction device for the testator who is more concerned about limiting the lifetime benefits flowing to his spouse than he is with respect to the distribution of the property after he and his spouse are both deceased. (Under applicable State law, a spouse who is dissatisfied with this arrangement may have a right to alter it by electing to take against the will, but such a possibility must be considered in connection with any restrictive testamentary provision for a spouse.)

The principal, and generally the most appropriate, use of the estate trust is not in the place of but in combination with a power of appointment trust. The choice of a particular form of gift for marital deduction purposes is not an either/or matter. Within the statutory limit—$250,000 or 50 percent of the adjusted gross estate, whichever is greater—any number of qualifying gifts can be made.

In relatively large estates, the estate tax advantage of the full marital deduction in the decedent's estate may be offset in some degree by the income tax cost of income distributions to the surviving spouse. For example, a $2,000,000 adjusted gross estate provides an allowable marital deduction of $1,000,000. If that sum were placed in a power of appointment trust and produced an annual income of $60,000, this income (by itself or "on top of" the spouse's other income) might exceed the normal living expenses of the surviving spouse. And yet she would have to receive and pay taxes on the entire $60,000.

She could make a gift of a portion of the trust principal, if permitted by the terms of the trust, but a substantial gift would involve current taxes at the new unified rates. She would lose the protection of the assets given and of the amount paid in taxes on the gifts.

If current trust income of $40,000 would be suitable for the surviving spouse in these circumstances, a solution would be to place two-thirds of the allowable marital deduction in a power of appointment trust and one-third in an estate trust. Each year the beneficiary would receive and pay taxes on $40,000, and the other $20,000 of trust income would be accumulated and taxed to the estate trust. With two taxpayers (spouse and trust), the total income taxes would be reduced without losing a single dollar of marital deduction.

To be sure, in the example given the annual income of the estate trust will be piled on top of the trust principal, which will be includible in the gross estate of the surviving spouse at the time of her death. But we had assumed that the income otherwise distributable from the power of appointment trust ($60,000) exceeded her requirements, so that the after-tax excess would presumably be accumulated and included in her gross estate anyway.

The estate trust may result in certain tax and expense disadvantages. In some States the assets of a power of appointment trust will escape inheritance tax at the death of the surviving spouse. The assets of the estate trust, however, will be added to her estate directly and lose the insulation of the trust. Depending on local rules or practices, a similar difference may also arise in the computation of various administration expenses in the estate of the surviving spouse.

Appendix C includes a will which utilizes an estate trust in combination with a power of appointment trust. A simple separate form of estate trust also appears in Appendix C.

Among the benefits of an estate trust are these:

☐ It can be extremely simple.

☐ Income can be taxed currently to the trust rather than to the testator's individual beneficiaries.

☐ It can provide the full marital deduction while total control of the trust property and its income is reserved during the lifetime of the surviving spouse.

☐ It can provide the full marital deduction while retaining in trust assets which might otherwise have to be made productive or be disposed of.

☐ Like the power of appointment trust, it can provide all the protections which trusts generally can provide, as well as professional management of the property involved.

Among the potential disadvantages are these:

☐ Ultimate distribution of the trust assets must be governed by the spouse's estate plan.

☐ The spouse's enjoyment and freedom of action wuth regard to the trust property, if any, are severely limited.

☐ Taxes and expenses in the estate of the surviving spouse may be increased.

☐ Costs of administration, as with all trusts, are involved.

[¶103.4]   Life Insurance Optional Settlements

Insurance policies commonly permit the insured or his beneficiary to have the proceeds paid at his death either in a lump sum or in various installment and deferred payment arrangements. The installment and deferred payment arrangements are called "optional settlements."

Proceeds payable to a surviving spouse in a lump sum qualify for the marital deduction, and the proceeds are not disqualified if she (rather than the insured) elects payments under a settlement option. The marital deduction is also available for proceeds payable in a lump sum to a trust which qualifies for the deduction under the criteria discussed above.

Where a settlement option has been elected by the insured, the proceeds payable to his surviving spouse will qualify for the marital deduction if they do not constitute a terminable interest (see ¶100.1) or if they meet the criteria for an exception to the terminable interest rule under Sec. 2056(b)(6) of the Code.

The commonly available optional settlements are:

☐ The interest option, under which the insurer retains the proceeds and pays interest to the primary beneficiary at a guaranteed rate. The principal may be subject to her right of withdrawal or it may be payable to a secondary beneficiary at the expiration of the option period.

☐ The life annuity option, under which the insurer makes fixed payments to the primary beneficiary until her death, or makes payments to her for life with a refund of any amount unpaid at her death, or makes payments for the lives of two beneficiaries and the survivor of them.

☐ The installment payment option under which the insurer makes fixed payments of principal and interest until the principal is exhausted. The primary beneficiary may have a right to withdraw the remaining installments at their commuted value, or any balance remaining at her death may be payable to a secondary beneficiary.

Where the surviving spouse is the sole beneficiary, or where the entire proceeds will be paid to the surviving spouse or her estate, there is no violation of the terminable interest rule.

One example is a nonrefund annuity: the surviving spouse alone receives the entire benefit of interest and principal. Another is the life annuity or installment option under which any amount due after the spouse's death is payable to her estate.

Section 2056(b)(6) of the Code provides an exception to the terminable interest rule for settlement options which meet the following criteria:

1. The proceeds must be held by the insurer subject to an agreement either to pay the proceeds in installments or to pay interest on the proceeds, and the installments or interest payable during the life of the surviving spouse must be payable only to her.

2. The installments or interest payable to the surviving spouse must be payable annually or more frequently, commencing not later than thirteen (13) months after the decedent's death.

3. The surviving spouse must have the power to appoint the amounts so held by the insurer to either herself or her estate.

4. The power in the surviving spouse must be exercisable by her alone and (whether exercisable by will or during life) must be exercisable in all events.

5. The amounts payable under such contract must not be subject to a power in any other person to appoint any part of them to any person other than the surviving spouse.

If or to the extent that these five criteria apply to a specific portion of the proceeds, the marital deduction is allowable for that portion. The similarity of these criteria to those which apply to a "power of appointment trust" will readily be noticed, and generally the corresponding principles discussed in ¶103.2 apply here as well.

Among the benefits obtainable through insurance settlements options are these:

☐ A high degree of security for the fund.

☐ Certainty as to the amount of annual payments.

☐ Certainty as to the duration of payments.

☐ Protection against various hazards of outright ownership or trust mismanagement.

Among the potential disadvantages, depending in part on the option selected, are these:

☐ Relative rigidity of the benefit flow.

☐ Failure of principal and income to keep pace with inflation.

☐ Minimal discretion and freedom of action with respect to the fund.

[¶104]　　MARITAL DEDUCTION FORMULAS
FOUR WAYS TO QUANTIFY THE MARITAL DEDUCTION

Whether the marital deduction gift is to be made in the form of an outright transfer, a power of appointment trust, or an estate trust, and whether the transfer is intended to take advantage of the maximum allowable marital deduction or some portion of it, it is necessary either to identify the gift assets or to specify the amount or portion of available assets which will constitute the gift.

If the testator wishes to give to his spouse, or to place in trust for her, a specific item of property, such as a parcel of real estate or his stock of a certain corporation, the task is simply to describe it. No formula is required.

More commonly, the testator's desire is to qualify a certain amount or a share of his estate for the marital deduction. There are various ways in which that can be done.

[¶104.1]　　Flat Sum

A gift of a fixed dollar amount, viz., "I give to my wife, Mary, the sum of $200,000," has two appealing features:

1. It is simple to state.
2. It is easy for testator, executor, and beneficiary to understand.

The major drawback of such a gift (except where a $250,000 gift is made and the adjusted gross estate is less than $500,000) is that the sum involved will amost always be less than or more than the precise amount which can qualify for the marital deduction. In a case of extreme estate stability, the figure employed may be expected to come close, and that may be deemed adequate. However, in cases of normal fluctuation of values and liabilities, the client will ordinarily desire greater assurance than the flat sum can provide that the gift will amount to, and will not exceed, the full marital deduction (or other desired quantum of this deduction).

The flat sum also involves the same problems as are presented by a pecuniary formula gift: (1) taxable gain if the bequest is satisfied with appreciated assets; (2) the "64-19" problem; and (3) failure to adjust for rising or falling values during the period of administration. These three problems are explained and discussed in ¶104.3.

The outright gift of a flat sum may be useful in combination with a formula marital deduction trust, as a compromise between the spouse's desire for full control and enjoyment of her inheritance and the testator's desire to provide the benefits and protuitions of a trust.

[¶104.2]   Simple Fraction or Percentage of Residue

A simple fraction or percentage of the residuary estate, given outright or in trust, may also be used for marital deduction purposes, viz., "I give one-half (or one-third, one-fourth, etc.) of all the rest of my estate to . . .," or "I give fifty percent (or forty percent, thirty percent, etc.) of all the rest of my estate to. . . ." (By "simple" we mean a percentage or fraction which, unlike those discussed in ¶104.3 and ¶104.4, is not keyed into the "adjusted gross estate" and involves no adjustment for other transfers by the decedent which qualify for the marital deduction.)

Like the flat sum, such a fraction or percentage gift is both simple and comprehensible. Moreover, it eliminates the problems which are inherent in pecuniary (flat sum or formula) gifts, as mentioned in the third paragraph of ¶104.1. But it is virtually impossible to choose a fraction or percentage which will not, after even a brief passage of time, either underqualify or overqualify the gift for marital deduction purposes.

The simple fractional or percentage gift would have its primary appeal where the gross estate includes no nontestamentary assets and where the Section 2053 deductions can be estimated with a high degree of accuracy.

[¶104.3]   Pecuniary Formula

To obtain precisely the desired quantum of marital deduction—not one penny less or one penny more—normally requires a formula.

A formula designed to yield a particular marital deduction requires two basic elements:

1. A provision for the deduction sought to be attained—50 percent of the adjusted gross estate, for a typical example—and

2. an adjustment to take into account other transfers which qualify for the marital deduction.

For example, assume that a testator's adjusted gross estate amounts to $1,000,000 and that a 50 percent marital deduction gift ($500,000) is desired. If the gross estate includes $200,000 of life insurance payable to the surviving spouse, $100,000 of real estate owned by testator and spouse as tenants by the entireties, and $30,000 of tangible personal property to be bequeathed to the surviving spouse, the formula gift should be reduced by the amount of these items (aggregating $330,000).

A formula which provides a gift of 50 percent of the adjusted gross estate minus the value of other assets which qualify for the marital deduction will yield the following (correct) result:

Adjusted gross estate		$1,000,000
50 percent of adjusted gross estate	$500,000	
Less other qualifying assets:		
Life insurance	$200,000	
Entireties property	100,000	
Tangible property	30,000	
	330,000	
Formula gift	$170,000	

The total of the formula gift ($170,000) and the other qualifying assets ($330,000) is $500,000, the desired 50 percent of the adjusted gross estate.

A formula gift which provided, in that example, 50 percent of the adjusted gross estate *without* reduction by the value of other qualifying assets would produce a formula gift of $500,000 (rather than $170,000). The total of the formula gift ($500,000) and the other qualifying assets ($330,000) would be $830,000. Of this total only $500,000 would qualify for the marital deduction, but the entire $830,000 would be added to the gross estate of the surviving spouse.

There are two basic types of formulas designed for precise marital deduction gifts—the fractional share formula and the pecuniary formula. The pecuniary formula was typically the estate planner's initial approach to the tax objective. And, with certain variations, it is probably still the most common approach.

The pecuniary formula is ordinarily identified by the word "amount" or "sum" or similar term implying a fixed number of dollars (e.g., "an *amount* equal to 50 percent of my adjusted gross estate, etc."), in contrast with language specifying a fractional share of the residuary estate or trust corpus. Before proceeding further, it is essential that this difference be understood.

In the preceding example, an appropriate pecuniary formula—an amount equal to 50 percent of the adjusted gross estate minus the value of other qualifying assets—yields the $170,000 figure calculated above. Assuming that all assets of the gross estate other than the $330,000 of nonformula qualifying assets comprised the testator's residuary estate, an appropriate fractional formula would multiply the value of the residuary estate by a fraction. The numerator of the fraction would be equal to 50 percent of the adjusted gross estate minus the value of other qualifying assets, or $170,000. The denominator would be equal to the value of the residuary estate calculated with reference to asset values and allowable deductions as determined for estate tax purposes: $670,000 ($1,000,000 minus $330,000).

With no change in value of the residuary estate as of the time of distribution of the marital deduction formula gift, the fractional formula would produce the same result as the pecuniary formula. Thus:

$$\frac{\$170,000}{\$670,000} \times \$670,000 = \$170,000$$

But if, for example, the value of the residuary estate were to double during the period of administration, the formula would be applied as follows:

$$\frac{\$170,000}{\$670,000} \times \$1,340,000 = \$340,000$$

And if the value of the residue were reduced by half, the formula would produce this result:

$$\frac{\$170,000}{\$670,000} \times \$335,000 = \$85,000$$

Under the fractional share formula, in short, the formula gift fluctuates in proportion to changes in asset values up to the time of distribution. In contrast, the pecuniary formula provides a fixed sum—$170,000 in the example given. If the residuary estate doubles in value, everything above $170,000 is allocated to the nonmarital portion. Conversely, if the residuary estate shrinks to $170,000 or less, the entire residue is allocated to the marital deduction gift.

The fixed dollar amount produced by the pure pecuniary formula has several significant implications and consequences:

☐ If the nonmarital portion of the residuary estate passes to beneficiaries other than the surviving spouse, the spouse and such others do not share proportionately in the vicissitudes of asset valuation.

☐ Where asset values decline prior to the time of distribution, the pecuniary formula adds to the gross estate of the surviving spouse a greater amount than is required in order to obtain the desired marital deduction in the estate of the first spouse to die.

☐ Once the pecuniary formula is applied to produce a fixed dollar amount, the results are the same as if the testator had simply bequeathed that precise amount. Thus, if the executor satisfies that gift with stocks and bonds or other noncash assets, the distribution of those assets to the spouse or to the trustee for her is equivalent to a sale of the assets for the stipulated amount. And if the assets have a "basis"[9] lower than such "sale" price, the estate realizes a taxable gain in the transaction. (See Rev. Rul. 56-270, 1956-1 Cum. Bull. 325; Rev. Rul. 60-87, 1960-1 Cum. Bull. 286, Regs. § 1.661(1)-2(e).)

☐ Attempts to avoid the above-mentioned capital gain problem may lead to total loss of the marital deduction under Rev. Proc. 64-19, 1964-1 CB 682. One "solution" to the capital gains problem is to direct that noncash assets be allocated to the pecuniary formula gift *at their values as finally determined for estate tax purposes*. As each asset's distribution value (the "price" received by the executor in the "sale" of the asset to the surviving spouse or trustee) is equal to its basis, no gain is realized in the transaction. The use of such a provision enabled executors, commonly with the consent of the surviving spouse, to allocate to the formula marital deduction gift assets which had declined in value. Thus the full marital deduction would be obtained while minimizing the gross estate of the surviving spouse.

---

[9]Prior to TRA 76, the basis of estate assets for the purpose of computing gain on their sale was presumed to be equal to their value as finally determined for estate tax purposes. Thus the values of a decedent's lower-basis assets were "stepped up" to their values as of the date of death (or alternate valuation date, if chosen). Although the stepped-up basis was, generally speaking, abolished by TRA 76, new Sec. 1040 of the Code preserves the pre-TRA 76 rules for this specific situation, i.e., on distribution of property under a pecuniary marital deduction formula, gain will be recognized only to the extent of appreciation over the value of such property as determined for estate tax purposes. Loss will not be recognized.

For example, assume an estate having the following assets, with values as determined (a) for estate tax purposes, and (b) as of the time of distribution:

	Estate Tax Value	Distribution Value
Asset A	$ 50,000	$ 25,000
Asset B	$ 50,000	$ 25,000
Asset C	$100,000	$150,000

And assume that the marital deduction amount determined by the pecuniary formula is $100,000. With a direction to allocate assets at estate tax values, the executor can satisfy the bequest with Asset A and Asset B. Result: there is no capital gain; the estate gets a $100,000 marital deduction; and the gross estate of the surviving spouse receives assets having a current value of only $50,000, thus reducing her potential estate tax expense.

But no! said IRS. In Rev. Proc. 64-19, the Service announced its refusal to allow the marital deduction in cases in which local law or the will (or other governing instrument) requires or permits the fiduciary to allocate noncash assets to the marital deduction gift using values as determined for estate tax purposes.

Let us be very clear about this.

Rev. Proc. 64-19 does not apply to:

☐ A fractional share formula.

☐ A pecuniary formula where the amount must be satisfied in cash.

☐ A pecuniary formula where the fiduciary has no discretion as to the selection of assets.

☐ A pecuniary formula where the noncash assets must be valued as of the date of distribution.

Moreover, the 64-19 problem is adequately overcome if State law or the will (or other governing instrument):

☐ requires the fiduciary to allocate to the marital deduction gift assets having an aggregate fair market value at the time of distribution amounting to no less than the amount of the pecuniary gift, or

☐ requires the fiduciary to allocate to the marital deduction gift assets fairly representative of appreciation or depreciation in value of all property available for distribution.

Sample provisions to implement each of these two solutions are included in Appendix C.

We can implement the first of these solutions by providing that each asset allocated to the formula marital deduction gift shall be allocated at its fair market value at the time of distribution or at its value as finally determined for estate tax purposes, whichever is the lesser. In such a case, the "price" received by the executor in distribution of an asset can never exceed the basis of the asset, so that there should be no capital gains tax. On the other hand, where most or all of the estate assets have appreciated, distribution of them at estate tax values (the "lesser" under the allocation formula) will result in giving to the surviving spouse more than her proportionate share of the assets available for distribution. And this will expose her estate to a greater potential estate tax liability than is necessary for obtaining the desired marital deduction in the first spouse's estate. Nevertheless, as between a present capital gains tax and a future estate tax, the latter exposure may be preferred.

If we use the second, or "fair allocation," solution to the 64-19 problem, again no capital gain should result as the assets are distributed at estate tax values and the amount of the gift (the "price" of the assets in distribution) is determined by the same values. Also, this device results in an equitable division between the marital deduction and nonmarital portions of the estate. Nevertheless, if the assets generally have appreciated, such an allocation gives the surviving spouse a greater share of the distributable assets than she would receive under a pure pecuniary formula, exposing her estate to a greater potential estate tax liability.

[¶104.4]   Fractional Share Formula

A marital deduction gift made via a pure pecuniary formula, as discussed above, is equivalent to a cash bequest of a certain number of dollars. The amount of the gift is unaffected by changes in the value of estate or trust assets during the period prior to satisfaction or distribution of the gift. A fractional share formula, in contrast, is designed to provide a certain share of whatever the principal fund will amount to at the time of division of the assets. The quantitative differences in the results of these two types of formula are illustrated in [¶104.3].

Correctly used, either type of formula, or one of the variants of the pecuniary formula discussed in [¶104.3], will provide the desired marital deduction. The selection may vary in particular cases as the estate planner weighs drafting considerations, capital gain probabilities, the concern or lack of concern for equity as between the marital and nonmarital portions, and the potential estate tax impact of the marital deduction gift in the estate of the surviving spouse.

The development of a fractional share formula which can be used with confidence is a matter of considerable art and delicacy. In the first place, the use of the term "fraction" or "fractional share" does not per se preclude interpretation of the formula as a pecuniary one.

For example, if one simply bequeaths (in substantially these terms) that fractional share of the residuary estate which, when added to other qualifying assets, will produce a marital deduction equal to one-half (or other stated portion) of the adjusted gross estate, the gift may be deemed a pecuniary bequest in fractional clothing. The interpretation presumably intended here is to use the amount required for the marital deduction as the numerator of a fraction which in turn will be applied to the residuary estate at the time of distribution. However, an alternate interpretation, resulting in a pecuniary formula, is simply to provide a gift of a portion of the residuary estate equal to the amount required for the desired marital deduction. In the latter interpretation, the use of the term "fractional share" is not material or operative.

To avoid such ambiguities, we recommend that the draftsman who elects a fractional share formula should specifically define the numerator and denominator of the fraction and the multiplicand (the principal fund to which the fraction is to be applied).

With a fractional share formula, the marital deduction portion and the nonmarital portion of the estate will share pro rata in increase or decrease in value of the fund up to the time of its division. The estate tax consequence of the gift for the estate of the surviving spouse will not be distorted in either direction. As there is no dollar amount to satisfy, distribution of the marital deduction share should produce no capital gains tax. As with all general residuary shares, in contrast with pecuniary bequests, the fractional share marital deduction gift results in distribution of distributable net income at the time of its satisfaction.

In an inter vivos trust, the numerator of a fractional share formula is somewhat more difficult to articulate than in a will by reason of the necessity to take into account qualifying testamentary gifts to the surviving spouse. In such cases, and probably as a useful safeguard in all cases, we recommend that the formula as drafted be tested with appropriate figures to verify that it will produce the intended result.

A suggested fractional share formula is included in Appendix C. An alternative fractional formula, developed for his own will by a client who is an engineer, is also included in that Appendix, as a matter of possible interest, under the caption "Engineer's Fractional Marital Deduction Formula."

[¶104.5]   Incorporating Vs. Tracking the Code

Whether a pecuniary or a fractional share formula is chosen, there are basically two approaches to the expression of it. You either "track" the relevant provisions of the Internal Revenue Code or you incorporate them by reference.

By "tracking" the Code we mean articulating the formula in specific terms which follow the relevant Code provisions and are sufficient in themselves to produce the desired marital deduction result. Rather than a broad statement of intent, e.g., to provide the maximum marital deduction, or to produce the lowest possible estate tax, the draftsman who tracks the Code specifies the desired portion of the adjusted gross estate and the requisite adjustments to it.

The sample formulas we have included in Appendix C exemplify the tracking approach. These formulas are more complicated than those which incorporate the Code by reference, and they may not be self-explanatory as far as the lay client is concerned. But we prefer them, for the several reasons explained below.

The draftsman who uses the tracking approach can avoid the awkwardness of introducing a cumbersome formula into the dispositive section of a will by relegating it to a position among the technical clauses. He then provides, in setting up the marital deduction gift, that the amount or the fractional share, as the case may be, will be determined in accordance with a formula set forth in a subsequent clause.

It is simpler, of course, to state your general purpose and then incorporate the Internal Revenue Code by reference. This practice is widely employed, and not only by the unsophisticated practitioner. There are two types of incorporation clauses in common use. One is the "lowest estate tax" type, such as:

> "If my wife, Mary, survives me, my executor shall place in a separate trust for her *that amount of the principal which will be exactly sufficient to reduce the federal estate tax to the lowest possible figure . . . "*

The other is the "maximum marital deduction" type, such as:

> "If my wife, Mary, survives me, my executor shall place in a separate trust for her *an amount equal to the maximum estate tax marital deduction . . ."*

In either case, the instrument commonly contains the following (or similarly worded) administrative power as well:

> "To treat administrative or other expenses as income tax or estate tax deductions or both, without regard to whether they were paid from principal or income *or whether the size of the marital trust for my wife will be affected thereby* and without requiring adjustments between principal and income for any resulting effect on income or estate taxes."

In our view, the incorporation approach involves several deficiencies and hazards:

☐ While the formulas which track the Code make it possible for the client—at least for the client who can remember what an "adjusted gross estate" is—to determine by reading his will approximately how his estate is to be divided and distributed, incorporation of the Code by reference requires the consultation of extraneous sources.

☐ Prior to TRA 76, it had been observed that the "maximum marital deduction" type provision effectively gives congress a general power of appointment over the testator's estate. Thus a change of the allowable marital deduction to less than or more than fifty percent of the adjusted gross estate, as was proposed from time to time, would automatically alter the estate plan in a drastic way, with unanticipated consequences as to both the quanta of beneficial interests and the taxation of them. Under TRA 76, this concern became a reality. For an adjusted gross estate of $300,000, the "maximum marital deduction" would now be $250,000, whereas the optimum marital deduction, and that intended by the testator, might still be $150,000. In order to avoid this result, Section 2002(d) of TRA 76 specifically provides that in a case in which (a) a decedent dies after December 31, 1976, and before January 1, 1979, (b) with a will or trust executed prior to January 1, 1977, which contains a formula of the "maximum marital deduction" type, (c) which formula is not amended between December 31, 1976, and the decedent's death, and (d) in the absence of an applicable State statute which construes the formula as referring to the marital deduction amount as enlarged by TRA 76, the old (pre-TRA 76) limit of fifty percent of the decedent's adjusted gross estate will apply. Two observations are in order: first, that the protection afforded by Section 2002(d) will expire on January 1, 1979, and second, that the hazard of further Congressional alterations of the "maximum marital deduction" remains so long as such expressions are utilized in wills and trust documents.

☐ Taken literally, the "maximum marital deduction" clause would seem to imply election of the alternate valuation date if asset values increase in the six-month period following death, as this election will increase the marital deduction, *even though the estate tax will also be increased.* Conversely, the "lowest estate tax" clause would seem to imply selection of the valuation date on which asset values are lower. A similar ambiguity may also arise as between (a) the direction to maximize the deduction or to minimize the estate tax and (b) the executor's power to deduct administration expenses either for income tax or for estate tax purposes.

Lest these difficulties be deemed facetious or fanciful, it should be noted that, following cases such as *Matter of Kennedy,* 39 Misc. 2d 688, 241 N.Y.S. 2d 894 (Surr. Ct. Westchester Co. 1963), which gave effect to

implications such as we have warned against, a 1965 New York statute
(New York EPTL, Sec. 11-1-2(C)) was passed in an effort to meet these
problems:

> "Unless otherwise provided by a will under which a disposition is
> made to or for the benefit of a surviving spouse of a decedent which
> qualifies for a marital deduction under any tax law of the state of New
> York or of the United States and the amount or size of such disposition is
> defined by the will in terms of the maximum marital deduction allowable
> under such tax laws, such definition shall not be construed as a direction by
> the decedent to the fiduciary to exercise any election respecting the deduc-
> tion of estate administration expenses or the determination of the estate
> tax valuation date, which the fiduciary may have under such tax laws, only
> in such manner as will result in a larger allowable estate tax marital deduc-
> tion than if the contrary election had been made."

Formulas which refer to "maximum marital deduction" or "lowest
possible estate tax" may in certain circumstances fail completely to pass
the intended estate interest to the surviving spouse. This danger is illustrated by *Kynett Estate,* 26 Fid. Rep. 230 (O.C. Phila., 1975). Kynett left a
will in which he provided a "power of appointment" type trust for his
wife, to which he gave "an amount exactly sufficient to reduce the Federal estate tax falling due because of my death to the lowest possible
figure . . ." He gave the residue of his estate to the Kynett Foundation, a
gift which qualified for a full charitable deduction under Section 2055
I.R.C. Since the latter bequest so qualified, no Federal estate tax saving
could result from funding the marital trust, and the Commonwealth of
Pennsylvania, as parens patriae, contended, on behalf of the charity, that
nothing passed under the will to the marital trust.

To avoid the result which the Commonwealth sought, the Court in
Kynett searched out the testator's intent within "the four corners" of the
will and in all the surrouding and attendant circumstances. To go
beyond the document required the Court to find the language involved
to be less than "clear and unequivocable" (sic), and the judicial strain is
evident in the adjudication. The widow's trust was sustained, and the
end may have justified the effort, but there is no guarantee of a happy
ending for every such case, and there is no good reason to invite the
hazards of such litigation. The lesson is clear: marital gifts framed
simply in terms of their expected tax results are inherently infirm.

☐ It is also possible, we believe, for an incorporation-type clause to
be attacked *as a terminable interest not susceptible of vesting within six months
after death, thereby losing the marital deduction in its entirety.* While this particular attack on marital deduction provisions has not yet become a reality, the danger signals were detected and reported more than a decade
ago. (See Christian M. Lauritzen, II, "Safeguarding the Marital Deduc-

tion," *Real Property, Probate and Trust Journal,* Vol. 1, No. 2, Summer 1966, p. 162, and Committee Report in same issue of the *Journal* at p. 164, "Vesting of Testator's Property as it Relates to the Marital Deduction."):

Based on the decision of the Supreme Court in *Jackson v. United States,* 376 U.S. 503, 84 S. Ct. 869 (1964), a case involving deductibility of a California widow's allowance, officials of the Treasury Department suggested that certain marital deduction formulas might fall under the terminable interest rule. One argument given for such failure was that a gift of "an amount equal to the maximum estate tax marital deduction, etc." is equivalent to: "If my estate is large enough so that it could qualify for a marital deduction, then and only in that event, I give to my surviving spouse an amount equal to the maximum marital deduction, etc." In other words, the bequest is conditioned upon the existence of an effective marital deduction. As such, it would arguably be a terminable interest. (In contrast, a gift of "one-half of my adjusted gross estate" would be effective even if little passed under it and even if no marital deduction resulted; the spouse's entitlement to the "one-half" would not turn on the marital deduction utility of the bequest.)

Lauritzen protested (*op.cit.,* page 162), with regard to this "vesting" attack, that it has "the same highly technical and strained approach as that employed in the old cases on the Rule against Perpetuities ..."[10] Nevertheless, the possibility of such an attack remains, and we have no assurance that it will not one day emerge with devastating effect.

If we consider not only the specific hints of such Treasury thinking, but also—

1. the entire history of strict and supertechnical surveillance of the marital deduction terrain (which, as a form of relief legislation, should have been liberally construed);

2. the fairly common testamentary ambiguities above mentioned as between the "maximum marital deduction" or "lowest estate tax" language and the executor's options as to (a) alternate valuation date and (b) deduction of administration expenses for income rather than estate tax purposes; and

3. Treasury disapproval of incorporation of the Code by reference in other areas (e.g., TIR 1334, released 1/8/75, disapproving incorporation for purposes of qualified employee benefit plans): Common pru-

dence would seem to dictate the use of a formula in which the amount or the fraction is explicit set forth in unambiguous terms. Not only should we "track" the Code in developing our formula, rather than endeavor to incorporate it by general reference, but we should also state that the interest of the surviving spouse shall vest in her immediately upon the testator's death (or, if a survivorship period is stipulated, that it shall vest in any event not later than six months following the date of the testator's death). For further discussion of time-delay and common disaster provisions, see ¶105.

[¶105]   **TIME DELAY AND COMMON
                              DISASTER CONDITIONS**

A transfer to a spouse which will fail if she does not survive for a certain period of time or if she and the testator die as a result of a common disaster is a "terminable interest" (see ¶100.1). Such a gift will not qualify for the marital deduction unless it falls within an exception to the terminable interest rule.

Section 2056(b)(3) of the Code provides an exception to the terminable interest rule to allow the marital deduction when (a) the gift to the spouse is conditioned on her surviving the decedent by a specified period not exceeding six months, or on her death as a result of a disaster which also resulted in the decedent's death, and (b) the condition does not in fact occur.

A six-month period, for the purpose of this exception, expires on the day of the sixth calendar month after the decedent's death, numerically corresponding to the day of the calendar month on which his death occurred. Rev. Rul. 70-400, 1970-2 CB 196. It should also be noted that if the condition involved (unless it relates to death as a result of common disaster) is one which may occur either within the six-month period or after the expiration, regardless of when it actually occurs, the exception will not apply. See, e.g., Rev. Rul 54-121, 1954-1 C.B. 196; *Eggleston v. Dudley*, 257 F. 2d 398 (3rd Cir., 1958).

Time delay or common disaster conditions may be useful to impose where the surviving spouse has her own estate and the addition to it of the marital deduction gift will be of dubious benefit unless she survives the testator for more than a minimal period. Of the two types of permissible conditions, the time-delay is much more frequently used. A common disaster condition is widely eschewed for fear of extended litigation as to whether or not the deaths of both spouses in fact resulted from a common disaster. It is also felt that most common disaster situations will be covered by a six-month, time-delay clause.

In many cases, especially where the testator's estate is much larger than that of his spouse, we would not wish to place the marital deduction under the cloud of any survival condition. Our computations may indicate that the total estate taxes of Spouse A and Spouse B will be less if the marital deduction is given effect than if it is not, even if B survives A only by one second.

For example, where a husband has an adjusted gross estate of $1,000,000 and his wife has no separate estate, the estate tax in the husband's estate without the marital deduction will be $265,000. Taking full advantage of the marital deduction will reduce his tax to $98,800. The tax in the surviving spouse's estate, assuming that the husband's marital deduction gift will comprise the wife's adjusted gross estate, would also amount to $98,800. The taxes in both estates, using the marital deduction, would aggregate $197,600, about $68,000 less than the tax in the husband's estate without the marital deduction. Thus, the effect of the marital deduction is to treat the $1,000,000 estate as if it were two $500,000 estates which are taxable at lower estate tax brackets.

In such a case it would be advantageous not only to avoid imposing a survival condition but also to create a presumption, in case of uncertainty, that the spouse with the lesser estate—or with no estate—is the survivor. Under Reg. Sec. 20.2056 (e)-2(e), where the facts as to survivorship cannot be ascertained, a presumption (whether provided by local law, by will, or otherwise) that the testator's spouse survived him will be considered the equivalent of survival in fact for marital deduction purposes. A suggested form of a clause to take advantage of this opportunity is as follows:

> *PRESUMPTION OF SURVIVORSHIP.* If my wife and I should die under such circumstances that the order of our deaths cannot be determined, I direct that my wife shall be presumed to have survived me, any provision of law to the contrary notwithstanding.

[¶106] CORRECTING MARITAL DEDUCTION DECISIONS— ELECTIONS AND RENUNCIATIONS

The utility of the marital deduction in any particular case cannot be determined once and forever. The estate planner who invites his clients to return for periodic reviews, and whose clients respond to those invitations, should regularly reconsider the marital deduction issue. But whether or not such periodic reviews occur, a final review should always be made immediately following a client's death.

The postmortem computation may indicate that the marital deduction should have been utilized where it was not, or that a greater marital deduction would be advantageous where the decedent used less than the maximum. In such cases attention should be given to the right of the surviving spouse under applicable State law to elect to take against the will or other conveyences involved. Such an election may result in giving the surviving spouse a share of the estate which will qualify for the marital deduction, either the maximum or a meaningful part of it. This may accomplish all or a significant part of the desired result. As more fully discussed in Chapter 10, the impact of such an election on the entire testamentary scheme must be considered.

Conversely, the postmortem facts may persuade us that elimination or reduction of the marital deduction gift would be advantageous. A typical case would be one in which the estate of the surviving spouse has grown substantially following the decision to use the marital deduction in the estate of the deceased spouse. As the marital deduction gift will be added to the estate of the surviving spouse for estate tax purposes, her projected estate tax as thus increased may far outweigh the estate tax saving which the marital deduction would produce in the deceased spouse's estate. This may be the case even when we consider the augmented income and the potential principal consumption factors mentioned in [¶102].

Where our analysis indicates that elimination or reduction of the marital deduction gift would be preferred, the opportunity of the surviving spouse to make lifetime gifts from her own separate assets, or from the marital deduction portion of the decedent's estate if the applicable provisions permit, may provide an adequate remedy.

Where a lifetime gift program does not afford an adequate remedy for an excessive marital deduction gift, the surviving spouse should consider renouncing the marital deduction gift. In a typical case the decedent's estate will have been divided into two portions, a marital deduction gift (outright or in trust for his spouse), and a nonmarital or residuary gift or trust designed to avoid estate taxation in the estate of the surviving spouse. The normal result of renouncing the marital deduction gift will be to add that portion of the estate to the nonmarital or residuary gift or trust.

If the surviving spouse is the income beneficiary of the nonmarital trust, so that she would have received the income of both the marital and nonmarital portions of the estate, after the former portion of the estate is added to the latter via renunciation she will still receive the income of the entire distributable estate. The total income will be reduced, however, as a result of the additional estate tax payable in the deceased spouse's estate by reason of its loss of the marital deduction.

On the other hand, in a case in which the nonmarital portion of the estate is given to children or other beneficiaries, excluding the surviving spouse, the result of her renunciation will be to increase the assets passing to those other beneficiaries. Depending on her relationship with such beneficiaries, the adequacy of her own estate, and the tax consequences of accepting or renouncing the marital deduction, the surviving spouse may or may not consider the renunciation to be desirable.

But total acceptance or renunciation may not be the only alternatives. Where our postmortem computations indicate an optimum marital deduction less than that which the decedent's will provides, it will be useful to determine whether a partial renunciation of the marital deduction gift will be effective.

If a partial renunciation would be helpful, and if the will makes no provision for it, it will be necessary to ascertain whether a partial renunciation will be recognized under applicable State law. If there is doubt on this point, you may have to make an all-or-nothing decision.

The estate planner who anticipates the possibility that a postmortem reduction of the marital deduction gift may be desired may pave the way for such a reduction in either of these ways:

1. He may provide in the will that the surviving spouse may renounce all or any portion of the marital deduction gift, and that in the event of a partial renunciation the gift will remain effective as to the portion not renounced.

2. In lieu of a single gift of 50 percent of the adjusted gross estate, he may provide one gift of, say, 20 percent, and another gift of 30 percent of the adjusted gross estate. Or any other combination that may seem useful. Following the testator's death, the surviving spouse can renounce one of these gifts in its entirety, leaving the other undisturbed.

Thus, two (or possibly more) marital deduction gifts may be utilized in order to permit the equivalent of a partial renunciation. Instead of attempting to renounce a part of a single marital deduction gift, the surviving spouse can renounce one of two smaller marital deduction gifts. In this way both State law questions as to effectiveness of a partial renunciation, and an I.R.S. "terminable interest" challenge to the marital deduction, should be avoidable.

If two or more gifts are designed to qualify for the marital deduction, and if the gifts are in the form of trusts on identical terms, it may be advisable to provide for the trusts to be combined into a single trust after a stipulated period if neither has been renounced. In this way the uneconomic administration of multiple trusts on the same terms for the same beneficiary can be avoided.

On the other hand, apart from the purpose of providing the equivalent of a partial renunciation, the use of two or more marital deduction gifts permits us to take advantage of two or more permissible forms of such gifts. We can use a power of appointment trust and an estate trust, or an outright gift and one or both of those trust devices. If there is no postmortem renunciation, the combination of such gift forms may be otherwise advantageous.

2

Charitable Deduction

[¶200]   **OPPORTUNITIES AVAILABLE—
THEIR NATURE AND SCOPE**

Our tax laws reflect an enduring Governmental policy of encouraging contributions to charitable organizations. Charity is seen as good for the character of the Nation and as relieving Government of the financing and administration of the functions carried out by various voluntary organizations. The Treasury itself has emphasized these positive benefits:

> "Private philanthropy plays a special and vital role in our society. Beyond providing for areas into which government cannot or should not advance (such as religion), private philanthropic organizations can be uniquely qualified to initiate thought and action, experiment with new and untried ventures, dissent from prevailing attitudes and act quickly and flexibly. In doing so they enrich the pluralism of our social order."[1]

Of course, not every "charitable" motivation or result of a gift is sufficient to produce a tax benefit for the donor or grantor. The first limitation, under Sec. 170(c) of the Code, is that the gift be made to or for the use of an organization which is in one of the following five categories:

1. A state, a possession of the United States, or any of their political subdivisions, the United States or the District of Columbia, but only if made for exclusively public purposes.
2. A corporation, trust, or community chest, fund or foundation:

---

[1]*Treasury Report on Private Foundations,* Committee on Ways and Means, U.S. House of Representatives, Washington: U.S. Printing Office, February 2, 1965, p. 5.

(a) created or organized in the United States or in any of its possessions or under the laws of the United States, any State, the District of Columbia, or any possession of the United States;

(b) organized and operated exclusively (and the contribution to be used only within the United States or its possessions) for religious, charitable, scientific, literary, or educational purposes, or to foster national or international amateur sports competition (but only if no part of its activities involves the provision of athletic facilities or equipment), or for the prevention of cruelty to children or animals;

(c) no part of which inures to the benefit of any private shareholder or individual; and

(d) which is not disqualified for tax exemption under Sec. 501(c)(3)[2] by reason of attempting to influence legislation, and which does not participate in, or intervene in (including the publishing or distributing of statements) any political campaign on behalf of any candidate for public office.

3. A post or organization of war veterans, or an auxiliary or society, or trust or foundation for, any such post or organization—

(a) organized in the United States or any of its possessions; and

(b) no part of the net earnings of which inures to the benefit of any private shareholder or individual.

4. A domestic fraternal society, order, or association, operating under the lodge system, but only if the contribution or gift is made by an individual and is to be used exclusively for religious, charitable, scientific, literary, or educational purposes, or for the prevention of cruelty to children or animals.

5. A cemetery company owned and operated exclusively for the benefit of its members, or any corporation chartered solely for burial purposes as a cemetery corporation and not permitted by its charter to engage in any business not necessarily incident to that purpose, if such company or corporation is not operated for profit and no part of the net earnings of such company or corporation inures to the benefit of any private shareholder or individual.

Also treated as charitable contributions under Section 170(c) are amounts paid to certain students as members of the taxpayer's household and treated under Section 170(g) as paid for the use of the charitable organizations described in paragraphs (2), (3) and (4), above.

Section 170(c) applies for income tax purposes. Most organizations described in 170(c) are also described in a similar, but not identical manner, in Sections 2055 and 2106(a)(2) as to estate taxes and Section 2522 for gift tax purposes. Nevertheless, every beneficiary ought to be examined in the light of the appropriate statute. The detailed interpretation of these statutory provisions goes beyond the scope of this book.

[2]See lobbying provisions of Sec. 501(c)(3) as liberalized under TRA 76.

For purposes of the estate planning considerations which follow, we will assume that gifts will be made only to organizations gifts to which are deductible (within statutory limits) for income, gift, and estate tax purposes. An organization which is a prospective donee can be asked for verification of its qualified status, and an inquiry can also be addressed to the IRS.

Our concern here is with charitable contributions as one of the ten best ways to save estate taxes. Our estate tax objective may be advanced by lifetime as well as by testamentary gifts. This means that the evaluation of a technique involving a lifetime transfer requires an understanding of its income and gift tax treatment as well as the estate tax result. Similarly, the evaluation of a testamentary device requires us to consider the income and gift tax treatment of inter vivos alternatives.

Further, although we are primarily concerned with the taxation of individual donors, we must allude at best briefly to charitable gifts by other entities. For example, the extent of an individual's indulgence in charitable transfers may be affected by the availability to him, and the tax treatment of contributions by, a corporation whose stock he owns.

[¶200.1]   Deduction Limitations

For individuals, the basic tax rules on gifts to or for the use of qualifying organizations are as follows:

☐ Estate tax: unlimited charitable deduction.

☐ Gift tax: unlimited charitable deduction.

☐ Income tax: depending principally upon the identity of the charitable donees, there are three operative percentage limitations:

A. The maximum deduction is 20 percent of the taxpayer's contribution base[3] for contributions which do not qualify for the 50 percent limitation according to the criteria set forth below. Essentially, the 20 percent limitation applies to (a) gifts to semipublic charities and private nonoperating foundations and (b) gifts "for the use of" any charitable organization. Further, the deduction for a gift of long-term capital gain property to a private nonoperating foundation is reduced by 50 percent[4] of the gain which would have been realized on sale of the property at its fair market value.

---

[3]Under Sec. 170(b)(1)(F) of the Code, the "contribution base" is the taxpayer's adjusted gross income computed without regard to any net operating loss carryback to the taxable year.

[4]62.5 percent in the case of a corporate donor.

A private nonoperating foundation is any organization exempt under Sec. 501 (c)(3) of the Code which is not (a) a semipublic charity (as described in the next paragraph) or (b) one of the four types of organization described below as qualifying for the 50 percent limitation.

A semipublic charity is an organization which is neither a private foundation as defined in Sec. 509(a) of the Code[5] nor a public charity as defined in Sec. 170(b)(1)(a). Semipublic charities consist of:

1. a post or organization of war veterans or an auxiliary unit or society, or trust or foundation for any such post or organization, organized in the United States, no part of the net earnings of which inure to the benefit of any private shareholder or individual;

2. a domestic fraternal society, order, or association, operated under the lodge system; and

3. a cemetery company owned and operated exclusively for the benefit of members, or any corporation chartered solely for burial purposes and not permitted by its charter to engage in any business not necessarily incident to that purpose, provided the corporation is not operated for profit and no part of its net earnings inures to the benefit of any private shareholder or individual.

B. Subject to election of alternate treatment as explained below, the maximum deduction where a gift is made of 30 percent capital gain property, is 30 percent of the taxpayer's contribution base, except that the limit will be 20 percent if the gift falls within the categories described in the preceding paragraph(A.) By "30 percent capital gain property" we mean property which would qualify for long-term capital gain treatment if sold on the date of the contribution and to which Sec. 170 (e) of the Code does not apply (i.e., those which do not have to be reduced by 50 percent of the gain).

If the taxpayer elects under Sec. 170(b)(1)(c)(iii) to reduce the fair market value of the gift property by 50 percent of the appreciation which would be gain if the property were sold (such election to apply to all 30 percent capital gain property), the gift will not be subject to the special 30 percent limitation.

C. The total of all deductible contributions cannot exceed 50 percent of the taxpayer's contribution base. The amount so deductible will be applied first to the gifts to (but not "for the use of"[6]) the following pub-

---

[5]See ¶203.9 of this Chapter for discussion of private foundations.

[6]As noted in paragraph (1), gifts "for the use of" any qualified charitable donee are subject to the 20 percent limitation. For the 50 percent limitation, the gift must be made "to" one of the organizations described in this paragraph (c). A gift in trust of an income interest is a gift "for the use of" the charity, but a gift of a remainder interest is a gift "to" the charity, provided the remainder passes outright following termination of the prior interests. Reg. Sec. 1.170A-8(a)(2).

lic charities, private operating foundations, distributing foundations, and pooling foundations:

1. Public charities, a class composed of:

(a) churches or conventions or associations of churches
(b) tax-exempt educational organizations with a regular faculty and curriculum and a regular student body attending resident classes
(c) tax-exempt hospitals
(d) under certain circumstances, organizations directly engaged in continuous medical research in conjunction with tax-exempt hospitals, and certain organizations operated exclusively to hold and administer property for State and local colleges and universities
(e) a State, a possession of the United States, or any political subdivision of a State or such possession, the United States, or the District of Columbia, if the contribution is made for exclusively public puposes
(f) an organization exempt as a charitable, religious, educational, scientific or literary organization, or an organization created to prevent cruelty to children or animals, if it normally receives a substantial part of its support (aside from income from the mentioned activities) from a governmental unit of the type above described or from direct or indirect contributions from the general public (i.e., from a representative number of people in the community, not just a few persons or families)

2. A private operating foundation, i.e., an organization which (a) spends at least 85 percent of its income directly for the active conduct of activities constituting its exempt purposes, and (b) meets one of the following tests:

(a) at least 65 percent of its assets are devoted directly to its exempt purpose or to functionally related businesses or both;
(b) it makes qualifying distributions directly for the active conduct of its exempt activities in an amount not less than two-thirds of its minimum investment return; or
(c) substantially all its support (other than gross investment income) is normally received from the general public and from five or more independent exempt organizations, and not more than 25 percent of its support (other than gross investment income) is normally received from any one such exempt organization, and not more than 50 percent of its support is normally received from gross investment income.

3. Certain private nonoperating foundations that distribute the contributions they receive to public charities and private operating foundations within 2½ months following the year of receipt.
4. Certain private foundations the contributions to which are pooled in a common fund and the income and principal of which are paid to public charities.

Within this 50 percent group, gifts of property subject to the 30 percent limitation will be covered to the extent the other gifts do not exhaust the deductible 50 percent. To the extent the gifts to charities in the 50 percent group (without regard to the special 30 percent limitation) exceed 30 percent of the contribution base, such excess will decrease the deduction allowable for gifts to which the 20 percent limitation applies.

Thus gifts subject to the 20 percent limitation are considered last for deduction purposes in this hierarchy. They are deductible only to the extent of the lesser of (a) 20 percent of the contribution base or (b) fifty percent of the contribution base minus the contributions for which the 50 percent deduction is allowable (without regard to the special 30 percent limitation). Also, gifts to which the 20 percent limitation applies are considered without regard to (i.e., will not be enlarged by) the 30 percent limitation.

A principal effect of the hierarchy relates to the carry-over of excess contributions. To the extent the contributions exceed 50 percent of the contribution base (or 30 percent where that limitation applies), the taxpayer may deduct the excess in each of the next five years (within the contribution limits applicable in those years). This carry-over privilege does *not* apply, however, to gifts within the 20 percent limitation.

In Publication 526 (1977 Rev.) IRS gives the following example, which may be helpful here:

The taxpayer's adjusted gross income for the year is $50,000. During the year he gives to his church cash in the amount of $2,000 and land (held for more than 6 months) with a fair market value of $30,000 and a basis of $10,000. He also gives $5,000 cash to a private foundation to which the 20 percent limitation applies.

The $2,000 cash donation to the church is considered first. The deduction for the gift of land is limited to 30 percent of his $50,000 adjusted gross income, i.e., $15,000, and the remaining $15,000 of this gift may be carried over to the following year.

Since the taxpayer gave more than $25,000 (50 percent of his $50,000 contribution base) to an organization to which the 50 percent limitation applies (disregarding for this purposes the 30 percent limitation on the gift of land), no deduction is available for his gift limited to 20 percent, and this $5,000 may not be carried over.

In this example, the taxpayer's deduction for the year in which the gifts are made is limited to $17,000 ($2,000 plus $15,000) and he has a $15,000 carryover.

If the taxpayer elects, as explained above, to eliminate the 30 percent limitation on the gift of his capital gain property, which means that he must subtract from its fair market value for deduction purposes 50 percent of the gain which would be realized on sale, his deduction for the land would be $20,000 ($30,000 minus 50 percent of the $20,000 appreciation). He would then be able to deduct the $2,000 cash gift to the church, $20,000 for the gift of land, and $3,000 of the $5,000 gift to the private foundation. In summary, his total deduction for the year would be $25,000 and there would be no carryover to later years.

The foregoing limitations apply to gifts by individuals. Deductions for contributions by partnerships are passed through to the partners. For corporations, deductions are limited to 5 percent of taxable income (computed without regard to any charitable deduction), and excess contributions can be carried forward for five years, regardless of the type of qualified charity.

[¶200.2]   Effect of Type of Property Donated

In ¶200.1 we alluded to the type of property involved, especially as affecting the special 30 percent limitation. Other aspects of the type of property donated are discussed in ¶203.1, below, in the context of the planning strategies reviewed there.

[¶201]   ESTATE TAX IMPACT AND HOW TO COMPUTE IT

As we indicated in ¶200, the gift tax and estate tax charitable deductions are unlimited as to amount. This means that a person can give his entire estate to charities[7] during lifetime or by will, incurring no gift tax and avoiding estate tax entirely. Of course, such a procedure will frequently be inhibited or limited by interrelated considerations of the size of the estate, the extent of the individual's charitable interests and inclinations, and the desire to provide for family members or other noncharity beneficiaries. These countervailing considerations are discussed in [¶202].

Where a person makes a charitable gift by will of less than his entire distributable estate, the charitable deduction is one of several deductions and credits which may be used to avoid or to reduce his estate tax.

Let us consider first an estate plan which involves no marital deduction. Assume the decedent's adjusted gross estate is $1,000,000 and that $300,000 is bequeathed to charity. The estate tax computation[8] would be as follows:

---

[7]For the balance of this chapter it is assumed that all gifts under discussion are to organizations recognized as charities for income, gift and estate tax purposes.

[8]In this and the examples that follow it is assumed that death occurs after 1980, so that the full unified credit is available.

Adjusted gross estate		$1,000,000
Less charitable deduction		300,000
Tentative tax base		700,000
Estate tax on tentative tax base		229,800
Less: credit for State death taxes (if paid)	$18,000	
Unified credit	47,000	
		65,000
Estate tax payable		$ 164,800

If the decedent had given the same $300,000 to charity during his lifetime (ignoring the increase in his estate due to the reduction in lifetime income taxes and assuming no change in his Sec. 2053 deductions), the estate tax computation would be as follows:

Adjusted gross estate		$ 700,000
Tentative tax base		700,000
Estate tax on tentative tax base		229,800
Less: Credit for State death taxes (if paid)	$18,000	
Unified credit	47,000	
		65,000
Estate tax payable		$ 164,800

The estate tax result, obviously, is the same, whether the $300,000 is given to charity during lifetime or at death. The lifetime gifts, however, subject to the limitations discussed in ¶200, provide the additional advantage of current deductions for income tax purposes.

A significant change occurs if we introduce the marital deduction into the picture. Let us now assume that the same individual's estate plan is designed to provide a maximum marital deduction gift (50 percent of his adjusted gross estate) to his wife as well as a $300,000 testamentary gift to charity. The resulting estate tax computation is this:

Adjusted gross estate		$1,000,000
Marital deduction	$500,000	
Charitable deduction	300,000	
Total deductions		800,000
Tentative tax base		200,000
Estate tax on tentative tax base		54,800
Less: Credit for State death taxes (if paid)	$ 1,200	
Unified credit	47,000	
		48,200
Estate tax payable		$ 6,600

If the decedent had given the $300,000 to charity during his lifetime (again assuming no change in his Sec. 2503 deductions), the estate tax computation would be as follows:

Adjusted gross estate		$ 700,000
Marital deduction		350,000
Tentative tax base		350,000
Estate tax on tentative tax base		104,800
Less: Credit for State death taxes (if paid)	$ 5,200	
Unified credit	47,000	
		52,200
Estate tax payable		52,600

Here we find that the election to make his charitable gifts during lifetime *results in an estate tax increase of $46,000* ($52,600 minus $6,600). This is due to the interplay between the marital deduction and the charitable deduction. Since the marital deduction (when the adjusted gross estate exceeds $500,000) is limited to 50 percent of the adjusted gross estate, the reduction of the adjusted gross estate by lifetime charitable gifts automatically reduces the marital deduction.

An understanding of the relationship between these two deductions is essential to effective tax planning for any substantial estate when the optimum utilization of both deductions is sought. To state the relationship precisely: so long as the adjusted gross estate exceeds $500,000[9], the amount of the allowable marital deduction is reduced by 50 percent of all amounts which are given away during lifetime and which are removed from the decedent's gross estate.

In the last example above presented, we noted the higher estate tax in the decedent's estate, through diminution of the marital deduction, where the gifts to charity were made during his lifetime. That, to be sure, is not the whole story. As explained in Chapter One, the reduced marital deduction may in turn mean a lesser estate tax in the estate of the surviving spouse. The estate tax cost in the first estate would also be offset to the extent of any income tax savings produced by the lifetime gifts.

Nevertheless, the larger marital deduction would provide a greater income for the decedent's wife during her lifetime, and the various techniques described in this book could be applied to reduce the taxes in

[9]Below that figure, a marital deduction up to $250,000 can be maintained, though a lesser marital deduction may be desired.

her estate. More important from the standpoint of his chapter, it will be possible in a variety of circumstances for a taxpayer *to obtain income tax benefits for lifetime transfers without losing the estate tax benefit of allowable marital and charitable deductions.* We will pursue this goal in [¶203].

[¶202]   WHEN SHOULD CHARITABLE TRANSFERS BE CONSIDERED FOR ESTATE TAX SAVINGS

1. *Size of Estate.* When the section 2053 deductions (for funeral expenses, costs of administration, and debts), the marital deduction (if its use is both desirable and feasible), and the unified credit, or one or two of these, are sufficient for an estate to avoid the estate tax, there is no estate tax reason to consider charitable transfers.

Where the other available deductions and credits do not eliminate the estate tax, gifts to charity represent one of several tax-saving techniques to be considered. For some, the solution will be found in a private annuity (Chapter Six). For others, in alteration of pension or profit-sharing pay-out arrangements (Chapter 8).

Where the lifetime transfer of assets appears to be a promising avenue, options include use of an irrevocable life insurance trust (Chapter 7) and other gifts to noncharity beneficiaries (Chapter 5), as well as gifts to charity. Income tax considerations may play a role in such decisions: gifts of income-producing property may divert income to lower bracket taxpayers; deductible gifts to charity may produce immediate spendable income for the donor.

Where gifts to charity would be useful in saving estate taxes, income taxes, or both, the relevant tax calculations will indicate the quantum of useful donation. But the extent of charitable giving, and the mode and timing of it, will depend also upon the nature and extent of the client's charitable interests and inclinations and competing concerns for family or other objects of his bounty.

2. *Charitable interests of client.* Normally the best candidates for a substantial charitable transaction, lifetime or testamentary, are those clients whose annual giving is more than nominal and those who are personally involved in one or more charitable organizations or activities. For those already committed to charitable endeavor, a more dramatic charitable transaction or a more ambitious charitable giving program will represent rather a fulfillment than an alteration of lifetime goals. In contrast, the client for whom "charity begins at home" (and ends there) may look upon the diversion of assets to charity as a dubious alternative to the payment of taxes.

3. *Family considerations.* For the client who has no family, or no

close family, or whose relatives' resources are already more than sufficient, charities may be in the forefront of potential beneficiaries. Such a
client may divide his entire estate among charitable donees, or he may
wish to make provisions for selected persons for life with charitable
remainders as discussed below in ¶203.10.

Most of our clients, of course, do have spouses, children, grandchildren, or some of these, and sometimes parents, siblings, and issue of
the latter. In these circumstances, the concerns for family and for charity
should be carefully weighed. A study of the tax considerations and the
variety of techniques covered in this chapter will assure that adequate
weight is given to the charitable possibilities in striking this balance.

[¶203]   HOW TO REDUCE ESTATE TAXES
VIA CHARITABLE TRANSFERS

We have considered the general scope of deductible charitable gifts
(¶201) and the several percentage limitations on gifts to qualified
charities (¶200.1). We have also reviewed the impact on the estate tax
of lifetime and testamentary gifts to charity, including the interplay of
marital and charitable deductions (¶201). In ¶202, we mentioned certain
nontax factors to be taken into account. We turn now to the development of strategies for charitable giving to maximize the tax advantages
of such gifts in the context of the foregoing considerations and limitations.

[¶203.1]   Strategies for Outright Lifetime Transfers

In the development of a charitable giving program, we are obviously not compelled to choose on an either/or basis between lifetime and
testamentary gifts. Nor are we restricted, within either of those broad
categories, to the selection of any particular mode of giving. Indeed, a
sound program may include a number of techniques, taking into account the client's charitable and family objectives, the types of property
available for a gift program, and his income and estate tax considerations.
    Even the most sophisticated program need not preclude the mak-
ing of lifetime gifts to charity of cash or other property, with no strings
attached. And even within this category of simple outright gifts, there
are strategic considerations.
    Cash gifts to qualified charities bring into play only the applicable
percentage limitations. Other types of property and interests in property

may involve potential losses or gains, the ramifications of which are discussed below.

[¶203.2]   Gifts of "Loss" Property

Where the taxpayer wishes to make a gift to charity of property which has declined in value, he should be advised to sell the property and contribute the proceeds instead. Assume, for example, that he has an asset with a market value of $1,000 and a cost basis of $2,000. If he contributes the property he will have a deduction of $1,000. If he sells the property and contributes the proceeds, he will have a deduction of $1,000, and he will also have generated a $1,000 loss.

[¶203.3]   Gifts of Ordinary Income
and Short-Term Gain Property

The deduction is limited to cost basis in the case of property which falls within one of these categories—

1. Property the sale of which would produce ordinary income, such as inventory, Section 306 stock, collapsible corporation stock, crops, art works created by the taxpayer.
2. Property the sale of which would produce a short term capital gain, e.g., securities, real estate, or taxable personal property held for less than one year.

When such property is given to charity the taxpayer deducts his cost basis[10] and not the full market value of the property. He will, however, avoid the tax on the ordinary income which sale of the asset would produce, and the charity will give him credit (toward his pledge or otherwise) for the full market value of the property.

[¶203.4]   Gifts of Long-Term Gain Property

Generally, capital assets held more than one year are deductible at full market value, regardless of cost, with no recognized gain on the appreciation. This combination of features can reduce substantially the cost of a charitable gift.

Consider the following illustration, involving a donor who is married and files a joint income tax return with his wife. He has an adjusted

[10]Different treatment is provided for corporations under Section 170(e)(3).

gross income of $250,000 and a taxable ordinary income (not subject to maximum tax on earned income, and after all deductions other than charitable deductions) of $200,000. He has securities, held more than six months, having a current market value of $60,000 which he acquired at a cost of $10,000.

If the taxpayer sells the securities during the taxable year his income tax will be as follows:

Tax on $200,000 or ordinary income	$110,980
Tax (at 25 percent) on long-term capital gain of $50,000	12,500
Income tax payable	$123,480

If he gives the securities to charity, instead of selling them, his income tax will be altered as follows:

Taxable ordinary income	$200,000
Deduction for gift to charity	60,000
Net taxable income	140,000
Income tax payable	$ 70,380

Compare the taxpayer's net cash position in those two situations —

Where taxpayer sells the securities:

Adjusted gross income		$250,000
Proceeds of sale of securities		60,000
		$310,000
Less: Tax on $200,000 net income	110,980	
Tax on $50,000 capital gain	12,500	
		123,480
Net cash retained		$186,520

Where taxpayer gives the secutities to charity:

Adjusted gross income	$250,000
Tax on net income of $140,000	70,380
Net cash retained	$179,620

Comparison:

Net cash retained—securities held	$186,520
Net cash retained—securities contributed	179,620
Cost of $60,000 donation	$ 6,900

The tax advantage above illustrated would be increased if State or local income taxes also apply, or if the taxpayer is unmarried and does not have the advantage of income splitting. Note, also, that the capital gains tax increases up to a maximum of 35 percent where a taxpayer's long-term capital gain in any taxable year exceeds $50,000.

In connection with gifts of appreciated property the following additional aspects and caveats should be borne in mind:

1. With a gift of real estate, it is important to ascertain that the property is a capital asset in the donor's hands. If the donor is a real estate dealer, his deduction would be limited to his cost basis, as with ordinary income property generally.

2. With a gift of tangible personal property, the deduction will be reduced by one-half of the unrealized gain unless the property is related to the tax-exempt function of the donee. If a painting is contributed to an art musuem, its full market value is deductible; if contributed to a church which plans to sell it and use the cash for other purposes, the deduction is reduced by one-half of the amount by which its market value exceeds its cost basis.

3. In a gift to a charity to which a 50 percent deduction is otherwise permitted, the 30 percent limitation on appreciated property presents no problem if it does not reduce the charitable giving intended by the donor. Otherwise, the deductible amount may be reduced either (a) to 30 percent of the contribution base or (b) by an amount equal to 50 percent of the gain which would be realized if the property were sold, whichever the taxpayer chooses (See ¶200.1). If reduction results in a substantial carryover of unused contributions, he may prefer to elect the (b) alternative.

Where the contribution would exceed the 30 percent limitation, the smaller the appreciation the greater is the advantage of electing the (b) alternative. For example, if the property has a market value of $10,000 and a cost basis of $9,990, the election will increase the percentage limitation for this property to 50 percent while the amount of the deduction will be $9,995, a reduction of only $5.

4. In a gift to a private nonoperating foundation to which the 20 percent deduction applies, the deduction is reduced by 50 percent[11] of

---

[11] 62.5 percent in the case of a corporate donor.

the amount of the gain which would have been long-term capital gain on sale of the property at its fair market value.

5. Where capital gain property also has an ordinary income aspect, such as property subject to the recapture of depreciation under Sec. 1245 or 1250 of the Code, the taxpayer will lose the amount of the recapture for deduction purposes.

Putting aside the special considerations we have noted with respect to tangible personal property and various types of ordinary income and short-term gain property, the planning considerations affecting gifts of appreciated property to charity involve mainly:

(a) the effects of the 20 percent, 30 percent and 50 percent limitations;
(b) the option of reducing the amount contributed by one-half of the appreciation by electing to raise the percentage limitation from 30 percent to 50 percent; and
(c) the effects of the carryover provisions.

On consideration of the foregoing discussion of these interrelated factors, certain guidelines may be offered:

1. Where the taxpayer wishes to give a certain amount to a charity to which the 50 percent deduction applies, a gift of appreciated long-term capital gain property[12] up to 30 percent of the taxpayer's contribution base is preferable to a gift of cash, if the appreciation has been substantial.

2. Where the desired gift of long-term capital gain property will exceed 30 percent of the donor's contribution base, generally the smaller the gain the greater the advantage of electing to raise the deduction limit to 50 percent at the cost of losing the deduction for 50 percent of the appreciation.

3. Where the taxpayer desires to maximize his current deduction in preference to a carryover, it is advisable to calculate the effect of contributing the appreciated property up to the 30 percent limit and selling appreciated property; then contributing the proceeds to the extent of the excess contribution desired. If the appreciated assets have different percentages of appreciation, selection of higher-basis assets for sale will minimize the recognized gain. Also, the sale will increase the taxpayer's adjusted gross income, thus enlarging his contribution base and the amount which is deductible for gifts to charity. Depending on all the facts, the result of a partial sale in lieu of an election may be more

[12]Other than tangible personal property unrelated to the donee's exempt purpose.

favorable than the alternative result of the election and carryover.

4. The taxpayer should not make a contribution to a 20 percent charity in a year in which his gifts of long-term capital gain property to 50 percent charities exceed 50 percent of his contribution base. Nor should his gifts to a 20 percent charity in any year exceed the amount by which 50 percent of his contribution base is greater than the amount of his gifts to 50 percent charities.

[¶203.5]   Bargain Sale of Long-Term Gain Property

In the heading of ¶203 we referred to "charitable transfers" rather than "charitable gifts" because certain transactions include nongift elements. Such a transaction is the so-called "bargain sale."

Prior to TRA 69, the bargain sale was a favored device for charitable deduction purposes. A taxpayer could sell appreciated property to a charity for a price equal to his cost basis, report no gain on the sale, and deduct the amount of the appreciation. On an asset having a cost basis of $10,000 and a market value of $30,000, the taxpayer would receive tax-free sale proceeds of $10,000 and a charitable deduction of $20,000.

TRA 69 required the taxpayer to allocate basis, thus eliminating the major element of the bargain sale's appeal. Basis must be allocated pro rata between the sale price and the contributed amount. This is the formula:

$$\frac{\text{Sale price}}{\text{Fair market value}} \times \text{Adjusted basis} = \text{Amount of basis apportioned to sale}$$

Applying this formula to the figures used in the preceding paragraph, we have:

$$\frac{10,000}{\$30,000} \times \$10,000 = \$3,333$$

The taxpayer would report a gain of $6,666 (sale price, $10,000, minus basis allocated to the sale transaction, $3,333).

Assuming the sale price covers the cost basis, there would be no charitable deduction in the case of ordinary income property. In the case of long-term capital gain property, the gift (nonsale) portion of the transaction is subject to all the rules and restrictions applicable to gifts to appreciated property where capital gain treatment would result from its sale. (For treatment of gifts of ordinary income property and capital gain property, see ¶203.3 and 203.4, above.)

A similar transaction is deemed to occur when a taxpayer transfers appreciated property subject to a mortgage or other debt, even if the transferee does not agree to pay or assume the indebtedness. The amount of the obligation is treated as if it were the bargain sale price, so that the donor is taxable on a gain computed in accordance with the example given above.

Where the taxpayer transfers property to a charity in exchange for an annuity, the bargain sale rules also apply. The difference between the present value of the annuity[13] and the market value of the property represents the charitable contribution. The basis of the property is apportioned between the sale price (present value of the annuity) and the contribution portion according to the formula set forth above. The resulting capital gain in the sale element of the transaction is reported by the taxpayer over a period of his life expectancy. The annual annuity payment multiplied by his life expectancy indicates the gross annuity proceeds. Of this amount, the present value of the annuity is excluded for tax purposes, and the percentage which the balance represents is applied to the annual payment and the resulting figure is reported annually as ordinary income.

Accordingly, for the period of the taxpayer's life expectancy, a portion of each annuity payment is exluded, a portion is taxed as capital gain, and a portion is taxed as ordinary income. If he lives beyond that period, he pays tax thereafter only on the ordinary income portion.

The bargain sale prior to TRA 69 was a useful device for the taxpayer who held appreciated property and was willing to give away his profit but not his investment. Or where the property otherwise exceeded either the allowable percentage limitation or the amount the taxpayer was willing to contribute. As noted above, he could accomplish his purpose without being taxed on any part of the appreciation. With the less favorable tax treatment which is now applicable, such a taxpayer may wish to consider as an alternative the use of a pooled income fund. This device permits a donor to enjoy an economic benefit from the transferred property, and to take a charitable deduction for the remainder interest, without incurring capital gains tax in the transaction. The pooled income fund is discussed in [¶203.10].

[¶203.6]   Gifts of Fractional Interests in Property

In the preceding sections we have dealt with transfers (gifts and bargain sales) of assets in their entirety. The taxpayer in our examples has transferred to charity a certain amount of cash or a certain number

---

[13]Determined in accordance with Sec. 101(b) of the Code, Reg. Sec. 1.101-2(e)(1)(iii)(b)(2), Reg. Sec. 1.102, and section 3 of Rev. Rul. 62-216, C.B. 1962-2,30.

of shares of stock or certain items of inventory or a certain parcel of land.

Where the amount or value of the property which the taxpayer donates exceeds the applicable deduction limits, the excess may in certain cases, as we have seen, be carried forward to the succeeding five years.

However, the five-year carryover has these limitations:

☐ If the intended donee is one to which the 20 percent limitation applies, no carryover will be permitted.

☐ If the taxpayer dies within the carryover period, the unused portion of it will be wasted.

☐ A taxpayer whose income fluctuates considerably cannot be certain that he will be able to utilize the excess contribution within the five-year period.

For these reasons, as an alternative to an excess contribution where the circumstances permit partial deferral of the gift, the taxpayer may be advised to donate the deductible amount in the current year and to make supplemental gifts in one or more following years. It is quite easy to do this with cash and it is normally feasible with securities. A tract of land presents greater difficulty. If it is feasible to divide the land into several parcels, the parcels can be donated seriatim. Where that is not feasible, it may be possible to solve the problem via gifts of fractional interests.

By deed conveying a fractional interest, e.g., an undivided one-fourth interest in the property, the donee becomes a tenant in common with the donor, who deducts the market value of the transferred interest.[14] In the following year or years, the donor may convey a similar or a different fraction, or the entire balance, depending on that year's deduction limits and his other charitible objectives. During the period of the tenancy-in-common the donor and the charity should divide the rentals or possession, as the case may be, in the proportion of their respective interests.

As to each gift of a fractional interest, of course, all of the rules and guidelines above set forth will apply. These include percentage limitations, and treatment of loss property, ordinary income and short-term gain property, and long-term gain property.

---

[14]*Caveat*—See ¶203.5 as to treatment of appreciated property subject to a mortgage.

[¶203.7]   Strategies for Lifetime Gifts
With Interests Retained

In connection with lifetime gifts to charity, there are two situations in which we are concerned as to includibility and deductibility for estate tax purposes:

☐ Where a simple outright gift will result in a diminished marital deduction, and a larger marital deduction would save estate taxes.

☐ Where the donor has retained such an interest in the transferred property that it will be includible in his gross estate, and the inclusion will result in higher taxes if the transfer is not deductible for estate tax purposes.

In situation (1) the chief problem is to arrange for the value of the transferred property to be *includible*. In situation (2), the primary goal is to assure that it will be *deductible*. Let us consider these matters further, in that order:

1. *The "includibility" cases.*

The charitable transfers discussed in ¶203.2 through 203.6 may produce estate tax savings simply by reducing the donor's gross estate. [We dealt mainly with the income tax treatment of those transfers because the income tax deduction is the only tax incentive (as distinguished from charitable incentive) to make such transfers during lifetime rather than at death.]

There are cases, however, in which the estate tax in the donor's estate will be greater if the gift is made during lifetime than it would be if the gift were deferred until death. As explained and illustrated in [¶201], this is due to the interrelation of the marital and charitable deductions. As we stated there, where the adjusted gross estate exceeds $500,000, the amount of the allowable marital deduction is reduced by 50 percent of all amounts which are given away during lifetime and which are *removed from the decedent's gross estate.*

The simple outright lifetime gift to charity creates no adverse estate tax effect where —

1. the Section 2503 deductions and the available credits will be sufficient to eliminate the estate tax, or

2. the marital deduction computed on the remaining estate, in combination with the other deductions and the available credits, will be sufficient to eliminate the estate tax, or

3. there will be no marital deduction, so that the issue of lifetime

vs. testamentary charitable transfers is a matter of indifference with respect to the estate tax.

Where the outright lifetime gift to charity does have an adverse estate tax effect, by reducing the allowable marital deduction, this occurs because the subject of the gift is removed from the donor's gross estate, so that 50 percent of the adjusted gross estate is a lower figure. The only remedies, therefore, are those which will cause the value of the transferred property to be *included* in the gross estate (such value also to be deductible for estate tax purposes).

The problem will be cured, though not by design, where the donor's death occurs within three years following the lifetime gift to charity. The transfer will then be included in the gross estate under Sec. 2035 of the Code.

Another cure, or course, is to defer the gift until death and accomplish it by will or other "testamentary" device. This decision requires the donor to weigh the estate tax advantage of deferral against the income tax benefits and the nontax advantages of a current lifetime gift.

In some cases, however, by attaching certain "strings" to the lifetime gift, the donor can cause the gift to be included in his gross estate (thus maximizing this marital deduction) and he can also enjoy the benefit of a current income tax deduction. Examples of such techniques are presented in [¶203.8 and 203.9].

2. *The "deductibility" cases.*

In the "includibility" section we were dealing essentially with cases in which the donor's desire was simply to make an outright lifetime gift to charity, but doing so might have an estate tax "cost" resulting from a diminished marital deduction. The problem was to keep the value of the gift property in the gross estate, either by deferring the gift or attaching appropriate "strings" to it.

In other cases, the donor may wish to make a lifetime gift and to obtain an income tax deduction for it, but he may also need or desire to retain an interest in the transferred property. He may wish, for example, to retain the income of the property for life or for a stated period, or he may wish to give the income or enjoyment to charity but have the entire property return to him or to his estate after a stated period or upon his death.

Such a donor gives to charity not "the property" as a whole but rather a present interest or a future interest in the property. Where the interest which he retains causes the value of the property (or some part of it) to be included in his gross estate, and deduction of all or part of it would reduce estate taxes, our goal is to assure that the amount so included is also deductible. Such split-interest gifts[15] and the criteria for deductibility are discussed in [¶203.10 through 203.15].

[¶203.8]   Gifts of Life Insurance Policies

Life insurance policies, like cash, securities and other property can be given to charity. For persons of modest means, life insurance is a device which makes it possible to make a substantial gift at relatively modest cost.

If the taxpayer makes an outright gift to charity of a policy which has cash value, he may deduct for income tax purposes the lesser of the cost basis (total premiums paid) or the policy's value as determined by Reg. Sec. 25.2512-6(a) (Rev. Rul. 59-145, 1959-1CB18). Any premiums subsequently paid by the taxpayer on such a policy can also be deducted. However, as there is a difference in percentage limitations as between gifts "to" and gifts "for the use of" charity (see ¶200.1), it may be advisable, where this is a concern, to make gifts of the premium amounts to the charity (which can then pay the premiums) rather than make payments directly to the insurer.

But where the taxpayer seeks both current income tax deductions and marital deduction maximization, he must so design the gift as to cause the insurance proceeds to be (a) includible in his gross estate and (b) deductible in computing his estate tax. In making noncharitable gifts of policies to individuals or trusts, where estate reduction is an objective, we must be certain that the insured retains no "incidents of ownership" in the policy (see Chapter 7). Here, our concern is the opposite: we must see that the taxpayer retains one or more incidents of ownership which will cause the policy to be included in his gross estate.

Assume that a taxpayer with a $1,200,000 adjusted gross estate and a 50 percent marital deduction desires to give a $200,000 policy on his life to charity. If he simply gives it to the charity, his estate tax would be calculated as follows:

Adjusted gross estate		$1,000,000
Marital deduction		500,000
Tentative tax base		500,000
Tax on tentative tax base		155,800
Less: Credit for State death taxes (if paid)	$10,000	
Unified credit	47,000	
		57,000
Estate tax payable		$ 98,800

---

[15]"Split-interest" gifts of this type are not to be confused with the fractional interest gifts discussed in ¶203.6. The latter are simple outright gifts where the subject of the gifts is an undivided interest in the property rather than the entire "fee."

If the taxpayer had given the policy to charity but retained suffi-cient "strings" to cause the proceeds to be includible in his gross estate, the estate tax calculation would be changed to this:

Adjusted gross estate		$1,200,000
Marital deduction	$600,000	
Charitable deduction	200,000	
		800,000
Tentative tax base		400,000
Tax on tentative tax base		121,800
Less: Credit for State death taxes (if paid)	$ 6,800	
Unified credit	47,000	
		53,800
Estate tax payable		$ 68,000

The second method gives the same $200,000 to charity but the donor's estate tax is reduced by $30,800 (98,800 minus $68,000).

If the policy involves annual premiums of $6,000 and the taxpayer is in a 50 percent income tax bracket, his actual cost under either ar-rangement is $3,000, as the amount of the premium is deductible. In the second arrangement, however, the estate tax saving of $30,800 will cover the actual cost of the premiums for ten years, so that his $200,000 gift to charity will cost him nothing if his death occurs within that period, and relatively little in any event.

But TRA 69, via amended Sec. 170(f)(3)(A) of the Code, has made it exceedingly difficult to obtain an income tax deduction for partial interest gifts to charity[16]. Specifically, with emphasis added:

"(A) In general—In case of a contribution (not made by a transfer in trust) of an interest in property which consists of *less than the taxpayer's entire interest in such property,* a deduction shall be allowed under this section only to the extent that the value of the interests contributed would be allowable under this section *if such interest had been transferred in trust* . . .

"(B) Exceptions—Subparagraph (A) shall not apply to a contribution of—

"(i) a remainder interest in a personal residence or farm, or

"(ii) *an undivided portion of the taxpayer's entire interest in property."*

And Reg. Sec. 1.170-7(b)(1)(i) adds:

"An undivided portion of a donor's entire interest in property must consist of a fraction or percentage of each and every right owned by the donor in such property and must extend over the entire term of the

[16]See Rev. Rul. 76-1 and Rev. Rul. 76-143.

donor's interest in such property and in other property into which such property is converted."

As a transfer of a policy in trust will not meet the requirements of Sec. 170(f)(2)(A), there will be no income tax deduction unless the gift either comprises the taxpayer's "entire interest" or fits within the above-quoted Sec. 170(f)(3)(B)(ii) exception.

The ultimate question is whether the taxpayer can reserve some kind of power over the policy which (a) will cause it to be included in his gross estate and (b) will not cause loss of the income tax deduction because the subject of the gift is only a partial interest in the policy. The powers most frequently suggested for retention are a power to select a settlement option for the charity and a power to change the charitable beneficiary or beneficiaries. Such powers should be effective to cause inclusion in the gross estate (possibly under Sec. 2038 rather than Sec. 2042(2) of the Code). And it is arguable that the gift subject to these powers is not a gift of less than the taxpayer's entire interest, as the donor cannot defeat the charity's interest and no economic benefit is reserved to the donor or his estate, so that the income tax deduction should not be lost. The counselor who attempts this combination of benefits must recognize, however, that the ground on which he takes his position is far from firm.

[¶203.9]   Gifts to a Family or Private Foundation

The taxpayer who is willing to make a substantial gift to charity, without retaining the income or any future interest for himself or others, can do so via a simple outright gift. If the amount involved exceeds the applicable percentage limitation, he can spread his gift over a number of years.

Such gifts, however, will not provide the maximum tax advantage, as explained in [¶203.7], for the taxpayer whose estate will be adversely affected by a diminished marital deduction.

To solve this problem the taxpayer can establish a trust (or corporation, as discussed below) and make gifts (within the 20 percent limitation) to that trust for the benefit of charity. If he retains such rights or powers as to cause the trust principal to be included in his gross estate under Sec. 2036 or 2038 of the Code, he will enjoy current income tax deductions and his marital deduction will not be diminished by the transfers. His power as trustee or co-trustee to designate the charitable beneficiaries from time to time will normally be sufficient for this purpose.

In such cases, the taxpayer enjoys the tax benefits without completely losing control of the transferred property. The selection of particular charities, and the selection of charitable interests or goals, need not be fixed at the time of the gift or gifts.

A taxpayer whose income fluctuates can make larger gifts in high income years while the trustees maintain an even flow of distributions to the objects of his bounty. The trust or corporation so established can also serve as a receptacle for gifts by family members and others, including the founder's corporation, and additional gifts can be made by will.

Also, while income accumulations are no longer permitted as a general rule (see paragraph 3 below), the taxpayer who wishes to make a major charitable contribution at some future time, and who would not ordinarily be able to do so on a current income or asset basis, can make annual deductible contributions to his private foundation which, at the appropriate time, can use its accumulated principal fund for a major charitable grant.

While the donors of private foundations sometimes prefer anonymity, others use their charitable trusts or corporations to heighten their profile of community involvement. Checks titled "The John Smith Foundation" or "The John and Mary Smith Foundation" can be a source of great satisfaction.

While such entities prior to TRA 69 were generally known as "family foundations" or "private foundations," these terms had no special tax status prior to that Act. Under TRA 69, however, a "private foundation" is subject to new taxes and to a variety of new requirements and sanctions.

Prior to TRA 69, foundations of the family or private type were not infrequently used or abused for private rather than charitable advantage. Common practices included various types of self-dealing, use of the foundation to control corporate businesses, and delay in the shift of funds to charitable uses. To correct these and other practices, TRA 69 imposed extensive regulations and severe sanctions on "private foundations," with penalties extending to the foundation and its managers, and, in some cases, to donors and related parties.

A "private foundation" is defined (in Sec. 509(a) of the Code) in terms of what is is *not*, i.e., as a 501(c)(3) organization which does not fall into any of these four categories:

☐ an organization which qualifies for the 50 percent limitation (see ¶200.1);

☐ a broadly based, publicly supported organization (including a membership organization) normally receiving more than one-third of its annual support from members and the general public and not more than one-third of its annual support from investment income;

☐ an organization organized and operated exclusively for the benefit of one or more organizations in the preceding two categories and controlled or operated by or in connection with one or more such organizations; or

☐ an organization organized and operated exclusively for testing for public safety.

A review of those four exceptions make it clear that most trusts and corporations of the type discussed in this ¶203.9 will be classed as, and governed by the rules pertaining to, "private foundations" under TRA 69.

It would take a book rather than a chapter fully to state and explain the taxes and rules which now govern private foundations. We can do no more here than mention the highlights, which are:

1. *Tax on net investment income.* For all taxable years beginning after December 31, 1969, an annual 4 percent excise tax is imposed on the net investment income of a private foundation (Sec. 4940 of the Code). Net investment income is gross investment income and net capital gain less expenses paid or incurred in earning the gross investment income. Gross investment income excludes unrelated business income (taxable under Sec. 511 of the Code), but includes interest, dividends, rents and royalties. Also included are capital gains and losses on capital assets used to produce gross investment income or unrelated business income, except to the extent they are used to compute unrelated business income tax.

2. *Prohibitions on self-dealing.* Under Sec. 4941 of the Code, these six types of transactions between a private foundation and a disqualified person are barred:

1. The sale, exchange or lease of property.
2. The lending of money or other extension of credit.
3. The furnishing of goods, services or facilities.
4. The payment of compensation or reimbursement of expenses to a disqualified person.
5. The transfer of foundation income or assets to, or use by or for the benefit of, a disqualified person.
6. The agreement by the private foundation to make any payment of money or other property to a government official (other than an agreement to employ him after termination of his government service if he is terminating it within a ninety day period).

There are certain exceptions to these prohibitions, such as:

(1) A disqualified person may lend money to the foundation if the loan does not require the payment of interest or any other charge and if the loan proceeds are used exclusively for Section 501(c)(3) purposes (See also Reg. Sec. 53.4941(d)-2(c)(2)).

(2) A disqualified person can furnish goods, services or facilities to the foundation if no charge is made and if they are used exclusively for Section 501(c)(3) purposes.

(3) The foundation can provide goods, services or facilities to a disqualified person where such furnishing is made on a basis no more favorable than that on which such items are made available to the general public.

(4) The foundation can pay reasonable compensnation to a disqualified person for personal services which are reasonable and necessary to carry out the exempt purposes of the foundation.

(5) Government officials may receive prizes, awards, scholarships, fellowships, and payment of certain domestic travel expenses.

A key element in several of the prohibited transactions is the disqualified person. Sec. 4946 defines a "disqualified person" as any of the following:

(1) a substantial contributor to the foundation (the creator of the trust *or* any other person [or corporation, trust, or other entity] who, alone or with a spouse, contributes or bequeaths, in the aggregate, more than $5,000 to the foundation, provided such amount exceeds 2 percent of the total gifts received by the foundation before the close of the tax year).

(2) a foundation manager (an officer, director or trustee, or a person with similar powers or responsibilities, or an employee with authority or responsibility for any of the acts within the self-dealing prohibitions).

(3) an individual who owns, directly or indirectly, more than 20% of a corporation of an interest in profits of a partnership or a trust or an unincorporated enterprise which is a substantial contributor to the foundation.

(4) a spouse, ancestor, lineal descendant, or spouse of a lineal descendant, of any of the persons above described.

(5) a corporation, partnership, trust or estate in which persons in any of the categories above described own or hold, directly or indirectly, more than a 35% interest.

(6) a government official.

Violations of the self-dealing prohibitions are subject to a graduated series of sanctions.

3. *Mandatory income payout.* Prior to TRA 69 (and despite the standards provided in Sec. 504 of the Code), it was frequently possible for a foundation to hold assets which produced little or no income or to delay for a considerable time the distribution of income to operating charities. As a result, the foundation's donor received a current deduction with no corresponding current benefit to charity.

Section 4942 of the code now prohibits most income accumulations. It imposes a graduated series of sanctions which compel the foundation to distribute its income and unrealized appreciation on a reasonably current basis.

To avoid the tax imposed on a percentage of its accumulated income, the foundation must distribute its income within the year received or the year following. Moreover, the payout (even if actual income is less) must be not less than a certain percentage of the foundation's aggregate noncharitable assets: TRA 69 provided 6 percent for 1970, the rate to be adjusted by IRS thereafter; TRA 76 sets it permanently at 5 percent.

The payments, to avoid penalties, must be "qualifying distributions" and reduce the foundation's "distributable amount" (Sec. 4942(g)(1) of the Code). If it distributes more than the required minimum in any year, the foundation is permitted to apply the excess against its payout requirements for the following five years (Sec. 4942(i) of the Code).

The mandatory pay-out rules can be avoided under certain circumstances. For taxable years beginning after 1974 (see Sec. 4942(g)(2) of the Code), a private foundation may "set aside" an amount for a special project and treat the amount as a qualifying distribution under the following conditions:

1. It must be established to the satisfaction of IRS that the amount will be paid for the project within five years and either:

(a) It is established to the satisfaction of IRS that the project is one that can better be accomplished by the set-aside than by immediate payment of funds, or

(b) the project will not be completed before the end of the year of the set-aside, and:

(1) In each taxable year beginning after 1975 (or, in the case of a newly created foundation, after the end of the fourth taxable year following the year of creation), the foundation must make charitable disbursements in an amount not less than the minimum required payment.

(2) During the four taxable years prior to its first taxable year beginning after 1975 (or, if later, after the end of the fourth taxable year after creation of the foundation), the foundation has distributed a total amount not less than the sum of the following:

—80 percent of the first preceding taxable year's regular required payout,

—60 percent of the second preceding taxable year's regular required payout,

—40 percent of the third preceding taxable year's regular required payout, and

—20 percent of the fourth preceding taxable year's regular required payout.

4. *Restrictions on unrelated business holdings.* By means of the provisions of Sec. 4943 of the Code, TRA 69 endeavors to end abuses

relating to private foundation interests in closely held businesses. Prior to TRA 69, it was frequently possible and extremely advantageous for a taxpayer to transfer to a private foundation shares of stock of a family business, taking a tax deduction for their value, retaining control of the business and all of his lifetime benefits, and avoiding estate tax on the transferred shares. With little or no benefit to charity, the taxpayer obtained substantial tax deductions and control of the business could be kept in the family indefinitely.

These games are somewhat, but not entirely, curtailed by Section 4943. As to stock held on or before May 26, 1969, the foundation and all disqualified persons can retain up to 50 percent ownership, and excess holdings (depending on amount) can be retained up to 10, 15 or 20 years. For newly acquired stock, the limit is 20 percent, but this is increased to 35 percent if unrelated third parties effectively control the business. If all disqualified persons own not more than 20 percent of the voting stock, the foundation may hold unlimited amounts of nonvoting stock.

Under Sec. 4943(d)(1), constructive ownership rules are introduced into the excess holding computations. Stock or other interests owned directly or indirectly by corporations, partnerships, trusts and estates are attributed proportionately to their respective shareholders, partners, and beneficiaries, in determining the interests held by the foundation or disqualified persons.

As in the case of other TRA 69 structures, multiple-level tax sanctions are imposed for violations.

An exception to the divestment rules is made for functionally related businesses (Sec. 4943(d)(4)(A) of the Code) and those in which 95 percent of the income is derived from passive sources (Sec. 4943(d)(4)(B)).

The new rules leave some room for foundation ownership of interests in family or other business interests unrelated to the charitable purpose. Where this is of interest to the client, the rules must be studied with great care.

5. *Prohibition against speculative investments.* Sec. 504 of the Code. repealed for taxable years after 1969, provided loss of exemption for foundations which invested their accumulated income in such manner as to jeopardize their tax exempt purposes. Section 4944 now imposes progressive tax sanctions (rather than loss of exemption) on foundations which make speculative investments of principal or accumulated income. Tax sactions are also imposed on a foundation manager who, without reasonable cause, willfully participates in making investments which jeopardize the foundation's exempt purpose.

A "prudent man" rule is applied to judge investments as of their dates of acquisition. A violation is cured when the investment is sold or otherwise disposed of and the proceeds are not again placed in jeopardy.

An exception is made for the use of funds to advance the exempt purpose (expenditures rather than investments), such as loans to needy students, small business loans, or investments in low-income housing.

6. *Political activities and private grants.* Under Sec. 170(c) of the Code, a deduction is not permitted for a gift to a foundation if the foundation is disqualified for tax exemption under Sec. 501(c)(3) by reason of attempting to influence legislation or participating or intervening in any political campaign on behalf of any candidate for public office. Section 501(c)(3) requires, apart from political campaigns, that no substantial part of a foundation's activities constitute the carrying on of propaganda or otherwise attempting to influence legislation. (Liberalized rules provided by TRA 76 appl; only to public charities.)

Lobbying and electioneering activities were further restricted by TRA 69 (Sec. 4945 of the Code), which also tightened the rules on grants by private foundations to individuals and to organizations other than public charities.

"Taxable expenditures" for lobbying, electioneering (including voter registration drives), grants to individuals (unless made in accordance with objective standards), grants to other organizations (unless the foundation accepts "expenditure responsibility"), and grants for any purpose not exempt under Section 501(c)(3), are penalized by multilevel taxes and other sanctions. We can do no more here than to counsel careful study of the applicable rules where any such expenditure is contemplated by or for a proposed or existing private foundation.

The private foundation, which is subject to the rules briefly summarized above, may be established in the form of a trust or a (nonprofit) corporation. Apart from the intial State contact on formation, which normally a corporation requires and a trust does not, the choice of entity may be affected by differences in the amount of governmental oversight and differences in the agencies having jurisdiction. These differences and others vary from State to State. Generally, distinctions between corporations and trusts with respect to powers, duties, and responsibilities of directors and trustees; their appointment, resignation and removal; investment standards; and amendment and termination of the foundation, can be eliminated in the preparation of the governing instruments.[17]

[17]For an excellent discussion of this subject, see Marion R. Fremont-Smith, *Foundations and Government: State and Federal Law and Supervision* (New York, Russell Sage Foundation, 1965), p. 154. See also Edith L. Fisch, "Choosing the Charitable Entity," 114 Trusts & Estates 874 (December 1975).

A foundation which meets the requirements of Sec. 501(c)(3) of the Code is not automatically exempt from income tax. It must first file an exemption application with IRS and obtain a favorable determination. Included in Appendix C are samples of a private foundation trust document, the related application to IRS, and an IRS determination letter.

When a private foundation is contemplated, for the requisite charitable purposes and for the tax benefits outlined in this Chapter, the estate planner should also study the rules relating to voluntary and involuntary termination of exempt status and the rules (expanded by TRA 69) for information reporting by private foundations and their managers.

[¶203.10]   Charitable Remainder Trusts

If the taxpayer transfers property to a charitable remainder annuity trust as described in Sec. 664(d)(1) of the Code, a charitable remainder unitrust as described in Sec. 664(d)(2), or a pooled income fund as described in Sec. 642(c)(5), the fair market value of the remainder interest[18] is deductible for income tax purposes under Sec. 170(f)(2)(A). The value of the remainder interest is also deductible for gift tax purposes (Sec. 2522 (c)(2)(A)).

If the taxpayer is the only noncharitable beneficiary (i.e., the "income" is reserved to him alone for life), the value of the remainder interest is includible in his gross estate under Sec. 2036 of the Code and deductible under Sec. 2055. Such a gift, therefore, provides a combination of lifetime income tax and portmortem estate tax benefits.[19]

The trusts which qualify for this tax treatment are these:

☐ Charitable remainder annuity trust. This is a trust from which a specified sum is to be paid, at least annually, to one or more persons[20] for a term of years (not exceeding 20) or for the life or lives of the individual or individuals. The specified sum must be not less than 5 percent of the initial fair market value of the property placed in trust.

---

[18]The value of a remainder interest in an annuity trust is determined under Reg. Sec. 1.664-2(c); the value of a remainder interest in a unitrust is determined under Reg. Sec. 1.664-4; and the value of a remainder interest in a pooled income fund is determined under Reg. Sec. 1.642(c)-6. If the value is dependent on the term of more than one life, a special factor may be found in Publication 723 or 723A.

[19]If another person succeeds the taxpayer as beneficiary, his interest would normally be subject to gift tax, and it would also be subject to estate tax in the donor's estate.

[20]At least one of which is not a Sec. 170(c) organization, and, in the case of individuals, only to an individual living at the time of the creation of the trust.

Except for these annuity payments, no amount may be paid from the trust to or for the use of any person other than a Sec. 170(c) charity. Upon termination of the annuity payments, the remainder interest must be transferred to or retained for the use of a Sec. 170(c) charity. And no property can be added to the trust following the initial contribution.

☐ Charitable remainder unitrust. This is a trust from which a fixed percentage (not less than 5 percent) of the net fair market value of the trust assets (valued annually) must be paid, at least annually, to one or more persons[20] for a term of years (not exceeding 20) or for the life or lives of such individual or individuals. Except for these percentage payments, no amount may be paid from the trust to or for the use of any person other than a Sec. 170(c) charity. Upon termination of the unitrust payments, the remainder interest must be transferred to or retained for the use of a Sec. 170(c) charity. Additional contributions can be made to the unitrust if the governing instrument so provides.

☐ Charitable remainder "income-only" unitrust. As a variant of the unitrust above described, the trust instrument may provide for the trustee to pay to the income beneficiary for any year (a) the lesser of (1) the trust income or (2) the percentage amount otherwise required to be distributed, and (b) whenever the trust income exceeds the percentage amount, so much of the excess as will make up any deficit incurred in prior years.[21] (Otherwise, the description of the unitrust set forth in the preceding paragraph applies.)

(NOTE: With respect to annuity trusts and unitrusts, Rev. Rul. 72-395, 1972-2 Cum. Bull. 340, a copy of which is included in Appendix B, provides sample provisions for meeting the mandatory requirements referred to in the Regulations. Also, the trust instrument must not include any provision which prevents the trustee from investing the assets in a manner which could result in the annual realization of a reasonable amount of income or gain from the sale or disposition of trust assets (Reg. Sec. 1.664-1(a)(3)). Normally, no capital gain is realized on the transfer of appreciated property to such a trust, but if the trustee has an express or implied obligation to sell or exchange such property and purchase tax-exempt securities, the donor will be deemed to have given the proceeds of the sale or exchange, so that the gain is includible in his gross income (Rev. Rul. 60-370, 1960-2 Cum. Bull. 203, 205)).

☐ Pooled income fund. This is a trust created by a charity, rather than a donor, in which the remainder interests of a number of donors are commingled. Such a trust has these characteristics[22]:

[21]The Code appears to require both (a) and (b). However, Reg. Sec. 1.664-3(b) and Sec. 7.01 of Rev. Rul. 72-395, 1972-2 Cum. Bull. 340, indicate that the "make-up" provision is not mandatory.

[22]For definitions of terms used below and for detailed requirements for qualification of such a fund, see Reg. Sec. 1.642(c)-(5).

1. The taxpayer transfers property to the trust, giving an irrevocable remainder interest to or for the use of an organization gifts to which qualify for the 50 percent limitation, and retains an income interest for the life or lives of one or more beneficiaries who are living at the time of the transfer.
2. The property so transferred is mingled with property similarly transferred by other donors.
3. The trust cannot have investments in tax-exempt securities.
4. The trust can hold only amounts received in accordance with the pooled income fund characteristics here listed.
5. The trust is maintained by the organization to which the remainder interest is given, and no donor or income beneficiary is a trustee of it.
6. Each income beneficiary receives income each year determined by the trust's rate of return for that year.

(NOTES: (1) Rev. Rul. 72-196, 1972-1 Cum. Bull. 194, a copy of which is included in Appendix C, provides forms for some pertinent provisions. (2) Generally no gain or loss is recognied on transfer of property to a pooled income fund, but if the transfer is made in exchange for property other than a life income interest, or if the transferred property is subject to an indebtedness, the bargain sale rules may apply. (See discussion of bargain sale, above, and Reg. Sec. 1.642(c)-5(a)(3).)

Under Sec. 4947 of the Code, the provisions of Sec. 507 (relating to termination of private foundation status, Sec. 508(e) (relating to governing instruments), and the private foundation restrictions against self-dealing (Sec. 4941), excess business holdings (Sec. 4943), jeopardy investments (Sec. 4944), and taxable expenditures (Sec. 4945), are applicable to the charitable remainder interests in the annuity trusts, unitrusts, and pooled income funds above described.

Prior to TRA 69, a taxpayer could make a transfer to or in trust for a charitable organization, retaining the income or a fixed annual sum for life. He could even provide for principal invasion in accordance with an ascertainable standard (if the probability of invasion was either remote or reasonably predictable). The taxpayer could do this and obtain a tax deduction for the value of the transferred property in excess of the interest retained by the donor. TRA 69 has limited the deductibility of charitable remainder interests (except in the case of a personal residence or farm, as discussed below) to the relatively rigid annuity trusts, unitrusts, and pooled income funds.

From the foregoing discussion, it will be clear that the criteria for deductibility of charitable remainder gifts are (a) extremely rigid and (b) highly technical. Nevertheless, such gifts continue to be useful in their income and estate tax aspects and beneficial in a variety of additional ways. They are of particular interest to the taxpayer who wishes to make substantial gifts but is unable or reluctant to give up the income produced by the property involved. Such gifts will be advisable if these criteria are met:

☐ There is an identifiable need for the income on the part of the donor or some other noncharitable party;

☐ the taxpayer will be able to make full use of the contribution deduction; and

☐ adequate provision can be made for his heirs (if any).

For the taxpayer who needs or desires a fixed annual dollar amount, the annuity trust is the ideal vehicle for a charitable remainder trust. He will receive each year a fixed percentage (not less than 5 percent) of the initial value of the trust principal. The "income" he receives will not keep pace with inflation, but neither will it fluctuate. Assuming other resources are available for increased expenses or emergency needs, this arrangement may be quite suitable.

The unitrust, in contrast, does provide a hedge against inflation. The donor receives a fixed percentage (not less than 5 percent) of the net fair market value of the trust principal, valued annually. Assuming the trust is established with $100,000, with 5 percent to be paid each year to the donor, and that the value of the principal for the first three years is $100,000, $105,000, and $110,000, the donor will receive $5,000, $5,250 and $5,500 for those years.

For a taxpayer who does not need additional income currently, but will need it after his retirement in several years, an "income only" unitrust with a "catch-up" provision may be the optimum device. Assume, for example, that a $100,000 trust specifying a 5 percent return is invested for five years prior to the donor's retirement in assets yielding a 2 percent return but growing at the rate of 8 percent per year. A deficiency of $17,600 will accumulate while the trust pays out its actual 2 percent return. If the trust assets are invested following the donor's retirement to yield 7 percent, the trust can pay 7 percent to the donor until the $17,600 deficiency has been made up. Thereafter the trust returns to paying its actual income each year but not more than 5 percent.

While the annuity trusts and unitrusts are relatively impractical for modest gifts, the pooled income fund is not. A gift to a pooled income fund is both easy and economical. And the pooling of many gifts makes it possible to invest them as part of a larger fund that can be diversified for the protection of all of the fund's donors.

All of these devices enable the donor to diversify the assets placed in trust without losing any of the property value through capital gains taxes. Except for the specific capital gains hazard above specified, the appreciation is not taxed to the donor at the time of the transfer, and neither he nor the trust incurs tax when the assets are sold. As a result, the full amount remains available to yield the income which the taxpayer has reserved.

Similarly, the transfer of low basis property which yields a modest return permits reinvestment in assets yielding a better return without loss of a portion of the fund through capital gains taxes.

For a tabular comparison of the four types of remainder trust gifts we have discussed, see George E. Thomsen, "Split Interest Gifts to Charity," 7 *Real Property, Probate and Trust Journal* 552, 560 (Fall 1972). For a comprehensive total-benefit approach to choosing between an annuity trust and a unitrust, and for selecting the terms of the vehicle selected, see John Petroff, "How to Choose the Right Charitable Remainder Trust," 114 *Trusts & Estates* 870 (December 1975).

[¶203.11]   Charitable Remainders—Homes and Farms

Where the subject of a proposed gift to charity is the taxpayer's personal residence or farm and the taxpayer desires to reserve a life estate, the unitrust, annuity trust and pooled income fund strictures described in ¶203.10 do not apply.

The value of the charitable remainder interest is deductible for income tax purposes (provided the interest retained is for the life of the donor or a term of years (Reg. Sec. 1.170A-7(b)(4)), and also for gift and estate tax purposes. (See Sec. 170(f)(3) of the Code; Reg. Sec. 1.170A-7(b)(3) and (4); Reg. Sec. 1.170A-12; and Code Sections 2522(c)(2) and 2055(e)(2). In determining the value of the remainder interest, cost depletion or straight-line depreciation which may affect the value must be taken into account, and a discount of 6 percent a year (or such other rate as the Government may determine) is applied for the period of the estate reserved to the donor (Sec. 170(f)(4) of the Code).

For purposes of tax deduction, a "personal residence" need not be the taxpayer's principal residence (Reg. Sec. 1.170A-7(b)(3)), and a "farm" means a farm used by the taxpayer or his tenant in the business of farming (Reg. Sec. 1.170A-7(b)(4)).

Remainder interests in homes and farms (unless they are placed in a unitrust, annuity trust or pooled income fund) will be deductible *only if the transfer is a nontrust gift.*

The purposes and criteria for using charitable remainder gifts as set forth in ¶203.10 apply to gifts of charitable remainder interests in homes and farms as well, so that they need not be repeated here.

[¶203.12]   Gifts of Income Interests

In ¶203.10 and ¶203.11 we considered split-interest gifts appropriate primarily to the taxpayer who is willing to give property to charity if he can do so without simultaneously surrendering the income it yields. Now we turn to the opposite case: the taxpayer who wishes to preserve property for himself or his heirs but is willing to pass its income to charity during his lifetime or for a certain period.

He may, as one option, establish a "Clifford Trust" under Sec. 673(a) of the Code. If the income is payable to charity for a period not less than ten years, the donor will avoid tax on the income for that period, and such income will pass tax-free to the charity. (If the period is less than ten years, the income will be taxed to the donor even though the charity receives it.)

In many cases, there is no advantage to be derived from a ten-year trust for charity. The income tax treatment is the same as if he had retained the property and contributed the income each year to charity, so long as his total contributions would not have exceeded his percentage limitations. In some cases, however, the trust will be useful because it permits the taxpayer to support a charity without regard to the applicable percentage limitations. His regular charitable giving can continue, except that the diversion of the trust income to charity will somewhat reduce his contribution base. However, unless the income interest qualifies as a guaranteed annuity interest or a unitrust interest as described below, its value will apparently not be deductible for gift tax or estate tax purposes.

In contrast with the above-described ten-year trust, which diverts income from the taxpayer to charity on an annual basis over the period involved, the taxpayer can obtain an immediate deduction for the value of an income interest passing to charity if he establishes one of the following types of trusts (and is taxed on the income thereof, as discussed below) with the required annual amounts passing to charity, to wit:

☐ A guaranteed annuity interest, with these characteristics (Reg. Sec. 1.170A-6(c)(2)(i)—

1. A guaranteed fixed amount;
2. The amount to be paid to the charity at least annually;
3. Payments to continue for the life or lives of a named individual or individuals or for a specified number of years;
4. If the present value of the annuity on the date of the gift exceeds 60 percent of the net value of the trust assets, the interest will not qualify as an annuity unless the trust instrument prohibits retention of assets which jeopardize the charitable purpose;
5. No amount may be paid for a private purpose before the charitable income interest terminates; and
6. Income in excess of the annuity amount may be payable to or for the use of charity.

☐ Unitrust with these characteristics (Reg. Sec. 1.170A-6(c)(2)(ii)—

7. A fixed percentage of the net fair market value of the trust assets, valued annually;

8. The amount to be paid to charity at least annually;

9. Payments to continue for the life or lives of a named individual or individuals or for a specified number of years;

10. If the present value of the annuity on the date of the gift exceeds 60 percent of the net value of the trust assets, the interest will not qualify as a unitrust unless the trust instrument prohibits the retention of assets which jeopardize the charitable purpose; and

11. Income in excess of the unitrust amount may be payable to or for the use of charity.

In addition to meeting the foregoing requirements, the donor must be taxed as owner of the trust assets (under Sec. 671 of the Code). If he ceases to be treated as owner (e.g., upon his death), he will be considered as having received income equal to the amount of any deduction he received reduced by the discounted value of all income earned by the trust and taxable to him before the time at which he ceased to be treated as the owner of the interest. (Sec. 170(f)(2)(B) of the Code and Reg. Sec. 1.170A-6(c)(4).)

The income tax deduction for the annuity or unitrust interest is limited to the minimum amount which the charity will receive (Reg. Sec. 1.170A-6(c)(3)(iii)). The gift is subject to the 20 percent limitation, with no carryover (Sec. 170(b)(1)(B) of the Code). As to valuation of such interests, see Reg. Sec. 1.170A-6(c)(3).

Such a transfer is deductible for gift tax purposes (Sec. 2522 (c)(2)(B) of the Code) and also for estate tax purposes (Sec. 2055(e)(2)(B)).

The gift of an annuity or unitrust interest to charity can usefully be timed to coincide with the realization of nonrecurring high income in a particular tax year. In this way the taxpayer can provide a steady flow of income to a charity over the years that lie ahead while taking his deduction in the year of greatest tax advantage.

[¶203.13]   Strategies for Testamentary Transfers

As compared with lifetime gifts to charity, the strategies involved in gifts to charity by will or other "testamentary" instrument are relatively simple. Virtually the same organizations[23] qualify as donees (see ¶200),

---

[23]There are minor differences, e.g., Sec. 2055(a)(2) includes "the encouragement of art" among the purposes of corporations, bequests to which are deductible for estate tax purposes, whereas that phrase does not appear in Sec. 170(c)(2) of the Code.

but there are no percentage limitations (see ¶200.1), and the income tax and gift tax concerns are out of the picture. Moreover, as compared with certain lifetime transfers (see ¶201 and ¶203.7), testamentary gifts to charity do not diminish the allowable marital deduction.

A gift of a decedent's entire estate to a qualified charity or charities will eliminate the estate tax entirely. The same tax avoidance can be attained through a combination of a marital deduction gift to the decedent's spouse and a gift of the balance to charity. Or by a nondeductible gift or gifts of the portion of the estate covered by the unified credit (approximately $175,000 after 1980), with gifts of the rest of the estate covered by the charitable deduction or by a combination of the marital and charitable deductions.

In most cases, to be sure, the limit of the client's charitable goals, or considerations of family or other competing interests, will dictate a less extensive use of the charitable deduction. In any case, it will be necessary to choose between outright gifts and split-interest gifts, and other decisions must be made within each of those categories, as discussed below.

[¶203.14]   Outright Testamentary Transfers

Where the intended gifts are not substantial, outright gifts are usually appropriate. And even for larger amounts, they will frequently be quite satisfactory. These may be gifts of stated dollar amounts. Or they may be gifts of stated percentages of the "estate" (i.e., the gross estate, the adjusted gross estate, the residuary estate, or any other fund deemed appropriate). Or the donor may make gifts of dollar amounts but provide for them to be reduced if they aggregate more than a stated percentage of the "estate".

Such bequests, however measured, may go to the indicated charities unconditionally. Or the testator may direct that the funds be applied to certain purposes (or to exclude certain purposes) within the donee's exempt activities. Or the testator may add a precatory expression of his desires as to application of the funds.

While such gifts may, or course, be made to public charities, they may also be made to a private foundation (as described in ¶203.9) and thus benefit public charities indirectly. With the obvious exception of the testator's own participation in its affairs, most of the advantages of a private foundation as listed in [¶203.9] apply to testamentary as well as lifetime gifts.

If the private foundation was established during the client's lifetime, it can simply be named as beneficiary of the outright gift. If the client desires to bequeath funds to a private foundation which is to come into existence after his death, he can by will direct his executors to establish and qualify such a foundation (in corporate or trust form) and he can designate the foundation so established to be the beneficiary of the outright gift.

In the case of a client who is a disqualified person (as explained in ¶203.9 with respect to the foundation, his gift to it is considered a prohibited sale or exchange under Sec. 4941(d)(2)(A) of the Code if the foundation assumes any mortgage or lien or takes subject to a mortgage or lien placed on the property by the client within ten years prior to the gift. Otherwise, any real or personal property may be the subject of the gift. The private foundation which is the beneficiary of the testamentary gift may be one established by the client (or pursuant to his will), or it may be one established by another person or persons. In the latter case, the client may still be a disqualified person under the definition set forth in ¶203.9.

[¶203.15]   Split-Interest Testamentary Transfers

For the client who would like to make a substantial gift to charity by his will but does not wish thereby to reduce the income available to his surviving spouse, or to some other object of his concern, a charitable remainder trust may provide the ideal solution.

If he establishes a charitable remainder annuity trust as described in Sec. 664(d)(1) of the Code or a charitable remainder unitrust as described in Sec. 664(d)(2), the specified annual sum will be paid to his designated beneficiary or beneficiaries for life (or stipulated term of not more than 20 years). The value of the remainder passing to charity will be deductible for estate tax purposes. The same results can be accomplished via a gift to a pooled income fund [as described in Sec. 642(c)(5)], with income reserved for the life or lives of one or more designated beneficiaries.

These charitable deduction vehicles are fully described, and the relevant strictures indicated, in ¶203.10, above, and need not be restated here.

It is important to recognize that the use of a charitable remainder trust does not merely preserve income for the intended beneficiary; it can actually increase the income available to him. It does so by reducing (or sometimes eliminating) the tax otherwise payable out of the estate.

Suppose, for example, that the client's sole heir is his son, who is to have an income for life before the estate passes to charity. Assume that the adjusted gross estate is $600,000, that the son is 50 years of age when the client dies, and that the client establishes a $400,000 5 percent unitrust for him with the remainder passing to charity, and gives the balance to his son outright, with the request that he pass the aftertax balance on to charity at his death.

The estate tax would be calculated as follows:

Adjusted gross estate		$600,000
Charitable deduction (35.9 percent of $400,000)		143,600
Tentative tax base		456,400
Tax on tentative tax base		140,976
Less: Credit for State death taxes (if paid)	$ 8,600	
Unified credit	47,000	
		55,600
Estate tax payable		$ 85,376

The son will receive an income of $20,000 per year from the unitrust. The income from the aftertax portion of the residuary estate ($200,000 less State taxes[24] of $8,600 and Federal estate tax of $85,376), assuming a 5 percent return, will provide additional income of about $5,300. The son's total income from the estate will be $25,300 per year.

Had the client given his entire estate to his son, with the request that he pass it on to charity at his death, the estate tax would be calculated as follows:

Adjusted gross estate (tentative tax base)		$600,000
Tax on tentative tax base		192,800
Less: Credit for State death taxes (if paid)	$14,000	
Unified credit	47,000	
		61,000
Estate tax payable		131,800

In the latter case, reduction of the adjusted gross estate by State death taxes ($14,000) and the Federal estate tax ($131,800) would leave a balance of $454,200. Again assuming a 5 percent return, the son's annual income from the estate would be $22,710, or about $2,600 less than with the use of the $400,000 unitrust. Also, the ultimate gift to charity would be reduced by about $52,000 of additional taxes incurred in the father's estate.

> NOTE: In order to qualify for estate tax deduction, the annuity trust or unitrust must function exclusively as such from the date of creation. it will be considered created at date of death, so that the value of the remainder interest will be deductible, even though the trust is not funded until the end of a reasonable period of estate administration, provided the obli-

---

[24]It is assumed in this example that State death taxes paid will be precisely equal to the Federal credit.

gation to make the stipulated payments begins as of the date of death (Reg. Sec. 1.664-1(a)(5)). It is important to check these regulations as to rules for payments during the interim period and adjustments required when the trust is funded.

Just as a charitable remainder trust can be established by the taxpayer during his lifetime or at death, a taxpayer who wishes to give a deductable income interest to charity may do so at either time. The requirements of annuity trusts and unitrusts for charity where the value of the income interest is deductable for income tax purposes are set forth in [¶203.12.] The same basic requirements apply for purposes of the estate tax deduction. The only exception is that for estate tax purposes the requirement that the donor be taxable on the trust income does not apply.

3

Generation-Skipping Trusts

[¶300] OPPORTUNITIES AVAILABLE—THEN AND NOW

In discussing the estate tax marital deduction (Chapter One), we alluded to the common practice where by the testator makes a separate gift of the optimum marital deduction portion of his estate to or for the benefit of his spouse and places the balance (nonmarital portion) in a trust for the surviving spouse (or for her and others) on such terms that the principal of this (nonmarital) trust will be excluded from the gross estate of the surviving spouse. The latter objective is ordinarily accomplished by giving the spouse limited trust benefits, the trust assets to be distributed after her death to the children or held in further trust for their benefit.

The principle involved, where estate tax on the nonmarital trust assets is avoided in the estate of the surviving spouse, is simply that inasmuch as she has neither the outright ownership of the property nor a general power of appointment over it, her interest expires with her. Nothing is considered to pass from her to the remainder beneficiaries within the meaning of the estate tax laws.

The same principle, obviously, would serve to keep the property out of the gross estates of the testator's children and subsequent descendants, via a series of consecutive life estates. And prior to TRA 76, this was indeed the case. Such "generation-skipping" trusts could be continued indefinitely, subject only to the requirement of eventual trust termination under the Rule against Perpetuities of the testator's domiciliary State. Termination might be postponed over 100 years.

Substantially increased family resources were obtainable in this way. Consider, for example, a testator who had a $1,000,000 taxable estate, the marital deduction being inapplicable or otherwise utilized. If he bequeathed this $1,000,000 to his wife, who left it outright to their only son, who passed it outright to his only child, from whom it passed to the testator's great-grandchildren, there would have been four taxable occasions along the way. Approximately the following estate taxes[1] (at pre-TRA 76 rates) would have been payable:

	Estate Tax
(1) At testator's death	$300,000
(2) At widow's death	195,000
(3) At child's death	128,000
(4) At grandchild's death	85,000
Total estate taxes	$708,000

The result is that the great-grandchildren would have received less than $300,000 ($1,000,000 minus $708,000) of the original $1,000,000. Actually, they might well have received a substantially smaller residue of the original fund, as the prior beneficiaries' other (nonmarital) assets might have pushed their estates into higher estate tax brackets.

Further, while the assumed series of events might have occurred over a period of many years, it might also realistically have taken place within 30 or fewer years. If, for example, the testator died at age 80, leaving a widow of 75 who died 10 years later, a son 55 who died 20 years later, and a grandson 30 who died within 30 years of the testator, the entire story would have been enacted in a relatively brief span.

Had the same $1,000,000 been placed in trust for the widow for life, then for the child for life, and then for the grandchild for life, with remainder to the testator's great-grandchildren, only the first of the above listed tax bites ($300,000) would have been imposed. $700,000, rather than $300,000, would have passed to the great-grandchildren. Also, the income on the funds paid out in the second and third of the listed tax payments would have been available to the testator's child and grandchild.

The preceding paragraph illustrates the traditional estate tax savings, with corresponding asset and income enhancement, of the generation-skipping trust. To which the Ways and Means Committee Report in connection with TRA 76 responds as follows:

---

[1]The calculations assume that State death taxes are equal to the federal credit in each case, that the after-tax balance comprises the recipient's adjusted gross estate, and that the credit for property previously taxed is eliminated by the lapse of at least 10 years between successive deaths.

"The purpose of the Federal estate and gift taxes is not only to raise revenue, but also to do so in a manner which has as nearly as possible a uniform effect, generation by generation. These policies of revenue raising and equal treatment are best served where the transfer taxes . . . are imposed, on the average, at reasonably uniform intervals. Likewise, these policies are frustrated where the imposition of transfer taxes is deferred for very long intervals, as possible, under present law, through the use of generation-skipping trusts.

"Present law imposes transfer taxes every generation in the case of families where property passes directly from parent to child, and then, from child to grandchild. However, where a generation-skipping trust is used, no tax is imposed upon the death of the child, even where the child has an income interest in the trust, and substantial powers with respect to the use, management, and disposition of the trust assets. While the tax advantages of generation-skipping are theoretically available to all, in actual practice these devices are more valuable (in terms of tax savings) to wealthier families. Thus, generation-skipping trusts are used more often by the wealthy.

"Generation-skipping results in inequities in the case of transfer taxes by enabling some families to pay these taxes only once every several generations, whereas most families must pay these taxes every generation. Generation-skipping also reduces the progressive effect of the transfer taxes, since families with modest levels of accumulated wealth may pay as much or more in cumulative transfer taxes (as) wealthier families who utilize generation-skipping trusts . . ."

And so on. While the Committee's rationale may not be flawless, we are bound by the legislative product. TRA 76 did indeed curtail the tax benefits to be derived from generation-skipping trusts. But it did not eliminate them. With the analysis that follows, we shall find that generation-skipping trusts still qualify as one of the ten best ways to save estate taxes.

[¶300.1]   Where Old Rules Still Apply

Although the tax saving properties of generation-skipping trusts generally are reduced under TRA 76, the pre-TRA tax benefits of such trusts will be preserved if they fall in one of these two categories:

☐ Generation-skipping transfers provided in trusts established *irrevocably* prior to May 1, 1976. (This exception does not extend to assets added to the trust on or after that date.)

☐ Generation-skipping transfers provided in a will or trust in existence on April 30, 1976, provided:

1. The provisions are not amended after that date in any way which will result in the creation of, or increasing the amount of, any generation-skipping transfer; and

2. The testator or grantor dies prior to 1982. (This "grace period" is extended in case of incompetency for a period of two years after the date on which competency to dispose of property is first regained.)

The two "provisos" to the "grandfathering" of wills and trusts in existence on April 30, 1976, are not as simple as they may at first glance appear. To take them in reverse order, "the date on which (the testator or grantor) first regains his competence to dispose of such property" may in many cases be difficult to establish. No bell rings.

Also, it is not presently clear—though regulations when issued may help—when an amendment will be considered to result in creating or increasing the amount of a generation-skipping transfer. A conservative position would eschew any amendment of any dispositive or administrative provision on the theory that the trust which embodies the amendment is not "the trust" which was in existence on April 30, 1976. Thus, the amendment "created" a generation-skipping transfer. A more flexible view (consistent with the statutory purpose and supported by statements of the Staff of the Joint Committee on Taxation in its *General Explanation of the Tax Reform Act of 1976,* p. 582 (1976)) would permit changes of trustees, changes of beneficiaries, and changes of the shares of beneficiaries. This could be done so long as these changes do not augment the amount previously subjected to generation-skipping or add any generations to be skipped.

Even more subtle questions may arise. Does the revocation of prior bequests *per se* increase the generation-skipping transfer? Suppose the revocation of a $10,000 bequest to charity is accompanied by a lifetime charitable gift of the same amount? The lifetime gift deprives the donor of the lifetime income on the gift amount, thus potentially reducing the funds eventually available for a residuary generation-skipping transfer. On the other hand, the income tax saving resulting from the lifetime gift may actually add to the principal of the generation-skipping trust.

Again, a literal reading of the statute would indicate that an amendment which converts one $100,000 generation-skipping trust for the benefit of A into two $50,000 trusts on the same terms, one for A and the other for B, would vitiate the protection of A's trust as well as B's. Although A's trust has simply been reduced, nevertheless, the amendment "will result in the creation of . . . (a) generation-skipping transfer," namely, the trust for B.

Until these questions are authoritatively answered, we recommend the avoidance whenever possible of any change to any will or revocable trust instrument existing prior to May 1, 1976, for which the statutory protection of one or more generation-skipping trusts is desired.

[¶300.2]   The TRA 76 Changes—An Overview

As to any transfer made after April 30, 1976, which gives an interest to a person of a generation younger than the transferor's[2] and gives a future interest to someone in a still younger generation, TRA 76 imposes a new tax (roughly equivalent to the estate tax) on termination of the income interest.

The amount of the tax is calculated as if the value of the future interest were a transfer from the parent (or some other persons in certain cases) of the person who receives it. Such parent is called the "deemed transferor." The tax is payable, however, not by the deemed transferor but from the future interest assets.

An exception, which now provides a major element of our planning with generation-skipping trusts, exempts from the new tax each $250,000 of property which skips a generation and passes to a set of the testator's or grantor's grandchildren. That is, it exempts up to $250,000 for the grandchildren descended from each child of the testator or grantor. In this connection, we should note at the outset that:

1. The $250,000 exemption applies to the future interests of grandchildren even if their parent is not the income beneficiary.
2. Future interests of great-grandchildren or subsequent issue are not covered by the exemption.
3. Outright gifts to any future generation are not subject to the generation-skipping tax.

Before proceeding to a close examination of this complex addition to the transfer tax laws, we should note that the testator who has a $1,000,000 taxable estate, who has four children, and who has grandchildren through each of his four children, can create a $250,000 trust for the life of each child, with remainder to the child's children, and the entire $1,000,000 will pass to the grandchildren and skip the children's estates for transfer tax purposes. No estate tax will be imposed in the children's estates and the generation-skipping tax will be avoided on the future interests (up to the stated $1,000,000) passing to the grandchildren.[3]

Suppose the spouse of the testator mentioned in the preceding paragraph also has a $1,000,000 taxable estate and is the mother of the

---

[2] Thus the new law does not affect trusts for the benefit of the testator's or grantor's spouse.

[3] We assume here that the trusts are so drawn that they would have been effective for generation-skipping purposes prior to TRA 76, i.e., the life tenants do not have general powers of appointment.

same four children. Can she create four more $250,000 generation-skipping trusts for the same beneficiaries and on the same terms, so that $2,000,000 will skip the children's estates under the mentioned generation-skipping tax exemption? The Ways and Means Committee Report says no, but the Code provision appears to say yes.

A footnote to the Committee Report states (with our emphasis added):

> "All trusts established by a grandparent *or his spouse* for any child's children would be attributed to that child as deemed transferor: thus, *only one* . . . ($250,000) exclusion is to be allowed to flow through a child of the grantor (for the ultimate benefit of the grandchildren), even if trusts involving that child (or that child's children) are established by the grantor, *and his spouse*. Your committee believes that the income from a . . . ($250,000) trust should be sufficient to provide for the needs of each child, even where that child might be the victim of disability or other hardship."

But Sec. 2613(b)(6) of the Code provides, in pertinent part (with our emphasis again):

> "In the case of any deemed transferor, the maximum amount excluded from the terms 'taxable distribution' and 'taxable termination' by reason of provisions exempting from such terms transfers to the grandchildren *of the grantor of the trust* shall be $250,000 . . ."

This can be read to allow a maximum of $250,000 per grantor, so that $500,000 would be permissible in the case of two grantors. We shall see.

[¶301]   THE GENERATION-SKIPPING TAX—CLOSE-UP

The generation-skipping tax is set forth in a new Chapter 13 which has been added to Subtitle B of the Code, relating to estate and gift taxes. Subchapter A of Chapter 13 covers imposition and calculation of the tax and liability for its payment. Subchapter B provides definitions and special rules. And Subchapter C deals with returns, extensions of time for payments, and additional special rules. As the definitions are a condition precedent to comprehension of the entire chapter, we will start with them:

[¶301.1]   Operative Terms Defined

The definitions which apply for purposes of the generation-skipping tax are as follows:

☐ A "generation-skipping trust" is any trust having younger generation beneficiaries who are assigned to more than one generation (according to rules summarized below).

☐ A "generation-skipping trust equivalent" is any nontrust arrangement which has substantially the same effect as a generation-skipping trust. Examples are legal life estates and remainders, estates for years, insurance and annuities, and split interests. (References to generation-skipping trusts in Chapter 13 of Subtitle B of the Code, and in this chapter of our book, include appropriate references to generation-skipping trust equivalents.)

☐ A "generation-skipping transfer" is any taxable distribution or taxable termination with respect to a generation-skipping trust.

☐ A "taxable distribution" (except as noted below) is any distribution, not out of the income (within the meaning of Section 643(b)) of the trust, from the trust to a younger generation beneficiary who is assigned to a generation younger than that of any other younger generation beneficiary of the trust.[4] (This would generally cover any principal distribution to a younger generation beneficiary where there is another beneficiary whose generation is younger than the grantor's and older than the distributee's. For a typical example, in a trust for the grantor's nephew for life, with remainder to the nephew's issue, a distribution of principal to any of the nephew's issue would be a taxable distribution.)

☐ A "taxable termination" (except as noted below) is the termination of the interest or power of any younger generation beneficiary who is assigned to a generation older than the generation assignment of any other younger generation beneficiary of the trust. (This would generally cover the expiration of the interest of a beneficiary whose generation is younger than the grantor's and older than that of a remainder beneficiary. For a typical example, in a trust for the grantor's nephew for life, with remainder to the nephew's issue, the death of the nephew would cause a taxable termination.)

☐ "Taxable distribution" and "taxable termination" exceptions: These terms do not apply to distributions to grandchildren of the grantor not in excess of $250,000 per deemed transferor. (The $250,000 exemption applies against transfers to grandchildren in the order in which they are made or deemed made.) Also excluded are transfers subject to tax under Chapter 11 (estate tax) or 12 (gift tax) of Subtitle B of the Code, for example, where a transfer is taxable because a younger generation beneficiary has a general power of appointment over the trust assets.

[4]Under a tier system provided in Sec. 2613 (a)(2), where income and principal distributions are made in the same year, income is deemed to have been received first by the older generation. This precludes giving income to the younger beneficiaries and principal to their parents to avoid a taxable distribution.

☐ A "deemed transferor" is (a) the parent of the transferee of the property who is more closely related to the grantor than the other parent (and a parent related to the grantor by blood or adoption is more closely related than a parent related by marriage); or (b) the parent having a closer "affinity" to the grantor, if neither parent is related to the grantor; or (c) the youngest ancestor of the transferee who is a younger generation beneficiary related to the grantor by blood or adoption, if neither parent is a younger generation beneficiary.

☐ The "transferee" is the person receiving the property, where a distribution is made. However, the identification of the "transferee" (and hence the identification of the deemed transferor) may present difficulties where a taxable termination does not result in outright distribution of the principal. Subject to regulations to be issued, the property in such a case is regarded as transferred pro rata to all beneficiaries in accordance with the amount each would receive under a maximum exercise of discretion in his behalf; and where the discretion is exercisable per stirpes or per capita, a per stirpes exercise would be presumed.

☐ A "younger generation beneficiary" is any beneficiary assigned (according to rules set forth below) to a generation younger than the grantor's generation.

☐ A "beneficiary" is any person who has a present or future interest or power in the trust.

☐ An "interest" is either a right to receive income or principal of the trust, or eligibility to receive it (as in a "sprinkling" or discretionary trust).

☐ A "power" is any power to establish or alter the beneficial enjoyment of interest or principal, other than a power (of a person who has no other present or future power) to distribute income or principal to descendents of the grantor assigned to a generation below that of the holder of the power.

[¶301.2]   Governing Rules

The application of the generation-skipping tax involves not only the special terminology specified above, but also the following special rules:

☐ For purposes of determining the generation to which a person belongs:

1. A lineal descendant of a grandparent of the grantor is assigned to a generation determined by comparing the generations between the grandparent and that descendant with the number of generations between the

grandparent and the grantor. If the descendant is separated from the grandparent by one more generation than the grantor, he is in the first younger generation; if separated by two more generations than the grantor, he is in the second younger generation; and so on.

2. A person who has been at any time married to the grantor is assigned to the grantor's generation, and a person who has been at any time married to a lineal descendant of a grandparent of the grantor is assigned to that descendant's generation.

3. A relationship by half blood or adoption is treated as a relationship by whole blood.

4. A person not related to the grantor is assigned to a generation based on the date of his birth: a person born not more than 12.5 years after the birth of the grantor is assigned to the grantor's generation; a person born more than 12.5 but not more than 37.5 years after the birth of the grantor is assigned to the first younger generation; and so on with consecutive 25-year generational intervals:

5. A person having an indirect interest or power through an estate, trust, partnership, corporation, or other entity is treated as a beneficiary of the trust and assigned to a generation under the foregoing rules.

☐ The occurrence of a taxable termination (as defined above) is governed by several special rules:

1. Where two or more younger generation beneficiaries are assigned to the same generation, except as otherwise provided in regulations to be issued, the transfer constituting the termination as to each such beneficiary is treated as occurring when the last termination at that level occurs.

2. Where a beneficiary has more than one interest or power, or has an interest and a power, except as otherwise provided in regulations to be issued, the termination as to each such interest or power is treated as occurring when the last of the beneficiary's powers or interests is terminated.

3. If at the time of termination of a power of interest of a younger generation beneficiary, a power or interest is still held by an older generation beneficiary, except as otherwise provided in regulations to be issued, the termination as to the younger generation beneficiary is treated as occurring when the last of the older generation beneficiary's powers or interests is terminated. In such a case, however, the generation-skipping tax is imposed as if the older generation beneficiary's termination occurred prior to the younger generation beneficiary's, and the value of the property taken into account in determining the tax on the younger beneficiary's termination is reduced by the tax on the older beneficiary's termination.

4. If a beneficiary assigned to the same generation as, or a higher generation than, that of the beneficiary whose interest or power terminates has a present power or interest "immediately after" and arising as a result of such termination, the termination of the younger beneficiary's interest or power is treated as occurring at the time of the termination of the interest or power arising "immediately after" such termination. If the latter power is held by an older generation benficiary, the tax rule set forth in the

second sentence of the preceding paragraph will also apply.

5. Where an occurrence (a) constitutes a taxable termination and (b) requires what would otherwise be a taxable distribution, the latter is disregarded in favor of the former.

6. An interest is to be taxed only once per generation, where the deemed transferor of property being transferred is a member of the same generation as, or a higher generation, than, any prior deemed transferor of the same property, and the transferee in the prior transfer is a member of the same generation as, or a higher generation than, the transferee of the current transfer. To the extent the prior transfer was taxable, the current transfer will not be treated as a taxable termination or distribution. The Ways and Means Committee Report offers the example of a trust which provides for the income to be distributed to the grantor's son for life, then to the grantor's great-grandchild A, then to the grantor's daughter, with remainder to great-grandchild B. The death of the grantor's son would be a taxable termination. But the death of the daughter would not be a taxable termination to the extent that the value of her terminated interest had previously been subject to tax upon the death of the son.

7. Regulations to be issued will govern the extent to which separate and independent shares of different beneficiaries in the trust will be treated as separate trusts. The special rules above summarized will presumably be modified by such regulations.

8. When a person has at no time held anything other than a future interest or power (or both) in the trust, the termination of such an interest is not a taxable termination.

[¶301.3]   Tax Calculation and Related Subjects

In the context of the definitions and rules we have outlined, let us examine the generation-skipping tax and related tax questions. The tax is, more or less, like the tax on a comparable gift made by the deemed transferor if living, or like the tax on such property as part of his gross estate if deceased. But the "more or less" requires further explication:

□ The new uniform rate schedule for estate and gift tax purposes applies for purposes of the generation-skipping tax.

□ In the case of a living deemed transferor, the value of the property subject to the tax is added to the amounts of his prior adjusted taxable gifts and deemed transfers, and the tax is calculated as if the deemed transfer were a current gift made by him.

□ In the case of a deceased deemed transferor, the value of the property subject to the tax is added to the amounts of his prior taxable gifts and deemed transfers and gross estate, and the tax is calculated as if the deemed transfer were an addition to the deemed transferor's gross estate.

□ In the case of a taxable distribution, the amount of any transfer tax paid by the trust is added to the value of the property actually distributed.

☐ In the case of a taxable termination, the full value of the principal with respect to which the younger generation beneficiary had any interest or power is includible for tax purposes, even though the interest or power may have been limited by an ascertainable standard, such as maintenance or support, or by a specific amount, such as a noncumulative power to withdraw the greater of $5000 or 5 percent of principal annually.

☐ If two or more transfers are attributable by reason of the same event to the same deemed transferor, the aggregate tax on such transfers is attributed to them in the proportion of the amounts transferred.

☐ In calculating the tax, an unlimited charitable deduction is allowable.

☐ If the transfer occurs at the time of, or after, the deemed transferor's death, any unused unified credit (not in excess of the generation-skipping tax) is allowable as a credit against the tax.

☐ The credit for tax on prior transfers is allowable to the extent it is not taken into account in computing the deemed transferor's estate tax.

☐ If the generation-skipping transfer occurs at the same time as, or within nine months after, the date of death of the deemed transferor, the deemed transferor's adjusted gross estate will be increased by the amount of the generation-skipping transfer for purposes of determining the allowable marital deduction.

☐ On a taxable termination at or after the death of the deemed transferor, debts, expenses and losses are deductible in computing the generation-skipping tax to the extent they would be deductible if the trust assets were part of the deemed transferor's gross estate and the deemed transferor had died immediately prior to the transfer.

☐ On a taxable distribution at or after the death of the deemed transferor, expenses incurred in the determination, collection, or refund of the tax are deductible.

☐ On a transfer occurring at or after the death of the deemed transferor, a credit for State death taxes is allowable, subject to certain limitations specified in Sec. 2602(c)(5)(C).

☐ The alternate valuation date may be elected with respect to (a) one or more taxable termination transfers from the same trust which have the same deemed transferor and occur at the time of his death, or (b) one or more taxable terminations occurring on the same day which would have occurred simultaneously with the deaths of the deemed transferors but for deferral of taxation under the special termination rules above set forth (involving two or more beneficiaries in the same generation or an unusual order of termination). If the election is made in situation (a), the alternate valuation date is calculated from the date of death of the deemed transferor; in situation (b), from the date on which the transfer occurred.

☐ Under regulations to be issued, the principles of Sec. 2035 of the Code are to be applied for inclusion of transfers made within three years preceding the death of the deemed transferor.

☐ The basis of assets transferred during the lifetime of the deemed transferor is increased (but not above fair market value) by the portion of the generation-skipping tax attributable to appreciation of the property over its pre-transfer adjusted basis.

☐ The basis of assets transferred at or after the death of the deemed transferor is adjusted as in the case of assets includible in the deemed transferor's gross estate, except that the $60,000 minimum basis adjustment (of Section 1023) (d) of the Code) does not apply.

☐ The transferee of income which is subject to the generation-skipping tax is entitled to deduct the tax in the same manner as he could deduct the estate tax attributable to income in respect of a decedent.

☐ For purposes of a Section 303 redemption, where stock is subject to the generation-skipping tax at or after the death of the deemed transferor, the generation-skipping tax is treated as estate tax; the stock is treated as if included in the gross estate of the deemed transferor; but the trust and the estate are treated spearately to determine qualification for redemption under Section 303. The distribution period is measured from the date of the generation-skipping transfer.

☐ The estate tax extension privilege for closely-held business assets under Sections 6166 and 6166A of the Code, and the special valuation method provided in Sec. 2032A for qualified farms and small business property, are unavailable for generation-skipping tax purposes.

[¶301.4]   Returns and Payment

Subject to regulations to be issued, returns for the generation-skipping tax are to be filed by:

1. The distributee, in the case of a taxable distribution.
2. The trustee, in the case of a taxable termination.

The time within which the return is required to be filed is:

1. In the case of a transfer occurring before the death of the deemed trans-

feror, on or before the 90th day after the close of the trust's taxable year in which the transfer occurred.

2. In the case of a transfer occurring on or after the death of the deemed transferor, on or before the 90th day following the due date (including extensions) of the deemed transferor's estate tax return, or within nine months following the date of the transfer, whichever limit expires later.

The generation-skipping tax constitutes a lien on the property transferred. If the tax is not paid when due[5] the distributee of the property is presumably liable up to the fair market value, determined as of the time of distribution, of the property received by him. And the trustee is also personally liable, except that the trustee is protected to the extent he relies on (a) tax rates forwarded to him by the Service as representing the rates applicable to the transfer and (b) the amount forwarded to him by the Service as representing the exclusion remaining for a transfer to a grandchild of the grantor.

No obligation is imposed on the deemed transferor or his estate with respect to filing of returns or payment of the tax.

[¶302]   WHEN TO USE GENERATION-SKIPPING TRUSTS

The decision as to whether a generation-skipping trust should be used in a particular situation, or as to the extent of its funding, will be influenced by a number of tax and nontax considerations, which are reviewed below.

[¶302.1]   Tax-Saving Criteria

Although the virtually limitless estate tax savings formerly available through generation-skipping are now severely limited by the new generation-skipping tax, such tax savings are not entirely eliminated. Four key points to remember are:

☐ In the case of a living deemed transferor, prior generation-skipping transfers are taken into account in determining the rate of tax applicable to a subsequent generation-skipping transfer. Prior generation-skipping transfers are not taken into account, however, in determining the rate of tax applicable to a gift made by a person who is a

---

[5]New Chapter 13 does not specify when the generation-skipping tax is due, but references in Sec. 2621 to subtitle F of the Code apparently indicate that the tax is due when the return is due (pursuant to Sec. 6151 of the Code), and returns are due as set forth in the preceding paragraph.

deemed transferor of such prior transfers, nor are they taken into account in determining the rate of tax applicable to his estate at death. This means that transfers which are taxable under the new law during the life of the deemed transferor will have a lesser estate tax impact than that of equivalent gifts made by him if the trust property had been given to the deemed transferor outright in lieu of the trust.

☐ The new tax applies only to trusts which divide benefits between two or more generations which are *younger than* the grantor's generation. A client who wishes to establish a trust for his wife for life, with remainder to his children, or a trust for his brother for life, with remainder to the brother's children, or a trust for his parents for life, and then for his siblings for life, with remainder to their children, can do so without inviting a generation-skipping tax.

☐ The new tax does not affect outright gifts (not involving a trust or trust equivalent) to members of any younger generation. A testator can still insulate property from tax in his children's estates via direct gifts to his grandchildren.

☐ Within the limitation of $250,000 per child of the grantor, the exemption of generation-skipping transfers to the grantor's grandchildren provides the major tax planning opportunity that remains available with respect to the new tax. Note, however, that the exclusion of $250,000 applies not to the amount placed in the generation-skipping trust, but rather to the amount which eventually passes to the grandchildren. Also, the testator or grantor who wishes to utilize this exclusion and also to make advance provision for possible future changes of the exclusion amount may utilize a provision along these lines:

> Notwithstanding the foregoing provisions of paragraph___, if at the time of the Grantor's death an amount other than Two Hundred Fifty Thousand Dollars is specified in Section 2613(b)(6) of the Internal Revenue Code as then in effect, the amount so specified in the Code shall be substituted for the figure of Two Hundred Fifty Thousand Dollars for the purpose of allocating assets to The_____ Trust pursuant to the first sentence of paragraph___of this Clause___.

[¶302.2]   Non-Tax Considerations

Let us now consider various factors other than estate tax avoidance, which bear on the use of generation-skipping trusts for children for life, with remainder to their issue. The application of these criteria may lead the client to eschew such trusts even within the sheltered $250,000 per child. Or to establish trusts designed to occupy that shelter. Or to establish such trusts with assets exceeding the sheltered amounts. The principal relevant factors are:

☐ Size of client's estate. Where the value of the assets available for such trusts is so modest that the normal expenses of trust administration over the anticipated trust period might approach or equal the potential tax savings, it would be difficult to recommend the use of generation-skipping trusts in the absence of significant non-tax considerations pushing in that direction. But in most cases where estate planning is a reasonable endeavor we will not be dealing with trusts in which administration expenses will weigh heavily in the balance. Moreover, we can provide, for borderline cases, that a trust of which the principal falls below a certain level can be terminated in favor of the income beneficiary or beneficiaries. For example:

> If at the inception or during the administration of any trust hereunder the principal assets of such trust have a fair market value less than Fifty Thousand Dollars, my Trustees are authorized, but shall not be required, to terminate such trust, in which event the trust assets shall be distributed to the beneficiary who would otherwise be currently entitled or eligible to receive the income of the trust, or, if there are two or more such beneficiaries, the trust assets shall be distributed to one or more of them in such proportions as my Trustees, in their sole discretion, may deem advisable.

☐ Family Considerations

1. *Ages of the children.* Where the client's assets are of substantial value and his children are relatively young, thoughts relating to the children's development, inexperience, and so on, may render the use of trusts appealing. Tax-saving concerns loom increasingly larger as the ages increase. The older the children, the more reliable are our tax projections, the more proximate and substantial the savings are likely to be, and the more contented the children are likely to be with a plan under which they forego outright inheritance for the ultimate benefit of the succeeding generation.

2. *Economic circumstances of children.* Generation-skipping trusts work their magic not for the estate of the client-testator but for the generation following. It is *their* estates, accordingly, which are the primary measure of the utility of this device for tax purposes. The larger the estates in each succeeding generation, the greater the tax benefit of such trusts. Also, the greater the resources available to the child directly, the less restricting is a trust in terms of the child's freedom and autonomy.

If distribution of all the trust income to the client's children appears to be unnecessary, and from an income tax standpoint unfortunate, the use of a "sprinkling" (or sprinkling and accumulation) trust may be advisable. For example:

> During the child's lifetime, my Trustees shall accumulate the net income, or distribute or apply all or any part of the current or accumulated net income to or for the benefit of the child and the child's children, or any of them, at such times, in such amounts or proportions, and in such manner, as the Trustees other than my children, in their sole discretion, may from time to time deem advisable.

Under such a provision, income can be made available to the child if needed. Otherwise, it can be diverted to the next generation, where there may be more than one beneficiary and the availability of lower income tax brackets. But *caveat:* the *accumulation* portion of such a provision carries a potential danger under present tax laws. The Tax Reform Act of 1969 replaced the five-year throwback rule which had been introduced in 1954 with an unlimited income throwback. The result, simply, is to treat the beneficiary who receives the accumulated income somewhat as if he had received it when the trustee received it. It is essential, therefore, to assure that we not direct distribution of the accumulated income to a taxpayer who will have to add it to his other income for high earning years. Probably the best way to handle this problem, where accumulation may be desirable, is by giving the child a nontaxable power of appointment.

3. *Children's family circumstances.* Where the projected estate and income tax savings to be attained by means of generation-skipping trusts are neither so trivial as to be meaningless nor so vast as to be compelling, considerations relating to each child's family circumstances may be determinative. For the child whose marriage appears to be unstable, or whose economic condition is fluctuating or at high risk, or whose concerns or capacities do not run to the competent utilization or preservation of material resources, the client may be inclined to structure his benevolence with the trust device, combining an element of protection with the tax saving objective.

4. *Philosophical criteria.* We alluded, in the preceding paragraph 3 to the "protection" of the client's children as one interest to be implemented through the trust device. Some of our clients, of course, place a low value on the notion of protection and a much higher value on their beneficiaries' freedom and autonomy, including the desire for their children to risk their resources and take responsibility for the outcome. Still others, in search of the "golden mean," will opt for a plan that provides substantial outright gifts but also establishes trusts to hold some

portion available indefinitely for the contingencies that life may bring.

In one unusual situation, a very dynamic corporate executive, who had single-handedly turned a modest inherited business into a vast commercial and industrial empire, provided for his son's share of his estate to be held in trust, the son to receive each year from the trust an amount equal to the amount he earned by his personal efforts. As an additional goad to his son's achievement, this client provided for his daughter to receive from her trust each year an amount equal to that paid to his son. We persuaded him to modify the game in the event the son should be disabled, but this arrangement illustrates the variety of non-tax uses which generation-skipping trusts can be made to serve.

□ *Specific asset criteria.* For the ordinary investment portfolio, the trust provides a vehicle for asset conservation and skilled management. A special utility may be added, however, in cases in which the estate is substantially invested in real estate or in a closely held business. And this is especially significant where there are two or more children who are to share in the benefits after the testator's death. In the real estate situation, the trust may be utilized to avoid the creation of tenancies in common, with their attendant problems of management and control, dispersion of title, and so on. For the closely held business, the trust may be so established and organized as to assure that various purposes of the testator (possibly involving employment of one or more children, dividend policy, unified control, etc.) will be carried out. In all such cases, it is important adequately to express the testator's purposes and special instructions, and the trustee's powers of retention, management, and disposition.

The client whose principal asset is the stock of the corporation of which he is also the chief executive may have problems of valuation, liquidity, and asset diversification. He may possibly have the difficulty of equalizing estate distribution between children who are interested and active in the business and those who are not. Several alternative solutions to these problems are discussed in Chapter Nine. By placing the stock of such a business in a generation-skipping trust, the client can provide for the business to be retained for his children and possibly for their descendants, while avoiding another tax (to the extent of the $250,000 per child shelter) on its possibly augmented value in the children's estates.

[¶303]   **HOW TO DESIGN THE**
                    GENERATION-SKIPPING TRUST

While a trust, apart from its tax-saving uses, may be employed as a device for the client to control his assets and rule his family from the grave, it need have no such purpose or effect. The testator who so desires can vest extensive powers and discretions in his trustees, and even in his beneficiaries, without losing any tax saving benefits of generation-skipping.

The testator who understands all of the possibilities open to him may overcome any reluctance he may have to govern by the "dead hand." And the beneficiary who perceives the flexibilities of a liberally drawn trust will not feel that his resources have been "tied up" for the benefit of a later generation. The elements of flexibility which may be considered, apart from broad trust management powers, include the following:

1. *Income sprinkling and accumulation techniques. The use of sprinkling and accumulation provisions has been discussed in* [¶302.2]. Such a power, in the hands of an independent trustee, can be used to alter the flow of income as the needs of a family fluctuate from time to time while at the same time reducing the total income tax bite.

2. *Principal invasion subject to ascertainable standard.* Where the trust principal is insulated by the $250,000 per child exemption or otherwise protected from the generation-skipping tax, we endeavor also to avoid estate tax in the life beneficiary's estate. If the beneficiary is given the power to withdraw principal, subject to an ascertainable standard relating to his health, education, support or maintenance[6], the power is not a general one and there is no adverse estate tax consequence to the possession, exercise or lapse of such a power. On the other hand, a power to use property for the comfort, welfare or happiness of the holder is not considered to be limited by the requisite standard. In determining whether an ascertainable standard applies, it is immaterial whether the beneficiary is required to exhaust his other income before exercising the power.

3. *Limited ($5,000 or 5 percent) principal invasion by beneficiary.* A trust beneficiary can be empowered to withdraw in each calendar year, on a noncumulative basis, the sum of $5,000 or 5 percent of the trust principal, whichever is greater. Although such a power constitutes a general power of appointment, lapse of the power so limited does not constitute a taxable release. Only the year-of-death value of the property subject to the unexercised power will be included in the holder's gross estate. Thus the beneficiary who requires or desires the additional amount in any year can withdraw it. If he does not, he can leave it

---

[6]But see Rev. Rul. 77-60, IRB 1977-11, which appears to contravene Reg. Sec. 20.2041-1(c)(2) where the donee is empowered to invade principal to maintain his customary standard of living.

in the trust with no significant tax consequence. (See Sec. 2041(a)(2), (b)(2), and Sec. 2514 (e) of the Code; Reg. Sec. 25.2511-2(a).) (But *caveat:* such a power may cause income or capital gains to be taxed to the holder, if not otherwise taxable to him, to the extent of the $5,000 or 5 percent, e.g., in an accumulation trust.) A suggested provision is the following:

> My trustees shall distribute to the child such portions of the principal as he or she may from time to time request in writing, provided that the aggregate of such distributions in any calendar year shall not exceed the sum of Five Thousand Dollars or five percent of the value of the principal of the child's trust, whichever is the greater, and provided, further, that the child's right to require such distributions of principal shall lapse to the extent it is not exercised in any such year. The "value of the principal of the child's trust" for the purpose of this paragraph shall mean the value of the trust principal determined as of the last day of the year plus the value of all trust principal previously distributed to the child during the year under the provisions of this paragraph.

A power of a beneficiary to withdraw principal in excess of the $5,000 or five percent limit will, if the power is not exercised, render the excess portion includible in the holder's gross estate as a transfer with income reserved. The lapse at year's end will, as to the excess portion, constitute a gift of a future interest (i.e., the amount the holder could have taken less the value of his life interest therein).

4. *Powers to distribute principal in trustees' discretion.* Maximum flexibility can be achieved if powers to invade principal are lodged in trustees. There is no need for an ascertainable standard of the type mentioned in paragraph 2 above. See, for sample, Rev. Rul. 76-368, IRB 1976-39, 9. Careful drafting, moreover, will inform the trustees and the beneficiaries as to what the appropriate grounds for invasion will be and whether the trustees are permitted or required, in exercising their discretion, to take into consideration the beneficiary's income from other sources, or the beneficiary's total resources, or both.

Typically, in trusts designed to provide for the possible tax advantages of generation-skipping without depriving the current beneficiary of financial assistance for any useful purpose, we would provide a broad discretionary power of invasion, for example:

> My trustees shall also distribute to the child, or apply for his or her benefit such portions of the principal as my Trustees in their sole discretion may from time to time deem advisable for the child's maintenance, for the child's education at any level, to enable or assist the child to purchase a home, to enable or assist the child to enter into a business or professional enterprise which my Trustees may approve, for a gift on the occasion of the child's marriage, or for the expenses of any accident, illness or emergency needs of the child or the child's spouse or issue.

A suggested supplemental provision with respect to the exercise of such powers is the following:

> In making any discretionary determinations provided in my Will with respect to the accumulation or distribution of income, or with respect to the distribution of principal, except as otherwise specifically provided, my Trustees shall take into consideration the income of the beneficiary from all other sources, and may, but shall not be required to, take into consideration the other assets or resources of the beneficiary. Moreover, whether or not such a restriction is imposed or omitted in any other provision of my Will, I direct that no Trustee who is currently entitled or eligible to receive distributions of income or principal of any trust established under Clause————shall participate in any discretionary determination with respect to the accumulation or distribution of income, or with respect to the distribution of principal, of that trust or of any other trust thereunder, nor shall such Trustee participate in the exercise of any administrative power which directly or indirectly effects an accumulation of income or involves the allocation or receipts or disbursements as between income and principal of any trust established under that Clause.

5. **Departure from equality.** Ordinarily the testator will wish to treat his children equally in the division or distribution of his estate. And, similarly, he will wish to treat a child's children equally in respect of assets passing to or in trust for the testator's grandchildren. Where there is a possibility or probability that the division may take place many years after the testator's death, as where wills are written for a relatively young married couple, the testator may wish to allow his independent trustees to disturb the pattern of equality, at least for the event of an intervening accident or illness which seriously affects one of his children.

A provision designed to provide for such reallocation, with a limit as to the extent of it, and with safeguards for protection of the other children, is the following:

> Notwithstanding the foregoing provisions, if it should appear to my Trustees, either at the time fixed for division of the trust principal pursuant to the ————— sentence of paragraph——, above, or at any time thereafter so long as there are two or more separate trusts in existence hereunder for the benefit of children of mine, that a child of mine is suffering from a physical, mental or emotional illness, disability or deficiency which is likely to be of long-continued or permanent duration, my Trustees may add to that child's trust, from the shares or trusts set aside or established for my other child or children hereunder, such amount or amounts as my Trustees, in their sole discretion, may deem appropriate to augment the share of the child who has such illness, disability or deficiency; provided, that not more than one-half of the share or trust of any other child may be diverted for the purpose above-described in this paragraph——. The determination of my Trustees under the foregoing provisions of this paragraph ————— shall be binding on all parties in in-

terest, and my Trustees shall have no liability to any current or future beneficiary as a result of such determination, provided my Trustees act in good faith on the basis of a written report of a duly licensed physician and an opinion of counsel that my Trustees' proposed determination appears to be a reasonable and proper exercise of their discretion hereunder.

Unless otherwise limited, of course, such a clause may divert to the disabled child's trust assets in excess of the $250,000 which is exempted from the generation-skipping tax.

6. *Special power of appointment.* A power of appointment can be given to an income beneficiary without causing the appointive property to be taxed as part of his estate (whether or not he exercises the power) so long as he cannot appropriate the property to himself or appoint it to his estate, his creditors, or creditors of his estate. Consequently, the successive beneficiaries of generation-skipping trusts can be given powers by will or otherwise to appoint the trust assets (outright or in further trust) to and among their issue, or the testator's issue, or a broader class or persons, or even to any beneficiaries other than themselves, their estates, or creditors of themselves or their estates.

Such a provision substantially dilutes the testator's hold on the future. If circumstances change so that his original testamentary design appears to be unfortunate or undesirable, his children or grandchildren have the opportunity to alter it without sacrificing the tax benefits originally conceived.

A special power of appointment may be granted not merely for testamentary exercise or effect, as discussed above, but also as a vehicle for inter vivos gifts by the holder of the power. An example of such a provision is as follows:

> During his or her lifetime, after the child has reached the age of twenty-one years, the child shall have the right at any time, and from time to time, to make gifts of the principal of his or her trust to and among his or her spouse and issue, or any of them, in such amounts or proportions, on such terms and conditions, and subject to such trusts or limitations, as the child may in writing set forth.

If no limit is imposed as to the extent to which such a power may be exercised, the holder of the power may use it to terminate the trust in favor of the succeeding generation, if he so desires. Whether he does so or not, the assets subject to the power will not be subject to estate tax at his death, but exercise of the power may cause taxable distributions or a taxable termination for purposes of the generation-skipping tax.

It should also be recognized that a lifetime or testamentary power which a child of the grantor may exercise via appointments which do not vest the property in his children may be used in such manner as to forfeit the $250,000 exemption from the generation-skipping tax otherwise available for transfer to the grantor's grandchildren.

An example of generation-skipping trusts will be found in the irrevocable life insurance trust which appears in Appendix C.

4

Joint Ownership

[¶400]   PROS AND CONS OF JOINT OWNERSHIP

Every estate tax saving technique involves a "cost" in terms of the loss or diminution of other values or advantages. The joint ownership of real or personal property may have one or more of the following advantages or utilities, the loss of which constitutes the "cost" of terminating such ownership:

□ *Speed of Transmission*—under the laws of most States, upon the death of one joint owner the survivor or survivors have immediate ownership and possession of the property involved. In some States, a clearance from the taxing authorities may be required as to all or a portion of the joint assets. The proceeds of insurance policies normally rival joint ownership in terms of ready access, but assets administered as part of a decedent's estate may be tied up for a number of months unless the personal representative is willing to make a "risk distribution."

□ *Inheritance tax savings*—State laws commonly give favored inheritance tax treatment to assets owned jointly as compared with assets administered as part of the decedent's estate.

For example, in Pennsylvania, property owned jointly by husband and wife passes to the surviving spouse free of inheritance tax. Property owned jointly by non-spouses is taxed only to the extent of the decedent's fractional interest. (This is not the case where the property is included in the taxable estate as a transfer in contemplation of death.)

□ *Reduced administration expenses* Where the compensation of executors or administrators is based on a percentage of the assets subject to administration in the decedent's estate, assets jointly owned are

115

excluded from that computation. Counsel fees which are computed on a percentage basis may exclude jointly owned assets in whole or in part, depending on variations in local and individual practice.

   ☐ *Other considerations.* Beyond the practical and monetary values, there is an appeal for some clients in the simplicity of the concept and the avoidance of complex documentation. For others, the joint owner- ship of a home, or in some cases the joint ownership of "all our assets," has sentimental value or may symbolize and reinforce the unity of their marriage and family structure. On the other hand, if the relationship deteriorates to the point of separation or divorce, at least one of the parties may have reason to reconsider his or her earlier enthusiasm for joint ownership.

   Too often counselors consider the termination of joint ownership to be a "nuisance." The problems may include:

1. Choosing the correct method of termination, as gift tax or other considera- tions may indicate, on the basis of the type of property, source of invest- ment, and even the date of acquisition.
2. The chances of error or omission in the processes of termination;
3. The difficulty of obtaining adequate compensation for work that may be tedious and time consuming with no visibly "packaged" result (See Chapter 11).

   All of these considerations tend to have a chilling effect on the counselor's ardor.

   Even worse, we have all too frequently seen the worthless "im- plementation" of an estate plan in the form of documents providing a marital deduction trust and a nonmarital trust, patently designed to achieve the estate tax savings described in Chapters 1 and 3, where the assets of husband and wife are entirely or mainly held by them in joint ownership. In such cases, as indicated below, the joint ownership re- moves all substance from the marital—nonmarital (or Trust A and Trust B) format.

   A final *caveat:* where joint ownership of property is for some reason desired, it is important to ascertain that it has in fact been established. For example, a number of States have legislated against joint ownership of real estate, at least to the extent that a grant to two or more persons will be construed as creating a "tenancy in common" unless the appropriate wording for joint ownership is used. The necessary language is also essential with respect to bank accounts and stocks and bonds.

   Beyond language, it is important to ascertain the requirements of state law with respect to actual or symbolic delivery in the establishment of a joint tenancy. Requirements in some states may be more rigid where the parties are not husband and wife. For example, we know of one case where a man who had by will directed distribution of his estate to four nephews in equal shares and subsequently decided to favor one of the nephews. He registered all of his securities in the names of himself and the favored nephew "as joint owners with right of survivorship". The uncle then retained the securities in his own box, deposited all the income to his own account, and gave his nephew no indication of the intended gift. Under applicable state court rulings, it was clear that the joint registration by itself was of no effect so that all of the securities passed under the uncle's will to the four nephews in equal shares.

[¶401] WHEN SHOULD JOINT OWNERSHIP BE TERMINATED?

As against the practical and sentimental values there are tax advantages which in certain cases will tip the balance in favor of termination of joint ownership.

[¶401.1]   Control of Joint Property

There are essentially two aspects to control of joint property: control during lifetime and control after death:

1. *Lifetime control.* In most jurisdictions, in tenancies by the entirety each tenant has an equal right to the income from the property and neither alone can encumber it or subject it to the claims of his creditors. In any case, it is as a practical matter difficult to dispose of any kind of jointly owned property or to manage it effectively without the collaboration or at least the consent of the other owner or owners.

With real estate, this problem extends to selling, mortgaging, improving, maintaining, leasing, or otherwise dealing with the property. With securities, it involves joint agreement on selling, borrowing, and reinvesting. Termination of the joint ownership, whatever mode of termination may be adopted, eliminates or reduces these problems.

2. *Control after death.* Control after death has two aspects. The first is the question, to whom ownership will pass. Where the property is jointly owned, the answer is simply that the survivor or survivors will own it, without regard to the decedent's will or other evidences of the decedent's desires. Moreover, the survivor's will—rather than the decedent's—will control the ultimate distribution of the property.

The second aspect involves outright ownership as compared with interests held in trust. Even if the surviving joint owner is the decedent's wife and she is the primary object of his bounty, the decedent (or both parties) may prefer that the property be placed in trust—for management reasons; for protection against claims of creditors; to save estate taxes; to divide income among several family members; or for other purposes—rather than pass to the survivor outright. Joint ownership precludes the imposition of a trust by the decedent; termination of the joint ownership enables him to place the property (or the portion received by him) in trust.

[¶401.2]   Tax in Estate of Surviving Spouse.

Where the client's potential estate tax is covered by the unified credit, and his spouse's estate will be shielded from tax, there is no estate tax disadvantage to their joint ownership of all the assets involved. Absent will be a different tax result due to lifetime transfers, if (a) the adjusted gross estate of the first spouse to die does not exceed the following amounts.

$120,666	if death occurs in	1977
$134,000	if death occurs in	1978
$147,333	if death occurs in	1979
$161,563	if death occurs in	1980
$175,625	if death occurs in	1981 or thereafter—

And (b) if the decedent's spouse has no separate estate, no tax will be payable by either estate, and joint ownership is from this standpoint harmless.

Although TRA 76 has replaced the prior $60,000 estate tax exemption with a credit, which will increase over a five-year period to an exemption equivalent of $175,625. However, estate tax savings will continue to be attained for many estates by taking advantage of the marital deduction in combination with a "nonmarital" or residuary trust. For example, $500,000 adjusted gross estate with no marital deduction involves estate tax of $98,000, whereas use of the full marital deduction would reduce the tax to $21,400. If the entire adjusted gross estate minus death taxes were to pass to a surviving spouse who has no estate of her own, her estate tax liability would be $64,000. On the other hand, if she is given only the portion of her husband's estate which qualifies for the marital deduction, the tax in her estate would be reduced to $21,400. Thus the combined taxes in both estates, utilizing the latter design, would amount to $42,800, as compared with the $162,600 that would have been payable if the surviving spouse had received her husband's entire distributable estate and died without consuming principal.

As a result of these considerations, it has become common practice for the spouse with the larger estate to direct that it be divided and distributed in two shares. The first share, equal to the maximum marital deduction, is given to the surviving spouse or is placed in a trust for her on terms which meet the criteria for the marital deduction.[1] The other share, diminished by estate and inheritance taxes, is placed in a trust which may provide income or other benefits for the surviving spouse during her lifetime and then passes to (or in trust for) children or other beneficiaries after her death, the trust being so designed as to avoid taxation of the principal at the death of the surviving spouse.

The result of this design, if the spouse with the substantial estate dies first, is that one-half of the estate (the nonmarital portion) will be subject to tax in his estate. The other one-half of his estate (the half that qualifies for the marital deduction) will be taxed in the estate of the second to die—rather than have the entire net estate taxed at the latter's death.

However, this division of an estate into marital deduction and nonmarital shares or portions cannot be accomplished where the entire gross estate is jointly owned. It is necessary in such cases, if the nonmarital portion is to be placed in trust, to place at least half of the adjusted gross estate in sole ownership so that it will pass under the client's will or other trust instrument. This means that it may be subjected to State inheritance taxes from which it might otherwise be exempt. And that it will be subject to administration expenses, such as commissions payable to the personal representative of the estate.

Where the client's adjusted gross estate exceeds $175,000 (or the lower exemption equivalent applicable in a year prior to 1981) it is necessary to weigh against the estate tax advantages of terminating joint ownership, the potential costs of State inheritance tax and administration expenses.

In the following examples, assume that:

(a) State law exempts from inheritance tax property passing to a surviving spouse through joint ownership;
(b) The applicable inheritance tax rate on assets passing by will is 6 percent;
(c) A personal representative is entitled to a commission of 5 percent on assets administered by him. No commission on assets jointly owned;
(d) Estate expenses otherwise will not vary as between jointly owned and testamentary assets;
(e) Deaths will occur after 1980.
(f) The adjusted gross estate will be the same as the gross estate (on the assumption that other allowable debts and deductions are nominal).

---

[1] The utility of this two-share (marital and nonmarital) scheme of distribution is explained in ¶101 of Chapter 1, and the criteria for qualification of the marital deduction gift are explained in ¶103 of that chapter.

If a client's (adjusted gross) estate consists entirely of $350,000 of assets owned jointly with his spouse but fully includible in the client's estate for estate tax purposes,[2] there will be no federal estate tax if he predeceases his spouse. One-half ($175,000) will qualify for the marital deduction, and the tax on the remaining $175,000 will be avoided by the unified credit. There will be no State inheritance tax and no commissions payable in his estate to an executor or administrator.

However, the client's surviving spouse will have the entire $350,000 adjusted gross estate. Assuming that she does not remarry and utilize the marital deduction, her estate will be subject to a federal estate tax of $52,600, State inheritance tax of $21,000 (6 percent of $350,000), and commissions of $17,500 (5 percent of $350,000), a total estate reduction of $91,100.

Had we terminated the joint ownership by transferring $175,000 of the joint assets to the sole ownership of the first spouse (A) to die (pursuant to the criteria for termination explained below), his adjusted gross estate would comprise $175,000 of joint assets and $175,000 of solely owned assets. By placing the latter in a trust for his spouse (B) for life, with remainder to the children, in such form that the principal would pass to the children at the death of the surviving spouse without being taxed in her estate, the estate tax results would be as follows:

In A's estate, $175,000 of his adjusted gross estate would qualify for the marital deduction and tax on the remaining $175,000 would be avoided by the unified credit. No estate tax.

In B's estate, estate taxes on the $175,000 received through joint ownership would be avoided by her unified credit. Her life estate in the $175,000 trust would simply terminate. No estate tax.

However the termination of joint ownership as to one-half of A's estate would result in State inheritance tax of $10,500 (6 percent of $175,000) in his estate, and commissions of $8,750 (5 percent of $175,000) for administering his estate, or total shrinkage of $19,250. In B's estate, the State inheritance tax would be $10,500 (6 percent of $175,000) and the commissions would be $8,750 (5 percent of $175,000). The total of the State inheritance taxes and commissions in both estates ($38,500) is substantially less than the shrinkage resulting from such taxes and commissions in B's estate ($91,000) where the entire estate passed to her through joint ownership.

The saving of $52,600 ($91,100 minus $38,500) achieved in this example is offset only by loss of income on the $19,250 of expenses accelerated into A's estate. At 6 percent the annual income of $19,250 is $1,155, so that it would take (ignoring tax on the income) more than 45

[2] As discussed in ¶401.3 below, this will continue to be so in a wide range of cases despite the fractional interest rule introduced by TRA 76.

years for this loss of income to offset the estate tax saving.

In the foregoing example, we have assumed that the joint ownership would be terminated only to the extent of one-half of the adjusted gross estate, in order for this one-half to be placed in a trust which will permit the principal to escape taxation in the estate of the surviving spouse. In this format the half of the estate that remains in joint ownership provides the full marital deduction. We avoid adding the remaining assets also to the taxable estate of the surviving spouse.

Your client may wish to go further, and terminate the joint ownership of all his assets. He may do this for at least two reasons: (1) to eliminate the burden (where the pre-TRA 76 rules still apply) of proving (see ¶401.3) the contribution to such investments of the spouse who survives; and (2) in order to increase his control of the property during lifetime and to impose trust provisions or other controls or limitations on the property by the terms of his will (as discussed in ¶401.1).

Termination of joint ownership of all of the jointly owned property doubles the State inheritance taxes and the costs of administration of the client's estate. This is true if we apply the same assumptions as to taxation and compensation as were applied in the earlier example.[3] This, in turn, raises the break-even point, in other words, the size of the adjusted gross estate above which the estate tax savings will be greater than the offsetting costs.

Not only is the break-even point raised, but for the same reasons the offsetting costs are correspondingly higher at all levels, and the net estate tax savings correspondingly reduced. However, the savings may remain substantial, and the elimination of the tracing problem and the acquisition of a greater degree of control over the property may well compensate for the reduction. Let us now consider with more particularity these matters of tracing and control.

[¶401.3]   Tracing problems.

Generally speaking, for State property law purposes, property which is placed in joint names by compliance with all requisite procedures is treated as jointly owned, without regard to the respective contributions of the parties. For estate tax purposes, property which the joint owners have acquired by gift or purchase is taxed in a deceased joint owner's estate only to the extent of his proportionate interest in the property. However, except as provided in TRA 76 (as specified below),

---

[3] In States which impose tax on a graduated scale, the tax could more than double, whereas the commissions of the personal representative would not double if local law or practice provides a declining scale for such compensation.

where the property was purchased in joint names by one or more of the joint owners, the entire value of jointly owned property is includible in the gross estate of the first to die of the joint owners except to the extent that the contribution of funds of the survivor can be proved. This means proof of the survivor's contribution of funds which were never derived from the decedent. A gift received by the survivor from the decedent and invested by her in the joint property will not be treated as the survivor's contribution. The only exception or limitation to this rule is that if the decedent, prior to acquisition of the joint property, made a gift to the other party of income-producing property, and if the income from that property belonged to the survivor and became her entire contribution to the purchase price of the joint property, the portion of the joint property attributable to that income contribution will be excluded from the decedent's gross estate. Reg. Sec. 20.2040-1(c)(5).

These rules impose the necessity of tracing, which in many cases becomes a Herculean task. Especially where spouses are involved, funds are commonly invested and reinvested over the years in real estate, securities, and bank accounts. Sometimes these investments are in joint names or in the names of one or the other spouse. Into the mix may go earnings of either or both, inheritances large or small, and gifts by each to the other. Even in the case of a single large purchase such as a home, the source of the down payment may be clear but the derivation of the mortgage installments, comprising the bulk of the purchase price, may vary from time to time.

In most of these cases, records that bear on contribution will be fragmentary at best, and records designed to establish the parties' respective contributions will be nonexistent, as most people are unfamiliar with the treatment of joint property for estate tax purposes and the eventual requirement of tracing. Those who are aware will normally avoid joint ownership, so that such records will not be needed.

Occasionally, the costs of tracing will be so high that little is saved by proving the contribution of the survivor. In other cases tracing will be impossible even though the parties know that there was a contribution.

This tracing problem will in many cases provide a strong incentive to terminate joint ownership. Not only can the tracing problem be eliminated by the termination, but in some cases the need for filing an estate tax return will also be eliminated.

For example, consider a case in which a husband and wife are joint owners of property having a value of $200,000 and no other assets. Upon the death of either spouse, an estate tax return must be filed. This is true even if it is claimed that the decedent made no contribution to the joint property. The avoidance of tax will depend on proof of the survivor's contribution. If the termination is accomplished by transferring title to all the joint property to the husband's name alone, and if no gift by the wife is involved in the transfer, no estate tax return will be required upon the wife's prior death.

Under TRA 76, in the following specified circumstances, the above-described "consideration furnished" test is replaced with a fractional interest or 50 percent rule:

☐ The property involved must have been owned by husband and wife with right of survivorship.

☐ The joint ownership must have been created by one or both of the joint tenants.

☐ The joint ownership must have been created after December 31, 1976.

☐ In the case of personal property, the creation of the joint interest must have been a completed transfer for gift tax purposes.

☐ In the case of real property, the donor must have elected (under Sec. 2515 of the Code discussed in ¶403.1 to treat the creation of the joint tenancy as a taxable event at that time by filing a timely gift tax return. (Such an election will also apply to additions to the value of the interest, such as mortgage payments.)

If the fractional interest rule applies under TRA 76, one-half of the value of the property owned in joint tenancy is includible in the decedent's gross estate regardless of which tenant furnished the consideration. (This may be helpful where the decedent furnished more than 50 percent of the consideration, but unfortunate where it can be proved that the surviving spouse furnished more than 50 percent of it.)

Unless the creation of the joint ownership meets the first three, and the fourth or fifth (whichever is pertinent) of the five requirements listed above, the "consideration furnished" test continues to apply, with its pre-TRA 76 burden of proof. This means that the old test remains in effect for the following cases:

☐ Property owned by non-spouses as joint tenants with right of survivorship.

☐ Property placed in joint ownership prior to January 1, 1977. (However, if the joint tenancy is severed, and recreated after December 31, 1976, it will be eligible for the new fractional interest treatment provided the other tests are met.)

☐ Personal property owned jointly by spouses where the creation of the joint ownership was not a completed gift for gift tax purposes. Examples are joint bank accounts from which either party may make withdrawals and U.S. Series E and Series H bonds which may be redeemed by either co-owner.

☐ Real property, where the creation of the joint tenancy was not duly reported as a gift.

☐ Real or personal property where the contribution of the parties was such that no gift was made in the creation of the joint ownership.

☐ Jointly owned property acquired by inter vivos or testamentary gift to the joint owners.

[¶402] ESTATE TAX SAVINGS THROUGH TERMINATION

Implicit in the discussion of "when to terminate" are three separate elements of potential estate tax savings.

[¶402.1] Avoidance of Over-Qualified Marital Deduction

In several examples we demonstrated that while joint ownership of the entire gross estate will provide the full marital deduction in the estate of the first spouse to die, it increases unnecessarily the taxable estate of the surviving spouse, who receives the entire estate minus the taxes payable therefrom. Joint ownership can be terminated as to the portion of the estate which is not intended to qualify for the marital deduction. This nonmarital portion of the larger estate, which is taxable at the owner's death, can be placed in a trust through which this portion will escape taxation in the estate of the surviving spouse.

The object is to give to the surviving spouse, and subject to estate tax in her estate, only the portion of the first spouse's estate which we desire to qualify for the marital deduction in his estate. Any more than this is an "overqualified" marital deduction.

By dividing the larger estate into two portions, the marital deduction and nonmarital portions, the effect is to divide one large estate (subject to double taxation as to the nonmarital portion) into two smaller estates for estate tax purposes. Moreover, since the estate tax is imposed on a graduated scale, the two smaller "estates" may be taxed at lower brackets than the single larger estate. Or these "estates" may be shielded from taxation by the applicable credits.

[¶402.2] Immediate Estate Reduction Without Gifts.

For the sake of simplicity we have assumed thus far that a joint estate of A and B valued at, say, $500,000, would, after termination, be the separate estate of A valued at $500,000, B having no estate at all.

Suppose the $500,000 consists of (a) real estate purchased with A's funds, not treated as a gift, and having a market value of $100,000, plus (b) securities purchased with A's funds prior to January 1, 1977, having a market value of $400,000. The decision may be to transfer title to the real estate to A and to divide the securities equally between A and B. None of these transfers would involve a gift cognizible for gift tax purposes (although taxable gifts may have been made when the securities were purchased in joint names). The result of the transactions would be that A would have a gross estate of $300,000 ($100,000 of realty and $200,000 of securities), and B would have a gross estate of $200,000. Use of the marital deduction for the excess over $175,000 (the exemption equivalent of A's credit) will eliminate A's estate tax if B survives him, and B's gross estate will be $325,000 (her $200,000 plus a marital deduction gift of $125,000) rather than $500,000 for estate tax purposes, thus reducing the tax in her estate also.

[¶402.3]   Avoidance of Unfair Taxation
Through Tracing Failure

Assume again, that A and B have jointly owned assets valued at $500,000, composed and acquired as already discussed, and that all of the property was purchased over the years with funds of A and funds of B given to her by A. If B should predecease A and A should fail to produce a persuasive tracing of the investment moneys, the entire $500,000 would be includible in B's estate, thus subjecting it to an "incorrect" and unnecessary estate tax of $21,400. To this tax may be added accounting or other costs involved in the unsuccessful attempt to trace. There may be increased legal fees by reason of the necessity to file a federal estate tax return and represent the estate in the audit. All of this can be avoided by appropriate termination measures.

[¶403]   HOW TO TERMINATE JOINT OWNERSHIP
WITHOUT TAXABLE GIFTS

If you have determined that estate tax savings or other objectives indicate termination of joint ownership, great care should be taken in selecting the method or methods of termination. Mistakes can be costly in terms of gift taxes, capital gains taxes, or both. The termination can be combined with a gift program, but it is also possible to terminate joint ownership without making taxable gifts.

In either case, it is essential to understand the gift tax treatment of the creation and the termination of joint ownership, which varies according to the nature of the assets involved. In the case of real estate, gift tax treatment depends on the date of acquisition and prior gift tax treatment. The gift tax aspects may be summarized as follows:

[¶403.1]   Entireties Real Property Acquired After 1954.

Where real property has been acquired after 1954 by husband and wife as joint tenants with right of survivorship or as tenants by the entirety, and no gift tax returns have been filed with respect to the property,[4] there will be no gift tax consequence on termination if each spouse receives a share equal to the value of his or her interest, depending upon contribution. The interest of each spouse is determined by applying a fraction, with a numerator equal to his or her contribution and a denominator equal to the total contributions of both spouses.

Thus, if the spouses contributed equally to the cost of the property, equal division of it will have no gift tax consequence. If one spouse provided the entire purchase price, transfer of the entire property to him or her will have no gift tax consequence.

If the spouses elected to report taxable gifts with respect to the Section 2515 property, its treatment for gift tax purposes on termination will be the same as the treatment of real property acquired prior to 1955.

[¶403.2]   Other Jointly Owned Real Property

Where real property has been acquired at any time in joint tenancy with right of survivorship by persons who are not husband or wife, a taxable gift was made if one owner contributed more than one-half of the total consideration. At termination, a taxable gift will be involved if one owner receives less than one-half of the total property.

Thus, if two such persons contribute equally to the purchase price of the property and on termination receive equal shares of it, no gift will have been made on creation or on termination of the joint tenancy.

However, if, one owner pays the entire purchase price and on termination receives the entire property, he will have made a gift to the other owner of one-half of the consideration at the time of purchase. The other owner will have made a gift to him of one-half of the value of the property on termination.

Where real property has been acquired by husband and wife as joint tenants with right of survivorship or as tenants by the entirety prior to January 1, 1955, or so acquired thereafter and reported for gift tax

[4]Such property will sometimes be referred to as "Section 2515 property."

purposes, the treatment discussed in the preceding paragraphs applies. However, the value of the spouses' respective interests in the property is determined actuarially. The factor so determined is substituted for the simple fraction mentioned in the preceding three paragraphs. (Use of such factors is illustrated in ¶403.6.)

[¶403.3]   Joint Bank Accounts

On the establishment of a joint bank account, the interests of the parties for gift tax purposes are considered to be proportionate to their contributions. Accordingly, no gift is recognized until one owner withdraws funds in excess of his or her contributions.

If A deposits $10,000 in the names of A and B jointly, A's withdrawals are not deemed gifts. Any withdrawal by B would be deemed a gift by A to B at the time of withdrawal.

If A and B deposit $5,000 each in their joint names, a gift would be made if and when the withdrawals by either exceed $5,000.

Accordingly, a termination of a joint account by which neither party receives (including his past withdrawals, if any) more than he contributed to the account involves no gift. Any other termination does involve a gift.

[¶403.4]   U.S. Savings Bonds

Series E bonds are issued at a discount and increase in value until maturity (or beyond). Series H bonds are issued at par and interest is payable semiannually. Either type of bond may be acquired in a form of co-ownership registered as "Mr. A or Mrs. A" In this form the bonds may be redeemed by either co-owner on request and presentation of the bond.

The purchase of these bonds (unlike other securities) in coownership does not result in a taxable gift. There is no gift unless and until the noncontributing co-owner surrenders the bond for redemption and has no obligation to account to his co-owner for the proceeds. Or the bond is reissued in the noncontributing co-owner's sole name.

If the purchasing co-owner redeems the bond or has it reissued in his own name, no gift will have occurred at the time of creation or at the time of termination of the co-ownership.

[¶403.5]   Other Securities

Where stocks or bonds (other than the above-mentioned U.S. savings bonds) are purchased in the names of two or more persons as joint

owners with right of survivorship, or in the names of two spouses as
tenants by the entireties, a gift is made if and to the extent that the value
of the interest received by a party exceeds his contribution to the purchase price.

Correspondingly, on termination of joint ownership or of a tenancy by the entireties, a gift is made to the extent that a party receives
less than the value of his interest at the time of termination.

Essentially, the same principles apply, with the same result, as in
subparagraph 403.2, with respect to real property acquired prior to
1955. There is a difference in the valuation of interests in securities as
well as pre-1955 real estate as between interests held by joint owners
with right of survivorship and interests held by spouses as tenants by the
entireties. The difference will be explained and illustrated in the following ¶403.6.

[¶403.6]   Joint Tenancies versus Tenancies by the Entirety

As we have seen, the gift tax rules are the same with respect to real
property acquired prior to 1955; real property acquired after 1954 and
reported for gift tax purposes; and personal property other than bank
accounts and United States Series E and H bonds. In all such cases, the
occurrence of a gift at the time of creation of joint ownership or entireties ownership turns on whether a party acquires an interest which is
greater than his or her contribution. The occurrence of a gift on termination turns on whether a party receives more than the value of his
interest at the time of termination.

The only difference between joint ownership and tenancy by the
entireties for these purposes involves the valuation of the parties' respective interests. In the case of joint ownership, the gift tax law recognizes
that under State law either joint owner may sever the joint tenancy and
transfer his fractional interest without the consent of the other. This
means that the value of each owner's interest is determined for gift tax
purposes by a simple fraction.

In the case of a tenancy by the entireties, however, the value of the
spouses' respective interests is determined by the use of actuarial factors
which take into account the probability of one spouse surviving the
other. Moreover, as these probabilities change with advancing age, it is
necessary to redetermine the interests of the spouses at the time of
termination. In each case, the actuarially determined value of the interest replaces the simple fraction that is used in a joint tenancy. (The
factor for the interest of the husband is the figure in the applicable
column for difference in ages determined according to the age of the

wife in Table ET6 of IRS Publication No. 723A, Supplement 1 (4-71).[5] The value of the wife's interest is determined by subtracing the value of the husband's interest from the value of the entire property. Table ET6 is reproduced in Appendix B of this book.)

The consequence of actuarial valuation will frequently be a figure other than a simple 50 percent. If the factor is .42911, for example, and if our purpose is to divide property according to the value of the interests in order to avoid a gift on termination, this would yield roughly a 43 percent and a 57 percent interest in real property, or, in the case of 100 shares of stock, 43 shares for one spouse and 57 for the other.

This awkwardness can frequently be avoided, however, because the gift that would be involved in a pure 50-50 split, depending on the values, may be covered by the annual gift tax exclusion. Or by the exclusion plus the gift tax marital deduction. Or may otherwise be a gift which the parties are willing to indulge in the circumstances.

But *caveat:* extreme care should be taken in advising people as how to divide their jointly owned securities. A common, and natural, impulse will be for them to do it on a "one for you, one for me" basis. In other words, where stocks of different companies have similar values, one spouse would take all the stock of company X and the other spouse would take all the stock of company Y, whereas we intend that they divide the stock of *each* company. For federal income tax purposes, trading assets ("one for you, one for me") is like selling them to each other; it is probable that the exchange will result in capital gains tax where the market values exceed basis.

We would suggest that the estate planner handle the division of securities directly with the transfer agents. Where this is not feasible, a letter should be given to the client for delivery to his broker, specifying precisely the splitting that is intended. And the results should be verified on completion.

Another *caveat:* where real estate is involved, whether or not the termination of the joint ownership involves a gift, it is important to ascertain whether the contemplated deed will involve state or local realty transfer taxes and, if so, to apprise the client of the additional cost involved.

Now, having reviewed the various types of property and their gift tax treatment, let us consider an illustrative case in which the parties desire to terminate all joint ownership without making substantial taxable

---

[5] Table ET6 is based upon interest at the rate of 6 percent per year. In the case of transactions from January 1, 1952, to December 31, 1970, the valuation tables were based upon interest at the rate of 3½ percent per year, were composite tables, and can be found in Table IX of IRS Publication No. 11. For transactions prior to January 1, 1952, interest was computed at 4 percent per year.

gifts in the process. A married couple, John (age 40) and Mary (age 37) have the following jointly owned assets, none of which is covered by the fractional interest rule of TRA 76:

Real property
1. Home—purchased with John's funds in 1960, no gift tax return $120,000
2. Seashore house—inherited by John and Mary from Mary's mother   80,000

Securities
3. Stocks—acquired with John's funds   160,000
4. E bonds—purchased by Mary with savings from her salary   20,000

Cash
5. Checking account—approximately equal funds of John and Mary   8,000
6. Savings account—Mary's savings   12,000
                                                                  $400,000

The assets should be distributed as follows:

1. Title to the home, which was acquired after 1954 and not then treated as a gift, can be transferred to John, who paid for it. His "contribution" was 100 percent, so that distribution to him of 100 percent involves no gift.

2. The interests of John and Mary in the seashore property, which they inherited jointly, must be actuarially determined. Based on Table ET6 of I.R.S. Publication No. 723A, Supplement 1 (4-71) (a copy of which is included in Appendix B), where the age of the wife is 37 years and the difference in age 3 years, the factor for the combined income and survivorship rights of the husband is .45023. Based on this factor, the value of John's rights in the property is $80,000 × .45023, or $36,018. The value of Mary's rights in the property is $80,000 minus $36,018, or $43,982. A 50-50 divisions will involve a gift to John of $3,982 ($40,000 minus $36,018.)

3. Although the stocks were acquired with John's funds (gifts having been made at the time of purchase), the only distribution not cognizible for gift tax purposes will be a division actuarially determined as in paragraph 2 above. Applying the same factor, John's interest amounts to $72,036 and Mary's amounts to $87,964. An equal division of the stocks will result in a gift to John of $7,964 ($80,000 minus $72,036).

4. The E bonds purchased with Mary's funds can be re-registered in Mary's name with no gift tax consequence.

5. If the checking account funds are divided equally between John and Mary and placed in separate accounts, neither party will have with-

drawn more than his or her contribution, so that no gift will have been made.

    6. The savings account, representing Mary's savings, can be transferred to her name alone without making a taxable gift.

If the joint ownership is terminated along the lines above suggested, the parties' estates will be composed as follows:

Real property	*John*	*Mary*
1. Home	$120,000	
2. Seashore house	40,000	$ 40,000
Securities		
3. Stocks	80,000	80,000
4. E Bonds		20,000
Cash		
5. Checking account	4,000	4,000
6. Savings account		12,000
GROSS ESTATE	$244,000	$156,000

    It should be noted that John's gross estate has been reduced from a "presumptive" $400,000 to a clear $244,000, eliminating the burden of tracing and proving Mary's contributions to items 3 through 6 and the risk of tax on failure of such proof. Mary's estate has been reduced from a "presumptive" $400,000 to a clear $156,000, eliminating the need to trace and prove John's contributions to items 1, 3 and 5 and the risk of tax on failure of such proof. (The equal division of items 2 and 3 involves gifts to John aggregating $11,946 [$3,982 plus $7,964]. (The gifts if made in one year will be covered by the gift tax marital deduction and Mary's annual exclusion.)

    Further, John can now arrange his estate so that if he predeceases Mary only the marital deduction portion of his estate (or perhaps less than the full marital deduction) will be added to Mary's estate and the balance can be held in trust without being taxed again at Mary's death. The ultimate devolution of that balance can now be determined by John's will rather than Mary's.

    In the foregoing example, we assumed that none of the jointly owned property was covered by the fractional interest rule of TRA 76. We should note, however, that if the stocks, for example, were covered by the rule, so that only 50 percent of their value would be includible in John's gross estate at death regardless of his 100 percent contribution to their cost, the termination of joint ownership as to the stocks would effect no estate tax saving, though it might be otherwise desirable.

[¶404]   HOW TO TERMINATE JOINT OWNERSHIP
WITH TAXABLE GIFTS

Termination involving gifts. We have discussed and illustrated the rules for terminating joint ownership without making taxable gifts. However, the estate planning that indicates termination may also indicate the advisability of making taxable gifts at the same time, for estate equalization or other goals.

For estate tax purposes, of course, Sec. 2036 of the Code pulls back into the gross estate transferred property, the income or enjoyment of which has been retained by the transferor. Where a home is transferred to one of two spouses and the other spouse continues to live in the house, the question arises whether there has been a transfer with enjoyment retained.

As might be anticipated, this question has been litigated. In the absence of proof of an agreement under which the transferor has reserved the right to reside in the home, the courts have thus far refused to construct the reservation of enjoyment upon the bare fact that the transferor continues to reside there. In *Estate of Allen D. Gutchess,* 46 T.C. 544 (1966), acq., 1967-1 C.B. 2, a husband transferred to his wife a residence in which both continued to reside until the transferor's death eleven years later. The court stated (p. 557) that the donor husband's continued occupancy did not diminish his wife's possession and enjoyment, and that such "post-transfer use is insufficient to indicate any prior agreement or pre-arrangement for retention of use by the transferor." See also *Stephenson v. U.S.,* 238 F. Supp. 660 (W.D. Va. 1965); *Estate of Binkley v. U.S.,* 358 F.2d 639 (3rd Cir. 1966); *Union Planters National Bank v. U.S.,* 238 F. Supp. 883 (W.D. Tenn. 1964), aff'd. 361 F.2d 662 (6th Cir. 1966); *Wier, Estate of Robert W.,* 17 T.C. 409, 422 (1951), and *Bridgforth v. U.S.,* 73-1 USTC Par. 12, 916 (S.D. Miss. 1973).

We suggest that the tranferor's position may be strengthened in such cases by including in the deed to his spouse a statement substantially as follows:

> "John Smith, one of the Grantors herein, renounces any and all right to the income, possession or enjoyment of the premises hereby conveyed."

The rules set forth in ¶403 with which we charted the course for gift-tax-free terminations of joint ownership, are also the rules that apply with respect to the several types of property and interests involved for determining the taxable amounts where gifts are intended to be made. Thus in the case of John and Mary, the transfer of the seashore home to her name, involving a $37,018 gift to her, would virtually equalize the two estates, enabling the parties to minimize potential estate taxes through well designed reciprocal wills.

5

Lifetime Gift Program

[¶500] IMPORTANT CONSIDERATIONS—THEN AND NOW

Gifts to charities are the subject of Chapter Two. Gifts involved in the creation and termination of joint ownership are fully discussed in Chapter Four. Transfers of the ownership of life insurance policies to irrevocable trusts are considered in Chapter Seven. This chapter deals mainly with the other elements that may be included in a thoughtful lifetime gift program: noncharitable gifts of assets other than life insurance. These will usually be gifts of real estate, securities, or cash to members of the donor's family. Such gifts can produce substantial estate tax savings.

Traditionally, one technique of estate planning has been to eliminate or to reduce a client's estate tax by reducing his gross estate. The gross estate can be reduced by consuming or wasting one's resources, but it can also be reduced by gifts of property to others, provided the donor completes the gifts, retaining no tax-adverse "strings" on the transferred assets, and the transfer is not includible in his gross estate by reason of its proximity to the date of death. As we shall see, notwithstanding extensive and drastic tax changes wrought by TRA 76, a lifetime gift program should still be considered one of the ten best ways to save estate taxes.

[¶500.1] Before TRA 76—Tax Background

The gift tax, related to the estate tax but having its own exclusions, exemptions and rates, was designed to mitigate the loss of tax revenues that might otherwise result from a program of lifetime giving. For reasons which will be apparent from the summary that follows, the gift tax provisions rarely imposed a serious impediment to significant tax avoidance. The present tax structure, as it affects lifetime transfers, can best be understood with reference to the gift tax law in effect prior to TRA 76. The principal elements of the "old law" were these:

☐ Transfers for less then full and adequate consideration in money or money's worth were subject to the gift tax provisions.

☐ The gift tax applied only to completed gifts.

☐ The gift tax was cumulative. Each year's tax was computed with reference to taxable gifts made in prior years, and the gift tax (like the estate tax) was imposed on a graduated scale, so that higher brackets were encountered as the total taxable gifts increased.

☐ The gift tax rates, ranging from 2½ percent to 57¾ percent, were three-fourths of the estate tax rates. (Moreover, this rate comparison does not fully depict the contrast, as the graduated gift tax rates began at the bottom of the scale while the property given away was removed from the top estate tax bracket.)

☐ An individual was permitted to make present interest gifts[1] up to $3,000 per year to any number of persons, regardless of relationship, without incurring gift tax liability. For a married donor, this annual exclusion was increased to $6,000 for gifts of community property or for gifts of separate property with the spouse's consent to gift-splitting.

☐ Each donor also had a $30,000 lifetime exemption, which could be used at one time or gradually during the donor's lifetime to cover gifts which were not covered by his $3,000 (or combined $6,000 as above mentioned) annual exclusions (either because they exceeded the exclusion amounts or because they were gifts of future rather than present interests). As in the case of the annual exclusion, a donor's gifts could be treated as made by the donor and his spouse in equal parts, in the case of gifts of community property or gifts of separate property with the spouse's consent to that treatment, so that the donor's lifetime exemption could be effectively increased to $60,000 in such cases.

☐ The donor was entitled to an unlimited deduction for gifts to qualified charities (as more fully discussed in Chapter Two).

☐ In the case of a gift to the donor's spouse, only one-half of the value of the transferred property was considered for gift tax purposes. In other words, there was a 50 percent gift tax marital deduction.

---

[1]Basically, a present interest gift is one in which the donee has the immediate right to possession or enjoyment of the property, either as outright owner or as a trust beneficiary. If possession or enjoyment is deferred, the donee has a future interest. The subject is more fully discussed in ¶503.4 below, as the distinction continues to apply under the current tax laws.

☐ Returns were due quarterly—on February 15, May 15, August 15 and November 15.

For a simple example of the tax utility of a gift program under the old law, consider a donor with an adjusted gross estate of $396,000 who desired to make outright present interest gifts to his two children and four grandchildren. With his spouse's consent to gift splitting, he could make tax-free gifts of $36,000 to each child and $6,000 to each grandchild, using exemptions and exclusions as follows:

Annual exclusions ($6,000 for each of six donees)	$36,000
Lifetime exemption (including spouse's)	60,000
	$96,000

These gifts, assuming they were not includible in his gross estate as gifts in contemplation of death, would reduce the donor's adjusted gross estate from $396,000 to $300,000. Utilizing a 50 percent estate tax marital deduction, the result would be to reduce the donor's estate tax (under pre-TRA 76 estate tax provisions) from $30,900 to $17,500, with no offsetting gift tax cost. It should also be noted that while the mentioned gifts exhausted the lifetime exemptions of the donor and his spouse, the annual exclusions for future years would permit the donor with his spouse's consent to make tax-free gifts to the same donees aggregating $36,000 per year so long as he might desire to do so.

In larger estates, of course, or in the absence of the estate tax marital deduction, the estate tax saving would be more dramatic. Also, it would frequently be beneficial to make gifts in excess of the available exemptions and exclusions, and pay gift tax on the excess, by reason of the very favorable tax rate differential which is mentioned above.

To recapitulate: Prior to TRA 76, a gift program could be designed to yield some or all of the following advantages:

1. Substantial gifts covered by the gift tax marital deduction, lifetime exemption(s), and annual exclusions could be utilized to reduce substantially the donor's taxable estate with *no* gift tax cost.

2. Gifts which were not covered by the above-mentioned gift tax "shelters" would be taxed (on a cumulative basis) in the lowest applicable gift tax brackets while relieving the donor's estate of tax in the highest applicable estate tax brackets.

3. The estate tax must be paid from the estate on which the tax is imposed, whereas the gift tax is normally payable from the remaining assets of the donor, thus yielding a greater differential than is revealed

by comparison of the corresponding tax brackets.

4. Use of the full gift tax exemption would not deprive the donor of any part of his (pre-TRA 76) $60,000 estate tax exemption.

5. Even if gifts made within three years prior to death were determined to be includible in the decedent's gross estate for estate tax purposes as gifts made "in contemplation of death," the gift taxes paid on such gifts were not added back to the gross estate, so that the estate tax was reduced as a consequence of any gift taxes paid.

6. Gifts of income-producing property to children or grandchildren might reduce substantially the total income taxes paid by the donor and his family. In some cases the income tax saving would in the first year or shortly thereafter exceed the gift tax cost of the transfer.

As we shall see, TRA 76 has put an end to some but not all of the gift program advantages outlined above.

[¶500.2]   The TRA 76 Changes—Estate Tax Saving vs. Gift Tax Costs

Several features of the old law have survived TRA 76, to wit:

1. The criteria for determining whether or not a transfer is in the taxable category—completed transfers for less than full consideration in money or money's worth.
2. Annual exclusions of $3,000 per donee for present interest gifts, with gift-splitting provisions for married donors.
3. Also, in the case of married donors, gift-splitting for gifts not covered by the annual exclusions.
4. Unlimited charitable deduction.

Beyond these elements, however, drastic changes have been made:

☐ TRA 76 discarded the exemptions provided in the old law for both lifetime gifts and transfers at death.

☐ A new unified (gift and estate tax) rate schedule has been provided. The rates range from 18 percent[2] on taxable amounts not over $10,000 to 70 percent for cumulative taxable transfers over $5,000,000, per the following schedule:

---

[2]As a result of applying the credit after the tentative tax is calculated, the tax actually starts in 1977 and 1978 in the 30 percent bracket.

UNIFIED FEDERAL ESTATE AND GIFT TAX RATES
Unified Rate Scedule

Amount with respect to which tentative tax is to be computed		Tentative tax	
Not over $10,000		18% of such amount	

Over–	But not over–	Tentative tax	of excess over–
$ 10,000	$ 20,000	$ 1,800 + 20%	$ 10,000
20,000	40,000	3,800 + 22%	20,000
40,000	60,000	8,200 + 24%	40,000
60,000	80,000	13,000 + 26%	60,000
80,000	100,000	18,200 + 28%	80,000
100,000	150,000	23,800 + 30%	100,000
150,000	250,000	38,800 + 32%	150,000
250,000	500,000	70,800 + 34%	250,000
500,000	750,000	155,800 + 37%	500,000
750,000	1,000,000	248,300 + 39%	750,000
1,000,000	1,250,000	345,800 + 41%	1,000,000
1,250,000	1,500,000	448,300 + 43%	1,250,000
1,500,000	2,000,000	555,800 + 45%	1,500,000
2,000,000	2,500,000	780,800 + 49%	2,000,000
2,500,000	3,000,000	1,025,800 + 53%	2,500,000
3,000,000	3,500,000	1,290,800 + 57%	3,000,000
3,500,000	4,000,000	1,575,800 + 61%	3,500,000
4,000,000	4,500,000	1,880,800 + 64%	4,000,000
4,500,000	5,000,000	2,205,800 + 69%	4,500,000
5,000,000		2,550,800 + 70%	5,000,000

☐ A new unified credit (in lieu of exemptions) has been provided. The unified credit of $47,000 is to be phased in over a five-year period, in the following stages and with the following exemption equivalents:

Year	Credit	Equivalent to Exemption of:
1977	$30,000	$120,667
1978	34,000	134,000
1979	38,000	147,333
1980	42,500	161,563
1981 (and after)	47,000	175,625

The credit is available for lifetime gifts to the same extent as for estate tax purposes (except that the credit was limited to $6,000 for gifts made after December 31, 1976, and before September 1, 1977. For gifts made after 1976, credit for pre-1977 gifts is based on the new unified schedule even though the gift tax actually imposed under the old rates was less[3].

☐ The marital deduction under the new law is unlimited for the first $100,000 of lifetime taxable transfers to a spouse; for the next $100,000 of such transfers there is no such deduction; and for interspousal gifts in excess of $200,000, a 50 percent deduction is allowed.

☐ To the extent that the lifetime gift tax marital deduction exceeds one-half of the amount of lifetime taxable interspousal gifts, the maximum estate tax marital deduction is reduced dollar-for-dollar.

☐ The new law changes the treatment of gifts made within three years prior to the donor's death. Under the old law, gifts made in that three-year period were presumed to have been made "in contemplation of death" and were includible in the decedent's gross estate unless the executor could rebut the presumption by showing lifetime gift motives. Moreover, even if such gifts were included in the gross estate, any gift taxes paid on them were excluded, so that the gross estate was reduced by the amount of gift tax if not by the value of the gift itself. Under the new law, gifts made within three years prior to death are added back to the gross estate regardless of motivation, and gift taxes paid on gifts made within the three-year period are also added back to the gross estate.[4] Excluded from this "add back," however, are the amounts attributable to the donor-decedent's annual exclusions (but not the exclusions attributed to his spouse as a result of gift-splitting) during the three-year period.

☐ New provisions with respect to the basis of inherited property do not change the treatment of lifetime gifts as such but alter the pre-TRA 76 contrast between lifetime and testamentary tranfers in this respect. Under the old law, property transferred during lifetime retained in the donee's hands the transferor's basis, augmented by any gift taxes paid in connection with the transfer. However, property passing from a decedent to his beneficiaries was received by the latter with a basis equal to the fair market value of the property on the date of the decedent's death or on the alternate valuation date, whichever was selected for estate tax purposes. Thus one "cost" of a lifetime gift of appreciated property was the transferee's loss of the stepped-up basis which would be

[3]The application of the new law to pre-1977 gifts is more particularly discussed in ¶500.3 below.

[4]Commentators generally refer to this as a "gross-up" of gift taxes. The authors prefer not to "gross up" their book with that expression.

available via a testamentary transfer of the property.

This differential which the old law provided in favor of transfer by inheritance is eliminated in some cases and reduced in others by the new carryover basis provisions. There provisions apply, under Sec. 1023 of the Code, to "carryover basis property." This includes all property other than income in respect of a decedent; life insurance proceeds; a joint and survivor annuity under which payments are taxable to the survivor under Sec. 72 of the Code; payments under a deferred compensation plan; property includible by reason of death within three years following a gift; property includible because of the decedent's power of revocation; property includible by reason of the decedent's general power of appointment; stock or stock options to the extent income in respect thereof is includible in gross income; and stock of a foreign personal holding company.

Carryover basis property is subject to the following four adjustments:

1. The adjusted basis of property which the decedent held (or is treated as having held) on December 31, 1976, is stepped up (for purposes of determining gain, but not loss) to the property's fair market value on December 31, 1976. For all property other than marketable securities, a special valuation method is provided. The adjustment to December 31, 1976, value is made by assuming that any appreciation occurring from the date of the decedent's acquisition of the property to the date of his death occured at the same rate per diem over the entire holding period. The appreciation so determined is reduced by the amount of any depreciation, amortization or depletion claimed by the decedent during the pre-1977 period. Any substantial improvement made after the acquisition date is treated as a separate property for the purpose of this adjustment.

2. The basis of appreciated carryover basis property that is subject to tax in the hands of its recipient is next increased on an asset by asset basis. It is increased by the amount that bears the same ratio to the federal and State estate taxes as the net appreciation in value of such property bears to the fair market value of all property subject to tax.

3. If the aggregate basis of all carryover basis property in the estate (after the foregoing adjustments) is less than $60,000, the basis of such property is stepped up pro rata (based on net appreciation) to $60,000. If the executor has elected, under Section 1023(b)(3)(A) of the Code, to exempt up to $10,000 of personal and household effects from the carryover basis rules, the basis of those assets is not counted in determining the $60,000 minimum basis.

4. A final adjustment is made for any portion of State estate, inheritance, legacy or succession taxes paid by the recipient of the prop-

erty for which the decedent's estate is not liable for or does not, in fact, pay and which is attributable to the net appreciation of the property.

The last three of the four adjustments above described may not increase the basis of the property above its fair market value. The adjustments are to be made in the order in which we have listed them.

☐ Under the new law, a donor is not required to file a gift tax return for any quarter until he has made taxable gifts of $25,000 during the calendar year. He must file a return by the 15th day of the second month following the end of the quarter in which that sum is reached or exceeded, or, if taxable gifts during the calendar year do not aggregate that amount, a return covering the year's taxable gifts must be filed by February 15 of the following year.

Before proceeding to analyze the utility of, and develop guidelines for, a lifetime gift program in the light of these sweeping changes, let us pause to grasp firmly the tax calculations which the new provisions require.

[¶500.3]   How to Calculate the Unified Tax on Gifts

Let us now reduce the tax law changes outlined above to the formulas which they indicate for calculation of taxes on transfers during lifetime and at death. For current lifetime gifts, the tax would be computed as follows:

(a)	Taxable gifts for the current quarter	(a)
(b)	Add taxable gifts for all previous quarters and years— including periods prior to January 1, 1977	+(b)
(c)	Total lifetime gifts of donor ((a) + (b))	(c)
(d)	Calculate tax (per unified rate schedule) on line (c) amount	(d)
(e)	Subtract tax (per unified rate schedule) on line (b) amount	−(e)
(f)	Gift tax liability before deducting unified credit ((d) minus (e))	(f)
(g)	Subtract available unified credit	−(g)
(h)	Gift tax liability ((f) minus (g))	(h)

The formula may be amplified helpfully with the following notes:

1. The amount of "taxable gifts" for line (a) is the amount remaining after subtracting any charitable deduction, marital deduction, and annual exclusions claimed.

2. The taxable gifts for line (b) are the amounts of prior quarters' and years'

gifts after substracting any deductions and exclusions claimed and allowable lifetime exemption.

3. The inclusion of all pre-1977 taxable gifts for line (b) will boost the marginal tax rate for post-1976 gifts. However, the reduction for tax on prior gifts (line (e)) will be calculated under the new rate schedule even for pre-1977 gifts.

4. The available unified credit is determined for line (g) by subtracing from the maximum allowable credit the amount of credit previously used for all post-1976 gifts. It should be noted that the allowable credit for gifts made in the first six months of 1977 may not exceed $6,000, and, further, that the credit otherwise available for post-1976 gifts must be reduced by 20 percent of the aggregate amount of specific exemption utilized by the donor for gifts made during the period September 8, 1976, to December 12, 1976.

For transfers at death, the tax would be computed as follows:

(a)	Gross estate—other than line (b) transfers	(a)
(b)	Add gifts within 3 years prior to death (minus exclusions allowed to donor) plus gift taxes paid thereon	+(b)
(c)	Gross estate	(c)
(d)	Subtract deductible debts and expenses	−(d)
(e)	Adjusted gross estate	(e)
(f)	Subtract allowable marital and charitable deductions	(f)
(g)	Taxable estate	(g)
(h)	Add adjusted taxable gifts	(h)
(i)	Tentative tax base	(i)
(j)	Estate tax on tentative tax base	(j)
(k)	Less credit for gift taxes paid	−(k)
(l)	Tax before unified credit	(l)
(m)	Subtract unified credit	(m)
(n)	Tax before credit for State death taxes	(n)
(o)	Subtract State tax credit	(o)
(p)	Estate tax payable	(p)

In connection with the preceding estate tax formula, we should note the following:

☐ Only taxable gifts made after December 31, 1976, are added (line (h)) in determining cumulative taxable transfers at death.

☐ In computing the estate tax, taxes paid on pre-1977 gifts are not subtracted (line (k)).

☐ The adjusted taxable gifts included in line (h) do not include any transfers which are includible in the gross estate via line (b) or otherwise.

☐ Where the entire value of a transfer subject to gift tax is included in the gross estate (line (b)), any gift tax which was paid by the decedent's spouse on such gifts under the split-gift provisions is subtracted (line (k)) in computing the estate tax.

☐ The unified credit (line (m)) must be reduced by 20 percent of any portion of the decedent's $30,000 lifetime exemption that was utilized for transfers made between September 9, 1976, and December 31, 1976.

☐ In the case of a decedent who made taxable gifts before and after 1977, some portion of the unified credit will always remain available for his estate. This is due to the fact that the gift tax computation takes pre-1977 gifts into account but the estate tax formula does not. Thus, if he made taxable gifts of $100,000 in 1975 and $150,000 in 1982, these gifts would fully utilize the $47,000 credit for gift tax purposes. For estate tax purposes, $8,200 of the credit would remain as only the 1982 gift of $150,000 would be includible in line (b) of the foregoing formula.

☐ The estate tax marital deduction (line (f)) otherwise allowable to the estate is reduced to the extent the gift tax marital deduction which the decedent utilized exceeded 50 percent of the value of the gifts made to his spouse after 1976[5]. Thus, where the lifetime gifts are less than $200,000, so that the $100,000 gift tax marital deduction exceeds 50 percent of the value of the gifts, the excess reduces the allowable estate tax marital deduction. It should be noted that:

(a) This rule has no application where the lifetime interspousal gifts exceed $200,000, as the gift tax marital deduction in such cases will not exceed 50 percent of the value of the gifts.

(b) Where the adjusted gross estate at death is $500,000 or more, application of the rule will have no effect on the aggregate estate and gift tax marital deductions (See column D, below).

(c) Where the interspousal gifts reduce the adjusted gross estate to less than $500,000, the maximum aggregate (estate and gift tax) marital deductions will be increased because the estate tax maximum ($250,000) exceeds one-half of the adjusted gross estate while the reduction for interspousal gifts does not exceed one-half of their value. See Columns A, B and C, below. (As explained in Chapter One, however, this maximization of the marital deduction will frequently be eschewed

---

[5]Note: If the decedent makes a gift to which this rule applies and dies within three years of the date of the gift, the value of the gift will be added back to his gross estate but the allowable marital deduction will be reduced by the excess of the gift tax marital deduction over 50 percent of the value of the gift. The lifetime gift in that case would result in increased estate tax.

because of the estate tax consequences of the higher amount in the estate of the surviving spouse.)

The marital deduction consequences set forth in the preceding paragraphs (b) and (c) are illustrated below:

Making Maximum Use of the Marital Deduction

	A	B	C	D
Total assets of taxpayer	400,000	525,000	735,000	1,050,000
Interspousal gifts	(100,000)	(150,000)	(250,000)	(150,000)
Debts and administration expenses	20,000	25,000	35,000	50,000
Adjusted Gross Estate at death	300,000	350,000	450,000	850,000
Potential maximum marital deduction	250,000	250,000	250,000	425,000
Reduction for gift tax marital deduction	(50,000)	(25,000)	(000)	(25,000)
Maximum estate tax marital deduction	200,000	225,000	250,000	400,000
Gift tax marital deduction	100,000	100,000	125,000	100,000
Total marital deductions	300,000	325,000	375,000	500,000
Maximum marital deduction if no gift made	250,000	250,000	350,000	500,000
Increase of total marital deduction by Interspousal gift	50,000	75,000	25,000	0

Before leaving the topic of gift and estate tax marital deductions, we should note that where a donor makes a gift to his spouse of less than $200,000, utilizing the gift tax marital deduction, and dies within three years after the gift, the estate tax marital deduction will be less than it would have been if the gift had not been made. No benefit will have been derived from the decedent's use of the gift tax marital deduction.

The credit for State death taxes (line (o) of the estate tax formula above provided) is continued as under the old law; the tabular rates for the credit are applied to the taxable estate reduced by $60,000.

[¶500.4]   Tax Treatment of Net Gifts

Where the total value of the gift property plus the gift tax thereon exceeds the amount which the donor wishes to surrender, or where the donor does not have sufficient liquid assets to pay the gift tax, the solution may be found in a "net gift." He may transfer the property to the donee on condition that the donee pay the gift tax. This arrangement has several actual and potential tax consequences:

Since the gift tax is imposed on what the donee receives, and the value of a gift subject to a gift tax liability is obviously less than the value of the gift free of tax, the reduced value of the gift and the tax must be calculated. An algebraic formula for this calculation is provided in Rev. Rul. 71-232, 1971-1 CB 275. Our current version of that formula is set forth on the next page. The authors' recent application of that formula appears on the page following the formula.

Net Tax Formula
$(T = \text{unknown gift tax})$

Gross transfers of donor for period
− Discount on gifts of fractional or
 Minority interests, if applicable
= Adjusted transfers for period − T
− Annual exclusion(s) and available credit
= Taxable gifts for period − T
+ Prior taxable transfers
= Aggregate taxable gifts − T

Bracket: Tax on bracket amount
Rate: + Tax on excess
                    = Tax on aggregate gifts
                    − Prior gift tax paid
                    = Tentative tax for period
                     − rate of tax × T

True Tax = $\dfrac{\text{Tentative Tax for period}}{1 + \text{rate of tax}}$

Proof

Adjusted transfers for period
− True tax
= Net transfers for period
− Annual exclusion(s)
= Taxable gifts for period
+ Prior taxable transfers
= Aggregate taxable gifts

Bracket: Tax on bracket amount
Rate: +   Tax on excess   _____
                              =   Aggregate gift tax
                              −   Prior gift tax paid   _____
                              =   True tax   ═══════════

Computation of Value of Taxable Gift Where Donees are Obligated to Pay the Gift Tax Due (pre-1977 Gift)

Gross transfers of donor for period	$1,435,491	
− Discount on gifts of fractional or minority interests	− 406,374	
= Adjusted transfers for period − T	1,029,144	− T
− Annual exclusion(s)	− 9,000	
= Taxable gifts for period − T	1,020,144	− T
+ Prior taxable transfers	+ 134,659	
= Aggregate taxable gifts − T	$1,154,803	− T

Bracket: 750,000   Tax on bracket amou .ι $174,900
Rate: 27¾%   + Tax on excess   + 112,333
                      = Tax on aggregate gifts   287,233
                      − Prior gift tax paid   −   23,323
                      = Tentative tax for period   263,910 −.2775T
                         − rate of tax × T

$$\text{True Tax} = \frac{\text{Tentative tax for period}}{1 + \text{rate of tax}} = \frac{263{,}910}{1.2775} = \$206{,}583$$

Proof

Adjusted transfers for period	$1,029,144
− True tax	− 206,583
= Net transfers for period	822,561
− Annual exclusion(s)	− 9,000
= Taxable gifts for period	813,561
+ Prior taxable transfers	+ 134,659
= Aggregate taxable gifts	$ 948,220

Bracket: 750,000   Tax on bracket amount $174,900
Rate: 27¾%   + Tax on excess   +   55,006
                      = Aggregate gift tax   229,906
                      − Prior gift tax paid   −   23,323
                      = True tax $206,583

The formula requires an adjustment if there is a change in the tax bracket after computing the tentative tax. The correct tax bracket may be readily apparent, and the tentative tax so computed. Otherwise, trial calculations will be necessary, moving from the bracket indicated by the tentative tax to the next lower bracket until the correct result is obtained (as confirmed by the "proof").

1. The IRS has asserted that if the donee's tax liability exceeds the donor's basis for the transferred property, the donor realizes gain equal to that excess. This contention has been rejected in *Richard H. Turner*, 49 T.C. 356 (1968), *aff'd*. 410 F. 2d 752 (6th Cir., 1969); *Kenneth W. Davis*, 30 T.C.M. 1363 (1971), aff'd 73-1 U.S.T.C. ¶9124 (5th Cir., 1972); and *Hirst v. Comm'r.*, 63 T.C. 307 (1974). But see *Joseph W. Johnson, Jr. v. Comm'r.*, 495 F. 2d 1079 (6th Cir., 1973).

2. Under Sec. 677 of the code, income realized by a trust donee between the date of the gift and the date of payment of the gift tax is taxable to the donor because it is income used to discharge a legal obligation of the donor (the gift tax being regarded as primarily the donor's obligation).

3. The donee's cost basis will be increased by the amount of the gift tax attributable to the appreciation included in the gift.

[¶501]   TAX BENEFITS OF A LIFETIME GIFT PROGRAM

Our review of the old law and the changes introduced by TRA 76 leads inevitably to this question: Since the lifetime gift tax exemption has been abolished, and lifetime gifts are taxed at the same rates as transfers at death and are added back to increase the estate tax bracket, and the unified credit at death is reduced to the extent it has been utilized by lifetime gifts, does any tax incentive remain for a lifetime gift program? The answer is that a number of significant tax incentives remain.

☐ Under the old law, the $3,000 annual exclusions were not allowed for gifts in contemplation of death. Now our client can make gifts up to $3,000 per year per donee, and the exclusions will be effective up to the moment of death. The client, for example, who makes annual gifts of $3,000 to each of his three children and their spouses and to his six grandchildren, can reduce his estate by $36,000 per year[6] with no gift tax involvement and no impairment of his unified credit. For gifts made more than three years prior to death, gift-splitting permits the donor to give $6,000 per year to each donee, thus doubling the permissible estate reduction during that period with no gift tax involvement and no im-

---

[6]*The General Explanation of the Tax Reform Act of 1976, Staff of the Joint Committee on Taxation,* 94th Cong., 2d Sess. 525 (1976), indicates that the gross estate will include any excess of the estate tax value over the $3,000 figure. Under this view, if a donor made a gift in 1977 of an asset worth $3,000 and died in 1978 when the asset was worth $13,000, the gross estate would include $10,000 thereof ($13,000 minus $3,000). This interpretation, however, is not justified by a reading of Sec. 2305(b)(2) of the Code, which appears to say that the entire $13,000 would be excluded from the gross estate in this example.

pairment of the donor's unified credit.

☐ For taxable gifts made more than three years prior to death, the amounts paid in gift taxes are removed from the gross estate, thus reducing the estate tax liability.

☐ As indicated above, the first $100,000 of gifts to a spouse are exempt from gift tax and 50 percent of interspousal gifts above $200,000 also qualify for gift tax marital deduction. Although the allowable estate tax marital deduction is reduced to the extent the gift tax marital deduction used exceeds one-half the value of interspousal gifts made after 1976, so that there will be a diminished estate tax marital deduction where the lifetime gifts are less than $200,000, utilization of the gift tax marital deduction can be advantageous where:

1. Interspousal gifts reduce the adjusted gross estate to less than $500,000 (as illustrated in ¶500.3 above).

2. The donor's spouse predeceases the donor, so that the donor would have no marital deduction but for the lifetime gifts.

3. The spouse's estate, but for the lifetime gifts, would not utilize her maximum unified credit. In such a case, shifting of assets covered by the donor's marital deduction will permit those assets to pass tax-free to his children.

☐ The unified credit, equivalent to a substantial exemption, can be used to avoid or to minimize the current payment of transfer taxes. The equivalent reduction or loss of the credit otherwise available at death will in many cases be outweighed by the removal of future appreciation of the transferred property from the donor's estate and the shift of taxable income to lower-bracket donees; each of the latter benefits is separately mentioned below.

☐ Where the donees—individuals or trusts—are in lower income tax brackets than the donor, gifts which shift substantial income, and hence substantial income taxes, to such donees can provide more usable income for the family as a whole. As mentioned above, the unified credit can minimize the cost of this income reallocation.

☐ Perhaps most important, where significant asset appreciation can be anticipated, is the elimination of future appreciation from the donor's gross estate. In our preceding tax comparisons we have calculated taxes in a static situation. To illustrate the present point, however, let us consider the example of a client who is forty years of age in 1980 and whose adjusted gross estate is then estimated at $1,500,000 and includes business assets valued at $1,000,000 which are likely to appreciate at the rate of 7 percent per annum. Let us assume, further, that his wife has no separate estate.

If this client holds his estate as presently composed for the balance of his 31 year life expectancy, the value of the business interest at his death will be $8,720,000. The estimated estate taxes would be:

(a) With full marital deduction
     Tax in client's estate $1,882,000
     Tax in wife's estate   1,758,000
     TOTAL TAXES $3,640,000

(b) With no marital deduction
     Tax in client's estate $4,509,000
     Tax in wife's estate   0
     TOTAL TAXES $4,509,000

If, however, the client at age 40 transfers interests in the appreciating asset to his two children, $181,000 to each, with his wife's joinder to make available their combined annual exclusions ($12,000) and unified credits ($350,000), the estimated tax results would be:

(a) With full marital deduction
     Tax in client's estate $1,077,000
     Tax in wife's estate   1,009,000
     TOTAL TAXES $2,086,000

(b) With no marital deduction
     Tax in client's estate $2,730,000
     Tax in wife's estate   0
     TOTAL TAXES $2,730,000

At the growth rate and over the time period we have assumed, the $362,000 interests given to the children have expanded to a total of $3,157,000—in *their* estates rather than in the donor's. The resulting tax savings, based on the figures shown above, for the donor and his wife are:

(a) With full marital deduction
     Total taxes without gifts $3,640,000
     Total taxes after gifts   2,086,000
     TAXES SAVED $1,554,000

(b) With no marital deduction
     Total taxes without gifts $4,509,000
     Total taxes after gifts   2,730,000
     TAXES SAVED $1,779,000

And these savings could be augmented by an annual giving program, utilizing the annual exclusions for the donor's children and eventually grandchildren, and possibly by further gifts on which lifetime transfer taxes are paid.

The new basis rules, summarized in ¶500.2 above, reinforce the utility of this type of gift program. For property acquired after 1976, except for (a) death taxes attributable to appreciation from date of acquisition to date of death and (b) the $60,000 minimum basis adjustment under Sec. 1023(d) of the Code, there is no basis advantage to lose by making a lifetime rather than a testamentary transfer. For property acquired prior to 1977 and held until death, there is a basis adjustment for any pre-1977 appreciation, but the adjustment, and hence the basis argument for retention, decreases with the passage of time. In many cases, the limited basis advantage of retention until death will be outweighed by the opportunity to shift future appreciation to the donees and the ability to shift current income to the donees. And the donative impulse will be further strengthened by the new unified credit, which permits substantial transfers to be made without immediate tax cost.

☐ The determination for gift tax purposes of the value of a business interest or an interest in real property, resulting from an audit of the gift tax return, may eliminate some of the uncertainty on that subject and provide a measure of guidance in planning for further lifetime gifts of such interests and in estimating estate taxes and estate liquidity needs.

☐ Many States tax transfers of property at death but impose no tax on lifetime transfers. The saving of State death taxes via lifetime gifts will in some situations be substantial. For a simple illustration, in Pennsylvania lifetime transfers of includible property aggregating $500,000, completed more than two years prior to death, will save $30,000 of inheritance tax (6 percent rate) if the assets are left to a spouse or to lineal relatives, or $75,000 of inheritance tax (15 percent rate) if the property is left to other persons.

☐ Finally, a gift program may be employed to enable the donor's interest in a closely held business to qualify for a Section 303 redemption, or for the special valuation method under Sec. 2032A of the Code, or for installment payments of the estate tax attributable to the business interest under Sec. 6166A or Sec. 6166 of the Code. This can be done by making sufficient gifts of other assets so that the retained business interest meet the applicable percentage standard or standards. (Conversely, a donor can forfeit the qualification of a closely held interest for one or more of the mentioned tax benefits by making gifts which reduce his interest in the business below the percentage required by the applicable Code section.)

[¶502]   ESTATE TAX HAZARDS AND DISADVANTAGES

The preceding ¶501 lists the varied and substantial tax benefits that may be derived from a lifetime gift program, notwithstanding the chill winds driven through this field of tax endeavor by TRA 76. There are, to be sure, certain pitfalls and potential disadvantages which a soundly designed program will endeavor to avoid. Beyond the technical hazards mentioned in the last section of [¶501], the countervailing considerations include these:

☐ Separation and divorce. Substantial interspousal gifts, made in a period of harmony, may be regretted in the event of a subsequent divorce or separation. Factors for the client to consider before making gifts to his spouse obviously include his assessment of the strength and durability of the relationship; the proportion of his estate which the proposed gift assets represent; and the connection, if any, of the assets involved with the donor's present earnings, retirement program, and other lifetime plans and objectives. To a certain extent, as discussed below, potential problems in this area can be avoided or reduced by the use of trusts.

☐ Reduced donor influence. The client's influence or potential influence on his children or other donees may be reduced by the shift of substantial assets to them during the donor's lifetime. This effect may vary in some degree according to the quantum of gift and the liquidity of gift assets, as well as the ages, life styles, and values of the persons involved. Again, trusts may be helpful in allaying concerns of this type.

☐ Diminished control of business. Gifts of stock of a solely or closely owned business will frequently be appealing, especially where the donor obtains his benefits entirely or primarily in the form of salary and fringe benefits, while the stock represents a nonliquid appreciating asset. The donee shareholders, however, will have their rights and may have to be dealt with. Such potential difficulties may be mitigated by a recapitalization to create a nonvoting class of stock for gift purposes (see Chapter Nine) or by the use of trusts and various contractual arrangements.

☐ Paralysis of real estate operations. The fragmentation of title to real property, through gifts of fractional or other interests resulting in tenancies in common or joint ownership may have seriously disabling effects. The requirement of unanimity for decisions on development, improvement, financing, leasing, sale, etc., may be rendered even more disruptive by the shifting of the donees' interests (by will or other transfers) to strangers, creditors, fiduciaries, minors, or other undesirable co-owners. These difficulties can be avoided or minimized by means of management agreements, powers of attorney, incorporation, formation of general or limited partnerships, cross-purchase agreements, or the use of trusts.

☐ Financial insecurity or dependency. We can have too much of any good thing, whether it is ice cream, jogging, or a gift program. Perhaps the saddest victim of a well-motivated lifetime gift program is the donor who carries his program to the point where his remaining resources are either insufficient for his personal feeling of financial security or actually inadequate for his comfortable maintenance. In time of need, his erstwhile donees may be indifferent, unavailable, or unable to help.

[¶503]   ELEMENTS OF A SOUND GIFT PROGRAM

A sound gift program, essentially, is one which provides one or more of the significant tax benefits listed in [¶501] and in which the potential disadvantages mentioned in [¶502] are either avoided in whole or in part or are accepted as a reasonable price to pay for the gains involved. Within that broad generalization, however, careful gift planning involves attention to the selection of assets, the selection of donees, the timing of transfers, the potential utility of trust arrangements, and transfers of income interests.

[¶503.1]   Selection of Assets

Certain criteria for the selection of gift assets are implicit in the preceding discussion. These and other considerations may be specified as follows:

☐ Where the deflection of income to other taxpayers is a significant feature of the gift program, assets with a high ordinary income yield should obviously be favored in the absence of countervailing considerations.

☐ For estate tax avoidance, assets with the greatest prospects for appreciation should be favored, other things being equal. (As in the case of income deflection, one or more of the hazards mentioned in ¶502 may lead to a different selection.)

☐ If the goal is to qualify (or not to forfeit the qualification of) closely held business assets for Section 303 redemption, for the special valuation method under Sec. 2032A of the Code, or for installment payments of estate tax under Sec. 6166A or 6166 of the Code, the selection of gift assets should be skewed in favor of those which move the closely held assets toward the percentage required by the applicable Code provisions or which maintain their qualifying percentage.

☐ For gifts of assets acquired after 1976, generally low basis assets should be selected in preference to high basis assets. For property acquired earlier, it will be necessary to consider the duration of prior ownership, the extent of prior appreciation, the donor's age and health, and the prospects for future appreciation. A long holding period with substantial appreciation pushes in the direction of retention, especially in the case of a donor of advanced age or failing health. Conversely, a short holding period in the case of a younger donor in good health tends to indicate suitability for gift, especially where significant future growth of the asset is anticipated.

☐ Property which might otherwise be suitable under the foregoing criteria may be deemed unsuitable if the gift will diminish the donor's control of a business enterprise or complicate the ownership and management of a real estate investment, as indicated in ¶502. The extent to which these problems can be handled satisfactorily by the use of trusts is discussed in ¶503.4.

[¶503.2]   Selection of Donees

The selection of donees should include, beyond the natural course of the donor's benevolence, the following considerations:

☐ In the case of interspousal transfers, the several factors mentioned in the third section of ¶501, above.

☐ Where income tax saving is a significant motive, the tax brackets of the suggested donees and their future income and tax bracket projections (as compared with those of the donor).

☐ In any case, the size of each proposed donee's estate and the potential impact of the gift on the donee's anticipated estate tax.

☐ In appropriate cases, the choice of grandchildren in preference to children as donees, bearing in mind that:

(a) The limitations imposed by TRA 76 on generation-skipping transfers have no application to direct gifts to grandchildren or more remote donees.
(b) The new unified rate schedule will make it more costly for the donor's children to make substantial property transfers to their children.

[¶503.3]   Timing of Gifts

Timing, as a family matter, involves making gifts when the needs of the donees or the potential benefits to them are the greatest. From the standpoint of taxes, timing may involve:

☐ Shift of relatively volatile assets to donees in advance of anticipated major appreciation.

☐ Making gifts generally at the earliest feasible time and making
substantial annual gifts as early as possible in January, by reason of the
provisions of Sec. 2035 of the Code for inclusion in the gross estate of
gifts made within three years of death plus gift taxes paid thereon.

☐ Death-bed gifts up to $3,000 per donee, which will reduce the
estate tax by reason of the exception to Section 2035 for gifts covered by
the annual exclusions.

[¶503.4]   Use of Trusts

In many cases the use of a trust will serve to provide one or more
advantages. It may assure the desired benefits of a gift to the donee;
maximize the potential income tax savings; avoid estate tax in a beneficiary's estate as well as the donor's; and avoid or reduce the hazards
and disadvantages mentioned in ¶502 above. Let us consider more
specifically some of the applicable trust techniques:

☐ Lifetime trusts can be used to provide benefits to the donor's
child, the balance to pass at the child's death to the donor's grandchildren. To the extent of $250,000 for each set of grandchildren, the trust
assets avoid the generation-skipping transfer tax, as more fully
explained in Chapter Three.

☐ The generation-skipping tax applies only to trusts which divide
benefits between two or more generations which are younger than the
grantor's generation. Thus a donor may establish a trust for his wife for
life, with remainder to his children; for his brother for life, with remainder to his brother's children; or for his parents for life, and then for his
brothers and sisters for life, with remainder to their children, without
involving a generation-skipping tax.

☐ Specific provisions can be made in the trust instrument for modification or termination of a spouse's beneficial interest in the event of
separation or divorce.

☐ Generally, trusts (with spendthrift provisions) can be effective to
protect the donor's beneficiaries from creditors' claims, spouses' elections, and their own improvidence.

☐ Provisions for the "sprinkling" of income among several beneficiaries in the trustee's discretion can be utilized to redetermine the
income allocation annually according to the beneficiaries' shifting tax
brackets.

☐ Combining the benefits mentioned in the preceding paragraphs, by means of a trust with sprinkling provisions for his wife and children, the remainder at death to pass to his grandchildren, the donor can attain the following advantages:

(1) In case of need, indirect benefit to the donor via discretionary distributions to his wife;
(b) Increase of after-tax income for the family via diversion of income to the lowest bracket taxpayers in the group;
(c) Removal of the property (and its future appreciation) from the donor's gross estate and his wife's also;
(d) Avoidance of tax on the transferred assets in his children's estates, to the extent of $250,000 per child;
(e) Professional management of the assets involved, if competent trustees are selected; and
(f) Protection of all concerned against the various vicissitudes of life.

☐ Prior to TRA 76, under the *Byrum*[7] case, it was possible for a donor to place closely held stock in trust and exclude it from his gross estate, even though he retained the rights to vote the stock; to veto the sale or transfer of trust assets; to approve investments; and to replace the corporate trustee with another corporate trustee. Section 2009(a) of TRA 76 amended Sec. 2036 of the Code to overrule *Byrum*. The amendment provides that the donor's reservation for life (or similar period) of the right to vote the stock will cause it to be included in his gross estate as a transfer with enjoyment retained.

Despite this amendment, closely held stock can be effectively removed from the gross estate, provided the voting rights are not retained by the donor, with the following advantages:

1. A number of persons can benefit from the transfer, while the stock is managed by a single trustee or set of trustees;
2. The *Byrum* rights, with the exception of voting rights, can be reserved to the donor;
3. Careful selection of trustees can reduce the discomfort of the shift of voting power; and
4. The other trust benefits above mentioned can also be obtained.

☐ Unified management and simplified title to real estate, despite divided beneficial interests, can also be provided by means of a trust. As indicated in the last section of ¶502 however, there are a number of alternate solutions to be considered for the client who desires to make gifts of fractional interests in real property.

For a discussion of nontax criteria respecting the use of trusts in

---

[7]*United States v. Byrum*, 408 U.S. 125 (1972).

family situations see ¶302.2. For suggested provisions, in the interest of flexibility and tax savings, see ¶303.

[¶503.5]   Trust Tax Hazards

The trust which is designed to keep the transferred assets out of the donor's gross estate as discussed in Chapter Seven also, has three pitfalls to avoid;

1. Death of the donor within three years following the transfer (Section 2035 of the Code).
2. Reservation to the donor of a life interest in the trust property or the right to designate the person or persons who are to enjoy the property or its income (Section 2036 of the Code). (This includes an unrestricted right of the donor to remove a Trustee and appoint himself as Trustee. Reg. Sec. 20.2036-1(b)(3)).
3. Reservation of a right to alter, amend or revoke the trust (Section 2038 of the Code).

The first of these hazards is essentially beyond our control, although expeditious completion of our work will reduce the hazard. We can sail safely past the other two by following these guidelines in the design of the trust:

☐ The trust should be irrevocable, the donor should have no right to amend it, and the trust instrument should so state.

☐ All income and principal should be currently and eventually distributable to persons other than the donor. No income or principal should revert to the donor or his estate on any occasion or in any event.

☐ The donor should have no right to designate current or eventual beneficiaries or to shift income or principal among the beneficiaries.

☐ The donor should have no voice in the management or administration of the trust property.

☐ The donor should have no right to substitute himself (or any person under his control) for another trustee or to appoint himself (or any person under his control) as a trustee in the event of a vacancy.

Any departure from this "safe" course, as in the case of the modified Byrum-type trust above mentioned, requires careful study of the applicable Code section or sections, the Regulations thereunder, and related rulings and court decisions.

Another tax peril, though frequently less severe in its impact than a failure to remove the gift assets from the donor's gross estate, is unan-

ticipated failure to qualify for annual exclusions. As indicated in
¶501, the $3,000 annual exclusions are available only for "present
interest" gifts. A present interest gift is one in which the donee has the
immediate right to possession or enjoyment of the property, either as
outright owner or as a trust beneficiary. If the possession or enjoyment is
deferred, the donee has a future interest, and a future interest does not
qualify for the annual exclusion.

Personal objectives of the donor, or competing tax objectives, may
dictate trust provisions in which the donor will voluntarily forego the
annual exclusion. But the distinctions between present and future interests for this purpose should be understood in order to avoid inadver-
tent loss of this tax benefit. Present interest gifts include the following:

☐ An outright gift.

☐ A gift of a life estate or other income interest (see Reg. Sec.
25.2503-3(b)). But see below.

☐ A transfer to a custodian under the Uniform Gifts to Minors
Act.

☐ A gift to certain trusts for minors as specified in Sec. 2503(c) of
the Code.

Gifts which do not so qualify, and are therefore classified as future
interest gifts, include:

☐ A gift of a remainder interest (see Reg. Sec. 25.2503(a)).

☐ A gift of an interest in a sprinkling trust (see Rev. Rul. 55-303,
1955-1 CB 471).

☐ A gift of an interest in an accumulation trust (see *U.S. v. Pelzer*,
312 U.S. 399 (1941).

☐ A gift of an interest in a discretionary trust (see *Fondren v.
Comm'r.*, 324, U.S. 18 (1945) and *Comm'r. v. Disston*, 325 U.S. 442 (1945).

☐ An "income" interest in unproductive property (see Rev. Rul.
69-344, 1969-1 CB 225 and *Berzon v. Comm'r.*, 37 AFTR 2d 76-1601).

The *Berzon* case indicates that the exclusion will be disallowed
where the lack of dividend history of the company whose stock is placed
in trust makes it impossible to put a value on the income beneficiary's
right to trust income and where restrictions on the stock prevent the
trustee from reinvesting in assets with a "normal" income yield.

The basic principle which can be drawn from the preceding clas-
sifications and distinctions (ignoring minor's trusts and custodianships)
is that an income interest in trust will qualify for the exclusion only if a
designated income beneficiary is entitled to current trust income or a
definite share of it, with mandatory and not discretionary distributions,

and the interest is "real" and not illusory.

One further distinction with regard to trust interests may be helpful. If the donor transfers assets in trust to pay the income to A for life, with remainder to B, B's remainder interest is a future interest. As such, it does not qualify for an annual exclusion. The result would be the same if the donor reserved the income to himself for life, with remainder to B. Let us consider the reverse situation: the trust income is payable to A for life, the principal to revert to the donor upon A's death. Some time after the creation of the trust, the donor transfers his reversionary interest to A: Is that a present interest gift?

In *Clark*, 65 TC No. 13, the creator of two Clifford (10 years plus 1 day) trusts for his sons subsequently conveyed to them his reversionary interest in certain of the trust securities and claimed gift tax exclusions in connection with those transfers. The court found that under applicable State law, the result of the transfers was a merger of the son's income interests with the reversionary (now remainder) interests, so that the trusts terminated as to the securities involved and the sons owned them outright. Under those circumstances, the transfer of a reversionary interest was held to be a present interest gift.

As indicated above, an outright gift normally qualifies for the annual exclusion. A donor will sometimes spread a proposed gift over several years in order to take greater advantage of his exclusions. While this can be done properly, a "sham" transaction will forfeit the exclusions. One case involved a grandfather who wished to give to two grandchildren parcels of realty worth $27,000 and $24,000. On the advice of counsel, he sold the property to his grandchildren in exchange for their noninterest-bearing notes which were equal to the annual gift tax exclusions, the notes to be forgiven as they came due. The Service ruled that the transaction was a disguised gift of the properties and not a bona fide sale because of the prearranged plan to forgive the notes; the notes did not constitute valuable consideration for the properties. Rev. Rul. 77-299, IRB 1977-34,14. The purpose could have been accomplished via annual gifts of fractional interests in the properties, although appreciation in value might cause the gift program to be extended over a longer period.

In addition to the hazards above mentioned, you should bear in mind that new Sec. 644 of the Code imposes tax at the donor's rates (rather than the trust's) on any gains realized by a trust within two years following the transfer of appreciated assets giving rise to the gain.

[¶503.6]   Transfers of Income Interests

Short-term trusts known as "Clifford" trusts have long been a favorite tax planning device, principally for income tax savings. Typically, a client in a high income tax bracket who is willing to part with the income of certain property but not to transfer to property permanently, establishes a Clifford trust for the benefit of a parent or a child or grandchild in a lower income tax bracket. If the trust is irrevocably established for a term which will not expire prior to the death of the income beneficiary or the expiration of ten years, whichever occurs earlier, the distributable net income of the trust will be taxed to the beneficiary and not to the grantor. (Capital gains, however, will be taxed to the grantor of the trust.)

The transfer of property to such a trust constitutes a gift of the commuted value of the income for the term of the trust. (See Sections 2511(a) and 2512(a) of the Code; Rev. Rul. 58-242, 1958-1 CB 251.) This is a present interest gift, qualifying for the annual exclusion.

Upon termination of the trust, the property is returned to the donor and is fully includible in his gross estate. If, however, the donor dies during the term of the trust, the value of his reversionary interest is included in his gross estate, that is, the value of the trust property reduced by the actuarial value of the income interest outstanding on the date of the donor's death (Sections 2031 and 2033 of the Code). To the extent of this differential, plus the amount of after-tax income, if any, which the donor would have accumulated in the absence of the trust, this income tax saving device serves also to reduce the donor's estate tax.

An even more promising technique, though its tax treatment has not been finally resolved at this writing, is the interest-free loan. The interest-free loan has no limit for tax purposes as to its duration, shifts taxable income as effectively as the Clifford trust, can produce substantial estate tax savings, and, if *Lester Crown*[8] is upheld, can accomplish all of these things *without incurring gift tax.*

A number of cases have held that the receipt of an interest-free loan does not result in taxable income to the recipient (E.g., *J. Simpson Dean*, 35 TC 1083 (1961); *Saunders v. U.S.*, 294 F. Supp. 1276 (1968); *Joseph Lupowitz Sons, Inc. v. Comm'r.*, 497 F. 2d 862 (3rd Cir., 1974)). For gift tax purposes, the case of *Johnson v. U.S.*, 254 F. Supp. 73 (N.D. Tex., 1966) had held that interest-free demand loans to family members were not gifts of the value of the use of the money. The position of the Service, which flatly refused to follow *Johnson,* is set forth in Rev. Rul. 73-61, 1973-1 CB 408:

> "The right to use property, in this case money, is itself an interest in property, the transfer of which is a gift within the purview of Section 2501 of the Code unless full and adequate consideration in money or money's worth is received. The tax . . . would be imposed on the value of the right to use the money . . ."

[8]6 TC No. 88 (3/31/77)

Lester Crown, supra, involved interest-free loans from a cash basis partnership to relatives and certain cash basis trusts for relatives of one or more of the partners. Some loans were on open account and others involved demand notes providing for interest at 6 percent per annum only after demand. The Tax Court followed *Johnson*. In finding that there was no taxable gift, the Court said:

> "Our income tax system does not recognize unrealized earnings or accumulations of wealth and no taxpayer is under any obligation to continuously invest his money for a profit. The opportunity cost of either letting one's money be idle or suffering a loss from an unwise investment is not taxable merely because a profit could have been made from a wise investment."

And further:

> "The courts have uniformly rejected every attempt by the Internal Revenue Service to subject the making of non-interest-bearing loans to income or gift taxes . . . If the making of non-interest-bearing loans is to become a taxable event, we think Congress, not the judiciary, should clearly say so."

Here, unless *Lester Crown* is reversed on appeal, we have a very flexible opportunity to shift taxable income to various donees (presumably using trusts in the case of minors) without incurring gift tax and without the donor permanently surrendering the transferred funds. In this connection, we note that the Tax Court referred to the value of the use of "money or property," so that loans of noncash property would presumably receive the same treatment.

As in the case of the Clifford trust, the potential estate tax savings arise from two sources. To the extent the donor would have accumulated the aftertax income of the "loaned" property, that accumulation is removed from his gross estate. And if the loan is a term loan, its value in the estate will involve discounting it at the market rate of interest for the period from the date of death to the due date of the obligation. The total estate tax savings can be substantial.

6

The Private Annuity

OPPORTUNITIES AVAILABLE

If any one of the estate tax saving techniques discussed in this book has been underused, it is probably the private annuity. Whether this is due to failure of client comprehension or counsel courage, or other causes, we cannot tell. But the device is quite simple of application, and when the facts are "right" (a condition we shall endeavor to describe) the results can be extremely advantageous to everyone but the Treasury.

A private annuity is an arrangement where one party transfers property to another—a transferee who is not in the business of selling annuities—in return for the latter's promise to make periodic payments of a fixed amount to the transferor for life.

Typically, an older person transfers property to a younger family member who promises to pay a stated sum to the older person each year (or more frequently) for the balance of the former's life. Alternatively, the transferee may be a corporation which redeems the transferor's stock of the corporation, making periodic payments to the transferor in exchange for his stock. (There are also "hybrids," which do not fit precisely into the private or commercial annuity molds, where a charitable or educational institution is the transferee; these lie beyond the scope of our treatment here.)

[¶600.1]   Chief Differences Of The Private From
The Commercial Annuity

☐ Commercial annuities are purchased, usually from a life insurance company, for cash, whereas the private annuity normally involves

160

the transfer of noncash property which has appreciated in value.

□ The transferee in the private annuity arrangement is not in the annuity business and is not subject to the rules and regulations governing commercial annuities with respect to permissible investments, maintenance of reserves, and the like.

□ Commercial annuity payments are determined by standard actuarial tables, whereas the private annuity payments are subject to negotiation and may include a gift element.

□ The transferee in the private annuity arrangement commonly lacks the financial resources and stability that characterize the commercial annuity transferee.

[¶601]   WHEN TO USE A PRIVATE ANNUITY

For reasons which will emerge from the ensuing discussion of the estate, gift and income tax treatment of the private annuity, and considering also the personal security of the propsed annuitant, the following circumstances may be regarded as favorable:

1. Transfer of the property involved would result in a saving of estate tax in the annuitant's estate.
2. The annuitant is willing to cede control of the transferred property.
3. The annuitant's health has not deteriorated to the point where use of the annuity table is manifestly inappropriate.
4. The annuity payments would be beneficial to the transferor and would not necessarily be accumulated and added to his gross estate.
5. The annuity payments would not be a hardship to the transferee.
6. The transferor has confidence in the integrity and financial soundess of the transferee.
7. Unforeseen loss of the annuity payments would not be a serious hardship to the annuitant.
8. Basis of the transferred assets is fairly close to current fair market value.

By properly using the private annuity you can remove a substantial asset from the transferor's estate while giving him an economic benefit similar to a life estate. This can be done without risk of inclusion in gross estate if death occurs within three years and without gift tax cost. Nonliquid assets can be sold in this way for a regular cash return and without immediate recognition of gain.

There are, to be sure, hazards involved. If the transferor dies much earlier than his life expectancy, the transferee will have a relatively low basis in the transferred property. On the other hand, if the transferor outlives his life expectancy, the acquisition may have cost the transferee more than acquisition by inheritance, assuming inheritance was the alternative. Further, for reasons explained below the transferor will normally eschew the retention of a security interest in the transferred property, so that he may be assuming a significant risk in relying on the transferee's unsecured promise. If the value of the property is substantial, or the transferor is of advanced age, or the property yields little or no income, or any combination of these circumstances is involved, the payments may be burdensome to the transferee. And, finally, where the value of the transferred property is very difficult to ascertain, the risk of liability for gift tax, or for estate tax if a gift is deemed to have been made within three years prior to death, cannot be totally removed.

Nevertheless, where we find in a given situation most of the eight favorable factors listed above, serious consideration should be given to the use of a private annuity. Although the considerations are obviously numerous and varied, there are many situations in which the advantages will clearly preponderate. There is no reason to limit our use of this device to larger estates. And the decision to use a private annuity is extremely simple to implement, as can be seen from the form of private annuity agreement which is included in appendix C.

[¶602]   **TAX TREATMENT**

[¶602.1]   Estate Tax Results

A primary purpose and the major advantage of most private annuity arrangements is the removal of the transferred property from the transferor's gross estate. If the annuity is properly computed and no endangering "strings" are attached, as mentioned below, the removal of the asset from the gross estate is total and immediate.

Consider for example, a married taxpayer who has a gross estate of $800,000 consisting of:

Cash	$ 50,000
Securities	100,000
Home	150,000
Life Insurance	200,000
Property "X"	300,000
	$800,000

Assuming use of the full marital deduction, assuming that the taxpayer dies after 1980, and using 5 percent of the gross estate for estimated allowable debts and deductions, the taxpayer's estate tax would amount to approximately $62,000. If he transfers Property "X" to his son in exchange for the latter's promise to make the appropriate annuity payments, the taxpayer's estate tax will be reduced to approximately $18,000,[1] a saving of $44,000. (As discussed below, the transfer avoids the substantial gift tax which a gift of Property "X" would involve, and it eliminates the estate tax cloud which would have hung over such a gift for three years.)

Property "X" in the foregoing example has been removed from the transferor's gross estate. The annuity itself, if it is a single life, non-refund type, will have no estate tax consequences for the annuitant's estate; it will simply terminate at his death and no value will pass by reason thereof.

To obtain this auspicious estate tax result, three technical and one practical hazard must be avoided:

First. The transfer must not be one which is intended to take effect in possession or enjoyment at the transferor's death (Section 2037 of the code). The retention of a security interest in the transferred property, whereby the transferor may repossess the property if the transferee defaults, should not subject the property to includibility under Section 2037, absent a donative intent (see *Seymour Johnson,* 10 BTA 411 (1928)). But it presents a hazard (Cf. *Tips v. Bass,* 21 F.2nd 460 (W.D. Tex. 1927)) that should be avoided. As discussed below, the avoidance of a security interest is also essential in order to obtain the desirable income tax treatment of the annuity payments, i.e., to avoid immediate tax on the value of the promised payments.

Second. The transferor must not retain a life estate in the property (Section 2036 of the code). The danger of includibility under Section 2036 is exemplified by *Lazarus v. Comm'r,* 58 T.C. 854 (1972), aff'd 513 F.2d 824 (9th cir., 1975). In *Lazarus,* following a comprehensive plan developed by counsel, the taxpayers (husband and wife) created a trust in the Bahamas and transferred to the trustee stock of a family corporation which owned a shopping center. As consideration for the transfer, the trustee agreed to pay the petitioners a joint and survivor annuity of $75,000 under an "annuity agreement." The trustee then sold the stock to a Bahamian corporation for the latter's $1,000,000 nonnegotiable promissory note due January 1, 1984. The note provided for the promisor to pay the trustee interest in the amount of $75,000 per year. The note had a 20-year term and the taxpayers had approximately a 21-year tabular life expectancy. Under the agreement, the trust would have no available cash principal until almost the end of the life expectancy period, so that the trust principal would presumably pass intact to the

---

[1] It might not be amiss to note that most of this remaining tax could be eliminated by effective transfer of the life insurance to an irrevocable trust, as discussed in Chapter 7.

grantor's issue as the designated beneficiaries.

The taxpayers reported the sale of the stock for a private annuity. It was their position that the private annuity arrangement governed the income tax treatment of the payments to them, and, further, that the assets would pass at their deaths to their children and grandchildren without any gift tax or estate tax having been incurred. IRS contended, *inter alia,* that the substance of the transaction was a transfer of property to a trust subject to the reservation of the income thereof. The Tax Court ruled that the trust declaration and the annuity agreement must be read as a single instrument. The Court held that the taxpayers should be treated as the owners of the trust property under Section 677(a), so that the income was taxable to them under Section 671; and that the taxpayers, having transferred the property to a trust, reserving $75,000 per year of the income thereof, made a gift to the trust of their remainder interest in the stock. (The Court's characterization of the transaction would also dictate includibility in the taxpayer's estate under Section 2036.)

In its affirmance, the 9th Circuit summarized and approved the factors which led the Tax Court to its conclusion as follows (513 F.2nd at 829):

"1. The trust had no assets other than the $1,000 with which it was initially funded by petitioners and the note received as consideration for the sale of the . . . stock. In effect the only source of petitioners' 'annuity' was property they had transferred to the trust—an arrangement more characteristic of a trust than a bona fide arms-length sale.

"2. Since the note was non-negotiable and could not be assigned, petitioners' 'annuity' payments of $75,000 a year could not be paid out of the corpus of the trust. The interest on the note, constituting the sole income of the trust, was exactly equal to the amount owing petitioners each year.

"3. The corpus of the trust will remain intact for ultimate distribution to the beneficiaries 'in precisely the same way as if petitioners had forthrightly cast the transaction in the form of a transfer in trust subject to a reservation of trust income.

"4. The arrangement did not give petitioners a down payment, interest on the deferred purchase price, or security for its payment—again more characteristic of a transfer in trust then a bona fide sale.

"5. There was a substantial disparity between the fair market value of the stock transferred and the actuarial value of the 'annuity' payments."

The court relied in part on *In Estate of Cornelia B. Schwartz,* 9 T.C. 229 (1947), and *Smith v. Commissioner,* 56 T.C. 263 (1971), in each of which the sole corpus of the trust from which the "annuity" was to be paid consisted of property given by the taxpayers to their children, who transferred the property to the trust in which they were the ultimate beneficiaries.

The taxpayers in *Lazarus* relied upon a footnote in *Fidelity–Philadelphia Trust Co. v. Smith,* 356 U.S. 274, 280, 78 S. Ct. 730, 733, 2 L. Ed. 2d 765 (1958), which reads:

> "Where a decedent, not in contemplation of death, has transferred property to another in return for a promise to make periodic payments to the transferor for his lifetime, it has been held that these payments are not income from the transferred property so as to include the property in the estate of the decedent. E.g., Estate of Sarah A. Bergen, 1 T.C. 543, Acq., 1943 Cum. Bull. 2; Security Trust & Savings Bank, Trustee, 11 B.T.A. 833; Seymour Johnson, 10 B.T.A. 411; Hirsch v. United States, 1929, 35 F.2d 982, 68 Ct. Cl. 508 cf. Welch v. Hall, 1 Cir., 134 F.2d 366. In these cases the promise is a personal obligation of the transferee, the obligation is usually not chargeable to the transferred property, and the size of the payments is not determined by the size of the actual income from the transferred property, at the time the payments are made."

Emphasizing the last quoted sentence, the 9th Circuit found that the footnote supported the conclusion of the Tax Court in *Lazarus* rather than the taxpayers.

From the *Lazarus* case and from Section 2036 principles generally, certain recommended guidelines emerge:

(a) The annuity payments should not be equal to or dependent upon the income available from the transferred property.
(b) The transferee should be personally liable for the annuity payments without regard to income from the transferred property and he should have other income or resources from which to make the annuity payments.
(c) The transferee should not be a trust of which the transferred property is the sole or principal asset.
(d) The transferor should relinquish control of the property entirely, retaining no voice in its disposition and no driect or indirect benefits from it beyond its function as consideration for the annuity promise.

Third. The third technical hazard to the desired estate tax treatment is that the taking of an annuity worth less than the fair market value of the transferred property may be considered a gift taxable under Section 2035 I.R.C. if death occurs within three years thereafter. There are, obviously, two sides to the necessary equivalence. First, it is necessary to ascertain the market value of the transferred property. Where marketable securities are involved, there is no problem. Where closely held stock or real estate is involved, an expert appraiser should be engaged.

Assuming the value of the transferred property has been adequately ascertained, the equivalent annuity payments must be developed. Use of the current estate and gift tax tables (Reg. Sec. 20.2031-10(f) Tables

A(1) and A(2), reproduced in Appendix B) is recommended on the basis of earlier cases in which the courts placed reliance upon the tables which preceded these. Others have suggested use of Treasury-approved values set out in Rev. Rul. 72-438, IRB 1972-38 for life annuity contracts issued on a sporadic basis after 9-18-72 by organizations other than insurance companies (for contracts issued prior to 9-18-72, values set forth in Rev. Rul. 62-216, 1962-2CB30).

Use of tables does not necessarily end the matter. The tables represent generalizations about life expectancy and fair investment return which may not apply in particular cases. An actuarial computation based on the transferor's life expectancy and a fair return in certain circumstances may result in a higher valuation of the annuity promise. Where this may be so, the engagement of a private actuary may be advisable, though the consequent increase of the transferor's capital gains tax may affect the estate and gift tax advantage of the higher annuity valuation.

The converse of this is that the Internal Revenue Service may be able to show in a particular case (Cf. *Leonard Rosen*, 48 T.C. 834 (1967)) that the tables should not apply, possibly because of a condition that may be expected to reduce the transferor's life expectancy. But the mere determination of a discrepancy between the value of the transferred property and the value of the annuity promise does not per se establish that there has been a gift. This subject is discussed further in the gift tax section of this chapter, below.

The anticipated estate tax saving to be derived from the transfer of property in a private annuity arrangement is also subject, as mentioned above, to a practical hazard: the possibility that the estate will be built up again, even possibly above the pre-annuity level, by accumulation of the annuity payments. This will not be the case, of course, where the annuity payments are simply consumed by the transferor. The estate tax impact of accumulation, where it occurs, will also be reduced to the extent the transferor fails to live to his life expectancy.

Where it appears that the annuity payments will not be fully consumed by the transferor, it may be possible to develop an advantageous compensatory gift program. Thus a taxpayer who enters into a private annuity transaction with his son, and who also has grandchildren, may wish to make annual gifts to his grandchildren covered by his annual gift tax exclusions and possibly his spouse's exclusions as well.

The foregoing estate tax discussion relates to a single life annuity. If the transaction provides for a joint and survivor annuity (payments to two persons so long as either survives), or a refund annuity (payments to aggregate not less than the annuity consideration if the annuitant dies before receiving that much), or an annuity for a term certain and life thereafter (payments to continue for a specified term if the annuitant dies before that term expires), the consequences are (a) that the annuity payments will be less, and (b) that a residual value may be includible in the transfer's gross estate at his death. The refund- and term-certain guarantees would be includible at the discounted value of any payments still to be made. The survivor benefit under a joint- and-survivor annuity would be includible at the cost of a comparable annuity of the gender and age of the survivor. If the annuitants are husband and wife, the interest of the surviving spouse would qualify for the marital deduction to the extent its value is included in the gross estate of the decedent and is within the applicable statutory limit as to the deductible amount.

[¶602.2]   Gift Tax Results

If the value of the annuity promise is equal to the value of the transferred property, no gift is made and there is no gift tax involvement in the case of a single life annuity.

Where, however, the value of the transferred property is found to exceed the value of the annuity promise, *and if donative intent is involved in the transaction,* the excess value constitutes a taxable gift. Before a gift tax can be imposed, there must be evidence that a transferor intended to make a gift. In *Beattie v. Comm'r.,* 159 F.2d 788 (6th Cir., 1947), the court found an absence of donative intent even though the annuity promise was worth only 30 percent of the value of the property transferred. In *Eva B. Hull,* T.C. Memo 1962-199, and *Stewart v. U.S.,* 63-1 USTC ¶9410 (D. Colo., 1963), the taxpayer successfully argued that the transferor had merely made a bad business bargain in agreeing to inadequate annuity payments.

Where the valuation discrepancy arises out of the taxpayer's presumably erroneous valuation of the transferred property, and where the property is of a type that has no readily ascertainable market value, it should be difficult to find a donative intent unless the valuation is baseless or erroneous to the point of absurdity.

Where a partial gift is in fact intended, it may be preferable clearly to separate the transfer into its two elements (a) a gift, precisely defined, and (b) a private annuity agreement with respect to the balance. This would have the effects of reducing the tranferor's capital gain, delimiting the portion subject to possible estate tax exposure on death within three years, and enabling you to compute and apply the appropriate tax treatment to an unclouded transaction. (Under Rev. Rul. 69-74, discussed below, the transferor's capital gain is simply reduced by the difference between the value of the property transferred and the value of the annuity interest.)

The foregoing gift tax discussion relates to a single life annuity. If a joint and survivor annuity is created, a gift will be made if the interest of either joint annuitant in the transferred property is less than the value of his or her annuity rights. Moreover, where the annuitants are husband and wife, such a gift (of a terminable interest) would not qualify for the gift tax marital deduction unless separate annuities are created in the transaction.

[¶602.3]   Income Tax Results

Prior to 1969, the income tax rules for private annuities were set forth in Rev. Rul. 239, 1953-2 Cum. Bul. 53. After failing to secure more restrictive legislation, the Service issued Rev. Rul. 69-74, 1969-1 Cum. Bul. 43. Although not yet fully tested in the courts, our conservative approach to the annuity transaction assumes that Rev. Rul. 69-74 will prevail.

The transaction is deemed "open" since the ultimate value of the promise to pay can not be determined, so that no taxable event occurred at the inception of the arrangement. Under Rev. Rul. 239, each annuity payment was deemed to include a tax-free return of basis and the balance was taxed as ordinary income. The fair market value of the property at time of transfer was the transferor's "investment in the contract." This was divided by the amount of the total payments to be made to the end of the transferor's life expectancy to determine the exclusion ratio. This ratio, multiplied against each payment, determined the portion of each payment that constituted return of basis, the balance of each payment being interest (ordinary income). Once the transferor's basis was fully recovered, the same portion of subsequent payments was taxed as a realized gain. Taxation of the excluded portions after all payments equalled the fair market value of the property transferred was not entirely clear. A question remained as to whether it would continue to be taxed as capital gain, would be converted into ordinary income, or would be tax-free.

Under Rev. Rul. 69-74, the transferor's "investment in the contract" is equal to his basis in the property. This ordinarily reduces the exclusion ratio and increases the income element. In addition, basis is not recovered first but is recovered over the entire term of the contract. Each annuity payment must be divided into three elements: (1) a recovery of basis, which is tax-free for the life of the contract even if the transferor outlives his life expectancy; (2) realized gain, which receives capital gains treatment for the period of the transferor's life expectancy and is treated as ordinary income thereafter; and (3) an annuity element, treated as the equivalent of interest and taxed as ordinary income under the usual annuity rules.

The elements under Rev. Rul. 69-74 are determined in this way: First, the exclusion ratio is determined in the same manner as under the prior rules except that the transferor's adjusted basis is substituted for the fair market value of the transferred property as the transferor's "investment in the contract." Expected return, again, is determined by multiplying the amount of the annual payment by the transferor's life expectancy (Table 1 of Reg. Sec. 1.72-9, reproduced in Appendix B). Application of the exclusion ratio to the amount of each payment indicates the recovery of basis element.

Next, the capital gain element is ascertained. The capital gain is the difference between the transferor's adjusted basis and the present value of the annuity promise (determined according to Table A(1) for males, or A(2) for females, of the estate and gift tax tables reproduced above. The capital gain element of each payment is determined by dividing the capital gain by the transferor's life expectacy. (As stated above, this element will be taxed as ordinary income after the entire capital gain has been taxed as such.)

By subtracting from the amount of the annual payment (a) the recovery of basis element and (b) the capital gain element, we ascertain the annuity amount, which is taxed as ordinary income for the balance of the transferor's life.

An example may be helpful. Assume that a woman 65 years of age transfers to her son a capital asset having an adjusted basis of $53,005 and a fair market value of $93,005 in exchange for the son's promise to pay her $10,000 per year for the balance of her life. The present value of the annuity promise under Table A(2) of Regs. Section 20.2031-10(f) is $93,005. The taxpayer's life expectancy, under Regs. Section 1.72-9, is 18.2 years, so that her expected return is $182,000 ($10,000 times 18.2). The tax consequences to the transferor under Rev. Rul. 69-74 are as follows:

(a) The exclusion ratio is 29.1 percent ($53,005 investment in the contract divided by $182,000 expected return). Of each annual payment, 29.1 percent, or $2,910, is excluded from income.

(b) A capital gain is realized in the amount of $40,000 ($93,005 present value of annuity promise minus $53,005 adjusted basis). This gain is reported ratably over the transferor's life expectancy, so that the annual capital gain element is $2,197 ($40,000 divided by 18.2).

(c) The balance of each payment, $4,893 ($10,000 minus $5,197 [$2,910 plus $2,197]), is taxed as ordinary income for the balance of the transferor's life.

(d) After the transferor has lived for 18.2 years, the capital gain portion of each payment, $2,197, will be taxed as ordinary income.

A simple worksheet for determination of the transferor's tax treatment is included in Appendix A.

The income tax treatment we have described is based on the premise that the transferee's promise to make the annuity payments is too uncertain to be valued at the time of the agreement. Otherwise, the transferor's profit in the transaction would be realized when the agreement is made and not deferred until payments are actually received. The criteria for the tax treatment we have described are:

1. The promise to pay the annuity must be an "unsecured" promise, that is, unfunded and not secured by a mortgage, pledge, or security agreement. (See *Commissioner v. Kann's Est.*, 174 F.2d 357 (3rd Cir., 1949); *J. Darsie Lloyd*, 33 B.T.A. 903 (1936), acq. 1950-2 Cum. Bul. 3.); and

2. The promisor must be an individual or an organization which does not issue annuities "from time to time."

Also, if the annuity agreement provides a refund feature or a guaranteed minimum number of payments, the computation would have to be adjusted for such variation.

A recent Tax Court case, *Bell Estate v. Commissioner*, 60 T.C. No. 52, (1973), with six dissents, involved in a private annuity transaction between parents and children, in which stock which was tranferred to the children in exchange for their annuity promise. The stock was placed in escrow to secure the children's promise, and a cognovit judgment against the transferee was entered in case of default. The Court held that capital gains were recognizable in the year of transfer by the parents, rather than over their lifetimes pursuant to Rev. Rul. 69-74. (It should also be noted that the court held the parents' "investment in the contract" to be the stock's fair market value rather than their basis in the stock as Rev. Rul. 69-74 prescribed.)

Further tax disadvantages occur where the transferee is a trust (even a trust which does not issue annuity contracts from time to time) and the transferor is the grantor of the trust. In such a case, if the trust has no significant income-producing assets other than the transferred property, the transferor will be treated as the owner of the trust under 677 (a)(1), so that the entire trust income will be taxed to him each year. Rev. Rul. 68-183, 1968-1 C.B. 308. See *Simon M. Lazarus, supra*. The transferor will also be considered to have retained a life estate in the property transferred, so that the property will be includible in his gross estate under Section 2036. The transferor may owe a gift tax on the fair market value of the property minus the value of the retained life estate. *Lazarus, supra*.

The transferee's income tax concerns relate primarily to the questions of his basis in the transferred property. The basic rules are essentially these:

(a) During the transferor's lifetime, the transferee's basis for depreciation purposes is the actuarial value of the annuity promise, or the total of the payments actually made, whichever is higher, less depreciation previously deducted. Following the transferor's death, the basis for depreciation is the total of the annuity payments made, less prior depreciation. Rev. Rul. 55-119, 1955-1 Cum. Bul. 352.

(b) If the property is sold prior to the transferor's death, the basis for computing *gain* is equal to the total payments actually made plus the actuarial value, as of the date of sale, of the payments to be made in the future. The basis for computing *loss* is the total amount of the payments made as of the date of sale. Payments made after a sale resulting in loss are deemed losses during the year in which they were made. Payments made after a sale resulting in a gain are deductible to the extent they exceed the actuarial value of the annuity promise at the time of the sale. If neither gain nor loss is realized (as where the sale price is less than the basis for determining gain but more than the basis for determining loss), the excess of the sale price over the annuity payments actually made will be income to the transferee upon the premature death of the annuitant. Rev. Rul. 55-119, *supra.*

(c) If the property is sold after the transferor's death, the transferee's basis for determining gain or loss will be the total of all payments made under the agreement. Rev. Rul. 55-119, *supra.*

Where the transferor has taken depreciation deductions on the property prior to its transfer, there may be a problem of depreciation recapture under IRC Section 1245 (for personalty) or Section 1250 (for realty). It will be necessary in such cases to determine, under the applicable Section, the amount of depreciation to be recaptured and also the timing of the recapture.

Where the transferee is a corporation which is redeeming its own stock via the annuity payments, special tax considerations are involved. Such a transaction may be attractive when (a) a stock redemption is preferable to a cross-purchase, so that the purchase price can be paid with funds which have not been taxed at both the corporate and individual levels; and (b) the selling shareholder would be more comfortable with an annuity than a terminable fixed sum.

The difficulty with corporate stock redemptions, via private annuity or otherwise, is that the distribution of cash by a corporation to a shareholder in exchange for stock will be treated as a dividend (to the extent of the corporation's current and accumulated earnings) unless the shareholder can escape dividend treatment under a specific statutory provision. Of the four tests applicable to stock redemptions, a redemption to pay death taxes (under section 303 of the Code) is not available for a lifetime transaction, and a redemption "not essentially equivalent to a dividend" is too small and infirm an aperture for our average camel to pass through. So we must attempt a redemption which is either "substantially disproportionate" (under section 302(b)(2)) or effects a "complete termination" of the shareholder's interest under section 302(b)(3)).

A substantially disproportionate redemption is accomplished if, as a result of the redemption, the shareholder's voting stock is reduced to less than 80 percent of the percentage of voting stock owned by him immediately prior to the redemption. Also, his percentage of all common stock (voting and nonvoting) must be reduced to less than 80 percent of the percentage of common stock owned by him immediately prior to the redemption. And after the redemption he must own less than 50 percent of the total voting power of all classes of stock outstanding. The difficulty of accomplishing all this is that Section 318 of the Code *attributes* to the redeeming shareholder the ownership of all shares on which he has a stock option and also shares owned by certain other shareholders, such as his spouse, children, grandchildren and parents. Also, a partnership of which the shareholder is a beneficiary; and a corporation of which he owns more than 50 percent in value of the stock. Under these attribution rules, it will be readily apparent that where some of the stock of the corporation involved is owned by persons or entities related to the redeeming shareholder in any of the enumerated ways, the "substantially disproportionate" test may be difficult to meet, even where the shareholder seeks to redeem all the shares actually owned by him.

The attribution rules also present a threshold problem where the shareholder seeks to escape dividend treatment via a "complete termination of his interest. For this purpose, however, a solution will be available in many cases through waiver of the family attribution rules (a waiver which is not available for purposes of a "substantially disproportionate" redemption). The attribution rules as to estates, trusts, partnerships and corporations continue to apply as above stated, but the rules will not apply as between family members if all of the stock owned by the shareholder is redeemed and the following conditions are met:

1. Immediately after the distribution the transferor must have no interest in the corporation (including an interest as an officer, director, or employee) other than an interest as a creditor;

2. The transferor must not acquire any such interest in the corporation (other than stock acquired by bequest or inheritance) within ten years from the date of the distribution;

3. The transferor must agree to notify IRS of any acquisition of the type described in the preceding paragraph (2) and to retain records

of the transaction; and

4. The transferor must not have given stock to or received stock from any person or entity designated in the attribution rules during the 10-year period preceding the redemption unless, in the case of stock so given by the transferor, that stock is also redeemed, or unless it can be shown that the stock was not received or given in an attempt to avoid income taxes.

Caveat. It would appear that the transferor's interest in a private annuity would normally be treated as that of a creditor. However, in Section 4.01(3) of Rev. Proc. 696, 1969-1 C.B. 396, IRS states that it will not ordinarily issue an advance ruling on the applicability of Section 302(b)(3) to a redemption in which the corporation gives the distributee a note having a duration of more than fifteen years. There would seem to be some danger that IRS would refuse to recognize the purely creditor status of a transferor-annuitant whose life expectancy exceeds fifteen years.

[¶603]   PRIVATE ANNUITY COMPARED WITH GIFT AND INSTALLMENT SALE

It may be helpful to compare the transfer of property in exchange for a private annuity with the transfer of the same property as a gift. Features favorable to the annuity are:

1. The annuity transaction avoids (a) the erosion or exhaustion of the estate and gift tax credit and (b) the gift tax which the gift transfer, depending on the amount, may involve.

2. The property transferred under a private annuity arrangement is immediately removed from the transferor's gross estate, whereas the property if transferred by gift is subject to the estate tax hazard of includibility under Section 2035 if death occurs within three years thereafter.

3. The annuity payments more than replace the normal income yield of the transferred property for the transferor's benefit, whereas a reservation to the transferor of income of property given to the transferee results in inclusion of the transferred property in the transferor's gross estate.

Comparisons more favorable to a transfer by gift are these:

1. Unless the annuity payments are consumed or given away, their accumulation will gradually erode the estate diminution benefit of the

transaction, whereas the gift more than three years prior to death, with no retained interest, effects a permanent estate reduction.

2. In the gift situation, the income from the transferred property is simply shifted from the donor to the donee. In the private annuity transaction, the transferee must make annuity payments out of after-tax dollars, and the transferor must include a portion of each payment in his taxable income. The burden is lessened for the transferee where depreciable property is transferred; and for the transferor where there is little difference between his basis and the fair market value of the transferred property.

Of course, while the foregoing comparison may be useful analytically, and you may indeed choose between a private annuity and a gift for transfer of a particular asset or class of assets, you will sometimes find complementary roles for annuity and gift transactions in connection with a client's estate planning. You may, for example, transfer an item of depreciable real estate in exchange for a private annuity, transfer policies of life insurance to an irrevocable trust as discussed in Chapter 7, and adopt a program of annual giving to use the client's annual exclusions as discussed in Chapter 5.

Comparison of the private annuity with an installment sale may be helpful. On the sale of real property or the casual sale of personal property other than stock in trade, gain from sale involving deferred payments may be reported on the installment method, if there is no payment in the year of sale or if payments in the year of sale do not exceed 30 percent of the selling price (Section 433(b)(2)(A) of the Code; Reg. Sec. 1.453-4). Where the gain on such a sale is reported on the installment method, and the property is a capital asset, the gain reported each year is short-term or long-term gain, depending on how long the property was held (Section 1233 of the Code). Interest or imputed interest in the transaction is ordinary income. Accordingly, such a transaction would involve the same three elements as the private annuity transaction: return of capital, capital gain, and ordinary income.

Assume for example, that on January 1, 1977, Property X, which the taxpayer had purchased in 1976 for $80,000, is sold by the taxpayer for $100,000, and that he receives $25,000 in cash and three notes for $25,000, one due January 1, 1978, another due January 1, 1979, and the third due January 1, 1980, with 6 percent simple interest payable annually. The payments would comprise the following elements:

	Payment	Return of Capital	Capital Gain	Ordinary Income
1977	$25,000	$20,000	$5,000	
1978	25,000	20,000	5,000	$1,500
1979	25,000	20,000	5,000	3,000
1980	25,000	20,000	5,000	4,500

The primary characteristics that distinguish the installment sale from the private annuity transaction, assuming no gift is involved in either case, are that in the former (1) the transferee's basis will be equal to his purchase price, which will not be affected by the length of the transferor's life, (2) the transferor may outlive the installment payments, and (3) the present worth of any installment remaining unpaid at the transferor's death will be includible in his gross estate for estate tax purposes.

Obviously, if we substitute for the simple, single life annuity a joint and survivor annuity, a refund annuity, or an annuity for a term certain and life thereafter, as discussed earlier in this chapter, a residual value may be includible in the transferor's gross estate and the difference from an installment sale is thereby diminished.

Where the transferor seeks a return for his lifetime, is motivated by the desire to reduce or avoid estate tax, and is not concerned to realize the full value of the transferred property (which is typically the case where the transferee is also a primary beneficiary of his estate plan), the annuity will normally be preferred to the installment sale. The same interest will normally indicate a preference for the simple annuity over the variants above mentioned.

7

Irrevocable Life Insurance Trust

[¶700]   **OPPORTUNITIES AVAILABLE**

The saving of estate taxes is normally the primary goal of the irrevocable life insurance trust. Such a trust presents no inordinate difficulty of draftsmanship or implementation. It is relatively "cheap" in its gift tax consequences. It offers numerous collateral advantages. There are hazards to be recognized, of course, but in most cases they can be accepted or overcome. And yet, whether from innate conservatism or overreaction to the word "irrevocable," planners often fail to recommend or propose this tax saving device to clients who could take advantage of it.

TRA 76 has heightened the significance of the irrevocable life insurance trust for tax planning purposes. TRA's removal of the "contemplation of death" issue under Sec. 2035 of the Code, when gifts are made within three years prior to death, will have a lesser impact on life insurance transfers than on other gifts, as the presumption was especially difficult to rebut in life insurance gifts anyway. More important, the unification of the estate and gift tax rates amplifies the "premium" built into the valuation of life insurance policies for gift tax purposes. (See ¶701).

[¶701]   **WHEN TO USE THE IRREVOCABLE
LIFE INSURANCE TRUST**

When we suggest irrevocable trusts to our colleagues for their clients, common responses are: "Isn't he too young to consider that?" and "Is his estate really large enough for that?"

176

The older client, to be sure, may be more "set" in his ultimate planning objectives, having a marriage that has lasted over the years and children who are grown and "established." The younger client, nevertheless, may be willing to adopt an irrevocable trust if it incoporates sufficient flexibility to meet future contingencies—through the trustees' discretionary powers, beneficiaries' special powers of appointment, and similar devices. He may wish to use it for some rather than all of his policies now, with the opportunity to add others later. Moreover, the transfer of the younger client's policies may be more advantageous than the transfer of the older client's in terms of the gift tax treatment of the accumulated cash values.

And, again, while there are more estate taxes to be saved through reduction of larger estates, this is no reason to forego the estate tax savings that can be accomplished in estates than are relatively modest.

Consider, for one example, an adjusted gross estate of $1,000,000, which includes $300,000 of life insurance which is to be transferred effectively to an irrevocable trust.

Assuming use of the full marital deduction, the estate taxes would be:

(a)	Prior to the transfer	$ 98,800
(b)	Following the effective transfer	52,600
	Tax Saving	$ 46,200

Assuming that the marital deduction will not apply, the estate taxes in that estate would be:

(a)	Prior to the transfer	$265,600
(b)	Following the effective transfer	164,800
	Tax saving	$100,800

For a more modest example, consider an adjusted gross estate of $500,000, including $150,000 of life insurance which is to be transferred effectively to an irrevocable trust.

Assuming use of the full marital deduction, the estate taxes would be:

(a)	Prior to the transfer	$ 21,400
(b)	Following the effective transfer	0
	Tax saving	$ 21,400

Assuming that the marital deduction will not apply, the estate taxes in that estate would be:

(a) Prior to the transfer	$ 98,800
(b) Following the effective transfer	$ 52,600
	$ 46,200

In the latter ($500,000 adjusted gross estate) example, the projected estate tax saving is "only" from $21,400 to $46,200. And yet these savings might have more meaning in terms of meeting the basic needs of this client's beneficiaries than the larger tax savings would have for the beneficiaries of the larger estate client. Also, the tax saving effected by the transfer will automatically expand with the increase in value of his retained estate as the years go by.

The irrevocable life insurance trust, in short, has applicability for many more clients and situations than estate planners have commonly recognized. Furthermore, the limitations imposed by TRA 76 on the tax savings to be attained through generation-skipping trusts (See Chapter 3) provide a new, additional reason to terminate foot-dragging for clients for whom the irrevocable life insurance trust may otherwise be in order.

The "democratization" of the irrevocable life insurance trust is long overdue. Such a trust should be considered as regularly and automatically—though it will not be adopted quite as frequently—as the marital deduction is considered in the estate planning process.

In considering the reduction of a client's taxable estate by means of lifetime gifts, certain advantages of life insurance policies over other assets for gift purposes should be considered, especially:

1. The entire face amount of a policy can be removed from the gross estate, whereas the value for gift tax purposes may be nominal or relatively low. Real estate, securities, or cash will have as great a value for gift tax purposes as they have at the time of the gift for estate tax purposes; indeed, where the values are fluctuating, the estate tax value of such assets when death occurs may be less than the value on which a gift tax was paid.

2. Ordinarily the proceeds of a life insurance policy are excluded from the beneficiary's gross income, so that the lifetime transfer does not involve concern as to the "basis" of the asset in the transferee's hands. With gifts of real estate or securities, in contrast, we must consider the potential income tax consequence to the donee through loss of the stepped-up basis that might otherwise be available at the time of the donor's death.

Prior to TRA 76, the basis of "inherited" property, for purposes of computing gain or loss, was its fair market value at the time of the decedent's death (or on the alternate valuation date, if the latter was applicable). However the basis of property acquired by lifetime gift (other than gifts deemed to be in contemplation of death) was the same as its basis in the donor's hands (increased in certain cases by gift tax paid on it) if subsequent sale resulted in a gain. TRA 76, however, abolished the "step-up" of basis at death, thus removing the distinction in this respect between lifetime and testamentary gifts, *except for a transitional rule.* Under the transitional rule, the basis for computing gain on property which the decedent is treated as holding on December 31, 1976, is increased by the excess of the fair market value of the property on December 31, 1976, over its adjusted basis on that date. While that limited step-up of basis will diminish in significance with the passage of time, it exists presently as a consideration in the lifetime transfer of real estate or securities. The lifetime transfer of a life insurance policy does not involve this potential income tax cost for the donee.

3. In contrast with most other assets, the life insurance policy is normally held for the funds it will produce at death and not for the owner's lifetime needs. Its transfer will not be considered as a current deprivation. If the donor is concerned about the loss of his access to a policy's cash values, he may reduce this loss (and correspondingly, of course, the projected estate tax saving) by borrowing the cash values prior to the gift. He may also indirectly have the potential benefit of future cash accumulations with the cooperation of the individual donee or, if the donee is a trust, by giving his spouse or other beneficiary the noncumulative right to withdraw $5000 (or 5 percent) a year from the trust principal. (If the power of withdrawal is so limited, failure to exercise it in any year will not be considered a gift by the holder of the power for gift tax purposes. Nor will it cause the property subject to the power to be included in the holder's gross estate for estate tax purposes.[1]

Just as life insurance is, for the reasons above mentioned, an excellent candidate for gift purposes, the irrevocable trust is in many cases the optimum transferee:

1. Use of the irrevocable trust enables us to eliminate the insurance proceeds from more than one estate. If an individual donee of a policy retains the policy and receives the proceeds at the donor's death, the entire proceeds are thus added to the donee's gross estate for estate tax purposes. The trust, however, can be so designed as to have the insurance proceeds made available to meet the beneficiary's needs without adding the proceeds to his or her gross estate. [See Chapter Three,

---

[1]Sections 2041(b)(2) and 2514(e) of the Code.

however, for limitations imposed by TRA 76 with respect to generation-skipping transfers.]

2. The irrevocable trust is a vehicle whereby the donor can direct the ultimate devolution of the insurance proceeds, whereas an individual donee of a policy may dispose of the proceeds in a manner not consistent with the donor's desires.

3. The irrevocable trust device enables the donor to provide for professional management of funds, or for multiple or group attention to the funds involved. These arrangements will be preferred in many cases to management by an inexperienced individual donee.

4. The trust gives the donor greater assurance that the insurance proceeds, which may be the donor's sole or major liquid asset, will be made available to meet the estate's liquidity needs. The trustees may be empowered, toward this end:

> "To purchase as an investment for any trust hereunder any assets of the Grantor's estate, provided that the price paid for such assets shall not exceed the fair market value thereof; to make loans to the Grantor's estate at a fair rate of interest and with adequate security; and to continue to hold assets so purchased or loans so made as investments hereunder."

An individual donee may or may not choose to make the proceeds available to the executors in any of those ways. On the other hand, in the light of the new carryover basis rules provided by TRA 76, consideration should be given to the potential capital gains consequences of transactions authorized by the above quoted provision.

5. In most jurisdictions a spendthrift provision in the trust instrument will be effective to protect the insurance proceeds and investments against claims of the beneficiaries' creditors. In the hands of an individual donee, the insurance proceeds are, of course, as vulnerable as the donee's others assets.

6. By the use of income accumulation and "sprinkling" provisions, the trust can also be used to effect income tax savings for the donor's beneficiary or beneficiaries over the years.

[¶702]   **TAX ASPECTS**

[¶702.1]   Estate Tax Results

The examples used in ¶701 show the estate tax savings to be attained on the assumption that the ownership of one or more insurance policies is effectively transferred to an irrevocable trust. In order to be effective for estate tax avoidance, the following criteria must be met:

(a) The transferor can retain no incidents of ownership in the policy. "Incidents of ownership" include powers to change the beneficiary; to surrender or cancel the policy; to assign the policy; to revoke an assignment; or to pledge the policy for a loan or obtain a loan from the insurer against the surrender value of the policy. There can be no requirement that the trustees pay debts and taxes of the transferor's estate out of the proceeds of the policy. Nor can there be the retention of a reversionary interest in excess of five percent of the value of the property immediately prior to death.

In the case of split-dollar insurance, where a corporation owns the cash surrender portion of the policy and an employee who is the controlling shareholder of the corporation owns the insurance in excess of cash value, the removal of the employee-owned portion of the policy from his gross estate is not so simple. Rev. Rul. 76-274, 1976-2 CB 278 covers three factual situations involving such arrangements, and this ruling should be reviewed when transfers or third-party acquisitions of such insurance are contemplated. The goal is to avoid includibility in the employee's gross estate by reason of his controlling interest in the corporation, where the employee's portion of the insurance is otherwise excludible. A key factor in achieving this is that the corporation have no rights other than the right to borrow against the cash value. The form or mode of the split-dollar arrangement (endorsement, collateral assignment, etc.) appears to be irrelevant.

(b) The transferor can retain no life interest in the trust property or right to designate the person or persons who shall enjoy the property or its income[2] In the latter connection, if the transferor reserves an unrestricted right to remove a Trustee at any time and appoint himself as Trustee, the transferor is considered as having the powers of the Trustee.[3]

(c) The transferor can retain no power to alter, amend or revoke the trust.[4]

(d) The policies must not be transferred or deemed to have been transferred within three years prior to the transferor's death.[5] This three year criterion is perhaps the greatest estate tax hazard; certainly it

---

[2]Section 2036 of the Code.
[3]Reg. Sec. 20.2036-1(b)(3).
[4]Section 2038 of the Code.
[5]Section 2035 of the Code.

is the one over which we have the least control. It should be considered in two phases:

(i) *Death within three years.* Under TRA 76, property transferred within three years prior to death will be includible in the transferor's gross estate under Section 2035 of the code regardless of motive.

This provision underscores the importance of arranging for the three-year period to run from the earliest possible date. It is suggested that a beneficiary change and transfer of ownership instrument be signed and mailed to each insurer involved on the same date as the trust instrument is executed. This is in order to take the position that that date is the effective date of transfer even if the insurer requests or insists that its own forms be signed and submitted thereafter. A suggested form is included in Appendix C.

Where new insurance is to be acquired with funds given to the trustees by the insured, it is arguable that purchase of the policy *by the trustees* with the transferred funds should eliminate the three-year hazard as to the policy (as distinguished from the transferred funds). In this case, the insured never owned the policy and, therefore, never "transferred" it. The Sixth and Ninth Circuits[6] have upheld the Internal Revenue Service in "looking through form to substance" and rejecting that contention. Nevertheless, this procedure should be considered until the issue is disposed of with finality.

Also, the "substance" might be more favorably developed if the transferred cash were applied in part to the purchase of insurance and in part to another type of investment, the proportion being determined by the trustees after they have received the funds.

And, finally, if the initial and subsequent premiums are paid with funds separately owned and contributed by the insured's spouse or other trust beneficiary, there should be no adverse "substance" to pursue from the standpoint of the insured's gross estate. In no way will the insured have transferred the insurance protection, directly or indirectly.

If it is determined that insurance premiums are to be paid by the trustees with funds given to the trustees by the grantor of the trust or by a trust beneficiary, and if it is desired to have these payments handled by one of several trustees (especially where there is a corporate trustee which is not receiving compensation during the grantor's lifetime), a provision for this purpose may be incorporated in the trust instrument. See Clause Seventeenth of the irrevocable life insurance trust included in Appendix C.

(ii) *Death after three years; payment of premiums within three years.* In Rev. Rul. 67-463, 1967-2 CB 327, IRS ruled that insurance proceeds attributable to premiums paid by the decedent within three years of his death were includible in his estate. In Rev. Rul. 71-497, CB 1971-2, 329, however, after a series of adverse court decisions, IRS adopted a position more favorable to the taxpayer: If a policy is transferred more than three yeas prior to death and the transferor continues to pay premiums on it

---

[6]*Detroit Bank & Trust Company v. United States,* 467 F.2d 964 (6th Cir., 1972); *First National Bank of Oregon v. United States,* 488 F.2d 575 (9th Cir., 1973).

until his death, only the premiums paid within three years prior to death are includible in his gross estate.

The recent case of *Silverman*[7] suggests the wisdom of having the trustees pay the premiums with funds given to them by the insured's spouse or other trust beneficiary for the period of three years following transfer of a policy to the trust. The Tax Court held in that case that if a transferee pays premiums with his own funds, that portion of the proceeds paid for by him (his premium payment as a percentage of total premium payments) will not be includible in the estate of the insured even if the transfer of the policy was made in contemplation of death. (This ruling would now apply under Section 2035, as amended by TRA 76, to all policies transferred within three years prior to death without regard to "contemplation of death" in the transfer.) Following the three-year period, the insured can and probably should resume payment of the premiums.

[¶702.2]   Gift Tax Results

(a) *On the policy.* The transfer of a policy to an irrevocable trust is, of course, a completed and taxable gift. If a policy is transferred immediately after it is issued, its value for the gift tax purposes is its cost[8]. If a single-premium or paid-up policy is transferred, its gift tax value is its replacement cost[9] (the amount the insurer would charge for a similar policy on a person the same age as the insured at the time of the transfer). In the more usual case, the policy on which premiums are payable on an on-going basis, the gift tax value is the interpolated terminal reserve (the amount the insurance company holds on reserve to cover its liability on the policy) plus prepaid premiums as of the date of the gift.[10]

(b) *On the premiums.* Following transfer of ownership of the policy, each premium paid on it by the transferor constitutes a taxable gift of the premium amount.[11] If the insured's employer pays the premiums on a group term life insurance policy which the employee has transferred to an irrevocable trust, each such payment is considered to be an indirect gift of the premium amount by the insured employee.[12] If a trust beneficiary pays premiums on the policy, he makes a taxable gift to

[7]*Estate of Morris R. Silverman,* 61 TC 338.
[8]Reg. Sec. 25.2512-6, Ex. (1).
[9]Reg. Sec. 25.2512-6, Ex. (3).
[10]Reg. Sec. 25.2512-6, Ex. (4).
[11]Reg. Sec. 25.2511-1(h)(8). Rev. Rul. 76-490, 1976-2 CB 300.
[12]Rev. Rul. 76-490, I.R.B. 1976-50, 28.

the extent of the actuarial value of the interests of other beneficiaries of the trust.[13]

(c) *Annual exclusions.* In computing the taxable gift of a donor in any taxable year, the first $3,000 of gifts of a *present interest* to each donee is excluded, but gifts of future interests are includible in their entirety. In order to qualify the policy and the premium payments for the present interest exclusion, it is suggested that a trust beneficiary be given, during the transferor's lifetime, the net income of the trust and the noncumulative right to withdraw in each calendar year the sum of $5,000 or an amount equal to 5 percent of the trust principal, whichever is greater. The trustees should also be directed, on demand of a current income beneficiary, to convert the policies into cash (which may be otherwise invested in accordance with the trustee's investment powers). Otherwise, if the trustees must await receipt of the proceeds at the time of the transferor's death, transfer of the policy and premium payments will constitute gifts of future interests.[14] (For purposes of the annual exclusion, if the transfer of the policy qualifies, future premium payments by the transferor will also qualify;[15] otherwise they will not.)

It might be advisable to go even further and require that the trust beneficiary be notified of each gift to the trust. Also, that an amount equal to the premium or $3,000, whichever is less, be retained uninvested through the end of the year, or for a stipulated period, subject to the beneficiary's annual withdrawal right. This would assure that the withdrawal right applies to the current gift (rather than to prior accumulations, in whole or in part), on a kind of last-in, first-out basis. For a provision along these lines, and court approval of it for annual exclusion purposes, see *Crummey v. Comm.*, 22 AFTR 6023, 397 F.2d 82 (9th Cir., 1968).

[¶703]   **HAZARDS AND DISADVANTAGES**

Apart from the gift tax treatment of the transactions involved, there are other "costs" which should be taken into account in deciding upon an irrevocable life insurance trust":

1. As with *all* trusts, we should weigh, as against the presumed tax

---

[13]*Commissioner of Internal Revenue v. Berger*, 201 F.2d 171 (2d Cir., 1953).
[14]Reg. Sec. 25.2503-3(c), Ex. (2).
[15]*Harbeck Halsted*, 28 TC 1069 (1957) (Acq. 1958-2 CB-5).

benefits and "control" benefits, the consequences to the beneficiaries in terms of the curtailment of their freedom and autonomy.

2. The compensation of trustees is an expense ordinarily involved in the administration of trusts. Related persons may be willing to serve without compensation, but generally we get what we pay for in this as in other aspects of life.

3. Use of the trust involves loss to a surviving spouse of the tax-free $1,000 interest element that would be available under Section 101(d) of the Code if a settlement option providing for installment payments were elected. On the other hand, as compared with election of a fixed insurance option, the trust can and should provide greater flexibility as to both investments and distributions.

4. The trust is irrevocable, and not subject to amendment or alteration by the transferor of the policies, and this feature can be a cause of concern to potential donors. There are, to be sure, cases in which this characteristic of the trust (considered in the context of the amount of projected estate tax savings, the ages of the parties concerned, the relative instability of the family situation, and other causes of apprehension) may lead to rejection or postponement of the irrevocable trust. But there are a number of extrinsic and intrinsic techniques and provisions which will in many cases relieve or mitigate the potential donor's concerns or apprehensions, especially:

(a) The grantor's spouse can be given a broad special power of appointment, which she may be willing to use to implement changes that may be desired by the donor following execution of the trust. Added flexibility can be attained by giving special powers of appointment to subsequent beneficiaries as well. Further, based on extensive research conducted several years ago, the authors have adopted the following provision, which appears to be unusual:

> During the lifetime of the Grantor, the Grantor's wife shall have the power at any time, and from time to time, to make gifts of the trust principal, without limitation, to or for the benefit of the Grantor, the Grantor's children, and the issue of the Grantor's children, or any of them, in such amounts or proportions, on such terms and conditions, and subject to such trusts or limitations, as the Grantor's wife may in writing set forth.

We are of the opinion that such a provision, in the first place, does not constitute a general power of appointment so as to draw the trust principal into the wife's gross estate. The reason is that the power is exercisable only in favor of "one or more designated persons or classes other than the decedent or (her) creditors, or the decedent's estate or creditors of (her) estate." Reg. Sec. 20.2041-1-c. Moreover, where the trust principal consists of insurance policies without substantial cash values, the question of includibility in the wife's gross estate, if she predeceases the grantor, is academic.

In the second and more important place, it is our opinion that the power of the grantor's wife to return transferred policies to the grantor is not sufficient to make them includible in the grantor's gross estate. He has not retained possession or enjoyment within the meaning of IRC Section 2036 of the Code. The grantor has not arranged by this device to meet his obligation to support dependents (Reg. Sec. 20.2036-1): see, e.g., *McCullough v. Granger,* 128 F. Supp. 611 (1955), and *Chrysler,* 44 TC 55, 62 (1966). Nor can we properly conclude that he had arranged for the trust assets to be applied "otherwise for his pecuniary benefit" (Reg. Sec. 20.2036-1) where he has no *right* but only a *chance* of having the policies restored to him. Otherwise, any outright gift would be subject to the same challenge, as there is always the chance that the donee will restore the gift property to the donor.

Nor can the concention that the wife's control is equivalent to the grantor's be supported. As the Court stated in *McCullough, supra,* at p. 616:

> "It is said that because the trustees were his wife and another son, that he, in effect retained control. As Judge Goodrich said in the *Douglas* case, 'We have no notion what the trustees would have done had such a request been made.' To assume that the donor controlled the trustees because they were his wife and another son is but to speculate. There is no indication that the donor did, in fact, exercise any control over the trustees during his lifetime."

Without a specific ruling or decision on the provision suggested above, each individual advisor must satisfy himself or herself and take responsibility for his or her decision to employ it. The opportunity which it provides for reversing an irrevocable trust transaction serves simultaneously (a) to invite concern and (b), in our judgment, to encourage its use as one of several safety valves to mitigate the rigors of the irrevocable trust.

(b) If the time should come when the trust provisions are not entirely satisfactory, the grantor of the trust may be able to effect adequate compensatory adjustments (in the proportions or timing of principal distributions, for example) via his will or other instruments or arrangements.

(c) A spouse's (or other beneficiary's) power to withdraw $5,000 or 5 percent of the principal each year, if the trust so provides, can be used to divert such amounts toward new or altered objectives.

(d) The trust instrument can be drawn to vest broad discretionary powers in the trustees with respect to income and principal distributions. It can provide flexibility in meeting the contingencies of an uncertain future.

(e) Policies transferred to the trust can be replaced with new ones purchased outside the trust (subject to higher rates, and conditioned on continued insurability), or can be simply dropped, if the grantor should decide to "disinherit" his trust beneficiaries. Merely by transferring policies to an irrevocable trust the donor does not obligate himself to pay future insurance premiums. As an alternative in the case of a spouse as beneficiary, the instrument can provide for termination of her service as a trustee (if she has been appointed), her powers of appointment, and also her beneficial interest, in the event of a separation or divorce. It is also possible, with careful draftsmanship, to make provision for a possible future spouse; it is generally advisable, however, for the trustees in such a case to be given very broad discretion as to income or principal distributions rather than to bestow fixed benefits on an unascertained future beneficiary.

In most cases, the elements of flexibility mentioned above will enable a client comfortably to adopt the irrevocable trust for all or part of his life insurance portfolio—at least in cases where he considers his family situation to be fairly stable and finds the projected estate tax savings attractive. He should be given at least the opportunity to make an informed decision.

A sample irrevocable life insurance trust is included in Exhibit C.

8

Qualified Pension and Profit-Sharing Plans

OPPORTUNITIES AVAILABLE

Although qualified pension and profit-sharing plans are frequently adopted in the pursuit of the income tax benefits which they provide, as well as other goals, they also furnish a major opportunity to reduce estate taxes. Qualification is available pursuant to Section 401 of the Internal Revenue Code.

[¶800.1]   Pension Plans

A pension plan is a plan by which an employer provides for retirement benefits for his employees on a regular, ongoing basis. Pension plans may be divided into two groups: defined-benefit plans and defined- contribution plans. Defined-benefit plans generally provide a retirement benefit which is equal to some percent of the employees' compensation, e.g., 30 percent. The benefit may be integrated with Social Security benefits so that the employee's projected Social Security benefit will serve as a base benefit. The benefit formula may be step-rated so that employees earning, for example, $8,000 or less receive a benefit of 30 percent and those earning in excess of $8,000 receive a benefit of 50 percent of the excess. Regardless of the benefit formula, the fundamental principal of the defined-benefit pension plan is to contribute sufficient funds annually to accumulate with compound interest a sum sufficient to purchase at retirement an annuity in the amount of the benefit. The benefit is the given quantity and the contributions are the variables which must be adjusted to them in accordance with investment experience. Obviously, the necessary calculations to set up such a plan require

188

the services of a qualified actuary.[1]

The defined-contribution pension plan provides for a contribution of a fixed sum or a fixed percent of an employee's compensation. The employer contributions are then accumulated together with compound interest and at retirement a retirement benefit is provided in accordance with the sum accumulated. Here the contribution is the given quantity and the benefit will vary with the investment experience. Each employee has a *share of each* employer contribution allocated to an account established by the trustees for him. The allocation method is usually based upon the percentage of total compensation which is attributable to each employee. (In the case of defined-benefit plans, in contrast, there is no allocation because the accumulations are of no consequence; the benefit is predetermined.)

[¶800.2]   Profit-Sharing Plans

Profit-sharing plans are much like the pension plans discussed above. However, employer contributions under a profit sharing plan may be made only from profits or accumulated earnings.[2] Further, a profit-sharing plan may be so designed as to permit the employer to determine annually if a contribution should be made, and if so, how much. Such a plan is known as a discretionary plan.

Both pension and profit-sharing plans provide for the employer contributions to be made to a trust established for the purpose of accumulating the funds and, at the appropriate time, paying the appropriate benefits. Some draftsmen prefer separate instruments and some prefer a single document embodying both the plan and trust. Aside from style, there would seem to be little to commend one form over the other.

[¶800.3]   Income Tax Treatment

Contributions to a qualified pension or profit-sharing plan are currently deductible payments by a corporation. Prior to the Employee Retirement Income Security Act of 1974 (referred to as ERISA) cash basis corporations were required to make their contributions prior to the end of their fiscal year in order to obtain a current deduction while accrual basis corporations had an additional 75 days (and more in certain cir-

---

[1] Now subject to enrollment and regulation by the IRS pursuant to Section 7701(a)(35) of the Code.
[2] Section 401 of the Code; Regs.Section 1.401-1(b)(1)(ii).

cumstances). Now, the 75 day grace period has been made available to all corporations.[3] With respect to contributions to profit-sharing plans which are discretionary, a corporate resolution is required in order to establish liability for the contribution prior to the year's end in support of the deduction.[4] From the viewpoint of the professional corporation, the deduction may be of particular interest because it enables the corporation to deduct and simultaneously save for the benefit of the principal shareholders such sums as would otherwise be taxable income. Thus the corporation may be operated at little or no federal income tax cost.

From the employee's point of view, the contributions made to either a pension or profit-sharing trust for his benefit are not taxable income until the time of distribution,[5] when lower tax rates will presumably apply. Thus tax deferral is made available. When distribution is made, its taxation will depend upon the method employed. If distribution is made in a lump sum, the Code now provides rules which offer either a combination of capital gains and 10-year averaging treatment to the sum distributed or treatment of the entire distribution as ordinary income subject to 10-year averaging.[6] If distribution is made in the form of installments, it is taxed as ordinary income, as received. Section 402(e)(4)(A) of the Code defines a lump-sum distribution as one "within one taxable year of the recipient of the balance of the credit of an employee which becomes payable to the recipient—

   (i)   on account of the employee's death
   (ii)   after the employee attains age 59½
   (iii)   on account of the employee's separation from service, or
   (iv)   after the employee has become disabled . . ."

In addition, the employee must have been a participant in the plan for five years prior to the distribution.[7]

The taxable portion of a lump-sum distribution is computed by reducing the total lump-sum distribution by the amount of employee contributions to the trust and unrealized appreciation of employer securities which form a part of the trust. ERISA, in 1974, changed the rules for taxation of lump-sum distributions and the Tax Reform Act of 1976 supplied an alternative method of taxation for such distributions. The ERISA method provided for separating the taxable portion of a lump-sum distribution into a capital gains portion and an ordinary in-

[3]Section 404(a)(6) of the Code.
[4]*Precision Industries, Inc. v. Com'r.*, 64 T.C. 901 (1975).
[5]Sections 402(a) and 403(a) of the Code.
[6]Sections 402(a); 402(e); 403(a) of the Code.
[7]Section 402(e)(4)(A) of the Code.

come portion which may be averaged over a 10-year period. That portion of a lump-sum distribution which is attributable to plan years commencing with 1974 is eligible for the special 10-year averaging provision. The remainder is the capital gains portion. The allocation of the distribution into two segments is achieved by multiplying it by a fraction, the numerator of which is the number of calendar years of participation after 1973 and the denominator of which is the number of years of total participation. (IRC §402(e) ERISA). The result of that computation is the ordinary income segment.

The alternative method of taxation of lump-sum distributions under the Tax Reform Act of 1976 involves an election (irrevocable after age 59½) to be taxed on the entire lump-sum distribution as ordinary income which qualifies for the special 10-year averaging provisions. Why would a distributee choose ordinary income rather than capital gains treatment? For several reasons:

(a) The minimum tax on tax preference items (capital gains) was increased in 1976 to 15 percent;

(b) The minimum tax exemption was reduced in 1976 from $30,000 to $10,000 or one-half of the Federal income tax otherwise paid for the year in question, whichever is greater.

(c) The amount subject to the 50 percent maximum tax is reduced dollar for dollar by the amount of the capital gain.

(d) The 10 year averaging provision may simply produce a lower tax than capital gains treatment.

For these reasons, the alternate method sometimes produces a lower tax on a lump-sum distribution. But State income tax provisions may produce results which counterbalance the federal tax saving. It is therefore necessary actually to compute the total federal and State income tax on such a distribution using both the original ERISA method and the alternate before an intelligent decision can be made.

Regardless of whether a distribution is made in the form of installments or as a lump-sum distribution with the two available methods of taxation, current tax deferral and preferential income tax rates make qualified pension or profit-sharing plans advantageous to the corporate employee.

Although the Tax Reform Act of 1976 reduced the estate tax advantages of qualified plans by subjecting lump-sum distributions to taxation, the exclusion of installment payments may nevertheless provide very significant savings. Prior to 1976, all types of distributions from qualified plans escaped federal estate taxation to the extent they were derived from employer contributions (Section 2039(c) of the code), so long as they were not payable to the personal representative of the employee's estate. Now, it is necessary to weigh many factors, both tax and nontax, to determine if the estate tax exclusion should be elected via installment payments. These factors are:

(a) The need of the beneficiary for the funds;
(b) The family situation of the beneficiary;
(c) The health of the beneficiary;
(d) The income tax applicable to installment payments which are estate tax excludible compared with the income and capital gains tax on lump-sum distributions.

A formula may be used to make the tax comparison as follows:

E.T.L.S. = estate tax resulting from lump sum distribution.
E.T.I.   = estate tax on installment payments.
E.T.S.   = estate tax saved by electing installment payments
             (E.T.L.S. minus E.T.I.).
I.T.I.   = income tax on total of installment payments.
I.T.L.S. = income tax on lump sum distribution, computed by
             whichever alternative is more favorable.
I.T.S.   = income tax saved by use of the lump sum distribution
             taxed on the most favorable method (I.T.I. minus I.T.L.S.).

If E.T.S. exceeds I.T.S., tax considerations point to the election of installment payments. If I.T.S. exceeds E.T.S., the tax factor points to a lump-sum distribution. Of Course, if the income tax on a lump-sum distribution exceeds the income tax on an installment distribution, the installment method is indicated without further consideration as the estate tax consequences will always be better under that method.

Changing lifetime circumstances will require a reevaluation of a decision to take a distribution in a particular way. For example, divorce or death of a spouse may call for a change in strategy. If the adjusted gross estate does not exceed $350,000, in years following 1980, $175,000 will be sheltered from federal estate tax by the credit which is equivalent to an exemption of approximately that amount. The remaining $175,000 can be sheltered from estate tax by the marital deduction. So long as the decedent has a spouse at the time of his death, the estate tax considerations will be nonexistent. On the other hand, should a divorce or death of a spouse take place, those considerations become important.

[¶801]   WHEN TO USE THEM

[¶801.1]   Business and Profession Considerations

Qualified pension and profit-sharing plans are available only to corporations or to nonowner employees of partnership or proprietorship businesses. Although H.R. 10 plans (for self-employed persons) provide estate tax treatment almost identical to that available under qualified corporate plans, more stringent limits are placed on contributions and benefits than are applicable to pension and profit-sharing plans. For persons earning substantial sums, pension and profit-sharing plans continue to be the best tax choice. This fact may often lead to the incorporation of an unincorporated business.

The corporate form itself presents problems which must be considered. Payroll taxes and accounting fees generally are somewhat higher for the corporate form of operation. The corporate form is somewhat less flexible in that the principals may find it necessary to agree on salaries without regard to the party responsible for production of business or completion of work. Also, the proper operation of the corporation calls for the formal keeping of records on a regular basis, not otherwise required. On the other hand, aside from the slightly increased costs, most of the corporate problems relating to rigidity and formality can be solved by properly drawn employment and stock redemption or cross-purchase agreements. The additional cost of corporate operation is generally offset by other benefits such as term life insurance for the group and medical reimbursement plans. Not altogether incidental is the fact that the corporate form provides limited liability, not otherwise available.[8] For these reasons, it is often worthwhile to incorporate and make available the full income and estate tax advantages of qualified plans.

Even if the business is in the corporate form, however, consideration must be given to a variety of other factors before adopting a qualified plan. Is the corporation's existence likely to continue indefinitely? If its business activity is one of short duration, such as a building project or other single contract operation, the tax-free build-up in the trust of contributions may not be sufficient to justify the costs involved. Qualification may also be endangered because a qualified plan must be intended as an ongoing affair,[9] and such a situation may lead to a conclusion that no such intention was present.

Further, in order to avoid the "double" taxation which results from corporate profit, it may be useful to have a corporation elect to be taxed pursuant to Subchapter S of the Internal Revenue Code. In that case there would be no tax at the corporate level, and the estate tax advantages would be available, but the amount of the contributions to a qualified pension or profit-sharing plan maintained by a Subchapter S cor-

---

[8] It should be noted that professional corporation statutes in most states provide for the continuing liability of the professional for his own acts. Even here, however, the professional in the corporation is not personally responsible for the separate unsupervised acts of the others.

[9] Regs. Section 1.401-1(b)(2).

poration is limited to those allowable under the self-employed or H.R. 10 Plans.[10]

Also, caution should be exercised if the corporation is relatively new and still requires an accumulation of funds for use as working capital. If the business is such that fairly large doses of working capital are required, obviously they should be accumulated first. On the other hand, if the corporation engages in service type business in which capital investment is minimal, a plan may appropriately be considered from the beginning. Pension and profit-sharing plans, of course, reduce corporate earnings and, therefore, reduce the risk of subjecting the corporation to the accumulated earnings tax pursuant to Section 531 of the Code.

[¶801.2]   Other Corporate Considerations

Pension plans require an ongoing commitment to make a contribution in good years and bad.[11] For this reason it is important to review the history of the corporation as well as its prospects for the future. You should make an effort to determine if it is likely to be in a position to afford the required contribution for the foreseeable future. Also, as noted above, profit-sharing contributions can only be made from profits or retained earnings, so that a review of the profitability of the corporation is appropriate before such a plan is adopted. A break-even enterprise (after salaries) would have little use for a profit-sharing plan.

[¶802]   HOW TO SELECT THE PLAN
BEST SUITED TO THE CLIENT

In selecting an appropriate plan it is necessary to consider a number of factors.

☐ History and stability of the business. The history and stability of the business is most important in determining if a pension plan is the proper vehicle. As has been noted above, a pension plan requires regular, ongoing contributions. A business which is new or which is subject to severe fluctuations in profit ought to be advised to consider the less rigid vehicle of a profit-sharing plan which can be adjusted to meet current cash flow requirements. On the other hand, a stable, well-established business can take larger deductions for contributions to a pension plan than those available for contributions to a profit-sharing plan. In some

---

[10]Section 1379(b)(1) of the Code.
[11]The IRC provides severe penalties for underfunding a pension plan.

cases, a combination of plans permits both flexibility and higher deductions (up to 25 percent of covered compensation).

☐ Ages of principal employees. If all principal employees are near retirement, a defined-benefit pension plan may be indicated. Although trust assets of defined-benefit plans are not allocated among participants, larger percentages of employer contributions will enure to the benefit of older employees than to younger employees because there will be less time to accumulate a fund to provide the required retirement annuity. On the other hand, if the principal employees are young, they would normally receive greater benefit from a defined-contribution profit sharing plan since a substantial preretirement period will permit a tax-free build-up of funds allocated to each employee.

☐ Type of investment vehicle. Because a defined-benefit pension plan must necessarily provide a fixed benefit at retirement, a conservative investment approach is called for. If fund values drop, the employer will be called upon to make additional contributions to fully fund the plan. A profit-sharing plan or other defined contribution plan will permit more flexibility in investment portfolio. One frequent approach to the defined-benefit plan funding problem is to purchase life insurance so that a death benefit can be paid and also in order that sufficient cash values can be accumulated during years of employment to permit the purchase of a retirement annuity.

Plans of either the defined-benefit or defined-contribution type may be designed to include provisions for loans to participants and also voluntary contributions (up to 10 percent of compensation) by participants so that they can built up their own fully vested accounts. Both provisions can be very useful to an employee. The first will provide cash when a commercial loan might be unavailable; the second permits tax-free buildup of savings, something not available with a savings account at a commercial bank.

We have described in general terms the types of retirement plans which are available and some of the provisions which they may contain, so that consideration will be given to selection of an appropriate plan for a particular set of circumstances. Another important factor is employee relations. Employees need to feel secure both in the present and in retirement. The defined-benefit plan produces a large measure of security through certainty of a specific retirement benefit. On the other hand, employers are desirous of having their employees reinforced financially in such a way that they will take a personal interest in the success of the business. Such reinforcement is provided by sharing the profits with the employees via a profit-sharing plan. Frequently in the rush to cut current taxation as well as to achieve a reduction of federal estate taxation, retirement plans are adopted without adequate consideration of these employee relationship concerns. Unless employee concerns are taken into account, a potentially useful opportunity may be lost.

[¶803]   PENSION REFORM ACT STRICTURES

In 1974, ERISA introduced a number of changes in both substantive and administrative retirement plan law. Not only were new forms developed for initial qualification applications, but also a number of additional reports and notices must now be prepared, distributed to participants, and filed with the Internal Revenue Service, the Department of Labor or both. Record keeping and preparation of these forms should be done by capable personnel; loss of qualification and severe penalties may result from failure to comply.

On the substantive side, ERISA prohibited blanket exculpatory provisions which previously insulated plan fiduciaries from liability.[12] In the post-ERISA era, all plans must specifically provide for the prudent man rule[13] as governing a fiduciary's duties. Fiduciaries may allocate among themselves certain responsibilities,[14] however, and either the plan or the corporation may purchase liability insurance.[15] The Department of Labor has determined that a corporation may indemnify plan fiduciaries against liability.[16]

Among the substantive ERISA changes are the following:

☐ Forfeitures. The old "bad boy" clauses which provided for forfeitures of rights upon the happening of certain events, such as conviction of a crime or competition by a participant, are no longer permitted.[17]

☐ Limits on benefits and contributions. Prior to ERISA there was no limit on benefits or contributions allocated to any one employee. Now, the maximum benefit which may be provided by a defined-benefit plan is the lesser of $75,000 (as adjusted for cost of living changes) or 100 percent of average compensation for the highest three consecutive years of employment.[18] Defined contribution plans may not allow annual additions to an employee's account to exceed the lesser of 25 percent of covered compensation or $25,000 (also as adjusted for cost of

[12]ERISA Section 401(a).
[13]ERISA Section 404(a)(1)(B).
[14]ERISA Section 405(b)(1)(B) and 405(C)(1).
[15]ERISA 401(b).
[16]29 C.F.R. § 2555.75-4.
[17]Section 411(a)(3) of the Code.
[18]Section 415(b)(1) of the Code.

living changes).[19] When an employer adopts both a defined-benefit plan and a defined contribution plan, an overall limitation is imposed to prevent benefits and contributions from each reaching 100 percent of their maximum. This is achieved by fixing the maximum combined percentages of the individual limits at 140 percent rather than 200 percent.[20]

☐ Participation. Prior to ERISA, it was possible to postpone participation in a plan for a number of years, Now participation must be open to employees who have attained age 25 or have completed one year of service, whichever is later.[21] One exception to this rule is the situation in which an employer provides for 100 percent immediate vesting upon participation. In such a case, an entry period of three years of service is permitted.[22]

☐ Service. Again, prior to ERISA, it was necessary to cover only those employees who were employed for more than five months per year and 20 hours per week. Now the test is built into the definition of a "year of service," which essentially is a twelve-month period during which an employee works more than 1,000 hours.[23]

☐ Vesting. Vesting standards have also been applied more stringently under ERISA. In order to meet the requirements for qualification, a plan must meet one of three minimum vesting schedules.[24]

1. *The Five to Fifteen Year Rule* provides than an employee's interest must be at least 25 percent vested after five years of participation and increased regularly thereafter so that it will be 100 percent vested after 15 years.

2. *The Ten Year Rule* provides for 100 percent vesting after 10 years of participation. No prior vesting is required.

3. *The Rule of 45* provides that an employee with five or more years of participation must be at least 50 percent vested when his age and years of service equal 45 and vesting must continue thereafter at the rate of 10 percent per year.

Despite ERISA's specific provisions on vesting, the practitioner should recognize that the Internal Revenue Service is authorized to require more rapid vesting and has been doing so.

The above are only some of the more important provisions of

---

[19]Section 415(c) of the Code.
[20]Section 415(e) of the Code.
[21]Section 410(a)(1)(A) of the Code.
[22]Section 410(a)(1)(B)(i) of the Code.
[23]Section 410(a)(3)(A) of the Code.
[24]Section 411(a) of the Code.

which the practitioner should be aware in considering the adoption of a qualified retirement plan. They will affect the cost and benefits available under various plans as well as the way in which a plan will relate to the employees.

[¶804]   PREPARATION, SUBMISSION TO INTERNAL REVENUE SERVICE, AND ADMINISTRATION OF PLAN AND TRUST

Once the specifications of a plan have been determined, the plan and trust should be prepared and executed by the employer and trustees. A copy should be kept at the corporate office together with all subsequent amendments. Employees, under ERISA, have a right to see the plan and trust and to make copies of it. A corporate resolution should be adopted in form sufficient to authorize execution of the plan and trust, to appoint the plan administrator or administrative committee which will operate the plan, and to appoint the trustees. Depending on the circumstances, the resolution may also include the necessary language to authorize an initial contribution.

To obtain qualification, it is necessary to submit the plan and trust, a copy of the corporate resolution, Form 5300 or 5301 (whichever applies), Form 5302 (employee census), and a power of attorney to the office of the District Director of Internal Revenue for the district in which the corporation's tax return is filed. Also, it is generally useful to enclose copies of the notice by which the adoption of the plan and trust were communicated to employees and the notice to interested parties which advises participants of their rights to object to the provisions of the plan. The notice to interested parties must be distributed prior to submission and should take the form which has been approved by the Service.[25] A copy of this form and other relevant forms may be found in Appendix C.

Commonly the Internal Revenue Service examiner to whom the plan and trust are assigned will contact the attorney making the submission and request amendments which are necessary, in his view, to meet the requirements of ERISA. Generally, it will be possible to agree to such amendments without doing violence to the intended plan. In the occasional situation in which that is not possible, the Code provides a declaratory judgment procedure in the Tax Court.[26]

Additional forms including EBS-1 and the Summary Plan Description must be submitted to the Department of Labor and to the

---

[25]Rev. Proc. 75-31, 1975-27 IRB §3.03.

employees of the adopting firm. Careful attention must be given to the preparation, distribution and filing of these forms as penalties and disqualification may otherwise result.

After a favorable letter of determination has been received the employer's attention should turn to placing the preparation of the various reporting forms and participant reports in the hands of a qualified administration firm. There are many independent firms in the business community which perform these services and frequently commercial banks and life insurance companies or their agencies perform similar functions. A decision to engage such a firm should involve a comparison of fees (some offer flat rates and others are based upon the number of participants), ability and staff, and reputation for integrity and privacy. The firm selected should work in close alliance with the corporation's attorney and accountant to achieve and maintain the income tax and estate tax advantages for which the plan was adopted.

[26]Section 7476 of the Code.

9

Close Corporation Recapitalization and Tax Saving Alternatives

[¶900]   **OPPORTUNITIES AVAILABLE**

From the estate-planning standpoint, the closely held corporation commonly presents a number of problems, especially when it comprises a significant portion of the estate. Among those problems are:

(1) The aftertax proceeds of sale of the business will in some cases be far less than the intrinsic value of the business if retained as a source of family income.

(2) It is difficult, and frequently impossible, for a shareholder during his lifetime to obtain funds from the corporation via a stock redemption without paying ordinary income tax on those funds.

(3) The fair market value of the stock may be difficult to ascertain for planning purposes. This makes it difficult to plan for installment payments of estate tax or for a Section 303 redemption or for adequate alternative liquidity provisions.

The continued growth of the company may exacerbate some or all of these problems.

We can frequently improve the position of the client who holds such stock by means of one or more of the techniques discussed in this chapter: a recapitalization, a stock purchase agreement, or sale to the

200

trustee under an ESOP. (A public offering is a fourth technique; it falls beyond the scope of our treatment.)

[¶901]   NATURE OF A RECAPITALIZATION

Sec. 368(a) of the Code covers six types of tax-free reorganizations. One of these, the Class "E" reorganization (Sec. 368(a)(1)(E)), is a "recapitalization." The primary characteristic of a recapitalization is that only one corporation is involved and as an enterprise it remains intact. That is, its name, situs, business, assets and management are undisturbed; only the capital interests are altered.

How are the capital interests of a corporation altered in a recapitalization? Let us recount the (principal) ways:

☐ Preferred or common stock is issued in exchange for bonds, debentures, or long-term notes.

☐ Preferred stock is issued in exchange for common (an "upstream" recapitalization).

☐ Common stock is issued in exchange for preferred (a "downstream" recapitalization).

☐ Preferred stock with dividend arrearages is replaced with a like amount of preferred plus additional preferred or common stock equal to the amount of the arrearages.

For tax planning purposes, we will be concerned primarily with the above-mentioned upstream recapitalization. Before examining the technical requirements, let us consider the objectives to be pursued via such a recapitalization.

From the inter-related viewpoints of business planning and estate planning, when stock of a closely held corporation comprises a major or substantial part of a client's estate, his death may pose a number of serious problems:

☐ Substantial estate taxes may be involved, with the closely held stock included at its "fair market value" (see Chapter Ten, ¶1006).

☐ If carryover basis is low, as commonly it is, disposition of the stock may pile capital gains taxes on top of the estate taxes. (For discussion of carryover basis see Chapter Five, ¶500.2.)

☐ A sale may be forced unless the stock qualifies for installment payments of estate tax (under Sec. 6166A or Sec. 6166 of the Code) or the necessary funds are otherwise provided.

☐ There may be a failure of adequate management continuity.

☐ Where one or more children are in the business and other children are not, it may be difficult to pass the business to the active heirs and "equalize" the others as to assets or income.

In many cases, a prudent recapitalization will pave the way to the solution of some or all of these problems.

[¶901.1]   Estate Tax Savings and Other Benefits

Let us consider this relatively simple example: Assume that a corporation has common stock (only) outstanding, of which 75 percent is owned by our client and 25 percent is owned by his son. The total value of the stock is $1,000,000. (Client also has a wife and a daughter, who own no shares.) By means of a recapitalization, client receives in exchange for his common 7500 shares of 6 percent cumulative preferred stock, worth $100 per share on redemption or liquidation, and his son receives 100 shares of common stock.

The current and potential benefits of the recapitalization are as follows:

☐ Future growth of the company will be reflected in the common stock, so that increases of valuation are shifted to the son's estate.

☐ The preferred stock can be easily valued for estate tax purposes. This provides an element of certainty which is helpful in:

(a) Planning for a Section 303 redemption.
(b) Planning for installment payments of estate tax under Sec. 6166A or Sec. 6166 of the Code.
(c) Planning to meet the estate's liquidity needs in other ways.

☐ The preferred stock can be easily valued for gift tax purposes.

☐ The preferred stock can be utilized for a lifetime gift program or retained for retirement income.

☐ The preferred stock can be utilized at death (a) to provide an income to the widow, and (b) to equalize the daughter's and son's shares of the estate without depriving the son of control of the business.

The preceding illustration involved the substitution of two classes of stock for one. We are not, however, limited to any particular number of classes. We can, for example, include nonvoting common stock[1] in the recapitalization. As in the case of the voting common, the nonvoting common can also serve to move future business growth to a younger generation or generations. And it can be used to spread ownership among a number of donees without diffusing control. With several classes of stock the client can give to various beneficiaries, during his lifetime or at death, interests tailored to their needs and their relationships to the business and to each other.

[¶901.2] Tax-Free Recap Requirements

In order for the recapitalization to be a taxfree reorganization under Sec. 368(a)(1)(E) of the Code, the following requirements must be met:

☐ A plan of reorganization must be adopted by the corporation. (See Sec. 354 (a)(1) of the Code and Reg. Sec. 1.354-1(a) and 1.368-1(c)). Also:

(a) A copy of the plan must be filed with the corporation's income tax return for the taxable year in which the recapitalization occurs.
(b) Each shareholder who receives stock pursuant to the reorganization must file with his return for the taxable year in which the recapitalization occurs a statement as to all facts pertinent to nonrecognition of gain or loss (Reg. Sec. 1. 368-3(a)(1), (b)).
(c) The corporation and each such shareholder are required to maintain permanent records of the transaction.

☐ The recapitalization must have a valid business purpose (Reg. Sec. 1.368-1(b)).

Making voting stock available to younger executives and concentrating common stock in the hands of active stockholders have been recognized by the courts and IRS as legitimate business purposes. See, e.g., *Hartzel*, 40 B.T.A. 492 (1939), acq, 1939-2 Cum. Bull. 16; *Dean*, 10 T.C. 19 (1948), acq. 1949-1 Cum. Bull. 1; and Rev. Rul. 74-269, 1974-1C.B. 87, superseding Rev. Rul. 54-13, 1954-1CB 109. For a discussion of the Hartzel-Dean type of recaptilization, see William H. Painter, *Corporate and Tax Aspects of Closely Held Corporations*, Sec. 6.6, p. 249 ff.

☐ Continuity of interest must be maintained, as set forth in Rev.

[1]But examine Rev. Ruls. 76-387, 1976-2 CB 96; and 76-386, 1976-2 CB 95.

Proc. 66-34, 1966-2 CB 1232. Where the stockholders before and after the recaptilization are the same persons, this requirement is met.

We recommend generally that a letter ruling be requested, affirming that the proposed recapitalization will qualify as a tax-free reorganization.

[¶901.3]   Income Tax Pitfalls

The recapitalization may result in ordinary income to a shareholder if the transaction does not meet the requirements outlined in ¶901.2. Additional income tax hazards are these:

☐ Ordinary income will be attributed to a shareholder if the transaction involves the payment of compensation to him. This would occur where the purpose is to give a shareholder-employee an equity interest or to increase his equity interest. See Rev. Rul. 74-269, 1974-1CB 87, superseding Rev. Rul. 54-13, 1954-1 CB 109.

☐ Preferred stock issued in the recapitalization may be Section 306 stock. Section 306 stock is a nontaxable preferred stock dividend paid on common stock. If the effect of a recapitalization is substantially the same as a stock dividend (for example, where the shareholders exchange their common for new common and preferred in the same percentages as the old common), the preferred will be Section 306 stock. See Reg. Sec. 1.306-3(d), Examples (1) and (2); Rev. Rul. 75-236, 1975-1 C.B. 106.

The consequence is that gain on subsequent sale of that stock will be treated as ordinary income. The taint may be "cured" in another recapitalization (provided there is no plan for a future exchange of the preferred for common at the time of the issuance of the preferred; Reg. Sec. 1.305-5(d), Examples (2) and (6)) or by a gift of the 306 stock to charity, and certain exceptions to ordinary income treatment are provided in Section 306(b). Also, a ruling can be requested on the applicability of Section 306 if the matter is in doubt.

☐ Under Sec. 305(b) of the Code, a recapitalization may be treated as a taxable distribution in any of these cases:

(a) A distribution, at shareholders' election, payable either (a) in stock or (b) in property (Section 305(b)(1)).
(b) A disproportionate distribution (Section 305(b)(2)).
(c) A distribution of common stock to some holders of common stock and preferred stock to other holders of common stock (Section 305(b)(3)).
(d) A distribution on preferred stock (other than an antidilution adjustment of convertible preferred) (Section 305(b)(4)).

(e) Certain distributions of convertible preferred, even if pro rata (Section 305(b)(5)).

Section 305 and the Regulations thereunder should be studied with care in connection with a proposed recapitalization.

☐ If stock is exchanged for stock plus bonds, debentures, or notes, the bonds, debentures, or notes are considered "boot." Gain on the transaction is taxed under Sec. 356(d) of the Code (provided there is gain), to the extent of the fair market value of such "boot." Further, under Sec. 356(a)(2), to the extent of the taxpayer's pro rata share of earnings and profits, the gain will be taxed as an ordinary dividend if the exchange has the "effect of the distribution of a dividend." Corporate obligations which are readily marketable, or are immediately callable (especially where the recipients have control of the corporation), may be deemed equivalent to a dividend for this purpose.

☐ If stock is exchanged for bonds, debentures, or notes only, the transaction will be treated as a distribution, redemption or liquidation under Sec. 301, 302, 331 or 346 of the Code and not as a recapitalization (See Reg. Sec. 1.354-1(d), Example (3)).

☐ Subchapter S treatment is not available to a corporation which has more than one class of stock.

[¶901.4]   Gift Tax Hazards

The alteration of capital interests in a corporation, especially where this takes place among related shareholders, may be found to involve a gift.

In the example set forth in [¶901.1], if a higher value than $1,000,000 should be attributed to the stock of the corporation, the result of the recapitalization would be to shift the father's share of that excess value to the son.

An IRS ruling that the proposed recapitalization is tax-free will not be extended to preclude gift tax treatment.

The only solution, where this is perceived to be a problem, is in a sound approach to valuation of the stock. Attention is invited to the guidelines for valuation set forth in [¶1006]. In some cases, the engagement of an independent appraiser may be deemed prudent.

[¶902]   STOCK PURCHASE AGREEMENTS

From the standpoint of estate taxes, an agreement by the corporation or the other shareholders to purchase your client's stock can do two useful things: (1) fix the value of the stock for estate tax purposes; and (2) provide money for payment of the tax. (It may also fail to do these things.)

The transaction when consummated, of course, may provide liquidity beyond tax needs. And it may permit diversification of the client's or the estate's holdings.

For the purchasers, the acquisition precludes undesirable demands or involvement on the part of a deceased shareholder's beneficiaries, and it eliminates a possible disqualification of the corporation for Subchapter S treatment due to a nonconsenting shareholder or a trustee shareholder.[2] For a purchase which is to take place at death, insurance on the deceased shareholder's life can render the acquisition relatively painless.

[¶902.1]   Choice of Purchaser

A nonshareholder executive may sometimes become a party to a stock purchase agreement, but the usual purchaser will be either the corporation itself or the other shareholder or shareholders.

Purchase by the corporation (a stock redemption) will frequently be advantageous to the remaining shareholders, when there is no Subchapter S election,[3] because the purchase will be made with corporate funds which have not been distributed and taxed to the shareholder.

From the seller's standpoint, the redemption arrangement will be satisfactory if it is treated as an "exchange," i.e., a capital transaction, and not as a dividend. A capital transaction will be recognized under Sec. 303 of the Code, in the case of a decedent's estate, to the extent of a payment not exceeding estate and inheritance taxes and deductible funeral and administration expenses. A capital transaction will be recognized under Sec. 302 (b) of the Code if it involves any of the following:

(a) a redemption "not essentially equivalent to a dividend;" or
(b) a "complete termination" of the shareholder's interest; or
(c) a "substantially disproportionate" redemption.

A disproportionate redemption of a shareholder's stock is recognized if as a result of the redemption all of the following tests are satisfied:

---

[2]Under TRA 76, a trust may be a shareholder if it is a trust treated as owned by the grantor under the grantor trust rules; a trust created primarily for voting of the stock placed in trust; or a trust that receives stock under a will, but only for 60 days after the stock is transferred to the trust.

[3]In the case of a Subchapter S corporation, whether a stock redemption or a cross-purchase is used, the funds available for purchase will be taxed only at the shareholder level.

(a) His proportion of voting stock is less than 80 percent of the proportion he held prior to his redemption. (If he owned 50 percent before the redemption, he must own less than 40 percent [80 percent of 50 percent] after it.)

(b) His proportion of all common stock (voting and nonvoting) must be less than 80 percent of the proportion he held prior to the redemption.

(c) After the redemption he must own less than 50 percent of the total voting power of the corporation.

 The difficulty of meeting these tests is far greater than appears on their face. That a distribution is not equivalent to a dividend can be argued when a redemption is challenged, but it is too vague and elusive a standard for reliance in planning a redemption. The troubles with the "substantially disproportionate" and "complete termination" tests derive principally from the attribution rules of Sec. 318 of the Code, under which stock owned by one party is attributed to (deemed to be owned by) another.

It will be readily apparent that a percentage of ownership test or a complete termination test that would be satisfied if we looked solely to shares actually owned by shareholder A might not be satisfied if A is treated as owning also the stock of shareholder B. The attribution rules cover the following relationships:

(a) Family members. A person is considered the owner of stock owned by his spouse, children, grandchildren and parents.

(b) Partnership and partners. Stock owned by a partner is considered owned by the partnership, and stock owned by a partnership is considered owned proportionately by the partners.

(c) Corporation and shareholder. A person who owns 50 percent or more in value of the stock of a corporation is considered to own proportionately the stock of another corporation owned by it, and any such stock owned by the person is considered owned by the corporation.

(d) Estate and beneficiary. Stock owned by an estate is considered owned proportionately by the beneficiaries of the estate, i e , those persons who have direct present (rather than future) interests in the estate. Stock owned by an heir or legatee is considered owned by the estate if it is subject to claims against the estate or administration expenses.

(e) Stock option holders. The owner of a stock option is deemed the owner of the stock which is subject to his option.

In connection with a complete termination, relief from the *family* attribution rules is available if all of the shareholder's stock is redeemed, he ceases to be interested in the company as a shareholder, officer, director or employee, and the following additional conditions are met: (1) the redeeming shareholder may not acquire any stock of the corporation within 10 years following the redemption, except by inheritance; (2)

with his tax return for the year in which the redemption occurs, the redeeming shareholder must file a statement that he has not acquired any such stock since the redemption and that he will notify the District Director within 30 days if he acquires any within 10 years following the redemption; (3) none of the stock redeemed was acquired during the preceding 10 years from his spouse, children, grandchildren, or parents; and (4) he did not dispose of any stock to any such persons within 10 years prior to the redemption, unless the avoidance of income tax was not a principal purpose of such disposition.

Where two or more unrelated persons own all of the stock of a corporation, a stock redemption agreement will normally present no difficulty. But where the principal shareholders are related to each other, or have given or sold shares to members of their families, a redemption agreement must be approached with caution, for the reasons already noted. We cannot here pursue all of the ramifications of the attribution rules in connection with stock redemptions. The reader is warned to study the redemption standards and attribution rules with care.

It is also possible, in appropriate circumstances, to avoid dividend treatment on a redemption which is part of a partial liquidation of a corporation terminating one of its business operations or contracting its business. Avoidance of dividend treatment is possible in a partial liquidation which is one of a series under a plan of complete liquidation.

The cross-purchase alternative will be attractive to the selling shareholder if it is not clear that a redemption will be treated as an "exchange" rather than a distribution of profits.

A cross-purchase arrangement will also be advantageous to the remaining shareholders to the extent it reduces their gain on a subsequent sale. In contrast with the redemption situation, shares purchased by the remaining shareholder acquire a new basis in the transaction. Prior to TRA 76, this was an important consideration only for shareholders who intended or contemplated a lifetime sale, as their stock would otherwise receive a "stepped-up" basis at death. With the new carryover basis rules, this feature of the cross-purchase arrangement will be entitled to greater weight.

In any event, where the purchase price is to be paid in installments and installment sale treatment is desired, it is important to assure in the agreement that the payments in the first tax year of the seller do not exceed 30 percent of the purchase price (Sec. 453 of the Code).

Whether the transaction involves redemption or cross-purchase, or a combination of these arrangements, under Sec. 1023 of the Code a postmortem transaction will involve gain or loss to the extent of the difference between the purchase price and carryover basis. (See ¶1004.)

[¶902.2]   Setting the Price

For a review of factors relevant to the valuation of closely held corporation stock, see [¶1006]. The stock purchase agreement may recognize a single factor for valuation, such as book value or capitalized earnings. It may provide a variant of one of these, such as book value altered by appraisals of certain assets and excluding good will, or earnings capitalized on a basis "weighted" in favor of the most recent years. Or there may be a formula involving a combination of several approaches to valuation.

Alternatively, the agreement may provide for the value to be set by an independent appraiser when the time arrives. A more common alternative is to fix a precise initial dollar value per share, with provisions for annual or other periodic review, the original or adjusted price per share to remain in effect until subsequently adjusted by agreement. The initial value may be arrived at by a formula or may be picked "out of the air" as a price per share at which the shareholders would currently be willing to sell the business.

[¶902.3]   Fixing the Value for Estate Tax Purposes

There are several basic types of stock purchase agreements, and they differ as to their binding effect for estate tax purposes:

☐ A right of first refusal. This is an agreement whereby each shareholder agrees that he or his estate will permit the corporation or the other shareholders to purchase his stock, if a decision is made to sell it. Usually the right of first refusal is exercisable at the price and on the terms accepted by a third party, although the agreement may stipulate book value or any other price and terms. Under such an agreement, there is no compulsion to sell or to buy.

☐ An option agreement. This is an agreement which gives the corporation or the other shareholders a right to purchase within a stipulated time after death, or on certain lifetime events, at a price fixed in or to be determined in accordance with the agreement. No one is required to purchase, but the shareholder or his estate is bound to sell at the stipulated time.

☐ A mandatory stock purchase agreement. This is an agreement whereby the corporation or the other shareholders are bound to purchase, and the estate of the deceased shareholder (or the shareholder himself on certain lifetime events) is bound to sell at a price fixed in or to be determined in accordance with the agreement.

There may also be a combination of these types of agreements, such as an agreement for mandatory purchase at death, but providing for either an option or a right of first refusal on a lifetime sale. Occasions commonly stipulated to trigger a lifetime sale, besides the appearance of a third party purchaser, are the retirement or disability of an active shareholder, or a shareholder's bankruptcy or other adverse creditor proceedings.

The various types of agreements are not equally effective to set a ceiling on the value of the stock for estate tax purposes. (There are corresponding variations in their effectiveness to provide an assured market for the stock.) In order for the agreement to be effective for estate tax purposes, the following requirements must be met:

☐ The price must be either fixed or determinable according to a formula.

☐ The estate must be obligated to sell at such a price upon the shareholder's death:

    (a) A mandatory stock purchase agreement satisfies this requirement.
    (b) An option agreement satisfies this requirement.
    (c) A right of first refusal does not.

☐ The obligation to sell must be binding on the decedent during his lifetime as well as upon his estate after death. (If the shareholder could have realized a higher price during his lifetime, the price binding at death will not control.)

☐ The agreement must be a bona fide business agreement and not a device to pass the decedent's shares to the natural objects of his bounty at less than adequate consideration in money or money's worth.

Such agreements, apart from their binding effect for estate tax purposes, have a number of significant elements which merit careful consideration, such as:

    (a) Timing and procedure for offers and acceptances and related notices.
    (b) Treatment of life insurance proceeds received by corporation or other shareholders.
    (c) Security arrangements for unpaid purchase installments.
    (d) Resolution of disagreements, and remedies for defaults.

Included in Appendix C are examples of a stock redemption agreement and a cross-purchase agreement. We recommend generally that such agreements be made binding upon both seller and buyer (in preference to option and first refusal arrangements). This is in order not only to fix the value for estate tax purposes but also to assure that the necessary liquidity will in fact be available to the deceased shareholder's estate.

Caveat: Stock purchase agreements sometimes give the corporation the right to purchase a decedent's shares and require the remaining shareholders to purchase the shares which the corporation does not elect to purchase. It is important, however, that the corporation not be required or permitted to purchase shares which the shareholders are already bound to purchase. If the corporation relieves the shareholders of their personal obligations, the corporate payments may constitute dividends to the shareholders so relieved.

[¶903]   ESOP

Though the stock bonus plan has been available for five decades as a form of qualified retirement plan, the ESOP (Employee Stock Ownership Plan, as it is called in the Pension Reform Act), or ESOT, as it is sometimes called,[4] is a relatively recent phenomenon, developed by lawyer-economist Louis O. Kelso. Despite the evangelism of Kelso, who conceived the ESOP as an instrument of workers' capitalism, the device was for a long time known and utilized almost exclusively on the West Coast. In a recent article, a California attorney confessed:

> "The writer's law office was among the relatively small group that felt that use of the plan has very great merit and that the substantial amount of research and development which the office has put into the plans would be recaptured best by not widely disseminating the idea."[5]

But the secret is out. Corporate officers, and especially shareholders of closely held corporations, are finding in the ESOP the solutions to old problems and the key to new opportunities. They are sometimes spurred by the desire to overcome the alienation of corporate employees. More often they are motivated by the desire to create a market for their shares of the company stock, or to buy out minority shareholders, or simply to obtain working capital on favorable terms.

In an economy in which the opportunity to obtain funds for growth and expansion by going public has shrunk dramatically; standard financing is less available and more restrictive; and profit-sharing plans have

---

[4]For simplicity I will use only the term ESOP, whether referring to the plan or the trust.
[5]Ralph Gano Miller, Jr., "Buying Closely Held Stock with Tax Deductible Dollars" *CLU Journal* (January, 1975). Reprinted by permission.

lost some of their sex appeal due to declining profits and a shaky stock market, the ESOP has emerged as a panacea. And if it is not panacea, surely it is panacea's twin brother.

What is an ESOP? It is a deferred retirement program, qualified—like a pension or profit-sharing plan—under Section 401(a) of the Internal Revenue Code. Like the other qualified plans, the ESOP provides tax benefits to all concerned—tax deductions to the corporate employer for its contributions, tax deferral to the employees, and tax exemption to the trust. It is the modern version of a stock bonus plan, which the Treasury Regulations define as a "plan established and maintained by an employer to provide benefits similar to those of a profit sharing plan except that the contributions by the employer are not necessarily dependent upon profits and the benefits are distributable in stock of the employer company."

The ten primary features of the ESOP are these:

1. The basic deduction limit is 15 percent of compensation (but deductions can aggregate 25 percent if a pension plan is added).

2. Contributions need not be dependent on profits.

3. Benefits must be distributable in employer stock.

4. The trust assets may (but need not be) entirely invested in employer stock.

5. The company stock need not pay dividends representing a fair return on capital.

6. The trust may buy corporate stock on an installment purchase from a controlling shareholder as a capital gain transaction.

7. The price paid for company stock must be equal to its fair market value.

8. The ESOP may borrow funds with which to buy employer stock if the company is sound, and the company or shareholders may guarantee the ESOP's repayment of the loan.[6]

9. Company stock distributed by the ESOP may be subjected to a right of first refusal in favor of the corporation, the ESOP, and other

---

[6]This is the so-called "leveraged ESOP," which raises problems under the prohibited transaction rules and fiduciary standards of ERISA. Proposed regulations on such plans, jointly issued by the Treasury and Labor Departments in 1976, were withdrawn following Congressional criticism in the Conference report on TRA76, and new regulations have been issued in their place. For a concise analysis of the issues in this unusual controversy, see Michael D. Savage, "The Attack on Proposed ESOP Regulations: A Battle Won at the Expense of the War?" 63 *American Bar Association Journal* 716, May 1977.

A plan may have all of the characteristics of an ESOP *except leveraging based on borrowing from or on the credit of an interested party,* if it is an Eligible Individual Account Plan (EIAP). See ERISA Sections 407(d)(3), 407(b)(1), 404(a)(2), 408(d), 408(e).

shareholders, or the distributee may be given a "put" to enable him to require the purchase of his shares. In the case of a leveraged ESOP, the stock *must* be subject to a "put" exercisable for fifteen months from the date of distribution.)

10. Distribution (on death, retirement, disability, etc.), may be in installments—taxable as ordinary income—or in a lump sum. Under ERISA, the portion of a lump-sum distribution attributable to pre-1974 service is taxed at long-term capital gains rates, and the balance at ordinary income rates subject to 10-year forward averaging. But TRA 76 permits the employee to elect the latter treatment as to the entire distribution. However, where company stock is distributed, the trustee's cost basis is taxed as ordinary income (with special averaging provisions). Appreciation in value of the stock is taxed as a capital gain when the employee sells the stock. Upon a participant's death, benefits payable to a named beneficiary are not subject to federal estate tax unless paid in a lump sum.

It may be helpful to compare the ESOP with a profit-sharing plan. The similarities are mainly these:

(a) Both are qualified plans.
(b) Both have basic limitations on contributions equal to 15 percent of the covered compensation.
(c) The same criteria apply generally as to nondiscrimination, termination, etc.

The major differences may helpfully be recapitulated as follows:

(a) Profit-sharing contributions are dependent on corporate profits; ESOP contributions need not be.
(b) The "exclusive benefit of employees" rule will frequently preclude a profit-sharing trust's investment in company stock. The very nature of a qualified stock bonus plan eliminates this problem for the ESOP. (A profit-sharing plan may be qualified to hold employer securities if it uses individual accounts and follows accounting and allocation rules similar to those of a stock bonus plan. But the profit-sharing authority passes to the fiduciary, which must compare the company stock with other investments [which the ESOP need not do]. Also, the profit-sharing trust cannot purchase on an installment basis from a substantial shareholder or borrow money with the loan guaranteed by the company or shareholders.)

While the features of the basic ESOP have been summarized above, there are certain special features which apply to the Tax Reduction Act ESOP, or "TRASOP." Section 301(d) of the Tax Reduction Act of 1975 (extended and amplified by TRA 76) provided for an extra 1 percent investment credit for a corporation which establishes an ESOP funded by transfer of corporate securities equal to 1 percent of the investment allowance. Such a Plan must meet various Treasury requirements not imposed on the regular ESOP, especially these:

1. Employer securities must be allocated to participants' accounts in proportion to compensation up to a maximum of $100,000 a year.

2. The plan must call for full immediate vesting.

3. The employees must have the right to vote the stock.

An additional one-half of one percent was provided by TRA 76 for cases in which employees contribute matching funds. Such contribution may not be made a condition of employment or of participation in the plan.

The role of life insurance in an ESOP or TRASOP is less clear at this time than we would wish. There are three ways in which life insurance may be useful to an ESOP:

1. To indemnify the ESOP and its participants for loss through death of a key man.

2. To fund stock purchase agreements whereby the ESOP can acquire the stock of shareholders at death.

3. To provide incidental death benefits for participants.

These are attractive avenues for the purchase of reasonable amounts of life insurance with funds deductible to the corporation. The question is, from the standpoint of the Internal Revenue Service, are these insurance purchases permissible ESOP investments?

The Treasury Department has issued Technical Information Release No. 1410 and T.I.R. No. 1413 dealing with ESOPs. These were its first official pronouncements subsequent to ERISA and the Tax Reduction Act of 1975. TIR No. 1410 deals entirely with Tax Reduction Act ESOPs and procedures for qualification and for claiming the extra 1 percent investment credit. TIR 1413 contains a series of questions and answers regarding ESOPs.

TIR 1410 tells District Directors not to issue determination letters with respect to any Tax Reduction Act ESOPs that permit the trustee to purchase key-man life insurance. Since one of the answers provided in TIR 1413 states the position essentially that Tax Reduction ESOPs cannot, by statute, hold assets other than employer securities, the "no key man" position in TIR 1410 may not apply to ESOPs generally. As long as the regular ESOP holds its funds invested "primarily" in employer securities, key-man insurance should be regarded as one type of prudent investment of the balance.

TIR 1413 also indicates that the ESOP may not enter into an agreement obligating it to purchase a shareholder's stock when he dies, apparently because the trustee cannot determine at this time the propriety of such a future investment. As an alternative to purchase of insurance by the ESOP for this purpose, the corporation might purchase insurance and lend the proceeds to the ESOP for such a stock purchase.

Question F-9 in TIR 1413 deals with the use of "incidental" life insurance in an ESOP where the proceeds are payable to the employee's designated beneficiaries. The Treasury acknowledges that such insurance is a proper investment, but a 25 percent limit is imposed on the amount of any individual's account which may be used to pay life insurance premiums, regardless of the type of insurance purchased.

These TIR's are, of course, not the end of the story. The insurance questions have not been fully or finally answered. The ESOP and its investment features are still being shaped by the Treasury.

[¶903.1]   Tax Savings and Improving the Debt-Equity Ratio

How does the ESOP work its magic? Its principal benefits, with an illustration of each, are as follows:

☐ Increased cash flow through contributions of stock.

Consider the case of Ace Manufacturing Company. Schedule A, below, shows three alternative "plans" for the Company. For the current year, Ace will have pre-tax earnings of $500,000—prior to a possible deduction for an ESOP or a profit-sharing plan. Assume Ace has a $2,000,000 qualified payroll, so that it may contribute up to $300,000 (15 percent of $2,000,000) to a trust under an ESOP or profit-sharing plan. If Ace makes no such contribution, its adjusted pre-tax earnings ($500,000) will be reduced by its estimated (54 percent) federal and State taxes ($270,000), leaving a balance os $230,000 of net worth increase and cash flow available to the business from earnings.

If Ace contributes the allowable $300,000 to a profit-sharing trust, its adjusted pretax earnings will be $200,000 ($500,000 minus $300,000), the estimated taxes will aggregate $108,000 (54 percent of $200,000), leaving $92,000 of net worth increase and cash flow available to the business from earnings.

If Ace contributes $300,000 to an ESOP rather than to a profit-sharing trust—either in stock of Ace or in cash which the ESOP pays to Ace for purchase of its stock—Ace's taxes will be the same as in the case

Schedule A

	(1) No profit-sharing or ESOP	(2) Profit-Sharing	(3) ESOP
Pre-tax earnings	500,000	500,000	500,000
Contribution —			
15 percent of $2,000,000	0	300,000	300,000
Adjusted pretax earnings	500,000	200,000	200,000
Estimated federal and state taxes (54 percent)	270,000	108,000	108,000
After tax earnings	230,000	92,000	92,000
Net worth increase	230,000	92,000	392,000[7]
Cash flow available to business from earnings and stock purchase	230,000	92,000	392,000

of the profit-sharing contribution. Its aftertax earnings will be similarly reduced to $92,000. But its net worth increase and cash flow available to the business *from earnings and from the ESOP's stock purchase* will be $392,000. *The entire $300,000 ESOP contribution becomes immediately available as cash to ACE.* (This, of course, is a one-year illustration, which can be repeated annually or from time to time.

□ New financing or refunding of outstanding debt so that principal as well as interest payments will be deductible from pretax income.

Assume that Best Service Company, a corporation paying top corporate taxes and having a $2,000,000 qualified payroll, wishes to borrow $1,000,000 from a bank, or to refinance an existing $1,000,000 bank loan. If Best establishes an ESOP, the ESOP can borrow the $1,000,000 with the corporation's guarantee of the loan. The ESOP can use the $1,000,000 to purchase Best stock, so that Best has the use of the borrowed funds. Best can then make fully deductible annual contributions of $300,000 to the ESOP, which in turn will use these contributions to repay the loan in installments.

As a result of its ESOP contributions, Best saves approximately $162,000 a year (54 percent of $300,000) which would otherwise have been paid in federal and State estimated taxes. Best's cash balance and shareholders' equity have been increased by the $1,000,000 received by

[7]Trust funds are used to buy stock from company, or stock is contributed to trust.

Best for its stock (the corporate guarantee of the ESOP loan being footnoted on the financial statement). Most significant, the bank indebtedness of $1,000,000 will be repaid entirely with pre-tax dollars. *Loan principal of $1,000,000 is repaid with $1,000,000 of corporate earnings rather than the $2,000,000 that would be required if the corporation itself had simply borrowed the money.*

☐ Acquisition of a subsidiary with pre-tax dollars.

Consider Cheerful Construction Company, which seeks to acquire a subsidiary, which we'll call "X." With cash contributed by Cheerful to the ESOP, or with such cash plus borrowed funds, the ESOP can purchase the stock or assets of X. The ESOP can then turn over the stock or assets so acquired to Cheerful in exchange for stock of the Company. Cheerful can continue to make cash contributions to the ESOP in amounts sufficient to pay off the acquisition debt.

Note that in the situation we have described the acquisition debt is paid off in pre-tax dollars, and the net worth of Cheerful is increased by the purchase price of the stock or assets of X when the exchange is made.

☐ Recapture of income taxes previously paid.

Assume that Dandy Sales Corporation had taxable income for the years 1975, 1976 and 1977 in the amounts of $50,000, $100,000 and $150,000, respectively (total $300,000), and paid corresponding taxes of $10,500, $34,500 and $58,500 (total $103,500). Assume, further, that 1978 is (otherwise) a break-even year for Dandy, and that Dandy in 1978 contributes $300,000 to an ESOP. As a result of that contribution, Dandy sustains a $300,000 loss, which can be carried back against taxable income for the preceding three years. The corporation will receive a $103,500 tax refund.

☐ Disposition of founder's stock in installment sales at capital gains rates.

Let us consider, finally, the case of Eddie Endeavor, founder and principal shareholder of Endeavor Corp. Eddie would like to sell some of his stock back to the company, thus obtaining a portion of its accumulated earnings and enabling Eddie to diversify his holdings and obtain some liquidity for estate purposes while retaining control of the corporation. But Eddie's advisers tell him that the Internal Revenue Service will regard the money he receives from the company as a dividend to him.

The company will get no deduction and the funds will be taxable to Eddie as ordinary income.

If, however, Endeavor Corp. establishes an ESOP, Eddie can accomplish his goals on a very favorable basis. The company can contribute to the ESOP cash in an amount equal to 15 percent of its qualified payroll. Eddie can then sell a portion of his stock to the ESOP. He can make a series of outright sales or a single sale on an installment basis and such sales will be reportable as long-term capital gains.[8] If desired, the ESOP can borrow money from a bank to purchase more of Eddie's stock than the company's annual contribution would permit.

By the adoption of an ESOP the company has created for Eddie's stock a market which might not otherwise have existed. Moreover, in the ESOP transaction, Endeavor Corp. deducts for tax purposes the amount of its annual contribution, so that the ESOP makes the purchase of Eddie's stock with pre-tax corporate dollars, thus costing the company only half of the amount that would be required for a comparable stock redemption. And Eddie retains control, obtains liquidity, diversifies his holdings, and can spread the sale of his stock over several years at capital gains rates. (It is important in such cases to avoid arrangements in which the facts of the case might support the inference of a step transaction that could be collapsed to yield dividend treatment.) Moreover, a portion of the stock is allocable to Eddie (as an employee) *in the ESOP.*

As in the case of other qualified plans, of course, the ESOP must be operated for "the exclusive benefit of the employees." But this standard does not preclude a corresponding or individual benefit to others, as the Service recognized in Rev. Rul. 69-65, 1969- 1 CB 114:

> "This requirement, (benefit of employees) however, does not prevent others from also deriving some benefit from a transaction with the trust. For example, a sale of securities at a profit benefits the seller, but if the purchase price is not in excess of the fair market value of the securities at the time of the sale and the applicable investment requisites have also been met, the investment is consistent with the exclusive benefit requirement."

[¶903.2] Basic Criteria for Adoption of an ESOP

What type of company should adopt an ESOP? There are three general characteristics on which most advisers would probably agree:

1. That the company be financially strong and growing.
2. That it be taxable under normal corporate tax provisions of the

---

[8]The attribution rules of Sec. 318 of the Code do not apply to a qualified employee's trust. See Sec. 318(a)(2)(B)(i).

Internal Revenue Code. (Subchapter S corporations do not qualify.)

3. That it be in a 48 percent tax bracket.

A fourth characteristic is sometimes suggested, namely, a stipulated minimum annual payroll of, say, $500,000. We would discourage the use of any such rule of thumb. Rather, we should consider in each case the objective or objectives which the ESOP may be designed to serve and the extent to which the annual contributions would serve to advance such specific aim or aims. The availability of funds which have already been accumulated in a profit-sharing plan, which may be convertible into an ESOP, may have some bearing on the decision. Also relevant may be the possibility of obtaining a refund of prior years' taxes as previously discussed.

[¶903.3]   ESOP Hazards

It is essential, of course, for the ESOP-minded to consider potential negative aspects. One of them is that a plan which can provide greater incentive and motivation for the employees than any other type of fringe benefit, and yield substantial rewards for all concerned, can also have a depressing effect on morale if things turn sour. Only a financially strong company with good prospects for growth should establish an ESOP or turn its profit-sharing plan into an ESOP.

Loss of control is often a concern, but there need be no shift of control. Initially, the trustee can be directed to vote the stock according to the instructions of a committee appointed by the board of directors. Or the ESOP may acquire only nonvoting stock. And repurchase arrangements will usually be effective to keep stock out of the hands of nonprincipal employees or their heirs, as they will normally prefer to obtain the cash value of their shares.

On the other hand, there will be some cases in which the shift of ownership and control will be precisely what is intended—the business is being sold to the employees.

Do contributions of stock to the ESOP dilute the principals' shares? Yes and no. If stock is contributed by the corporation at its fair market value, as it must be, the result is the same as issuance of the stock for cash. The capital is cut into more slices, but only after the size of the pie has been increased proportionately.

On the other hand, at the end of a fiscal year in which shares have been contributed to an ESOP, an increase of net worth will be allocable to a larger number of shares than in the absence of the ESOP, so that a larger net worth increase in the company may yield (after the ESOP contribution) a lesser increase in the book value per share. This effect may or may not be offset by an increase in productivity. Also, in the case of a shareholder who is also an employee, this decline of per share increase may or may not be counterbalanced by the allocation of shares to his account *within* the ESOP.

[¶903.4]   ESOP Prospects

At this writing, the potential "negatives" appear to have had little effect in stemming the tide of ESOP excitement. ERISA, with its new provisions for accelerated funding and plan-termination insurance, has increased the costs of a mandatory pension plan and has in many ways burdened the administration of traditional pension and profit-sharing plans. At the same time, the Act has given separate status to the ESOP, and extremely favorable treatment, including specific approval to financing arrangements for the trust to borrow funds.

Kelso, the inventor and chief advocate of the ESOP, has found an enthusiastic ally in Senator Russell Long, chairman of the Senate Finance Committee. It was Long who added the provision for the extra 1 percent investment credit to the Tax Reduction Act of 1975. He has stated: "I want to see the day when every corporate employee will own stock of his employer which will provide him with a good source of supplemental income and a comfortable retirement base."

10

Postmortem Options

[¶1000]   **OPPORTUNITIES AVAILABLE**

Let us first define the scope of this Chapter. While postmortem planning frequently includes a variety of income tax choices for the estate, for related trusts, and for individual beneficiaries, as well as certain gift tax decisions, our subject is the estate tax, and we will deal with other taxes only as they are affected by the estate tax options presented here.

The subject of this Chapter is neither a single tax-saving technique (like the private annuity as described in Chapter Six), nor a variety of techniques to utilize a particular deduction as in the case of the marital deduction (Chapter One) or the charitable deduction (Chapter Two).

We are dealing here essentially with an approach which embraces a variety of measures which can alter estate tax computations. These measures include the choice of valuation date, the timing of sale of distribution of property, and several devices which can change the amount of the marital deduction or the charitable deduction. In this context, we are concerned not only with the tax payable in the estate of the decedent, but also with the estate tax situations of the surviving spouse and other beneficiaries.

The approach which we consider appropriate begins with the recognition that the termination of an individual's life does not mean the termination of tax planning in relation to his resources and beneficiaries. When a client dies, we do not put away the tax books and mechanically carry out the terms of his will. Rather, the inception of the estate marks the beginning of a new and major tax-planning phase.

As a consequence of the decedent's death we can now represent and plan for a new client. Or, if the decedent was married, we can plan for two "new" clients. The decedent's *estate,* in the first place, is not the decedent. And the widow (or widower[1]) is no longer the decedent's spouse. Each of them—estate and widow—may have its or her own income, gift and estate tax problems and opportunities. These may derive from or be related to the decedent's, but they are not the same as the corresponding tax problems and opportunities which the decedent, or the decedent and his spouse, had while he was alive. They should not be swept under the rug of the tax planning that was done during the decedent's lifetime.

The shift from a living client to a decedent's estate is sharp and clear. A completely new taxpayer is created with the probate of the Will. The estate planning options of the living client were limited only by the extent of his resources, beneficiaries, and imagination (as informed by your counsel). The tax planning options of the executors are narrowed by the decedent's lifetime decisions, but they are still many and varied.

The shift from wife to widow may be less apparent but is just as real. We seem to see the same "person," Mrs. Jones, but we can be helped by T.S. Eliot's injunction:

> What we know of other people
> Is only our memory of the moments
> During which we knew them. And they have
>   changed since then.
> To pretend that they and we are the same
> Is a useful and convenient social convention
> Which must sometimes be broken. We must also
>   remember
> That at every meeting we are meeting a stranger.[2]

The "widowhood" of reality is never precisely the same as the widowhood that was imagined in estate planning sessions. The quiet house, the terminated salary, altered family and social relationships, new responsibilties, and the emotional climate in which these things emerge, raise new questions. And they may cast a shadow on various decisions with which the widow agreed, or in which she acquiesced, when the decedent was alive.

Not only are we planning for new clients, in the senses suggested above, but the gross estate of the decedent will normally vary from the gross estate as constituted when the estate plan was adopted. In the course of time assets are disposed of, others are acquired, and property

---

[1]For simplicity, we will refer to "widow" and omit "widower" for the balance of this discussion.

[2]T.S. Eliot, *The Cocktail Party,* Harcourt, Brace and Company (New York, 1947), pages 71-72.

values rise and fall. Similarly, indebtedness may be altered and various contractual obligations assumed or terminated. And, of course, the relevant provisions of the tax laws may not be the same as those in effect when the lifetime planning was done.

For all of these reasons, tax planning should be a major, if not the primary, aspect of our postmortem counseling. From the several elections and options discussed below, significant estate tax savings may in many cases be derived.

[¶1001]   ELECTION TO TAKE AGAINST THE WILL

The right of a spouse to take a specified share of a decedent's estate in lieu of the benefits provided in his will is a creature of statute. Nearly all States provide for such an election, and it is usually available to either spouse. In most cases the election provides an outright share for the surviving spouse, though in a few States only a form of "dower" or "curtesy" in realty is provided. In some cases the election applies not only to the probate estate but also to certain lifetime conveyances of the decedent.

Statutes commonly provide an elective share of one-third or one-half of the estate, depending on the number of issue, sometimes with a fixed dollar minimum. Usually this share applies to both real and personal property. Other benefits, such as homestead rights, or widow's and family allowances, may affect the computation.

Obviously, it is necessary to consult applicable State law as to the nature, scope and extent of election available to the surviving spouse. State law will also indicate whether it may be exercised by such spouse's personal representative or guardian; the time within which it must be exercised; the prescribed method of exercising it; and possibilities of extension of time for the election and withdrawal of an election.

While an elective share comprising a life estate will not qualify for the marital deduction, the outright fractional share provided by most jurisdictions will qualify, as a statutory interest in lieu of dower or curtesy under Sec. 2056(e)(3) of the Code. (See Reg. Sec. 20.2056(e)-2(c).) This is the most significant feature of the spouse's election for estate tax planning purposes. (Again, State law must be consulted as to whether the statutory share must bear its pro rata share of the estate tax or will pass free of estate tax.)

[¶1001.1]   When to Exercise Election

Subject to countervailing considerations mentioned below, the following are appropriate cases for an election to be considered:

1. *Where there is no marital deduction.* In some cases, lifetime computations indicate that use of the marital deduction would not be advantageous. (See Chapter One, especially ¶101.) Postmortem computations may show that a marital deduction in the amount of the elective share would be advantageous. As explained in ¶101, such a determination involves not only the tax result in the decedent's estate but also the tax treatment of the marital deduction as part of the gross estate of the surviving spouse. Where these new calculations favor use of the marital deduction, the election should be seriously considered.

The decedent may have eschewed the marital deduction for personal rather than tax reasons. He may have preferred the additional estate tax to giving his spouse either lifetime or testamentary powers to dispose of substantial assets. Where State law provides an election, and the surviving spouse is not precluded by contract from exercising it, she may decide to obtain the marital deduction for the decedent's estate in this way.

Attention is invited to *Estate of Harter,* 39 T.C.511 (1962). The surviving spouse, who received nothing under the will, elected to take his statutory share, which he gave immediately to the children of his wife's son. (The son was the beneficiary under her will). The marital deduction was allowed for the husband's elective share. Gift tax of $5,000 was paid, but $22,000 of estate tax was saved in the wife's estate, and the transfer to the son's children avoided estate taxes in the son's estate.

2. *Where the marital deduction is inadequate.* The statutory share available through election may be greater than the marital deduction share provided in the decedent's will.[3] Where the latter is less than (a) the statutory share and (b) the maximum marital deduction, and postmortem computations favor a larger deduction, the election may be indicated.

3. *Where the marital deduction is uncertain.* Where there is a question, for technical reasons, whether the marital deduction gift as drafted (presumably by your predecessor) will pass muster at the estate tax audit, it may be advisable for the surviving spouse to substitute a statutory share by electing against the will. Even if the statutory share will be a lesser amount than the testamentary gift, a smaller share which qualifies may be prefereed to a larger one that may not.

4. *Where the marital deduction gift is deemed too rigid.* If the decedent chose to obtain the marital deduction via a power of appointment trust [see ¶103.2] in which provisions for lifetime invasion of principal are

---

[3]Whenever the elective share provided by statute is compared with a formula marital deduction gift which is related to the "adjusted gross estate," bear in mind that the gross estate, and hence the adjusted gross estate, may take into account life insurance proceeds or other assets not reached by the statutory election.

nonexistent or very restrictive, or if the decedent used an estate trust [¶103.3] in which the surviving spouse may even be denied the trust income during her lifetime, she may prefer to obtain an outright statutory share by electing against the will. Such a share may be preferred even if it results in a reduced marital deduction.

Similarly, the marital deduction trust may be sufficiently flexible to meet the needs of the surviving spouse herself, but not to permit diversion of principal by her to others. If a lifetime gift program would be helpful, e.g., to save taxes in the estate of the surviving spouse, the election of an outright share would put her in the position to make gifts of the assets involved.

Again, a spouse who would be adequately maintained from the marital deduction trust or otherwise, and who is not precluded by the trust from pursuing a desirable gift program, may reject the trust concept *per se* and elect a statutory share in order to increase her personal autonomy and control.

5. *Where the marital deduction gift is excessive.* The marital deduction gift provided in the decedent's will may be excessive in any or all of these ways:

(a) It may exceed the allowable marital deduction.

(b) It may add to the gross estate of the surviving spouse a greater amount than is desirable when the tax results in both estates are considered. [See ¶101].

(c) It may provide excessive income (and income taxes) for the surviving spouse [See ¶103.3].

In such a case, it may be possible to substitute a desirable lesser share of the estate by an election against the will.

[¶1001.2]   Acceleration of Remainder Interests

The spouse's election substitutes her statutory share for any legacies and beneficial interests provided in the will (or other conveyances subject to the election). When she is designated as the income beneficiary of a trust or trusts, the question arises whether the elimination of her life estate will result in accelerating the remainder interests. This is a question of State law, which must be examined in each case. Some jurisdictions appear to bar acceleration generally. In others, acceleration will be prevented only if the will so provides or if the remainder interests are contingent rather than vested. In still others, the usual result is to accelerate the remainder, whether vested or contingent, unless acceleration would subvert special purposes of the testator.

A case which involved acceleration as well as several of the benefits described in [¶1001.1] occurred in the writers' practice shortly before the advent of TRA 76. The decedent's will, which may have been sensible when written, provided very traditional marital and nonmarital trusts. The widow was the sole income beneficiary of each. Barring appointment otherwise of the marital trust principal, the entire estate would pass outright to the son upon the widow's death. The estate consisted almost entirely of marketable securities, and the son had handled his parents' investments for a number of years.

With an adjusted gross estate of about $600,000, the annual income of the two trusts would substantially exceed the widow's customary income needs, thus yielding excessive income taxes and potential accumulation of income in the widow's estate. In addition, the marital deduction principal would remain intact, to be included (probably at a higher figure) "on top of" the widow's separate property as part of her gross estate for estate tax purposes.

With only one child, the elective share was one-half of the distributable estate, virtually the same portion of the estate that would otherwise be placed in the marital deduction trust. As a consequence of the election which we recommended in that case:

1. The widow's taxable income was reduced to a more appropriate level; and
2. The son's remainder interest in the nonmarital trust was accelerated, so that both testamentary trusts (which had no nontax purpose in this case) were eliminated.

At the time of distribution of the estate, we arranged a private annuity contract between the widow and her son (see Chapter Six). With this device the widow immediately transferred to her son and removed from her gross estate sufficient assets to eliminate the estate tax which would otherwise be payable at the time of her death. To the extent the annuity payments exceed her income needs, she makes annual gifts (covered by her $3,000 exclusions) to her several grandchildren, thus avoiding the build-up of her estate and "skipping" her son's estate also.

[¶1001.3]   Gift Tax Consequences

Where the result of a spouse's election is to increase the value of residuary shares, or of remainder interests which are accelerated, the question arises whether the spouse has made a taxable gift to those who are so enriched. Under Reg. Sec. 25.2511-1(c), it seems clear that such increased or accelerated interests will be treated as passing from the decedent, and not from the electing spouse. The election, however, may be deemed to include the spouse's "disclaimer" of any benefits inconsistent with her election. Such a disclaimer, in order to avoid gift and estate taxes, will presumably have to meet the requirements of Sec. 2518 of the Code as set forth below in ¶1002.

[¶1002]   RENUNCIATIONS AND DISCLAIMERS

The terms "renunciation" and "disclaimer" are synonymous. A disclaimer or renunciation is a refusal to accept ownership of a property or interest which would otherwise pass to the disclaiming or renouncing party. These terms should be distinguished from an election (right of a spouse to claim a statutory share, as discussed in [¶1001), a release (relinquishment of an interest which has already been accepted by a beneficiary), and a compromise (settlement of a bone fide dispute). We will use the term disclaimer for the balance of this discussion.

A designated beneficiary may disclaim outright bequests. income interests, remainders, and nontestamentary property such as life insurance proceeds. Thus, the reach of the disclaimer is broader than that of the usual spouse's election, and it is available regardless of relationship to the testator or donor, so that the disclaimer is a substantially more versatile planning tool than the election.

Prior to TRA 76, the effectiveness of a disclaimer for estate and gift tax purposes was governed to a large extent by State law. A disclaimer had to be unconditional, irrevocable, and unequivocal. It had to be exercised within a reasonable time after the disclaiming party learned of the transfer, and there could be no conduct indicating acceptance of the disclaimed property (or it would be a release, leaving the estate tax treatment unaltered and constituting a taxable gift). And the disclaimer had to be effective under applicable State law. (See Reg. Sec. 25.2511-1(c)).

Generally, State law required a disclaimer to be clear and unequivocal. It was also necessary to determine whether the interest involved (e.g., the interest of a surviving joint tenant, or an interstate share) could be disclaimed. The permissible timing of the disclaimer (e.g., the time of vesting of a contingent future interest or the time of its receipt), the formal requirements (whether established by will or by statute), the validity of a partial disclaimer, and the capacity of a personal representative or guardian to exercise it, were all issues to be determined under the law of the jurisdiction involved.

In order to eliminate the variations in estate and gift tax treatment caused by local law differences, TRA 76 provides uniform rules in new Sec. 2518 of the Code.[4] Under the new rules, *whether or not the disclaimer*

[4]These rules apply for purposes of gift tax (Sec. 2518) and also for estate and generation-skipping tax purposes (Sec. 2045).

would be recognized as such under State law, Federal tax law will apply as if the interest had never been transferred to the designated beneficiary who makes a qualified disclaimer. A "qualified disclaimer" is an irrevocable and unqualified refusal by a person to accept an interest in property, provided these four conditions are met:

☐ the refusal is in writing;

☐ the writing is received by the transferor of the interest, his legal representative, or the holder of the legal title to the property to which the interest relates within 9 months after the later of—

(a) the date on which the transfer creating the interest is made, or
(b) the day on which the person disclaiming reaches age 21;

☐ The person disclaiming has not accepted the interest or any of its benefits; and

☐ As a result of the refusal, the interest passes to a person other than the person making the disclaimer (without any direction on the part of the disclaiming person).

Further, a disclaimer of an undivided portion of an interest will be treated as a qualified disclaimer of that portion if the foreging requirements are met as to the portion (Sec. 2518(c)(1)). And a power with respect to property is treated as an interest in property for this purpose (Sec. 2518(c)(2)).

As we shall see, the qualified disclaimer can be used to save estate taxes in a variety of ways.

[¶1002.1]   When to Make a Disclaimer

A disclaimer[5] can be used to obtain estate tax savings in the following ways:

1. *Where there is no marital deduction.* Where the decedent did not provide a gift to his spouse which qualifies for the marital deduction, and where a marital deduction appears after his death to be desirable, a remedy can sometimes be found in a spouse's statutory election to take against the will (see paragraph (1) of ¶1001.1, above). But if the elective share in the jurisdiction involved does not qualify for the marital deduction, or if the tranfers subject to the election are insufficient to provide an adequate marital deduction, a useful alternative can sometimes be found in a disclaimer.

---

[5]For purposes of this discussion, we assume that disclaimers will be qualified disclaimers as defined in Sec. 2518 of the Code.

An interest disclaimed by a third party in favor of the surviving spouse will be treated as an interest passing from the decedent to his spouse for marital deduction purposes, under Section 2056(d)(2) of the Code.

2. *Where the marital deduction is inadequate.* Similarly, where the decedent has provided (by will or otherwise) tranfers to his wife which utilize less than the maximum marital deduction, and postmortem computations indicate that a larger marital deduction would be advantageous, it will sometimes be possible to obtain the increase via a third party disclaimer which increases the share of the surviving spouse. Also, where less than the maximum marital deduction has been used, the relative rigidity of the marital deduction arrangements may provide a nontax incentive to obtain a supplemental gift by means of such a renunciation.

3. *Where the marital deduction is uncertain.* If there is doubt as to whether one or more transfers to the surviving spouse qualify for the marital deduction, a third party disclaimer in her favor may be an appropriate method of obtaining all or part of the desired deduction.

4. *Where the marital deduction is excessive.* As explained in paragraph (5) of [¶1001.1], postmortem analysis may indicate that a lesser marital deduction gift than that provided under the decedent's estate plan would be preferable. The desired result can be obtained by means of a partial disclaimer by the surviving spouse, assuming a partial disclaimer is permissible under applicable State law.[6] (In such cases, and in any other case where marital deduction planning is involved, whether it is lifetime or postmortem planning, it is important to consider the tax impact of the marital deduction transfer not only in the estate of the decedent but also in the estate of the surviving spouse.)

5. *To save or increase a charitable deduction.* Where the decedent has provided a trust with both charitable and noncharitable interests, and the charitable interest does not qualify for the deduction as a unitrust, annuity trust, or pooled income fund [see ¶203.10 and 203.15], the defect can be cured and the charitable deduction obtained via renunciation of the noncharitable interest, e.g., a life estate prior to a charitable remainder.

---

[6]It was clearly the intent of Sec. 2009 of TRA 76, in adding Sec. 2518 of the Code, that a refusal to accept property is to be given effect for estate and gift tax purposes even if local law does not characterize the refusal as a disclaimer or if local law considers the refusing person to have been the owner of the property prior to his refusal. The authors assume, however, that local law will still apply to determine whether a person may refuse a part of a transfer while retaining the balance.

Where the disclaimer of other transfers will increase the residuary estate, and all or part of the residuary estate passes to charity, the disclaimer can be utilized to increase the residuary estate and thereby increase the charitable deduction.

Another alternative to the disclaimer of an interest in favor of charity is for the individual beneficiary to accept the interest and then release it in favor of charity. A disclaimer operates on the premise that the interest was never received by the disclaiming party. In contrast, if the interest is first accepted and then given away, the beneficiary-donor may be able to obtain an income tax deduction which the disclaimer does not provide. He may also choose a charitable beneficiary other than the one(s) which would benefit from a disclaimer. And he may be able to arrange a combination of income and estate tax benefits via the techniques discussed in Chapter Two.

Where the last mentioned alternative is of interest, it will be necessary to consider the qualification of the interest for the income tax charitable deduction, applicable percentage limitations and carryover provisions. Also, the value of the income tax deduction (and estate tax charitable deduction in the beneficiary's estate, if applicable) to the beneficiary as compared with the value of the estate tax charitable deduction in the estate of the deceased transferor.

6. *To avoid tax in the beneficiary's estate.* To the extent an interest passing to a decedent's spouse qualifies for the marital deduction, a disclaimer to avoid adding the interest to the spouse's gross estate will decrease the marital deduction in the decedent's estate. This means that competing estate tax and related income considerations must be weighed. To the extent the spouse's "inheritance" exceeds the marital deduction allowable in the decedent's estate, as where the decedent gives his entire estate to his wife, the excess can be disclaimed without a corresponding estate tax cost.

Others may also wish to disclaim in order to avoid estate taxes. A child of the decedent, for example, may wish to disclaim his interest where the consequence will be to pass the interest to (or in trust for) his issue. He can thus keep the disclaimed interest out of his gross estate, and do so without incurring gift tax, and possibly reduce the taxes payable on the income to be derived from the property.

Where the beneficiary's interest is not an outright gift to him but rather an interest in trust which would be includible in his gross estate by reason of a power over the trust (or would have adverse income tax consequences by reason of a power), the beneficiary can disclaim the troublesome power while retaining other beneficial interest (Sec. 2518(c)(2) of the Code).

7. *Other uses of disclaimers.* Although we are concerned here primarily with federal estate tax savings, it might be helpful to note in passing that disclaimers can be used for other purposes, such as:

☐ To save State inheritance and estate taxes.

☐ To shift income and income taxes to others.

☐ To protect the property or interest from the beneficiary's creditors.

[¶1003]   OPTIONS WITH RESPECT TO DEDUCTIONS

The two principal options affecting the estate tax, as far as deductions are concerned, are these:

☐ Medical expenses of the decedent which are paid out of the estate within one year following the date of death can be deducted on the decedent's lifetime return(s) for the year or years in which the expenses were incurred. Alternatively, they may be deducted on the estate tax return. (See Sec. 2053 and Sec. 213(d) of the Code, and Reg. Sec. 1.213-1(d).)

☐ Allowable expenses of administering the estate (Sec. 2053 of the Code) and casualty losses (Sec. 2054) may be deducted on the fiduciary income tax return(s) for the year or years in which the expenses are paid. Alternatively, they may be deducted on the estate tax return. (See Sec. 642(g) of the Code.)

[¶1003.1]   How to Evaluate Deduction Options

With respect to each of those options, it is necessary to compare the value of the estate tax deduction with the value of the income tax deduction. The comparison will be based on the marginal tax rates applicable to each return. Bear in mind that:

☐ The effective estate tax rate will be affected by the percentage of the estate which qualifies for the marital or charitable deduction.

☐ The effective income tax rates for medical expenses will be those applicable to the lifetime return or returns for the year(s) in which the expenses were incurred.

☐ The effective income tax rate for administration expenses or losses will be that applicable to either:

(a) The estate's return for the taxable year during which the expense or loss
     was incurred, if incurred prior to the year of termination, or

(b) The return(s) of the beneficiary or beneficiaries for their taxable year in
     which the expense or loss was incurred, if incurred during the year of
     termination of the estate. (If an estate has deductions in excess of gross
     income during its last taxable year, the excess deductions can be passed
     on to the beneficiaries who succeed to the property of the estate. See
     Reg. Sec. 1.641(b)-3(a).)

□ Use of medical expenses for income tax purposes increases the
estate tax not only by loss of the corresponding estate tax deductions but
also by reducing the income tax liability, which is itself deductible as a
debt of the decedent.

□ Use of deductions for fiduciary income tax purposes benefits
the income beneficiaries to the detriment of the remaindermen, who
bear the estate tax cost.

□ The deductions for medical expenses and for administration
expenses and losses can be divided between the estate tax return and the
applicable income tax returns when such division will produce the optimum result. (Deductible items can be divided, or some items can be
allocated for estate tax purposes and others for income tax purposes.)

If the estate's income includes tax-exempt income, Sec. 265(1) of
the Code may bar the income tax deduction of a pro rata portion of the
administration expenses. Where use of the deduction for income tax
purposes is otherwise desirable, the nondeductible portion can be
utilized for estate tax purposes. Alternatively, it may be desirable to
distribute the tax-exempt securities in a year prior to the year in which
the expenses are paid.

Caveat: The decision to deduct the items discussed above for income tax or estate tax purposes will affect the amount of the adjusted
gross estate and also the amount of the taxable estate. Thus the decision
may determine whether or not a closely held business interest will qualify
for payment of estate tax in installments under either Sec. 6166A or
6166B of the Code. It may also affect the opportunity to redeem corporate stock without dividend treatment under Sec. 303 of the Code, and it
will (by altering the amount of estate tax) alter the amount which can be
paid out in a Section 303 redemption.

[¶1003.2]   How to Exercise Deduction Elections

In order to deduct medical expenses, administration expenses or
casualty losses for income tax purposes, the executor must file in dupli-

cate a statement that the amount claimed as a deduction has not been allowed as a deduction under Sec. 2054 of the Code in computing the decedent's taxable estate. Or, in the case of losses, that it has not been allowed as a deduction under Sec. 2053. The statement must also indicate that the right to have such amount allowed at any time as a Sec. 2053 (or Sec. 2054 if applicable) deduction is waived.

The statement need not be filed with the return. It may be filed at any time prior to the expiration of the statuory period of assessment. No waiver is required for estate tax purposes. As a consequence, the deductions can be tentatively claimed on income tax and estate tax returns, so long as a timely decision is eventually made. So long as the deductions have not been finally allowed for estate tax purposes (i.e., when a deficiency assessment is barred by a closing agreement, the statute of limitations, or otherwise), an income tax election within the time above mentioned can be made.

In order for these options to be meaningful with respect to administration expenses, it is important to see that payments are made in the taxable year or years of the estate in which the income tax deductions may be deemed desirable.

[¶1004]   **ALTERNATE VALUATION**

Where the gross estate on the date of death is large enough to require the filing of an estate tax return, the assets comprising the gross estate are valued for estate tax purpose as of that date unless the executor elects the alternate valuation date under Sec. 2032 of the Code. If the executor so elects, normally by checking a box provided for that purpose on the estate tax return, the assets will be valued as follows:

☐ as of the date of sale, distribution or other disposition of assets which are retained by the executor for less than six months after the date of death; and

☐ as of the date six months after the date of death in the case of assets not disposed of within the intervening six-month period.

Caveat: The election of the alternate valuation method can be made only if it is done on or before the date on which the return is due or within the period of any extension of the due date. It is, therefore, essential that the election, if desired, be timely, and it is advisable that a receipt showing timely filing of the return be obtained.

Prior to TRA 76, assets inherited from a decedent received a "stepped-up" basis. That is, the recipient's basis in the property was the fair market value of the property on the date of death, or on the alternate valuation date if the latter was elected, regardless of the decedent's acquisition cost.

Under the pre-TRA 76 rules, as between the date of death and alternate valuation method, that producing the *higher* asset valuation would sensibly be chosen, in the interest of obtaining a higher stepped-up basis, in these situations:

(a)   where the allowable deductions and exemption eliminated the estate tax.

(b)   where (i) sale of the property was not unlikely and (ii) the income tax bracket on capital gains would be higher than the effective estate tax bracket resulting from the higher valuation of the gross estate.

TRA 76 substituted "carryover basis" for the earlier stepped-up basis.[7] This means that assets inherited from a decedent retain the decedent's pre-death adjusted basis, further adjusted (but not in excess of estate tax values) principally as follows:

(a)   For purposes of determining gain, the basis of marketable securities will be stepped-up to their value on December 31, 1976, and the basis of other assets will be stepped-up to the value determined by prorating appreciation from the date of acquisition to December 31, 1976.

(b)   Basis is increased by the amount of federal and State death taxes attributable to *appreciation* of the property.

(c)   The estate's aggregate carryover basis has a $60,000 minimum, allocable to particular assets in proportion to their appreciation.

Under TRA 76, it would seem that the adjustments to carryover basis will rarely produce a situation in which the choice of the higher valuation date will yield an income tax (on capital gains) saving which outweighs the estate tax cost. In short, the elimination of the pre-TRA 76 stepped-up basis generally means that the alternate valuation method will henceforth be elected only where the effect will be to reduce the value of the gross estate.

Caveat: The election of the alternate valuation method will affect the amount of the adjusted gross estate and the amount of the taxable estate as well as the value of the estate's closely held business interests. Thus the decision may determine whether or not a closely held business interest will qualify for payment of estate tax in installments under either Sec. 6166A or Sec. 6166 of the Code. It may also affect the opportunity to redeem corporate stock without dividend treatment under Sec. 303 of the Code, and it will (by altering the amount of estate tax) alter the amount which can be paid out in a Section 303 redemption.

---

[7]Under Sec. 1040(a) of the Code, however, the old stepped-up basis is reintroduced to determine gain on distribution of property by an executor in satisfaction of a pecuniary bequest (e.g., a pecuniary marital deduction formula gift).

[¶1004.1]   How to Maximize the Alternate
Valuation Tax Saving

Where alternate valuation is elected in the interest of reducing the estate tax, the valuation of particular assets will depend on whether they are retained by the executor for six months following the date of death or are sold or distributed within that period.

Where property is to be sold to meet the estate's liquidity needs, sale within the six-month period may be preferable to sale at a later date. A low sale price within the period will result in a lower estate tax and a reduced price thereafter will not. (Where sale is not otherwise required, it is not generally advisable to sell at a loss merely in the interest of estate tax saving. Retention may result in a higher price later.)

Where assets have declined below date-of-death values, distributions during the six-month period may be wise, especially if an increase within the period is considered likely. However, as against the use of distributions to maximize the estate tax advantage of alternate valuation, the fact that the income of the tranferred property will be shifted from the estate to the beneficiaries must be considered.

[¶1005]   VALUATION OPTIONS—FARM AND SMALL
BUSINESS PROPERTY

Assets of the gross estate are includible at fair market value as of the applicable valuation date—date of death or alternate valuation date [¶1004]. Fair market value is the price at which the property would pass from a willing seller to a willing buyer, each having knowledge of the relevant facts and neither being under any compulsion to enter into the transaction.

The fair market value of a farm or other business property would normally mean valuation at its highest and best use. This might be the value at which the property could be sold to a developer, even though it was not in fact being sold or held for development and its actual farm or business profitability would not justify such a valuation.

As relief legislation, Section 2032A of the Code now permits the executor to value land for estate tax purposes on the basis of its actual current use, rather than its highest and best use. The reduction of the gross estate which can be effected by this "use valuation" is limited to $500,000. And this method may be used only when the following conditions are met:

☐ The decedent was a citizen or resident of the United States at the time of his death;

    ☐ At the time of the decedent's death the property was being used for a qualified use, i.e., use as a farm or for farming purposes[8] or use in a trade or business[9] other than farming.

    ☐ For periods aggregating at least five years during the eight-year period ending on the date of the decedent's death, the property was owned by the decedent or a member of his family[10] and used for a qualified use, with material participation by the decedent or a member of his family in the operation of the farm or other business;

    ☐ The value (determined without regard to Section 2032A) of the farm or business assets in the decedent's estate, including real and personal property, reduced by mortgages or indebtedness attributable to such assets, is at least 50 percent of the decedent's gross estate (determined without regard to Section 2032A[11]) less Section 2053(a)(4) deductions;

    ☐ The value (determined without regard to Section 2032A) of the farm or business real property, reduced by mortgages or indebtedness attributable to it, is at least 25 percent of the decedent's gross estate (determined without regard to Section 2032A[11]) less Section 2053(a)(4) deductions;

    ☐ The qualifying property must pass to a qualified heir, that is, a member of the decedent's family as defined in Sec. 2032A(e)(2) of the Code; and

    ☐ Each person in being who has an interest in the property (whether or not in possession) must sign an agreement consenting to the application of the recapture provisions of Sec. 2032A(c) of the Code, as summarized below.

Where the decedent's ownership of the property interest is indirect, i.e., through an interest in a partnership, corporation or trust which is an interest in a closely held business within the meaning of Sec. 6166(b)(1) of the Code, the Treasury is directed to issue regulations as to the application of the special valuation rules.

---

[8]See definitions of "farm" and "farming purposes" in Sec. 2032A(e)(4) and (5) of the Code.

[9]An interest in a closely held business for purposes of Sec. 2032A is the same as for deferred payment purposes under Sec. 6166(b) of the Code.

[10]Member of the family means the individual's ancestor or lineal descendant, a lineal descendant of the individual's grandparent, the spouse of the individual, or the spouse of any such descendant, and an adopted child of an individual is treated as a child of the individual "by blood." (Sec. 2032A(e)(2))

[11]Note that for purposes of the 50 percent test and the 25 percent test the assets involved must be valued at highest and best use to determine eligibility; if eligible under all criteria, the special valuation methods mentioned below will apply to fix the values actually to be used for inclusion of the realty in the gross estate.

[¶1005.1]   Valuation Methods

The special method for valuing farms is as follows: the last five years' average annual gross rentals (less average annual real estate taxes) of comparable farm properties in the area is divided by the average effective interest rate for all new Federal Land Bank Loans.

The above-mentioned farm method applies unless (a) it is established that there is no comparable land from which the annual gross rentals can be determined, or (b) the executor elects to use the closely held business method.

The closely held business method (which applies to eligible closely held businesses and to certain farms described in the preceding paragraph) is a combination of the following factors:

(a) capitalization of anticipated annual earnings,
(b) capitalization of fair rental value for farm or closely held business use,
(c) assessed value if the State provides for use assessment as farm or small business property,
(d) comparable sales of property in the area far enough removed from a metropolitan or resort area that nonagricultural use is not a significant factor in the sale price, and
(e) any other factor which fairly values the farm or closely held business value of the property.

[¶1005.2]   How to Elect

The Section 2032A election must be made by the executor (in a manner to be prescribed by regulations) on or before the due date of the estate tax return (including any extensions). The election must be accompanied by a written agreement signed by every person in being who has an interest (whether or not in possession) in property for which the special use valuation is elected, wherein each such person consents to the recapture provisions of Section 2032A(c), as summarized in ¶1005.3, below.

[¶1005.3]   Recapture

The estate tax benefits of the special valuation option for farm and small business property are subject to total or partial recapture if within 15 years after the decedent's death and before the death of a qualified heir:

(a) the qualified heir disposes of any interest in the property other than to a member of his family, or

(b) the qualified heir ceases to use the property for a qualified use.[12]

In such a case, the "adjusted tax difference," that is, the amount by which the estate tax which would have been due but for the application of Section 2032A exceeds the estate tax determined with its use, is potentially subject to recapture, If the event as described by (a) or (b), above occurs within ten years of the decedent's death, the recapture is limited to the lesser of (i) the "adjusted tax difference" or (ii) the excess of the amount realized with respect to the interest (or its fair market value, in lieu of an arm's length sale or exchange) over the value of the interest determined under the special use valuation provisions. If the event occurs between 10 and 15 years after the decedent's death, the amount subject to recapture is reduced ratably on a monthly basis.

If more than one heir receives an interest in qualified property subject to special use valuation, the "adusted tax difference" is allocated among such interests in proportion to their respective reductions in estate tax value according to the values finally determined in the audit of the estate tax return or subsequent proceedings. If there is more than one recapture event with respect to a property interest, as where the heir first changes the use and then sells the property, recapture applies only to the first event.

A qualified heir is made personally liable for any recapture tax imposed with respect to his interest in qualified property. Also, a special lien is imposed with respect to all property to which the special use valuation is applied; this extends until the tax benefit is recaptured or the period of potential recapture expires.

Caveat: Section 2032A is riddled with ambiguities and rife with administrative problems. For a useful and more extended discussion, with examples, see John D. Wheeler, "New valuation provisions for farms and other property can reduce estate as much as $500,000," *Taxation for Accountants,* July 1977, p. 42.

[¶1006]   VALUATION OF CLOSELY HELD CORPORATION STOCK

Whether the assets includible in a decedent's gross estate are valued as of the date of his death or pursuant to the alternate valuation method

---

[12]The cessation of a qualified use occurs if (a) the property ceases to be used for the qualified use under which the property qualified for the special valuation or (b) during any eight-year period ending after the decedent's death and prior to the death of a qualified heir, there are periods aggregating three years in which there was or is no material participation by the decedent or a member of his family and no material participation by the qualified heir or a member of his family in the operation of the farm or other business.

[¶1004], it is obvious that the amount of estate tax will vary according to the valuation of assets as finally determined. The desire to qualify a particular asset for Section 303 redemption, or for installment payments of estate tax, will sometimes motivate a higher valuation preference with respect to that asset, by reason of the percentage tests provided in the Code for those purposes. In the absence of those special considerations, the executor's effort normally will be to establish values which will result in estate tax savings.

Assets are includible at their fair market value (see introductory paragraph of ¶1005). In the case of regularly traded securities, that value is readily ascertainable. Where it is not, the question of an asset's value may leave considerable room for disagreement. While the establishment of value in such cases is not a postmortem "option" precisely, it is certainly a postmortem opportunity.

For such items as real estate and tangible personal property, the executor must normally turn for assistance to an independent "outside" appraiser, that is, a qualified person who is not one of his estate counselors. But where the asset involved is stock of a closely held corporation, the executor may engage an organization which is in the business of evaluating business interest or he may find the requisite expertise in one or more of his professional staff: attorney, accountant, trust company, or others.

While an entire volume could usefully be devoted to this topic, the guidelines set forth in the following paragraph may be helpful in those cases in which the appraisal report (or memorandum of valuation) is to be prepared by the estate's professional aides. Before turning to the criteria for valuation, we offer two observations:

☐ Prior to TRA 76, the opportunity of the estate counselors and their staffs to make an in-depth study of all aspects of the subject corporation, to develop alternate ratio comparison with selected publicly held companies, to study alternative approaches to valuation, and generally to build their "case," far exceeded the corresponding opportunity (and interest, in many cases) of the estate tax examiner with his heavy caseload and his time pressures. The new unifed credit, however, with the exemption equivalent rising to $175,000 by 1980, should substantially lighten those case-loads, and this may serve to reduce the strategic imbalance on valuation issues. A more exhaustive analysis of closely held businesses should certainly be a high priority for use of the examiner's released time.

☐ The appraisal of estate assets should not, in the writers' opinion, be regarded as part of the regular representation of the estate by the executor's attorneys or other consultants. The fees charged for such services by outside appraisers are substantial, and we suggest that a substantial separate fee be charged to the estate when the executor's regular advisers undertake this responsibility. The knowledge, diligence, and presentational skills involved will considerably affect the tax results, and the value of these professional attributes should be recognized by all concerned.

[¶1006.1]   How to Determine Value

Reg. Sec. 20.2031-2(f) gives some general guidance: Shares not actively traded, say the Regs., should be valued on the basis of the company's net worth, prospective earning power, and dividend-paying capacity. Also mentioned as relevant are the company's goodwill, economic outlook of the industry, the selling price of companies in similar lines of business, and "other facts in each case."

Treasury rulings have gone into more detail. The first was issued in 1920 (A.R.M. 34) and provided:

1. Net tangible assets are to be valued and a reasonable return (8-10 percent) allowed.
2. Any remaining income (above the 8-10 percent return) is then capitalized at 15 or 20 percent—i.e., goodwill.

Example:

Net tangible assets		300,000
Average net income for 5 years	$50,000	
Fair (10 percent) return on assets	30,000	
Excess above fair return	20,000	
20 percent capitalization of excess (5 × excess)		100,000
Total value including goodwill		$400,000

A.R.M. 34 has had some recognition in the cases since 1920. The authors, in their practice, have never seen an estate tax examiner use it, nor do we consider it useful. A 1965 ruling states that it can now be used only when no better basis exists for determining the fair market value of goodwill.

The next significant Treasury pronouncement was Rev. Rul. 54-77 (1954), which listed the factors then deemed relevant. These are largely repeated in the latest, and still applicable, Rev. Rul. 59-60, 1959-1 C.B. 237:

1. The nature of the business and the history of the enterprise since its inception.

In a recent case, we used this approach and held the Government to a book value of $19,000, where capitalization of earnings indicated a valuation of several hundred thousand dollars. We showed that the major customers of the business had been gradually lost; only one remained, which could be lost at any time. The profits at the moment were high, but they hung by a single thread.

2. The economic outlook in general and the condition and outlook of the specific industry in particular.

On the industry as a whole, commercial and governmental sources (e.g., the Department of Commerce) offer boundless information. The client, of course, is usually a major source.

Also, the ability of the corporation to compete within its industry should be studied. For example, where a company has not had competition in the past, its high percentage of profits may attract competitors.

3. The book value of the stock and the financial condition of the business.

Book value is determined by subtracting the liabilities from the assets and dividing the remainder by the number of outstanding shares of stock. Assets of an investment type are to be recomputed on basis of market price and book value adjusted. Book value is deemed especially significant where the corporation is of an investment or holding-company type, as distinguished from sales of products or services.

Book value may produce various distortions, because it is based on historical cost. Machinery with a certain book value may be worth several times that amount because the company used accelerated depreciation or because of inflation. Or the machinery may be worth much less than its book value because it has become totally obsolete.

Receivables may be worth more than book because the client tended to be pessimistic, or worth less than book because he was too optimistic (having his banker in mind).

There are also certain things which may be left off the balance sheet, such as contingent liabilities in possible lawsuits, assets already written off, and, of course, good will.

4. The earning power of the company.

In considering this factor, the profit and loss statements may have to be reinterpreted:

(a) The owner may have paid himself an excessive salary, or worked for next to nothing (which a purchaser might not be willing to do).
(b) The owner may have permitted the business to occupy a building he owned with little or no rent, or he may have charged it excessive rent.

Income taxes are, of course, a cost of doing business, so that after-tax earnings are normally considered.

5. Dividend-paying capacity.

The interest of the Government here is in the capacity to pay dividends, not dividends actually paid—since small companies frequently find better ways to pay out corporate funds. This is not usually an important factor in an audit, as it is too elusive.

6. Whether or not the corporation has good will or other intangible value.

Factors involved in the search for good will are:

(a) Prestige and renown of the business.
(b) Ownership of a trade or brand name.
(c) A record of successful operation over a prolonged period.

Where stock is valued according to actual market or sales price, the element of goodwill is reflected automatically. In a closely held company, absent a sale, it is determined mainly on the basis of earning capacity.

The straight capitalization method is most frequently used to arrive at a valuation that will include good will. The average net earnings for five years are capitalized at a factor reflecting a fair return. The excess over book value is good will.

How are earnings "capitalized?" The earnings multiplier is the reciprocal of the capitalization rate. If, for example, a potential purchaser would expect an 8 percent return on his investment, the price he should pay on that basis would be 12.5 times expected earnings (100 ÷ 8). $100,000 of expected earnings multiplied by 12.5 would be $1,250,000. Correspondingly, an 8 percent return on $1,250,000 would be $100,000.

Before capitalizing, adjustments should be made for unusual or nonrecurring items, excessively high or low salaries, and so on.

What capitalization factor should be used? Rev. Rul. 59-60, Sec. 6, offers the following discussion:

> "In the application of certain fundamental valuation factors, such as earnings and dividends, it is necessary to capitalize the average or current results at some appropriate rate. A determination of the proper capitalization rate presents one of the most difficult problems in valuation. That there is no ready or simple solution will become apparent by a cursory check of the rates of return and dividend yields in terms of the selling prices of corporate shares listed on the major exchanges of the country. Wide variations will be found even for companies in the same industry. Moreover, the ratio will fluctuate from year to year depending upon economic conditions. Thus, no standard tables of capitalization rates applicable to closely held corporations can be formulated. Among the more important factors to be taken into consideration in deciding upon a capitalization rate in a particular case are: (1) the nature of the business; (2) the risk involved; and (3) the stability or irregularity of earnings."

Based on the stability or irregularity of earnings, the following factors have been suggested:

(a) Very narrow profit variation—e.g.,
     retail food sales; tobacco   10 ×
(b) Moderate variation—e.g.,
     amusements, alcoholic beverages   9 ×
(c) Moderately wide variation—e.g.,
     advertising, household products   7 ×
(d) Very wide variations—e.g.,
     automobiles, construction   6 ×

Another approach:
(a) Where company's earnings are good
     and rising—   10 to 12 ×
(b) Where its earnings are stable—   8 to 9 ×
(c) Where earnings are poor—   5 to 7 ×

Estate tax examiners frequently start with 10 times earnings as a "rule of thumb" and leave it to you to influence them away from it.

The Rev. Rul. recognizes that if there is a trend of increasing or decreasing income, greater weight may be given to the most recent years' profits. In a case of declining profits, a considerable valuation advantage can sometimes be derived from the "weighted" average approach.

7. Sales of stock and the size of the block to be valued.

Prior sales may help to establish the value, but this depends on surrounding circumstances. If the sales are not recent, or are not at arms length, or if they are forced or distress sales, or if a controlling interest was involved and the decedent's was a minority interest, or vice versa, prior sales are not very helpful.

8. The market price of stocks of corporations engaged in the same or a similar line of business whose stocks are actively traded.

Here, you take one or several of the most similar publicly held companies and determine[13] their price-earnings, price-dividends, and price-book value ratios, and apply these to the company being valued. The following differences must be taken into account:

1. Stock in a closely held corporation is normally difficult to sell and may represent a substantial or total interest.

2. A public company frequently has a more stable history and much more management depth.

(A factor similar to (8) but not specifically listed in the Rev. Rul. is a generally recognized customary valuation formula in the industry, as in

[13]From Moody's Industrial Averages or similar sources.

magazine distribution, taprooms, medical and dental practices, or cable tv.)

Which factors are most often used—how many are used—and which are most important?

Standard Research Consultants[14] examined all (77) Tax Court cases from 1955 through June 1966 (and a writer[15] in 1972 finds no significant differences thereafter). The results (with our emphasis):

A.   *Number of factors used*

14	11	10	9	8	7	6	5	4	3	2	1

Number of cases in which these factors were used

1	2	4	2	3	2	5	9	7	7	19	16

Which factors were most used
Sales price was used in 33 of the 77 cases.
Book value was used in 24 of the 77 cases.
Earning power was used in 17 of the 77 cases.
(Expert testimony was used in 50 percent of the cases.)

C.   *Conclusions*
   1. In most cases few factors are used.
   2. Lacking reliable sales, book value and earnings are the factors chiefly used.
   3. The results nearly always look like a compromise between the taxpayer's and the Treasury's positions.

For another helpful discussion of this ¶1006 topic we suggest John S. Furst and Cordell B. Moore, "Valuation of Closely Held Corporate Stock," a pamphlet published by Coopers & Lybrand, 1975.

[¶1007]   PRIVATE ANNUITY TRANSACTIONS

The postmortem options discussed in the preceding sections of this Chapter are creatures either of State law or of the Internal Revenue Code. Additional postmortem options may be created by the testator in his will or other estate planning documents. One such option is a power of the decedent's fiduciaries to enter into private annuity transactions.

A private annuity, as explained in Chapter Six, is an arrangement whereby one party transfers property to another, a transferee who is not in the business of selling annuities, in return for the latter's promise to make periodic payments of a fixed amount to the transferor for life.

If the annuity is properly computed and there are no endangering

[14]Corporate Security Values as Determined by the Tax Court (New York, 1966).

[15]Spencer J. Martin, "Factors the IRS and the courts are using today in valuing closely held shares," *The Journal of Taxation*, February 1972, p. 118.

"strings" attached (see Chapter Six for full discussion of technical aspects), the transferred property is immediately removed from the transferor's estate. In the case of a single life annuity, no gift is made and there is no gift tax involvement. Under Rev. Rul. 69-74 the annuity payments received by the transferor will normally include three elements: interest, capital gain, and tax-free recovery of basis.

If a beneficiary of the decedent's estate, such as his widow, has a gross estate which will be subject to estate tax at her death (as a result of a marital deduction gift to her or otherwise), and if the basis of her assets is fairly close to current market value, a private annuity may be an excellent device to reduce or eliminate her estate tax while preserving an adequate life income for her.

And a residuary trust under the decedent's will may be the ideal second party to the annuity transaction. Its resources will normally be confined to prudent investments, and the trustee is normally less likely than an individual transferee to lose the transferred property by incurring unforeseen liabilities. If the assets of the trust are adequate, the annuity payments can be made without hardship to any interested party.

Where the widow's assets are of such magnitude that an election against the Will [see ¶1001] or a total or partial disclaimer of the marital deduction gift [see ¶1002] may be contemplated in order to avoid a disadvantageous increase of her gross estate, a private annuity transaction may be a useful alternative. By accepting the marital deduction gift and then transferring the marital deduction assets or other property in exchange for a private annuity, she can reduce her gross estate without increasing the estate tax in the estate of the deceased spouse.

If there is no special power or direction, the trustee of the residuary trust may be reluctant to enter into such an arrangement. If the widow (or other beneficiary-annuitant) lives beyond life expectancy, the ultimate beneficiaries of the trust will bear the excess cost of the annuity payments, and the trustee may be fearful of criticism or possible surcharge in those circumstances.

It is recommended, therefore, where the possible utility of a private annuity is envisaged, that the trustee be specifically authorized to enter into such transactions. The potential annuitant or class of annuitants should be identified. And the trustee should be relieved of liability to any current or future party in interest provided the annuity calculation and the terms of the annuity contract are approved by counsel to the trustee.

11

How to Multiply Your Estate Planning Fees by Ten

[¶1100]   **HOW TO MULTIPLY THE VALUE**
OF YOUR SERVICES BY TEN

Let us begin this chapter by stating unequivocally that our objective in writing it here is not to urge you to charge a $2,000 fee for $200 worth of services. Our purpose is to correct those situations in which you render services worth $2,000 but are reluctant to issue the appropriate bill. Even worse from the standpoint of our professional responsibility, are cases in which counsel provides only a fraction of the appropriate services because of his fear that he will not be able to charge the full value of his work if performed.

We have the firm impression that adequate billing for competent estate planning services has traditionally been and remains exceptional in the legal profession. This impression is based on the principal author's experience over the years through association and membership in several law firms, large, medium-sized, and small, and also from the reports of life insurance agents and bank trust officers.

The now-defunct Minimum Fee schedule of the Philadelphia Bar Association, adopted by its Board of Governors on March 23, 1971, provides a similar set of figures, with interesting opening and closing comments:

I Estate planning: The fee for such planning should take into account the size of the estate and the intricacy of the problems involved.

II Minimum will and its execution	$ 50.
III Will without trust provisions and its execution	$ 75.
IV Will with trust provisions and its execution	$100.

246

   V Will with marital deduction provisions and its execution $150.
  VI If husband and wife execute similar and separate wills, add 50%
of the cost of one will as additional charge for drawing second will
and its execution.
 VII Living trust agreement and its execution $100.
VIII Living trust agreement with marital deduction provisions and its
execution $150.
    Note: Estate planning should be separately compensated, in addition to the
charge for drafting documents, wherever substantial planning is involved.

About such schedules, there are several things to be said:

First, they relegate "estate planning," which is or ought to be the heart of the matter, to a casual or pious foreword or afterthought. What the client fundamentally needs, whether or not he is sophisticated enough to request it in these words, is estate planning, not pieces of paper. The plan may require pieces of paper—wills, trusts, deeds, beneficiary changes, and so on—but they are, so to speak, only the "tail" of the estate planning dog.

The quoted fee schedules speak as if estate planning were something that may occasionally occur in connection with a will. The schedules, taken literally, do permit the charge of a substantial estate planning fee in addition to a modest fee for drawing documents, but in fact the common practice is for the "planning," if any, to be casually done and its compensation simply absorbed in the scheduled fee for document preparation.

Second, for the attorney who recognizes that his primary service is in the planning phase of his engagement, the reference in these schedules to a separate charge for estate planning (whether determined on an hourly basis or otherwise) gives the attorney no guidance whatsoever, for himself or for advising his client, as to the appropriate charge for the major undertaking.

And third, assuming that the appropriate estate plan was in some way selfevident or "given," without the need for conferences, computations, and analysis, so that the development, preparation and execution of appropriate documents become the entire task of counsel, the above-quoted schedules, even adjusting for several years of inflation, would be inadequate to the point of absurdity.

[¶1101]   **HOW TO GET FULL VALUE
FOR YOUR SERVICES**

The American Bar Association's Code of Professional Responsibility, Disciplinary Rule 2-106, dealing with "Fees for Legal Services," lists the "factors to be considered as guides in determining the reasonableness of a fee. . . ." They include the following:

1. The time and labor required, the novelty and difficulty of the question involved, and the skill requisite to perform the legal service properly.
2. The likelihood, if apparent to the client, that the acceptance of the particular employment will preclude other employment by the lawyer.
3. The fee customarily charged in the locality for similar legal services.
4. The amount involved and the results obtained.
5. The time limitations imposed by the client or by circumstances.
6. The nature and length of the professional relationship with the client.
7. The experience, reputation, and ability of the lawyer or lawyers performing the services.
8. Whether the fee is fixed or contingent.

For our purposes item (8) of that list has no application. Generally speaking, item (3) is an obstacle to be overcome. Items (2) and (6) should have no special significance. One may or may not wish to increase the charges, as suggested by item (5), where the client or the situation requires a "crash program."

Item (4) presents a certain amount of difficulty. Generally speaking, we do not agree that the size of a client's estate should *in itself* affect the fee for his estate planning. For a simple example, if the same amount of work is done for a client with a $300,000 estate and another with a $600,000 estate, it is our view that the latter client should not receive a larger bill merely because of the larger amount of his estate.

On the other hand, the larger estate is more likely to present a broader range of estate planning opportunities. It is more likely than the smaller estate for example, to be accessible to significant estate tax savings through the various techniques discussed in the preceding chapters of this book. As a result, it will invite more extensive analysis, more creative recommendations, and, frequently, a more comprehensive and extensive set of implementing documents. The fee relating to such services will not be a "tax" on the client's wealth, but will be a function of the increased time and skill necessarily involved. This will in turn normally correspond in a high degree with the results obtained.

The "results obtained," as mentioned in item (4), is an elusive concept. In terms of estate tax savings, the "results" of an estate plan can be projected for a relatively stable situation with a high degree of reliability. The tax savings should indeed be projected for the client, as part of the estate planning memorandum suggested below. The indication of substantial tax savings will normally increase or reinforce the client's willingness to pay an appropriate fee for the services involved. It is less clear that the amount of projected savings *per se* should play a significant role in determining the fee that is appropriate. Moreover, the "results" of skillful estate planning include much more in terms of implementing a client's goals than the saving of a certain amount of taxes. The "much more" is not susceptible of precise valuation.

There will, of course, be cases in which the value of the results obtained are so far disproportionate to the professional time expended that the time involvement cannot be a significant consideration. We were recently consulted for example, by an attorney who proposed to us for consideration a variety of devices—corporation, trust, nominee arrangements, etc.—for the acquisition of a house by a corporate client's key employee. The key employee's personal situation required that title be presently held by a party other than himself. Our suggestion that the corporate employer purchase the home eliminated a number of complications and was adopted. The consultation lasted not more than three minutes, and clearly the time charge for three minutes was not in that case an adequate key to the appropriate counsel fee.

The use of a private annuity furnishes perhaps a more useful example. This device is almost universally ignored in estate planning, and its implementation when adopted involves one of the simplest of all legal documents. The results can be quite dramatic in particular cases, if not fantastic. Here a decent respect for the novelty of the solution, the creativity of the counselor, and the results obtained, would in our view indicate a fee substantially disproportionate to the time involved.

By and large, however, the appropriate charge for our estate planning services will be a function of item (1) of the elements above listed. In other words, it is principally the time expended, as affected by item (7), the experience, reputation and the ability of the lawyer performing the services. Subject to variations for local overhead cost differentials, we suggest that the hourly charge of the attorney highly skilled in estate planning matters should not be less than $75-100. It will frequently be considerably more, depending on his reputation, competing uses of his available time, and other imponderables. The attorney who becomes familiar with the techniques discussed in the preceding chapters of this book and gains some experience in applying them should soon qualify as highly skilled in such matters.

Essentially, we are trying to arrive at a fee that fairly reflects the value of the services rendered. In the estate planning area, we suggest that that fee should reflect a mix of the following elements:

(1) Time involved.

(2) Taxes saved.

(3) Originality and creativity.

(4) Client satisfaction.

We have discussed principally the first three of these elements. In chapter [1102] we will offer specific recommendations for the development of a fee schedule which will fairly reflect all of the relevant ingredients in most cases. The matter of client satisfaction, however, is extremely subtle, and also vital, so that we might usefully give further attention to the development of this subject.

If we pause here to state the obvious, it is because the obvious often and paradoxically eludes perception in the kaleidoscope of our professional vision. What is, or ought to be, obvious is that client satisfaction is at once the goal and the measure of our professional effort. By the term "client satisfaction" we mean simply the business of meeting the needs and desires of each particular client, a separate unique human person.

This is the spirit and the substance of our professional responsibility in relation to our clientele. "While the term 'responsibility' is frequently used with a negative or even punitive connotation, we are using the term here in its more fundamental affirmative sense. Thus, before the professional can be 'held' responsible, he 'assumes' responsibility. He assumes it in taking the professional posture, and he assumes it in case after case as clients engage him.[1]"

To "respond in responsibility": the root term is *response*. The client calls upon us to design and to provide the conditions under which certain needs and desires may be fulfilled. In the spirit and quality of our response lies the opportunity for client satisfaction. And yet, while this is true for all aspects of our professional endeavor, we suggest that the proper role of the lawyer in estate planning differs in certain respects from our role in other areas of counseling. Let us consider our role in three stages: basic approach, plan design, and drafting.

[¶1101.1] Basic Approach

In advising the client in his business affairs, for example, we tend to be interested, frank, positive. This is what seems to be called for, this is the kind of people we lawyers are, and this is what the client comes to expect. When we take up his estate planning, the client expects nothing

---

[1]Gilbert M. Cantor, "The Case for Modesty in Estate Planning," American Bar Association Journal, Feb. 1961, p. 147. Reprinted with permission from the American Bar Association Journal.

less or different, and we tend to operate in the same manner. The result, however, in many cases is not the same.

If you examine a number of wills prepared by each of several lawyers, you will in all probability discern patterns. The wills of each of them will exhibit certain common substantive features. In one case there will be a recurrence of sprinkling trusts. In another the gifts or trusts will be separate and equal. A third set will feature a period of trust administration limited only by the Rule against Perpetuities, while another will favor outright distributions to beneficiaries at early ages. The wills of a fifth lawyer may emphasize restrictive trust provisions for female beneficiaries only.

If you should ask the first lawyer why many of his wills provide sprinkling trusts, he will tell you, "That's what most of my clients seem to want." The separate-trust man will say the same thing, and so will the long-term trust man and the outright-gift man and the wife-and-daughter-protector. They may be entirely honest in this response, or just slightly disingenuous.

While different client groups may have certain problems or needs that set them apart from each other, nevertheless, among client groups whose affluence is sufficient to require their lawyer to say, "We should attend to the planning of your estate," rather than, "You ought to have a will," we doubt the existence of differences that would account for the pattern of substantive preferences which we have noted.

We suggest that each lawyer's estate planning pattern reflects, to a substantial degree, his own experiences, values, judgments and preferences, which his clients seem to desire. The manner and general approach which have worked well in the area of business counseling often result in domination of the client by his lawyer when they take up the ultimate devolution of the client's worldly goods. The reasons for this are not difficult to supply.

In the first place, in this area lawyer and client are less evenly matched. In the give and take of business conferences the client can meet the lawyer's proposals and advice with the knowledge and practical experience of his regular business activities. In the area of estate planning, the client has a very limited idea of the possibilities that are available to him; he has few conceptions of the applicable tax laws and those few are most often inaccurate; and his experience of estate planning has been intermittent, if he has had any at all.

Not only is the client a comparative innocent in this field, but in many cases he exhibits a willingness to abdicate entirely if the lawyer will take over for him. He would like to be told what others do, what he should do. He behaves as if the dispositive questions posed by the lawyer are making their debut in his consciousness, as if he had never before imagined the life and needs of his family as they might follow the event of his death. As if he had not had a hundred relevant fantasies of this order just on his way to your office!

Perhaps he has turned away from these fantasies because it is painful to hold before him the single prospect which gives them meaning: the event of his death. We may speak of "lifetime planning," using the latest jargon, but it remains lifetime planning with the end in view:

> I have seen the moment of my greatness
> flicker
> And I have seen the eternal Footman hold
> my coat, and snicker,
> And in short, I was afraid.[2]

Has he also pictured his wife using his estate to support a new husband, some dapper ne'er-do-well? Or his children merrily squandering the wealth he has spent his life's energy to accumulate? Are these fantasies unbearable? And do they arouse in him feelings of hostility that he does not wish to recognize? Or has he perhaps cherished great and generous hopes and foreseen their failure when he does not remain to nourish them? We can only guess what these fantasies may have been, but we cannot believe that a mind on its way to a meeting set aside for the contemplation of his death can arrive innocent of the possibilities that must be confronted. We may surmise that the uncomfortable fantasies, though repressed, lie not too far from consciousness, and moreover, that their useful residue of impulses, wishes and thoughts may be brought into play if the lawyer does not acquiesce in the client's desire to abandon the operation to him.

Let us now face the question: why on earth should you not tell the client what he ought to do with his estate—as you might tell him with respect to a proposed lease, a new class of stock, a profit-sharing plan or anything else? Why shouldn't you take the positive and firm position that the client has come to expect of you? Why should not all of your knowledge, experience, judgment and skill be made directly and forcefully available to the helpless client? If the client is relatively ignorant, if he has strong impulses to avoid the issues himself, if he wants to know what others do, what he should do, is it not senseless cruelty for you to withhold the comforting assurance that lies so near at hand?

Everything is pushing and pulling us in the same direction. We have the apparent ability easily to supply what the client seems to need, yet we recommend that you resist all of these pressures and behave as we shall soon describe, in a different way. We urge a kind of reserve or

[2]T.S. Eliot, "The Love Song of J. Alfred Prufrock", in COLLECTED POEMS 1909-1935 (New York, Harcourt, Brace and Company, 1947), p. 15. Reprinted by permission.

modesty, for three basic reasons:

First: In the field of business counseling, as contrasted with that of estate planning, we are planning primarily for the client himself. If the welfare of anyone else is a consideration, it is his welfare through the client, or his welfare insofar as it is linked with the client's, that is involved. But in estate planning we are organizing an economic system that will affect the client not at all, or only incidentally insofar as we tinker with his assets while he is alive. The primary impact of our work will fall upon others, the beneficiaries who will have to live with it when the testator is gone. Yet these beneficiaries, whose lives and relationships may be drastically affected, have ordinarily no voice in what is done. They may even be, for planning purposes, virtually unknown to us.

Have then we the right—is it not arrogance—to intrude our own values, preferences and biases into the plan for these people? How shocked some beneficiaries might be to dicover in what shortness of time, on what terms, and by whose formulation their testamentary rights and interests were determined!

Second: Let us contrast business planning with estate planning in yet another way. In the theatre of commerce, the client's objectives can ordinarily be assumed. In the equation of his business career, the goal is "the given," only the path is "the unknown." The client is economic man and we are projecting his interests in a competitive situation, helping him to preserve his gains and to grow as against the multiple forces of attrition. But when we turn to the eventual devolution of his property, the man whom we have known so well, to whom we have related so effectively in his business affairs, becomes a stranger to us—a stranger in the sense that we now have no working idea of his objectives. In the equation of his estate planning the goal and the path are both unknowns.

Often, indeed, the client seems unable to help us beyond the vaguest generalities. He wishes to give his heirs the greatest possible enjoyment of his estate. But what follows from that? He may wish to treat the members of his family fairly. Does this imply equality? How do you confer equal benefits upon people whose circumstances and capacities are not alike? Or does fairness imply that adjustments are to be made for merit or the lack of it? What then is merit and how does one measure its proper claims? Does the client mention justice as a prelude to petty revenge? Is someone to receive "protection" which smacks of punishment? We do not mean that the client is to be psychoanalyzed, unmasked or judged. We suggest only that the goals of estate planning are his goals, and therefore, he should be brought to the point of decision.

And third: As soon as we get down to the substantive details of the estate plan, we recognize or should recognize—that we have gone beyond the area in which we have superior knowledge. We do have superior knowledge of the types of gifts that can be made and of their tax consequences, but for predicting what other advantages or harms will flow from different approaches or choices we have less knowledge than we sometimes admit. We may have convictions and strong feelings as to how a family's wealth should be divided, held or distributed, and what harmful effects should be avoided. But if we are honest with ourselves, and then with the client, we recognize that most of our judgments are based on cases or incidents that have had dramatic impact on us either because they were extreme or because they involved us. Our generalizations have no statistical corroboration, and even if they had, even if we could say, for example, "giving a young man a large amount of money generally has a bad effect on his character, and moreover, he is likely to lose it," nevertheless, our generalization has less pertinency in predicting for the testator's particular family than his intimate lifetime knowledge of the persons involved. Besides, may he not prefer to grant the opportunity to do something important as against the danger to character, may he not prefer the challenge to wisdom and maturity as against the risk of loss?

All of these considerations lead to the same conclusion, that your true and proper purpose should be to discover and implement the client's testamentary desires and not to foist your preferences upon him—even if he asks you to.

In myriad cases the courts have said: "In the construction of wills the great general and controlling rule is that the intent of the testator shall prevail."[3] Should not the same rule apply at the planning stage? We suggest it should, with this single but significant qualification, namely, that since the testator's intent is then still viable, we have the duty to insure that it will be an informed intent, for a choice made in ignorance is no choice at all. Thus we are in the position of a government which submits an issue to popular election though it also controls the media of education and communication. Without the most delicate balance and restraint, this is tyranny.

We may have sound general ideas as to how property should devolve as a matter of economics or sociology. Such notions, however, should be taken to the legislature, and not directed at particular clients. We might, to reflect on an analogous situation, think that long-term capital gains should be taxed as ordinary income, but we would not urge our clients to complete their tax returns in that way as long as the law is otherwise. The right to dispose of property in accordance with one's will is neither unlimited nor constitutionally guaranteed. But to the extent

[3]*Woelpper's Appeal*, 126 Pa. 526, 572 (1889).

the law empowers a person freely to dispose of his estate, we have no right to crush this freedom under the weight of our professional wisdom.

We have a great power in this relationship, but in consideration of the client's proper freedom, the rights of the unrepresented heirs, and our basic inability to supply another man's goals and to assure their attainment, we suggest that this power should be exercised with the most self-conscious restraint.

It is our job, then, fairly to give the client the information he needs, and to present the possibilities available to him. We should be as frank with him in these matters as we are in his other affairs, but the frankness will have a different content. We should frankly explain to him why he alone can make the essential choices involved in his estate plan. And we should proceed to discover the client's thoughts, preferences and goals. We suggested earlier that the client may not be as innocent and helpless as he appears, that he has doubtless "put out of his mind" innumerable fantasies which involve his fears and wishes relating to the life of his family and to disposition of his wealth after his death. If you are persistent, a considerable fund of this testamentary material may become available. If the client is compelled to face the issues and to make the necessary decisions, we submit that these decisions will not be as superficial or "off the cuff" as they may appear.

You should undertake not to solve the testator's estate planning problems, but to make possible their intelligent solution by the testator. If you approach the planning with the modest restraint that we have urged, and if you receive the client's ideas with an open mind, you may have the benefit of a broader range of experience which will multiply the possibilities available to your clients of the future.

[¶1101.2]   How to Design A Plan

With the client's basic goals in mind, your next task is to design a plan for the implementation of these goals. This involves, of course, not merely the design of documents which will govern the devolution of property after death, but also the arrangements and possible transfer of property during lifetime, both for lifetime and after-death purposes. The accumulation, rearrangement and disposition of the client's resources must be considered.

The lifetime purposes of estate planning may include some or all of the following:

(a) Facilitating the disposition of property.
(b) Altering the distribution of income or the proceeds of sale of property.

(c) Minimizing taxes on the income or proceeds of sale of property.
(d) Providing for the event of retirement or disability.
(e) Diversification of assets and resources.
(f) Protection of property from claims of creditors.
(g) The pursuit of charitable or philanthropic goals.
(h) Various family objectives, such as the education of children or grandchil-
     dren, or the support of dependent parents.

After-death objectives of our planning may include:

(a) Assuring the financial security of surviving spouse, descendants, or
     heirs, and various particular objectives for them.
(b) Provision for disposition or continuation of a business, possibly including
     the employment or other involvement of family members.
(c) The pursuit of charitable or philanthropic goals.
(d) Simplifying estate administration.
(e) Minimization of estate and inheritance taxes.

The listed objectives, of course, are not separate but are interrelated in various ways, and an overarching goal is the development of a suitable accomodation among conflicting and competing aims.

Estate tax saving, the object of this volume, is listed last but will in most cases have a serious impact on the form and content of the overall design and its implementation. This impact is not a simple and single one. On one hand, the saving of taxes enlarges the resources available for the pursuit of various family and philanthropic ends. On the other hand, the tax saving techniques available in a particular case—a gift program, the creation of generation-skipping trusts, and so on—may conflict in some degree with personal desires and philosophies of the client. This requires the sorting out of priorities and, in some case, the articulation of a satisfactory compromise.

In working toward the accommodation of conflicting or competing estate planning aims, we can helpfully be guided and give some guidance to our clients by attending to several principles which are inherent in the trite expression: "It's only money." The first implication of this aphorism is that financial resources and legal documents cannot be expected to do the jobs of education, training, and character development. The complex and restrictive provisions that can be written into wills, trusts, and insurance settlements cannot adequately substitute for the thoughtful training of one's beneficiaries in the responsible management and use of their resources and expectancies.

The second implication of the adage, for our purposes, is that our clients should not strain to do absolute justice with their wordly goods. By and large, we should avoid planning for infinitely delicate readjustments of income and shares of trust principal, for example, based on all conceivable contingencies extending into the distant future. Rather than justice or equality, such complexities are likely to create misunderstandings, ambiguities, and administrative difficulties, and may even pave the way for wasteful litigation. Equality of distribution, indeed, does not guarantee equality of benefit; life is too complex and varied for that.

The third and most important meaning for us of the concept "It's only money" is that we should not allow tax-saving concerns to overwhelm our clients and ourselves. The temptation to do so arises partly from the fact that of all the estate planning objectives tax saving alone is susceptible of computation and demonstration. Utilizing the techniques described in the preceding ten chapters, we can in most cases produce substantial tax savings. The numbers are clear and impressive. In a relatively stable situation the projected results are highly reliable. And the measures which the savings dictate are difficult to resist.

Indeed, the pursuit of tax savings can become a kind of game, an endless battle of wits in which any money received by the Government is tacitly regarded as money down the drain. We can become so fascinated with the process of threading our way through the complexities of the tax laws, to save the ultimate penny from the Government's grasp, that we forget we are planning for the benefit of particular human beings.

A number of countervailing considerations should always be kept in mind. One of them is the fact that our clients vary considerably in their capacities to comprehend and comfortably to endure sophisticated tax analysis and complicated property arrangements. Life is aleady too complex for many of us, and the pursuit of tax savings, if carried too far, can add painfully to its complication. A program of inter vivos gifts, multiple family trusts, business recapitalization, and so on, may be utterly fascinating to one client. It may impose on another a diminished conception of his own resources and the extent to which he has retained or yielded control of them. The question in each case is whether the tax saving involved justifies the means employed.

Another countervailing consideration is that of the beneficiaries' freedom and autonomy. Where the choice, for example, lies between an outright marital deduction gift and a "power of appointment" trust, the value of the surviving spouse's freedom and autonomy with respect to this portion of the estate, as provided by the outright gift, may outweigh the additional savings of state inheritance tax and administration expenses which may be attained through use of the trust. On the other hand, the interest in various aspects of protection and security for the surviving spouse will reinforce the tax oriented selection of the trust.

These observations may appear, at first, to represent a radical retrenchment on the authors' part, following ten chapters devoted to the vigorous pursuit of estate tax savings. Actually, our intent here is simply to put the matter of estate tax saving into its proper human perspective. It is an essential part of our professional responsibility in estate planning to be aware of the available tax saving techniques and their proper application, and also fully to inform our clients with respect to their planning options and their probable tax "value." But, as we stated earlier in this chapter, *client satisfaction* is our primary goal and the ultimate measure of our professional effort. In our experience, the truly satisfied or "happy" client is one who recognizes that *all* of his concerns have been carefully explored and thoughtfully met, utilizing those tax saving techniques, but only those, *which will significantly advance his basic objectives.*

The plan we design, of course, must have an adequate factual foundation. We must have complete and accurate family data and asset and liability information. Our client (together with his accountant, insurance counselor, and other advisors) is the primary source. He should be asked to complete a comprehensive estate planning questionnaire, which counsel should design for this purpose. Adequate questionnaires can sometimes be obtained from accounting firms, banks, or insurance companies.

In addition to the completed questionnaire, our client should be asked to furnish the following documents or copies of them:

(a) Deeds to all real estate in which he has an interest.
(b) Antenuptial or postnuptial agreements, and separation or divorce agreements and decrees in which he or his spouse is involved.
(c) All policies of insurance on the life of the client and his spouse.
(d) Partnership agreements, stock redemption agreements, and buy-sell agreements to which the client or his spouse is a party.
(e) Pension plans, profit-sharing plans, ESOPs, stock options, deferred compensation agreements, and employment agreements involving the client or his spouse as a participant or a party.
(f) Inter vivos trust instruments involving the client or his spouse as a grantor, trustee or beneficiary, and decedents' wills under which the client or his spouse is a trustee or beneficiary.
(g) Current wills and codicils of the client and his spouse.
(h) Balance sheets and income statements for last five fiscal years of each closely held business in which the client or his spouse has a financial interest.
(i) Individual or joint income tax returns for the last three years.
(j) All gift tax returns which have been filed by the client or his spouse.

Whenever the situation permits, we suggest that the client be asked to complete and furnish all of this information and documentation *in advance of your initial conference,* for several reasons:

First: The review of this data will give you a preliminary view of the client's entire situation and the planning opportunities that may be worth exploring. This preview will also enable you to estimate and predict for the client the counsel fee, or the potential range of fees, in which your work for him may fall according to your firm's fee schedule.

Second: In most cases, your inquiry will exceed in breadth and depth anything that the client will have experienced in prior estate planning or will-drafting episodes. He will perceive that he is initiating a process that will be thorough and comprehensive.

Third: Your initial conference will be one in which you are relatively well informed. Rather than spend the time in superficial inquiries, you can clear up any omissions, ambiguities or apparent conflicts in the data you have received and then concentrate on discovering your client's basic concerns, objectives, and attitudes. Indeed, it may not be amiss, in requesting the preliminary data, to advise your client that you are asking him to collect and organize the necessary materials on his own in order to avoid spending your valuable (expensive) professional time on such clerical tasks as the listing of assets and liabilities.

There is a great deal to be learned about the client in the initial interview, so that we recommend that the estate planner work in this phase primarily with his ears rather than his mouth. We need to develop quickly and accurately a picture not only of the client's articulated concerns and goals, but also his relationships with his family, and his partners or employees, if any. Also, his attitudes toward his estate in general and particular assets, and the extent or degree of his intelligence, sophistication, generosity, personal security, and other attributes.

Some of the emerging material may be utilized for purposes of a will or trust preamble, as described below, but it will serve primarily to guide us in developing a plan that represents not merely a tax saving scheme for a client in the abstract but rather a set of measures suitable in all respects to this particular person. We may wish to touch all the bases, so to speak, and even to mention all of the techniques which we have considered for their potential applicability to the client's situation, but our emphasis and recommendations should involve those elements which are compatible with the philosophy, attitudes, and life style of the client whom we are learning to know.

The accumulated data and our intitial recommendations should be embodied in a complete estate planning memorandum. Samples of two such memoranda appear in Appendix A. These involve the planning for a father and son who have interests in the same business enterprise.

While our tax-saving projections are normally based on current data as to the client's assets and liabilities, we can in appropriate cases also project the long-term impact of our recommendations. Where, for example, the client has an investment portfolio, the income of which he expects to save and reinvest over the years, we can compute the value of his estate as augmented through that program over the client's life expectancy and then recompute the estate tax impact of our suggestions as applied to his augmented estate.

If, for example, the client's gross estate has a $200,000 investment-savings element of the type described, and if the client is fifty years of age and has a twenty-three year life expectancy, and if a 7 percent growth factor appears to be a reasonable assumption, the $200,000 portfolio will have an estimated value of $948,000 at the end of the twenty-three year period. The tax projections, recomputed on that basis, will be more impressive in a dramatically heightened degree. Included in Appendix B is a table of "Estate Projections" for the life expectancies of males, showing the value at the end of life expectancy per $100,000 of current value, assuming growth rates of 5 percent, 7 percent, and 9 percent over the periods involved.

The estate planning memorandum, properly done, serves several purposes:

1. It gives the client an opportunity to correct any erroneous impression you may have received with respect to the factual data involved.

2. If mailed to the client in advance of discussion, it helps him to prepare for the necessary review and improves the quality of that review.

3. It provides an agenda for orderly coverage of the planning elements.

4. It forces you to make complete and accurate tax computation and appropriate judgments as affected by their outcome.

5. It shifts the emphasis from the ultimate documents (wills, etc.) to the planning process, which is the heart of the matter. [It also strengthens the client's case for deducting a major portion of your fee for tax planning services, a subject discussed below.]

6. It demonstrates to the client, in a clear and impressive way, the quality and the quantity of the work you have done and for which your fee will be appropriate as well as substantial.

7. For future reference, it provides for the client and you, and for any other advisers who may be involved, a record of the ideas and techniques that were considered, as well as the reasons for your recommending those which will finally have been adopted.

[¶1101.3]   Drafting An Instrument

Having considered our basic approach, and the matter of plan design, let us turn to the subject of the drafting of instruments. Some of our tax saving techniques, of course, can be accomplished by the client without our assistance, e.g., gifts made by delivery of bearer bonds or the issuance of a check. Others may require documentation of a simple, formal nature, e.g., a deed, stock assignment form, or annuity contract.

But our work will commonly include wills and trust instruments which are extensive and to a significant degree drafted for each client.

These drafting assignments, representing the implementation of at least a significant portion of our planning endeavor, involve a challenge and an opportunity of a very high order. We agree with the authors of a book on will drafting: "A lawyer never faces a more intellectually demanding, or a more spiritually rewarding task than the drafting of a will." If the job is undertaken with the attitude and the goals we are suggesting, this will frequently be true.

Earlier in this chapter, we stated that client satisfaction is at once the goal and the measure of our professional effort. We alluded next to the subject of responsibility, and the root word "response," stating that the spirit and quality of our response to the client's needs and drives hold the key to client satisfaction. Let us now consider a third related concept, that of *style*.

An effective response to any situation involves, for the professional as for others, two intertwined elements: (a) power and (b) style. The basic need is the *power* to attain the desired end. "The first thing," as Whitehead tells us, "is to get there . . . solve your problem, justify the ways of God to man, administer your province, or do whatever else is set before you."[4] In estate planning terms, the power to accomplish major tax-saving (and hence estate preservation) results may be derived from the first ten chapters of this book.

But what of the "style" of that accomplishment? What do we mean by style, and how does it relate to our professional responsibility? Let Pascal, a renowned "stylist," point the way:

"Let no one say that I have said nothing new; the arrangement of the subject is new. When we play tennis, we both play with the same ball, but one of us places it better."

"Eloquence is an art of saying things in such a way-(1) that those to whom we speak may listen to them without pain and with pleasure; (2) that they feel themselves interested, so that self-love leads them more willingly to reflection upon it."[5]

The nature or meaning of style is presented even more plainly by Whitehead:

"Style in art, style in literature, style in science, style in logic, style in practical execution have fundamentally the same aesthetic qualities,

[4]Whitehead, Alfred North, *The Aims of Education and Other Essays* (The Free Press, New York, 1967), p. 12. Reprinted by permission.
[5]From Pascal's *Pensees*, by Blaise Pascal, translated by W.F. Trotter. Published by E.P. Dutton, New York, 1958, pp. 6-7, and reprinted with their permission.

namely, attainment and restraint . . .

"Style, in its finest sense, is the last acquirement of the educated mind; it is also the most useful. It pervades the whole being. The administrator with a sense for style hates waste; the engineer with a sense for style economises his material; the artisan with a sense for style prefers good work. Style is the ultimate morality of mind.

". . . with style the end is attained without side issues . . . With style your power is increased, for your mind is not distracted with irrelevancies, and you are more likely to attain your object. Now style is the exclusive privilege of the expert. Whoever heard of the style of an amateur painter, the style of an amateur poet? Style is always the product of specialist study, the peculiar contribution of specialism to culture."[6]

Style, then involves economy of means; it is the cutting edge of power; as such, it is the key to effectiveness, in our profession as in the arts.

To prepare a will, of course, is not the work of an artist, yet there are esthetic considerations. The relation of the form or manner of expression to its meaning is so intimate that these considerations may not be ignored as matters of decoration or embellishment.[7]

In the drafting of wills we are insistently made aware of two outstanding characteristics of the human condition: isolation and mortality. Neither of these presents itself only in this context but each of them has a special impact on the approach to testamentary language.

First, human isolation: by which we mean the inability ever wholly to communicate anything to anybody; the lamentable extent to which each person, whether he breaks into a dance, bursts forth in song, writes eighty volumes of words, or lunges with a bayonet, remains always and irretrievably an island.

"We start then from the natural isolation and severance of minds. Their experience at best, under the most favorable circumstances, can be but similar."[8]

In our efforts to communicate the testator's plan, which is to become effective at his death, we do not have the most favorable circumstances, even as compared with other legal drafting situations. This for three reasons: first, the lapse of time between the drafting and the publication of the will; second, the departure of the communicant prior

[6]Whitehead, *op. cit.*, pp. 12-13.

[7]"For we are blundering into an old and absurd quarrel when we try to consider 'form' apart from 'matter'; the truth is that they are, or should be, the same thing." Andre Gide, *Imaginary Interviews*, translated by Malcom Cowley (Alfred A. Knopf, New York, 1949), pp. 38-39. Reprinted by permission.

[8]I.A. Richards, *Principles of Literary Criticism* (Routledge & Kegan Paul Ltd., London, 1948), p. 177. Reprinted by permission.

to publication of his words; and third, the fact that the will, at the time of its preparation, has not ordinarily the benefit of a truly hostile scrutiny.

We must, therefore, make a sepcial effort to achieve clarity and precision in the testamentary language. We are all aware of the failures: the many contests involving the construction of wills and the many occasions on which counsel, in presenting the account of an executor or trustee, asks the court to confirm the accountant's interpretation of the will. Some of these, of course, are failures of imagination, failures to anticipate the changes in assets, in survival, and in human relationships, that the future holds in store; others, however, result from opacity of the language used.

If one drafts a provision that contains several exceptions, provisos, counter-provisos, and, perhaps cross-allusions among the parts, there is likelihood of omission or of harmful ambiguity. It would be better, even if repetitious, to present in extended series the alternative situations which such a provision is designed to encompass, than so to condense and interpolate as to sacrifice clarity.

One sometimes reads a clause relating to the incidence and adjustment of succession taxes, or the powers of the fiduciary with respect to assets of an estate or trust, expressed with elaborate complexity. In such cases, its justification in the mind of the draftsman can only have been that from such an ample jumble of verbiage he would eventually be able to draw whatever authorizations might be needed. The pitfall is evident.

In the interest of precision, I think we should consider it axiomatic that there are not two ways of expressing exactly the same thing. "Slightly alter the expression and you slightly alter the idea . . . A writer, having conceived and expressed an idea, may and probably will, 'polish it up'. But what does he polish up? To say that he polishes up his style is merely to say that he is polishing up his idea, that he has discovered faults or imperfections in his idea, and is perfecting it."[9]

Second, human mortality. Of course, we require of a will that it be effective to carry out the plan that the testator has adopted and that it do so with the least possible diminution of the estate through avoidable taxes and expenses of administration. Beyond this, however, a will, like any other expression, should be suited to the occasion that calls it forth. In the case of a will, that occasion is death and bereavement. It is fitting, then, that a will be expressed with dignity, grace and order.

A will is more than an instrument for disposing of interests in property, like a deed or mortgage. It is also a final communication delivered to the testator's family at a sensitive, sometimes a crucial, time. From the standpoint of the family the effect of the will may be divisive

[9] Arnold Bennett, *Literary Taste*, (Penguin Books Limited, England, 1939), p. 64. Reprinted by permission of A.P. Watt & Son, London.

and disastrous, at one extreme, or soothing and sustaining, at the other. Consideration of these possibilities is part of the responsibility of the draftsman. It is, consequently, important that in spite of the various technical expressions that a lawyer may consider to be essential, the will should remain recognizably a human document.

This is not to say that will should be conversational in tone, but rather than it should reflect something of the testator's pattern of thought and feeling. Something of his personal philosophy, of his individuality, should be perceptible. If this can rarely be achieved in significant measure, perhaps for this reason it provides a suitable ideal. To the extent that this ideal can be attained, the draftsman will not only have created a more satisfying instrument for the testator and his family, but in many cases he will also have reinforced the substantive effectiveness of the will.

If we cannot ordinarily closet ourselves with a client for weeks, as William J. Duane is said to have done with Stephen Girard, to discuss "cabbages and kings," we can at least permit a testator whom we do not know intimately to ramble on a little about his proposed arrangements. We can encourage him to express some of his thoughts about the essential decisions throughout the planning stage. Then, in drafting, we can give appropriate emphasis to matters that most deeply concern him.

Too often a comment suggested by the testator is rejected on the ground that his meaning is implicit in the substantive language of our dispositive provision. Or that his thought relates to property that does not pass as part of the testamentary estate. The rejected statement might have made the scheme of distribution more sensible to the testator's family and even to the testator himself. In preserving the austere formality of a will, we may give up something of real if unmeasurable value.

Of course, a variety of pressures militate against the development of wills that are "personalized" to a significant degree: the time pressures that afflict lawyers at least as much as others; the need to keep fees at a reasonable level; the myriad technical provisions dictated by the complexities of modern tax laws; and also the natural inclination to repeat what we have done before rather than to create and to innovate. Nevertheless, the creation of a distinctly individual document should continue to be the goal.

In a recent magazine article, a New York Circuit Judge was quoted as saying; "The average will today is a few pages of dry legal phraseology, airtight, impersonal and dull. All those wills we used to see in the old days, the ones that sounded human and gave you an interesting reflection of the personality of the man who wrote it—what's happened to them?" With the exception of the word "few," we agree with the judge's lament.

One of the wills which the judge cited as a will worth reading was that of the late John B. Kelly of Philadelphia. When Kelly's will was probated a few years ago and quoted in the newspapers, requests for copies flooded the office of the Register of Wills, who had the will reproduced in response to the popular demand. Kelly's will began with the following recital:

> "For years I have been reading Last Wills and Testaments, and I have never been able to clearly understand any of them at one reading. Therefore, I will attempt to write my own will with the hope that it will be understandable and legal. Kids will be called "kids" and not "issue", and it will not be cluttered up with "parties of the first part", "per stirpes", "perpetuties", "quasi judicial", "to wit" and a lot of ther terms that I am sure are only used to confuse those for whose benefit it is written.
>
> "This is my Last Will and Testament and I believe I am of sound mind. (Some lawyers will question this when they read my Will, however, I have my opinion of some of them, so that makes it even.)" And so on.

Actually, we suspect that Mr. Kelly's recital of his own draftsmanship may have been slightly disingenous though no less charming for that, as subsequent portions of his will contain technical clauses in precisely the kind of language that lawyers commonly employ. The will appears to be an unusually happy blend of individual expression and legal attention, producing a result which has received wide approbation.

Of course, the client or the lawyer who has a flair for that kind of thing is relatively rare. The Kelly Will required a personality and a touch than cannot be forced. Nevertheless, even without the humor of that particular example, a distinctly personal flavor or imprint can sometimes be provided by means of a brief "preamble" to the document. In cases in which the client has been fairly articulate with regard to his philosophy or his goals, we have sometimes written them into a kind of foreword which, with any changes or additions the client may offer, tells those concerned something about the thoughts behind the bequests and the technicalities. An example (with names altered):

> "These introductory paragraphs, which are designated as a Preamble, are intended to provide for my beneficiaries, and for those charged with the administration of my estate and trusts, an understanding of certain basic ideas and attitudes that underlie the design of my estate plan as embodied principally in my will and The John Smith Irrevocable Trust.
>
> "The primary objects of my concern, as the documents reflect, are my wife, Helen, and my three children, Harry, Walter, and Susan. It is my

intent that Helen, if she survives me, shall have such protection and benefits as she may need for the balance of her lifetime. Having provided for my children to the best of my ability in their earlier years, including the opportunity and encouragement of each to pursue such education as he or she might wish, I have for the most part deferred the 'inheritance' which my children may anticipate until such time as my wife and I are both deceased.

"On the other hand, I do not wish to prolong unduly the benefits which my children are to receive from my estate. Accordingly, I have included in my will a provision whereby Helen can, with certain restrictions, make gifts of principal to or for the benefit of my children and grandchildren. And in my irrevocable trust I have permitted my Trustees to make distributions to or for the benefit of my children and grandchildren even during Helen's lifetime. In each case, however, it is my assumption and my intent that such distributions will be made only if and to the extent that Helen's security for the balance of her life, for her comfortable maintenance and for any emergencies that may arise, will clearly be protected.

"It is hoped that the foregoing comments will be helpful to those concerned. This Preamble is not intended to modify in any way the provisions of the above-mentioned trust or the succeeding provisions of my Will, nor shall it be used for purposes of legal interpretation of either document."

Another example, this one taken from an Indenture of Trust rather than a Will, reproduced here without the opening and closing paragraphs (which are similar to those of the preamble quoted above):

"The primary objects of the Grantor's concern are his wife, MARY HAMILTON, and their sons, WALTER HAMILTON and FRED HAMILTON, and the children of WALTER and FRED. The fact that the Grantor's wife is not designated as a major beneficiary of the Grantor's estate reflects no lack of love and affection for her, but simply the fact that her own income and resources are quite ample for her maintenance in health and comfort, and it is her wish also that the Grantor's estate be disposed of primarily for the benefit of the children and other descendants of the Grantor and his wife.

"The Grantor's sons also have participated in the development of the estate plan represented by the mentioned documents, and their ideas have contributed to the planning process, in keeping with the relationship which has been developed in the Hamilton family over the years as well as the Grantor's desire to adopt an arrangement for property devolution which is, insofar as possible, in harmony with the ideas, objectives and circumstances of the succeeding generation. It is the Grantor's hope and expectation that the trusts which are established under this Indenture for his sons and their families will be understood and utilized not as restrictive devices but rather as vehicles to advance the happiness and well-being of the trust beneficiaries.

"A word also with regard to the gifts to charitable beneficiaries provided below. The selection of the mentioned organizations reflects in part the Grantor's lifetime work and interest in the field of medicine, but primarily his desire to contribute to the work of organizations which have a broad educational impact in the community, especially with young people, opening up to them interests and life possibilities that might otherwise elude them."

In each such case, the document is raised to a new level in terms of communication to the client's beneficiaries. It also raises the document to a new level of satisfaction for the client, for whom the whole matter is thus "pulled together" in a few paragraphs, and who perceives that someone has paid attention to him and has enabled him to express himself in a major, and possibly the final, document or documents of his life.

A more subtle but also helpful measure toward the same end is the arrangement of the testamentary provisions so that the matters which are of most immediate interest to the client—his estate "personnel" (executors, trustees, guardians) and his dispositive provisions are placed "up front" and the "technicalities" (marital deduction formula, tax clause, management powers, etc.) are relegated to the back pages. The documents appended to this book reflect such arrangements.

[¶1102]   PLANNING FEES VS. ESTATE FEES

Early in their legal careers we were informed by our elders that it was customary to charge small or nominal fees—in some cases no fees at all—for estate planning or will drafting because the lawyer who prepared the will would in due course represent the estate. The fee for this would be more than adequate to cover the earlier efforts as well. The "logic" of this approach was selfreinforcing, in the sense that clients became accustomed to small fees and would presumably come to regard a reasonable fee for estate planning as outrageous.

Fortunately for our clients as well as ourselves, a number of social and professional developments have opened the way for a realistic fee system. (A number of firms and practitioners still cling to the old way, nevertheless.) Among the developments helping to bring about the change have been these:

1. Increasing mobility. In a geographic sense, our clients are much more mobile than they were a few decades ago. Executives are transferred frequently, businessmen pursue opportunities wherever they arise, and even professionals evince an unwonted readiness to relocate. And within the community, it is our impression that clients have much more mobility among their professional counselors than was formerly

the case. There has been a loosening of traditional ties and old loyalties. Professionals, like the suppliers of other services and goods, are regarded as essentially competitive and replaceable. As a consequence we find, for example, that a substantial number of the decedents' estates in administration in our firm involve wills prepared elsewhere. We assume that a corresponding number of our estate planning clients will become clients of other firms. In these circumstances, the preparation of a will is far from binding as to the engagement of estate counsel.

2. Estate fee limitations. Traditionally, counsel fees in connection with estate administration have been set (whether by bar associations or lawyers) in terms of a percentage of the value of the estate. The percentage normally diminishes as the value of the estate increases but substantial estates provide substantial fees on this basis. If a fee of $10,000 or $20,000 or $90,000 lies ahead in the foreseeable future, who can blame the attorney who fears to jeopardize it by charging a large estate planning fee?

But two clouds have drifted over the estate fee scene. There has been mounting criticism of the percentage fees. Despite the talk of the "responsibility" involved, it has become increasingly difficult for courts and others to perceive why fees for estate legal services should not be related primarily to the amount of professional time involved. On the other side of the coin, so to speak, modern time-record systems disclose that in many if not most cases, at least in our firm's experience, our substantial estate percentage fees are actually earned on a time basis.

From either vantage point, it becomes clear that the postulated cushion or profit in estate counsel fees, which should make up for the years of low-fee estate planning, is or will soon be fictional or illusory.

3. Consequences of effective estate planning. Anyone who has read the preceding chapters will recognize that the successful application of our tax saving techniques will tend to reduce the client's gross estate and also his probate estate. Whichever you may take as the base for estate counsel fee computation, the reduced estate will yield a reduced percentage fee. As a result, the attorney who seeks to be compensated by the estate for his lifetime estate planning efforts is working at cross-purposes with himself.

The conflict of interest is readily apparent. The greater the attorney's estate planning success—through an annual gift program, irrevocable life insurance trust, private annuity, etc.—the less will be his eventual compensation. Indeed, if he were wholly successful he would receive no compensation at all from the decedent's estate.

4. Impact of compensation deferral. Just as the conflict mentioned in the preceding paragraph carries a negative incentive to effective estate planning, so does the bare fact of compensation deferral. The op-

portunity to receive a presumably substantial estate fee at some date in the indefinite future, subject to a variety of intervening hazards, necessarily creates pressure on the busy attorney to do the presentable minimum at the estate planning stage.

Such a system is simply wrong. It erodes professional responsibility. It is unfair to the client and to his attorney. The system can and must be abandoned. Current services should be currently and adequately compensated, and rare indeed, in our experience, is the client who thinks otherwise when the subject is properly presented. The client who thinks otherwise can and should be abandoned if he cannot be converted.

[¶1103]   **SUGGESTED FEE SCHEDULE**

We suggested near the beginning of this chapter that the fees for estate planning services should reflect a mix of the following elements: (1) time involved; (2) taxes saved; (3) originality and creativity; and (4) client satisfaction. But how do we translate these generalities into a fee schedule?

We did the translation for our firm mainly by working backward from the final estate planning documents. Ignoring special items, such as deeds, annuity contracts, and others, we recognized easily that our clients' documentation would normally fall into several categories— simple wills, wills with marital and nonmarital trusts, wills with revocable inter vivos trusts, wills with irrevocable trusts, etc. Each such documentary classification would involve, in turn, a corresponding extent and complexity of the estate planning memorandum, number and duration of conferences with client, and follow-up activities with banks, insurers, and the like.

Having made that classification, we then selected several typical clients in each category and reviewed the clients' time records. This review gave us a figure for each category that would provide a fee or fee range appropriate at least for the average client whose estate planning would fall in that zone.

For the case that is exceptional in its time requirements because the client is unusually discursive or indecisive, we reserve the right to charge for the unanticipated hours. For the case that is exceptional in the sense that a great and unusual result can be attained by a very simple device, as, for example, where we accomplish large tax savings by use of a private annuity, our fee schedule permits a special charge which relates rather to our special knowledge and creativity than to our time involvement.

The fee schedule produced in this way, which we offer for your consideration, is the following:

Suggested Fee Schedule

Estate and Tax Planning

Codicil to will (1-2 pages)	$ 40.00
Tax planning; simple will- reciprocal will for spouse	200.00
Tax planning; will with one or two trusts—simple will for spouse	500.00 to $750.00
Tax planning; pour-over will and revocable life insurance trust— simple will for spouse	750.00 to $1,000.00
Tax planning; will with marital deduction provisions and pour-over residuary gift, with irrevocable life insurance trust— simple will for spouse	1,800.00 to $3000.00
Ten-year or minority trust	400.00
Family foundation (passive)— prepare and qualify	600.00
Family foundation (active—prepare and qualify	1,200.00
Additional billing at hourly rates for asset transfers, joint ownership termin- ations, preparation of gift tax returns, and other supplemental services.	

One of the merits of this fee schedule, apart from the amounts involved, is that it can usefully be shown to the client in many cases. The client will quickly recognize that his fee is being set in accordance with some kind of system, and not arbitrarily or by whim. He will also perceive that the charge is keyed to the documentation involved and the effort behind it and is not simply a "tax" levied according to the size of his estate.

[¶1104]   **WHEN AND HOW TO DISCUSS FEES**
WITH CLIENT

When should the estate planning fee be discussed with the client? Without exception, at the first meeting. All of your rationalizations for deferring that discussion—he's an old client; he's a new client; it's too crass; etc.—should be rejected.

The client has a right to know, and he wants to know, at least approximately how much this endeavor will cost and when he will be expected to pay. And the lawyer has a right to know, and should want to know, that the client is aware of the fee and agrees to pay it. Any other approach is a silly game which is likely to lead in some cases to bad feelings and in others to financial loss.

The fee discussion may usefully include, as prelude or supplement to the statement of amount, the following educational elements:

1. As emphasized above, the fee includes necessary documents (wills, etc.), but the charge is primarily for tax planning, which will involve many hours of professional time in computations, in the preparation of a memorandum of your recommendations and the reasons for them, and in conferences with the client for analysis, decision-making, and document review.

2. The client and his family and their resources are in a sense analogous to a business enterprise. They have assets and liabilities, income and expenses, and taxes of various kinds, and yet they engage only sporadically, if at all, in the kind of professional counseling that even a modest business enterprise commonly obtains on an on-going basis. Our effort in estate planning may be viewed as a comparable effort to put the family's economic affairs in order.

3. As a third way of saying the same thing, the estate-planning enterprise is not a matter of listing gifts for distribution of whatever will be left when the client is deceased—as in mere will writing. The effort, rather, is *to increase what will be left and to enhance the ultimate utility of it.*

[¶1105]   WHEN SHOULD FEES BE BILLED?

The estate-planning fee should be paid in installments over the period in which the services are performed. In our experience, this normally lasts two to four months. Our clients readily accept the notion that their payments and our labors should move forward together. They frequently consider it helpful to have a period over which to pay the fee in installments.

This billing arrangement should be explained as part of the initial fee discussion. It may be confirmed by a letter accompanied by a bill for the first installment. It has several advantages for the lawyer or law firm:

1. It virtually eliminates collection problems. You no longer spend hundreds or thousands of dollars worth of professional time only to discover that the client, though pleased with your work, has more pressing demands on his financial resources. And when a client whose pay-

ments are delayed finds that your progress also is delayed, a very useful silent communication has taken place.

2. The pay-as-you-go system also improves the firm's cash flow, relieving the lawyer of the burden of financing his client's legal expenses. Under the old system, still widely followed, in which completion of the work is followed by billing and eventual payment, not infrequently the inception of services and the receipt of payment are separated by a period of six months to one year. As the use of money is itself expensive, the fees charged in that system are obviously worth substantially less than face value.

[¶1106]   **HOW SHOULD FEES BE BILLED**

We suggest that the final statement be issued in a form which will reflect the nature of the services rendered; the total fee involved; the payments which have been made and the balance due; and the portion of the fee which you consider to be deductible for income tax purposes. A typical final statement might be as follows:

[Name and address of client]	[Date]
Tax planning; preparation of wills	$800.00*
Payments on account	600.00
Balance	$200.00

  *Of this amount, $640.00 is attributable to the tax planning portion of the services rendered and may properly be deducted for income tax purposes.

Section 212 of the Code provides:

"In the case of an individual, there will be allowed as a deduction all the ordinary and necessary expenses paid or incurred during the taxable year—

"(1). for the production or collection of income;

"(2). for the management, conservation, or maintenance of property held for the production of income; or

"(3). in connection with the determination, collection, or refund of any tax."

Reg. Sec. 1.212-1 (1) provides:

"(e) Expenses paid or incurred by an individual in connection with the determination, collection, or refund of any tax, whether the taxing authority be Federal, State, or municipal, and whether the tax be income, estate, gift, property, or any other tax, are deductible. Thus, expenses paid or incurred in connection with the preparation of his tax returns or in connection with any proceeding involved in determining the extent of his tax liability or in contesting his tax liability are deductible."

The Internal Revenue Service appears to concede that amounts paid for tax planning advice in the estate planning process are deductible under Section 212 (3) as expenses incurred "in connection with the determination, collection, or refund of any tax," and to recognize the deductibility of counsel fees for advance tax planning even if there is no contested liabililily. See *Sidney Merians*, 60 T.C. No. 23 (1973), *acq.*, Rev. Rul. 72-545, 1972 IRB 4-6; *Carpenter v. United States*, 338 F. 2d 366 (1964 Ct. Claims). The cost of tax advice in estate planning may also be deductible under 213 (2) as an expense for the "management, conservation or maintenance of property held for the production of income." See *Nancy Reynolds Bagley*, 8 T.C. 130, 133, 135 (1947), *acq.*, 1947 — 1 C.B. 1.

On the other hand, the charge for the preparation of wills and trusts is not deductible. *Estate of Helen S. Pennell*, 4 B.T.A. 1039 (1926); also *Bagley, supra*. As a consequence, deductibility of the tax advice fee requires that we indicate in our statements a breakdown of the services performed and the amounts allocated to them. In *Merians, supra*, where the lawyer's bill and his "vague" testimony did not include an itemization of services and time spent, the Court allowed only 20 percent to be allocated to tax advice.

There are several possible bases of allocation. One method is to allocate purely on the basis of the firm's time records. Another is to allocate pursuant to a fee schedule containing a dollar or percentage apportionment to which the client has agreed. We have taken the view that will and trust drafting, unless there are very unusual drafting problems, cannot account for more than 15-20 percent of the value of the estate planning effort, being relatively routine and ancillary to the principal subject of our engagement. We believe that this approach is strongly reinforced by the use of tapes, forms, and preprinted documents as described below.

The client will normally appreciate the tax notation on his bill, which shows that you are concerned about his tax advantage even when involved in collecting your own fee.

[¶1107]   ANCILLARY EQUIPMENT AND TECHNIQUES

1. *Word-processing equipment.* Extremely useful in the estate planning process are MT/ST, Wang, CPT and similar machines which provide information storage and enable an electric typewriter to reproduce this information without having an operator actively work the keys.

The provisions frequently used in your will drafting can be put on tape in this way and can be applied over and over again without new drafting and without new typographical errors. For each basic type of will used in our office we have a set of cassettes and a corresponding photocopy of the recorded material. The photocopy of a particular model may contain one or several of each type of provision that may be desired, with blank spaces throughout for names and figures. To "draft" a will on such a form one merely fills in the necessary blanks, crosses out the provisions which are not needed or desired, and writes or dictates any provisions which are special or unique. This marked up form is given to the operator, most of whose work is then quickly completed via the automatic typewriter with the appropriate cassettes.

To "carve" a will out of such a form or model can be done with several times the speed of building up a comparable document. We are also less likely to omit an essential or a helpful technical clause. And the opportunities for typographical errors are substantially reduced. For a helpful study of automatic typing and its applications, see Chapter 13 of Altman and Weil, *How to Manage Your Law Office*, Matthew Bender (New York, 1974).

2. *Preprinted documents.* For a study of the use of preprinted pages, see Keydel, " 'Preprinted Page' Techniques for Estate Planning," 8 *Real Property, Probate and Trust Journal* 300, Summer 1973, Vol 8/No.2. This technique involves the use of previously produced "standard pages" together with currently produced "special pages" to assemble a finished document. Keydel's article provides a complete preprint system, with samples.

3. *Paralegal assistants.* Estate planning has several functions for the paraprofessional. In the preliminary stage of planning, he or she may be given the assignment of summarizing the client's life insurance policies, as to type and amount, ownership, beneficiary arrangements, cash values, etc. If preprinted pages are used, the assistant can assemble the document as directed in your instruction sheet. In the "clean-up" period, the paralegal can process insurance ownership and beneficiary changes, stock transfers, and similar matters.

The three ancillary techniques or systems previously mentioned in this section serve to reduce the amount of lawyer time devoted to standard document provisions and routine processes. At the same time this system generally improves, the quality and appearance of the final product. Moreover, *while photocopies, tapes and cassettes, and preprinting convey at first blush the aura of mechanization and depersonalization, their proper impact is quite the opposite.* By mechanizing the prompt and accurate production of the *ordinary* portions of our documents, we are freed to devote our valuable drafting time to those provisions which are creative, special, and personal to the client. Among these more creative efforts will be, in appropriate cases, the development of a suitable preamble along the lines suggested in an earlier portion of this chapter.

In our experience, the client whose estate planning and whose personal interests and concerns receive the kinds of attention and treatment we have endeavored to describe will recognize the value of the professional services rendered and also the reasonableness of the relatively substantial fees we have suggested. The goal of client satisfaction will have been attained. We will have "responded in responsibility" to our client. No lesser effort is worthy of our professional life.

APPENDIX A

FORMS TO HELP YOU
Develop the Estate Plan

APPENDIX A—INTRODUCTION

The materials included in this Appendix are designed to facilitate estate planning purposes and to illustrate the development and presentation of specific recommendations.

The careful and thoughtful use of the forms and models that follow will help:

(1) to avoid errors and omissions in the planning process

(2) to enhance the client's understanding and evaluation of the available tax saving opportunities

(3) to provide ample background information for future reference.

FORM A-1

Private Annuity Worksheet

Form A-1 can be used to determine the transferor's income tax treatment in a simple single-life private annuity transaction, pursuant to Rev. Rul. 69-74, as discussed in Chapter 6, [¶602]. See reference to this form at page 169.

Taxation of a Private Annuity

1.	Age of transferor.	—
2.	Transferor's basis in the property transferred.	$—
3.	Fair market value of such property at the time of transfer.	$—
4.	Annual payments to the transferor.	$—
5.	The annuity factor under Table A(1) or A(2) of Reg. Sec. 20.2031-10(f).	—
6.	Fair market value of the annuity. (Line 4 multiplied by Line 5.)	$—
7.	(If Line 3 exceeds Line 6, the excess represents a gift.	$—)
8.	The transferor's life expectancy under Table 1 of Reg. Sec. 1.72-9.	—
9.	The expected return. (Line 4 multiplied by Line 8.)	$—
10.	Exclusion ratio. (Line 2 divided by Line 9.)	—%
11.	Excluded amount. (Line 4 multiplied by Line 10.)	$—
12.	Capital gain portion (Line 6 less Line 2.)*	$—
13.	Annual capital gain portion. (Line 12 divided by Line 8.)	$—
14.	Ordinary income portion. (Line 4 less the total of Line 11 plus Line 13.)**	$—

---

*After the capital gain portion has been fully taxed (upon the transferor attaining his life expectancy), that portion will be subsequently taxed as ordinary income.

**The total of Lines 11, 13 and 14 should equal the annual payment to the transferor (Line 3).

FORM A-2

Estate Planning Memorandum

Form A-2 is a sample of the type of estate planning memorandum which is recommended in Chapter 11, [¶1101.2], at page 259. This sample was selected as a model because it includes recommendations based on several of the tax-saving techniques discussed in this book. Estate planning was done simultaneously for this client and for his father, and the memorandum to this client's father is included as Form A-3.

Memorandum to John Smith

**ESTATE PLANNING REVIEW
AND
RECOMMENDATIONS**

Gilbert M. Cantor, Esquire
Sixth Floor
1700 Sansom Street
Philadelphia, Pennsylvania 19103

Table of Contents

Smith Family Information

Name	Age
John Smith	34
Mary Smith	34
Betsy Smith	12
Susan Smith	8

Home address: 123 South Market Street, Philadelphia, Pa. 19103

John's brother, Edward Smith, is 23 years of age and unmarried.

Both of John's parents, William Smith and Jenny Smith, age 57, are living.

Social Security Numbers:

    John:

    Mary:

Estate Inventory

Assets owned individually by John:

Interest in Gorgeous Country Enterprises, Inc.	1,020,000	
Interest in Arden Enterprises	36,000	
Interest in Purple Knoll	4,000	
Qualified profit-sharing interest	10,000	
Life insurance ($300,000 presumably excludible)	60,000*	
		$1,130,000

Assets owned jointly by John and Mary:

Home	$175,000		
Less mortgage	89,000		
Equity		$86,000	
Vacation condominium		12,000	
Cash in banks		4,000	
Tangible personal property		34,000	
			$ 136,000**
GROSS ESTATE			$1,266,000

Unsecured liabilities—$40,000

---

*We have received conflicting information as to whether or not a $300,000 policy has been transferred to John's 1974 irrevocable trust. Pending clarification of that issue, we have treated this $300,000 as excluded from the gross estate. We recommend, however, that the trust, and also the insurance if transferred to it, be replaced, for reasons set forth below.

**Assuming your jointly owned assets were so acquired prior to 1/1/77, their value will be fully includible for estate tax purposes in the estate of the first spouse to die, except to the extent the funds invested in those assets can be traced to the separate property of the spouse who survives. With the understanding that these items represent the investment of your funds and not Mary's, I have included their values in your gross estate and not hers. You would be well advised, however, to develop a written tracing of these funds now, and to avoid joint ownership in the future unless we specifically recommend it.

REVIEW AND RECOMMENDATIONS

1. TAX-GUIDED FAMILY PLANNING

A. *CURRENT ESTATE PLAN.* For reference in certain of the following portions of this memorandum, I will briefly summarize the main provisions of your previously executed documents:

(1) Will of John Smith

Executors: Solid Bank, Mary Smith, and Jerry Smith. Larry Smith is successor to Jerry Smith.

Guardian: Robert Berg is Guardian of the persons of minor children, with authority to appoint his own substitute or successor.

Distribution Plan: Tangible personal property is given to Mary, with an alternate gift to the children. All the rest of the estate is to be added to the revocable trust described below.

(2) Revocable Trust of John Smith (5/25/73):

Trustees: Solid Bank, Mary Smith, and Jerry Smith. Larry Smith is successor to Jerry Smith.

Distribution Plan: A Marital Trust (presumably 50% of your adjusted gross estate) is established for your wife. She is to receive the income. If the aggregate annual income of the marital deduction and the residuary trust amounts to less than $15,000 (as adjusted for cost of living increases), Mary is to receive the amount of the deficiency from principal. She has the power to appoint the principal remaining at her death, by her own Will, to whomever she may select; failing such appointment, the after-tax balance of principal is to be added to the Residuary Trust.

A Residuary Trust is to receive the balance of the trust assets. Mary is to receive the income. If the Marital Trust is exhausted, the principal invasion provisions above mentioned shift to this trust. After you and Mary are both deceased, and until such time as your youngest child reaches age 22, there is a "sprinkling" trust for your issue. Thereafter separate trusts are established for your children (including issue of deceased children), the beneficiaries to receive income currently, with the rights to withdraw principal, 1/3 at age 26, 1/2 of the balance at age 32, and the balance at age 38. On death of a child, trusts continue for the child's issue until age 21. If you should die without spouse or issue surviving, a number of individual and charitable gifts are provided.

(3) Irrevocable Trust of John Smith (3/8/74):

Trustee: William Smith. When he ceases to act as Trustee, the Solid Bank, Clarence C. Johnson, and Jerry Smith are designated to succeed him. Larry Smith is named as successor to Clarence C. Johnson or Jerry Smith. The successor individuals are qualified only so long as they are employed by Gorgeous Country Enterprises, Inc. If, during William Smith's lifetime, there are less than two qualified successors available, he is authorized to name a substitute successor. Further successors, after William Smith ceases to serve, can be named by the remaining Trustees.

Distribution Plan: Although designated as an insurance trust, provision is made for William Smith to make distributions of Gorgeous Country Enterprises, Inc.* to his issue and their spouses with a limit on the shares distributable to William Smith and his spouse. Further and complex provisions, not useful to itemize, are set forth for the benefit of William Smith his issue and spouses of issue, and for your issue, with your children having the right to withdraw their shares, 1/2 at age 25 and the balance at age 30.

(4) Will of Mary Smith:

Executor: John Smith. Solid Bank is named as successor. (Clause Eighth refers to her Executors *and Trustees*, but the Will establishes no trusts.)

Guardian: Same as in John's Will.

Distribution Plan: Tangible personal property is given to John with an alternate gift to the children.

---

*Per 3/8/74 stock purchase agreement, the Trustee is to purchase from your estate, to the extent of the insurance proceeds he receives, the stock remaining after a Section 303 redemption. Any shares that still remain may be purchased by (a) William (b) Edward Smith and shares not purchased are to be "given" (how?) to the Revocable Trust.

All the rest of the estate is given to John with an alternate gift to the Trustees of John's revocable trust.

B. *JOHN'S WILL–CHANGES TO CONSIDER.* I recommend that consideration be given to the following:

(1) The selection of guardians of the persons of your children should be reviewed now and at regular intervals in the future. If possible, one or two alternate guardians (or pairs of alternate guardians) should be named in the Will. Should Mr. Berg's wife be included?

(2) You have selected the "top" corporate fiduciary, in my opinion, but your choice of individual Executors and their successors should also be reviewed now and at regular intervals in the future.

(3) Guardians of property passing to minors should also be designated in the Will.

(4) Full and adequate administrative powers should be given to your Executors.

(5) If we transfer to an irrevocable trust the ownership of the insurance policies which are now payable to your revocable trust, the marital deduction trust can be shifted from the latter to your will and the revocable trust would be eliminated entirely.

C. *MARITAL DEDUCTION TRUST—CHANGES TO CONSIDER.* Whether the marital deduction provisions are retained in a revocable trust or are shifted to your Will as above mentioned, certain possible changes should be reviewed.

First, let me refresh your recollection of the marital deduction "basics." Under pertinent provisions of the Internal Revenue Code as amended by the Tax Reform Act of 1976, you may leave to your wife, free of federal estate tax, the greater of $250,000 or one-half of your "adjusted gross estate." The "adjusted gross estate" is the gross estate (see estate inventory above) minus debts, funeral expenses, and the costs of administering the estate. In your case, assuming an adjusted gross estate of about $1,200,000, one-half, or $600,000, can qualify for the marital deduction if you so choose and if Mary survives you.

This marital deduction portion of your estate, to the extent it remains at the death of your surviving spouse, is includible in her estate for estate tax purposes. Thus, the applicability of the estate tax to the marital deduction "half" of the estate is deferred rather than totally avoided. Nevertheless, the tax in the second spouse's estate may be imposed in lower brackets; the taxable assets may decline in value or, if the Will or Trust permits, may be wholly or partly consumed or given away in the second spouse's lifetime; and, in any event, she enjoys the income on the funds which would have been paid in taxes if the marital deduction had not been utilized.

The figures involved indicate to me that the *full* marital deduction should be used as a part of your estate plan. Assuming that both you and Mary will survive beyond 1980, and using the figures above mentioned, the federal estate taxes in your estate and Mary's, computed with and without the marital deduction, would be approximately as follows:

(a) Without marital deduction:
    (1) In your estate $336,000
    (2) In Mary's estate   0
       Total taxes $336,000
(b) With full marital deduction:
    (1) In your estate $132,000
    (2) In Mary's estate   117,000
       Total taxes $249,000
       Tax saving (as compared
       with (a), above) $87,000

After determining the amount of marital deduction that is desirable, we should consider the mode or modes of obtaining it:

(1) *"Power of appointment" trust provisions*. While the marital deduction may be obtained via an outright gift to the surviving spouse, use of an appropriate trust for this purpose can provide several advantages, particularly in asset management and protection of beneficiaries, as well as Pennsylvania inheritance tax avoidance. The most common form of trust which qualifies for the marital deduction is the so-called "power of appointment" trust. This is the type which appears in your revocable trust document. In order for such a trust to qualify, there are two statutory requisites: (1) The surviving spouse must receive all of the trust income at least annually; and (2) the surviving spouse must have a general power of appointment over the trust principal, that is, the power to dispose of the principal remaining at her death as if the assets were owned by her outright.

Beyond the above mentioned criteria for such a trust to qualify for the marital deduction, the Will or trust instrument can (without affecting the marital deduction) include a variety of provisions for principal invasion during the lifetime of the surviving spouse. If we use a power of appointment trust for all or part of the marital deduction for your estate, the following principal invasion options might be considered (as alternatives to those of your present Trust):

(a) Provision for Mary to have a guaranteed after-tax "spendable income" of a specified amount, that amount to be adjusted with changes in the consumer price index. Your present marital trust directs a principal distribution to the extent trust income is less than $15,000 (with cost of living increases), but (1) this distribution is mandatory, whereas it could be left to Mary's discretion annually, (2) it ignores her other income, (3) it ignores her income taxes, and (4) I understand that you now consider the base figure to be inadequate.

(b) Provision for Mary to receive principal over and above the amount set forth in subparagraph (a), above, in the Trustees' discretion, for any emergency needs and to maintain her customary standard of living. The figure used for the purpose of paragraph (a), no matter how generously conceived, may turn out to be inadequate. Moreover, illness or accident may deprive Mary of the ability to make principal withdrawals or to use the funds for her own benefit.

(c) Authority for Mary to make gifts of trust principal to your children and their issue (and perhaps to charities), with power to direct payment out of trust principal of any related transfer taxes. In connection with such an authorization, the approval of the other Trustees could be required. Bear in mind that the marital deduction trust principal is taxable at Mary's death, and the suggested provision would permit planning to reduce her estate taxes.

(2) *Estate trust introduced.* The "estate trust" is the least frequently employed form of marital deduction gift, and is not widely known, but is worthy of consideration in your case. Simply, a trust may qualify for the marital deduction even though the Trustees are empowered to accumulate all or a portion of the trust income, provided the trust is for the sole benefit of the surviving spouse and if, upon her death, the remaining principal and accumulated income must be paid over to her estate.

The estate trust has three principal advantages, each of which could be meaningful in your case:

(1) Assuming Mary has adequate income from other sources, the "excess" income of the estate trust can be professionally invested and managed along with the principal. (This will depend in part on arrangements for Mary to receive a salary from Gorgeous Country Enterprises, qualified retirement plan benefits, and so on.)

(2) Bearing in mind that Mary will eventually lose the advantage of the joint income tax rates you presently enjoy, it could be useful to have any excess income taxed to the estate trust—a separate taxpayer—rather than to Mary (subject to a throwback rule which would have no adverse effect in this case).

(3) In the "power of appointment" trust, the widow must have the right to compel the Trustees to make the trust principal produce a reasonable income for her or to reinvest it in assets which will produce a reasonable income. In contrast, she need have no such right in an estate trust, so that vacant land, business interests, or other assets yielding little or no income could properly be retained in this trust. Gorgeous Country stock may be an example of this type of asset.

The estate trust has two potential disadvantages which must also be considered. One is that the principal and accumulated income added to

Mary's estate would be subject to Pennsylvania inheritance tax in her estate. The other is that in the absence of a suitable antenuptial agreement, a second husband who survived Mary could exercise his statutory right to receive a share of Mary's estate, which would include the assets of the estate trust.

We could provide for the marital deduction "half" of your estate to be further divided into two (equal or unequal) portions, one portion to be placed in a power of appointment trust for Mary and the other to be placed in an estate trust for her, with provision in either or both trusts for invasion of principal in the event of any accident, illness or other emergency needs. Pending further discussion, I can not make a firm recommendation on this issue.

D. *"NON-MARITAL" TRUST(S)—CHANGES TO CONSIDER.* Assuming that one-half of your adjusted gross estate will be allocated to one or more trusts which qualify for the marital deduction, we should consider the disposition of the balance of your estate assets.

Preliminarily, I would note that your irrevocable trust contains various provisions with respect to your brother, especially dealing with stock of Gorgeous Country. The information furnished to me thus far indicates that those provisions have a questionable relation to your goals and desires. Nor is that trust necessarily the appropriate vehicle for dealing with that stock. Taking the foregoing into account, as well as (a) the failure of integration of the irrevocable trust with the balance of your estate plan, (b) the absence of provision for transferred policies to be returned to you if needed, (c) the lack of a specific provision for purchase of assets from your estate or the lending of funds to your estate (for liquidity needs), (d) the many drafting improvements that can be made, and (e) your age as affecting insurance premiums: I recommend that the $300,000 policy be replaced and that the present irrevocable trust be discarded. I will return to this subject below.

Passing that, and turning to your evident concerns to provide for Mary's security and to provide the maximum benefits eventually to your children, I would suggest that the first element of your revocable trust be continued, that is, to place the non-marital "half" of your estate in a trust so designed that the trust assets will be held for Mary's benefit during her lifetime and will eventually pass to or for the benefit of your children without being taxed again at Mary's death.

In contrast with your present trust instrument, however, I would recommend providing, in this second or "non-marital" trust, for the income to be "sprinkled" among Mary and your children and their issue, or accumulated, as an independent Trustee or Trustees from time to time consider advisable. Such a provision can accomplish two tax-saving purposes: (1) avoid giving excessive taxable income to Mary (to whom joint tax rates may not then be available); and (2) encourage consumption of marital deduction trust principal (which is taxable, as noted above, in Mary's estate) and possible enhancement of the non-marital trust principal (thus in effect exchanging tax-free for taxable assets each year). I will explain this concept further when we meet.

We can provide for principal distributions from this trust to meet Mary's needs if the marital trust(s) should be exhausted. Income and principal of the non-marital trust could also be used to provide for various needs of your children and eventually grandchildren, though you may wish to specify that the Trustees give primary consideration to Mary's welfare when they consider principal invasions during her lifetime.

After you and Mary are both deceased, there are still many estate planning options available. The use of a "sprinkling" trust for your children should be reconsidered. Except in small estates, separate equal trusts are attractive in their simplicity and do relatively little "injustice." On the other hand, you may wish to permit your Trustees to depart from equality, within limits, in favor of any child who develops a serious long-term disability.

To the extent that assets are held in trust for a child for life and pass thereafter to her children, trusts can be so designed that the assets will not be subject to estate or inheritance taxes in the child's estate. In other words, we can arrange to "skip" a generation with respect to tax on these assets.

Under the Tax Reform Act of 1976, a ceiling has been placed upon the amount which can be sheltered from estate tax via such generation-skipping trusts. That amount has been set at $250,000 per child, so that you can effectively shelter $500,000 in this manner for your two children.

Further, to the extent income can be diverted from a child to her issue, or can be accumulated, we can have multiple taxpayers for the trust income, with multiple exemptions and lower aggregate tax brackets.

One way to accomplish all of these objectives without totally depriving your children of the benefits and responsibilities of direct control of their own resources would be to establish two trusts for each child. In one trust, we would require the Trustees to distribute the income to the child currently, and we would permit the child to withdraw the principal in two or more installments at stated ages. In the other trust we would permit the Trustees to "sprinkle" the income among the child and her issue, or to accumulate it, as the Trustees from time to time deem advisable, and the principal would remain in trust for the child's lifetime and pass on to her children.

In any of the trusts above mentioned, we can provide for invasion of principal for various purposes, using first the trusts which are not designed for generation-skipping. The Trustees could be empowered to distribute principal for the child's maintenance, for a gift on the occasion of a wedding or the birth of a child, for the purchase of a home, for investment in a business or professional enterprise, and so on. We can also give each child limited powers to appoint the principal remaining at her death.

And, finally, you may also wish to establish charitable remainder trusts for Mary or your children along the lines mentioned below.

E. *LIFE INSURANCE TRANSFERS—IRREVOCABLE TRUSTS.* Currently you own insurance policies on your life with a face value of $60,000, the beneficiary of which is your revocable trust. This means that this $60,000 will be includible in your estate for estate tax purposes, the revocable trust being merely a convenience device.

By transferring ownership of these policies to Mary, your estate would be reduced by $60,000, with a resultant estate tax saving of $25,000 with no marital deduction, or $11,000 using a full marital deduction. Mary's estate, if she predeceases you, would be increased only by the amount of any cash values accumulated in the policies. However, if Mary survives you, the proceeds of the life insurance policies, to the extent they are not consumed, would be taxed in Mary's estate, "on top of" her marital deduction share.

You can accomplish the tax saving on these policies in your estate and also avoid having the proceeds taxed in Mary's estate by transferring ownership of the policies to an irrevocable trust rather than to Mary. Considering your estate tax brackets, I would recommend that you establish such a trust (to replace the present one). Gift tax returns may have to be filed for this transfer, but, again, the gift would involve only the amount of any accumulated cash values.

While the irrevocable trust avoids estate taxes, it also involves *some* loss of flexibility with respect to insurance beneficiary arrangements, and this concern must be weighed in the balance when we consider the utility of this device. On the other hand, a great deal of flexibility can be built into the trust itself, as I have already suggested and will explain further when we meet.

Apart from the $60,000 of life insurance above mentioned, I have suggested that your $300,000 policy be replaced. If you were simply to purchase a $300,000 policy, adding it to your gross estate, it would involve additional estate tax of $123,000 in the absence of the marital deduction or $53,000 if the full marital deduction is obtained. I would suggest, therefore, that the policy be purchased, not by you, but by the

Trustees of your new irrevocable trust,* so that it will not be part of your gross estate and, arguably, will never have been transferred by you to the trust (and thus possibly excludible even if you die within three years following the policy purchase).

If such a trust is established, it can also serve as a "receptacle" for the entire non-marital portion of your estate, so that we would provide a marital deduction trust or trusts in your Will and simply add the balance of your estate to the irrevocable trust. This would simplify the estate plan and produce administrative economies.

In connection with both marital and non-marital trusts, we should review your selection of original and successor Trustees.

F. *MEETING LIQUIDITY NEEDS.* The following schedules A, B and C reflect your estate liquidity needs and Mary's, (a) if Mary survives you, and (b) if she does not, assuming that deaths occur after 1980 and at least 10 years apart, and assuming that present asset values are maintained and you do not reduce your taxable estate(s) by means of the charitable gifts, family gift program, and life insurance transfers that are suggested in this memorandum.

One question, however, is whether we should look at current or at future liquidity needs. Although your own growth projections might be more useful, if we assume for illustrative purposes that assets totaling $1,000,000 will appreciate in your estate at the rate of 5% per annum for the period of your life expectancy, a very different picture emerges: your gross estate would in that way increase from approximately $1,200,000 to about $5,400,000, and the increase would presumably be in non-liquid assets. Schedules D, E and F reflect the altered liquidity needs of that situation.

---

*If purchased on minimum deposit basis, we will give further advice on current law as to deductibility of interest, possibly utilizing split-dollar arrangement with cash value portion owned by Mary and interest payable by her.

Schedule A

The following is a projection of the administration expenses, estate and inheritance taxes in your estate assuming Mary survives you, that a full marital deduction is utilized, and that you both live beyond 1980.

Gross Estate		$1,300,000
Less estimated debts and deductions allowed by law		100,000
ADJUSTED GROSS ESTATE		$1,200,000

Taxes Payable

FEDERAL ESTATE TAX	$132,000	
PENNSYLVANIA INHERITANCE TAX	70,000	
TOTAL TAXES		$ 202,000

Summary of Projected Taxes and Costs

TAXES	$202,000	
DEBTS AND DEDUCTIONS	100,000	
TOTAL		$ 302,000

Schedule B

The following is a projection of the administration expenses, estate and inheritance taxes in Mary's estate assuming that Mary survives you and that you both live beyond 1980.

Gross Estate		$600,000
Less estimated debts and deductions allowed by law		45,000
ADJUSTED GROSS ESTATE		$555,000

Taxes Payable

FEDERAL ESTATE TAX	$117,000	
PENNSYLVANIA INHERITANCE TAX	33,500	
TOTAL TAXES		$150,500

Summary of Projected Taxes and Costs

TAXES	$150,500	
DEBTS AND DEDUCTIONS	45,000	
TOTAL		$195,500

Schedule C

The following is a projection of the administration expenses, estate and inheritance taxes in your estate assuming that you survive Mary and that you live beyond 1980.

Gross Estate		$1,300,000
Less estimated debts and		
deductions allowed by law		100,000
ADJUSTED GROSS ESTATE		$1,200,000

Taxes Payable

FEDERAL ESTATE TAX	$336,000	
PENNSYLVANIA INHERITANCE TAX	72,000	
TOTAL TAXES		$ 408,000

Summary of Projected Taxes and Costs

TAXES	$408,000	
DEBTS AND DEDUCTIONS	100,000	
TOTAL		$ 508,000

Schedule D

The following is a projection of the administration expenses, estate and inheritance taxes in your estate assuming that you live to your current life expectancy, that your assets appreciate at the rate of 5% per annum over that period, and that Mary survives you and a full marital deduction is utilized.

Gross Estate		$5,400,000
Less estimated debts and		
deductions allowed by law		415,000
ADJUSTED GROSS ESTATE		$4,985,000

Taxes Payable

FEDERAL ESTATE TAX	$837,000	
PENNSYLVANIA INHERITANCE TAX	290,000	
TOTAL TAXES		$1,127,000

Summary of Projected Taxes and Costs

TAXES	$1,127,000	
DEBTS AND DEDUCTIONS	415,000	
TOTAL		$1,542,000

Schedule E

The following is a projection of the administration expenses, and inheritance taxes in Mary's estate assuming that you live to your life expectancy, that your assets appreciate at the rate of 5% per annum over that period, and that Mary survives you.

Gross Estate		$2,492,500
Less estimated debts and		
deductions allowed by law		124,500
ADJUSTED GROSS ESTATE		$2,368,000

Taxes Payable

FEDERAL ESTATE TAX	$786,000	
PENNSYLVANIA INHERITANCE TAX	142,000	
TOTAL TAXES		$ 928,000

Summary of Projected Taxes and Costs

TAXES	$928,000	
DEBTS AND DEDUCTIONS	124,500	
TOTAL		$1,052,500

Schedule F

The following is a projection of the administration expenses, estate and inheritance taxes in your estate assuming that you live to your current life expectancy, that your assets will appreciate at the rate of 5% per annum over that period, and that you survive Mary.

Gross Estate		$5,400,000
Less estimated debts and		
deductions allowed by law		415,000
ADJUSTED GROSS ESTATE		$4,985,000

Taxes Payable

FEDERAL ESTATE TAX	$2,104,000	
PENNSYLVANIA INHERITANCE TAX	299,000	
TOTAL TAXES		$2,403,000

Summary of Projected Taxes and Costs

TAXES	$2,403,000	
DEBTS AND DEDUCTIONS	415,000	
TOTAL		$2,818,000

There are several possible approaches to these requirements:

(1) Under certain sections of the Internal Revenue Code, the portion of the estate tax attributable to interests in business assets which meet the standards to be deemed "closely held" and which comprise a certain prescribed portion of your gross, adjusted gross, or taxable estate can be deferred: (a) for a period up to 10 years if the value exceeds 35% of your gross estate or 50% of your taxable estate, and (b) up to 15 years if the value exceeds 65% of your adjusted gross estate. There is also a discretionary deferral for "reasonable cause." We hesitate to rely on any of these provisions, however, because we do not know whether the business interest will continue to be "closely held," we do not know what portion of your resources they will represent, and we find that Congress now displays a willingness to tinker with these sections of the Code, so that we do not know what the criteria will be when the time comes. And, as indicated above, only a portion of the estate tax can be so deferred in any event.

(2) Again, a favorite way in the past to meet estate liquidity needs, as in your 1974 stock purchase agreement, was the Section 303 stock redemption, assuming adequate corporate funds will be made available. The funds to cover taxes and expenses could be withdrawn from a closely held corporation without the divided treatment that might otherwise apply, and the transaction would be free of capital gains tax, because the stock received a stepped-up basis at death. Now, however, not only have the Section 303 requirements been changed, but the basis for the stock will not be stepped up beyond its 12/31/76 level, so that the transaction in the case of a growing company will result in a taxable gain. Apart from taxes, such a redemption may also change the stock ownership proportions in a way that is not desired.

(3) A third way, of course, is to provide for all or some of the anticipated liquidity needs via life insurance. Such insurance may be acquired in connection with qualified retirement plans or separately, and Mr. Dean's advice will be helpful in this connection. The important tax considerations here is that such insurance be acquired, owned, and made payable in such ways that the insurance will not itself add to the liquidity needs which it is designed to meet. The irrevocable trust discussed in this memorandum is one technique for attaining this objective.

Of course, while we endeavor to meet anticipated liquidity needs, we should strive at the same time to restrict or to reduce those requirements. Section G, below, is addressed to that subject.

G. *GIFT PROGRAM—RECAPITALIZATION*. One of the most effective ways to reduce taxes is to give away assets which are taxable. In your case, apart from life insurance (which I have already discussed) and your home, your resources are largely concentrated in closely held business enterprises, especially Gorgeous Country Enterprises, Inc. In making the following suggestion, I am anticipating and intruding into the area which Mr. Johnson and his associates in our corporate group should consider in due course, but my thought is that we might usefully recapitalize the corporation, in a tax-free reorganization, to create two or three classes of stock.

For purposes of your estate planning, the substitution of a non-voting common stock for a portion of the voting common would leave the present voting rights undisturbed, but the nonvoting common would give you a vehicle for an annual gift program.

Under such a program annual gifts could be made to Mary and the children (and eventually grandchildren), outright or in trust,* thus continually reducing your estate without reducing your voting power or your current liquid resources.

To be sure, any shareholder, voting or not, can create difficulties. Also, if the stock were sold to an outside purchaser, to the extent of prior gifts the proceeds would go to your donees rather than to you. Nevertheless, the tax saving potential is significant and should be considered. At your present tax level, each $100,000 given away would save approximately the following estate and inheritance taxes:

 (a) With full marital deduction $24,500
 (b) Without marital deduction $47,000

The future growth of the stock so given would occur outside your estate. Dividends on such stock would be shifted to lower bracket taxpayers.

A third class of stock might be a cumulative preferred stock, to be exchanged for William Smith's common stock. The purpose of such an exchange would be to give him a security which has a reasonable level income yield but which will not grow in value and increase his taxable estate. Such stock might be "Section 306" stock, but not necessarily. There are other income tax hazards, and also gift tax hazards, to be dealt with. Further, such stock might advantageously be used by William Smith in implementing his desire to give stock to Edward Smith. Again, I would ask our corporate group to pass on the feasibility of this device and to suggest a specific recapitalization pattern as part of their corporate review.

Obviously, the existing stock purchase agreement would have to be

---

*The recent *Berzon* case in the Second Circuit indicates that the $3,000 annual gift tax exclusion may be disallowed where the dividend history—or lack of it—makes it impossible to put a value on the beneficiary's rights to trust income and where restrictions on the stock prevent the Trustee from reinvesting in assets with a "normal" income yield.

replaced in order for any of these things to occur. It should be replaced anyway.

Apart from Gorgeous Country, other business interests for which substantial future growth is anticipated should be considered for a family gift program. With proper attention, it should be possible for you to retain control, and to be compensated for services, while shifting asset growth and taxable income to the next generation.

Even if your gift program exhausts your unified gift and estate tax credit, so that no credit remains at your death, and even if you incur gift tax in connection with your gift program, these costs may be far outweighed, in the case of volatile assets, by preventing or limiting the increase of taxable values in your estate (plus potential income tax savings).

II. *TAX-GUIDED CHARITABLE PLANNING*

A. *BASIC CONSIDERATIONS*. It would take a book to explain in full all of the available techniques for lifetime and post-mortem charitable giving. As your tax return reflects substantial gifts to charity, and there are other indications that charities are within the scope of your interests, I will mention here certain basic tax information and two devices which may be interesting to you and also feasible.

The basic tax rules on gifts by individuals to or for the use of qualifying organizations are as follows:

1. Estate tax: Unlimited charitable deduction.

2. Gift tax: Unlimited charitable deduction.

3. Income tax: Depending principally upon the identity of the charitable donees, there are three operative percentage limitations (20%, 30%, and 50% of adjusted gross income). Mainly, the 50% limitation is available for gifts to public charities and several other types of donee; the 20% limitation applies to gifts to donees (such as a private foundation) which do not qualify for the 50% limitation; and the 30% limitation applies to long-term capital gain property (unless you elect to reduce the fair market value of the gift by 50% of the appreciation).

As the gift tax and estate tax charitable deductions are unlimited as to amount, you could give your entire estate to qualified charities during your lifetime or by Will, incurring no gift tax and avoiding estate tax entirely. Of course, such a procedure would be outweighed by your desire to provide for your family. I mention it to clarify the tax rules.

The two devices which I wish to bring to your attention are these:

(1) *Private Foundation*. By establishing a private foundation, you can

create a convenient channel for all of your charitable gifts. The foundation would disburse gifts to various objects of your charity. As above mentioned, you may make gifts to your foundation which for tax purposes may be deducted up to 20% of your adjusted gross income each year. A corporation may also deduct the amount of its gifts to your foundation up to 5% of its taxable income, and excess corporate contributions can be carried over for up to five years. The charitable objects permitted for your foundation will be as broad as those for which you may take a deduction if you make the gifts directly.

If your income, and thus your ability to make gifts to charity, may fluctuate, your foundation will be able to provide a steady cash flow to the objects of your charity. They will not be severely affected in years of lower income when you may be unable to make a gift as substantial as you would wish, or in years of higher income, *when you may wish to take full or substantial advantage of the 20% limitation without all of the money so given passing at once out of your control.* Your foundation can also finance long term projects which you could not otherwise undertake. Further, such a foundation can heighten your family profile of community involvement extending beyond generations now living.

Private foundations may no longer engage in the abusive practices which under the Tax Reform Act of 1969 led to some curtailment of their use as an income tax planning device. Relationships between the foundation, its creator, substantial contributors, and directors, are, under present law, regulated to prevent private foundations from providing amenities to the founder, controlling family businesses, making interest free loans, and paying excessive salaries to related persons and the like.

Generally, all income of such a foundation must be distributed promptly for charitable purposes. Under current rules an amount equal to 5% of the fair market value of the foundation's assets must be distributed each year. An annual 4% excise tax is imposed on the net investment income of a private foundation.

If your foundation is properly designed, the asets may be includible in your gross estate, so that these assets will enlarge your marital deduction and they will also be deductible for estate tax purposes.

If you wish to pursue this subject futher, I will outline for you the various provisions of the foundation document, and we can consider your selection of Trustees and other related topics.

We would obtain recognition of the exempt status of your foundation by applying to the Internal Revenue Service for a ruling. A determination will normally (but not always) be made on the basis of our statement of proposed operations in sufficient detail to permit the Service to conclude that your foundation will meet the requirements of the law. In order to maintain exempt status, there are various reporting requirements, compliance with which on a regular and careful basis is necessary.

(2) *Charitable remainder trusts.* If you wish to provide current benefits to your wife or children (or anyone else, for that manner) and simultaneously make provision for charity, you can accomplish both purposes by establishing a trust to pay the income to your individual beneficiary or beneficiaries for life or a term of years, the principal thereafter (called the "remainder") to pass to charity.

Under current law applicable to "charitable remainder" trusts, as the above-described trusts are called, an estate tax deduction is allowable to your estate for the value of the charitable remainder only in the case of a pooled income fund, an annuity trust, or a unitrust.

A *pooled income fund* is a trust created by a charity rather than the donor, in which the remainder interests of a number of donors are commingled, and the donor reserves an income for the life or lives of designated beneficiaries who are living at the time of the gifts.

An *annuity trust* is one which specifies an annual dollar amount (which must be not less that 5% of the initial value of the trust) to be paid to the individual beneficiary.

A *unitrust* is one which specifies a certain percentage (not less than 5%) of the value of the trust assets each year to be paid to the individual beneficiary.

An annuity trust or a unitrust may be established by will or during your lifetime. The value of the remainder interest is deductible for income, estate and gift tax purposes. Moreover, if done by Will, the entire principal is includible in your gross estate for purposes of computing the marital deduction, so that your estate receives a marital deduction based on the entire trust principal and also receives a charitable deduction for the value of the charitable remainder interest. Moreover, you can increase the charitable deduction by reducing the duration of the trusts involved, that is, by limiting each trust to a relatively short term of years rather than the life of a child or other beneficiary.

If you establish a charitable remainder annuity trust or a charitable remainder unitrust, the specified annual sum will be paid to your designated beneficiary or beneficiaries for life (or stipulated term of not more than 20 years) and the value of the remainder passing to charity will be deductible for estate tax purposes. The same results can be accomplished via a gift to a pooled income fund with income reserved for the life or lives of one or more designated beneficiaries. Further, if you establish a private foundation, as discussed in Section D, above, the charitable remainder can be given to your foundation.

If you would like to make a substantial gift to charity by will but do not wish thereby to reduce the income available to Mary or to your children, a charitable remainder trust may provide the ideal solution. It is important to recognize that the use of a charitable remainder trust does not merely preserve income for the intended beneficiary; it can actually increase the income available to her. It does so by reducing the tax otherwise payable out of the estate at the time of your death.

If you are interested in this subject, I can make appropriate tax calculations. The feasibility of such trusts for you will depend in part on the eventual composition of your trust assets.

GILBERT M. CANTOR

DATED: December 12, 1977

FORM A-3

Estate Planning Memorandum

Form A-3 is a sample of the type of estate planning memorandum which is recommended in Chapter 11, [¶1101.2], at page 259. Estate planning was done simultaneously for this client and his son, and the memorandum to this client's son is included in Form A-2. Although these two models are interrelated and similar in scope, they also differ noticeably because the son requested full particulars and calculations for review, whereas the father preferred that we touch on the highlights and omit unnecessary details.

Confidential Memorandum to William Smith

**ESTATE PLANNING REVIEW
AND
RECOMMENDATIONS**

Gilbert M. Cantor
Sixth Floor
1700 Sansom Street
Philadelphia, Pennsylvania 19103

Table of Contents

Smith Family Information

Name	Age*
William Smith	57
Jenny Smith	57
John Smith	34
(Wife: Mary Smith)	
Betsy Smith	12
Susan Smith	8
Edward Smith	23

Residence: 234 Front Street
　　　　　　 Philadelphia, Pa. 19103

Social Security numbers:
　　William:
　.　Jenny:

---

*Ages to be verified.

Estate Inventory

Assets owned individually by William Smith:

Cash in bank		$ 35,000	
Life insurance	50,000		
less policy loans	12,000		
		38,000	
Loans receivable		30,000	
Business interests		1,017,000	
			$1,120,000

Assets owned jointly by William Smith and Jenny Smith:

Cash in bank		2,000	
Residence	107,000		
Less mortgage	48,000		
		59,000	
Tangible personal property		10,000	
			71,000
GROSS ESTATE			$1,191,000

Notes payable—$34,000

Review and Recommendations

I. *INTRODUCTION*

Estate and tax planning are meaningful only insofar as they relate usefully to your goals and desires. For our preliminary analysis, our understanding of your objectives has been gleaned from the estate planning and business documents which you previously adopted and from discussions with your son John and the others who have been involved in the planning process.

Accordingly, as we have not yet had the advantage of personal discussion of the ends and means which you would regard as desirable, this memorandum is designed to present to you in summary form the main planning elements to which I would invite your attention. We can next pursue in greater depth, and endeavor to implement, those courses of action which are of greatest interest to you.

The main planning techniques which I would urge you to consider, as discussed in the balance of the memorandum, are these:

Estate tax marital deduction
Irrevocable trust
Lifetime gift program
Corporate recapitalization
Private annuity
Charitable foundation

II. *ESTATE TAX MARITAL DEDUCTION*

The Internal Revenue Code permits you to leave to Mrs. Smith, free of federal estate tax, up to one-half of your "adjusted gross (or net) estate." Assuming that you have an adjusted gross estate estimated at $1,100,000, assets aggregating $550,000 can be given to Mrs. Smith free of estate tax in your estate.

This marital deduction portion of your estate, to the extent it is not diminished, would eventually be includible in Mrs. Smith's estate for estate tax purposes. Nevertheless, the tax in her estate would presumably be imposed in lower brackets; the assets may decline in value or may be wholly or partially consumed or given away in Mrs. Smith's lifetime; and, in any event, she would have the benefit of the increased income generated by the funds which would have been paid in taxes at the time of your death if the marital deduction had not been utilized.

The difference in taxes—with and without the marital deduction—may be summarized as follows:

A. With no marital deduction (and nothing added to Mrs. Smith's gross estate):

Tax at your death	$301,000	
Tax at Mrs. Smith's death	0	
Total taxes		$301,000

B. With full marital deducation:

Tax at your death	$113,000	
Tax at Mrs. Smith's death	105,000	
Total Taxes		218,000
Tax saving via marital deduction		$ 83,000

Accordingly, I recommend full use of the estate tax marital deduction in your Will. Your present Will purports to establish a marital deduction trust for Mrs. Smith, *but*:

(1) For technical reasons we regard the type of formula used as unfortunate.

(2) I would suggest a broader range of principal distribution provisions for that trust.

(3) Your 1974 stock purchase agreement, relating to your shares of Gorgeous Country Enterprises, Inc., requires your unredeemed shares to be given to your two sons. The last sentence of Clause FIFTH of your Will also precludes allocating such stock to the marital trust. *The balance of your assets would be insufficient to provide the full marital deduction.*

This means that the stock purchase agreement should be altered and that your marital deduction trust should be amplified in both its technical and its "beneficial" aspects.

III. *LIFE INSURANCE—IRREVOCABLE TRUST*

I suggest that you consider the prompt establishment of an irrevocable life insurance trust for two reasons:

(1) By transferring ownership of your present life insurance policy (net of loans) to an irrevocable trust you can remove the net proceeds from your gross estate for estate tax purposes, provided you live at least

three years following the transfer. Further, if the trust is properly designed:

(a) The insurance proceeds can be made available to help meet your estate liquidity needs *without* having the insurance itself increase those needs.

(b) The proceeds will be excluded not only from your gross estate but from Mrs. Smith's gross estate as well.

(c) Although the trust would be "irrevocable," a great deal of flexibility can be built into it.

(2) Your liquid assets are grossly insufficient to cover the taxes and expenses that will be payable at the time of your death, not to mention those payable on the subsequent death of Mrs. Smith.

The Internal Revenue Code permits deferral of estate tax where closely held business interests comprise certain percentages of your gross estate, adjusted gross estate, or taxable estate. However, the applicable sections of the Code were altered in 1976, and may be altered again. Further, only a portion of the tax may be so deferred.

A Section 303 redemption, as provided in your 1974 stock purchase agreement, was previously considered a useful technique for extracting the needed funds from the corporation. Now, however, apart from the question whether the corporation will have the necessary funds, the Tax Reform Act of 1976 limits the basis of your stock to its 12/31/76 value, so that subsequent appreciation will result in capital gains tax in the Section 303 redemption. Thus there would be capital gains tax piled on top of the federal estate tax and the State inheritance tax. Under these circumstances, you may be well advised to reconsider the Section 303 redemption.

If life insurance is chosen, and it should be seriously considered as the primary way to meet your estate liquidity needs and Mrs. Smith's, it would be purchased by the Trustees of your irrevocable insurance trust. As in the case of your "old" insurance transferred to the trust, the insurance proceeds could be used for taxes and expenses without adding those proceeds to your taxable estate.

IV. *LIFETIME GIFT PROGRAM*

A common and excellent way to reduce one's taxable estate is to give away assets which are subject to tax. The preceding section III of this memorandum described one type of gift recommended for that purpose. While the Tax Reform Act has taken some of the advantages out of lifetime giving, it is still possible to effect substantial savings in this way.

Your wife and children and grandchildren provide you with a number of potential donees. Gifts can be made to them now and annually hereafter, outright or in trust. Gifts of what? I suggest for consideration gifts of two categories of non-liquid assets:

(1) Interests in those of your investments (other than Gorgeous Country stock) which are likely to increase in value, so that the increase will take place outside your estate.

(2) Gifts of shares of Gorgeous Country Enterprises, Inc., the growth of which would also take place outside your estate.

NOTE: To the extent you shift income producing assets to lower-bracket taxpayers, you effect an increase of the family's after-tax income in addition to the estate tax saving.

V. *CORPORATE RECAPITALIZATION*

If it is possible—and I would refer this question to our corporate department if you wish to pursue it—to effect a tax-free reorganization in which you would exchange your present Gorgeous Country stock for a new class of preferred stock, several potential advantages could be made available:

(a) The value of the preferred stock would be more readily ascertainable for estate tax purposes.

(b) The future growth of the corporation would be attributed to the common stock and thus occur outside your estate.

(c) The preferred stock dividends could eventually provide a part of your retirement income and Mrs. Smith's.

(d) Such stock might advantageously be used as part of the gift program suggested in section III, above. It could be distributed without diffusing control.

VI. *PRIVATE ANNUITY*

Shares of Gorgeous Country Enterprises, Inc. or other investments in your portfolio could be sold to your sons (or to the business entities involved) for a "private annuity." A private annuity is an arrangement whereby one party transfers property to another (a transferee not in the business of selling annuities) in return for the transferee's promise to make periodic payments of a fixed amount to the transferor for life.

The tax consequences are quite complex and I will not spell them out in detail at this preliminary stage. Basically, you as the annuitant would receive payments consisting of three elements determined by a formula: interest, capital gain, and tax-free recovery of basis. The transferee's basis varies depending on whether the asset is sold during your lifetime or thereafter, and differs for computing gain as compared with loss.

The transferee's promise to make the payments must be unsecured. Essentially, he must make them out of his after-tax income, so that it may be necessary to augment his income or to find other sources of funds if the required payments are substantial.

Properly handled, the annuity transaction is a sale and not a gift (though it can be combined with a gift). Therefore:

(1) There is no gift tax or loss of your unified gift and estate tax credit.

(2) The transferred assets are immediately removed from your gross estate*, without the three year "cloud" that hangs over a gift.

If a $500,000 annuity transaction (or set of them), for example, would be feasible in your case, the potential estate tax saving would be:

(a)   With full marital deduction $137,800
(b)   Without marital deduction $155,200

VII. CHARITABLE FOUNDATION

While other charitable transactions can be considered, if you wish, I would invite your attention preliminarily to the idea of a private non-operating charitable foundation.

To the extent of 20 percent of your adjusted gross income, you can make deductible gifts to your own private or family foundation. In this way, you will enjoy the tax benefits of the charitable deduction without completely losing control of the transferred property. Gorgeous Country could also make deductible contributions to it. The selection of particular charities, and the selection of charitable interests or goals, need not be fixed at the time of the gift or gifts but can be determined on an annual or more frequent basis. Such a foundation might be called, for example, "The William Smith Foundation" or "The William and Jenny Smith Foundation" or "The Smith Family Foundation."

One use of such a foundation, which may be of interest to you, is to finance major charitable projects which you could not otherwise undertake. By making regular contributions to your foundation in excess of the foundation's regular disbursements, a substantial accumulation can be effected for major future goals.

In the case of a private foundation, gifts of assets other than cash are deductible to the extent of their basis plus, in the case of long-term capital assets, one-half of any appreciation over basis. (The purpose is to put the taxpayer in approximately the same position as if he sold the property and contributed the proceeds to charity.) Subject to review of the highly technical restrictions which the 1969 Tax Reform Act imposed in this area, it might be possible to use some of your Gorgeous Country preferred stock, if the above-mentioned recapitalization takes

---

*If you reserve a joint and survivor annuity for yourself and Mrs. Smith, rather than an annuity for yourself alone, the survivor benefit would be includible in your gross estate at the cost of a comparable annuity at the gender and age of the survivor.

place, for gifts to your own foundation. Thus the stock could be kept in the hands of family Trustees while generating substantial annual income tax savings for you.

If we establish a private foundation for you, we will apply to the Internal Revenue Service for a determination as to the exempt status of your foundation prior to your making substantial transfers to it. A determination will normally, though not always, be made in advance of operations, on the basis of our statement of proposed operations in sufficient detail to permit the Service to conclude that the foundation will meet the requirements of the law. In some cases, the Service will insist upon a year of operation prior to a determination of exempt status. In order to maintain exempt status, there are various reporting requirements, compliance with which on a regular and careful basis is necessary, and, of course, it is necessary to operate in accordance with the tax laws and either the trust instrument or the corporate charter and by-laws, as the cases may be.

VIII. *SUPPLEMENTAL CONSIDERATIONS*

Other tax-saving techniques may be discussed after the foregoing has been reviewed. I have omitted the topic of generation-skipping trusts from this memorandum, for example, because it would represent a radical departure from the thinking embodied in your present Will. Also, the gift in Clause THIRD B of your Will appears to be inconsistent with the provisions of the stock purchase agreement with respect to redemption of Gorgeous Country stock, and this should be reviewed.

Gilbert M. Cantor

DATED: December 14, 1977

APPENDIX B

TABLES TO HELP YOU
Develop the Estate Plan

APPENDIX B—INTRODUCTION

The tables included in this Appendix are for use in connection with certain calculations discussed in Chapters 4, 6 and 11. (We have not endeavored to cull from the Regulations the numerous additional tables which tax planning analysis will involve from time to time.)

TABLE B-1

Table ET6 of IRS Publication No. 723A, Supplement 1(4-71)

This table is to be used to determine the value of a husband's interest in property owned by husband and wife as tenants by the entireties where relevant to the gift tax treatment of the termination of such tenancies as discussed in Chapter 4. (The value of the wife's interest is determined by subtracting the value of the husband's interest from the value of the entire property.)

Tables to Help You Develop the Estate Plan

Table ET6
Tenancy by the entirety. Interest at 6 percent

Factors for the combined income and survivorship rights of husband
as a tenant by the entirety (see note below)

Age of Wife	Husband OLDER than wife by						
	0 Yrs.	1 Yrs.	2 Yrs.	3 Yrs.	4 Yrs.	5 Yrs.	6 Yrs.
30	.47691	.47283	.46856	.46410	.45946	.45464	.44963
31	.47585	.47154	.46705	.46236	.45749	.45244	.44721
32	.47471	.47018	.46545	.46054	.45543	.45015	.44468
33	.47350	.46874	.46378	.45863	.45329	.44777	.44207
34	.47223	.46722	.46203	.45664	.45106	.44530	.43938
35	.47088	.46564	.46020	.45457	.44875	.44277	.43662
36	.46947	.46399	.45831	.45243	.44638	.44016	.43379
37	.46800	.46227	.45634	.45023	.44395	.43750	.43089
38	.46647	.46049	.45432	.44797	.44146	.43477	.42793
39	.46487	.45865	.45224	.44565	.43890	.43197	.42489
40	.46322	.45676	.45011	.44328	.43628	.42911	.42178
41	.46153	.45482	.44792	.44084	.43359	.42618	.41860
42	.45978	.45282	.44567	.43834	.43084	.42317	.41538
43	.45799	.45077	.44337	.43578	.42803	.42014	.41215
44	.45617	.44869	.44102	.43317	.42519	.41709	.40893
45	.45431	.44657	.43863	.43055	.42236	.41409	.40577
46	.45242	.44441	.43624	.42795	.41958	.41114	.40265
47	.45051	.44225	.43387	.42539	.41685	.40824	.39955
48	.44860	.44013	.43155	.42290	.41418	.40537	.39645
49	.44672	.43805	.42930	.42046	.41154	.40249	.39330
50	.44490	.43605	.42711	.41806	.40889	.39956	.39009
51	.44314	.43411	.42495	.41565	.40619	.39658	.38682
52	.44147	.43221	.42279	.41321	.40345	.39354	.38352
53	.43987	.43035	.42064	.41075	.40068	.39051	.38029
54	.43835	.42853	.41851	.40830	.39797	.38758	.37719
55	.43693	.42679	.41645	.40597	.39542	.38485	.37429
56	.43559	.42513	.41451	.40381	.39307	.38234	.37161
57	.43436	.42361	.41277	.40187	.39097	.38006	.36915
58	.43324	.42226	.41123	.40016	.38907	.37797	.36685
59	.43225	.42108	.40987	.39861	.38733	.37601	.36466
60	.43141	.42006	.40865	.39719	.38568	.37413	.36255
61	.43072	.41917	.40756	.39587	.38411	.37232	.36049
62	.43020	.41844	.40658	.39464	.38264	.37059	.35849
63	.42987	.41787	.40576	.39356	.38129	.36895	.35654
64	.42976	.41750	.40513	.39265	.38009	.36743	.35466
65	.42993	.41740	.40475	.39198	.37908	.36605	.35290
66	.43041	.41761	.40465	.39154	.37827	.36484	.35128
67	.43121	.41811	.40481	.39131	.37763	.36378	.34980
68	.43231	.41885	.40516	.39125	.37713	.36284	.34844
69	.43360	.41975	.40563	.39127	.37671	.36198	.34714

Age *of* *Wife*	Husband OLDER than wife by						
	0 Yrs.	*1 Yrs.*	*2 Yrs.*	*3 Yrs.*	*4 Yrs.*	*5 Yrs.*	*6 Yrs*
70	.43502	.42074	.40617	.39134	.37632	.36115	.34584
71	.43656	.42182	.40677	.39148	.37599	.36033	.34453
72	.43824	.42302	.40750	.39173	.37574	.35955	.34327
73	.44005	.42434	.40834	.39205	.37551	.35883	.34219
74	.44196	.42576	.40922	.39237	.37532	.35826	.34140
75	.44395	.42720	.41009	.39270	.37525	.35795	.34120
76	.44607	.42875	.41108	.39329	.37559	.35841	.34208
77	.44842	.43053	.41246	.39442	.37686	.36014	.34419
78	.45090	.43262	.41431	.39643	.37936	.36305	.34698
79	.45345	.43493	.41679	.39945	.38284	.36643	.34946

Note.—The above factors assume that each spouse is entitled to one-half of the income while both are living.

ⒸInstitute for Business Planning, Inc.

Table ET6
Tenancy by the entirety. Interest at 6 percent

Factors for the combined income and survivorship rights of husband as a tenant by the entirety (see note below)

Age *of* *Wife*	Husband OLDER than wife by						
	7 Yrs.	*8 Yrs.*	*9 Yrs.*	*10 Yrs.*	*11 Yrs.*	*12 Yrs.*	*13 Yrs.*
30	.44445	.43910	.43359	.42792	.42210	.41614	.41003
31	.44180	.43622	.43049	.42461	.41858	.41241	.40609
32	.43905	.43325	.42730	.42121	.41497	.40858	.40206
33	.43621	.43019	.42403	.41772	.41126	.40467	.39793
34	.43330	.42706	.42068	.41415	.40747	.40066	.39372
35	.43031	.42385	.41724	.41049	.40360	.39657	.38944
36	.42725	.42057	.41373	.40676	.39964	.39242	.38513
37	.42413	.41721	.41015	.40295	.39564	.38825	.38081
38	.42093	.41378	.40649	.39908	.39160	.38407	.37650
39	.41765	.41027	.40277	.39519	.38756	.37989	.37220
40	.41430	.40671	.39903	.39130	.38353	.37573	.36787
41	.41091	.40313	.39529	.38742	.37950	.37154	.36350
42	.40750	.39955	.39157	.38354	.37547	.36731	.35905
43	.40409	.39600	.38786	.37966	.37139	.36300	.35452
44	.40072	.39247	.38415	.37575	.36724	.35862	.34990
45	.39739	.38895	.38042	.37178	.36303	.35417	.34525
46	.39409	.38543	.37665	.36776	.35876	.34970	.34063
47	.39076	.38185	.37282	.36367	.35446	.34523	.33604
48	.38740	.37822	.36893	.35956	.35018	.34083	.33153
49	.38398	.37453	.36500	.35546	.34594	.33648	.32706

Age of Wife	Husband OLDER than wife by						
	7 Yrs.	*8 Yrs.*	*9 Yrs.*	*10 Yrs.*	*11 Yrs.*	*12 Yrs.*	*13 Yrs.*
50	.38049	.37080	.36109	.35141	.34177	.33218	.32263
51	.37697	.36709	.35723	.34742	.33764	.32791	.31822
52	.37348	.36344	.35344	.34348	.33356	.32367	.31381
53	.37007	.35989	.34974	.33962	.32953	.31947	.30945
54	.36682	.35647	.34616	.33587	.32560	.31536	.30516
55	.36376	.35324	.34274	.33225	.32180	.31138	.30100
56	.36090	.35019	.33948	.32881	.31816	.30754	.29693
57	.35823	.34731	.33640	.32552	.31467	.30381	.29296
58	.35571	.34458	.33346	.32236	.31126	.30015	.28903
59	.35330	.34195	.33060	.31924	.30786	.29647	.28506
60	.35096	.33936	.32773	.31608	.30440	.29271	.28102
61	.34864	.33675	.32482	.31285	.30085	.28885	.27687
62	.34634	.33412	.32186	.30955	.29722	.28491	.27264
63	.34405	.33148	.31885	.30619	.29354	.28091	.26833
64	.34180	.32886	.31586	.30285	.28986	.27690	.26399
65	.33964	.32631	.31294	.29958	.28623	.27291	.25969
66	.33761	.32389	.31015	.29641	.28268	.26903	.25561
67	.33572	.32161	.30747	.29332	.27924	.26537	.25184
68	.33396	.31942	.30485	.29032	.27600	.26200	.24862
69	.33222	.31723	.30226	.28746	.27299	.25914	.24612
70	.33044	.31502	.29975	.28480	.27046	.25697	.24425
71	.32867	.31293	.29749	.28266	.26868	.25549	.24270
72	.32708	.31115	.29582	.28135	.26768	.25440	.24099
73	.32579	.30997	.29502	.28086	.26708	.25314	.23956
74	.32510	.30967	.29503	.28075	.26627	.25213	.23835
75	.32530	.31020	.29543	.28040	.26569	.25132	.23738
76	.32653	.31129	.29572	.28045	.26548	.25093	.23711
77	.32850	.31243	.29661	.28106	.26589	.25146	.23814
78	.33044	.31411	.29800	.28224	.26720	.25329	.24061
79	.33266	.31603	.29971	.28409	.26960	.25636	.24430

NOTE.—The above factors assume that each spouse is entitled to one-half of the income while both are living.

Table ET6
Tenancy by the entirety. Interest at 6 percent

Factors for the combined income and survivorship rights of husband as a tenant by the entirety (see note below)

Age of Wife	Husband OLDER than wife by						
	14 Yrs.	*15 Yrs.*	*16 Yrs.*	*17 Yrs.*	*18 Yrs.*	*19 Yrs.*	*20 Yrs.*
30	.40378	.39740	.39088	.38423	.37747	.37064	.36375
31	.39964	.39306	.38634	.37951	.37261	.36566	.35867
32	.39540	.38861	.38172	.37474	.36772	.36066	.35357

Age of Wife	Husband OLDER than wife by						
	14 Yrs.	15 Yrs.	16 Yrs.	17 Yrs.	18 Yrs.	19 Yrs.	20 Yrs.
33	.39107	.38409	.37705	.36995	.36282	.35565	.34843
34	.38666	.37954	.37236	.36515	.35791	.35061	.34324
35	.38223	.37497	.36768	.36035	.35298	.34552	.33797
36	.37778	.37040	.36299	.35553	.34799	.34035	.33261
37	.37334	.36584	.35829	.35066	.34293	.33510	.32716
38	.36891	.36126	.35353	.34571	.33778	.32975	.32166
39	.36445	.35662	.34870	.34067	.33254	.32435	.31615
40	.35994	.35191	.34378	.33554	.32725	.31894	.31066
41	.35536	.34711	.33876	.33036	.32194	.31355	.30520
42	.35068	.34222	.33369	.32516	.31666	.30819	.29977
43	.34592	.33727	.32862	.31999	.31141	.30287	.29437
44	.34112	.33233	.32357	.31486	.30620	.29757	.28897
45	.33633	.32743	.31858	.30978	.30103	.29230	.28360
46	.33159	.32260	.31365	.30475	.29589	.28705	.27825
47	32690	.31781	.30876	.29974	.29076	.28181	.27290
48	.32228	.31307	.30390	.29476	.28566	.27660	.26757
49	.31769	.30835	.29905	.28978	.28056	.27137	.26220
50	.31312	.30364	.29420	.28481	.27545	.26610	.25677
51	.30855	.29893	.28935	.27981	.27029	.26077	.25125
52	.30400	.29422	.28449	.27477	.26506	.25535	.24564
53	.29947	.28953	.27961	.26969	.25978	.24986	.23997
54	.29501	.28487	.27473	.26460	.25447	.24436	.23428
55	.29063	.28027	.26990	.25954	.24920	.23889	.22864
56	.28633	.27573	.26513	.25454	.24399	.23349	.22305
57	.28211	.27125	.26040	.24960	.23885	.22815	.21751
58	.27790	.26679	.25571	.24469	.23373	.22282	.21202
59	.27366	.26230	.25099	.23974	.22855	.21747	.20659
60	.26935	.25774	.24618	.23469	.22331	.21213	.20127
61	.26494	.25306	.24124	.22953	.21804	.20687	.19622
62	.26042	.24825	.23620	.22437	.21286	.20189	.19162
63	.25580	.24338	.23118	.21932	.20801	.19741	.18747
64	.25118	.23859	.22634	.21466	.20372	.19344	.18353
65	.24670	.23404	.22197	.21065	.20002	.18977	.17949
66	.24253	.23004	.21832	.20732	.19669	.18604	.17574
67	.23891	.22678	.21538	.20436	.19331	.18261	.17226
68	.23605	.22423	.21280	.20133	.19022	.17945	.16910
69	.23385·	.22199	.21007	.19851	.18732	.17654	.16640
70	.23193	.21953	.20751	.19585	.18462	.17404	.16436
71	.22980	.21729	.20513	.19342	.18238	.17226	.16310
72	.22795	.21528	.20305	.19151	.18093	.17135	.16268
73	.22634	.21357	.20150	.19043	.18040	.17132	.16318
74	.22500	.21238	.20079	.19028	.18076	.17222	.16457

Age of Wife	Husband OLDER than wife by						
	14 Yrs.	15 Yrs.	16 Yrs.	17 Yrs.	18 Yrs.	19 Yrs.	20 Yrs.
75	.22417	.21203	.20100	.19101	.18204	.17400	.16667
76	.22439	.21282	.20233	.19290	.18445	.17673	.16915
77	.22602	.21500	.20510	.19621	.18809	.18010	.17246
78	.22906	.21867	.20934	.20081	.19240	.18434	.17663
79	.23342	.22366	.21471	.20588	.19741	.18929	.18151

Note.—The above factors assume that each spouse is entitled to one-half of the income while both are living.

Table ET6
Tenancy by the entirety. Interest at 6 percent

Factors for the combined income and survivorship rights of husband as a tenant by the entirety (see note below)

Age of Wife	Husband OLDER than wife by						
	21 Yrs.	22 Yrs.	23 Yrs.	24 Yrs.	25 Yrs.	26 Yrs.	27 Yrs.
30	.35683	.34986	.34285	.33575	.32854	.32123	.31380
31	.35164	.34456	.33740	.33013	.32276	.31527	.30772
32	.34642	.33919	.33186	.32442	.31687	.30926	.30162
33	.34113	.33373	.32622	.31861	.31092	.30322	.29553
34	.33576	.32818	.32049	.31274	.30497	.29721	.28947
35	.33030	.32254	.31471	.30686	.29903	.29123	.28345
36	.32476	.31685	.30892	.30101	.29313	.28528	.27745
37	.31916	.31115	.30315	.29519	.28726	.27936	.27147
38	.31356	.30547	.29742	.28941	.28142	.27345	.26549
39	.30797	.29983	.29172	.28364	.27559	.26754	.25952
40	.30242	.29421	.28604	.27789	.26976	.26164	.25355
41	.29689	.28862	.28037	.27214	.26393	.25574	.24758
42	.29139	.28303	.27469	.26638	.25810	.24983	.24157
43	.28589	.27744	.26902	.26063	.25226	.24389	.23551
44	.28040	.27186	.26335	.25487	.24639	.23790	.22940
45	.27493	.26630	.25769	.24909	.24049	.23187	.22324
46	.26948	.26074	.25201	.24328	.23454	.22579	.21704
47	.26403	.25516	.24629	.23742	.22854	.21966	.21079
48	.25856	.24954	.24053	.23150	.22248	.21348	.20452
49	.25303	.24386	.23468	.22551	.21636	.20725	.19818
50	.24743	.23809	.22876	.21945	.21019	.20096	.19177
51	.24174	.23223	.22275	.21332	.20392	.19457	.18530
52	.23595	.22628	.21667	.20709	.19757	.18812	.17885
53	.23010	.22029	.21052	.20080	.19117	.18172	.17252
54	.22425	.21427	.20435	.19452	.18486	.17547	.16652
55	.21844	.20829	.19824	.18837	.17878	.16963	.16106
56	.21267	.20238	.19229	.18247	.17311	.16435	.15612
57	.20698	.19664	.18659	.17701	.16803	.15961	.15148

Age of Wife	Husband OLDER than wife by						
	21 Yrs.	22 Yrs.	23 Yrs.	24 Yrs.	25 Yrs.	26 Yrs.	27 Yrs.
58	.20142	.19112	.18130	.17210	.16347	.15514	.14679
59	.19602	.18594	.17651	.16765	.15911	.15054	.14226
60	.19092	.18122	.17213	.16335	.15456	.14605	.13782
61	.18625	.17689	.16786	.15882	.15008	.14161	.13348
62	.18198	.17268	.16337	.15436	.14565	.13728	.12940
63	.17787	.16826	.15897	.14999	.14135	.13323	.12580
64	.17360	.16400	.15471	.14579	.13740	.12972	.12279
65	.16955	.15993	.15069	.14201	.13406	.12688	.12040
66	.16576	.15618	.14717	.13893	.13148	.12476	.11874
67	.16231	.15295	.14438	.13664	.12965	.12340	.11781
68	.15937	.15045	.14240	.13512	.12861	.12279	.11748
69	.15711	.14872	.14113	.13434	.12827	.12274	.11733
70	.15559	.14767	.14058	.13425	.12847	.12282	.11743
71	.15482	.14740	.14078	.13473	.12882	.12318	.11782
72	.15492	.14798	.14164	.13545	.12954	.12391	.11854
73	.15590	.14926	.14275	.13655	.13064	.12500	.11962
74	.15759	.15076	.14424	.13802	.13209	.12643	.12100
75	.15947	.15260	.14605	.13980	.13383	.12811	.12259
76	.16190	.15498	.14838	.14207	.13602	.13019	.12447
77	.16515	.15817	.15149	.14509	.13891	.13286	.12672
78	.16925	.16219	.15541	.14887	.14246	.13597	.12893
79	.17405	.16689	.15997	.15318	.14632	.13890	.12986

Note.—The above factors assume that each spouse is entitled to one-half of the income while both are living.

Table ET6
Tenancy by the entirety. Interest at 6 percent

Factors for the combined income and survivorship rights of husband as a tenant by the entirety (see note below)

Age of Wife	Husband YOUNGER than wife by						
	14 Yrs.	13 Yrs.	12 Yrs.	11 Yrs.	10 Yrs.	9 Yrs.	8 Yrs.
35	.52205	.51972	.51725	.51460	.51174	.50864	.50531
36	.52360	.52115	.51853	.51569	.51260	.50928	.50573
37	.52522	.52263	.51981	.51674	.51344	.50990	.50612
38	.52689	.52410	.52106	.51777	.51425	.51048	.50650
39	.52855	.52554	.52228	.51878	.51503	.51106	.50685
40	.53020	.52697	.52349	.51976	.51581	.51162	.50719
41	.53183	.52838	.52468	.52075	.51658	.51216	.50749
42	.53345	.52978	.52588	.52173	.51733	.51267	.50777
43	.53506	.53119	.52707	.52270	.51806	.51317	.50801
44	.53670	.53262	.52827	.52366	.51879	.51364	.50823

Age of Wife	Husband YOUNGER than wife by						
	14 Yrs.	_13 Yrs._	_12 Yrs._	_11 Yrs._	_10 Yrs._	_9 Yrs._	_8 Yrs._
45	.53836	.53405	.52948	.52463	.51950	.51411	.50844
46	.54004	.53551	.53069	.52560	.52023	.51457	.50865
47	.54175	.53697	.53191	.52657	.52094	.51503	.50884
48	.54347	.53845	.53314	.52755	.52166	.51549	.50905
49	.54520	.53994	.53438	.52852	.52237	.51595	.50926
50	.54694	.54143	.53562	.52950	.52311	.51643	.50947
51	.54870	.54293	.53686	.53050	.52385	.51691	.50969
52	.55047	.54445	.53813	.53152	.52461	.51741	.50992
53	.55228	.54602	.53945	.53258	.52541	.51794	.51018
54	.55418	.54767	.54085	.53372	.52629	.51855	.51051
55	.55620	.54944	.54237	.53498	.52728	.51927	.51095
56	.55835	.55135	.54402	.53637	.52840	.52010	.51153
57	.56065	.55339	.54580	.53789	.52963	.52110	.51230
58	.56306	.55555	.54770	.53951	.53102	.52226	.51329
59	.56556	.55779	.54967	.54124	.53254	.52360	.51446
60	.56811	.56008	.55173	.54309	.53422	.52512	.51579
61	.57071	.56245	.55390	.54510	.53606	.52679	.51725
62	.57342	.56496	.55625	.54729	.53809	.52861	.51881
63	.57628	.56767	.55881	.54970	.54030	.53057	.52047
64	.57939	.57065	.56164	.55233	.54269	.53266	.52224
65	.58281	.57392	.56474	.55520	.54526	.53492	.52417
66	.58656	.57751	.56810	.55828	.54804	.53737	.52635
67	.59062	.58136	.57167	.56156	.55100	.54007	.52885
68	.59492	.58540	.57544	.56502	.55421	.54309	.53172
69	.59939	.58959	.57933	.56867	.55768	.54643	.53493
70	.60397	.59389	.58339	.57257	.56145	.55009	.53845
71	.60866	.59836	.58772	.57678	.56558	.55409	.54232
72	.61356	.60313	.59239	.58137	.57007	.55847	.54653
73	.61874	.60823	.59743	.58634	.57494	.56318	.55107
74	.62423	.61368	.60283	.59165	.58012	.56821	.55593
75	.63005	.61946	.60855	.59727	.58560	.57354	.56108
76	.63627	.62564	.61464	.60326	.59147	.57926	.56661
77	.64294	.63226	.62118	.60970	.59779	.58543	.57254
78	.64996	.63923	.62808	.61651	.60448	.59191	.57875
79	.65716	.64639	.63518	.62351	.61129	.59847	.58500
80	.66440	.65358	.64230	.63047	.61803	.60492	.59110
81	.67142	.66054	.64912	.63707	.62435	.61090	.59670
82	.67810	.66709	.65546	.64315	.63009	.61627	.60165
83	.68456	.67336	.66148	.64885	.63543	.62121	.60617
84	.69131	.67990	.66774	.65478	.64101	.62639	.61085

Note.—The above factors assume that each spouse is entitled to one-half of the income while both are living.

Table ET6
Tenancy by the entirety. Interest at 6 percent

Factors for the combined income and survivorship rights of husband
as a tenant by the entirety (see note below)

Age of Wife	Husband YOUNGER than wife by						
	7 Yrs.	6 Yrs.	5 Yrs.	4 Yrs.	3 Yrs.	2 Yrs.	1 Yrs.
30	.50010	.49740	.49450	.49139	.48807	.48454	.48082
31	.50052	.49762	.49451	.49117	.48763	.48389	.47996
32	.50091	.49779	.49445	.49090	.48714	.48319	.47905
33	.50123	.49789	.49433	.49056	.48659	.48243	.47806
34	.50151	.49795	.49417	.49019	.48601	.48162	.47702
35	.50175	.49796	.49397	.48978	.48537	.48075	.47592
36	.50194	.49795	.49375	.48932	.48468	.47983	.47476
37	.50213	.49792	.49348	.48883	.48395	.47885	.47353
38	.50229	.49785	.49318	.48829	.48316	.47781	.47225
39	.50242	.49774	.49283	.48769	.48232	.47672	.47090
40	.50251	.49760	.49244	.48705	.48142	.47557	.46950
41	.50258	.49741	.49200	.48636	.48047	.47437	.46805
42	.50260	.49719	.49152	.48562	.47948	.47312	.46655
43	.50259	.49692	.49100	.48484	.47844	.47183	.46502
44	.50256	.49663	.49045	.48403	.47739	.47052	.46345
45	.50251	.49632	.48988	.48321	.47631	.46919	.46185
46	.50245	.49601	.48932	.48239	.47522	.46784	.46024
47	.50239	.49569	.48874	.48155	.47412	.46647	.45859
48	.50234	.49538	.48817	.48071	.47301	.46508	.45693
49	.50229	.49507	.48758	.47985	.47188	.46367	.45527
50	.50224	.49475	.48700	.47899	.47073	.46227	.45364
51	.50220	.49443	.48639	.47810	.46959	.46090	.45208
52	.50215	.49410	.48578	.47723	.46849	.45961	.45060
53	.50213	.49380	.48522	.47644	.46750	.45843	.44922
54	.50218	.49359	.48478	.47580	.46668	.45740	.44797
55	.50236	.49354	.48454	.47537	.46605	.45655	.44685
56	.50272	.49371	.48452	.47516	.46561	.45584	.44584
57	.50330	.49411	.48473	.47515	.46533	.45526	.44493
58	.50411	.49473	.48513	.47528	.46515	.45475	.44409
59	.50509	.49550	.48563	.47548	.46502	.45429	.44334
60	.50622	.49635	.48618	.47569	.46490	.45388	.44269
61	.50741	.49725	.48674	.47592	.46483	.45357	.44219
62	.50867	.49817	.48733	.47621	.46489	.45343	.44187
63	.51000	.49917	.48803	.47668	.46516	.45352	.44175
64	.51144	.50031	.48895	.47740	.46571	.45387	.44189
65	.51308	.50174	.49019	.47847	.46658	.45453	.44231
66	.51505	.50353	.49182	.47991	.46783	.45554	.44306
67	.51739	.50572	.49383	.48174	.46942	.45688	.44414
68	.52011	.50828	.49621	.48390	.47134	.45854	.44553
69	.52318	.51117	.49890	.48635	.47354	.46048	.44717

Age *of* *Wife*	Husband YOUNGER than wife by						
	7 Yrs.	6 Yrs.	5 Yrs.	4 Yrs.	3 Yrs.	2 Yrs.	1Yrs.
70	.52655	.51435	.50185	.48906	.47599	.46264	.44899
71	.53023	.51782	.50509	.49205	.47871	.46501	.45096
72	.53424	.52162	.50866	.49536	.48167	.46759	.45311
73	.53859	.52576	.51255	.49892	.48485	.47035	.45540
74	.54326	.53019	.51666	.50267	.48819	.47322	.45780
75	.54820	.53484	.52096	.50656	.49163	.47619	.46028
76	.55346	.53977	.52551	.51067	.49527	.47935	.46295
77	.55909	.54503	.53036	.51507	.49921	.48282	.46588
78	.56496	.55051	.53541	.51968	.50337	.48644	.46892
79	.57084	.55599	.54046	.52429	.50745	.48995	.47187

Note.—The above factors assume that each spouse is entitled to one-half of the income while both are living.

TABLE B-2

Reg. Sec. 20.2031-10(f)
Tables A(1) and A(2)

Table B-2 should be used, as explained in Chapter 6, to determine the present value of the annuity promise in order to ascertain the tax treatment of a client's private annuity.

REGULATIONS

Valuation Table-Estate Tax (Regs. 20.2031-10(f)
(Note: Gift Tax Regs. 25.2512-9(f) are identical)

Table A(1)

*Table, single life male, 6 percent, showing
the present worth of an annuity, of a life
interest, and of a remainder interest*

(1)	(2)	(3)	(4)	(1)	(2)	(3)	(4)
		Life	Remain-			Life	Remain-
Age	Annuity	estate	der	Age	Annuity	estate	der
0	15.6175	0.93705	0.06295	37	13.6036	.81622	.18378
1	16.0362	.96217	.03783	38	13.4591	.80755	.19245
2	16.0283	.96170	.03830	39	13.3090	.79854	.20146
3	16.0089	.96053	.03947	40	13.1538	.78923	.21077
4	15.9841	.95905	.04095	41	12.9934	.77960	.22040
5	15.9553	.95732	.04268	42	12.8279	.76967	.23033
6	15.9233	.95540	.04460	43	12.6574	0.75944	0.24056
7	15.8885	.95331	.04669	44	12.4819	.74891	.25109
8	15.8508	.95105	.04895	45	12.3013	.73808	.26192
9	15.8101	.94861	.05139	46	12.1158	.72695	.27305
10	15.7663	.94598	.05402	47	11.9253	.71552	.28448
11	15.7194	.94316	.05684	48	11.7308	.70385	.29615
12	15.6698	.94019	.05981	49	11.5330	.69198	.30802
13	15.6180	.93708	.06292	50	11.3329	.67997	.32003
14	15.5651	.93391	.06609	51	11.1308	.66785	.33215
15	15.5115	.93069	.06931	52	10.9267	.65560	.34440
16	15.4576	.92746	.07254	53	10.7200	.64320	.35680
17	15.4031	.92419	.07581	54	10.5100	.63060	.36940
18	15.3481	.92089	.07911	55	10.2960	.61776	.38224
19	15.2918	.91751	.08249	56	10.0777	.60466	.39534
20	15.2339	.91403	.08597	57	9.8552	.59131	.40869
21	15.1744	.91046	.08954	58	9.6297	.57778	.42222
22	15.1130	.90678	.09328	59	9.4028	.56417	.43583
23	15.0487	.90292	.09702	60	9.1753	.55052	.44948
24	14.9807	.89884	.10116	61	8.9478	.53687	.46313
25	14.9075	.89445	.10555	62	8.7202	.52321	.47679
26	14.8287	.88972	.11028	63	8.4924	.50954	.49046
27	14.7442	.88465	.11535	64	8.2642	.49585	.50415
28	14.6542	.87925	.12075	65	8.0353	.48212	.51788
29	14.5588	.87353	.12647	66	7.8060	.46836	.53164
30	14.4584	.86750	.13250	67	7.5763	.45458	.54542
31	14.3528	.86117	.13883	68	7.3462	.44077	.55923
32	14.2418	.85451	.14549	69	7.1149	.42689	.57311
33	14.1254	.84752	.15248	70	6.8823	.41294	.58706
34	14.0034	.84020	.15980	71	6.6481	.39889	.60111
35	13.8758	.83255	.16745	72	6.4123	.38474	.61526
36	13.7425	.82455	.17545	73	6.1752	.37051	.62949

(1) Age	(2) Annuity	(3) Life estate	(4) Remain- der	(1) Age	(2) Annuity	(3) Life estate	(4) Remain- der
74	5.9373	.35624	.64376	92	2.3917	.14350	.85650
75	5.6900	.34194	.65806	93	2.2801	.13681	.86319
76	5.4602	.32761	.67239	94	2.1802	.13081	.86919
77	5.2211	.31327	.68673	95	2.0891	.12535	.87465
78	4.9825	.29895	.70105	96	1.9997	.11998	.88002
79	4.7469	.28481	.71519	97	1.9145	.11487	.88513
80	4.5164	.27008	.72902	98	1.8331	.10999	.89001
81	4.2955	.25773	.74227	99	1.7554	.10532	.89468
82	4.0879	.24527	.75473	100	1.6812	.10087	.89913
83	3.8924	.23354	.76646	101	1.6101	.09661	.90339
84	3.7029	.22217	.77783	102	1.5416	.09250	.90750
85	3.5117	.21070	.78930	103	1.4744	.08846	.91154
86	3.3259	.19955	.80045	104	1.4065	.08439	.91561
87	3.1450	.18820	.81130	105	1.3334	.08000	.92000
88	2.9703	.17872	.82178	106	1.2452	.07471	.9252
89	2.8052	.16831	.83169	107	1.1196	.06718	.93282
90	2.6536	.15922	.84078	108	.9043	.05426	.94574
91	2.5162	.15097	.84903	109	.4717	.02830	.97170

Table A(2)

Table, single life female, 6 percent, showing the present worth of an annuity, of a life
interest, and of a remainder interest

(1) Age	(2) Annuity	(3) Life estate	(4) Remain- der	(1) Age	(2) Annuity	(3) Life estate	(4) Remain- der
0	15.8972	0.95383	0.04617	18	15.7620	.94572	.05428
1	16.2284	.97370	.02630	19	15.7172	.94303	.05697
2	16.2287	.97372	.02628	20	15.6701	.94021	.05979
3	16.2180	.97308	.02692	21	15.6207	.93724	.06276
4	16.2029	.97217	.02783	22	15.5687	.93412	.06588
5	16.1850	.97110	.02890	23	15.5141	.93085	.06915
6	16.1648	.96989	.03011	24	15.4565	.92739	.07261
7	16.1421	.96853	.03147	25	15.3959	.92375	.07625
8	16.1172	.96703	.03297	26	15.3322	.91993	.08007
9	16.0910	.96541	.03459	27	15.2652	.91591	.08409
10	16.0608	.96365	.03635	28	15.1946	.91168	.08832
11	16.0293	.96176	.03824	29	15.1208	.90725	.09275
12	15.9958	.95975	.04025	30	15.0432	.90259	.09741
13	15.9607	.95764	.04236	31	14.9622	.89773	.10227
14	15.9239	0.95543	0.04457	32	14.8775	.89265	.10735
15	15.8856	.95314	.04686	33	14.7888	.88733	.11267
16	15.8460	.95076	.04924	34	14.6960	.88176	.11824
17	15.8048	.94829	.05171	35	14.5989	.87593	.12407

(1) Age	(2) Annuity	(3) Life estate	(4) Remain- der	(1) Age	(2) Annuity	(3) Life estate	(4) Remain- der
36	14.4975	.86985	.13015	73	7.0568	.42341	.57659
37	14.3915	.86349	.13651	74	6.7645	.40587	.59413
38	14.2811	.85687	.14313	75	6.4721	.38833	.61167
39	14.1663	.84998	.15002	76	6.1788	.37073	.62927
40	14.0468	.84281	.15719	77	5.8845	.35307	.64693
41	13.9227	.83536	.16464	78	5.5910	.33546	.66454
42	13.7940	.82764	.17236	79	5.3018	.31811	.68189
43	13.6604	.81962	.18038	80	5.0195	.30117	.69883
44	13.5219	.81131	.18869	81	4.7482	.28489	.71511
45	13.3781	.80269	.19731	82	4.4892	.26935	.73065
46	13.2290	.79374	.20626	83	4.2398	.25439	.74561
47	13.0746	.78448	.21552	84	3.9927	.23956	.76044
48	12.9147	.77488	.22512	85	3.7401	.22441	.77559
49	12.7496	.76498	.23502	86	3.5016	.21010	.78990
50	12.5793	.75476	.24524	87	3.2790	.19674	.80326
51	12.4039	.74423	.25577	88	3.0719	.18431	.81569
52	12.2232	.73339	.26661	89	2.8808	.17285	.82715
53	12.0367	.72220	.27780	90	2.7068	.16241	.83759
54	11.8436	.71062	.28938	91	2.5502	.15301	.84699
55	11.6432	.69859	.30141	92	2.4116	.14470	.85530
56	11.4353	.68612	.31388	93	2.2901	.13741	.86259
57	11.2200	.67320	.32680	94	2.1839	.13103	.86897
58	10.9980	.65988	.34012	95	2.0891	.12535	.87465
59	10.7703	.64622	.35378	96	1.9997	.11998	.88002
60	10.5376	.63226	.36774	97	1.9145	.11487	.88513
61	10.3005	.61803	.38197	98	1.8331	.10999	.89001
62	10.0587	.60352	.39648	99	1.7554	.10532	.89468
63	9.8118	.58871	.41129	100	1.6812	.10087	.89913
64	9.5592	.57355	.42645	101	1.6101	.09661	.90339
65	9.3005	.55803	.44197	102	1.5416	.09250	.90750
66	9.0352	.54211	.45789	103	1.4744	.08846	.91154
67	8.7639	.52583	.47417	104	1.4065	.08439	.91561
68	8.4874	.50924	.49076	105	1.3334	.08000	.92000
69	8.2068	.49241	.50759	106	1.2452	.07471	.92529
70	7.9234	.47540	.52460	107	1.1196	.06718	.93282
71	7.6371	.45823	.54177	108	.9043	.05426	.94574
72	7.3480	.44088	.55912	109	.4717	.02830	.97170

TABLE B-3

Reg. Sec. 1.72-9, Table I

Table B-3 should be used, as explained in Chapter 6, to determine the taxpayer's life expectancy for calculation of his expected return (annual payment multiplied by life expectancy) to ascertain the tax treatment of a client's private annuity.

Table I—
Ordinary Life Annuities—One Life—
Expected Return Multiples

Ages		Multiples	Ages		Multiples	Ages		Multiples
Male	Female		Male	Female		Male	Female	
6	11	65.0	41	46	33.0	76	81	9.1
7	12	64.1	42	47	32.1	77	82	8.7
8	13	63.2	43	48	31.2	78	83	8.3
9	14	62.3	44	49	30.4	79	84	7.8
10	15	61.4	45	50	29.6	80	85	7.5
11	16	60.4	46	51	28.7	81	86	7.1
12	17	59.9	47	52	27.9	82	87	6.7
13	18	58.6	48	53	27.1	83	88	6.3
14	19	57.7	49	54	26.3	84	89	6.0
15	20	56.7	50	55	25.5	85	90	5.7
16	21	55.8	51	56	24.7	86	91	5.4
17	22	54.9	52	57	24.0	87	92	5.1
18	23	53.9	53	58	23.2	88	93	4.8
19	24	53.0	54	59	22.4	89	94	4.5
20	25	52.1	55	60	21.7	90	95	4.2
21	26	51.1	56	61	21.0	91	96	4.0
22	27	50.2	57	62	20.3	92	97	3.7
23	28	49.3	58	63	19.6	93	98	3.5
24	29	48.3	59	64	18.9	94	99	3.3
25	30	47.4	60	65	18.2	95	100	3.1
26	31	46.5	61	66	17.5	96	101	2.9
27	32	45.6	62	67	16.9	97	102	2.7
28	33	44.6	63	68	16.2	98	103	2.5
29	34	43.7	64	69	15.6	99	104	2.3
30	35	42.8	65	70	15.0	100	105	2.1
31	36	41.9	66	71	14.4	101	106	1.9
32	37	41.0	67	72	13.8	102	107	1.7
33	38	40.0	68	73	13.2	103	108	1.5
34	39	39.1	69	74	12.6	104	109	1.3
35	40	38.2	70	75	12.1	105	110	1.2
						106	111	1.0
36	41	37.3	71	76	11.6	107	112	.8
37	42	36.5	72	77	11.0	108	113	.7
38	43	35.6	73	78	10.5	109	114	.6
39	44	34.7	74	79	10.1	110	115	.5
40	45	33.8	75	80	9.6	111	116	0

TABLE B-4

Estate Projections

This table provides estate projections for males, showing the value at the end of life expectancy per $100,000 of current value, assuming growth rates (asset appreciation plus income accumulation) of 5 percent, 7 percent and 9 percent. The use of these projections is discussed in Chapter 11, [¶1101.2], at page 260.

Estate Projections
(Assuming No Withdrawals of Income)

Approximate Value At End of Life Expectancy
Per $100,000 Current Value
(Includes Appreciation of Assets and
Accumulation of Income)

Current Age	Life Expectancy	Low Growth (5%)	Medium Growth (7%)	High Growth (9%)
35	36 years	$579,000	$1,142,000	$2,225,000
36	35	552,000	1,068,000	2,041,000
37	34	525,000	998,000	1,873,000
38	33	500,000	933,000	1,718,000
39	32	477,000	872,000	1,576,000
40	31	454,000	872,000	1,576,000
41	30	432,000	761,000	1,327,000
42	29	412,000	711,000	1,217,000
43	29	412,000	711,000	1,217,000
44	28	392,000	665,000	1,117,000
45	27	373,000	621,000	1,025,000
46	26	356,000	581,000	940,000
47	25	339,000	543,000	862,000
48	24	323,000	507,000	791,000
49	24	323,000	507,000	791,000
50	23	307,000	474,000	726,000
51	22	293,000	443,000	666,000
52	21	279,000	414,000	611,000
53	21	279,000	414,000	611,000
54	20	265,000	387,000	560,000
55	19	253,000	362,000	514,000
56	18	241,000	338,000	472,000
57	18	241,000	338,000	472,000
58	17	229,000	316,000	433,000
59	16	218,000	295,000	397,000
60	16	218,000	295,000	397,000
61	15	208,000	276,000	364,000
62	15	208,000	276,000	364,000
63	14	198,000	258,000	334,000
64	13	189,000	241,000	307,000
65	13	189,000	241,000	307,000
66	12	180,000	225,000	281,000
67	12	180,000	225,000	281,000
68	11	171,000	211,000	258,000
69	11	171,000	211,000	258,000
70	10	163,000	197,000	237,000

*Based Upon United States Life Tables For Men (1968)

APPENDIX C

FORMS TO CARRY OUT

The Estate Plan

APPENDIX C—INTRODUCTION

This Appendix provides a number of forms and models, most of which are taken from the authors' law practice. These should be helpful in implementing the estate plans which you develop with the guidance of this book. Obviously, you should satisfy yourself, before using or adapting any of these forms or models, as to its adequacy under applicable State law, its general efficacy for the intended tax purpose, and its specific efficacy or desirability for the particular client involved. While the authors have used these forms, they assume no responsibility for any consequences of your employment or adaptation of them.

FORM C-1

Sample Power of Appointment Trust for Marital Deduction

This form provides the dispositive provisions (omitting the formula) of a power of appointment marital deduction trust. It includes a variety of principal invasion provisions (paragraphs B through E), although only paragraphs A and F of the form are required for marital deduction purposes. In some cases, you will wish to provide for the surviving spouse to withdraw principal at will, with no limitation; in such case, paragraphs B and E of this form should be omitted, but paragraphs C and D should be retained for use in case of a disability that prevents the spouse from exercising her withdrawal power. The mandatory and optional provisions of a power of appointment trust are discussed in Chapter 1, ¶103.2.

Sample of Power of Appointment Trust
for Marital Deduction

THE MARITAL DEDUCTION TRUST. I give the Marital Deduction Portion of my residuary estate to my Trustees, who shall hold it in a separate trust to be known as "The Marital Deduction Trust" and dispose of the net income and principal as follows:

A. My Trustees shall distribute all of the net income to my wife, Mary Smith, during her lifetime, in annual or more frequent periodic installments. (The term "net income" in this paragraph A shall be construed to include all items or amounts within the meaning of the term "income" in the estate tax marital deduction provisions of the Internal Revenue Code in effect at the time of my death.)

B. For each calendar year in which my wife's income from this trust and from all other sources (including as "income" for this purpose any periodic payments to her under policies of insurance on my life and any Social Security payments she may receive), minus the amount of the income tax due by her for that year, amounts to less than
Thousand Dollars, my Trustees shall distribute to my wife from the principal of this trust, if she so requests in writing by the thirtieth day of April of the following year, a sum equal to the amount of such deficiency; provided, however, that the right of my wife to require such principal distributions shall lapse to the extent it is not so exercised for any such year.

Notwithstanding the foregoing provisions, my Trustees shall compare the Consumer Price Index for Urban Wage Earners and Clerical Workers—U.S. City Average, all items (1976 equals 100), which is published by the Bureau of Labor Statistics of the United States Department of Labor, as of the end of each calendar year with such Index as of the end of the year 197 , and the figure of   Thousand Dollars above mentioned shall be adjusted upward or downward, prospectively, for purposes of this paragraph B, in proportion to the changes in the Index as so determined. If publication of the Consumer Price Index is discontinued, my Trustees shall apply comparable cost of living statistics as computed by an agency of the United States Government or by a responsible financial periodical, my Trustees' selection of such statistical data to be binding on all concerned.

The amount of principal which may be distributed to my wife under the provisions of this paragraph B for the year in which my death occurs shall be proportionate to the part of that year then remaining.

C. My Trustees shall also distribute to my wife, or apply for her benefit, such portions of the principal as my Trustees in their sole discretion may from time to time deem necessary for payment of the expenses of any accident, illness, or emergency needs of my wife.

D. My Trustees shall also distribute to my wife, or apply for her benefit, such portions of the principal as my Trustees in their sole discretion may from time to time deem necessary in order to provide for the maintenance of my wife in accordance with the standard of living to which she shall be accustomed at the time of my death.

E. During her lifetime, my wife shall have the right at any time, and from time to time, to make gifts of the principal, without limitation, to and among my children, and the issue of my children, or any of them, in such amounts or proportions, on such terms and conditions, and subject to such trusts or limitations, as my wife may in writing set forth, provided that no such distribution shall be made without the prior written approval of the then serving Trustee or Trustees other than my wife.

In addition, my wife shall have the right to withdraw from the principal, on her request in writing, any amounts that may be required for the payment of any transfer taxes that may be incurred as a result of such gifts.

F. Upon the death of my wife, the principal of this trust then remaining shall be distributed to such beneficiary or beneficiaries, in such amounts or proportions, on such terms and conditions, and subject to such trusts or limitations, as my wife may appoint in her Will, or by other instrument delivered to my Trustees during her lifetime, making specific reference to this power of appointment in such Will or other instrument. In the exercise of this power of appointment, my wife may designate her estate to receive all or any portion of the trust principal. The power of appointment granted to my wife in this paragraph F shall be exercisable by her alone and in all events.

G. Upon the death of my wife, any principal then remaining of this trust with respect to which she fails to exercise effectively the power of appointment which is given to her in the preceding paragraph F shall be disposed of as follows:

(1) My Trustees shall pay out of such unappointed principal the amounts of any increase in federal and state estate and inheritance taxes and administration expenses in my wife's estate which are attributable to the inclusion therein of such unappointed principal, and my Trustees may accept as correct a written statement by my wife's personal representatives as to the amounts so payable; and

(2) My Trustees shall distribute the balance of such unappointed principal to . . .

FORM C-2

Sample Estate Trust for Marital Deduction

This form provides the dispositive provisions (omitting the formula) of an estate trust qualifying for the marital deduction. For an estate trust with provision for invasion of principal during the lifetime of the surviving spouse, see paragraph B of Clause ELEVENTH of Form C-3. The mandatory and optional provisions of an estate trust are discussed in Chapter 1, ¶103.3.

Sample Estate Trust for Marital Deduction

THE MARITAL DEDUCTION TRUST. I give the Marital Deduction Portion of my residuary estate to my Trustees, who shall hold it in a separate trust to be known as "The Marital Deduction Trust" and dispose of the net income and principal as follows:

A. My Trustees shall either accumulate the net income or distribute all or any part of the current or accumulated net income to my wife, , as the Trustees other than my wife, in their sole discretion, may from time to time deem advisable.

B. Upon the death of my wife, the principal and any accumulated and undistributed income of this trust then remaining shall be distributed to her personal representatives, to be disposed of as part of my wife's estate.

FORM C-3

Complete Will with Power of
Appointment Trust and Estate Trust
for Marital Deduction Purposes

Form C-3 provides for division of the marital deduction fractional share of the estate into two trusts, a power of appointment trust and an estate trust, as discussed in ¶103.2 and ¶103.3, respectively, of Chapter 1. For establishment of the trusts, see Clauses Tenth and Eleventh. The formula is provided in Clause Fourteenth, and special restrictions to protect the deduction are set forth in Clause Fifteenth. Specially adapted to a marital deduction will be the tax clause (Eighteenth) and paragraphs D and R of Clause Nineteenth.

WILL
OF

Table of Contents

I,   , declare
this to be my Will.

PRIOR INSTRUMENTS

FIRST: REVOCATION. I revoke all of my prior wills and codicils.

APPOINTMENT OF MY FIDUCIARIES

SECOND: GUARDIANS OF PERSONS OF MINOR CHILDREN. If
my wife,   , does not survive me, I appoint as Guardians of
the persons of my minor children
                . If   should
for any reason fail or cease so to serve, I appoint
                    as such Guardians.

THIRD: GUARDIANS OF MINORS' ESTATES. I appoint my wife,
                    as Guardian of any property which passes to a minor
(under the provisions of my Will or otherwise) and with respect to which
I am authorized by law to appoint such Guardian and have not otherwise
done so. If   should for any reason fail or cease to serve, I
appoint   as such Guardian.

The Guardians of each minor's estate are authorized to use principal as well as income thereof for the minor's maintenance, education and
welfare, as the Guardians, in their sole discretion, may from time to time
deem advisable. In addition, such Guardians shall have the same management powers with respect to each minor's estate as are granted to my
Executors and Trustees under subsequent provisions of this Will.

FOURTH: EXECUTORS. I appoint
                    and
as Executors of my Will.

FIFTH: TRUSTEES. I appoint as my Trustees hereunder
and

SIXTH: COMPENSATION. My original corporate Trustee and each corporate successor shall be compensated from time to time for its services in the administration of the trust hereunder in accordance with its schedule of fees in effect during the period over which such services are rendered.

Each individual Trustee shall be entitled to receive compensation from time to time during the period of his or her services hereunder equal to one-half of the compensation payable during that period to the corporate Trustee, such compensation to be in addition to that of the corporate Trustee.

SEVENTH: CHANGE OF CORPORATE TRUSTEE. The individual Trustee other than my wife is authorized at any time, and from time to time, by instrument in writing delivered to the other Trustee or Trustees then serving, to remove the corporate Trustee without stating any reason for such action, provided he simultaneously by written instrument appoints another corporate Turstee in its place.

EIGHTH: WAIVER OF BOND. I direct that no Guardian, Executor or Trustee serving at any time hereunder shall be required to file bond or give security in any jurisdiction, any rule or law to the contrary notwithstanding.

DISPOSITION OF MY ESTATE

NINTH: TANGIBLE PERSONAL PROPERTY. I give to my wife, , if she survives me, my jewelry, clothing and other articles of personal use, household furniture and furnishings, and automobiles, and all policies of insurance relating to those things.

If   does not survive me, my Executors shall sell any of the items described in the preceding paragraph which they, in their sole discretion, do not consider suitable for current or eventual distribution to my children, the proceeds to be part of my residuary estate. The items which are not so disposed of I give to my children who survive me, to be divided between or among them in shares as nearly equal in value as may be practicable, as my Executors in their sole discretion shall determine. My Executors are authorized (a) to hold or store such property for a minor during his or her minority, making arrangements for payment out of my residuary estate of any storage, insurance and other related charges, or (b) to deliver any or all of the items to the minor, or to the Guardians of the minor's person or estate, or to any other person or persons selected by my Executors to hold such property for the minor, as and when my Executors may deem appropriate. The receipt or receipts given to my Executors by the minor or other distributee or distributees shall be fully effective to release and discharge my Executors with respect to such distributions.

    TENTH: DIVISION OF MY RESIDUARY ESTATE. If my wife,
, survives me, my residuary estate shall be divided into two fractional portions, the Marital Deduction Portion and the Non-Marital Portion, the division to be made in accordance with the formula provided in Clause FOURTEENTH, and the beneficial interest of my wife in the trusts provided in Clause ELEVENTH shall vest in her immediately upon my death. If   does not survive me, my entire residuary estate shall be disposed of under the provisions of my Will relating to the Non-Marital Portion.

    ELEVENTH: THE*
TRUSTS. I give the Marital Deduction Portion of my residuary estate to my Trustees, who shall allocate two-thirds thereof to a separate trust to be known as"*
Trust A," and one-third to a separate trust to be known as"*
Trust B."

    A.   *Trust A.* My Trustees all dispose of the net income and principal of   Trust A as follows:

    (1) My Trustees shall distribute all of the net income to my wife,
, during her lifetime, in annual or more frequent periodic installments. (The term "net income" in his paragraph A shall be construed to include all items or amounts within the meaning of the term "income" in the estate tax marital deduction provisions of the Internal Revenue Code in effect at the time of my death.)

    (2) For each calendar year in which my wife's income from this trust and from all other sources (including as "income" for this purpose any periodic payments to her under policies of insurance on my life and any Social Security payments she may receive), minus the amount of the income tax due by her for that year, amounts to less than
Thousand Dollars, my Trustees shall distribute to my wife from the principal of this trust, if she so requests in writing by the thirtieth day of April of the following year, a sum equal to the amount of such deficiency; provided, however, that the right of my wife to require such principal distribution shall lapse to the extent it is not so exercised for any such year.

    Notwithstanding the foregoing provisions, my Trustees shall compare the Consumer Price Index for Urban Wage Earners and Clerical Workers—U.S. City Average, all items (1967 equals 100), which is published by the Bureau of Labor Statistics of the United States Department of Labor, as of the end of each calendar year with such Index as of the end of the year 1975, and the figure of

*Use of wife's full name is suggested.

Thousand Dollars above mentioned shall be adjusted upward or downward, prospectively, for purposes of this subparagraph A(2), in proportion to the changes in the Index as so determined. If publication of the Consumer Price Index is discontinued, my Trustees shall apply comparable cost of living statistics as computed by an agency of the United States Government or by a responsible financial periodical, my Trustees' selection of such statistical data to be binding on all concerned.

My Trustees may rely upon any statements of my wife as to the amounts of her income (as above defined in this subparagraph) from sources other than trusts under my Will, and as to the amounts of her income taxes, and my Trustees shall not be required to verify any such figures.

The amount of principal which may be distributed to my wife under the provisions of this subparagraph A(2) for the year in which my death occurs shall be proportionate to the part of that year then remaining.

(3) My Trustees shall also distribute to my wife, or apply for her benefit, such portions of the principal as my Trustees in their sole discretion may from time to time deem necessary for payment of the expenses of any accident, illness or emergency needs of my wife.

(4) My Trustees shall also distribute to my wife, or apply for her benefit, such portions of the principal as my Trustees in their sole discretion may from time to time deem necessary in order to provide for the maintenance of my wife in accordance with the standard of living to which she shall be accustomed at the time of my death.

(5) During her lifetime, my wife shall have the right at any time, and from time to time, to make gifts of the principal, without limitation, to and among my children, and the issue of my children, or any of them, in such amounts or proportions, on such terms and conditions, and subject to such trusts or limitations, as my wife may in writing set forth, provided that no such distribution shall be made without the prior written approval of the then serving Trustee or Trustees other than my wife. In addition, my wife shall have the right to withdraw from the principal, on her request in writing, any amounts that may be required for the payment of any gift taxes that may be incurred as a result of such gifts.

(6) Upon the death of my wife, the principal of this trust then remaining shall be distributed to such beneficiary or beneficiaries, in such amounts or proportions, on such terms and conditions, and subject to such trusts or limitations, as my wife may appoint in her Will, or by other instrument delivered to my Trustees during her lifetime, making specific reference to this power of appointment in such Will or other instrument. In the exercise of this power of appointment, my wife may designate her estate to receive all or any portion of the trust principal.

The power of appointment granted to my wife in this subparagraph A(6) shall be exercisable by her alone and in all events.

(7) Upon the death of my wife, any principal then remaining of this trust with respect to which she fails to exercise affectively the power of appointment which is given to her in the preceding subparagraph A(6) shall be disposed of as follows:

(1) My Trustees shall pay out of such unappointed principal the amounts of any increase in federal and State estate and inheritance taxes and administration expenses in my wife's estate which are attributable to the inclusion therein of such unappointed principal, and my Trustees may accept as correct a written statement by my wife's personal representatives as to the amounts so payable; and

(2) My Trustees shall distribute the balance of such unappointed principal to the then serving Trustee or Trustees of The Irrevocable Trust, which is more fully described in Clause TWELFTH, to be held, administered and disposed of in accordance with the provisions of that Trust.

B.   *Trust B.* My Trustees shall dispose of the net income and principal of   Trust B as follows:

(1) My Trustees shall either accumulate the net income or distribute all or any part of the current or accumulated net income to my wife   , as the Trustees other than my wife, in their sole discretion, may from time to time deem advisable.

(2) If the principal of   Trust A should be exhausted, my Trustees shall make distributions of principal of this trust for the same purposes as provided in subparagraphs A(3) and A(4), above; provided, however that my wife shall not participate as a Trustee in any of the discretionary determinations for which provision is made in those subparagraphs.

(3) Upon the death of my wife, the principal and any accumulated and undistributed income of this trust then remaining shall be distributed to her personal representatives, to be disposed of as part of my wife's estate.

TWELFTH: GIFT TO THE   IRREVOCABLE TRUST. I give the Non-Marital Portion of my residuary estate (or my entire residuary estate if my wife,   , does not survive me) to the Trustee or Trustees serving at the time of my death under a certain Indenture of Trust executed by and between myself as Grantor and

,   , and   , *as* Trustees, dated June 1, 1976, and entitled "The   Irrevocable Trust," to be held, administered and disposed of in accordance with the provisions of that Trust.

THIRTEENTH: DISCRETIONARY DETERMINATIONS. In making any discretionary determinations provided in my Will with respect to the accumulation or distribution of income, or with respect to the distribution of principal, except as otherwise specifically provided, my Trustees shall take into consideration the income of the beneficiary from all other sources, and may, but shall not be required to, take into consideration the other assets or resources of the beneficiary. Moreover, whether or not such a restriction is imposed or omitted in any other provision of my Will, I direct that my wife as a Trustee of the trust established under paragraph B of Clause ELEVENTH shall not participate in any discretionary determinations with respect to the accumulation or distribution of income, or with respect to the distribution of principal, of that trust, nor shall she participate in the exercise of any administrative power which directly or indirectly effects an accumulation of income or involves the allocation of receipts or disbursements as between income and principal of that trust.

MARITAL DEDUCTION MATTERS

FOURTEENTH: MARITAL DEDUCTION FORMULA. My residuary estate shall be divided for the purpose set forth in Clause TENTH according to the following provisions:

A. The fraction to be applied to the value of my residuary estate in order to determine the Marital Deduction Portion (the balance of my residuary estate to comprise the Non-Marital Portion) shall consist of the following:

(1) The numerator shall be equal to (a) fifty percent of the value of my "adjusted gross estate" (as that term is defined in the federal estate tax laws in effect on the date of my death), computed according to the valuations determined and the deductions allowed in the final determination of the federal estate tax liability of my estate (b) less the value, as finally determined for such tax purposes, of all items in my gross estate which pass or have passed from me to my wife either outside of my Will or under the provisions of Clause NINTH of my Will and which qualify for the marital deduction.

(2) The denominator shall be equal to the value of my residuary estate as composed on the date of my death and computed on the basis of the valuations fixed in the final determination of the federal estate tax liability of my estate.

B. The foregoing fraction shall be applied to my residuary estate taken as a whole (rather than to the individual assets comprising it), and such fraction shall be applied to my residuary estate valued and composed as of the date of division thereof between the Marital Deduction Portion and the Non-Marital Portion, plus the amount of any estate, inheritance, transfer or succession taxes paid prior thereto, so that the value of my residuary estate shall not be diminished by any such taxes for the purpose of this computation. My "residuary estate" for the purpose of the fraction's denominator shall likewise be determined without diminution by the amount of any such taxes.

C. Notwithstanding the foregoing provisions in the division of my residuary estate between the Marital Deduction Portion and the Non-Marital Portion, only property which qualifies for the federal estate tax marital deduction shall be allocated to the Marital Deduction Portion. It is implicit in the formula above provided that the division shall be made in such manner that the two Portions shall share proportionately in any appreciation or depreciation in the value of the property available for such division from the value thereof as finally determined for federal estate tax purposes.

FIFTEENTH: MARITAL DEDUCTION RESTRICTIONS. In accordance with my desire and intent that the Marital Deduction Portion shall qualify for the federal estate tax marital deduction, I direct that, notwithstanding any other provision of my Will:

A. My fiduciaries, in the administration of my estate and the

Trusts, and in the exercise of any power relating thereto, shall use the degree of judgment and care which a prudent man would exercise if he were the owner of the estate and trust assets.

B. If any property of the Marital Deduction Portion or

Trust A is or becomes unproductive or under-productive, my wife shall have the right, which may be exercised by instrument in writing, to require my fiduciaries within a reasonable time either to make such property productive of a reasonable income or to dispose of it and invest the proceeds in property which is productive of a reasonable income.

C. My fiduciaries shall not have any rights, powers, duties, privileges or immunities which would disqualify the Marital Deduction Portion for the marital deduction, and all provisions of my Will shall be construed in such manner, and the powers and discretions herein conferred shall be exercised only to the extent and in such manner, as to assure compliance with the estate tax marital deduction provisions of the Internal Revenue Code in this respect, and any provision of my Will which is incapable of being so construed or applied shall be applicable.

MISCELLANEOUS PROVISIONS

SIXTEENTH: PRESUMPTION OF SURVIVORSHIP. If my wife and I should die under such circumstances that the order of our deaths cannot be determined, I direct that my wife shall be presumed to have survived me, any prosivions of law to the contrary notwithstanding.

SEVENTEENTH: PROTECTIVE PROVISION. As long as any income or principal to which any beneficiary under my Will may be entitled remains in the possession of my fiduciaries and is not actually distributed to the beneficiary, such income or principal shall not be subject to anticipation or alienation by the beneficiary by assignment or by any other means (except as specifically authorized herein), and it shall be free and clear of the beneficiary's debts and obligations and shall not be taken, seized or attached by any process whatsoever.

EIGHTEENTH: TAXES. All inheritance, estate, transfer and succession taxes, federal, state and foreign, payable by reason of my death, and any interest or penalties thereon, with respect to all property includible for such tax purposes, whether or not passing under my Will, excepting, however, any property over which I may have a general power of appointment at the time of my death, shall be paid out of the Non-Marital Portion of my residuary estate, without apportionment between temporary estates and remainders, and, except as aforesaid, with no right of reimbursement from the beneficiary or owner of any other property. No assets, forming part of any trust, which are not includible in my estate for federal estate tax purposes shall be used to pay any inheritance, estate, transfer or succession taxes which may be payable by reason of my death. I authorize my Executors to compromise, settle and adjust all such taxes and, insofar as the law may permit, to pay such taxes at such time or times as they may deem advisable.

The decisions of my Executors as to (a) the date or dates which shall be selected for the valuation of property in my estate for federal estate tax purposes, and (b) whether certain deductions shall be claimed as income tax deductions or as estate tax deductions (without the necessity for adjustment of income or principal accounts of my estate or any trust), shall be conclusive on all concerned.

My Executors, acting in my place, may join with my wife in her individual capacity, or with her personal representatives, in joint income tax returns, or in gift tax returns for any gifts made by her prior to my death, without requiring my wife or her personal representatives to indemnify my estate against liability to it for tax attributable to her.

NINETEENTH: MANAGEMENT POWERS. In addition to the powers conferred upon them by law or other provisions of my Will, my Executors and Trustees (and their successors) shall have, respectively, for the management of my estate and each trust established hereunder, the following powers, which they may exercise as often as they may deem advisable, without application to or approval by any court, and without liability for loss or depreciation in value resulting therefrom:

A. *Retention.* To retain all or any part of the property comprising my estate at the time of my death, or received by my Trustees from my Executors, as long as they may deem advisable.

B. *Sale or Exchange.* To sell at public or private sale, grant options on, exchange or otherwise dispose of any property held hereunder, at such times and on such terms, conditions, prices and considerations, including credit, with or without security, as they may deem advisable, to give good and sufficient instruments of transfer thereof, and to receive the proceeds of any such disposition.

C. *Investment.* To invest and reinvest estate and trust funds (including any income accumulations) in such preferred stocks, common stocks, bonds, obligations, shares or interests in any common trust fund or funds administered by the corporate Trustee, investment companies, investment trusts, or other real or personal property, as they may select, without the requirement of diversification, and without regard to restrictions upon estate or trust investments imposed by any present or future statutes, rules of court or court decisions of any jurisdiction. The foregoing investment powers include the authority to exercise any stock options acquired as a result of my lifetime employment or otherwise. Subject to the restrictions set forth in the succeeding paragraph D, the purchase of life insurance and annuities for the benefit of my estate or any trust hereunder is also authorized.

D. *Payment of Premiums.* To pay out of income or principal the premiums which may become due from time to time on any life insurance or annuity policies owned by my estate or any trust or acquired for the benefit of my estate or any trust; provided, however, with respect to my estate or   Trust A, that such premium payments, during my wife's lifetime, shall be made only upon the written direction of my wife.

E. *Real Property Management.* To take possession of any real property or interest in real property held hereunder; manage, operate, maintain, collect the rentals of, and pay the taxes, mortgage interest and other charges against, such property; and to partition, develop, or subdivide such property and make repairs, replacements and improvements, structural or otherwise, thereto.

F. *Leases.* To lease any real or personal property held hereunder, with or without options to purchase, on such terms and conditions and for such periods as they may deem advisable, even though the period or periods of the lease or leases may extend beyond the term of any trust and without regard to any statutory limitations on the duration of such leases; to reserve in such leases fixed rentals, rentals based upon the amount of business or profits of the lessors, or rentals based upon any other conditions; and to renew, cancel, amend or extend, and consent to the assignment or modification of any lease, on such terms as they may deem advisable.

G. *Borrowing.* To borrow money from themselves or others for the purpose of paying debts of my estate, taxes, or estate or trust administration expenses, or for the protection or improvement of any property held hereunder, to execute promissory notes or other obligations for amounts so borrowed, and to secure the repayment thereof by mortgage or pledge of any property held hereunder.

H. *Renewals and Extensions.* To renew or extend the time for payment of any obligation, secured or unsecured, for such period or periods, and on such terms, as they may deem advisable.

I. *Rights and Voting.* To exercise, sell or abandon all conversion, subscription or other rights, options, powers and privileges pertaining to, or to vote in person or by proxy upon, any stocks, bonds, or other securities, all as might be done by an individual holding a similar interest in his own right.

J. *Corporate Changes.* To oppose or to assent to and to participate in any reorganization, recapitalization, readjustment, merger, voting trust, consolidation or exchange affecting any corporation or association the securities of which are held hereunder, and in connection with any such proceeding to deposit securities with any custodian, agent, protective or similar committee, or trustee, and to pay any fees, expenses or assessments incurred in connection therewith, and exchange property, all as might be done by an individual holding a similar interest in his own right.

K. *Claims and Suits.* To adjust, settle, compromise, arbitrate or abandon, or sue on or defend, any claims by or against my estate or any trust hereunder.

L. *Agents.* To employ and compensate such attorneys, accountants, brokers, investment counsel and other agents and services as they may deem necessary or advantageous to my estate or any trust hereunder.

M. *Custodians.* To employ as custodian or agent for my estate a bank or trust company; to have securities registered in the name of such bank or trust company or its nominee without designation of fiduciary capacity; to appoint such bank or trust company agent to receive and disburse any income; and to pay the charges and expenses of such custodian or agent.

N. *Nominees.* To cause the securities which may from time to time be held hereunder to be registered in the name of a nominee, or to hold such securities unregistered and to retain them in such condition that they will pass by delivery.

O. *Bank Accounts and Safe Deposit Boxes.* To select one or more depositories and to authorize payment out of any accounts on checks signed by such person or persons as they may designate in writing, and to delegate to such person or persons as they may designate in writing access to any safe deposit box or boxes which they may rent.

P. *Insurance Coverage.* To obtain and keep in force such fire, theft, liability, casualty or other insurance as they may deem advisable for the protection of my estate or any trust hereunder.

Q. *Consolidated Trust Funds.* To hold, manage and account for separate trusts established hereunder either as separate funds or in one or more consolidated funds in which each trust shall have an undivided interest, provided that no such holding shall defer the vesting of any interest in possession or otherwise.

R. *Distribution in Kind.* To make distribution of my estate or any trust hereunder in cash or in kind, or partly in cash and partly in kind, and to allocate specific assets among the beneficiaries (including any trust or trusts) in such proportions as my fiduciaries may think best, so long as the total market value of any beneficiary's share is not affected by such allocation, and provide that nothing in this paragraph shall be deemed to modify any of the provisions above set forth with respect to allocation of assets to the   Trusts.

S. *Business Interests.* In dealing with the stock of any closely held corporation or any other business interest forming a part of my estate or any trust hereunder:

(1) To disregard any principle of investment diversification and to retain all or any part of such interest as long as they may deem advisable;

(2) To sell all or any part of such interest at such time or times, for such prices, to such persons (including persons who are fiduciaries hereunder), and on such terms and conditions, as they may deem advisable;

(3) To do anything that may seem advisable with respect to the operation or liquidation of any such business or any change in the purpose, nature or organization of any such business;

(4) To participate directly in the conduct or management of such business, or render professional services thereto, and receive reasonable compensation therefor, regardless of any rule with respect to conflict of interest;

(5) To delegate authority to any stockholder, director, manager, agent, partner or employee, and to approve payment from the business of adequate compensation to any such person;

(6) To borrow money from the banking department of the corporate Trustee, regardless of any rule with respect to conflict of interest; and

(7) To make additional investments in or advances to any such business if such action appears to be in the best interests of my estate or any trust hereunder and the beneficiaries thereof.

TWENTIETH: DISINTERESTED PARTIES. No person dealing with my Executors or Trustees, or their successors or survivors, shall be bound to see to the application of any purchase money or other consideration or to inquire into the validity, necessity or propriety of any transaction to which such fiduciaries may be parties.

TWENTY-FIRST: ACCOUNTING BY TRUSTEES. My Trustees shall be entitled at any time to seek a judicial settlement of their accounts in any court of competent jurisdiction selected by my Trustees. As an alternative, my Trustees may at any time settle their account of any trust hereunder by agreement with the income beneficiary who is not under any legal disability; and such agreement shall bind all persons, whether or not then in being or sui juris, then or thereafter entitled to any portion of the trust, and shall effectively release and discharge the Trustees for the acts and proceedings so accounted for.

TWENTY-SECOND: INTERPRETATIONS. Wherever appropriate in this Will, the singular shall be deemed to include the plural, and vice versa; and the masculine shall be deemed to include the feminine, and vice versa, and each of them to include the neuter, and vice versa.

For all purposes hereunder, the word "property" shall be deemed to include real and personal property and any interests of any kind in any real or personal property; and the word "give" shall be taken to include the words "devise" and "bequeath" wherever appropriate in order to effectuate the testamentary transfer of real or personal property.

For all purposes hereunder, the terms "Executor," "Trustee," "Guardian," and "fiduciary," and the plurals thereof, shall apply, respectively, to those who are then entitled and qualified to act as such, whether originally appointed, remaining, substituted or succeeding.

For all purposes hereunder, each adopted child of any person shall have the same status and benefits as if he or she were a child born to that person.

All references to "my wife" or to   shall be deemed to be references to   , to whom I am married at the time of execution of this Will.

TWENTY-THIRD: HEADINGS. The headings or titles preceding the sections, clauses and certain paragraphs of this Will are provided only for convenience of reference and shall not be used to explain or restrict the meaning, purpose or effect of any of the provisions to which they refer.

IN WITNESS WHEREOF, I have hereunto set my hand and seal this   day of   , 19

_____ (SEAL)

In our presence the above named Testator signed this instrument and declared it to be his Will, and now, at his request, in his presence and in the presence of each other, we sign as witnesses.

Name _____ Address _____

Name _____ Address _____

FORM C-4

Pecuniary Marital Deduction Formula

Form C-4 is a simple pecuniary marital deduction formula, the attributes and consequences of which are discussed in Chapter 1, ¶104.3.

Pecuniary Marital Deduction Formula

I give to my wife,   , (or, I give to my Trustees), free of all inheritance, estate, transfer and succession taxes, an amount equal to (a) one-half of the value of my adjusted gross estate as finally determined for federal estate tax purposes,* (b) less an amount equal to the value (as so determined) of all other property or interests in my gross estate which shall pass or have passed to my wife, either outside of my Will or under the provisions of Clause
hereof, and which qualify for the federal estate tax marital deduction.

---

*In cases in which the $250,000 marital deduction provided by TRA 76 is to be used, insert here: "or $250,000, whichever is greater."

FORM C-5

Alternate Provisions to Avoid 64-19 Problem with Pecuniary Marital Deduction Formula

The tax problem posed by Rev. Proc. 64-19 is discussed in Chapter 1, ¶104.3. Two "solutions" to the 64-19 problem, as discussed in ¶104.3, are provided in Form C-5.

Alternate Provisions to Avoid 64-19 Problem
with Pecuniary Marital Deduction Formula

Alternate No. 1

In assigning to the gift provided in Clause
assets sufficient to satisfy the amount determined under the
foregoing formula, each item allocated in kind to that gift shall be allocated at the lesser of (a) its value as finally determined for federal estate tax purposes (or its adjusted income tax basis if acquired after my death) or (b) its fair market value determined as of the time of such allocation.

Alternate No. 2

In assigning to the gift provided in this Clause
assets sufficient to satisfy the amount determined under the
foregoing formula, assets shall be assigned only at values finally determined for estate tax purposes; provided, however, that the assets shall be so selected that the cash and other property allocated to this gift shall have an aggregate fair market value fairly representative of this gift's proportionate share of the appreciation or depreciation in value from the federal estate tax valuation date to the date or dates of distribution of all property then available for distribution.

FORM C-6

Fractional Marital Deduction Formula

Form C-6 is a fractional marital deduction formula, as discussed in Chapter 1, ¶104.4. In ¶104.3, pecuniary and fractional formulas are contrasted.

Fractional Marital Deduction Formula

If my wife,   , survives me, my residuary estate
shall be divided into two fractional portions, the Marital Deduction Portion and the Non-Marital Portion, the division to be made in accordance
with the formula provided in the ensuing paragraphs of this Clause
                . If my wife does not survive me, my entire residuary
estate shall be disposed of under the provisions of my Will relating to the
Non-Marital Portion.

The fraction to be applied to the value of my residuary estate in
order to determine the Marital Deduction Portion (the balance of my
residuary estate to comprise the Non-Marital Portion) shall consist of the
following:

(1) The numerator shall be equal to (a) fifty percent of the value of
my "adjusted gross estate" (as that term is defined in the federal estate
tax laws in effect on the date of my death), computed according to the
valuations determined and the deductions allowed in the final determination of the federal estate tax liability of my estate,* (b) less the value, as
finally determined for such tax purposes, of all items in my gross estate
which pass or have passed from me to my wife either outside of my Will
or under the provisions of Clause   of my Will
and which qualify for the marital deduction.

(2) The denominator shall be equal to the value of my residuary
estate as composed on the date of my death and computed on the basis
of the valuations fixed in the final determination of the federal estate tax
liability of my estate.

---

*In cases in which the $250,000 marital deduction provided by TRA 76 is to be used, insert
here "or $250,000, whichever is greater."

The foregoing fraction shall be applied to my residuary estate taken as a whole (rather than the individual assets comprising it), and such fraction shall be applied to my residuary estate valued and composed as of the date of division thereof between the Marital Deduction Portion and the Non-Marital Portion, plus the amount of any estate, inheritance, transfer and succession taxes paid prior thereto, so that the value of my residuary estate shall not be diminished by any such taxes for the purpose of this computation. My "residuary estate" for the purpose of the fraction's denominator shall likewise be determined without dimunution by the amount of any such taxes.

FORM C-7

"Engineer's" Fractional Marital
Deduction Formula

Form C-7 is the alternate fractional formula mentioned in the last sentence of ¶104.4 of Chapter 1. It may be disconcerting to those who are not mathematically inclined, but it has the combined virtues of clarity and precision.

"Engineer's" Fractional Marital Deduction Formula

My residuary estate shall be divided for the purpose set forth in Clause   in accordance with the following formula:

$$(M.D.P.) = (Rt_2) \times \frac{(A.G.E.) - 2 \times (Q.P.)}{2 \times (Rt_1)}$$

In the said formula:

(M.D.P.) × the Marital Deduction Portion, which passes under the provisions of Clause

(A.G.E.) = the value of my "adjusted gross estate" as that term is defined in the federal estate tax laws in effect on the date of my death, said value to be computed according to the valuations determined and the deductions allowed in the final determination of the federal estate tax liability of my estate.

(Q.P.) = the value, as finally determined for federal estate tax purposes, of all items in my gross estate which pass or have passed from me to my wife either outside of my Will or under the provisions of Clause   of my Will and which qualify for the estate tax marital deduction ("Qualifying Portion").

(Rt_1) = the value of the assets in my residuary estate as of the date of my death, computed on the basis of the valuations established in the final determination of the federal estate tax liability of my estate.

(Rt₂) =   the value of my residuary estate as of the date of division thereof between the Marital Deduction Portion and the Non-Marital Portion.

Also, in the said formula, the following mathematical symbols shall have their usual mathematical meanings, as follows:

× means "times" or "multiplied by"
− means "minus" or "diminished by taking away"
= means "is equal to"

_____ is a fraction bar denoting the numerical division of the net quantity above the fraction bar by the numerical value of the quantity beneath the fraction bar.

Neither (Rt₁) nor (Rt₂) shall be diminished, for the purpose of the formula above set forth, by the amount of any estate, inheritance, transfer or succession taxes which may have been paid prior to the application of the said formula. In allocating specific assets to the Marital Deduction Portion, in order to implement the formula above provided for the division of my residuary estate, only property which qualifies for the federal estate tax marital deduction shall be selected for the Marital Deduction Portion. It is inherent in the formula that the division shall be made in such manner that the two Portions shall share proportionately in any appreciation or depreciation in the value of the property available for such division from the valuation thereof as finally determined for federal estate tax purposes.

FORM C-8

Private Foundation

This form provides a relatively simple trust qualifying as a private charitable foundation, as discussed in Chapter 2, [¶203.9]. The Trust Agreement is followed by the related Form 1023 (Application for Recognition of Exemption), Form SS-4 (Application for Employer Identification Number), Form 2848 (Power of Attorney), and the determination letter issued by the Internal Revenue Service.

Trust Agreement
of
The Mary and John Smith Foundation

This Trust Agreement is made this 1st day of January, 1978, by and between John Smith, as Donor, and Mary Smith and John Smith, as Trustees.

1. *Name of Trust.* The name of this Trust is The Mary and John Smith Foundation. The Trustees may change the name of the Trust from time to time.

2. *Purposes of Trust.* The purposes of this Trust are to devote and apply the trust property and the income to be derived therefrom exclusively for charitable, religious, scientific, literary or educational purposes, directly or by contributions to organizations which are duly authorized to carry on charitable, religious, scientific, literary or educational activities and which are exempt from taxation under section 501(c)(3) of the Internal Revenue Code (hereinafter called "the Code"). No part of this trust fund shall enure to the benefit of any private shareholder or individual, and no part of the direct or indirect activities of this Trust shall consist of carrying on propaganda, or otherwise attempting, to influence legislation, or of participating in any political campaign on behalf of any candidate for public office. Notwithstanding any other provision hereof, the Trust shall not carry on any activities forbidden to be carried on by an organization exempt under section 501(c)(3) of the Code or by an organization contributions to which are deductible under section 170 of the Code.

3. *Trust Fund.* The property to constitute this Trust and Foundation as herein provided shall consist of cash in the amount of Twenty-five Dollars ($25.00), which the Donor has given to the Trustees, and

such other money and other property as the Donor or any other person or corporation may from time to time hereafter transfer to the Trustees and be accepted by them. Such money and other property shall be transferred to the Trustees to be held by them in trust and be disposed of as herein provided.

4. *Use of Trust Fund.* The Trustees, except as herein limited, shall have the power and authority and are directed to distribute from time to time exclusively for the purposes described in paragraph 2, each year, such amounts of income or principal as they in their discretion may determine; provided that the Trustees shall distribute income annually at such time and in such manner as not to incur the tax on undistributed income imposed by section 4942 of the Code.

5. *Actions and Meetings of Trustees.* The Trustees shall meet on notice given to all Trustees. A majority of the then Trustees shall constitute a quorum at any meeting of the Trustees, but less than a majority may adjourn any such meeting from time to time and from place to place until a quorum shall be present. A majority vote of all Trustees present at a meeting where there is a quorum shall be necessary and sufficient to authorize or ratify any acts by the Trustees. The Trustees shall keep a permanent record of all proceedings and acts taken at their meetings.

Notwithstanding the foregoing, if any act is desired to be taken without a meeting, such act shall be valid for all purposes as a resolution adopted at a Trustees' meeting if a resolution of such act is signed by all of the then Trustees.

If a corporation becomes a Trustee hereunder, it shall not be counted toward a majority or quorum, nor shall its vote or consent be necessary to any action by the Trustees. Such corporate Trustee shall serve as Trustee solely for the convenience of securing a depository for the money and other property in this Trust, keeping the books, and giving financial advice on investments. Such corporate Trustee is authorized, empowered and directed to act or not to act, from time to time, in accordance with the written instructions of the other Trustees, or, if a corporation is organized as provided in paragraph 12 hereof, in conformity with the written instructions of a duly authorized officer of such corporation, and such corporate Trustee shall be fully protected in so acting or not acting.

6. *Powers of Trustees.* The Trustees shall have all of the common law and statutory powers of Trustees and the powers set forth herein are in extension and not in limitation thereof. However, notwithstanding any other provision hereof, the Trustees may not jeopardize the status of this Trust as exempt under section 501(c)(3) of the Code, nor shall the Trustees engage in any act of self-dealing as defined in section 4941(d) of the Code, retain any excess business holdings as defined in section 4943(c) of the Code, make any investments in such manner as to incur tax under-

section 4944 of the Code, or make any taxable expenditures as defined in section 4945(d) of the Code.

Subject to the foregoing, the Trustees shall have the following powers:

(a) To retain for such period as they shall deem proper any money or other property of any kind contributed to this Trust by the Donor or others, although some or all of the property so retained is of a kind or size which, but for this express authority, would not be considered a proper trust investment.

(b) To invest and reinvest the principal and income of the Trust in such property, real, personal, and in such manner as they shall deem proper, and from time to time to change investments as they shall deem advisable; to invest in or retain any stocks, shares, bonds, notes, obligations or other real or personal property (including without limitation any interests in or obligations of any corporation, association, business trust, investment trust, common trust fund or investment company), although some or all of the property so acquired or retained is of a kind or size which, but for this express authority, would not be considered a proper trust investment, and although all of the trust funds are invested in the securities of one company.

(c) To make distributions in cash or in specific property, real or personal, or an undivided interest therein, or partly in cash and partly in such property.

(d) To sell, lease, or exchange any real or personal, property, at public auction or by private contract, for such considerations and on such terms as to credit or otherwise, and to make such contracts and enter into such undertakings related to the trust property, as they consider advisable, although some or all of such leases or contracts may extend beyond the duration of the Trust.

(e) To borrow money in such amounts, for such periods, at such rates of interest and upon such terms and conditions as the Trustees consider advisable, and, as security for such loans, to mortgage or pledge any real or personal property with or without power of sale; to acquire or hold any real or personal property subject to any mortgage or pledge; and to assume any mortgage or pledge on or of property acquired or held by this Trust.

(f) To execute and deliver deeds, assignments, transfers, mortgages, pledges, leases, covenants, contracts, promissory notes, releases and other instruments, sealed or unsealed, incident to any transaction in which they engage.

(g) To vote, to give proxies, to participate in the reorganization, merger or consolidation of any concern, or in the sale, lease, disposition, or distribution of its assets; to join with other security holders in acting through a committee, depository, voting trustees, or otherwise, and in this connection, to delegate authority to such committee, depository, or trustee, and to deposit securities with them or transfer securities to them; and to pay assessments levied on securities or to exercise subscription rights in respect of securities.

(h) To employ and compensate such attorneys, accountants, brokers, investment counsel and other agents and services as they may deem necessary or advantageous to the Trust.

(i) To defend suits at law or in equity or before any tribunals, affecting the Trust; to begin suits and prosecute such suits to final judgment decree; and to compromise claims or suits or submit them to arbitration.

(j) To carry insurance at trust expense against such risks and for such amounts and upon such terms as they may determine, with mutual insurers or otherwise.

(k) To select one or more depositories, and to authorize payment out of any accounts upon checks or withdrawal forms signed by such person or persons as the Trustees may from time to time designate in writing, and to delegate to any such person access to any safe deposit box or boxes which the Trustees may rent.

7. *Appointment of Trustees.* The Donor hereby nominates and appoints Mary Smith and John Smith as the Trustees of this Trust and Foundation. The original Trustees or the survivor of them may in writing appoint such additional Trustees as they see fit, provided that there shall be no more than seven Trustees. Any Trustee may resign by writing delivered to the other Trustee or Trustees or may be removed for cause by a majority of the Trustees. Any vacancy that occurs may be filled by the remaining Trustee or Trustees. Each additional or successor Trustee shall have all the power and authority conferred by this instrument upon the original Trustees.

8. *Chairman and Other Officers and Employees.* The Donor hereby designates John Smith as the first Chairman of the Trustees, to serve for one year from the date hereof and thereafter until a successor may be elected by the Trustees. The Trustees may appoint such other officers and fix the duties of such other officers as they shall from time to time see fit, and may engage an executive director or such other employee as they shall from time to time see fit for the performance of services to the Foundation.

9. *Compensation and Expenses.* The Trustees may from time to time fix whatever, if any, reasonable compensation shall be paid to the Trustees or their employees, but in no event shall any compensation be paid to any person after he has made a transfer of property to the Trust as a contribution. The Trustees may incur any other expense or do any other act which they consider necessary and proper to the effective administration of the Trust. The expenses and compensation of the Trustees, if

any, and of their employees, and all other expenses of administration of this Trust, shall first be paid each year, or provision made therefor, out of the income of the Trust before any distribution is made therefrom for that year.

10. *Accounting.* The Trustees shall make a report annually of their administration of this Trust, and shall provide a copy thereof to the Donor and each Trustee. The Trustees may also publish such reports or distribute copies thereof in such manner as they see fit.

11. *Contributions from Others.* The Trustees may receive gifts and bequests from any person or corporation at any time, and apply the principal and income therefrom to the purposes and under the terms hereof, provided such gifts or bequests are not made upon any terms or conditions that would conflict with the provisions or administration of this Trust.

12. *Organization of Corporation.* The Trustees may organize a corportion for the purposes hereof, to administer and control the affairs of the Foundation and carry out the uses, objects and purposes of this Trust. Upon organization of such corporation, the Trustees may deliver to it all the money and other property of the Foundation, and such corporation shall take the place of the Trustees as if named hereunder originally. The corporation shall have the same powers and authorities as are hereby vested in the Trustees, subject to the same limitations and restrictions. The Trustees then serving shall be the incorporators of the corporation, together with such other persons as they may choose, and such Trustees and other persons shall be the first directors of such corporation. The charter and by-laws of such corporation shall be determined by the Trustees, provided that the corporation shall be so organized and operated as to qualify for exemption under section 501(c)(3) of the Code.

13. *Duration and Amendment of the Trust.* This Trust shall continue until its principal is exhausted or a corporation is established under paragraph 12 hereof. This Trust Agreement shall be irrevocable, but the Trustees may amend it in writing from time to time in any manner consistent with the trust purposes in order to obtain or continue exempt status under section 501(c)(3) of the Code, or to qualify any gift or bequest made to the Trust as a charitable contribution for tax purposes.

14. *Miscellaneous.* This Trust Agreement has been executed in the Commonwealth of Pennsylvania and shall be governed in accordance with the laws thereof. The principal office of the Foundation shall be Suite 100, 500 Main Street, Philadelphia, Pennsylvania 19100, or such other place as the Trustees may from time to time select. The headings before the text of the paragraphs hereof are for convenient reference

and shall not be used to restrict or amplify the meaning of such text. The undersigned Trustees hereby accept the Trust herein created and agree that they shall carry out the provisions hereof and faithfully discharge all the duties of their office.

IN WITNESS WHEREOF, the Donor and the Trustees have executed this Trust Agreement the day and year first above written.

_____(SEAL)
John Smith, Donor

_____(SEAL)
Mary Smith, Trustee

_____(SEAL)
John Smith, Trustee

COMMONWEALTH OF PENNSYLVANIA   :
                                : SS.
COUNTY OF PHILADELPHIA   :

    BEFORE ME, this 1st day of January, 1978, personally appeared John Smith, who acknowledges having executed the foregoing Trust Agreement for the purposes therein set forth as his free act and deed.
    WITNESS my hand and Notarial seal the day and year aforesaid.

                                                      ————————————————————
                                                           Notary Public

Form **1023**

(Rev. November 1972)

Department of the Treasury
Internal Revenue Service

Application for Recognition of Exemption

Under Section 501(c)(3) of the Internal Revenue Code

To be filed in the District in which the organization has its principal office or place of business.

This application, when properly completed, shall constitute the notice required under section 508(a) of the Internal Revenue Code in order that organizations may be treated as described in section 501(c)(3) of the code, and the notice under section 508(b) appropriate to those organizations claiming not to be private foundations within the meaning of section 509(a).

Part I.—Identification (See instructions)

1 Full name of organization	2 Employer identification number (If none, attach Form SS-4)
The Mary & John Smith Foundation	Application pending

3(a) Address (number and street)

500 Main Street, Suite 100

3(b) City or town, State and ZIP code	4 Name and phone number of person to be contacted
Philadelphia, Pennsylvania 19103	

5 Month the annual accounting period ends	6 Date incorporated or formed	7 Activity Codes (see instructions)
December	January 1, 1978	602		

Part II.—Organizational Documents (See instructions)

1 Attach a conformed copy of the organization's creating instruments (articles of incorporation, constitution, articles of association, deed of trust, etc.).

2 Attach a conformed copy of the organization's by-laws or other rules for its operation.

3 If the organization does not have a creating instrument, check here (see instructions) . . . . ☐

Part III.—Activities and Operational Information (See instructions)

1 What are or will be the organization's sources of financial support. List in order of magnitude. If a portion of the receipts is or will be derived from the earnings of patents, copyrights, or other assets (excluding stock, bonds, etc.), identify such item as a separate source of receipt. Attach representative copies of solicitations for financial support.

Contributions from John Smith, Mary Smith, and Acme Enterprises, Inc.

2 Describe the organization's fund-raising program and explain to what extent it has been put into effect. (Include details of fund-raising activities such as selective mailings, formation of fund raising committees, use of professional fund raisers, etc.)

There is no fund raising program presently in effect or planned.

I declare under the penalties of perjury that I am authorized to sign this application on behalf of the above organization and I have examined this application, including the accompanying statements, and to the best of my knowledge it is true, correct and complete.

	Trustee	2/18/78
(Signature)	(Title or authority of signer)	(Date)

Form 1023 (Rev. 11-72)   Page 2

Part III.—Activities and Operational Information (Continued)

3   Give a narrative description of the activities presently carried on by the organization, and also those that will be carried on. If
    the organization is not fully operational, explain what stage of development its activities have reached, what further steps re-
    main for the organization to become fully operational, and when such further steps will take place. The narrative should spe-
    cifically identify the services performed or to be performed by the organization. (Do not state the purposes of the organization
    in general terms or repeat the language of the organizational documents.) If the organization is a school, hospital, or medical
    research organization, include sufficient information in your description to clearly show that the organization meets the defi-
    nition of that particular activity that is contained in the instructions for Part VII–A on page 3 of the instructions.

    The Foundation is newly established. As soon as significant funds are
received, the Trustees will meet to consider gifts to be made to further the
purposes of the Foundation as set forth in the trust agreement submitted here-
with.

    For the foreseeable future, the Trustees' intent is to make direct dis-
tributions to existing exempt organizations only, and there will be no Trustees'
fees or substantial expenses of administration of any sort whatsoever.

Forms to Carry Out the Estate Plan

Form 1023 (Rev. 11–72)

Part III.—Activities and Operational Information (Continued)

4 The membership of the organization's governing body is:

(a) Names, addresses, and duties of officers, directors, trustees, etc.	(b) Specialized knowledge, training, expertise, or particular qualifications
The Trustees are: John Smith 123 Apple Street Philadelphia, PA 19100 Mary Smith 123 Apple Street Philadelphia, PA 19100	The Trustees are long-time residents of their community, are fully familiar with and sensitive to the charitable needs of the community, as well as the needs of others beyond the immediate community.

(c) Do any of the above persons serve as members of the governing body by reason of being public officials or being appointed by public officials? . . . . ☐ Yes ☒ No

If "Yes," please name such persons and explain the basis of their selection or appointment.

(d) Are any members of the organization's governing body "disqualified persons" with respect to the organization (other than by reason of being a member of the governing body) or do any of the members have either a business or family relationship with "disqualified persons"? (See specific instructions 4(d).) . . ☐ Yes ☒ No

If "Yes," please explain.

5 Does the organization control or is it controlled by any other organization? . . . . ☐ Yes ☒ No

Is the organization the outgrowth of another organization, or does it have a special relationship to another organization by reason of interlocking directorates or other factors? . . . . ☐ Yes ☒ No

If either of these questions is answered "Yes," please explain.

6 Is the organization financially accountable to any other organization? . . . . ☐ Yes ☒ No

If "Yes," please explain and identify the other organization. Include details concerning accountability or attach copies of reports if any have been rendered.

7 What assets does the organization have that are used in the performance of its exempt function? (Do not include income producing property.) If any assets are not fully operational, explain what stage of completion has been reached, what additional steps remain to be completed, and when such final steps will be taken.

The trust currently has property consisting of $25.00 cash and will become operational as stated at line 3, above.

Part III.—Activities and Operational Information (Continued)

8 **(a)** What benefits, services, or products will the organization provide with respect to its exempt function?

Cash distributions will be made to exempt organizations.

(b) Have the recipients been required or will they be required to pay for the organization's benefits, services, or products? . . . . ☐ Yes ☒ No

If "Yes," please explain and show how the charges are determined.

9 Does or will the organization limit its benefits, services or products to specific classes of individuals? . . . ☐ Yes ☒ No

If "Yes," please explain how the recipients or beneficiaries are or will be selected.

10 Is the organization a membership organization? . . . . ☐ Yes ☒ No

If "Yes," complete the following:

(a) Please describe the organization's membership requirements and attach a schedule of membership fees and dues.

(b) Are benefits limited to members? . . . . ☐ Yes ☒ No

If "No," please explain.

(c) Attach a copy of the descriptive literature or promotional material used to attract members to the organization.

11 Does or will the organization engage in activities tending to influence legislation or intervene in any way in political campaigns? . . . . ☐ Yes ☒ No

If "Yes," please explain.

Part IV.—Statement as to Private Foundation Status (See instructions)

1 Is the organization a private foundation? . . . . ☒ Yes ☐ No

2 If question 1 is answered "No," indicate the type of ruling being requested as to the organization's status under section 509 by checking the applicable box below:

☐ Definitive ruling under section 509(a)(1), (2), (3), or (4) — complete Part VII.

☐ Advance or extended advance ruling under section 509(a)(1) or (2) — See instructions.

3 If question 1 is an answered "Yes," and the organization claims to be a private operating foundation, check here ☐ and complete Part VIII.

Form 1023 (Rev. 11-72) Page 5

Part V.—Financial Data (See instructions)

Statement of Receipts and Expenditures, for period ending October 31, , 19 77

Receipts

1	Gross contributions, gifts, grants and similar amounts received	25.00
2	Gross dues and assessments of members	
3	Gross amounts derived from activities related to organization's exempt purpose	
	Less cost of sales	
4	Gross amounts from unrelated business activities	
	Less cost of sales	
5	Gross amount received from sale of assets, excluding inventory items (attach schedule)	
	Less cost or other basis and sales expense of assets sold	
6	Interest, dividends, rents and royalties	
7	**Total receipts**	25.00

Expenditures

8	Contributions, gifts, grants, and similar amounts paid (attach schedule)	
9	Disbursements to or for benefit of members (attach schedule)	
10	Compensation of officers, directors, and trustees (attach schedule)	
11	Other salaries and wages	
12	Interest	
13	Rent	
14	Depreciation and depletion	
15	Other (attach schedule)	
16	**Total expenditures**	0
17	Excess of receipts over expenditures (line 7 less line 16)	25.00

SPECIMEN FORM

Balance Sheets

		Beginning date October 1, 1977	Ending date October 21, 1977
	Assets		
18	Cash (a) Interest bearing accounts	25.00	25.00
	(b) Other		
19	Accounts receivable, net		
20	Inventories		
21	Bonds and notes (attach schedule)		
22	Corporate stocks (attach schedule)		
23	Mortgage loans (attach schedule)		
24	Other investments (attach schedule)		
25	Depreciable and depletable assets (attach schedule)		
26	Land		
27	Other assets (attach schedule)		
28	**Total assets**	25.00	25.00
	Liabilities		
29	Accounts payable		
30	Contributions, gifts, grants, etc., payable		
31	Mortgages and notes payable (attach schedule)		
32	Other liabilities (attach schedule)		
33	**Total liabilities**	0	0
	Fund Balance or Net Worth		
34	Total fund balance or net worth	25.00	25.00
35	Total liabilities and fund balance or net worth (line 33 plus line 34)		

Part VI.—Required Schedules for Special Activities (See instructions)

		If "Yes," check here.	And, complete schedule
1	Is the organization, or any part of it, a school?		A
2	Does the organization provide or administer any scholarship benefits, student aid, etc.?		B
3	Has the organization taken over, or will it take over, the facilities of a "for profit" institution?		C
4	Is the organization, or any part of it, a hospital?		D
5	Is the organization, or any part of it, a home for the aged?		E
6	Is the organization, or any part of it, a litigating organization (public interest law firm or similar organization)?		F

Form 1023 (Rev. 11–72)   Page **6**

Part VII.—Non-Private Foundation Status (Definitive ruling only)

A.—Basis for Non-Private Foundation Status

The organization is not a private foundation because it qualifies as:

	✓	Kind of organization	Within the meaning of	Complete
1		a church	Sections 509(a)(1) and 170(b)(1)(A)(i)	
2		a school	Sections 509(a)(1) and 170(b)(1)(A)(ii)	
3		a hospital	Sections 509(a)(1) and 170(b)(1)(A)(iii)	
4		a medical research organization operated in conjunction with a hospital	Sections 509(a)(1) and 170(b)(1)(A)(iii)	
5		being organized and operated exclusively for testing for public safety	Section 509(a)(4)	
6		being operated for the benefit of a college or university which is owned or operated by a governmental unit	Sections 509(a)(1) and 170(b)(1)(A)(iv)	Part VII.–B
7		normally receiving a substantial part of its support from a governmental unit or from the general public	Sections 509(a)(1) and 170(b)(1)(A)(vi)	Part VII.–B
8		normally receiving not more than one-third of its support from gross investment income and more than one-third of its support from contributions, membership fees, and gross receipts from activities related to its exempt functions (subject to certain exceptions)	Section 509(a)(2)	Part VII.–B
9		being operated solely for the benefit of or in connection with one or more of the organizations described in 1 through 4, or 6, 7 and 8, above	Section 509(a)(3)	Part VII.–C

B.—Analysis of Financial Support

		(a) Most recent taxable year 19	**(b)** 19	**(c)** 19	**(d)** 19	**(e)** Total
			(Years next preceding most recent taxable year)			
1	Gifts, grants, and contributions received					
2	Membership fees received					
3	Gross receipts from admissions, sales of merchandise or services, or furnishing of facilities in any activity which is not an unrelated business within the meaning of section 513					
4	Gross income from interest, dividends, rents and royalties					
5	Net income from organization's unrelated business activities					
6	Tax revenues levied for and either paid to or expended on behalf of the organization					
7	Value of services or facilities furnished by a governmental unit to the organization without charge (not including the value of services or facilities generally furnished the public without charge)					
8	Other income (not including gain or loss from sale of capital assets)—attach schedule					
9	Total of lines 1 through 8					
10	Line 9 less line 3					
11	Enter 2% of line 10, column (e) only					

12 If the organization has received any unusual grants during any of the above taxable years, attach a list for each year showing the name of the contributor, the date and amount of grant, and a brief description of the nature of such grant. Do not include such grants in line 1 above. (See instructions)

For clear copy on both parts, please **typewrite** or print with ball point pen and press firmly
(See Instructions on pages 2 and 4)

Form **SS-4** (Rev. 8-76) Department of the Treasury Internal Revenue Service	**Application for Employer Identification Number** (For use by employers and others as explained in the Instructions)	

1 Name (True name as distinguished from trade name. If partnership, see Instructions on page 4)
The Mary & John Smith Foundation

2 Trade name, if any (Enter name under which business is operated, if different from item 1) None	**3** Social security number, if sole proprietor N/A

4 Address of principal place of business (Number and street) 500 Main Street , Suite 100	**5** Ending month of accounting year December

6 City and State Philadelphia, Pennsylvania	**7** ZIP code 19100	**8** County of business location Philadelphia

9 Type of organization
☐ Individual ☐ Partnership ☒ Other (specify)
☐ Governmental (See Instr. on page 4) ☐ Nonprofit organization (See Instr. on page 4) ☐ Corporation Trust

10 Date you acquired or started this business (Mo., day, year) 10/17/77

11 Reason for applying
☐ Started new business ☐ Purchased going business ☒ Other (specify) Acquired by Trust

12 First date you paid or will pay wages for this business (Mo., day, year) No Wages

13 Nature of business (See Instructions on page 4)
Charitable Foundation

14 Do you operate more than one place of business? ☐ Yes ☒ No

15 Peak number of employees expected in next 12 months (if none, enter "0") ►
Nonagricultural 0 | Agricultural 0 | Household

16 If nature of business is manufacturing, state principal product and raw material used
N/A

17 To whom do you sell most of your products or services?
☐ Business establishments ☐ General public ☒ Other (specify) Charitable Foundation

18 Have you ever applied for an identification number for this or any other business? ☐ Yes ☒ No
If "Yes," enter name and trade name (if any). ►
Also enter the approximate date, city, and State where you first applied and previous number if known.

Date 10/18/77	Signature and title Attorney	Telephone number (215) LO3-6060

Please leave blank ►	Geo.	Ind.	Class	Size	Reas. for appl.	Part I

SPECIMEN FORM

Form 2848
(Rev. Dec. 1974)
Department of the Treasury
Internal Revenue Service

Power of Attorney

(See the separate Instructions for Forms 2848 and 2848–D.)

Name, identifying number, and address including ZIP code of taxpayer(s)

The Mary and John Smith , Foundation
Suite 100 , 500 Main Street, Philadelphia, Penna. 19100

hereby appoints (Name, social security number, address including ZIP code, and telephone number of appointee(s)) (If the appointee has no social security number, so state.)

Gilbert M. Cantor; Nancy Rothkopf

Cantor/Franklin/Grodinsky   (215) LO3-6060
2000 Market Street, Suite 1200
Philadelphia, Penna. 19103

as attorney(s)-in-fact to represent the taxpayer(s) before any office of the Internal Revenue Service with respect to the following Internal Revenue tax matters (specify the type(s) of tax and year(s) or period(s)):

Form 1023 application for exemption

Said attorney(s)-in-fact (or either of them) shall, subject to revocation, have authority to receive confidential information and full power to perform on behalf of the taxpayer(s) the following acts with respect to the above tax matters:
(Strike through any of the following which are not granted.)
   To receive, but not to endorse and collect, checks in payment of any refund of Internal Revenue taxes, penalties, or interest. (See "Refund checks" on page 2 of the separate instructions.)
   To execute waivers (including offers of waivers) of restrictions on assessment or collection of deficiencies in tax and waivers of notice of disallowance of a claim for credit or refund.
   To execute consents extending the statutory period for assessment or collection of taxes.
   To execute closing agreements under section 7121 of the Internal Revenue Code.
   To delegate authority or to substitute another representative.

   Other acts (specify) ....
Copies of notices and other written communications addressed to the taxpayer(s) in proceedings involving the above matters should be sent to (Name, social security number, address including ZIP code, and telephone number):

the appointees named above

and

This power of attorney revokes all prior powers of attorney and tax information authorizations on file with the same Internal Revenue office with respect to the same matters and years or periods covered by this instrument, except the following:

no exceptions
....
(Specify to whom granted, social security number, date, and address including ZIP code, or refer to attached copies of prior powers and authorizations.)

Signature of or for taxpayer(s)
If signed by a corporate officer, partner, or fiduciary on behalf of the taxpayer, I certify that I have the authority to execute this power of attorney on behalf of the taxpayer.

.... Trustee   2/18/78
      (Signature)   (Title, if applicable)   (Date)

.... Trustee   2/18/78
      (Signature)   (Title, if applicable)   (Date)

(The applicable portion of the back page must also be executed.)   Form **2848** (Rev. 12–74)

Form 2848 (Rev. 12–74)   Page 2

If the power of attorney is granted to an attorney, certified public accountant, or enrolled agent, this declaration must be completed.

I declare that I am not currently under suspension or disbarment from practice before the Internal Revenue Service, that I am aware of Treasury Department Circular No. 230 as amended (31 C.F.R. Part 10), and that:

I am a member in good standing of the bar of the highest court of the jurisdiction indicated below; or
I am duly qualified to practice as a certified public accountant in the jurisdiction indicated below; or
I am enrolled as an agent pursuant to the requirements of Treasury Department Circular No. 230.

Designation (Attorney, C.P.A., or Agent)	Jurisdiction (State, etc.) or Enrollment Card Number	Signature	Date
Attorney	PA		10/18/77
Attorney	PA		10/18/77

If the power of attorney is granted to a person other than an attorney, certified public accountant, or enrolled agent, it must be witnessed or notarized below.

The person(s) signing as or for the taxpayer(s): (Check and complete one.)

[ ] is/are known to and signed in the presence of the two disinterested witnesses whose signatures appear here:

....
(Signature of Witness)   (Date)

....
(Signature of Witness)   (Date)

[ ] appeared this day before a notary public and acknowledged this power of attorney as his/her/their voluntary act and deed.

....   NOTARIAL SEAL
(Signature of Notary)   (Date)   (If required)

E.I. #25-1231452

PHI-50-78-54   P. O. Box 959
                                                   Scranton, Pa. 18501

                          E. O. Determination Section (717) 342-3141

                                                   EO:7212:DAC

The Mary and John Smith
  Foundation
500 Main Street - Suite 100
Philadelphia, Pa. 1910   March 24, 1978

Gentlemen:

Based on information supplied, and assuming your operations will
be as stated in your application for exemption, we have determined you
are exempt from Federal income tax under section 501(c)(3) of the
Internal Revenue Code.

We have further concluded that you are a private non-operating
foundation as defined in section 509(a) of the Code as explained below:
failure to meet the "income" test. To qualify as an operating foundation,
a private foundation must satisfy the "income" test and one of three
additional tests termed respectively the "assets" test, "endowment" test
and "support" test.

If your purposes, character, or method of operation is changed,
you must let us know so we can consider the effect of the change on your
exempt status. Also, you must inform us of all changes in your name or
address. You are required to file Form 990PF (Return of Private Foundation Exempt from Federal Income Tax) and 990AR (if at any time
during the year the organization had at least $5,000 of assets) by the
fifteenth day of the fifth month after the end of your annual accounting
period. The law imposes a penalty of $10 a day, up to a maximum of
$5,000 for failure to file a return on time.

You are not required to file Federal income tax returns unless you
are subject to the tax on unrelated business income under section 511 of
the Code. If you are subject to this tax, you must file an income tax
return on Form 900T. In this letter, we are not determining whether any
of your present or proposed activities are unrelated trade or business as
defined in section 513 of the Code.

Donors may deduct contributions to you as provided by section 170
of the Code. Bequests, legacies, devises, transfers, or gifts to you or for
your use are deductible for Federal estate and gift tax purposes under
sections 2055, 2106, and 2522 of the Code.

You are not liable for Federal Unemployment taxes. You are liable
for social security taxes only if you have filed a waiver of exemption
certificate, Form SS-15, as provided in the Federal Insurance Contributions Act.

In view of the fact that you are a private foundation, you are subject to the excise taxes under Chapter 42 of the Code.

If you do not agree with these conclusions, you may, within 30 days from the date of this letter, appeal by complying with the procedures explained in the enclosed Form 892, Exempt Organization Appeal Procedures for Unagreed Issues.

If you do not protest this proposed determination in a timely manner, it will be considered by the Internal Revenue Service as a failure to exhaust available administrative remedies. Section 7428(b)(2) of the Internal Revenue Code provides in part that, "A declaratory judgement or decree under this section shall not be issued in any proceeding unless the Tax Court, the Court of Claims, or the District Court of the United States for the District of Columbia determines that the organization involved has exhausted administrative remedies available to it within the Internal Revenue Service."

If we do not hear from you within 30 days from the date of this letter, this determination will become final.

Sincerely yours,

James T. Rideoutte
District Director

cc. Gilbert M. Cantor
    Nancy Rothkopf

lm

FORM C-9

Rev. Rul. 72-395, 1972-2 C.B. 340

Form C-9 is a Revenue Ruling which sets forth certain mandatory and optional provisions for charitable remainder annuity trusts and charitable remainder unitrusts. Such trusts are discussed primarily in Chapter 2, ¶203.10.

Rev. Rul. 72-395

Table of Contents

Section 1. Purpose

The purpose of this Revenue Ruling is to set forth illustrative sample provisions for inclusion in the governing instrument of a charitable remainder trust that may be used to satisfy the requirements of section 664 of the Internal Revenue Code of 1954 and the Income Tax Regulations application thereto.

Sec. 2. Background

.01 The Tax Reform Act of 1969 Public Law 91-172, C.B. 1969-3, 10, imposed new requirements which must be satisfied by a charitable remainder trust in order for an income, gift, or estate tax deduction to be allowed for the transfer of a remainder interest to charity. The new requirements are contained in section 664 of the Code and in the regulations promulgated thereunder, T.D. 7207, page 106.

.02 In general, a charitable remainder trust is a trust which provides for a special distribution at least annually for life or a term of years, to one or more beneficiaries, at least one of which is not a charity, with an irrevocable remainder interest to be held for the benefit of, or paid over to, charity. In order to qualify under section 664 of the Code, the trust must satisfy the requirements of either a charitable remainder annuity trust or a charitable remainder unitrust.

Sec. 3. Instructions to Taxpayers

.01 This Revenue Ruling contains sample illustrative provisions that may be included in the governing instrument of a charitable remainder annuity trust and a charitable remainder unitrust. These sample provisions include the mandatory provisions and certain permissible optional provisions referred to in the regulations. Provisions corresponding to these sample provisions will be accepted by the Internal Revenue Service in the absence of any showing that they are not enforceable under applicable local law.

.02 The language and format of the sample provisions included in this Revenue Ruling are merely examples of provisions which comply with the requirements and options in the regulations. There is no fixed language or format which must be used, and any other language or format that satisfies the requirements of the regulations will be acceptable. Incorporation of a regulatory requirement in the governing instrument of the trust by a short, specific, and descriptive reference to the requirement and its citation in the regulations will also be acceptable if such a reference incorporating the regulatory requirement into the governing instrument is effective under local law. However, a general provision stating that the grantor or testator intends to create a charitable remainder trust and incorporating by general reference all necessary requirements of the Internal Revenue Code and regulations will not, by itself, be sufficient.

.03 The trust instrument must create a valid trust under applicable local law in order to qualify as a charitable remainder trust. Thus, in addition to complying with the regulations, the trust instrument should incorporate any additional provisions relating to charitable trusts that are required under applicable local law.

.04 The trust instrument may contain provisions in addition to those provisions which are intended to satisfy the requirements of the regulations, but care should be taken to determine that such provisions are not in conflict with the regulations.

Sec. 4. Charitable Remainder Annuity Trust; Mandatory Provisions

.01 Under section 1.664-2(a)(1) of the regulations, one of the requirements of a charitable remainder annuity trust is that the governing instrument of the trust provide that the trust shall pay a sum certain not less often than annually to one or more persons described in section 1.664-2(a)(3) for the period specified in section 1.664-2(a)(5). Section 1.664-2(a)(2)(i) requires that the annuity amount must be at least 5 percent of the initial net fair market value of the assets placed in trust. Section 1.664-2(a)(3) provides that the sum certain must be payable to or for the use of a named person or persons, at least one of which is not an organization described in section 170(c) of the Code. Section 1.664-2(a) (5) provides that the sum certain may be payable for either the life or lives of a named individual or individuals or for a term of years not to exceed 20 years. The following is a sample provision for inclusion in the governing instrument which satisfies the requirements of the mandatory provision described in this subsection:

> The trustee shall pay to *A* during his life an annuity amount of $*Y* in each taxable year of the trust. The annuity amount shall be paid in equal quarterly installments from income and, to the extent that income is not sufficient, from principal. Any income of the trust for a taxable year in excess of the annuity amount shall be added to principal.

The following comments pertain to the sample provision described above:

(1) *5 Percent test.* The annuity amount must be at least 5 percent of the initial net fair market value of the assets placed in trust.

(2) *Annuity amount stated as a fraction or percentage.* If the annuity amount is stated as a fraction or percentage rather than as a dollar amount, a provision must be included in the governing instrument regarding incorrect valuations. See section 5.01.

(3) *Source of payment.* The annuity amount may be paid from trust income or principal, but it must be paid from either of the two in all events. It should be noted that in many jurisdictions, the payment of the annuity amount is restricted to the income of the trust unless otherwise indicated. In such jurisdictions, it is necessary that such restrictions be removed by the governing instrument of the trust. The above provision removes such restrictions. Any income of the trust in excess of the annuity amount may, but need not, be added to principal. Care should be taken, however, to assure that, under applicable local law, such excess income is retained by the trust. The above provision so provides.

(4) *Payment of annuity amount in installments.* The annuity amount

may be paid to the recipient annually or in equal or unequal installments throughout the year. The first and each succeeding installment should fall due at the end of the period to which it applies. The amount of the charitable deduction will be affected by the frequency of payment, by whether the installments are equal or unequal, and by whether each installment must await the end of the period for which it is paid.

(5) *Terms of years.* As an alternative to the payment of the annuity amount for the recipient's life, the annuity amount may be paid to the recipient for a term of years (not to exceed 20 years). See section 1.664-2(a)(5)(i).

(6) *Concurrent or successive recipients.* The annuity amount may be paid to concurrent or successive recipients so long as the 5 percent test is met. See section 1.664-2(a)(5).

(7) *Payment of a portion of the annuity amount to charity.* Any part, but not all, of the annuity amount may be paid to charity instead of to a noncharitable recipient. See section 1.664-2(a)(3)(i).

.02 Under section 1.664-2(a)(6)(i), the entire corpus of the trust must be irrevocably transferred to or for the use of one or more organizations described in section 170(c) of the Code or retained for such use upon the termination of all noncharitable interests. The following is a sample provision for inclusion in the governing instrument which satisfies the requirements of the mandatory provision described in this subsection:

> Upon the death of *A*, the trustee shall distribute all of the then principal and income of the trust, other than any amount due *A*, to *M* charity.

The following comments pertain to the sample provision described above:

(1) *Permissible remaindermen.* M charity must be an organization described in section 107(c) of the Code at the time of the transfer to the charitable remainder annuity trust. See section 1.664-2(a)(6)(i). If a deduction is sought under section 2055 or 2522 of the Code, M charity must also be an organization described in section 2055(a) or 2522(a) or (b), respectively, of the Code.

(2) *Permissible dispositions of remainder interest.* Upon the termination of the noncharitable interests, the charitable remainder may be distributed outright to one or more charities, may be held in further trust for one or more charities, may be held in further trust for charitable purposes, or any combination of the foregoing. See section 1.664-2(a)(6)(i).

.03 Under section 1.664-2(a)(6)(iv), the governing instrument of the trust shall provide that, in the event that an organization to or for the use of which the trust corpus is to be transferred or retained is not an organization described in section 170(c) of the Code at the time when any amount is to be irrevocably transferred to or for the use of such organization, such amount shall be transferred to or for the use of, or retained for the use of, one or more alternative organizations which are described in section 170(c) at such time. The following is a sample provision for inclusion in the governing instrument which satisfies the requirements of the mandatory provision described in this subsection:

> If *M* charity is not an organization described in section 170(c) of the Internal Revenue Code of 1954 at the time when any principal or income of the trust is to be distributed to it, the trustee shall distribute such principal or income to one or more organizations then described in section 170(c) as the trustee shall select in his sole discretion.

The following comments pertain to the sample provision described above:

(1) *Manner of selection of alternative charitable remainderman.* One or more alternate charities may be selected in any manner provided in the trust instrument. See section 1.664-2(a)(6)(iv).

(2) *Cross references.* See comments (1) and (2) in section 4.02.

.04 Under section 1.664-2(a)(1)(iv)(*a*), the governing instrument shall provide that, in the case of a taxable year which is for a period of less than 12 months, the annuity amount required to be paid shall be the sum certain multiplied by a fraction the numerator of which is the number of days in the taxable years of the trust and the denominator of which is 365 (366 if February 29 is a day included in the numerator). Section 1.664-2(a)(1)(iv)(*b*) provides that, in the case of the taxable year in which occurs the termination of the noncharitable interests, the annuity amount required to be paid shall be the sum certain multiplied by a fraction the numerator of which is the number of days between the beginning of such taxable year and the termination of such noncharitable interests and the denominator of which is 365 (366 if February 29 is a day included in the numerator). The following is a sample provision for inclusion in the governing instrument which satisfies the requirements of the mandatory provision described in this subsection:

> In determining the annuity amount, the trustee shall prorate the same, on a daily basis, for a short taxable year and for the taxable year of *A*'s death.

.05 Under section 1.664-2(b), the governing instrument shall provide that no additional contributions may be made to the trust after the initial contribution. The following is a sample provision for inclusion in the governing instrument which satisfies the requirements of the mandatory provision described in this subsection:

No additional contributions shall be made to the trust after the initial contribution.

The following comment pertains to the sample provision described above:

Property passing by reason of death. All property passing to the trust by reason of the death of the grantor shall be considered one contribution. See section 1.664-2(b).

.06 Section 4947(a)(2) of the Code makes section 508(e) of the Code applicable to a charitable remainder annuity trust to the extent that other provisions of chapter 42 of the Code are also made applicable to such a trust. Section 4947(a)(2) of the Code makes sections 4941, 4943, 4944, and 4945 of the Code applicable to such trusts except for the payment of the annuity amount to the income beneficiary. Section 4947(b)(3)(B) of the Code excludes such trusts from the application of sections 4943 and 4944 of the Code in cases where a deduction was allowed for amounts going to every remainder beneficiary but not to any income beneficiary. The following is a sample provision for inclusion in the governing instrument which satisfies the requirements of the mandatory provision described in this subsection:

Except for the payment of the annuity amount to *A*, the trustee is prohibited from engaging in any act of self-dealing as defined in section 4941(d) of the Internal Revenue Code of 1954, from retaining any excess business holdings as defined in section 4943(c) of the Code which would subject the trust to tax under section 4943 of the Code, from making any investments which would subject the trust to tax under section 4944 of the Code, and from making any taxable expenditures as defined in section 4945(d) of the Code. The trustee shall make distributions at such time and in such manner as not to subject the trust to tax under section 4942 of the Code.

The following comments pertain to the sample provision described above:

(1) *Rule if part of the annuity amount is paid to charity.* The governing instrument of the trust must prohibit the trustee from engaging in activities described in sections 4943 and 4944 of the Code during any period in which any part of the annuity amount is paid to charity. The above provision satisfies this requirement.

(2) *Application of provisions after the trust ceases to be a charitable remainder annuity trust.* To retain its exempt status after the trust ceases to be a charitable remainder annuity trust, the trust's governing instrument must also prohibit the trustee from engaging in any activities described in sections 4943 and 4944 of the Code and must require the trustee to distribute property at such times and in such manner as not to subject

the trust to tax under section 4942 of the Code during any period after the date the trust is no longer treated as a trust described in section 4947(a)(2) of the Code and the regulations thereunder. The above provision satisfies this requirement. See section 1.664-2(a)(6)(ii).

(3) *Application of state law.* See section 13.8(b) of the Temporary Income Tax Regulations under the Tax Reform Act of 1969 providing for the satisfaction of the requirements of section 508(e) of the Code by applicable provisions of state law. If these requirements are satisfied by applicable provisions of state law, there is no need specifically to refer to them in the trust agreement.

Sec. 5. Charitable Remainder Annuity Trust; Optional Provisions

.01 Under section 1.664-2(a)(1)(iii) of the regulations, the sum certain may be expressed as a fraction or a percentage of the initial net fair market value of the property irrevocably passing in trust as finally determined for Federal tax purposes if the governing instrument also provides that, in the event that such value is incorrectly determined by the fiduciary, the trust shall pay to the recipient (in the case of an undervaluation) or be repaid by the recipient (in the case of an overvaluation) an amount equal to the difference between the amount which the trust should have paid the recipient if the correct value were used and the amount which the trust actually paid the recipient. The following is a sample provision for inclusion in the governing instrument which satisfies the requirements of the optional provision described in this subsection:

> The trustee shall pay to A in each taxable year of the trust during his life an annuity amount equal to Y percent of the initial net fair market value of the assets constituting the trust. In determining such value, assets shall be valued at their values as finally determined for Federal tax purposes. If the initial net fair market value of the assets constituting the trust is incorrectly determined by the fiduciary, then within a reasonable period after such final determination, the trustee shall pay to A in the case of an undervaluation or shall receive from A in the case of an overvaluation an amount equal to the difference between the annuity amount properly payable and the annuity amount actually paid. The annuity amount shall be paid in equal quarterly installments from income and, to the extent that income is not sufficient, from principal. Any income of the trust for a taxable year in excess of the annuity amount shall be added to principal.

The following comments pertain to the sample provision described above:

(1) *5 Percent test.* The annuity amount percentage must be at least 5 percent. See section 1.664-2(a)(2)(i).

(2) *Annuity amount expressed as the greater of two amounts.* The annuity amount may also be expressed as the greater of a stated dollar amount or

a fixed percentage (not less than 5 percent) of the initial value of the assets placed in trust.

(3) *Provisions replaced.* The optional provision set forth above may be used in lieu of the provision set forth in section 4.01.

(4) *Cross references.* See comments (3) through (7) in section 4.01.

.02 Section 1.664-1(a)(5)(i) provides, in effect, that a deduction is not allowable under section 2055 or 2106 of the Code unless the obligation to pay the annuity amount with respect to the property passing in trust at the date of death begins as of the date of death of the decedent. Nonetheless, the requirement to pay such amount may be deferred until the end of the taxable year of the trust in which occurs the complete funding of the trust if such deferral is permitted by applicable local law or authorized by the provisions of the governing instrument. The following is a sample provision for inclusion in the governing instrument which satisfies the requirements of the optional provision described in this subsection:

> All the rest, residue and remainder of my property and estate, real and personal, of whatever nature and wherever situated, I give, devise, and bequeath to my trustee in trust, to invest and reinvest the same during the life of *A* and in each taxable year of the trust to pay to *A* an annuity amount equal to *Y* percent of the initial net fair market value of the assets constituting the trust. In determining such value, assets shall be valued at their values as finally determined for Federal tax purposes. If the initial net fair market value of the assets constituting the trust is incorrectly determined by the fiduciary, then within a reasonable period after such final determination, the trustee shall pay to *A* (in the case of an undervaluation) or shall receive from *A* (in the case of an overvaluation) an amount equal to the difference between the annuity amount properly payable and the annuity, amount actually paid. The annuity amount shall be paid in equal quarterly installments from income and, to the extent that income is not sufficient, from principal. Any income of the trust for a taxable year in excess of the annuity amount shall be added to principal.
>
> The obligation to pay the annuity amount shall commence with the date of my death but payment of the annuity amount may be deferred from the date of my death to the end of the taxable year in which occurs the complete funding of the trust. Payment of the annuity amount so deferred, plus interest computed at 6 percent a year, compounded annually, shall be made within a reasonable time after the occurrence of said event.

The following comments pertain to the sample provision described above:

(1) *Deferral of annuity amount for period of administration.* The second paragraph of the above provision may be included in cases where funds pass to a charitable remainder annuity trust by reason of death, but the

actual amount passing in trust may not be known until the trust has been completely funded.

(2) *Provisions replaced.* The optional provision set forth above may be used in lieu of the provision set forth in section 4.01 and the optional provision set forth in section 5.01.

(3) *Cross references.* See comments (3) through (7) in section 4.01 and comments (1) and (2) in section 5.01.

.03 Under section 1.664-2(a)(3)(ii), a trust is not a charitable remainder trust if any person has the power to alter the amount to be paid to any named person, other than an organization described in section 170(c) of the Code, if such power would cause any person to be treated as the owner of the trust, or any portion thereof, if subpart E (section 671 through 678 of the Code) were applicable to the trust. Consequently, it is possible to grant to the trustee the power to allocate the annuity amount among members of a class if such power comes within the exception to section 674(a) of the Code provided in section 674(c). The following is a sample provision for inclusion in the governing instrument of such a power:

> The trustee shall pay an annuity amount of Y in each taxable year of the trust to such member or members of a class of persons consisting of A, B, and C in such amounts and proportions as the trustee in its absolute discretion shall from time to time determine until the last to die of A, B, and C. The trustee may pay the annuity amount to any one member of said class or may apportion it among the various members in such manner as the trustee shall from time to time deem advisable. The annuity amount shall be paid first from income and, to the extent that income is not sufficient, from principal. Any income of the trust for a taxable year in excess of the annuity amount shall be added to principal.

The following comments pertain to the sample provision described above:

(1) *Gifts to a class.* A, B, and C must be individuals living at the creation of the trust. The annuity amount may also be allocated among members of a class such as "children" or "issue" for their lives, provided that the class is closed and all members of the class are living and ascertainable at the creation of the trust. The annuity amount may also be allocated among the members of such a class for a term of years (not to exceed 20 years), in which event the members of the class need not be living or ascertainable at the creation of the trust. See section 1.664-2(a)(3)(i).

(2) *Type of power.* The power to allocate the annuity amount among members of a class must not cause any person to be treated as the owner of any part or all of the trust under the rules of sections 671 through 678 of the Code.

See section 1.664-2(a)(3)(ii).

(3) *Power to delay payment not permitted.* The power to allocate the annuity amount may not include a power to delay payment of the annuity amount, *i.e.,* the entire annuity amount must be paid out for each taxable year of the trust. See section 1.664-2(a)(1)(i).

(4) *Provisions replaced.* The optional provision set forth above may be used in lieu of the provision set forth in section 4.01.

(5) *Cross reference.* See comments (1) through (7) in section 4.01.

.04 Under section 1.664-2(a)(1)(i), the stated dollar amount must be the same either as to each recipient or as to the total amount payable for each year of the term of years or the lives of the recipients. However, under sections 1.664-2(a)(1)(i) and 1.664-2(a)(2)(ii), the stated dollar amount may be reduced at the death of a recipient or expiration of a term of years if: (1) the reduced amount is the same either as to each recipient or as to the total amount payable each year for the balance of the period during which annuity amounts are to be paid, (2) there is a distribution to an organization described in section 170(c) of the Code at the death of the recipient or expiration of the term of years, and (3) the total amounts payable each year after such distribution are not less than a stated dollar amount which bears the same ratio to 5 percent of the initial net fair market value of the trust assets as the net fair market value of the trust assets immediately after such distribution bears to the net fair market value of the trust assets immediately before such distribution. The following is a sample provision for inclusion in the governing instrument which satisfies the requirements of the optional provision described in this subsection:

> During the joint lives of A and B, the trustee shall, in each taxable year of the trust, pay to A an annuity amount of $\$X$ and pay to B an annuity amount of $\$Y$. The annuity amounts shall be paid in equal quarterly installments from income and, to the extent that income is not sufficient, from principal. Any income of the trust for a taxable year in excess of the annuity amounts shall be added to principal. Upon the death of the first to die of A and B, the trustee shall distribute $\$Z$ (or P percent of the trust assets) to M charity, and thereafter the trustee shall pay, in equal quarterly installments, to the survivor of A and B, for his life, an annuity amount, in each taxable year of the trust, which bears the same ratio to 5 percent of the initial net fair market value of the trust assets as the net fair market value of the trust assets, valued as of the date of distribution, less $\$Z$ (or P percent of the trust assets bears), to such fair market value as of the date of distribution.

The following comments pertain to the sample provision described above:

(1) *5 Percent test.* The sum of $\$X$ and $\$Y$ must not be less than 5

percent of the initial net fair market value of the assets placed in trust. See section 1.664-2(a)(2)(i).

(2) *Annuity amount larger than minimum amount provided above.* The above provision provides a formula to calculate the minimum annuity amount which must be paid to the survivor of A and B. The annuity amount paid to the survivor of A and B may be greater than that provided, but in no event may it exceed the annual aggregate annuity amount paid to A and B during their joint lives.

(3) *Provision replaced.* The optional provision set forth above may be used in lieu of the provision set forth in section 4.01.

(4) *Cross reference.* See comments (2) through (7) in section 4.01. See section 5.05 for rules requiring that the adjusted basis of assets distributed to charity in kind be fairly representative of the adjusted basis of all assets available for distribution on the date of distribution.

.05 Under section 1.664-2(a)(4), the governing instrument may provide that any amount, other than the annuity amount, shall be paid (or may be paid in the discretion of the trustee) to an organization described in section 170(c) of the Code provided that, in the case of distributions in kind, the adjusted basis of the property distributed is fairly representative of the adjusted basis of the property available for payment on the date of payment. The following is a sample provision for inclusion in the governing instrument which satisfies the requirements of the optional provision described in this subsection:

> During the life of A, the trustee may pay to M charity any income of the trust in excess of the annuity amount payable to A for the taxable year of the trust in which the income is earned. The adjusted basis for Federal income tax purposes of any trust property which the trustee distributes in kind to charity during the life of A must be fairly representative of the adjusted basis for such purposes of all trust property available for distribution on the date of distribution.

The following comment pertains to the sample provision described above:

Permitted distributions to charity. The governing instrument may permit or require distributions of trust assets to charity prior to the termination of all noncharitable interests. In such cases, the above provision with respect to adjusted basis is mandatory unless the governing instrument prohibits the trustee from satisfying such distribution in kind.

.06 Under section 1.664-2(a)(5)(i), the payment of the annuity amount may terminate with the regular payment next preceding the termination of all noncharitable interests. The following is a sample provision for inclusion in the governing instrument of the optional provision described in this subsection:

> The trustee shall pay to A during his life an annuity amount of $\$Y$ in each taxable year of the trust. However, the obligation of the trustee to pay such annuity amount shall terminate with the payment next preceding the death of A. The annuity amount shall be paid in equal quarterly installments from income and, to the extent that income is not sufficient, from principal. Any income of the trust for a taxable year in excess of the annuity amount shall be added to principal.

The following comments pertain to the sample provision described above:

(1) *Provisions replaced.* The optional provision set forth above may be used in lieu of the provision set forth in section 4.01.

(2) *Cross references.* See comments (1) through (7) in section 4.01.

.07 Under section 1.664-2(a)(4), the grantor of the trust may retain the power, exercisable only by will, to revoke or terminate the interest of any recipient other than an organization described in section 170(c) of the Code. The following is a sample provision for inclusion in the governing instrument of the optional provision described in this subsection:

> The trustee shall pay to the settlor during his life an annuity amount of $\$Y$ and upon the death of the settlor, if B survives him, the trustee shall pay to B during her life an annuity amount of $\$Y$. The settlor hereby expressly reserves the power, exercisable only by his will, to revoke and terminate the interest of B under this trust. Upon the first to occur of (i) the death of the survivor of the settlor and B or (ii) the death of the settlor if he effectively exercises his testamentary power to revoke and terminate the interest of B, the trustee shall distribute all of the then principal and income of the trust, other than any amount due A or B, to M charity. The annuity amount shall be paid in equal quarterly installments from income and, to the extent that income is not sufficient, from principal. Any income of the trust for a taxable year in excess of the annuity amount shall be added to principal.

The following comments pertain to the sample provision described above:

(1) *Provisions replaced.* The optional provision set forth above may be used in lieu of the provisions set forth in sections 4.01 and 4.02.

(2) *Cross references.* See comments (1) through (7) in sections 4.01 and comments (1) and (2) in section 4.02.

.08 Under section 1.664-1(a)(3), the provisions of the trust may not include any provisions which restrict the trustee from investing the trust assets in a manner which could result in the annual realization of a reasonable amount of income or gain from the sale or disposition of trust assets. The following is a sample provision for inclusion in the trust instrument which insures that the requirement described in this subsection is met:

Nothing in this trust instrument shall be construed to restrict the trustee from investing the trust assets in a manner which could result in the annual realization of a reasonable amount of income or gain from the sale or disposition of trust assets.

.09 Under section 1.664-1(a)(4), in order for a trust to be a charitable remainder annuity trust, the trust must function exclusively as a charitable remainder annuity trust from its creation. Consequently, a revocable inter vivos trust which is used to administer the estate of the decedent can never qualify as a charitable remainder annuity trust. However, the regulations permit the revocable inter vivos trust to distribute assets to another trust which does qualify as a charitable remainder annuity trust. The following is a sample provision for inclusion in the governing instrument of the revocable inter vivos trust which provides that the revocable inter vivos trust will be used to partially administer the estate of the decedent and then distribute assets to another trust which is a charitable remainder annuity trust:

The trustee shall pay to *A* all of the income from the trust assets for *A*'s life, during which the trust shall be fully revocable by *A* Upon *A*'s death the trust shall become irrevocable and the trustee shall pay all debts, taxes and other expenses of the administration of *A*'s estate. After the payment or satisfaction of all such debts, taxes and expenses, the trustee shall transfer all of the then principal and income of the trust to the trustee of the charitable remainder annuity trust hereinafter established to be held, administered and distributed in the manner and according to the terms and conditions hereinafter provided.

The following comments pertain to the sample provisions described above:

(1) *Trust provisions during life.* There are no restrictions on the dispositive provisions of the above trust during the period it is fully revocable.

(2) *Provisions for both trusts in same instrument.* The same governing instrument may provide for both the revocable inter vivos trust and the charitable remainder annuity trust, and both trusts may have the same trustee.

Sec. 6. Charitable Remainder Unitrust; Mandatory Provisions

.01 Under section 1.664-3(a)(1)(i)(*a*) of the regulations, one of the requirements of a charitable remainder unitrust is that the governing instrument of the trust provide that the trust shall pay, not less often than annually, a fixed percentage of the net fair market value of the trust assets, determined annually, to one or more persons described in section 1.664-3(a)(3) for the period specified in section 1.664-3(a)(5). Section 1.664-3(a)(2)(i) provides that the fixed percentage must be at least 5 percent. Section 1.664-3(a)(3) provides that the fixed percentage of such value must be payable to or for the use of a named person or persons, at least one of which is not an organization described in section 170(c) of the Code. Section 1.664-3(a)(5) provides that the fixed percentage of such value may be payable for either the life or lives of a named individual or individuals or for a term of years not to exceed 20 years. The following is a sample provision for inclusion in the governing instrument which satisfies the requirements of the mandatory provision described in this subsection:

> The trustee shall pay to *A* in each taxable year of the trust during his life a unitrust amount equal to *Y* percent of the net fair market value of the trust assets valued as of the first day of each taxable year of the trust. The unitrust amount shall be paid in equal quarterly installments from income and, to the extent that income is not sufficient, from principal. Any income of the trust for a taxable year in excess of the unitrust amount shall be added to principal.

The following comments pertain to the sample provision described above:

(1) *5 Percent test.* The unitrust percentage must be at least 5 percent. See section 1.664-3(a)(2)(i).

(2) *Source of payment.* The unitrust amount may be paid from trust income or principal, but it must be paid from either of the two in all events. It should be noted that, in some jurisdictions, the payment of the unitrust amount may be restricted to the income of the trust unless otherwise indicated. In such jurisdictions, it is necessary that such restrictions be removed by the governing instrument of the trust. The above provision removes such restrictions. Any income of the trust in excess of the unitrust amount may, but need not, be added to principal. Care should be taken, however, to assure that, under applicable local law, such excess income is retained by the trust. The above provision so provides.

(3) *Payment of the unitrust amount in installments.* The unitrust amount may be paid to the recipient annually or in equal or unequal installments throughout the year. The first and each succeeding installment should fall due at the end of the period to which it applies. The amount of the charitable deduction will be affected by the frequency of payment, by whether the installments are equal or unequal, and by whether each installment must await the end of the period for which it is paid.

(4) *Terms of years.* As an alternative to the payment of the unitrust amount for the recipient's life, the unitrust amount may be paid to the recipient for a term of years (not to exceed 20 years). See section 1.664-3(a)(5)(i).

(5) *Concurrent or successive recipients.* The unitrust amount may be

paid to concurrent or successive recipients so long as the 5 percent test is met. See section 1.664-3(a)(5)(i).

(6) *Payment of a portion of the unitrust amount to charity.* Any part, but not all, of the unitrust amount may be paid to charity instead of to a noncharitable recipient. See section 1.664-3(a)(3)(i).

(7) *Valuation date.* The governing instrument may provide that the trust assets be valued, for example, as of the first business day of each taxable year. See section 1.664-3(a)(1)(iv).

(8) *Amount of charitable deduction.* The amount of the charitable deduction will be affected by the period of time between the valuation date and the payment date or dates and by the frequency of payment. See section 1.664-4.

.02 Under section 1.664-3(a)(6)(i), the entire corpus of the trust must be irrevocably transferred, in whole or in part, to or for the use of one or more organizations described in section 170(c) of the Code or retained, in whole or in part, for such use upon the termination of the noncharitable interests. The following is a sample provision for inclusion in the governing instrument which satisfies the requirements of the mandatory provision described in this subsection:

> Upon the death of *A*, the trustee shall distribute all of the then principal and income of the trust, other than any amount due *A*, to *M* charity.

The following comments pertain to the sample provision described above:

(1) *Permissible remaindermen.* M charity must be an organization described in section 170(c) of the Code at the time of the transfer to the charitable remainder unitrust. See section 1.664-3(a)(6)(i). If a deduction is sought under section 2055 or 2522 of the Code, *M* charity must also be an organization described in section 2055(a) or 2522(a) or (b), respectively, of the Code.

(2) *Permissible dispositions of remainder interest.* Upon the termination of the noncharitable interest, the charitable remainder may be distributed outright to one or more charities, may be held in further trust for one or more charities, may be held in further trust for charitable purposes, or any combination of the foregoing. See section 1.664-3(a)(6)(i).

.03 Under section 1.664-3(a)(6)(iv), the governing instrument of the trust shall provide that, in the event that an organization to or for the use of which the trust corpus is to be transferred or retained is not an organization described in section 170(c) of the Code at the time when any amount is to be irrevocably transferred to or for the use of such organization, such amount shall be transferred to or for the use of or retained for the use of one or more alternative organizations which are described in section 170(c) at such time. The following is a sample provision for inclusion in the governing instrument which satisfies the requirements of the mandatory provision described in this subsection:

> If *M* charity is not an organization described in section 170(c) of the Internal Revenue Code of 1954 at the time when any principal or income of the trust is to be distributed to it, the trustee shall distribute such principal or income to one or more organizations then described in section 170(c) as the trustee shall select in his sole discretion.

The following comments pertain to the sample provisions described above:

(1) *Manner of selection of alternative charitable remainderman.* One or more alternate charities may be selected in any manner provided in the trust instrument. See section 1.664-3(a)(6)(iv).

(2) *Cross references.* See comments (1) and (2) in section 6.02.

.04 Under section 1.664-3(a)(1)(iii), the governing instrument of the trust shall provide that, in the case where the net fair market value of the trust assets is incorrectly determined by the fiduciary, the trust shall pay to the recipient (in the case of an undervaluation) or be repaid by the recipient (in the case of an overvaluation) an amount equal to the difference between the amount which the trust should have paid the recipient if the correct value were used and the amount which the trust actually paid the recipient. The following is a sample provision for inclusion in the governing instrument which satisfies the requirement of the mandatory provision described in this subsection:

> If the net fair market value of the trust assets is incorrectly determined by the fiduciary for any taxable year, then within a reasonable period after the final determination of the correct value, the trustee shall pay to *A* in the case of an undervaluation or shall receive from *A* in the case of an overvaluation an amount equal to the difference between the unitrust amount properly payable and the unitrust amount actually paid.

.05 Under section 1.664-3(a)(1)(v)(*a*), the governing instrument shall provide that, in the case of a taxable year which is for a period of less than 12 months, the unitrust amount required to be paid shall be the fixed percentage of the net fair market value of the trust assets for such year multiplied by a fraction of the numerator of which is the number of days in the taxable year of the trust and the denominator of which is 365 (366 if February 29 is a day included in the numerator). Section 1.664-3(a)(1)(v)(*b*) provides that, in the case of the taxable year in which occurs the termination of the noncharitable interests, the unitrust amount required to be paid shall be the fixed percentage of the net fair market value of the trust assets for such year multiplied by a fraction the numerator of which is the number of days between the beginning of such taxable year and the termination of such noncharitable interests and the denominator of which is 365 (366 if February 29 is a day included in the numerator). The following is a sample provision for inclusion in the governing instrument which satisfies the requirements of the mandatory provision described in this subsection:

> In determining the unitrust amount, the trustee shall prorate the same, on a daily basis, for a short taxable year and for the taxable year of *A*'s death.

The following comment pertains to the sample provision described below:

(1) *Valuation date.* If a valuation date other than the first day of the taxable year is selected, section 1.664-3(a)(1)(v)(*a*)(*3*) and (*b*)(*1*)(*iii*) provides that the governing instrument of the trust must also provide that where no valuation date occurs in a taxable year of the trust which is a short taxable year or which is the taxable year in which the noncharitable interests terminate, the trust assets shall be valued as of the last day of such short taxable year or as of the day on which such noncharitable interests terminate.

.06 Under section 1.664-3(b), the governing instrument shall provide either that no additional contributions may be made to the trust after the initial contribution or that the unitrust amount for the taxable year of a contribution shall be computed by multiplying the fixed percentage by the sum of (1) the net fair market value of the trust assets (excluding the value of the additional contribution and any earned income from and any appreciation on such property after its contribution) and (2) that proportion of the value of the additional property (that was excluded under (1)) which the number of days in the period which begins with the date of contribution and ends with the earlier of the last day of such taxable year or the last day of the period described in section 1.664-3(a)(5) bears to the number of days in the period which begins with the first day of such taxable year and ends with the earlier of the last day of such taxable year or the last day of the period described in section 1.664-3(a)(5). If additional contributions are not prohibited, section 1.664-3(b) also provides that the governing instrument shall provide that, where no valuation date occurs after the time of the contribution and during the taxable year in which the contribution is made, the additional property shall be valued as of the time of contribution. The following is a sample provision for inclusion in the governing instrument which satisfies the requirements of the mandatory provision described in this subsection:

If any additional contributions are made to the trust after the initial contribution in trust, the unitrust amount for the taxable year in which the assets are added to the trust shall be Y percent of the sum of (a) the net fair market value of trust assets (excluding the assets so added and any income from, or appreciation on, such assets) and (b) that proportion of the value of the assets so added that was excluded under (a) which the number of days in the period which begins with the date of contribution and ends with the earlier of the last day of the taxable year or A's death bears to the number of days in the period which begins on the first day of such taxable year and ends with the earlier of the last day in such taxable year or A's death. In the case where there is no valuation date after the time of contribution, the assets so added shall be valued at the time of contribution.

The following comments pertain to the sample provision described above:

(1) *No additional contributions.* In lieu of the above provision, the governing instrument may provide that no additional contribution shall be made to the trust.

(2) *Property passing by reason of death.* All property passing to the trust by reason of death of the grantor shall be considered one contribution. See section 1.664-3(b).

.07 Section 497(a)(2) of the Code makes section 508(e) of the Code applicable to a charitable remainder unitrust to the extent that other provisions of chapter 42 of the Code are also made applicable to such a trust. Section 4947(a)(2) makes sections 4941, 4943, 4944, and 4945 of the Code applicable to such trusts except for the payment of the unitrust amount to the income beneficiary. Section 4947(b)(3)(B) of the Code excludes such trusts from the application of sections 4943 and 4944 of the Code in cases where a deduction was allowed for amounts going to every remainder beneficiary but not to any income beneficiary. The following is a sample provision for inclusion in the governing instrument which satisfies the requirements of the mandatory provision described in this subsection:

Except for the payment of the unitrust amount to A, the trustee is prohibited from engaging in any act of self-dealing as defined in section 4941(d) of the Internal Revenue Code of 1954, from retaining any excess business holdings as defined in section 4943(c) of the Code which would subject the trust to tax under section 4943 of the Code, from making any investments which would subject the trust to tax under section 4944 of the Code, and from making any taxable expenditures as defined in section 4945(d) of the Code. The trustee shall make distributions at such time and in such manner as not to subject the trust to tax under section 4942 of the Code.

The following comments pertain to the sample provision described above:

(1) *Rule if part of the unitrust amount is paid to charity.* The governing instrument of the trust must prohibit the trustee from engaging in activities described in sections 4943 and 4944 of the Code during any period in which any part of the unitrust amount is paid to charity. The above provision satisfies this requirement.

(2) *Application of provisions after the trust ceases to be a charitable remainder unitrust.* To retain its exempt status after the trust ceases to be a charitable remainder unitrust, the trust's governing instrument must also prohibit the trustee from engaging in any activities described in sections 4943 and 4944 of the Code and must require the trustee to distribute property at such times and in such manner as not to subject the trust to tax under section 4942 of the Code during any period after the date the trust is no longer treated as a trust described in section 4947(a)(2) of the Code and the regulations thereunder. The above provision satisfies this requirement. See section 1.664-3(a)(6)(ii).

(3) *Application of state law.* See section 13.8(b) of the Temporary Income Tax Regulations under the Tax Reform Act of 1969 providing for the satisfaction of the requirements of section 508(e) of the Code by applicable provisions of state law. If these requirements are satisfied by applicable provisions of state law, there is no need specifically to refer to them in the trust agreement.

Sec. 7. Charitable Remainder Unitrust; Optional Provisions

.01 Under section 1.664-3(a)(1)(i)(*b*), the trust may pay, instead of the regular unitrust amount (the fixed percentage of the net fair market value of the trust assets, determined annually), either the first of the following amounts or the sum of the first and second of the following amounts:

(1) The amount of trust income (as defined in section 643(b) and the regulations thereunder) for the taxable year to the extent that such amount is not more than the amount required to be distributed as the regular unitrust amount for that taxable year.

(2) The amount of the trust income for a taxable year which is in excess of the regular unitrust amount for that taxable year to the extent that the aggregate of the amounts paid in prior years was less than the aggregate of the regular unitrust amounts for those prior years.

Section 1.664-3(a)(1)(v)(*a*)(2) and (*b*)(*1*)(*ii*), in effect, provides that in a short taxable year and in the taxable year in which the noncharitable interests terminate, the amount determined under section 1.664-3(a)(1)(i)(*b*) shall be computed on the basis of the income for the taxable year and the prorated regular unitrust amount. The prorated regular unitrust amount is determined under section 1.664-3(a)(1)(v)(*a*)(*1*) and (b)(1)(i). The following is a sample provision for inclusion in the governing instrument which satisfies the requirements of the optional provision described in this subsection:

> The trustee shall pay to A in each taxable year of the trust during his life an amount equal to the lesser of (a) the trust income for such taxable year (as defined in section 643(b) of the Internal Revenue Code of 1954 and the regulations thereunder) and (b) Y percent of the net fair market value of the trust assets valued as the first day of such taxable year decreased as elsewhere provided in the case where the taxable year is a short taxable year or is the taxable year in which A dies and increased as elsewhere provided in the case where there are additional contributions in the taxable year. If the trust income for any taxable year exceeds the amount determined under (b), the payment to A shall also include such excess income to the extent that the aggregate of the amounts paid to A in prior years is less than Y percent of the aggregate net fair market value of the trust assets for such years. Payments to A shall be made in quarterly installments. Any income of the trust in excess of such payments shall be added to principal.

The following comments pertain to the sample provision described above:

(1) *Makeup of deficiencies not required.* If it is desired to use the above provision, the second sentence, increasing the unitrust amount by the income in excess of the fixed percentage to the extent of deficiencies between the income and the regular unitrust amount in prior years, is optional.

(2) *Computation of charitable deduction.* It should be noted that, notwithstanding the above provision, the computation of the charitable deduction will be determined on the basis that the regular unitrust amount will be distributed in each taxable year of the trust.

(3) *Provisions replaced.* The optional provision set forth above may be used in lieu of the provision set forth in section 6.01. In addition, the above provision assumes that the governing instrument does not prohibit additional contributions. See section 6.06.

(4) *Cross references.* See comments (1) through (8) in section 6.01.

.02 Section 1.664-1(a)(5)(i) provides, in effect, that a deduction is not allowable under section 2055 or 2106 of the Code unless the obligation to pay the unitrust amount with respect to the property passing in trust at the date of death begins as of the date of death of the decedent. Nonetheless, the requirement to pay such amount may be deferred until the end of the taxable year of the trust in which occurs the complete funding of the trust if such deferral is permitted by applicable local law or authorized by the provisions of the governing instrument. The following is a sample provision for inclusion in the governing instrument which satisfies the requirements of the optional provision described in this subsection:

> All the rest, residue and remainder of my property and estate, real and personal, of whatever nature and wherever situated, I give, devise, and bequeath to my trustee in trust, to invest and reinvest the same during the life of A and in each taxable year of the trust to pay, in equal quarterly installments, to A, a unitrust amount equal to Y percent of the net fair market value of the trust assets valued as of the first day of each taxable year of the trust. The unitrust amount shall be paid from income and, to the extent income is not sufficient, from principal. Any income of the trust for a taxable year in excess of the unitrust amount shall be added to principal.
>
> The obligation to pay the unitrust amount shall commence with the date of my death, but payment of the unitrust amount may be deferred from the date of my death to the end of the taxable year of the trust in which occurs the complete funding of the trust. Within a reasonable time after the occurrence of said event, the trustee shall pay the amount determined under the method described in section 1.664-1(a)(5)(ii) of the Federal Income Tax Regulations less the sum of any amounts previously distributed and interest thereon, computed at 6 percent a year, compounded annually, from the date of distribution to the occurrence of said event.

The following comments pertain to the sample provision described above:

(1) *Deferral and computation of unitrust amount for period of administration.* The second paragraph of the above provision may be included in cases where funds pass to a charitable remainder unitrust by reason of death, but the actual amount passing in trust may not be known until the trust has been completely funded. The cited section of the regulations contains a formula under which the unitrust amount may be retroactively computed during a reasonable period of administration or settlement.

(2) *Incorporation by reference.* If the reference to the regulations is not effective under the law governing the trust to incorporate the regulatory provision into the governing instrument, the formula contained in the regulations should be restated in the governing instrument.

(3) *Provisions replaced.* The optional provision set forth above may be used in lieu of the provision set forth in section 6.01.

(4) *Cross references.* See comments (1) through (8) in section 6.01.

.03 Under section 1.664-2(a)(3)(ii), a trust is not a charitable remainder trust if any person has the power to alter the amount to be paid to any named person, other than an organization described in section 107(c) of the Code, if such power would cause any person to be treated as the owner of the trust, or any portion thereof, if subpart E (sections 671 through 678 of the Code) were applicable to the trust. Consequently, it is possible to grant to the trustee the power to allocate the unitrust amount among members of a class if such power comes within the exception to section 674(a) provided in section 674(c). The following is a sample provision for inclusion in the governing instrument of such a power:

> The trustee shall pay, in each taxable year of the trust, a unitrust amount equal to Y percent of the net fair market value of the trust assets valued as of the first day of such taxable year to such member or members of a class of persons consisting of A, B, and C in such amounts and proportions as the trustee in its absolute discretion shall from time to time determine until the last to die of A, B, and C. The trustee may pay the unitrust amount to any one member of said class or may apportion it among the various members in such manner as the trustee shall from time to time deem advisable. The unitrust amount shall be paid first from income and, to the extent that income is not sufficient, from principal. Any income of the trust for a taxable year in excess of the unitrust amount shall be added to principal.

The following comments pertain to the sample provision described above:

(1) *Gifts to a class.* A, B, and C must be individuals living at the creation of the trust. The unitrust amount may be allocated among members of a class such as "children" or "issue" for their lives, provided that the class is closed and all members of the class are living and ascertainable at the creation of the trust. The unitrust amount may also be allocated among the members of such a class for a term of years (not to exceed 20 years), in which event the members of the class need not be living or ascertainable at the creation of the trust. See section 1.664-3(a)(3)(i).

(2) *Type of power.* The power to allocate the unitrust amount among members of a class must not cause any person to be treated as the owner of any part or all of the trust under the rules of sections 671 through 678 of the Code. See section 1.664-3(a)(3)(ii).

(3) *Power to delay payment not permitted.* The power to allocate the unitrust amount may not include a power to delay payment of the unitrust amount. Thus, the entire unitrust amount must be paid out for each taxable year of the trust. See section 1.664-3(a)(1)(i).

(4) *Provisions replaced.* The optional provision set forth above many be used in lieu of the provision set forth in section 6.01.

(5) *Cross references.* See comments (1) through (8) in section 6.01.

.04 Under section 1.664-3(a)(1)(i), the fixed percentage amount must be the same either as to each recipient or as to the total of the percentages payable for each year of the term of years or the lives of the recipients. However, under sections 1.664-3(a)(1)(ii) and 1.664-3(a)(2)(ii), the fixed percentage may be reduced at the death of a recipient or expiration of a term of years if: (1) the reduced percentage is the same either as to each recipient or as to the total percentage payable each year for the balance of the period during which unitrust amounts are to be paid, (2) there is a distribution to an organization described in section 170(c) of the Code at the death of the recipient or expiration of the term of years, and (3) the total of the percentages payable each year after such distribution are not less than 5 percent. The following is a sample provision for inclusion in the governing instrument which satisfies the requirements of the optional provision described in this subsection:

> During the joint lives of A and B, the trustee shall, in each taxable year of the trust, pay to A a unitrust amount equal to X percent of the net fair market value of the trust assets valued as of the first day of such taxable year and pay to B a unitrust amount equal to Y percent of the net fair market value of the trust assets valued as of the first day of such taxable year. The unitrust amounts shall be paid in equal quarterly installments from income and, to the extent that income is not sufficient, from principal. Any income of the trust for a taxable year in excess of the unitrust amounts shall be added to principal. Upon the death of the first to die of A and B, the trustee shall distribute $\$Z$ (or P percent of the trust assets) to M charity, and therefore the trustee shall pay to the survivor of A and B for his life a unitrust amount in each taxable year of the trust equal to 5 percent of the net fair market value of the trust assets valued as of the first day of such taxable year.

The following comments pertain to the sample provision described above:

(1) *5 Percent test.* The sum of X and Y must not be less than 5 percent. See section 1.664-3(a)(2)(i).

(2) *Unitrust amount larger than minimum amount provided above.* The above provision describes the minimum unitrust amount which must be paid to the survivor of A and B. The unitrust amount paid to the survivor of A and B may be greater than that provided, but in no event may it exceed the total of the percentages paid to A and B during their joint lives.

(3) *Provisions replaced.* The optional provision set forth above may be used in lieu of the provisions set forth in sections 6.01 and 6.02.

(4) *Cross references.* See comments (2) through (8) in section 6.01 and comments (1) and (2) in section 6.02. See section 7.05 for rules requiring the adjusted basis of assets distributed to charity in kind to be fairly representative of the adjusted basis of all assets available for distribution on the date of distribution.

.05 Under section 1.664-3(a)(4), the governing instrument may provide that any amount, other than the unitrust amount, shall be paid (or may be paid in the discretion of the trustee) to an organization described in section 170(c) of the Code provided that, in the case of distributions in kind, the adjusted basis of the property distributed is fairly representative of the adjusted basis of the property available for payment on the date of payment. The following is a sample provision for inclusion in the governing instrument which satisfies the requirements of the optional provision described in this subsection:

> During the life of A, the trustee may pay to M charity any income of the trust in excess of the unitrust amount payable to A for the taxable year of the trust in which the income is earned. The adjusted basis for Federal income tax purposes of any trust property which the trustee distributes in kind to charity during the life of A must be fairly representative of the adjusted basis for such purposes of all trust property available for distribution on the date of distribution.

The following comment pertains to the sample provision described above:

Permitted distributions to charity. The governing instrument may permit or require distributions of trust assets to charity prior to the termination of all noncharitable interests. In such cases, the above provision with respect to adjusted basis is mandatory unless the governing instrument prohibits the trustee from satisfying such distributions in kind.

.06 Under section 1.664-3(a)(5)(i), the payment of the unitrust amount may terminate with the regular payment next preceding the termination of all noncharitable interests. The following is a sample provision for inclusion in the governing instrument of the optional provision described in this subsection:

> The trustee shall pay to A in each taxable year of the trust during his life a unitrust amount equal to Y percent of the net fair market value of the trust assets valued as of the first day of such taxable year. However, the obligation of the trustee to pay such unitrust amount shall terminate with the payment next preceding the death of A. The unitrust amount shall be paid in equal quarterly installments from income and, to the extent that income is not sufficient, from principal. Any income of the trust for a taxable year in excess of the unitrust amount shall be added to principal.

The following comments pertain to the sample provision described above:

(1) *Provisions replaced.* The optional provision set forth above may be used in lieu of the provision set forth in section 6.01.

(2) *Cross references.* See comments (1) through (8) in section 6.01.

.07 Under section 1.664-3(a)(4), the grantor of the trust may retain the power, exercisable only by will, to revoke or terminate the interest of any recipient other than an organization described in section 107(c) of the Code. The following is a sample provision for inclusion in the governing instrument of such a power:

> The trustee shall pay to the settlor during his life a unitrust amount equal to Y percent of the net fair market value of the trust assets valued as of the first day of each taxable year of the trust and upon the death of the settlor, if B survives him, the trustee shall pay to B during her life a unitrust amount equal to Y percent of the net fair market value of the trust assets valued as of the first day of each taxable year. The settlor hereby expressly reserves the power, exercisable only by his will, to revoke and terminate the interest of B under this trust. Upon the first to occur of (i) the death of the survivor of the settlor and B or (ii) the death of the settlor if he effectively exercises his testamentary power to revoke and terminate the interest of B, the trustee shall distribute all of the then principal and income of the trust, other than any amount due A or B, to M charity. The unitrust amount shall be paid in equal quarterly installments from income and, to the extent that income is not sufficient, from principal. Any income of the trust for a taxable year in excess of the unitrust amount shall be added to principal.

The following comments pertain to the sample provision described above:

(1) *Provision replaced.* The optional provision set forth above may be used in lieu of the provisions set forth in sections 6.01 and 6.02.

(2) *Cross references.* See comments (1) through (8) in section 6.01 and comments (1) and (2) in section 6.02.

.08 Under section 1.664-3(a)(3), the provisions of the trust may not include any provisions which restrict the trustee from investing the trust assets in a manner which could result in the annual realization of a reasonable amount of income or gain from the sale or disposition of trust assets. The following is a sample provision for inclusion in the trust instrument which insures that the requirement described in this subsection is met:

> Nothing in this trust instrument shall be construed to restrict the trustee from investing the trust assets in a manner which could result in the annual realization of a reasonable amount of income or gain from the sale or disposition of trust assets.

.09 Under section 1.664-1(a)(4), in order for a trust to be a charitable remainder unitrust, the trust must function exclusively as a charitable remainder unitrust from its creation. Consequently, a revocable inter vivos trust which is used to administer the estate of the decedent cannot qualify as a charitable remainder unitrust. However, the regulations permit the revocable inter vivos trust to distribute assets to another trust which does qualify as a charitable remainder unitrust. The following is a sample provision for inclusion in the governing instument of the revocable inter vivos trust which provides that the revocable inter vivos trust will be used to partially administer the estate of the decedent and then distribute assets to another trust which is a charitable remainder unitrust:

> The trustee shall pay to *A* all of the income from the trust assets for *A*'s life, during which the trust shall be fully revocable by *A*. Upon *A*'s death the trust shall become irrevocable and the trustee shall pay all debts, taxes and other expenses of the administration of *A*'s estate. After the payment or satisfaction of all such debts, taxes and expenses, the trustee shall transfer all of the then principal and income of the trust to the trustee of the charitable remainder unitrust hereinafter established to be held, administered and distributed in the manner and according to the terms and conditions hereinafter provided.

The following comments pertain to the sample provision described above:

(1) *Trust provisions during life.* There are no restrictions on the dispositive provisions of the above trust during the period it is fully revocable.

(2) *Provisions for both trusts in same instrument.* The same governing instrument may provide for both the revocable inter vivos trust and the charitable remainder unitrust, and both trusts may have the same trustee.

Sec. 8. Requests for Rulings

Requests for rulings on the governing instruments of charitable remainder trusts should be submitted in compliance with the general procedures contained in Revenue Procedure 72-3, C.B. 1972-1, 698, pertaining to the issuance of rulings, and should be addressed to the Assistant Commissioner (Technical), Attention: T:PS:T (T:I:I), Internal Revenue Service, 1111 Constitution Avenue, N.W., Washington, D.C., 20224.

FORM C-10

Rev. Rul. 72-196, 1972-1 C. B. 194

Form C-10 is a Revenue Ruling which sets forth sample provisions for the governing instruments of pooled income funds. Pooled income funds are discussed in Chapter 2, ¶203.10.

Rev. Rul. 72-196

Section 1.

The purpose of this Revenue Ruling is to set forth illustrative sample provisions for inclusion in a Declaration of Trust and an Instrument of Transfer that may be used to satisfy the requirements of section 642(c)(5) of the Internal Revenue Code of 1954 with respect to a pooled income fund. These sample provisions, which are set forth in sections 3 through 10, assume the establishment of the Y Pooled Income Fund by the Declaration of Trust and a transfer of property to such fund pursuant to an Instrument of Transfer in which an income interest is retained for the lives of the donor and his spouse and an irrevocable remainder interest in such property is contributed to the Y Public Charity. The donor has retained the power to terminate by will the income interest for the life of his spouse.

Sec. 2.

.01 Section 1.642(c)-5(b) of the Income Tax Regulations sets forth specific requirements for qualification of a pooled income fund.

02. By virtue of section 4947(a)(2) of the Code, a pooled income fund is subject to the governing instrument requirements of section 508(e) of the Code. For sample provisions of governing instruments meeting the requirements of section 508(e), see Rev. Rul. 70-270, C.B. 1970-1, 135, but note exception contained in section 4947(b)(3)(B) of the Code with respect to a pooled income fund. See also Rev. Rul. 72-103, page 152, for a list of states that have enacted legislation pursuant to which the governing instruments of private foundations under the jurisdiction of such states are considered to have been amended as required by section 508(e) of the Code.

.03 Section 1.642(c)-5(a)(5)(iii) of the regulations provides that the term "governing instrument" means either the governing plan (referred to in this Revenue Ruling as the Declaration of Trust) under which the pooled income fund is established and administered or the Instrument of Transfer, as the context requires.

Sec. 3.

.01 Section 1.642(c)-5(b)(1) of the regulations requires that each donor must transfer property to a pooled income fund and contribute an irrevocable remainder interest in such property to or for the use of a public charity. Under this provision, a contingent remainder interest is not treated as an irrevocable remainder interest.

.02 The following is a sample provision for inclusion in a Declaration of Trust which satisfies the requirement described in sec. 3.01:

> Each donor transferring property to Y Pooled Income Fund shall contribute an irrevocable remainder interest in such property to or for the use of Y Public Charity.

.03 The following is a sample provision for inclusion in an Instrument of Transfer which satisfies the requirement described in sec. 3.01:

> Upon the death of either the Donor or the Donor's wife, whichever is later, or upon the death of the Donor if the Donor exercises his power to terminate the life income interest upon his death, the trustee of Y Pooled Income Fund shall sever from the Fund an amount equal to the value of the remainder interest in the property upon which the income interest is based and transfer it to Y Public Charity.

Sec. 4.

.01 Section 1.642(c)-5(b)(2) of the regulations requires that each donor must retain for himself for life an income interest in the property transferred to the pooled income fund, or create an income interest in such property for the life of one or more beneficiaries, each of whom must be living at the time of the transfer of the property to the fund. The donor may retain the power exercisable only by will to revoke or terminate the income interest of any designated beneficiary other than the public charity. The governing instrument must specify at the time of the transfer the particular beneficiary or beneficiaries to whom the income is payable and the share of income distributable to each person so specified. No charitable contributions deduction is allowed to the donor for the value of an income interest of which the public charity is a beneficiary or for the amount of any income paid by the fund to such organization.

.02 The following is a sample provision for inclusion in a Declaration of Trust which satisfies the requirement described in sec. 4.01:

Each donor transferring property to Y Pooled Income Fund shall retain for himself for life an income interest in the property transferred, or create an income interest in such property for the life of one or more named beneficiaries, each of whom must be living at the time of the transfer of the property to the Fund by the donor. Such income interest shall be represented by units of participation in the Fund. In the event more than one beneficiary of the income interest is named, such beneficiaries may enjoy their shares of income concurrently, consecutively, or both concurrently and consecutively. Y Public Charity may also be designated as one of the beneficiaries of the income interest. The donor need not retain or create a life interest in all the income from the property transferred to the Fund provided any income not payable to an income beneficiary under the terms of the Instrument of Transfer is contributed to, and within the taxable year of the Fund in which it is received is paid to, Y Public Charity.

.03 The following is a sample provision for inclusion in an Instrument of Transfer which satisfies the requirement described in sec. 4.01:

The Donor hereby retains for himself for and during his life an income interest in the property transferred to Y Pooled Income Fund. In the event that Donor's wife (insert name) survives the Donor, there is hereby retained and created an income interest in such property to commence on the Donor's death for the Donor's wife for and during her life. However, the Donor hereby reserves the right to appoint and direct by will that the income interest retained or created in such property shall terminate upon his death, whether or not the Donor's wife survives the Donor. Such income interest shall consist of—units of participation in Y Pooled Income Fund, and payments of income thereon shall be made in accordance with the Declaration of Trust attached hereto.

Sec. 5.

.01 Section 1.642(c)-5(b)(3) of the regulations requires that the property transferred to a pooled income fund by a donor must be commingled with, and invested or reinvested with, other property transferred to the fund by other donors satisfying the requirements described in secs. 3.01 and 4.01. The governing instrument must contain a provision requiring compliance with this requirement on commingling and investing of property. A pooled income fund shall not be disqualified because any portion of its properties is invested or reinvested jointly with other properties, not a part of the pooled income fund, which are held by, or for the use of, the public charity which maintains the fund.

.02 The following is a sample provision for inclusion in a Declaration of Trust which satisfies the requirement described in sec. 5.01:

The property transferred to Y Pooled Income Fund by each donor must be commingled with, and invested or reinvested with, other property transferred to the Fund by other donors satisfying the requirements of this instrument and of section 642(c)(5)(A) of the Internal Revenue Code of 1954 or corresponding provision of any subsequent Federal tax law. The

Fund shall not include property transferred under arrangements other than those specified in this instrument and section 642(c)(5) of the Internal Revenue Code of 1954 or corresponding provision of any subsequent Federal tax law. All or any portion of the Fund may, however, be invested or reinvested jointly with other properties, not a part of the Fund, which are held by, or for the use of, Y Public Charity. When such joint investment or reinvestment occurs, detailed accounting records shall be maintained by the trustee of the Fund specifically identifying the portion of the total fund which is owned by Y Pooled Income Fund and the income earned by, and attributable to, such portion.

Sec. 6.

.01 Section 1.642(c)-5(b)(4) of the regulations prohibits a pooled income fund from accepting from a donor, or investing in, any securities the income from which is exempt from Federal income tax. The governing instrument of the pooled income fund must contain specific prohibitions against accepting or investing in such securities.

.02 The following is a sample provision for inclusion in a Declaration of Trust which satisfies the requirement described in sec. 6.01:

> The property transferred to Y Pooled Income Fund by any donor shall not include any securities the income from which is exempt from the taxes imposed by Subtitle A of the Internal Revenue Code of 1954 or corresponding provision of any subsequent Federal tax law, and the trustee of the Fund shall not accept or invest in any such security as part of the Fund.

Sec. 7.

.01 Section 1.642(c)-5(b)(5) of the regulations requires that the pooled income fund must be maintained by the same public charity to or for the use of which the irrevocable remainder interest is contributed. The requirement of maintenance will be satisfied where the public charity exercises control directly or indirectly over the pooled income fund.

.02 The following is a sample provision for inclusion in a Declaration of Trust which satisfies the requirement described in sec. 7.01:

> Y Public Charity shall always maintain Y Pooled Income Fund or exercise control, directly or indirectly, over the Fund. Y Public Charity may resign as Trustee of the Fund and designate a new Trustee or Trustees of the Fund. Y Public Charity retains the power to remove such Trustee or Trustees and to designate a new Trustee or Trustees.

Sec. 8.

.01 Section 1.642(c)-5(b)(6) of the regulations prohibits a pooled income fund from having as a trustee a donor to the fund or a beneficiary (other than the public charity to or for the use of which the remainder interest is transferred) of an income interest in any property transferred to the fund. It is also required that the governing instrument contain such a prohibition. The fact that the donor of property to the fund, or a beneficiary of the fund, is a trustee, officer, director, or other official of the public charity to or for the use of which the remainder interest is contributed ordinarily will not prevent the fund from complying with this prohibition.

.02 The following is a sample provision for inclusion in a Declaration of Trust which satisfies the requirement described in sec. 8.01:

> Y Pooled Income Fund shall not have as a Trustee a donor to the Fund or a beneficiary (other than Y Public Charity) of an income interest in any property transferred to the Fund. No donor or beneficiary (other than Y Public Charity) shall have, directly or indirectly, general responsibilities with respect to the Fund which are ordinarily exercised by a Trustee.

Sec. 9.

.01 Section 1.642(c)-5(b)(7) of the regulations contains the following requirements with respect to the income of a beneficiary of a pooled income fund:

(1) Each beneficiary entitled to income of any taxable year of the fund must receive such income in an amount determined by the rate of return earned by the fund for such year with respect to his income interest.

(2) On each transfer of property to the fund by a donor one or more units of participation in the fund must be assigned to the beneficiary or beneficiaries of the income interest in such property, determined by dividing the fair market value of the property by the fair market value of a unit of participation at the time of the transfer.

(3) The fair market value of a unit of participation is to be determined by dividing the fair market value of all property in the fund by the number of units of participation in the fund at the time of the transfer.

(4) If a transfer of property to a fund occurs on other than a determination date, the number of units of participation assigned to the income interest in such property may be determined by using the fair market value of the property in the fund on the determination date immediately preceding the date of transfer, with appropriate adjustments on the next succeeding determination date.

(5) A determination date is each day of the taxable year of the fund on which there is a valuation of property in the fund, being the first day of such year and at least 3 other days, with no more than 3 calendar months between two consecutive determination dates.

(6) The share of income allocated to each unit of participation is to be determined by dividing the income of the fund for the taxable year by the outstanding number of units in the fund at the end of such year, with appropriate adjustment for units outstanding during only a part of such year.

(7) The governing instrument of the fund shall direct the trustee to distribute income currently or within the first 65 days following the close of the taxable year in which the income is earned.

(8) The governing instrument shall provide that the income interest of any designated beneficiary shall either terminate with the last regular payment which was made before the death of the beneficiary or be prorated to the date of his death.

(9) The term "income" has the same meaning as it does under section 643(b) of the Code and the regulations thereunder.

.02 The following are sample provisions for inclusion in a Declaration of Trust which satisfy the requirements described in sec. 9.01:

> The taxable year of Y Pooled Income Fund shall be the calendar year. To each beneficiary entitled to income of any taxable year of the Fund, the trustee of the Fund shall pay such income in the amount determined by the rate of return earned by the Fund for such year with respect to the beneficiary's income interest, payment to be made at least once in the taxable year in which the income is earned. Until the trustee determines that payments shall be made more or less frequently or at other times he shall make income payments to the beneficiary or beneficiaries entitled thereto in four quarterly payments on or about March 31, June 30, September 30, and December 31, of each year. An adjusting payment, if necessary, will be made during the taxable year or within the first 65 days following its close to bring the total payment to the actual income to which the beneficiary or beneficiaries are entitled for that year.
>
> On each transfer of property by a donor to the Fund, there shall be assigned to the beneficiary or beneficiaries of the income interest retained or created in such property the number of units of participation equal to the number obtained by dividing the fair market value of the property transferred by the fair market value of a unit in the Fund immediately before such transfer. The fair market value of a unit in the Fund immediately before the transfer shall be determined by dividing the fair market value of all property in the Fund at such time by the number of units then in the Fund. All units in the Fund shall always have equal value.
>
> If a transfer of property to the Fund by a donor occurs on other than a determination date, the number of units of participation assigned to the income interest in such property shall be determined by using the average fair market value of the property in the Fund immediately before the transfer, which shall be deemed to be the average of the fair market values of the property in the Fund on the determination dates immediately preceding and succeeding the date of transfer. For the purpose of determining such average fair market value, the property transferred by the donor and any other property transferred to the Fund between such preceding and succeeding dates, or on such succeeding date, shall be excluded. The

fair market value of a unit in the Fund immediately before the transfer shall be determined by dividing the average fair market value of the property in the Fund at such time by the number of units then in the Fund.

A determination date means each day within the taxable year of the Fund on which a valuation is made of the property in the Fund. The property of the Fund shall be valued on January 1, April 1, July 1, and October 1 of each year.

The amount of income allocated to each unit of participation in the Fund shall be determined by dividing the income of the Fund for the taxable year by the outstanding number of units in the Fund at the end of such year, except that income shall be allocated to units outstanding during only part of such year by taking into consideration the period of time such units are outstanding during such year.

For purposes of this trust, the term "income" has the same meaning as it does under section 643(b) of the Internal Revenue Code of 1954, or corresponding provision of any subsequent Federal tax law, and the regulations thereunder.

The income interest of any beneficiary of the Fund shall terminate with the last regular payment of income which was made before the death of the beneficiary. The trustee of the Fund shall not be required to prorate any income payment to the date of the beneficiary's death.

Sec. 10.

.01 Section 1.642(c)-5(b)(8) of the regulations provides that, upon the termination of the income interest retained or created by any donor, the trustee of the pooled income fund shall sever from the fund an amount equal to the value at such time of the remainder interest in the property upon which the income interest is based. The value of the remainder interest shall be either (1) its value as of the determination date next succeeding the termination of the income interest or (2) its value as of the date on which the last regular payment was made before the death of the beneficiary if the income interest is terminated on such payment date.

.02 The following is a sample provision for inclusion in a Declaration of Trust which satisfies the requirement described in sec. 10.01:

Upon the termination of the income interest of any designated beneficiary or beneficiaries, the trustee of Y Pooled Income Fund shall sever from the Fund an amount equal to the value of the remainder interest in the property upon which the income interest is based. The value of the remainder interest for such purpose shall be its value as of the date on which the last regular payment was made before the death of the beneficiary. The amount so severed from the fund shall be paid to Y Public Charity.

Sec. 11.

.01 The sample provisions in sections 3 through 10 are set forth merely as a guide in developing governing instruments for specific pooled income funds and in no way preclude the use of other provisions conforming to the requirements of section 642(c)(5) of the Code and the regulations thereunder.

.02 Provisions corresponding to these sample provisions will be accepted by the Internal Revenue Service in the absence of any showing that they are not enforceable under applicable local law.

Sec. 12.

Requests for rulings on declarations of trust and instruments of transfer should be submitted in compliance with the general procedures contained in Revenue Procedure 72-3, page 698, pertaining to the issuance of rulings, and should be addressed to the Assistant Commissioner (Technical), Attention: T:PS:T (T:I:I), Internal Revenue Service, 1111 Constitution Avenue, N.W., Washington, D.C., 20224.

FORM C-11

Irrevocable Life Insurance Trust

This form is designed to provide a sample of the irrevocable life insurance trust which is the subject of Chapter 7. It includes, in paragraph C of Clause Seventh, generation-skipping trusts as discussed in Chapter 3.

THE THOMAS JONES IRREVOCABLE TRUST

Table of Contents

THE THOMAS JONES IRREVOCABLE TRUST

This Indenture of Trust, entitled "The Thomas Jones Irrevocable Trust," is made this 1st day of June, 1976, by and between Thomas Jones as Grantor, and Sally Jones, Walter Grant and the Solid Bank as Trustees.

TRUST ASSETS

FIRST: INITIAL GIFT. The Grantor hereby transfers to the Trustees the policy of insurance on the Grantor's life which is identified on Schedule A, which is attached to this Indenture and shall be deemed part of it.

SECOND: ADDITIONAL ASSETS. The Trustees shall also accept such insurance policies and other property as the Grantor or any other person may, by Will or other instrument making appropriate reference to this Indenture, transfer or make payable to the Trustees from time to time hereafter.

TRUSTEES

THIRD: TRUSTEES AND GUARDIANS. Sally Jones, Walter Grant, and Solid Bank are the original Trustees. If Walter Grant should for any reason cease to serve, he shall be succeeded by Phoebe Grant.

The grantor hereby appoints SALLY JONES as Guardian of any property which passes to a minor hereunder. If SALLY JONES should fail or cease so to serve, she shall be succeeded by WALTER GRANT. If he also should fail or cease so to serve, MARY SMITH is appointed as such Guardian. The Guardian of each survivor's estate is authorized to make demands of behalf of the minor under the provisions of subparagraph A(5) of Clause SEVENTH if the minor is unable to do so by reason of any legal or other disability, and to apply principal as well as income for the minor's maintenance, education, and welfare, as the Guardian, in his or her sole discretion, may from time to time deem advisable.

FOURTH: COMPENSATION. The original corporate Trustee and each corporate successor shall be compensated from time to time for its services under this Indenture in accordance with its schedule of fees in effect during the period over which such services are rendered.

Each individual Trustee shall be entitled to receive compensation from time to time during the period of his or her services as a Trustee equal to one-half of the compensation payable during that period to the corporate Trustee, such compensation to be in addition to that of the corporate Trustee.

FIFTH: CHANGE OF CORPORATE TRUSTEE. The individual Trustee other than the Grantor's wife is authorized at any time, and from time to time, by instrument in writing delivered to the other Trustees or Trustee then serving, to remove the corporate Trustee without stating any reason for such action, provided he or she simultaneously by written instrument appoints another corporate Trustee in its place.

SIXTH: WAIVER OF BOND. No Trustee serving at any time under this Indenture shall be required to file bond or give security in any jurisdiction, any rule or law to the contrary notwithstanding.

DISPOSITION OF TRUST ASSETS

SEVENTH: INCOME AND PRINCIPAL DISTRIBUTIONS. The Trustees shall hold in trust the assets comprising the initial gift described in Clause FIRST and any additional assets received in accordance with Clause SECOND, and shall dispose of the net income and principal as follows:

A. During the Grantor's lifetime:

(1) The Trustees shall distribute the net income to the Grantor's wife, Sally Jones, from the date of this Indenture, in annual or more frequent periodic installments.

(2) The Trustees shall also distribute to the Grantor's wife such portions of the principal as she may from time to time request in writing, provided that the aggregate of such distributions in any calendar year shall not exceed (a) the sum of Five Thousand Dollars or five percent of the value of the trust principal, whichever is greater, (b) minus the amount, if any, which she is entitled to withdraw during the year under the provisions of subparagraph A(5); and provided, further, that the right of the Grantor's wife to require such distributions of principal shall lapse to the extent it is not exercised in any such year. The "value of the trust principal" for the purpose of this subparagraph shall mean the value of the trust principal determined as of the last day of the year.

(3) During her lifetime, the Grantor's wife shall have the power at

any time, and from time to time, to make gifts of the trust principal, without limitation, to or for the benefit of the Grantor, the Grantor's children, and the issue of the Grantor's children, or any of them, in such amounts or proportions, on such terms and conditions, and subject to such trusts or limitations, as the Grantor's wife may in writing set forth.

(4) Following the death of the Grantor's wife, if the Grantor survives her, the Trustees shall distribute the net income, in annual or more frequent periodic instalments, in equal shares to the Grantor's children living at the time of each such distribution, and the Trustees may distribute or apply so much of the principal of the trust as the Trustees, in their sole discretion, may from time to time deem necessary to provide for the maintenance, for the education at any level, and for any emergency needs, of the Grantor's children, or any of them.

(5) From the property comprising the Grantor's initial transfer described in Clause FIRST, and from the property which is the subject of each subsequent transfer from the Grantor to the Trustees, each person who is at the time of the transfer entitled to receive all or any portion of the current net income of the trust, pursuant to subparagraph A(1) or A(4), as the case may be, shall be entitled to receive from the transferred property (a) the sum of Three Thousand Dollars or (b) his proportionate share (equivalent to his current share of the trust income) of the cash or other property transferred if the amount or fair market value of the transferred property is less than Three Thousand Dollars. Upon the receipt of each transfer which is subject to the provisions of this subparagraph, the Trustee who receives the transferred property shall promptly give notice thereof to the current income beneficiary or beneficiaries, and also to the Guardian of his estate in the case of each minor, and each beneficiary shall have thirty days following receipt of such notice within which to demand the distribution herein provided. In the case of a beneficiary who is a minor at the time of the transfer, and who is unable to make such demand by reason of any legal or other disability, the demand may be made on behalf of the minor by the Guardian of such beneficiary's estate. Each distribution required to be made hereunder shall be made immediately on receipt by the Trustees of the beneficiary's or Guardian's written demand (which may be presented to the Trustee from whom the beneficiary receives notice of the transfer involved) and in any event not later than December 31 of the year in which the transfer involved was made.

B. Following the death of the Grantor, if his wife survives him:

(1) During the lifetime of the Grantor's wife, the Trustees shall accumulate the net income or distribute or apply all or any part of the current or accumulated net income to or for the benefit of the Grantor's wife, the Grantor's children, and the issue of the Grantor's children, or any of them, at such times, in such amounts or proportions, and in such manner, as the Trustees other than the Grantor's wife, in their sole

discretion, may from time to time deem advisable. In the exercise of this discretion, however, the welfare of the Grantor's wife shall be given primary consideration.

(2) The Trustees shall also distribute to the Grantor's wife, or apply for her benefit, such portions of the principal as the Trustees other than the Grantor's wife, in their sole discretion, may from time to time deem necessary for payment of the expenses of any accident, illness or emergency needs of the Grantor's wife.

(3) The Trustees shall also distribute to the Grantor's wife, or apply for her benefit, such portions of the principal as the Trustees other than the Grantor's wife, in their sole discretion, may from time to time deem necessary in order to provide for the maintenance of the Grantor's wife in accordance with the standard of living to which she shall be accustomed at the time of the Grantor's death.

(4) The Trustees may distribute to the Grantor's wife, or to any other person or persons whom the Trustees may select for this purpose, such portions of the principal as the Trustees other than the Grantor's wife, in their sole discretion, may from time to time deem advisable for the maintenance, for the education at any level, and for the expenses of any accident, illness or emergency needs, of the Grantor's children, or any of them. However, in determining whether or not to make such distributions for the benefit of the Grantor's children, and in determining the amount of any such distribution, primary consideration shall be given to the welfare of the Grantor's wife.

C. Upon the death of the Grantor's wife, if she survives the Grantor, the principal and any undistributed income then remaining shall be distributed to or for the benefit of the Grantor's children, and the issue of the Grantor's children, or any of them, in such amounts or proportions, on such terms and conditions, and subject to such trusts or limitations, as the Grantor's wife may appoint in her Will, making specific reference therein to this power of appointment. To the extent the Grantor's wife fails to exercise effectively the foregoing power of appointment, or on the death of the Grantor if his wife does not survive him, the principal and any undistributed income then remaining shall be divided into as many equal shares as there are children of the Grantor then living and children of the Grantor then deceased who have left issue then living; the share of each such deceased child shall be distributed to his or her issue then living, per stirpes; and the share of each child then living shall be held in a separate trust for such child, the net income and principal of each such trust to be disposed of as follows:

(1) The Trustees shall distribute the net income to the child, in annual or more frequent periodic installments.

(2) The Trustees shall also distribute to the child, or apply for his or

her benefit, such portions of the principal as the Trustees, in their sole discretion, may from time to time deem advisable for the child's maintenance, for the child's education at any level, to enable or assist the child to purchase a home, to enable or assist the child to enter into a business or professional enterprise which the Trustees may approve, for a gift on the occasion of the child's marriage, or for the expenses of any accident, illness or emergency needs of the child or the child's spouse or issue.

(3) Upon the death of the child, the principal and any undistributed income then remaining shall be distributed to the child's issue then living, per stirpes, or, if there are no such issue, to the Grantor's issue then living, per stirpes; provided, however, that the share of each child of the Grantor who is then the beneficiary of a separate trust hereunder shall be added to the principal of that trust, to be held, administered and disposed of in accordance with all the provisions relating thereto.

D. If at the time fixed for the termination of any trust hereunder there is no beneficiary living to whom, or to whose trust, the principal then remaining is distributable under the foregoing provisions, such principal and any undistributed income then remaining shall be distributed to the Grantor's sister, Mary Jones, or, if she is not then living, to her issue then living, per stirpes.

EIGHTH: DISCRETIONARY DETERMINATIONS. In making any discretionary determinations under the provisions of Clause SEVENTH of this Indenture, with respect to the accumulation or distribution of income, or with respect to the distribution of principal, except as otherwise specifically provided, the Trustees shall take into consideration the income of the beneficiary from all other sources, and may, but shall not be required to, take into consideration the other assets and resources of the beneficiary. Moreover, whether or not such a restriction is imposed or omitted in any other provision, no Trustee who is currently entitled or eligible to receive distributions of income or principal of any trust hereunder shall participate in any discretionary determinations with respect to the accumulation or distribution of income, or with respect to the distribution of principal, of that trust or of any other trust hereunder, nor shall such Trustee participate in the exercise of any administrative power which directly or indirectly effects an accumulation of income or involves the allocation of receipts or disbursements as between income and principal of any trust hereunder.

NINTH: PREMATURE TERMINATION OF TRUSTS. If at any time after the death of the Grantor or during the administration of any trust hereunder, the principal assets of such trust shall have a fair market value less than Twenty-five Thousand Dollars, the Trustees are authorized, but shall not be required, to eliminate or terminate such trust, in which event the assets which are in or would have been allocated to such trust shall be distributed instead to the beneficiary who would otherwise be currently entitled or eligible to receive the income of the trust, or, if there are two or more such beneficiaries, the trust assets shall be distributed to one or more of them in such proportions as the Trustees, in their sole discretion, may deem advisable. Twenty-one years after the death of the last survivor of the Grantor's wife and those of his issue who are living on the date of this Indenture, each trust hereunder which is then in existence shall terminate and the principal thereof shall vest in and be distributed to the beneficiary who is then entitled or eligible to receive the income of the trust.

PROVISIONS RESPECTING LIFE INSURANCE

TENTH: TRUSTEES' RIGHTS IN POLICIES. For purposes of the trusts provided in this Indenture, all right, title and interest in and to each policy of life insurance which may be transferred to the Trustees or purchased by them are hereby vested in the Trustees, and they are authorized and empowered as Trustees to exercise and obtain any or all options, benefits, rights, privileges and interests under the policies. Any receipts, releases or other instruments executed by the Trustees in connection with the policies shall be binding and conclusive as to the insurance companies involved and all beneficiaries under this Indenture.

ELEVENTH: PAYMENT OF PREMIUMS. The Trustees shall have no obligation to pay premiums, dues, assessments or other charges which may be or become due or payable with respect to any of the policies, nor to see that such payments are made by the Grantor or any other person, nor to notify the Grantor or any other person that such payments are or will become due, and the Trustees shall have no liability to any person or persons if such premiums, dues, assessments or other charges are not paid, nor for any result of such non-payment, nor shall the Trustees have any responsibility with respect to any indebtedness of the Grantor to any of the insurance companies involved or to any lending institution with which the Grantor may have deposited any of the policies as collateral.

TWELFTH: COLLECTION OF INSURANCE PROCEEDS. Upon the maturity of any policy by reason of the death of the Grantor or otherwise, the Trustees shall receive such sum or sums as may be paid to them as beneficiaries, and they are hereby authorized to execute all necessary receipts and releases to the insurance company concerned. The Trustees shall have the duty, upon being advised of the Grantor's death, to endeavor to collect such sums as may appear to be due upon any policies of insurance on the Grantor's life then owned by the Trustees or payable to them as beneficiaries. The receipts of the Trustees shall fully discharge the insurance companies issuing the policies, and upon payment of the insurance proceeds to the Trustees the insurance companies shall be free of all liability as to the proper application of the trust funds. The Trustees shall not be required to institute suit or maintain any litigation to collect the proceeds of any policy of insurance owned by them or payable to them unless they are in possession of funds sufficient for that purpose or unless they have been indemnified to their sole satisfaction for their counsel fees, costs, disbursements and all other expenses and liabilities to which they may in their sole judgment be subjected by such action on their part. The Trustees may, however, utilize any cash in their hands to meet expenses incurred in connection with enforcing payment of any such obligation to them.

MISCELLANEOUS PROVISIONS

THIRTEENTH: PROTECTIVE PROVISION. As long as the income or principal to which any beneficiary may be entitled is in the possession of the Trustees and not actually distributed by them, such beneficiary shall not have the right to anticipate or alienate such income or principal by assignment or by any other means (except as specifically provided herein), and it shall be free and clear of the beneficiary's debts and obligations and the Grantor's debts and obligations and shall not be taken, seized or attached by any persons whatsoever.

FOURTEENTH: PROVISION FOR DISABILITY. If at the time fixed in this Indenture, or selected by the Trustees under the provisions hereof, for any distribution of income or principal, any beneficiary entitled thereto shall be less than twenty-one years of age, or shall have been adjudicated an incompetent, or shall be, in the sole judgment of the Trustees, otherwise unable to apply such income or principal to his or her own best interest and advantage, the title to the property to be distributed shall vest in such beneficiary, but during the existence of such condition or disability the income or principal to which the beneficiary is entitled may be retained by the Trustees, who in that event shall hold, invest or reinvest it and use as much of such income or principal as the Trustees, in their sole discretion, may deem appropriate for the beneficiary's maintenance in health and comfort, or for his or her education, or for any emergency needs of the beneficiary, either by the payment of bills directly or by payments to such person or persons as the Trustees may select, without the intervention of a guardian, committee or other fiduciary. The receipts of such payees shall completely discharge the Trustees with respect to such payments. Upon the termination of the condition or disability, the unexpected income and principal shall be distributed to the beneficiary. If a beneficiary dies during the existence of the condition or disability, any unexpended income and principal held for such beneficiary hereunder shall be distributed to the personal representative of his or her estate. Notwithstanding the foregoing provisions, no Trustee who is also a beneficiary with respect to whose interests the provision of this Clause could, if appropriate, be currently invoked, shall participate in the exercise of any discretionary determinations under the provisions of this Clause.

As an alternative, the Trustees may also, in their sole discretion, distribute the share of any minor beneficiary to the minor's parents or surviving parent as guardian of the estate of such minor.

FIFTEENTH: MANAGEMENT POWERS. In addition to the powers conferred upon them by law or other provisions of this Indenture, the Trustees (and their successors) shall have, for the management of each trust hereunder, the following powers, which they may exercise as often as they deem advisable, without application to or approval by any court, and without liability for loss or depreciation in value resulting therefrom:

A. *Retention.* To retain all or any part of the property comprising any trust hereunder as long as they may deem advisable.

B. *Sale or Exchange.* To sell at public or private sale, grant options on, exchange or otherwise dispose of any property held hereunder, at such times and on such terms, conditions, prices and considerations, including credit, with or without security, as they may deem advisable, to give good and sufficient instruments of transfer thereof, and to receive the proceeds of any such disposition.

C. *Investment.* To invest and reinvest trust funds (including any income accumulations) in such preferred stocks, common stocks, bonds, obligations, shares or interests in any common trust fund or funds administered by the corporate Trustee, investment companies, investment trusts, or other real or personal property, as they may select, without the requirement of diversification, and without regard to restrictions upon trust investments imposed by any present or future statutes, rules of court or court decisions of any jurisdiction. The foregoing investment powers include the authority to exercise any stock options acquired as a result of the Grantor's lifetime employment or otherwise.

D. *Life Insurance.* To retain any life insurance policies transferred to the Trustees or acquired pursuant to the succeeding paragraph E, or, in their discretion, to convert such policies into cash and to reinvest such cash in other types of investments under the authority hereinbefore set forth; provided, however, that on demand of any current income beneficiary the Trustees shall convert such policies into cash and reinvest the cash as hereinbefore set forth.

E. *Payment of Premiums.* To purchase life insurance and annuity contracts for the benefit of any trust hereunder and to pay out of income or principal the premiums which may become due from time to time upon life insurance and annuity contracts owned by any trust or acquired for the benefit of any trust.

F. *Transactions with Grantor's Estate.* To purchase as an investment for any trust hereunder any assets belonging to the Grantor's estate, provided that the price paid for such assets shall not exceed the fair market value thereof; or to make loans to such estate for adequate security and at a fair rate of interest; and to continue to hold assets so purchased or loans so made as investments hereunder.

G. *Real Property Management.* To take possession of any real property or interest in real property of any trust; manage, operate, maintain, collect the rentals of, and pay the taxes, mortgage interest and other charges against, such property; and to partition, develop, or subdivide such property and make repairs, replacements and improvements, structural or otherwise, thereto.

H. *Leases.* To lease any real or personal property of any trust, with or without options to purchase, on such terms and conditions and for such periods as they may deem advisable, even though the period or periods of the lease or leases may extend beyond the term of any trust, and without regard to any statutory limitations on the duration of such leases; to reserve in such leases fixed rentals, rentals based upon the amount of business or profits of the lessees, or rentals based upon any other conditions; and to renew, cancel, amend or extend, and consent to the assignment or modification of any lease, on such terms as they may deem advisable.

I. *Borrowing.* To borrow money from themselves or others for payment of trust administration expenses or for the protection or improvement of any property held hereunder, to execute promissory notes or other obligations for amounts so borrowed, and to secure the repayment thereof by mortgage or pledge of any property held hereunder.

J. *Renewals and Extensions.* To renew or extend the time for payment of any obligation, secured or unsecured, for such period or periods, and on such terms, as they may deem advisable.

K. *Rights and Voting.* To exercise, sell or abandon all conversion, subscription or other rights, options, powers and privileges pertaining to, or to vote in person or by proxy upon, any stocks, bonds or other securities, all as might be done by an individual holding a similar interest in his own right.

L. *Corporate Changes.* To oppose or to assent to and to participate in any reorganization, recapitalization, readjustment, merger, voting trust, consolidation or exchange affecting any corporation or association the securities of which are held hereunder, and in connection with any such proceeding to deposit securities with any custodian, agent, protective or similar committee, or trustee, and to pay any fees, expenses or assessments incurred in connection therewith, and exchange property, all as might be done by an individual holding a similar interest in his own right.

M. *Claims and Suits*. To adjust, settle, compromise, arbitrate or abandon, or sue on or defend, any claims by or against any trust.

N. *Agents*. To employ and compensate such attorneys, accountants, brokers, investment counsel and other agents and services as they may deem necessary or advantageous to any trust.

O. *Nominees*. To cause the securities which may from time to time be held hereunder to be registered in the name of a nominee, or to hold such securities unregistered and to retain them in such condition that they will pass by delivery.

P. *Insurance Coverage*. To obtain and keep in force such fire, theft, liability, casualty or other insurance as they may deem advisable for the protection of any trust hereunder.

Q. *Consolidated Trust Funds*. To hold, manage and account for separate trusts established hereunder either as separate funds or in one or more consolidated funds in which each trust shall own as undivided interest, provided that no such holding shall defer the vesting of any interest in possession or otherwise.

R. *Distribution in Kind*. To make distribution of any trust in cash or in kind, or partly in cash and partly in kind, and to allocate specific assets among the beneficiaries (including any trust or trusts) in such proportions as the Trustees may think best, so long as the total market value of any beneficiary's share is not affected by such allocation.

S. *Business Interests*. In dealing with the stock of any closely held corporation or other business interest held hereunder:

(1) To disregard any principle of investment diversification and to retain any part of all of such interest as long as they may deem advisable;

(2) To sell all or any part of such interest at such time or times, for such prices, to such persons (including persons who are Trustees hereunder), and on such terms and conditions, as they may deem advisable;

(3) To do anything that may seem advisable with respect to the operation or liquidation of any such business or any change in the purpose, nature or structure of any such business;

(4) To participate directly in the conduct or management of such business, or render professional services thereto, and receive reasonable compensation therefor, regardless of any rule of law with respect to conflict of interest;

(5) To delegate authority to any director, stockholder, manager, agent, partner, or employee, and to approve payment from the business of adequate compensation to any such person;

(6) To borrow money from the banking department of the corporate Trustee, regardless of any rule of law with respect to conflict of interest; and

(7) To make additional investments in or advances to any such business if such action appears to be in the best interests of any trust or trusts hereunder and the beneficiaries thereof.

SIXTEENTH: DISINTERESTED PARTIES. No person dealing with the Trustees, or their successors or survivors, shall be bound to see to the application of any purchase money or other consideration or to inquire into the validity, necessity or propriety of any transaction to which the Trustees may be parties.

SEVENTEENTH: CUSTODY OF TRUST ASSETS. The assets comprising the intial gift or any subsequent gift to the Trustees may be delivered by the Grantor or any other donor to any Trustee selected by him, and such delivery shall constitute delivery to all the Trustees, none of whom shall have any liability to the Grantor or to any beneficiary or other person as a consequence of not obtaining possession of such assets.

Moreover, notwithstanding any other provision of this Indenture, during the lifetime of the Grantor he or any other person may give cash or other assets to Walter Grant, or to any successor to him, in trust for the purposes of this Indenture, and such individual Trustee is authorized, during the Grantor's lifetime, to hold, administer, apply or distribute such funds or other assets and any income thereof pursuant to the terms of this Indenture (including responsibility for all notices and distributions provided in paragraph A of Clause Seventh), as if he were the sole Trustee hereunder, and for that purpose he may maintain such accounts as he may deem advisable, in banks or otherwise, without the necessity of specific reference to this Indenture or to his co-Trustees, and no other Trustee at any time serving hereunder, and no bank or other organization in which any such account may be established, shall have any liability to the Grantor or to any beneficiary or other person with respect to such funds or other assets.

Upon the death of the Grantor, any such cash or other assets then remaining in the hands of Walter Grant or any successor to him shall remain in trust under this Indenture, and shall thereafter be administered by the Trustees subject to all the then applicable provisions hereof, and none of the other Trustees then or thereafter serving hereunder shall have any responsibility to investigate or to obtain an accounting with respect to any prior receipts, disbursements or distributions, nor shall any such Trustee have any liability to any beneficiary or other person with respect to such funds or other assets.

EIGHTEENTH: INTERPRETATIONS. Wherever appropriate in this Indenture, the singular shall be deemed to include the plural, and vice versa; and the masculine shall be deemed to include the feminine, and vice versa; and each of them to include the neuter, and vice versa.

For all purposes hereunder, the word "property" shall be deemed to include real and personal property and any interests of any kind in any real or personal property.

For all purposes hereunder, the term "Trustees" shall mean the Trustees who at the time are entitled and qualified to act as such, whether originally appointed, remaining, substituted or succeeding.

All provisions of this Indenture for the benefit of the Grantor's children shall be equally applicable to any children who may be born to the Grantor or adopted by him after the date of this Indenture, so that any later born or adopted child shall be provided for in the same manner as the Grantor's children living on the date of this Indenture.

Without intending to affect the interpretation of any provision of this Indenture, Grantor wishes to record that he has, at this time, three children, namely, John Jones, Janet Jones, and Sidney Jones.

All references in this Indenture to the Grantor's wife shall be deemed to refer to Sally Jones to whom the Grantor is married on the date of this Indenture.

All references in this Indenture to "the policies" shall be deemed to refer to any policies hereafter transferred to Trustees or purchased by them, as well as the policy identified on Schedule A.

NINETEENTH: ACCOUNTING BY TRUSTEES. The Trustees shall be entitled at any time to seek a judicial settlement of their accounts in any court of competent jurisdiction selected by the Trustees. As an alternative, the Trustees may at any time settle their account of any trust hereunder by agreement with the income beneficiaries who are not under any legal disability and those persons not under any legal disability who would be entitled to receive a share of the principal if the trust were to terminate at the time of such agreement (disregarding for this purpose potential beneficiaries under any powers of appointment herein granted), and such agreement shall bind all persons, whether or not then in being or sui juris, then or thereafter entitled to any portion of the trust, and shall effectively release and discharge the Trustees for the acts and proceedings so accounted for.

TWENTIETH: SITUS OF TRUSTS. This Indenture has been executed and accepted in the Commonwealth of Pennsylvania, which is hereby designated as the situs of the trusts herein provided, and all questions pertaining to the validity and construction of this Indenture or the administration of the trusts hereunder shall be determined in accordance with the laws of Pennsylvania, regardless of the jurisdiction in which the trusts may at any time actually be administered.

TWENTY-FIRST: HEADINGS. The headings or titles preceding the sections, clauses and certain paragraphs of this Indenture are provided only for convenience of reference and shall not be used to explain or restrict the meaning, purpose or effect of any of the provisions to which they refer.

TWENTY-SECOND: TRUST IRREVOCABLE. This trust shall be irrevocable and not subject to any amendment or alteration.

TWENTY-THIRD: ACCEPTANCE OF TRUSTS. The Trustees accept the trusts hereby created and agree to carry out the provisions of this Indenture.

IN WITNESS WHEREOF, Thomas Jones, the Grantor, and Sally Jones, Walter Grant, and the Solid Bank, the Trustees, have hereunto set their hands and seals the day and year first above written.

SIGNED, SEALED and
    DELIVERED
    in the presence of:

_____   _____(SEAL)
                                   Thomas Jones, Grantor

_____   _____(SEAL)
                                   Sally Jones, Trustee

                                  _____(SEAL)
                                   Walter Grant, Trustee

                                   Solid Bank

                                   By: _____
                                   Attest: _____
                                                      Trustee

COMMONWEALTH OF PENNSYLVANIA   :
                                : SS.
COUNTY OF PHILADELPHIA   :

    BEFORE ME, this 1st day of June, 1976, the subscriber, a Notary Public in and for the Commonwealth of Pennsylvania, personally appeared the within named Thomas Jones, the Grantor in the foregoing Indenture of Trust, and acknowledged the same to be his act and deed and desired that it might be recorded as such.
    WITNESS my hand and seal the day and year aforesaid.

                         _____

                              Notary Public

SCHEDULE A

INSURER	POLICY NUMBER
General Mutual Life Insurance Company	356743

FORM C-12

Private Annuity Agreement

Form C-12 is a simple single life private annuity agreement, exemplifying the tax saving technique which is the subject of Chapter 6.

PRIVATE ANNUITY AGREEMENT

This Agreement is made this 15th day of February, 1976, by and between HILDA KRAUSS, who resides at   , Philadelphia, Pennsylvania (hereinafter called the "Transferor"), and ARTHUR KRAUSS, who resides at   , Philadelphia, Pennsylvania (hereinafter called the "Transferee").

PREAMBLE

The Transferor is the owner of the assets listed on Schedule "A," which is attached hereto and made part hereof.

The transferor desires to be assured of a fixed annual income for the remainder of her life, without being limited to her dividend and interest receipts.

The Transferee desires to acquire the assets listed on Schedule "A" and is willing to make fixed annual payments to the Transferor in exchange therefor.

The Transferor and the Transferee have agreed that the securities listed on Schedule "A" have the fair market values therein set forth and that the assets transferred hereby have an aggregate fair market value of $ .00.

NOW, THEREFORE, in consideration of the mutual covenants contained herein, and intending to be legally bound, the parties agree to the following:

CONTRACTUAL PROVISIONS

1. The Transferor hereby sells, transfers and assigns absolutely to the Transferee the assets listed on Schedule "A."

2. The Transferor represents and warrants that she has good title

to the assets transferred hereunder, and that such assets are free and clear of all liens, pledges and encumbrances whatsoever.

3. The Transferor represents and warrants that she was born on , 19

4. In consideration of the Transferor's sale, transfer and absolute assignment of the assets listed on Schedule "A," the Transferee hereby agrees to pay to the Transferor the sum of $ .00 per year for the remainder of the Transferor's life, the first such payment to be made on February 15, 1977.

5. Upon the written request of the Transferor, the Transferee may from time to time make advance payment of the amounts due under this Agreement. Any such advances shall be promptly repaid by the Transferor. If the Transferor should die with advances due and owing the Transferee, such advances shall be repaid by the Transferor's estate.

6. The parties agree that the Transferee's obligation to make the payments provided in paragraph 4 shall terminate upon the death of the Transferor, and no heir, legatee, creditor or beneficiary of the Transferor's estate, nor such estate itself, shall have any rights under this Agreement.

7. The Transferee shall be absolutely liable for the payments due under paragraph 4 of this Agreement, and such payments shall not be contingent on the Transferee's future earnings from the transferred assets.

8. The Transferor retains no security interest, lien or pledge with respect to any of the assets transferred under this Agreement.

9. The Transferor agrees that the Transferee may apply for the benefit of the Transferor all or any portion of any payment due hereunder rather than pay such amount directly to the Transferor. If any amounts are applied as provided in this paragraph, the Transferee shall, within a reasonable time after such application, notify the Transferor in writing of the amounts so paid and the party or parties to whom such amounts were paid.

IN WITNESS WHEREOF, this private annuity agreement is signed, sealed and delivered on the date first above written.

Signed, sealed and delivered
   in the presence of:

_____   _____ (SEAL)
                            HILDA KRAUSS

_____   _____ (SEAL)
                            ARTHUR KRAUSS

SCHEDULE "A"

TOTAL _____

FORM C-13

Owner and Beneficiary Designations

Form C-13 is designed to provide for transfer of ownership of an insurance policy to the trustees of an irrevocable life insurance trust, and designation of the trustees as "beneficiary" of the policy, as discussed in Chapter 7, ¶701, at page 176. Some insurance companies will accept this form; others will request execution of their own ownership and beneficiary forms.

Owner and Beneficiary Designations

(Name of insurer) _____

_____

Re: Policy No. _____ (hereinafter called "the policy") on the life of

_____

FIRST: Designation of Beneficiary.
    The undersigned hereby designates as primary beneficiary of the policy: _____

_____

_____ ,

Trustees under Indenture of Trust of _____ ,
Grantor, dated _____ , 197_, and entitled "The _____
Irrevocable Trust," hereby revoking, as of the date of this instrument, any beneficiary designation or designations now in effect and any settlement agreement or optional method of settlement election now in effect with respect to the policy.

                _____
                          (Signature of Insured)
Witnessed by:

_____   _____
                               (Date)

SECOND: Transfer of Ownership.
    The undersigned hereby gives and transfers to: _____

_____

_____ , Trustees under Indenture of
Trust of _____ , Grantor, dated _____ ,
197 , and entitled "The _____ Irrevocable Trust," all of his right, title and interest in and to the policy, hereby designating said Trustees, their successors and assigns as the owner of the policy, and vesting in them all incidents of ownership of the policy, so that they may, without the consent of the insured and to the exclusion of the insured, exercise all rights, privileges and options, and receive all benefits, conferred by the policy, anything in the policy to the contrary notwithstanding. Further, the undersigned certifies that his signature at the end of Clause FIRST, above, was subscribed prior to his signature at the end of this Clause SECOND.

                _____
                          (Signature of Insured)
Witnessed by:

_____   _____
                               (Dated)

FORM C-14

Profit Sharing Plan Trust

Pension and profit sharing plans are the subject of Chapter 8. Form C-14 comprises a profit sharing plan and the related trust agreement as designed for a client.

ATLAS CONSTRUCTION CO., INC.
PROFIT SHARING PLAN

(Amended and Restated as of October 1, 1976)

Gilbert M. Cantor, Esquire
Sixth Floor
1700 Sansom Street
Philadelphia, Pennsylvania 19103

ATLAS CONSTRUCTION CO., INC.
PROFIT SHARING PLAN

Table of Contents

ATLAS CONSTRUCTION CO., INC.
PROFIT SHARING PLAN
(Amended and Restated as of October 1, 1976)

Atlas Construction Co., Inc., a corporation organized under the laws of the State of Pennsylvania, in order to comply with the provisions of the Employee Retirement Income Security Act of 1974, does hereby amend and restate its profit sharing plan as set forth below, effective October 1, 1976.

ARTICLE I
Definitions

When used in this Plan and the accompanying Trust Agreement, the following words and phrases shall have the following meaning:

1.01 "Account" shall mean the entire interest of a Participant in the Trust Fund as of the date of reference. A Participant's Account shall consist of his Employer Contribution Account and his Voluntary Contribution Account(s).

1.02 "Age" shall mean the chronological age attained by the Participant at his most recent birthday or as of such other date of reference as is set forth in the Plan.

1.03 "Anniversary Date" shall mean the last day in each Plan Year.

1.04 "Board of Directors" shall mean the board of directors of the Employer.

1.05 "Break in Service" shall mean any Plan Year during which an Employee has not completed more than five hundred (500) Hours of Service. Any Break in Service shall be deemed to have commenced on the first day of the Plan Year in which it occurs. A "Break in Service" shall not be deemed to have occurred during the first twelve (12) calendar months of an Employee's Service merely because of the failure to complete five hundred (500) Hours of Service during any one Plan Year occurring in part during such twelve-month period if the Employee completes one thousand (1000) Hours of Service during such twelve-month period. A Break in Service shall not be deemed to have occurred during any period of Excused Absence if the Employee returns to the Service of the Employer within the time permitted pursuant to the provisions of this Plan setting forth circumstances of Excused Absence. A Break in Service shall not be deemed to have occurred merely because an Employee fails to complete more than five hundred (500) Hours of Service during a Plan Year solely because of his or her retirement or death during such Plan Year.

    1.06 "Compensation" shall mean the total remuneration paid or accrued on behalf of the Participant during the fiscal or Plan Year to which reference is made. "Compensation" shall include basic salary or wages, overtime payments, bonuses, commissions, and all other direct current compensation, but shall not include Employer contributions to Social Security, contributions to this or any other retirement plan or program or the value of any other fringe benefits provided at the expense of the Employer.

    1.07 "Contract" shall mean any annuity, pension, income or insurance policy or contract providing benefits under the Plan.

    1.08 "Earliest Retirement Date" shall mean the date on which the Participant has attained Age 60.

    1.09 "Early Retirement Date" shall mean the date of the Participant's actual retirement at or after his Earliest Retirement Date, but prior to his Normal Retirement Date.

    1.10 "Effective Date" shall mean October 1, 1976.

    1.11 "Employee" shall mean any person employed by the Employer.

    1.12 "Employee Retirement Income Security Act of 1974" shall mean the Act known by that name (P. L. 93-406), including all amendments thereto.

    1.13 "Employer" shall mean Atlas Construction Co., Inc., or any successor entity thereto which adopts this Plan and joins in the corresponding Trust. The term "Employer" shall also include any other entity which, with the consent of the board of directors, adopts this Plan and joins in the corresponding trust agreement.

    1.14 "Employer Contribution Account" means so much of a Participant's Account as is attributable to Employer contributions, reallocated forfeitures, and the earnings and accretions of the trust fund generated by such employer contributions and reallocated forfeitures.

1.15 "Entry Date" shall mean October 1, 1976 and April 1, 1977 and every October 1st and April 1st thereafter during which this Plan remains in effect.

1.16 "Excused Absence" means any of the following:

(a) Absence on leave granted by the Employer for any cause for the period stated in such leave, or, if no period is stated, then for six (6) months and any extensions that the employer may grant in writing. For the purpose of this subparagraph, the employer shall give equal treatment to all employees in similar circumstances.

(b) Absence in any circumstance so long as the employee continues to receive his regular compensation from the employer.

(c) Absence in the armed forces of the United States or government service in time of war or national emergency.

(d) Absence by reason of illness or disability.

An "Excused Absence" shall cease to be an "Excused Absence" and shall be deemed a Break in Service (unless the employee has more than 500 Hours of Service in such Plan Year) as of the first day of such absence if the Employee fails to return to the Service of the employer (1) within five (5) days of expiration of any leave of absence referred to in paragraph (a) hereof, (2) at such time as the payment of regular compensation is discontinued as referred to in paragraph (b) hereof, (3) within three (3) months after his discharge or release from active duty, or, if the employee does not return to service with the employer within the said three (3) months period by reason of a disability incurred while in the armed forces, if he returns to service with the Employer upon the termination of such disability as evidenced by release from confinement in a military or veterans hospital, or (4) upon recovery from illness or disability. The Employer shall be the sole judge of whether or not recovery from illness or disability has occurred for this purpose.

1.17 "Fund" or "Trust Fund" shall mean all of the assets of the Plan held by the Trustee (or any nominee thereof) at any time under the Trust Agreement.

1.18 "Hour of Service" shall have the following meanings:

(a) For an Employee paid on an hourly basis or for whom hourly records of employment are required to be maintained: Each hour for which the Employee is directly or indirectly paid or entitled to payment.

(b) For an Employee paid on a non-hourly basis or for whom hourly records of employment are not required to be maintained: Each week for which the Member is directly or indirectly paid or entitled to payment shall be equal to 45 Hours of Service.

(c) An Employee shall receive an Hour of Service for each hour for which back pay has been awarded or agreed to by the Employer, provided that each such hour shall be credited to the Applicable Computation Period to which it pertains, rather than the Applicable Computation Period in which the awards or agreement shall have the effect of crediting an Hour of Service for any hour for which the Employee previously received credit under (a) or (b) above.

1.19 "Internal Revenue Code" means the Internal Revenue Code of 1954 as the same presently exists, and as it may hereafter be amended.

1.20 "Named Fiduciary" shall mean the Employer, the Trustee, the Plan Administrator and the Named Appeals Fiduciary. Each Fiduciary shall have only those particular powers, duties, responsibilities and obligations as are specifically given him under this Plan and/or the Trust Agreement.

1.21 "Net Income" shall mean the current and accumulated earnings of the Employer, as determined by the Employer's regularly engaged accountant upon the basis of the Employer's books of account, in accordance with generally accepted accounting principles, but without any deduction being taken from any of the following: (1) depreciation, (2) extraordinary losses resulting from the sale of assets not in the ordinary course of business, (3) casualty losses in excess of recovery, (4) contributions to this or any other qualified retirement plan, or (5) Federal, state, county or city income taxes.

1.22 "Normal Retirement Date" shall mean the Anniversary Date occurring in the Plan Year in which the Participant attains age 65.

1.23 "Participant" shall mean any person who has been or who is an Employee and who has been admitted to participation in this Plan pursuant to the provisions of Article II hereof. The term "Participant" shall include Active Participants (those who are Employees currently and who are eligible to share in Employer contributions to the Plan), Retired Participants (those former Employees presently receiving benefits under this Plan) and Vested Participants (former Employees who have incurred a Break in Service and who are entitled at some future date to the distribution of benefits from this Plan).

1.24 "Plan" shall mean the Atlas Construction Co., Inc. Profit Sharing Plan as set forth herein, and as the same may from time to time hereafter be amended.

1.25 "Plan Administrator" shall mean the person or committee named as such pursuant to the provisions of Article XI hereof.

1.26 "Plan Year" shall mean the twelve-month period commencing October 1st and ending on the subsequent September 30th.

1.27 "Total Disability" shall mean a physical or mental condition of such severity and probable prolonged duration as to entitle the Participant to disability retirement benefits under the Federal Social Security Act.

1.28 "Trust Agreement" shall mean the Atlas Construction Co.,

Inc. Profit Sharing Plan Trust Agreement as the same presently exists and as it may from time to time hereafter be amended.

1.29 "Trustee" shall mean the party or parties so designated pursuant to the Trust Agreement.

1.30 "Valuation Date" shall mean the Annual Valuation Date, being the last day of each Plan Year, and each interim date on which a valuation of the Trust Fund is made.

1.31 "Year of Service" shall have the following meanings when used in this Plan:

(a) When applied to the eligibility provisions of Article II, a "Year of Service" shall mean a Plan Year in which an Employee completes one thousand (1000) Hours of Service. Notwithstanding the foregoing, any Employee who completes one thousand (1000) Hours of Service within twelve (12) calendar months of his most recent date of hire shall be credited with a "Year of Service" for eligibility purposes.

(b) When applied to vesting provisions, a "Year of Service" shall mean any Plan Year during which an Employee has one thousand (1000) or more Hours of Service or, for years prior to the effective date of the Plan, consecutive calendar years during which an Employee was employed on a full time salaried basis. However, a "Year of Service" will not be credited for any period of Excused Absence after the Employee incurs a Break in Service during such absence from the service of the Employer."

ARTICLE II
Participation and Entry Date

2.01 *Initial Eligibility.*

Every Employee shall be eligible to become a Participant on the Entry Date coincident with or next following the date on which he completes one (1) Year of Service, provided, however, that no Employee shall be admitted to this Plan if he is no longer an Employee on the Entry Date as of which his admission to participation would otherwise have become effective.

2.02 *Procedure for and Effect of Admission.*

Each Employee who becomes eligible for admission to participation in this Plan shall complete such forms and provide such data as are reasonably required by the Plan Administrator as a precondition of such admission. By becoming a Participant, each Employee shall for all purposes be deemed conclusively to have assented to the provisions of the Plan, the corresponding trust agreement and to all amendments to such instruments.

2.03 *Waiver of Participation.*

An Employee, once having become eligible for participation in this Plan, shall not have the right to waive such participation unless the Plan Administrator, in his sole discretion, determines to allow written waivers of participation. If such waivers are permitted, they shall be permitted on a non-discriminatory basis and shall be effective on a year-to-year basis only. The Plan Administrator retains the right not to permit waivers in any year or years, even if such waivers have been permitted in prior years.

2.04 *Re-employment after Break in Service.*

In the event a Participant ceases to be an Employee by reason of a 1-year Break in Service, and subsequently again becomes an Employee, he shall be readmitted as an Active Participant on the Entry Date next following his completion of one Year of Service after such Break in Service; provided, however, that if an Employee has a vested interest in the Trust or if his Years of Service exceed his consecutive one year Breaks in Service, he shall participate as of his reemployment commencement date."

ARTICLE III
Employer Contributions

3.01 *Determination of Amount.*

Employer shall, out of current or accumulated Net Income, make such contributions to the Trust in respect of the fiscal year of the Employer during which this Plan is first adopted and in respect of each fiscal year thereafter during which this Plan is in effect, in such amounts as the board of directors of the employer, in its absolute discretion, shall determine by resolution adopted on or before the last day of the fiscal year with respect to which any contribution is being made. This provision shall not be construed as requiring employer to make contributions in any specific fiscal year, whether or not there exists net income out of which such contributions could be made.

3.02 *Timing of Contributions.*

Employer shall pay its contribution made with respect to any fiscal year to the Trustee on or before the date established for the filing of the employer's Federal income tax return (including any extensions of such date) for the fiscal year with respect to which such contribution is made.

3.03 *Contingent Nature of Contributions.*

Each contribution made by Employer pursuant to the provisions of Section 3.01 hereof is hereby made expressly contingent on the deductibility thereof for Federal income tax purposes for the year with respect to which such contribution is made. Each contribution is further contingent upon the maintenance of qualified status by the Plan for the year with respect to which such contribution is made.

3.04 *Exclusive Benefit; Refund of Contribution.*

All contributions made by the Employer are made for the exclusive benefit of the Participants and their beneficiaries, and such contributions shall not be used for nor diverted to purposes other than for the exclusive benefit of the Participants and their beneficiaries (including the costs of maintaining and administering the Plan and Trust). Notwithstanding the foregoing, amounts contributed to the Trust by the Employer may be refunded to the Employer under the following circumstances and subject to the following limitations:

(a) *Initial Non-qualification.* If the plan fails initially to satisfy the qualification requirements of Section 401(a) of the Internal Revenue Code, and if Employer declines to amend the Plan to satisfy such qualification requirements, contributions made prior to the determination that the Plan has failed to qualify shall be returned to the Employer.

(b) *Disallowance of Deduction.* To the extent that a Federal income tax deduction is allowed for any contribution made by Employer, Trustee shall immediately refund to the Employer the amount so disallowed upon presentation, within one (1) year of the date of such disallowance, of evidence thereof and a demand by Employer for such refund.

(c) *Loss of Qualified Status.* If it is determined that the Plan does not constitute a qualified plan for any Plan Year, there shall be returned to Employer upon demand any contribution made by Employer with respect to any year in which qualified status is denied, provided that demand is made by the Employer and refund is made by the Trustee within one (1) year of the date of denial of qualification of the Plan.

(d) *Mistake of fact.* In the case of a contribution which is made in whole or in part by reason of a mistake of fact, so much of such contribution as is attributable to the mistake of fact shall be returnable to Employer on demand, upon presentation of evidence of the mistake of fact to the Trustee and of calculations as to the impact of such mistake. Demand and repayment must be effectuated within one (1) year after the payment of the contribution to which the mistake applies.

In the event that any refund is paid to the Employer hereunder, such refund shall be made without interest and shall be apportioned among the Accounts of the Participants as an investment loss except to the extent that the amount of the refund can be attributed to one or more specific Participants (as in the case of certain mistakes of fact, disallowances of compensation resulting in reduction of deductible contributions, etc.) in which case the amount of the refund attributable to each Participant's Account shall be debited directly against such account.

Notwithstanding any other provision of this paragraph, no refund shall be made to Employer which is specifically chargeable to the Account(s) of any Participant(s) in excess of 100% of the amount in such Account(s) nor shall a refund be made by the Trustee of any funds, otherwise subject to refund hereunder, which have been distributed to Participants and/or beneficiaries. In the case that such distributions become refundable, Employer shall have a claim directly against the distributees to the extent of the fund to which it is entitled.

All refunds pursuant to Sections 3.04(b), (c) and (d) shall be limited in amount, circumstance and timing to the provisions of Section 403(c) of The Employee Retirement Income Security Act of 1974.

ARTICLE IV
Contributions By Participants

4.01 *Mandatory Contributions.*

No contributions shall be required of any Participant under this Plan.

4.02 *Voluntary Contributions.*

(a) *Permissibility.* The Plan Administrator may, in his sole discretion, elect to provide all Participants with the opportunity to contribute to the Trust for each Plan Year an amount not less than fifty dollars ($50.00) nor more than six percent (6%) of such Participant's Compensation for such Plan Year. If, with respect to the Plan Year, six percent (6%) of the Participant's Compensation is less than fifty dollars ($50.00), the maximum and the minimum contribution acceptable from such Participant shall be six percent (6%) of such Compensation. Contributions hereunder shall be aggregated with contributions made by the Participant to all other plans for the purposes of applying the limitations hereunder.

(b) *Date of Payment.* The amount of each Participant's voluntary contribution in respect of any Plan Year shall be paid by the Participant to the Trustee not later than the last day of such Plan Year and shall be credited to his Voluntary Contribution Account as of the first day of the Plan Year next following the Plan Year in which such contribution is received by the Trustee. The Plan Administrator may, in his sole discretion, determine that voluntary Participant contributions shall be accepted only if made pursuant to a payroll withholding method or similar reasonable administrative device.

(c) *Withdrawal.* A Participant may withdraw from the Trust as of any Valuation Date, an amount not to exceed the lesser of (i) the aggregate of the voluntary contributions he has made to date, reduced, however, by any prior withdrawals therefrom, or (ii) the net asset value of his

Voluntary Contribution Account. Earnings and appreciation in excess of the aggregate of the Participant's contributions are not withdrawable, and shall remain fully vested in the Participant for distribution at such time as the Participant is or would be entitled to a distribution of his vested interest, if any, from his Employer Contribution Account.

4.03 *Rollover Contributions.*

(a) *Direct Inter-Plan Transfers.* Any Participant may, with the written consent of the Plan Administrator, direct the appropriate funding agency or fiduciary of any qualified retirement plan of a former employer to distribute directly to the Trustee such Participant's entire interest in the distributing plan, exclusive of contributions made by the Participant as an employee or participant thereunder. Upon receipt of such a distribution, the Trustee shall establish a segregated account on behalf of the Participant in whose behalf such distribution was received. The account so established shall be considered a Voluntary Contribution Account of the Participant on whose behalf it is established, and it shall be subject to the terms and conditions of Section 4.02 hereof, except, however, that no withdrawals will be permitted pursuant to Section 4.02(c). Any amount presented by a Participant to the Trustee within sixty (60) days of the receipt thereof as a distribution from any other qualified retirement plan shall be treated, upon receipt by the Trustee, as having been received directly from the appropriate disbursing officer or fiduciary of the distributing plan.

(b) *IRA Rollovers.* Any Participant who has established an Individual Retirement Account (pursuant to the provisions of Section 408 of the Internal Revenue Code) solely for the purpose of serving as a repository for total distributions received from qualified retirement plans of former employers, exclusive of amounts contributed by the employee as a participant therein, and who has not made any contributions to such Individual Retirement Account on his own behalf, may, with the consent of the Plan Administrator, transfer all of the assets of such Individual Retirement Account to the Trustee, which assets shall then be placed in a segregated account on behalf of the Participant. The account so established shall be considered a Voluntary Contribution Account of the Participant on whose behalf it is established, and it shall be subject to the terms and conditions of Section 4.02 hereof, except, however, that no withdrawals will be permitted pursuant to Section 4.02(c).

(c) *Rollover Account Conditions and Limitations.* The trustee shall not accept a rollover distribution from any other plan or Individual Retirement Account unless all of the following conditions are met:

(i) The amount so received shall constitute the Participant's entire interest in the distributing plan (or Individual Retirement Account), exclusive of contributions made to such plan by the Participant;

(ii) The Participant shall present a written certification, in form satisfactory to the Plan Administrator, to the effect that (A) the amount so received is the full amount standing to that participant's credit in such other plan; (B) no portion of such amount consists of contributions made by the Participant; and (C) if such amount is being paid by the Participant personally, it was received within the prior sixty (60) calendar days as a total distribution from such other plan.

(iii) No rollover contributions will be accepted, directly or indirectly, from: (A) any Individual Retirement Account to which the Participant contributed on his own behalf or (B) any plan for self-employed persons or any plan containing assets previously a part of a plan for self-employed persons. No rollover contribution will be accepted which consists, in whole or in part, or insurance contracts with respect to which future premium payments are or may become due unless the Plan Administrator is satisfied that there are sufficient other segregatee account assets being transferred so as to make maintenance of such contract(s) feasible without violation of any limitations on assets which may be applied for that purpose.

(d) *Investment of Rollover Accounts.* Rollover accounts shall be segregated Voluntary Contribution Accounts and shall be held in interest-bearing passbook accounts until the Valuation Date next following the date of receipt by the Trustee. Thereafter, such accounts shall be held, at the Trustee's option, either as segregated interest-bearing accounts or as separate Voluntary Contribution Accounts in the Trust Fund as though contributed pursuant to the provisions of Section 4.02(a) hereof.

(e) *Vesting of Rollover Accounts.* All rollover accounts shall be fully vested in the Participant on whose behalf they are established.

(f) *Withdrawal of Rollover Accounts.* There shall be no withdrawals of any portion of any rollover account by any Participant until such time as he is otherwise eligible to receive his vested interest attributable to Employer contributions under this Plan (or would have been eligible, had he been vested in any part of his Employer Contribution Account).

(g) *Distribution of Rollover Accounts.* The assets held on behalf of any Participant in a rollover account shall be aggregated with any other vested interest he may have in this Plan for the purpose of distribution and shall be distributed at the same time as the remainder of his vested interest in this Plan, and, to the extent feasible, by the same method of distribution of benefits.

4.04 *Restoration Contributions.*

Any former Participant who once again qualifies as an Active Participant and who has received a "cash out" of his vested interest attributable to his prior participation in this Plan, may, upon reinstatement as an Active Participant or within sixty (60) days after such reinstatement, restore to the Trustee the full amount of the "cash out" he previously received. All such amounts received by the Trustee shall be credited to the Participant's Employer Contribution Account as of the Valuation Date coincident with or next following his restoration to Active Participant status, but such amount shall be established in a separate subaccount. Any Participant who fails to make his restoration contribution within sixty (60) days of his again becoming an Active Participant shall be deemed to have waived his right to make such a contribution.

ARTICLE V
Allocation of Contributions and Forfeitures

5.01 *Employer Contributions.*

As of each Anniversary Date, there shall be allocated to the Employer Contribution Account of each Participant an amount determined by multiplying (a) the sum of (i) the Employer's contribution for its fiscal year ending with or immediately prior to such Anniversary Date and (ii) forfeitures occurring during such Plan Year by (b) a fraction, the numerator of which is the Participant's Compensation during such fiscal year, and the denominator of which is the aggregate Compensation of all Participants for such fiscal year.

For the purposes hereof, any Participant who is absent on an Excused Absence, has retired, suffered Total Disability or died during the Plan Year shall be deemed a Participant on such Anniversary Date, and shall share in the allocation on the basis of actual Compensation with respect to the subject fiscal year. Participants who voluntarily leave the employ of the Employer or who are discharged during the Plan Year shall not share in such allocations if they occasion a Break in Service during such Plan Year. Any Participant who remained in the employ of the Employer through the end of the Plan Year or fiscal year for which the contribution is made, but who changed from an eligible to an ineligible classification during the Plan Year shall be deemed an Active Participant for such Plan Year, but only with respect to his Compensation while in an eligible status.

5.02 *Forfeitures.*

Forfeitures shall be allocated as additional Employer contributions pursuant to the provisions of Section 5.01 hereof. No portion of a Participant's Account shall be deemed forfeited until he has incurred a 1-year Break in Service.

5.03 *Annual Additions Limitations.*

Notwithstanding the provisions of Sections 5.01 and 5.02 hereof, in no event shall the annual addition to the Participant's Employer Contribution Account exceed the lesser of $25,000 or 25% of such Participant's Compensation (or such greater limit as may be permissible pursuant to the provisions of Section 415 of the Internal Revenue Code and regulations issued thereunder). Any excess resulting from these limits shall be reallocated among the remaining Participants in the same manner as provided in Section 5.01. For the purposes hereof, the amounts contributed to any defined contribution plan maintained by the Employer (or any related business entity under common control) shall be aggregated with contributions made by the Employer under this Plan for any Employee in computing his annual additions limitation. Moreover, in no event shall the amount allocated to the Employer Contribution Account of any Participant be greater than the maximum amount allowed pursuant to Section 415 of the Internal Revenue Code with respect to combinations of plans without disqualification of any such plan. If the reallocation of contributions to other Participants is impossible without causing them or any of them to have annual additions violations under said Section 415 of the Internal Revenue Code, the amount that cannot be reallocated without occasioning such a violation shall be considered as having been contributed pursuant to a mistake of fact. For purposes of this Section, the Plan Year shall be the limitation year.

5.04 *Voluntary Employee Contributions.*

Voluntary contributions made by Participants shall be allocated directly to their respective accounts.

5.05 *Rollover Contributions.*

Rollover contributions shall be credited directly to the segregated accounts of the Participants on whose behalf they are received.

5.06 *Restoration Contributions.*

Restoration contributions shall be credited directly to the Employer Contribution Accounts of the respective Participants on whose behalf they are received.

ARTICLE VI
Administration of Funds

6.01 *Investment of Assets.*

All contributions shall be paid over to the Trustee and shall be invested by the Trustee in accordance with the Plan and Trust Agreement.

6.02 *Valuations.*

The Fund shall be valued by the Trustee at fair market value annually as of the close of business on the Annual Valuation Date. A similar valuation of the Fund may occur at the end of any calendar month upon direction of the Plan Administrator.

6.03 *Crediting of Contributions.*

(a) *Employer Contributions.* Any contribution made in respect of any Plan Year (or fiscal year ending during a Plan Year) by the Employer shall be deemed to have been made immediately after the valuation occurring at the end of the Plan Year with respect to which such contribution was made or during which such fiscal year ended.

(b) *Voluntary Contributions.* Contributions made by Participants pursuant to Section 4.02 hereof during any Plan Year shall be credited immediately after the annual Valuation Date occurring at the end of the Plan Year during which such contribution is made. Notwithstanding the foregoing, if the Participant becomes entitled to receive the entire amount standing to his credit during any Plan Year and such amount is distributed to him (or to his beneficiary), the distribution shall include all amounts contributed by him during the Plan Year in which the distribution occurs, as though the same were credited to his Account as of the date of distribution.

(c) *Rollover and Restoration Contributions.* Rollover and restoration contributions made pursuant to Section 4.03(a) and 4.03(b) hereof shall be credited to segregated accounts established on behalf of the Participant on whose behalf they are contributed, as promptly as practicable following receipt thereof by the Trustee. This paragraph (c) of this Section 6.03 is subject, however, to the provisions of Section 4.03(d) of this Plan. If the Participant becomes entitled to receive the entire amount standing to his credit during any Plan Year and such amount is distributed to him (or his beneficiary), the distribution shall include all amounts contributed as rollover or restoration contributions on his behalf during such Plan Year, whether or not formally credited to his Account prior to the date of distribution.

6.04 *Crediting of Investment Results.*

(a) *Contract Surrender Values and Dividends.* Increases in cash surrender values of Contracts and dividends payable with respect to Contracts shall be allocated directly to the Accounts of the Participants for whose benefit the respective Contracts are maintained.

(b) *Segregated Accounts.* To the extent that the Trustee maintains segregated accounts on behalf of any Participant or beneficiary, there shall be credited to the Account of such Participant or beneficiary all earnings and accretions generated by the segregated account since the immediately preceding Valuation Date, and there shall be debited from such Account all identifiable separate expenses incurred in the operation and maintenance of such Account.

(c) *General.* As of any Valuation Date, the earnings and accretions of the Trust Fund attributable to investment of Fund Assets, reduced by losses experienced (whether or not realized) and expenses incurred since the preceding Valuation Date shall be credited to the Accounts of the Participants and beneficiaries who had unpaid balances in their Accounts as of such Valuation Date in proportion to the balances in such Accounts as of the prior Valuation Date, after reducing such prior Valuation Date balances by the amounts withdrawn by or distributed to the Participant or beneficiary since such Valuation Date, if any. For the purposes of this paragraph, the balance in any Participant's or beneficiary's account shall not include values contained in Contracts. Where there is maintained for any Participant or beneficiary, in addition to the Employer Contribution Account, sub-accounts such as one or more Voluntary Contribution Accounts, each such sub-account shall be considered a separate Account for the purposes of credited investment results pursuant to Section 6.04.

6.05 *Investments in Life Insurance.*

(a) *Limitations.* The Trustee, if so instructed by the Plan Administrator, shall invest an amount less than 50% of the Employer's contribution allocable to each Participant for the year in which such instruction is first given in the purchase of an ordinary life insurance contract for such Participant's Account, provided, however, that:

(1) The aggregate premiums for life insurance in the case of each Participant shall be less than one-half of the aggregate of the Employer contributions allocated to him at any particular time, and

(2) the Trustee shall:

(A) convert the entire value of any life insurance at or before retirement into cash, or

(B) purchase an annuity contract which is not assignable and not commutable in the hands of the Participant to provide periodic income so that no portion of the value of the life insurance contract may be used to continue life insurance protection beyond retirement, or

(C) distribute the life insurance contract or contracts to the Participant.

No instruction for purchase of life insurance shall be given by the Plan Administrator unless a request therefor has been made by the Participant or an application therefor has been completed by the Participant. The Plan Administrator may thereafter give, or refrain from giving, such instruction to the Trustee and shall have sole discretion in regard thereto.

(b) *Maintenance of Insurance Contracts.* In the event the Employer's contribution allocable to any Participant's Account in any Plan Year is not sufficient to pay the annual premium on all life insurance held by the Trustee for such Participant, the Trustee shall apply the Employer's contribution as allocated to each Participant's Account, to the extent permissible and available, to the payment of such premiums, and, if additional funds are required, shall insofar as possible pay the same from any other assets in its possession to the extent of the respective Participant's interest therein and by borrowing on such life insurance for the benefit of the insured thereunder to the extent of the cash value where necessary. In any following year in which the Employer's contribution as allocated to each Account exceeds the amount necessary to pay the premiums on the life insurance held for such accounts, the Trustee shall repay outstanding loans against each Participant's life insurance to the extent of such excess funds in such Participant's account. The provisions of this paragraph shall not be construed to impair the Trustee's right to borrow available cash surrender values for the purposes of investing the proceeds of such loans for the benefit of the respective Accounts of the Participants whose policies are so borrowed against.

(c) *Ownership and Beneficiary Designation under Life Insurance Contracts.* Each life insurance contract purchased by the Trustee shall designate the Trustee as the sole owner and beneficiary thereof subject to the terms and provisions of the Trust Agreement. All dividends on life insurance purchased by the Trust shall be allocated to the account of the Participant for whose benefit the life insurance was issued.

6.06 *Loans to Participants.*

(a) Loans to Participants shall be allowed if, and only if, the Plan Administrator determines that such loans are to be made. The determination as to whether or not Participant loans are to be allowed shall be completely within the discretion of the Plan Administrator.

(b) Subject to such uniform and nondiscriminatory rules as may from time to time be adopted by the Plan Administrator after it has been determined that loans to Participants shall be allowed, the Trustee, upon application by a Participant on forms approved by the Plan Administrator, may make a loan or loans to such Participant for the purposes of enabling a Participant to meet emergency conditions in his financial affairs, such as may result from the illness or disability of the Participant, illness or death in the Participant's immediate family, unemployment or severe curtailment of income of the Participant due to reasons beyond his control, or establishing or preserving the health of the Participant or his immediate family. A loan may also be made for the purpose of providing a college education, including graduate studies, for a child of a Participant, or for special schooling required due to a disability of such child. A loan may also be made in connection with the acquisition of a residence for the Participant or in accordance with major capital expenses in connection with such a residence.

6.07 *Limitations on Loans to Participants.*

(a) *Individual.* No Participant shall, under any circumstance, be entitled to loans in excess of the value of his vested interest in his Account as of the Valuation Date coincident with or immediately preceding the date on which the loan is made. Any amount withdrawn by a Participant from his Account while a loan is outstanding shall be immediately applied to reduce such loan.

(b) *General.* Loans shall be available to all Participants on a reasonably equivalent basis, provided, however, that the Trustee may make reasonable distinctions among prospective borrowers on the basis of credit worthiness. Loans shall not be made available to highly compensated Participants in an amount greater than the amount available to other Participants. Thus, the same percentage of a Participant's vested balance in his Account may be loaned to Participants with both large and small amounts of vested benefits, if such vested benefit is security for the loan.

6.08 *Loans as an Investment of the Trust Fund.*

(a) *Adequacy of Security.* All loans to Participants made by the Trustee shall be secured by the pledge of the Participant's vested interest in the Trust Fund and by the pledge of such further collateral as the Trustee, in its discretion, deems necessary or desirable to assure repayment of the borrowed amount and all interest payable thereon in accordance with the terms of the loan.

(b) *Rates of Interest.* Interest shall be charged at one percent (1%) per annum in excess of the prime commercial lending rate in force in the community on the date of the loan, provided, however, that in no event shall the interest rate charged be in violation of any applicable usury law.

(c) *Term of Loan.* Loans shall generally be for a term of three (3) years, or for such lesser term as the Plan Administrator and Trustee agree is appropriate. The Trustee, with the consent of the Plan Administrator, may extend or renew loans if the conditions qualifying the Participant for the initial loan continue beyond the loan due date, provided, however, that such extensions and renewals shall be on a year-to-year basis. To the extent that a Participant or beneficiary becomes entitled to payments of benefits or withdraws all or a portion of the Participant's Account, the payments or withdrawals as the case may be shall be immediately applied against the balance outstanding, including the interest on the loan, and such amount shall then be deemed immediately due and payable.

(d) *Remedies in the Event of Default.* If not paid as and when due, any such outstanding loan or loans may be deducted at retirement, death, disability or other termination of employment from any benefit to which such Participant (or his beneficiary) is entitled under this Plan, and any other security pledged shall be sold as soon as is practicable after such default by the Trustee at private or public sale. The proceeds of such sale shall be applied first to pay the expenses of conducting the sale, including reasonable attorneys' fees, and then to pay any sums due from the borrower to the Trust Fund, with such payment to be applied first to accrued interest and then to principal. The Participant shall remain liable for any deficiency, and any surplus remaining shall be paid to the Participant.

ARTICLE VII
Retirement Benefits and Disability Benefits

7.01 *Normal Retirement Benefit.*

The Normal Retirement Benefit shall be payable with respect to any Participant retiring at his Normal Retirement Date, and shall be equal to 100% of the net asset value of the Participant's Account as of the Valuation Date coincident with or next following the Participant's Normal Retirement Date.

7.02 *Early Retirement Benefit.*

The Early Retirement Benefit shall be payable with respect to any Participant retiring at his Early Retirement Date, and shall be equal to 100% of the net asset value of the Participant's Account as of the Valuation Date coincident with or next following the Participant's retirement prior to his Normal Retirement Date.

7.03 *Deferred Retirement Benefit.*

The Deferred Retirement Benefit shall be payable with respect to any Participant retiring after his Normal Retirement Date, and shall be equal to 100% of the net asset value of the Participant's Account as of the Valuation Date coincident with or next following the Participant's actual retirement.

7.04 *Disability Benefit.*

The Disability Benefit shall be payable with respect to any Participant who has suffered Total Disability and who is separated from service of the Employer by reason of such disability, and shall be equal to 100% of the net asset value of the Participant's Account as of the Valuation Date coincident with or next following the Participant's disability separation date.

7.05 *Mandatory Retirement, Extensions.*

Every Participant shall be required to retire on his Normal Retirement Date unless the Employer consents in writing to his remaining an employee. Such consent, if granted, shall be granted on a year-to-year basis. Any Participant may retire without the consent of the Employer or may be retired by the Employer at any time on or after his Earliest Retirement Date.

ARTICLE VIII
Death Benefits

8.01 *Pre-Retirement Death Benefits.*

In the event of the death of an Active Participant or of a Vested Participant prior to the commencement of benefit payments, there shall be paid an amount equal to 100% of the net asset value of the Participant's Account.

8.02 *Post-Retirement Death Benefits.*

In the event of the death of a Retired Participant or of a Vested Participant who is receiving benefits, there shall be paid only such death benefit as is determined by the method of distribution of benefits or settlement option then in force with respect to the Participant. If no such method of distribution of benefits or settlement option is in force, then the death benefit shall be 100% of the undistributed balance of the Participant's Account.

8.03 *Timing of Distribution.*

Distributions becoming payable pursuant to Section 8.01 hereof shall be paid as promptly as practicable following the Valuation Date coincident with or next following the death of the Participant. Distributions becoming payable pursuant to Section 8.02 hereof shall be paid pursuant to any annuity or other arrangement in force on the Participant's life at the time of his death, or if there be none, then as promptly as practicable following the Valuation Date coincident with or next following the Participant's death.

8.04 *Beneficiary Designation.*

Each Participant shall have the right by written notice to the Plan Administrator, in the form prescribed by the Plan Administrator, to designate, and from time to time to change the designation of, one or more beneficiaries and contingent beneficiaries to receive any benefit which may become payable pursuant to the provisions of Section 8.01 hereof. Benefits becoming payable pursuant to the provisions of Section 8.02 hereof shall be governed in this respect by the terms and provisions of any contract or policy in force on the life of the Participant pursuant to which benefits are being paid at the time of his death, except that if there be no such contract or contracts, and if a benefit be payable pursuant to Section 8.02, then such benefit shall be treated as being payable pursuant to the provisions of Section 8.01 hereof for beneficiary designation purposes.

In the event that the Participant fails to designate a beneficiary to receive a benefit that becomes payable pursuant to the provisions of Section 8.01, or in the event that the Participant is predeceased by all designated primary and contingent beneficiaries, the death benefit shall be payable to the following classes of takers, each class to take to the exclusion of all subsequent classes, and all members of each class to share equally:

(a) surviving spouse;

(b) lineal descendants (including adopted and step-children), per stirpes;

(c) surviving parents;

(d) Participant's estate.

ARTICLE IX
Vesting and Separation from Service

9.01 *Voluntary Contribution Accounts.*

All Participants shall at all times be fully vested in their respective Voluntary Contribution Accounts, if any.

9.02 *Employer Contribution Accounts.*

(a) Every Participant shall at all times be fully vested in so much of his Employer Contribution Account as consists of "restoration contributions" made pursuant to the provisions of Section 4.04, and the earnings and accretions, if any, attributable thereto.

(b) The Employee's vested interest in the remainder of his Employer Contribution Account shall be determined as of the date on which he incurs a Break in Service. The amount of such vested interest shall be determined pursuant to the following table:

Employee's Years of Service	*Vested Percentage*
Fewer than 2 years	None
2 Years but fewer than 3	10%
3 Years but fewer than 4	20%
4 Years but fewer than 5	30%
5 Years but fewer than 6	40%
6 Years but fewer than 7	50%
7 Years but fewer than 8	60%
8 Years but fewer than 9	70%
9 Years but fewer than 10	80%
10 Years but fewer than 11	90%
11 Years but fewer than 12	100%

(c) For the purposes of Section 9.02(b), the term "Years of Service" shall not include service:

(1) during any Plan Year in which the Employee has fewer than

1,000 Hours of Service, whether or not a Break in Service occurs during such Plan Year;

(2) during any Plan Year prior to the Plan Year in which the Participant had his most recent Break in Service, if the Participant had no vested interest in his Employer Contribution Account (other than an interest therein by reason of the provisions of Section 9.02(a)) at the time of his Break in Service, and such Break or Breaks in Service extended continuously for a period equal to or longer than his prior period of service."

ARTICLE X
Method and Timing of Benefit Distributions

10.01 *Retirement Benefits, Disability Benefits.*

(a) *Commencement Date.* Should a Participant become entitled to benefits pursuant to the provisions of Article VII of this Plan, unless the Participant elects otherwise, such benefits shall commence not later than the 60th day after the latest of the close of the Plan Year in which (i) the date on which the Participant attains age 65 or (ii) occurs the 10th anniversary of the year in which the Participant commenced participation in the Plan, or (iii) the Participant terminates service with the Employer.

(b) *Normal Form of Benefits.*

(1) In the case of a Participant who is married as of the date such benefits commence, the normal form of benefit shall be a Qualified Joint-and-Survivor Annuity with a periodic benefit payable to the surviving spouse, if any, equal to the periodic benefit payable to the retired Participant.

(2) In the case of a Participant who is not married as of the date such benefits commence, the normal form of benefit shall be a Straight Life Annuity.

(c) *Alternate Forms of Benefits.* Any Participant becoming entitled to benefits may elect to receive, in lieu of the normal form of benefit set forth in paragraph (b) above, an actuarially equivalent benefit in any of the following forms, all such elections to be subject to the approval and consent of the Plan Administrator:

(1) A Qualified Joint-and-Survivor Annuity providing a specified periodic benefit to the retired Participant for life, with a benefit payable to the Participant's surviving spouse, if any, equal to less than 100%, but in no event less than 50%, of the periodic benefit payable to the retired Participant prior to his or her death;

(2) A Joint-and-Survivor Annuity naming any dependent or related person as a contingent annuitant, provided that at the time of purchase, 60% or more of the value of the annuity applies to the provision of benefits for the retired Participant;

(3) A Straight Life Annuity;

(4) A Period Certain Annuity, with payments guaranteed for a period of 5, 10 or 15 years, as determined by the Participant with the consent of the Plan Administrator;

(5) Payments in installments as nearly equal as possible over a period of 5, 10 or 15 years, but in no event over a period exceeding the Participant's life expectancy or the joint life expectancy of the Participant and his spouse, as of his benefit commencement date;

(6) An investment or variable annuity, provided that no such annuity may be of an "interest only" variety;

(7) A lump-sum distribution; or

(8) Any combination of the foregoing.

(d) *Special Rules and Definitions.*

(1) As used herein, the term-

(A) "Qualified Joint-and-Survivor Annuity" means an annuity benefit payable monthly (or if monthly benefits would be less than $25, then payable at the shortest periodic intervals which would generate a benefit of not less than $25, provided that such intervals shall be not less frequent than annual) for the life of the Participant, and continuing after the death of the Participant to the person who was the spouse of the Participant as of the Participant's benefit commencement date (whether or not such person remains the Participant's spouse), if then living, for the remainder of such spouse's life.

(B) "Straight Life Annuity" means an annuity benefit payable monthly (or if monthly benefits would be less than $25, then payable at the shortest periodic intervals which would generate a benefit of not less than $25, provided that such intervals shall be not less frequent than annual) commencing as of the benefit commencement date hereinabove specified and ending with the payment made on the day coincident with or the payment immediately preceding the Participant's death.

(C) "Period Certain Annuity" means an annuity payable to the Participant only during his lifetime, as in (B) above, provided, however, that in the event of the Participant's death prior to the receipt of the number of installments specified by the period of the guarantee (the "period certain"), installments shall be continued after the Participant's death for the remainder of the period certain only (or the commuted value of such payments) and shall be paid to the Participant's designated beneficiary.

(2) Under no circumstances shall a Participant elect any "interest only" optional form of benefit, nor shall any distributed Contract offer other optional modes of payment.

(3) Elections out of the Qualified Joint-and-Survivor Annuity pursuant to the provisions of Section 10.01(c) must be made in writing on forms provided by the Plan Administrator prior to the Participant's benefit commencement date, are irrevocable subsequent to such benefit

commencement date, and are effective only if the Participant has been advised in writing of the consequences of such an election.

(4) Elections of any alternative form of benefit pursuant to the provisions of Section 10.02(c) shall be made:

(A) in writing;

(B) on forms provided by the Plan Administrator; and

(C) not less than sixty (60) days prior to the Participant's benefit commencement date,

and shall be revocable at any time prior to the Participant's benefit commencement date, but shall become irrevocable on the Participant's benefit commencement date.

(5) Except in the case of a joint-and-survivor annuity (whether or not a Qualified Joint-and-Survivor Annuity), the Participant shall retain the right to change the designation of beneficiaries with respect to any amounts becoming payable by reason of his death.

(6) A Participant's statement of his marital status shall be absolutely dispositive thereof, and the Plan Administrator may rely thereon. The Plan Administrator is not required at any time to inquire into the validity of any marriage, the effectiveness of a common-law relationship or the claim of any alleged spouse which is inconsistent with the Participant's report of his or her marital status and the identity of his or her spouse.

(7) Benefits provided hereunder may be provided by the purchase of annuity contracts or may be paid directly from the Trust Fund. In the event that an annuity contract is purchased and distributed to the Participant, such annuity contract shall be a single premium non-transferrable annuity issued by a legal reserve life insurance company. In the event such benefits are to be paid directly from the Trust Fund, the Trustee shall segregate the Participant's Account from the Trust Fund (except as may otherwise be required with respect to variable or investment annuities) and shall hold the same in an interest-bearing savings account or other segregated assets of a similar nature providing security of principal and a stated rate of return. The Plan Administrator shall stipulate appropriate mortality tables to determine life expectancies, if relevant, with respect to any method of providing benefits enjoyed hereunder.

10.02 *Death Benefits.*

(a) *Commencement Date.*

(1) Should a Participant die prior to retirement so that benefits become payable pursuant to the provisions of Section 8.01 hereof, such benefits shall be paid as promptly as practicable after the Valuation Date coincident with or next following the date of the Participant's death.

(2) Benefits becoming payable pursuant to Section 8.02 hereof shall be paid in accordance with the terms of the annuity contract or policy in

force at the time of the Participant's death. If the Participant's retirement benefit was being paid directly from the Trust Fund, then the undistributed balance of the Participant's Account shall be paid as promptly as practicable after the Valuation Date coincident with or next following the date of the Participant's death.

(b) *Normal Form of Benefits.*

(1) Benefits payable pursuant to the provisions of Section 8.01 or, if there be no governing annuity contract in force, pursuant to section 8.02, shall be paid as a lump-sum unless the Participant requested otherwise in writing on forms provided by the Plan Administrator. If the Participant did file such a request with the Plan Administrator, and did not revoke such request prior to his death, the Plan Administrator shall attempt to comply with such request, but shall not be liable for failing to do so, and may in any event discharge all obligations of the fund by a lump-sum payment.

(2) Benefits payable pursuant to an annuity contract in force at the time of the Participant's death shall be paid in accordance with the terms of such contract.

10.03 *Vested Benefits.*

(a) *Commencement Date.* Benefits shall commence as of the Valuation Date of the Plan coincident with or next following the earliest of (1) the Participant's death, (2) the date determined pursuant to Section 10.01(a), or (3), if the Participant so elects, the date on which his Earliest Retirement Date occurs. Notwithstanding the foregoing, the Plan Administrator shall have the right to pay any benefit to which a Vested Participant is entitled pursuant to Article IX at any earlier date if—

(1) The Participant consents to such benefit distribution in writing, or

(2) the total value of the Participant's Account is less than (A) $1,750 or (B) such smaller sum as may be prescribed by the Secretary of Labor as the maximum amount that may be distributed without the Participant's consent.

(b) *Normal Form of Benefits.*

The normal form of benefit payment shall be as provided pursuant to the provisions of Section 10.01(b), subject to the provisions of Section 10.01(c), and, if an annuity starting before Normal Retirement Date, actuarially reduced to reflect the commencement of benefits prior to Normal Retirement Date.

10.04 *Post-Distribution Credits.*

In the event that after the purchase of an insurance or annuity contract there shall remain in the Participant's Account any funds, or any funds shall be subsequently credited thereto, such funds shall be paid to the Participant (or to the beneficiary of a deceased Participant) in cash within one (1) year. In the event that after a lump-sum distribution has been made, funds shall be credited to the Participant's Account, such funds shall be paid to the participant (or to the beneficiary of the deceased Participant) in cash within one (1) year. In the event that after an installment payout directly from the Trust Fund has commenced, funds are credited to the Retired (or deceased) Participant's Account, the Plan Administrator shall direct adjustments to the remaining installment payouts so as to include such credited sums, as nearly evenly as possible, in the remaining installment payments.

ARTICLE XI
The Plan Administrator

11.01 *Appointment and Tenure.*

The Plan Administrator shall consist of a committee of three (3) members who shall serve at the pleasure of the Board of Directors. Any committee member may be dismissed at any time, with or without cause, on ten (10) days' notice from the Board of Directors. Any Committee member may resign by delivering his or her written resignation to the Employer. Vacancies arising by the death, resignation or removal of a committee member shall be filed by the Board of Directors. If the Board fails to act, and in any event, until the Board so acts, the remaining members of the Committee may appoint an interim committee member to fill any vacancy occurring on the committee. If no person has been appointed to the committee, or if no person remains on the committee, the Employer shall be deemed to be the Plan Administrator.

11.02 *Meetings, Major Rule.*

Any and all acts of the Plan Administrator shall be by majority rule. The Plan Administrator may act by vote taken in a meeting, or by action taken in writing without the formality of convening a meeting.

11.03 *Delegation.*

The Plan Administrator may, by written majority decision, delegate to each or any one of its number or to the Secretary to it authority to sign any documents on its behalf, or to perform ministerial acts, but no person to whom such authority is delegated shall perform any act involving the exercise of any discretion without first obtaining the concurrent of a majority of the members of the committee, even though he or she alone may sign any document required by third parties. If at any time there will be less than three (3) members of the committee in office, pending the appointment of a successor to fill an existing vacancy, the remaining members shall have the authority to act as Plan Administrator.

The Plan Administrator shall elect one of their number to serve as chairman. The chairman shall preside at all meetings of the committee or shall delegate such responsibility to another committee member. The committee shall elect one person to serve as secretary to the committee. The secretary may, but need not, be a member of the committee. All third parties may rely on any communication signed by the secretary, acting as such, as an official communication from the plan Administrator.

11.04 *Authority and Responsibility of the Plan Administrator.*

The Plan Administrator shall have the following duties and responsibilities:

(a) to maintain and retain records relating to Plan Participants, former Participants and each of their beneficiaries;

(b) to prepare and furnish to Participants all information required under Federal law or provisions of this Plan to be furnished to them;

(c) to prepare and furnish to the Trustee sufficient employee data and the amount of contributions received from all sources so that the Trustee may maintain separate Accounts for Participants and make required payments of benefits;

(d) to prepare and file or publish with the Secretary of Labor, the Secretary of the Treasury, their delegates and all other appropriate government officials all reports and other information required under law to be so filed or published;

(e) to provide directions to the Trustee with respect to the purchase of life insurance, methods of benefit payment, valuations at dates other than Annual Valuation Dates and on all other matters where called for in the Plan or requested by the Trustee;

(f) to construe the provisions of the Plan, to correct defects therein and to supply omissions thereto;

(g) to engage assistants and professional advisers;

(h) to arrange for bonding; and

(i) to provide procedures for determination of claims for benefits, all as further set forth herein.

11.05 *Reporting and Disclosure.*

The Plan Administrator shall keep all individual and group records relating to Plan Participants, former Participants and beneficiaries, and all other records necessary for the proper operation of the Plan. Such records shall be made available to the Employer and to each Participant and beneficiary for examination during business hours except that a Participant or beneficiary shall examine only such records as pertain exclusively to the examining Participant or beneficiary and the Plan and Trust Agreement. The Plan Administrator shall prepare and shall file as required by law or regulation all reports, forms, documents and other items required by the Employee Retirement Income Security Act of 1974, the Internal Revenue Code, and every other relevant statute, each as amended, and all regulations thereunder. This provision shall not be construed as imposing upon the Plan Administrator the responsibility or authority for the preparation, preservation, publication or filing of any document required to be prepared, preserved or filed by the Trustee or by any other Named Fiduciary to whom such responsibilities are delegated by law or by this Plan.

11.06 *Construction of the Plan.*

The Plan Administrator shall take such steps as are considered necessary and appropriate to remedy any inequity that results from incorrect information received or communicated in good faith or as the consequence of an administrative error. The Plan Administrator shall interpret the Plan and shall determine the questions arising in the administration, interpretation and application of the Plan. He shall endeavor to act, whether by general rules or by the particular decisions, so as not to discriminate in favor of or against any person and so as to treat all persons in similar circumstances uniformly. The Plan Administrator shall correct any defect, reconcile any inconsistency or supply any omission with respect to this Plan.

11.07 *Engagement of Assistants and Advisers.*

The Plan Administrator shall have the right to hire, at the expense of the Employer, such professional assistants and consultants as he, in his sole discretion, deems necessary or advisable, including, but not limited to:

(1) investment managers and/or advisers;

(2) accountants;

(3) actuaries;

(4) attorneys;

(5) consultants;

(6) clerical and office personnel;

(7) medical practitioners.

To the extent that the costs for such assistants and advisers are not paid by the Employer, they shall be paid from the Trust Fund as an expense of the Fund at the direction of the Plan Administrator.

11.08 *Bonding.*

The Plan Administrator shall arrange for such bonding as is required by law, but no bonding in excess of the amount required by law shall be considered required by this Plan.

11.09 *Compensation of the Plan Administrator.*

The Plan Administrator shall serve without compensation for his services as such, but all expenses of the Plan Administrator shall be paid or reimbursed by the Employer, and if not so paid or reimbursed, shall be proper charges to the Trust Fund and shall be paid therefrom.

11.10 *Indemnification of the Plan Administrator.*

Each member of the committee constituting the Plan Administrator shall be indemnified by the Employer against expenses (other than amounts paid in settlement to which the Employer does not consent) reasonably incurred by him in connection with any action to which he may be a party by reason of his service as Plan Administrator except in relation to matters as to which he shall be adjudged in such action to be personally guilty of negligence or willful misconduct in the performance of his duties. The foregoing right to indemnification shall be in addition to such other rights as the committee member may enjoy as a matter of law or by reason of insurance coverage of any kind. Rights granted hereunder shall be in addition to and not in lieu of any rights to indemnification to which the committee member may be entitled pursuant to the by-laws of the Employer. Service on the committee as a Plan Administrator shall be deemed in partial fulfillment of the committee member's function as an employee, officer and/or director of the Employer, if he serves in such other capacity as well.

ARTICLE XII
Allocation of Authority and Responsibilities

12.01 *Authority and Responsibilities of Employer.*

The Employer, as Plan sponsor, shall serve as a "Named Fiduciary" having the following (and only the following) authority and responsibility:

(a) To establish and communicate to the Trustee a funding policy for the Plan;

(b) To appoint the Trustee and the Plan Administrator and to monitor each of their performances;

(c) To appoint an investment manager (or to refrain from such appointment), to monitor the performance of the investment manager so appointed, and to terminate such appointment. More than one investment manager may be appointed and in office at any time pursuant thereto;

(d) To communicate such information to the Plan Administrator and to the Trustee as each may need for the proper performance of its duties; and

(e) To provide channels and mechanisms through which the Plan Administrator and/or the Trustee can communicate with Participants and their beneficiaries.

In addition, the Employer shall perform such duties as are imposed by law or by regulation and shall serve as Plan Administrator in the absence of an appointed Plan Administrator.

12.02 *Authority and Responsibilities of the Plan Administrator.*

The Plan Administrator shall have the authority and responsibilities imposed by Article XI hereof. With respect to the said authority and responsibility, the Plan Administrator shall be a "Named Fiduciary," and as such, shall have no authority or responsibility other than as granted in this Plan, or as imposed as a matter of law.

12.03 *Authority and Responsibilities of the Trustee.*

The Trustee shall be the "Named Fiduciary" with respect to investment of Trust Fund assets and shall have the power and duties set forth in the Trust Agreement.

12.04 *Limitations on Obligations of Named Fiduciaries.*

No Named Fiduciary shall have authority or responsibility to deal with matters other than as delegated to it under this Plan, under the Trust Agreement, or by operation of law. A Named Fiduciary shall not in any event be liable for breach of fiduciary responsibility or obligation by another fiduciary (including Named Fiduciaries) if the responsibility or authority of the act or omission deemed to be a breach was not within the scope of the said Named Fiduciary's authority or delegated responsibility.

ARTICLE XIII
Claims Procedure

13.01 *Applications for Benefits.*

All applications for benefits shall be submitted in writing on forms provided by the Plan Administrator. Such application shall include all information and exhibits deemed necessary by the Plan Administrator to properly evaluate the merit of the claim for benefits and to make such determinations as are necessary with respect thereto.

13.02 *Appeals of Denied Claims for Benefits.*

In the event that any claim for benefits is denied in whole or in part, the Participant or beneficiary whose claim for benefits has been so denied shall be notified of such denial in writing by the Plan Administrator. The notice advising of the denial shall specify the reason or reasons for denial, make specific reference to pertinent Plan provisions, describe any additional material or information necessary for the claimant to perfect the claim (explaining why such material or information is needed), and shall advise the Participant or beneficiary, as the case may be, of the procedure for the appeal of such denial. All appeals shall be made by the following procedure:

(1) The Participant or beneficiary whose claim has been denied shall file with the Plan Administrator a notice of desire to appeal the denial. Such notice shall be filed within sixty (60) days of notification by the Plan Administrator of claim denial, shall be made in writing, and shall set forth all of the facts upon which the appeal is based. Appeals not timely filed shall be barred.

(2) The Plan Administrator shall, within thirty (30) days of receipt of the Participant's or beneficiary's notice of appeal, establish a hearing

date on which the Participant or beneficiary may make an oral presentation to the Named Appeals Fiduciary in support of his appeal. The Participant or beneficiary shall be given not less than ten (10) days notice of the date set for the hearing.

(3) The Named Appeals Fiduciary shall consider the merits of the claimant's written and oral presentations, the merits of any facts or evidence in support of the denial of benefits, and such other facts and circumstances as the Named Appeals Fiduciary shall deem relevant. If the claimant elects not to make an oral presentation, such election shall not be deemed adverse to his or her interest, and the Named Appeals Fiduciary shall proceed as set forth below as though an oral presentation of the contents of the claimant's written presentation has been made.

(4) The Named Appeals Fiduciary shall render a determination upon the appealed claim which determination shall be accompanied by a written statement as to the reasons therefor. The determination so rendered by the Named Appeals Fiduciary shall be binding upon all parties.

13.03 *Appointment of the Named Appeals Fiduciary.*

The Named Appeals Fiduciary shall be the person or persons named as such by the board of directors, or if no such person or persons be named, then the person or persons named by the Plan Administrator as the Named Appeals Fiduciary. Named Appeals Fiduciaries may at any time be removed by the board of directors, and any Named Fiduciary named by the Plan Administrator may be removed by him. All such removals may be with or without cause and shall be effective on the date stated in the notice of removal. The Named Appeals Fiduciary, if there be more than one determining the merits of any appeal, shall act by a majority vote on each matter coming before it. The Named Appeals Fiduciary shall be a "Named Fiduciary" within the meaning of the Employee Income Security Act of 1974, and, unless appointed to other fiduciary responsibilities, shall have no authority, responsibility or liability with respect to any matter other than the proper discharge of the functions of the Named Appeals Fiduciary as set forth herein.

ARTICLE XIV
Amendment, Termination, Mergers and Consolidations of the Plan

14.01 *Amendment.*

The provisions of this Plan may be amended at any time and from time to time by the Employer, provided, however, that:

(a) no amendment shall increase the duties or liabilities of the Plan Administrator or of the Trustee without the consent of such party;

(b) no amendment shall deprive any Participant or beneficiary of a deceased Participant of any of the benefits to which he is entitled under this Plan with respect to contributions previously made, nor shall any amendment decrease the balance in any Participant's Account;

(c) no amendment shall provide for the use of funds or assets held to provide benefits under this Plan other than for the benefit of Employees and their beneficiaries or to provide that funds may revert to the Employer.

Each amendment shall be approved by the board of directors by resolution. Notwithstanding the foregoing, any amendment necessary to initially qualify this Plan under Section 401(a) of the Internal Revenue Code may be made without the further approval of the board of directors if signed by the proper officers of the Employer.

14.02 *Plan Termination.*

(a) *Right Reserved.* While it is the Employer's intention to continue the Plan indefinitely in operation, the right is, nevertheless, reserved to terminate the Plan in whole or in part. Termination or partial termination of the Plan shall result in full or immediate vesting in each Participant of the entire amount standing to his credit in his Account, including his Employer Contribution Account, and there shall not thereafter by any forfeitures with respect to any Participant for any reason. Plan termination or partial termination shall be effective as of the date specified by resolution of the board of directors.

(b) *Effect on Retired Persons, etc.* Termination or partial termination of the Plan shall have no effect upon payment of installments and benefits to former Participants, their beneficiaries and their estates, whose benefit payments commenced prior to Plan termination or partial termination. The Trustee shall retain sufficient assets to complete any such payments, and shall have the right, upon direction by the Employer, to purchase annuity contracts to assure the completion of such payments or to pay the value of the remaining payments in a lump-sum distribution.

(c) *Effect on Remaining Participants, etc.* The Employer shall instruct the Trustee either (1) to continue to manage and administer the assets of the Trust for the benefit of the Participants and their beneficiaries pursuant to the terms and provisions of the Trust Agreement, or (2) to pay over to each Participant (and vested former Participant) the value of his vested interest, and to thereupon dissolve the trust.

14.03 *Permanent Discontinuance of Employer Contributions.*

While it is the Employer's intention to make substantial and recurrent contributions to the Trust Fund pursuant to the provisions of this Plan, the right is, nevertheless, reserved to at any time permanently discontinue Employer contributions. Such permanent discontinuance shall be established by resolution of the board of directors and shall have the effect of a termination of the Plan, as set forth in Section 14.02, except that the Trustee shall not have authority to dissolve the Trust Fund except upon adoption of a further resolution by the board of directors to the effect that the Plan is terminated and upon receipt from the Employer of instructions to dissolve the Trust Fund pursuant to Section 14.02(c) hereof.

14.04 *Suspension of Employer Contributions.*

The Employer shall have the right at any time, and from time to time, to suspend Employer contributions to the Trust Fund pursuant to this Plan. Such suspension shall have no effect on the operation of the Plan except as set forth below:

(a) If the board of directors determines by resolution that such suspension shall be permanent, a permanent discontinuance of contributions will be deemed to have occurred as of the date of such resolution or such earlier date as is therein specified.

(b) If such suspension continues uninterrupted for five (5) consecutive years during which the Employer had net income out of which contributions could have been made which would have been deductible and would have otherwise satisfied the contingencies and conditions upon which such contributions are made under this Plan, a permanent discontinuance of contributions will be imputed. In such case, the permanent discontinuance shall be deemed to have occurred on the earlier of:

(1) the date specified by resolution of the board of directors or established as a matter of equity by the Plan Administrator, or

(2) the last day of the Plan Year in which there occurred the fifth consecutive failure of the Employer to make contributions as set forth above.

In determining whether or not five years of failure to contribute have occurred, there shall be omitted from such calculations any years in which the Employer was unable to contribute by reason of lack of net income or in which no contribution was made because if such contribution had been made, it would have been refundable to the Employer pursuant to Section 3.03 and/or 3.04 of this Plan.

14.05 *Mergers and Consolidations of Plans.*

In the event of any merger or consolidation with, or transfer of assets or liabilities to, any other plan, each Participant in the event of termination shall have a normal retirement benefit in the surviving or transferee plan (determined as if such plan were then terminated immediately after such merger, etc.) that is equal to or greater than the normal retirement benefit he would have been entitled to receive immediately before such merger, etc. in the Plan in which he was then a Participant (had such Plan been terminated at that time). For the purposes hereof, former Participants and beneficiaries shall be considered Participants.

ARTICLE XV
Miscellaneous Provisions

15.01 *Non-Alienation of Benefits.*

(a) *General.* Except as provided in paragraph (b) of this Section 15.01, none of the payments, benefits or rights of any Participant or beneficiary shall be subject to any claim of any creditor, and, in particular, to the fullest extent permitted by law, all such payments, benefits and rights shall be free from attachment, garnishment, trustee's process, or any other legal or equitable process available to any creditor of such Participant or beneficiary. Except as provided in paragraph (b) of this Section 15.01, no Participant or beneficiary shall have the right to alienate, anticipate, commute, pledge, encumber or assign any of the benefits or payments which he may expect to receive, contingently or otherwise, under this Plan, except the right to designate a beneficiary or beneficiaries as hereinbefore provided.

(b) *Exception.* All loans made by the Trustee to any Participant or beneficiary shall be secured by a pledge of the borrower's interest in the Trust Fund, which pledge shall give the Trustee a first lien in such interest to the extent of the entire outstanding amount of such loan, unpaid interest thereon, and all costs of collection.

15.02 *No Contract of Employment.*

Neither the establishment of the Plan, nor any modification thereof, nor the creation of any fund, trust or account, nor the payment of any benefits shall be construed as giving any Participant or Employee, or any person whomsoever, the right to be retained in the service of the Employer, and all Participants and other Employees shall remain subject to discharge to the same extent as if the Plan had never been adopted.

15.03 *Severability of Provision.*

If any provision of this Plan shall be held invalid or unenforceable, such invalidity or unenforceability shall not affect any other provisions hereof, and this Plan shall be construed and enforced as if such provisions had not been included.

15.04 *Heirs, Assigns and Personal Representatives.*

This Plan shall be binding upon the heirs, executors, administrators, successors and assigns of the parties, including each Participant and beneficiary, present and future.

15.05 *Headings and Captions.*

The headings and captions herein are provided for reference and convenience only, shall not be considered part of the Plan, and shall not be employed in the construction of the Plan.

15.06 *Gender and Number.*

Except where otherwise clearly indicated by context, the masculine and the neuter shall include the feminine and the neuter, the singular shall include the plural, and vice versa.

15.07 *Controlling Law.*

This Plan shall be construed and enforced according to the laws of the Commonwealth of Pennsylvania to the extent not preempted by Federal law, which shall otherwise control.

15.08 *Funding Policy.*

The Plan Administrator, in consultation with the Employer, shall establish and communicate to the Trustee a funding policy consistent with the objectives of this Plan and of the corresponding Trust. Such policy will be in writing and shall have due regard for the emerging liquidity needs of the Trust. Such funding policy shall also state the general investment objectives of the Trust and the philosophy upon which maintenance of the Plan is based.

15.09 *Title to Assets.*

No Participant or beneficiary shall have any right to, or interest in, any assets of the Trust Fund upon termination of his employment or otherwise, except as provided from time to time under this Plan, and then only to the extent of the benefits payable under the Plan to such Participant or out of the assets of the Trust Fund. All payments of benefits as provided for in this Plan shall be made from the assets of the Trust Fund, and neither the Employer nor any other person shall be liable therefore in any manner.

15.10 *Payments to Minors, etc.*

Any benefit payable to or for the benefit of a minor, an incompetent person or other person incapable of receipting therefore shall be deemed paid when paid to such person's guardian or to the party providing or reasonably appearing to provide for the care of such person, and such payment shall fully discharge the Trustee, the Plan Administrator, the Employer and all other parties with respect thereto.

IN WITNESS WHEREOF, and as evidence of the adoption of this Plan, Employer has cause the same to be executed by its duly authorized officers and its corporate seal to be affixed this 1 day of May, 1976.

ATLAS CONSTRUCTION CO., INC.

By:_____
President

(CORPORATE SEAL)

Attest:_____
Secretary

ATLAS CONSTRUCTION CO., INC.
PROFIT SHARING TRUST AGREEMENT

(Amended and Restated as of October 1, 1976)

Gilbert M. Cantor, Esquire
Sixth Floor
1700 Sansom Street
Philadelphia, Pennsylvania 19103

ATLAS CONSTRUCTION CO., INC.
PROFIT SHARING TRUST AGREEMENT

Table of Contents

ATLAS CONSTRUCTION CO., INC.
PROFIT SHARING TRUST AGREEMENT
(Amended and Restated as of October 1, 1976)

This Agreement is made as of the 1st day of May 1976, by and among Atlas Construction Co., Inc., a Pennsylvania corporation, (hereinafter called "Company," which term shall include all successors thereto which have adopted the Atlas Construction Co., Inc. Profit Sharing Plan and agreed to be bound by this Trust Agreement) and John Smith, as Trustee.

PREAMBLE

WHEREAS, Company has this day adopted a profit-sharing plan for its employees (hereinafter called the "Plan"); and

WHEREAS, under the Plan, funds will be contributed to the Trustees by the Company to be held as a trust fund for the benefit of the participating employees (hereinafter called the "Participants"); and

WHEREAS, Company has appointed a Plan Administrator as provided in the Plan; and

WHEREAS, Company desires the Trustees to hold and invest such funds, and to pay the benefits contemplated by the Plan, and the Trustees are willing to do so under the terms provided herein;

NOW, THEREFORE, in consideration of the premises and the mutual covenants herein contained, it is agreed by and between the Company and the Trustees as follows:

ARTICLE I
Establishment of the Trust

1.1 The Company hereby establishes with the Trustees a trust consisting of such sums of money or property as shall from time to time be paid to the Trustees under the Plan, and such earnings, profits, increments, additions and appreciation thereto and thereon as may accrue from time to time. All such sums of money, all investments made therewith or proceeds thereof, and all earnings, profits, increments, appreciation and additions thereto and thereon, less the payments which shall have been made by the Trustees, as authorized herein, to carry out the Plan, are referred to herein as the "Fund."

1.2 The Trustees shall not be responsible for the collection of any funds required by the Plan to be paid by the Company to the Trustees.

1.3 It shall be the duty of the Trustees hereunder:

(a) To hold, to invest, to reinvest, to manage, and to administer the Fund for the exclusive benefit of the Participants and their beneficiaries in accordance with the provisions of this Agreement, and

(b) From time to time, on the written direction of the Plan Administrator, to make payments out of the Fund to such persons, in such manner, in such amounts, and for such purposes as may be specified in such written direction. The Trustees shall be under no liability for any payment made by them pursuant to such a direction.

1.4 Except as hereinafter provided in Section 1.5, the Company shall not have the right, title, interest, claim or demand whatsoever in or to the Fund held by the Trustees, other than the right to a proper application thereof and accounting therefor by the Trustees as provided herein, nor shall any funds revert to the Company.

1.5 Neither the provisions of Section 1.4 hereof nor any other provision of this instrument or of the Plan shall prohibit any of the following transactions, each of which is specifically authorized hereby, to the extent permitted by Section 403(c) of the Employee Retirement Income Security Act of 1974:

(a) The return to Company of all or any part of one or more contributions made by Company by reason of mistake of fact if such return is made within one (1) year after payment of such contribution;

(b) The return to Company of all or any part of one or more contributions made by Company if all of the following conditions apply: (i) the contribution was conditioned on the qualification of the Plan under Section 401, 403(a) or 405(a) of the Internal Revenue Code of 1954 (or successor provisions of that or other statutes of similar intent), (ii) the Plan is found not to so qualify, and (iii) the contribution(s) is/are returned to Company within one (1) year of the date of denial of qualification of the Plan; and

(c) The return to Company of any contribution for which deduction is wholly or partially disallowed under Section 404 of the Internal Revenue Code of 1954 (or successor provisions of that or other statutes of similar intent), to the extent of such disallowance, if (i) the contribution, when made, was conditioned upon its deductibility and (ii) the return of the contribution occurs within one (1) year after the disallowance of the deduction.

1.6 Whenever payments to a Participant or beneficiary are to be made by the Trustees in installments pursuant to the directions of the Plan Administrator, the Trustees shall withdraw from the Fund the amount to which such Participant or his beneficiary is entitled under the Plan and deposit the same, less such amounts as the Trustees deem necessary for current payments, in their names in such savings banks or institutions as may be selected by the Trustees with the approval of the Plan Administrator. The installments shall thereafter be withdrawn from such savings banks or institutions by the Trustees in such amounts as the Trustees deem necessary for current payments due to such Participant or his beneficiary. All interest received or accrued on such amount shall be added to the principal thereof and included in the payments made to the Participant or his beneficiary.

1.7 Whenever payments to a Participant or beneficiary are to be made in the form of an annuity based upon one or more lives or life expectancies, the Trustees shall have the option of making the required payments directly from the Fund as and when they become due or at any time purchasing from any legal reserve insurance company a single premium or other annuity contract providing for the payment of the benefits.

ARTICLE II
Investment of the Fund

2.1 The Trustees shall invest and reinvest the principal and income of the Trust and keep the same invested without distinction between principal and income. The selection and retention or disposition of any investment shall be determined by the Trustees, who shall have the exclusive authority to manage and control the assets of the fund except to the extent that (a) the Plan provides that the Trustees are subject to the investment direction of a named fiduciary or (b) the authority to acquire, manage, retain and dispose of assets to the Fund has been delegated to an appointed investment manager.

2.2 The Trustees shall have the following powers in addition to the powers customarily vested in Trustees by law and in no way in derogation thereof:

(a) With any cash at any time held by them, to purchase or subscribe for any authorized investment, and to retain such authorized investment in trust.

(b) To sell for cash or on credit, convert, redeem, exchange for another authorized investment, or otherwise dispose of, any authorized investment at any time held by them.

(c) To retain uninvested all or any part of the Fund and to deposit the same in any banking or savings institution.

(d) To exercise any option appurtenant to any authorized investment in which the Fund is invested for conversion thereof into another authorized investment, or to exercise any rights to subscribe for additional authorized investments, and to make all necessary payments therefor.

(e) To join in, consent to, dissent from, oppose, or deposit in connection with, the reorganization, recapitalization, consolidation, sale, merger, foreclosure, or readjustment of the finances of any corporations or properties in which the Fund may be invested, or the sale, mortgage, pledge or lease of any such property or the property of any such corporation upon such terms and conditions as they may deem wise; to do any act (including the exercise of options, making of agreements or subscriptions, and payment of expenses, assessments, or subscriptions) which may be deemed necessary or advisable in connection therewith; and to accept any authorized investment which may be issued in or as a result of any such proceedings, and thereafter to hold the same.

(f) To vote, in person or by general or limited proxy, at any election of any corporation in which the Fund is invested, and similarly to exercise, personally or by a general or limited power of attorney, any right appurtenant to any authorized investment held in the Fund.

(g) To sell, either at public or private sale, option to sell, mortgage, lease for a term of years less than or continuing beyond the possible date of the termination of the Trust created hereunder, partition or exchange any real property which may from time to time or at any time constitute a portion of the Fund, for such prices and upon such terms as they may deem best, and to make execute and deliver to the purchasers thereof good and sufficient deeds of conveyance thereof and all assignments, transfers and other legal instruments, either necessary or convenient for passing the title and ownership thereof to the purchaser, free and discharged of all trusts and without liability on the part of such purchasers to see to the proper application of the purchase price.

(h) To repair, alter or improve any buildings which may be on any real estate forming part of the Fund or to erect entirely new structures thereon.

(i) To renew or extend or participate in the renewal or extension of any mortgage, upon such terms as may be deemed advisable, and to agree to a reduction in the rate of interest on any mortgage or to any other modification or change in the terms of any mortgage or of any guarantee pertaining thereto, in any manner and to any extent that may be deemed advisable for the protection of the Fund or the preservation of the value of the investment; to waive any default, whether in the performance of any convenant or condition of any mortgage or in the performance of any guarantee, or to enforce any such default in such manner and to such extent as may be deemed advisable; to exercise and enforce any and all rights of foreclosure, to bid on property in foreclosure, to take a deed in lieu of foreclosure with or without paying a consideration therefor, and in connection therewith to release the obligation on the bond secured by such mortgage; and to exercise and enforce in any action, suit or proceeding at law or in equity any rights or remedies in respect to any mortgage or guarantee.

(j) To purchase authorized investments at a premium or discount.

(k) To employ suitable agents, actuaries, accountants, investment advisors or managers and counsel and to pay their reasonable expenses and compensation.

(l) To borrow, raise or lend moneys, for the purposes of the Trust, in such amounts and upon such terms and conditions as the Trustees in their absolute discretion may deem advisable, and for any such moneys so borrowed to issue their promissory note as Trustees and to secure the repayment thereof by pledging or mortgaging all or any part of the Fund. No person lending money to the Trustees shall be bound to see to the application of the money lent or to inquire into the validity, expediency or propriety of such borrowing.

(m) To cause any investment in the Fund to be registered in, or transferred into, their names as Trustees or the name of their nominee or nominees or to retain them unregistered or in form permitting transfer by delivery, but the books and records of the Trustees shall at all times show that all such investments are part of the Fund, and the Trustees shall be fully responsible for any misappropriation or defalcation in respect to any investment held by their nominee or held in unregistered form and shall cause the indicia of ownership to be maintained within the jurisdiction of the district courts of the United States.

(n) To do all acts which they may deem necessary or proper and to exercise any and all powers of the trustees under this Agreement upon such terms and conditions which they may deem are for the best interests of the Fund.

(o) To apply for, purchase, hold, transfer, pay premiums on, surrender, and exercise all incidents of ownership of any life insurance, retirement income or annuity contract which they are directed to purchase by the Plan Administrator, provided, however, that if Trustees shall borrow against the cash surrender values of any insurance contracts for the general purposes of the Fund, they shall borrow and repay the amounts so borrowed on a pro rata basis so as to preclude discrimination.

2.3 "Authorized Investment" as used in this Article II shall mean bonds, debentures, notes, or other evidences of indebtedness; stocks (regardless of class), or other evidences of ownership, in any corporation, common trust fund, mutual investment fund, investment company, association, or business trust; life insurance, retirement income or annuity contracts; and real and personal property of all kinds, including leaseholds on improved and unimproved real estate; provided, however, that as long as the Fund is invested in a common trust fund available only to pension and profit-sharing trusts which meet the requirements of Section 401(a) of the Internal Revenue Code of 1954 or corresponding provisions of subsequent income tax laws of the United States, such common trust fund shall constitute an integrel part of this Trust and of the Plan. "Authorized investments" shall not be limited to that class of investments which are defined as legal investments for trust funds under the laws of the Commonwealth of Pennsylvania or of any other jurisdiction. Obligations or securities of the Company shall not be excluded from the term "authorized investments," provided, however, that this provision shall not be construed as purporting to exempt employer securities (or employer real estate) from any limitation of investment imposed thereon by federal statute.

2.4 (a) The Trustees shall have the right, but not the obligation, to establish on behalf of any Participant or former Participant at their request one or more separate, segregated account(s) in which to place, hold and invest (i) funds received as voluntary or required contributions from the Participant under the Plan, (ii) funds received from the Participant or from the trustee(s) of any other qualified retirement plan as a distribution from such qualified retirement plan (commonly called a "rollover") if such funds are certified to be the full amount standing to the Participant's credit under such other plan exclusive of the Participant's contributions thereto or (iii) the value of the Participant's vested, accrued benefit (or account balance) in the case of any who has ceased to be an Active Participant. The amount so segregated shall be invested in passbook savings accounts, certificates of deposit or other interest bearing assets, and the interest generated thereby shall be credited to the segregated account by which generated.

(b) The Trustees shall have the right, but not the obligation, upon the request of any Participant, to apply all or a portion of that Participant's segregated account to the payment of premiums on ordinary life insurance contracts provided that the Trustees are designated the sole owners and beneficiaries thereof, and provided that any dividends paid with respect to such contracts for any period during which premiums are so paid shall be credited to the Participant's segregated account from which the premiums were so paid.

(c) The provisions of paragraph (b) of this Section 2.4 shall not be construed as giving to any Participant the right to direct the purchase or maintenance of life insurance contracts except as the Trustees grant such option as a privilege, nor shall the Trustees grant such option except within such limitations as may be applicable to the purchase of life insurance by qualified plans.

(d) Segregated accounts shall not be considered a part of the Fund for the purpose of allocating earnings, accretions and losses generated by those assets not held in segregated accounts.

(e) Any active Participant who has attained age 60 may request that the net asset value of his account be established as a segregated account as of the Valuation Date next following (or coincident with) the later of his attainment of age 60 or his attainment of full vesting. In the event that such a request is made and the Trustees approve thereof, the entire interest of the Participant under the Plan shall be established as a segregated account to be invested as set forth in paragraph (a) and (b) of this Section 2.4. All amounts thereafter allocable to the Participant, regardless of source, shall be credited to such segregated account and all benefits payable to the Participant and his beneficiaries shall be paid from the segregated account(s) held by the Trustees for the benefit of the Participant.

ARTICLE III
Accounts to be Kept and Rendered by the Trustees

3.1 The Trustees shall keep accurate and detailed accounts of all investments, receipts and disbursements and other transactions hereunder, including such specific records as shall be required by law and such additional records as may be agreed upon in writing between the Plan

Administrator and the Trustees. All accounts, books and records relating thereto shall be open to inspection and audit by any person or persons designated by the Plan Administrator or the Company at all reasonable times.

3.2 Within ninety (90) days following the close of each year of the Plan or the receipt of the Company's contribution for such year, whichever is the later, and within ninety (90) days after the effective date of the removal or resignation of the Trustees, and the Trustees shall file with the Plan Administrator a written account, setting forth all investments, receipts and disbursements, and other transactions effected by them during such year of the Plan or during the period from the close of the last preceding year of the Plan to the date of such removal or resignation, including a description of all securities and investments purchased and sold with the cost of net proceeds of such purchases or sales, and showing all cash, securities and other property held at the end of such year or as of the date or removal or resignation, as the case may be. The Trustees shall include in such report a valuation of the Fund in accordance with Section 3.4. Neither the Company nor the Plan Administrator nor any other person shall have the right to demand or to be entitled to any further or different accounting by the Trustees, except as may be required by statute or by regulations published by federal government agencies with respect to reporting and disclosure.

3.3 Except with respect to alleged breaches of fiduciary responsibility under the Employee Retirement Income Security Act of 1974 (and amendments thereto), upon the expiration of ninety (90) days from the date of filing such annual or other account, the Trustees shall be forever released and discharged from any liability or accountability to anyone as respects the propriety of their acts or transactions shown in such account, except with respect to any acts or transactions as to which the plan Administrator shall within such ninety-day period file with the Trustees a written statement claiming negligence or other breach of fiduciary duty on the part of the Trustees. In the event such a statement is filed, the Trustees shall, unless the matter is compromised by agreement between the Plan Administrator and the Trustees, file their account covering the period from the date of the last annual account to which no objection was made, in any court of competent jurisdiction for audit or adjudication. With respect to alleged breaches under the Employee Retirement Income Security Act of 1974 (and amendments thereto), the Trustees shall be entitled to rely upon the statements of limitations set forth therein.

3.4 The Trustees shall maintain one or more separate accounts on their books for each Participant in the Plan and shall allocate to such Participants' accounts the Company's contributions to the Fund, the contributions made by each Participant (including rollover contributions), if any (such Participants' contributions to be credited directly to the accounts of the respective contributing Participants), and the net income and losses of the Fund and any forfeitures as provided in the Plan. The Trustees shall determine the fair market value of the Fund and of each Participant's interest therein as of the 30th day of September in each year, commencing with the year 1976, and at such other times as may be necessary under the Plan.

ARTICLE IV
The Trustees

4.1 The Trustees accept the Trust hereby created and agree to perform the duties hereby required of them, subject, however, to the following conditions:

(a) The Trustees shall incur no liability to anyone for any action taken pursuant to a direction, request or approval given by the Plan Administrator or by any other party to whom authority to give such directions, requests or approvals is delegated under the powers conferred upon the Plan Administrator, or such other party under the Plan or this Trust Agreement. Any such direction, request, or approval shall be evidenced by delivery to the Trustees of a statement in writing signed by the authorized initiator thereof.

(b) The Trustees shall receive as compensation for their services such amounts as may be agreed upon at the time of execution of this Agreement, subject to change at any time and from time to time by agreement between the Plan Administrator and the Trustees. The Trustees' compensation shall be paid by the Company. Any other proper expense of the Trustees for the Fund (unless payable out of the Trustees' compensation) including all real and personal property taxes, income taxes, transfer taxes and other taxes of any and all kinds whatsoever that may be levied or assessed under existing or future laws of any jurisdiction upon or in respect of the Trust hereby created, or any money, property or securities forming a part thereof shall be paid out of the Fund.

(c) The Trustees shall not be answerable for any action taken pursuant to any direction, consent, request, or other paper or document on the belief that the same is genuine and signed by the proper person if such direction, consent, request or other paper or document relates to a matter with respect to which the purported initiator or signatory has authority under the Plan or Trust.

(d) The Trustees shall be indemnified by the Company against their prospective costs, expenses, and liability in connection with all litigation relating to the Plan, the Trust Agreement or the Fund, except where the litigation is occasioned by the fault of the Trustees or involves a question of their fault.

(e) Nothing in this Agreement shall preclude the purchase by or for the Trustees of one or more policies of insurance to protect each Trustee from liability for breach of fiduciary or co-fiduciary responsibility, provided, however, that if such insurance shall be purchased by the Fund utilizing the assets thereof to pay premiums, such insurance must permit recourse by the insuror against the Trustee in the case of a breach by that Trustee of his fiduciary responsibilities.

4.2 Upon the appointment of the Plan Administrator and upon any change in the Plan Administrator, the Company shall advise the Trustees in writing thereof, and the Trustees shall be fully protected in assuming that there has been no change until so advised by the Company.

4.3 Company may, by action of the board of directors of company, from time to time change the number of Trustees hereunder and appoint additional Trustees to fill the vacancies caused by any such increase. The Trustees may be members of the board of directors of the company, officers or employees of the company, or any other person.

4.4 Any Trustee acting hereunder may resign at any time by giving sixty (60) days' written notice to the Plan Administrator and may be removed at any time, with or without cause, by the board of directors of Company. Upon the death, resignation or removal of any Trustee, a successor Trustee may be appointed by the board of directors of Company, and such successor Trustee, upon qualifying as such by delivering a written acceptance of such appointment to the Plan Administrator, shall, without further act, become vested with all the rights, powers, discretion and duties of his predecessor Trustee, with the same effect as if he had originally been named as a Trustee herein.

4.5 The Trustees may act by a majority of their number, either at a meeting, or by writing, telegram, cablegram or other communication without a meeting. The Trustees may elect a chairman from among their number and may appoint a secretary who need not be a trustee. Any act of the Trustees shall be sufficiently evidenced if certified by not less than a majority of the trustees then serving or by the person then holding the office of secretary. Any trustee may authorize any other Trustee to act in his stead and on his behalf in his absence.

4.6 No person shall serve or continue to serve as a Trustee in violation of Section 411 of the Employee Retirement Income Security Act of 1974.

4.7 Each Trustee shall be bonded to the extent required by law, and the premiums for such bonds shall be treated as expenses of the Plan.

ARTICLE V
Delegation of Duties and Responsibilities

5.1 With the consent of the Plan Administrator, the Trustees may appoint one or more investment managers or investment advisors to manage, acquire or dispose of assets of the Fund. Such managers and/or advisors appointed by the Trustees shall be subject to dismissal by the Trustees, and the fees charged by such person for their services shall be considered expenses, of the Fund. The Trustees shall be authorized to enter into such agreements with such investment managers and advisors as they deem necessary or desirable, included, but not limited to, conpensation agreements.

5.2 The Trustees may enter into a written agreement among themselves, subject to the approval of the Plan Administrator, to allocate specific responsibilities, obligations and duties among themselves, in which event those Trustees to whom a specific responsibility, obligation or duty has not been delegated shall be free from liability for breach of the same by a co-fiduciary to the fullest extent permitted by law.

5.3 To the extent that any Participant or beneficiary exercised control over the assets in his account(s), the Trustees shall not be liable for any loss or by reason of any breach which results from each Participant's or beneficiary's exercise of control.

ARTICLE VI
Concerning Insurance Companies

6.1 If, on any occasion as provided in the Plan, the Trustees shall be directed to purchase a life insurance, retirement income or annuity contract from an insurance company, no such insurance company shall be deemed a party to this Agreement. It shall have no obligation to determine that any person with respect to whom the Trustees make an application for a contract is, in fact, eligible for benefits or participation under the Plan, nor shall the insurer have any obligation to determine any fact, the determination of which is necessary or desirable for the proper issuance of such contracts, and it shall be fully protected in acting upon any advice, representation or other instrument executed by the Trustees. In no event shall the insurer be responsible for any lack or failure of proper authority in the establishment or maintenance thereof. The responsibilities of the insurer shall be limited to the terms of its policies. Notice of modification, change or termination of this Agreement shall not be effective notice to the insurer until actual receipt thereof at its home office. The insurer may expect this Trust to continue in force as is, and the named Trustees to continue as the Trustees of this Trust until notified otherwise in writing at its home office.

6.2 A certification in writing to the insurer by the Trustees or Plan

Administrator as to the occurrence of any event contemplated by the Trust Agreement or the Plan shall constitute conclusive evidence of such occurrence, and the insurer shall be fully protected in accepting and relying upon such certification and shall incur no liability or responsibility for so doing.

6.3 The insurer shall not be responsible to see that any action taken by the Trustees with respect to any contract is authorized by the terms of the Trust Agreement or the Plan. Any change made or action taken by the insurer under any contract upon the written direction of the Trustees shall fully discharge such insurer from all liability with respect thereto, and the insurer shall not be obligated to see to the distribution or further application of any moneys paid by it to the Trustees or in accordance with the written direction of the Trustees.

ARTICLE VII
Amendments to Trust Agreement–Discontinuance of Plan

7.1 The provisions of this Agreement may be amended at any time and from time to time by the Company provided that:

(a) No such amendment shall be effective unless the Plan and the Trust Agreement, as so amended, shall be for the exclusive benefit of the employees of the Company or their respective beneficiaries.

(b) No such amendment shall operate to deprive a Participant of any rights or benefits irrevocably vested in him under the Plan or Trust Agreement prior to such amendment.

(c) No such amendment which may effect the Trustees shall be effective until the Trustees have consented thereto.

(d) Each such amendment shall be effective when adopted by the board of directors of company, and filed with the Trustees, except that where the consent of the Trustees is required, any such amendment shall not become effective until the Trustees have given their consent by approving the copy of the amendment filed with them.

7.2 In the event of termination of this Agreement, the Trustees shall continue to hold the Fund in trust to be applied and distributed in accordance with the Plan.

ARTICLE VIII
Internal Revenue Code of 1954 Initial Non-Qualification

8.1 Anything in this Trust to the contrary notwithstanding, if the Internal Revenue Service determines that this Trust does not initially meet the requirements of Section 501(a) of the Internal Revenue Code of 1954 (as part of a Plan meeting the requirements of Section 401(a) thereof):

(a) The Company and the Trustees shall execute and deliver an agreement amending this Trust so that it will meet such requirements, if they both approve such amendment, or the Company shall execute an agreement amending the Plan so that it will meet such requirements, but

(b) If the Company or the Trustees notify the other that it does not approve such amendment of the Trust or the Company notifies the Trustees that it does not approve a required amendment of the Plan:

(1) This Trust shall be cancelled as of, and shall be null and void from, the date of the execution and delivery hereof;

(2) The rights and interests of all Participants hereunder shall be cancelled and terminated as of such date; and

(3) The Trustees shall:

(i) surrender any policies purchased to the insurer for cancellation and recover the premiums less the insurer's charge for cancellation, and

(ii) pay and deliver to the Company all amounts so recovered from the insurer and all other moneys and property then constituting the assets of the Trust, except for contributions that may have been made by the Participants, which contributions shall be returned to the respective contributing Participants.

ARTICLE IX
Miscellaneous Provisions

9.1 Any person dealing with the Trustees may rely upon a copy of this Agreement and any amendments thereto, certified to be a true and correct copy by the secretary of the trustees.

9.2 Other than as provided in Section 1.5 hereof, in no circumstances, whether upon amendment or termination of this Agreement, or otherwise, shall any part of the Fund be used for or diverted to any purposes other than the exclusive benefit of employees of the Company who are Participants under the Plan, or their beneficiaries.

9.3 The Plan and each provision thereof is hereby incorporated by reference and shall, for all purposes, be deemed a part of this Trust Agreement, provided, however, that in the event of any conflict between the provisions of the Plan and the Trust Agreement, the latter shall control.

9.4 The term "Plan" whenever used herein shall mean the Plan as amended from time to time, and the Company will cause a copy of any amendment or a copy of the Plan, as amended, revised or changed, in any way and from time to time to be delivered to the Trustees for incorporation herein by reference.

9.5 Company shall have the right, on behalf of all its employees at any time having any interest in the Fund, to approve any action taken or omitted by the Trustees.

9.6 Any term used herein which is defined in the Plan shall be considered to have the same meaning as in the Plan unless the contrary is clearly indicated.

9.7 This Agreement shall be construed, enforced and regulated under federal law, and to the extent (if any) not preempted thereby, under the laws of the Commonwealth of Pennsylvania. The Trust created hereby shall be known as the Atlas Construction Co., Inc. Profit Sharing Trust.

IN WITNESS WHEREOF, the Company has caused this Agreement to be executed and its corporate seal to be hereunto affixed and attested and the Trustees have hereunto set their hands and seals as of the day and year first above written.

ATLAS CONSTRUCTION CO., INC.

By:_____
                                        President

(CORPORATE SEAL)

Attest:_____
                                        Secretary

WITNESS:

_____ (SEAL)
John Smith, Trustee

COMMONWEALTH OF PENNSYLVANIA :

                                                 : SS.

COUNTY OF PHILADELPHIA

On the 1st day of May, 1976, before me, the subscriber, a Notary Public in and for the Commonwealth of Pennsylvania, County of Philadelphia, personally appeared John Smith, the Trustee above-named, and in due form of law acknowledged the foregoing Trust Agreement to be his voluntary act and deed and desired the same might be recorded as such.

WITNESS my hand and notarial seal the day and year aforesaid.

_____

Notary Public

COMMONWEALTH OF PENNSYLVANIA   :
                                                          : SS.
COUNTY OF PHILADELPHIA

On the 1st day of May, 1976, before me, the subscriber, a Notary Public, personally appeared Mary Smith as Secretary of ATLAS CONSTRUCTION CO., INC. who, being duly sworn according to law, says that she was personally present at the execution of the foregoing Trust Agreement and saw the common or coporate seal of ATLAS CONSTRUCTION CO., INC. duly affixed thereto; that the seal so affixed thereto is the common or corporate seal of the said corporation that the foregoing Trust Agreement was duly sealed and delivered by JOHN SMITH, as President of the said corporation for the uses and purposes therein mentioned, and that the name of this deponent as Secretary and of JOHN SMITH, as President of the said corporation, subscribed to the foregoing Trust Agreement in attestation of its due execution and delivery, are in their and each of their respective handwritings.

_____
                                                           Secretary

SWORN and subscribed before
me the day and year aforesaid
WITNESS my hand and seal.

_____
        Notary Public

FORM C-15

Pension Plan and Trust

Pension and profit sharing plans are the subject of Chapter 8. Form C-15 comprises a pension plan and the related trust agreement, followed by the related letter to IRS requesting a favorable determination; From 5300 (Application for Determination for Defined Benefit Plan); Form 5302 (Employee Census); Form 2848 (Power of Attorney); certification that the submitted copies of Plan and Trust are true and correct copies of the originals; certified copies of corporate resolutions; and notice (with covering letter) to employees. Also attached is the related summary plan description (with covering letter) distributed to the employees and submitted to the Department of Labor.

**JONES STATIONERY SUPPLY COMPANY
PENSION PLAN**

Gilbert M. Cantor, Esquire
Sixth Floor
1700 Sansom Street
Philadelphia, Pennsylvania 19103

JONES STATIONERY SUPPLY COMPANY
PENSION PLAN

Table of Contents

JONES STATIONERY SUPPLY COMPANY
PENSION PLAN
(Amended and Restated as of June 1, 1976)

Jones Stationery Supply Company, a corporation organized under the laws of the Commonwealth of Pennsylvania, in order to comply with the provisions of the Employee Retirement Income Security Act of 1974, does hereby amend and restate its pension plan as set forth below, effective June 1, 1976.

ARTICLE 1
Definitions

When used in this Plan and the accompanying Trust Agreement, the following words and phrases shall have the following meaning.

Section 1.01—*Accrued Benefit* shall mean an amount as of any specified date on or before a Participant's Normal Retirement Date which is equal to his annual normal retirement benefit as computed in Section 3.2 of the Plan, calculated on the assumption that he continued to earn annually until his Normal Retirement Date the same rate of compensation which he earned on the benefit accrual date, multiplied by a fraction, the numerator of which is the number of Years of Service accumulated to such date and the denominator of which is the number of Years of Service he would have had had he continued in the employment of the Company until his Normal Retirement Date.

Section 1.02—*Act* shall mean the Employee Retirement Income Security Act of 1974.

Section 1.03—*Actuarial Equivalent* shall mean a benefit of equal value when computed in accordance with the actuarial tables last adopted by the Committee and approved by the Actuary for the Plan.

Section 1.04—*Actuary* shall mean an enrolled actuary selected by the Committee to provide actuarial service for the Plan.

Section 1.05—*Age* shall mean age at nearest birthday.

Section 1.06—*Average Annual Compensation* of an Employee shall mean the total Compensation received by the Employee from the Company during his most highly paid three consecutive calendar Years of Service during which the Employee was a Participant, divided by three.

Section 1.07—*Board of Directors or Board* shall mean the Board of Directors of Jones Stationery Supply Company.

Section 1.08—*Break in Employment* shall mean any Plan Year during which an Employee has not completed more than five hundred (500) Hours of Service. Any Break in Employment shall be deemed to have occurred on the first day of the Plan Year in which such Break in Employment occurs. A "Break in Employment" shall not be deemed to have occurred during the first twelve (12) months of an Employee's employment merely because of the failure to complete five hundred (500) Hours of Service during any one Plan Year occurring in part during such twelve-month period if the Employee completes one Thousand (1,000) Hours of Service during such twelve-month period. A Break in Employment shall not be deemed to have occurred during any period of Excused Absence unless the Employee fails to return to employment at the expiration of his Excused Absence nor shall it be deemed to occur because an Employee fails to complete more than five hundred (500) Hours of Service during a Plan Year solely because of his or her retirement, disability or death during such Plan Year.

Section 1.09—*Code* shall mean the Internal Revenue Code of 1954, as amended, or as it may be amended from time to time.

Section 1.10—*Committee* shall mean the Administrative Committee as described in Article II.

Section 1.11—*Company* shall mean Jones Stationery Supply Company, a corporation with its principal office in Philadelphia, Pennsylvania.

Section 1.12—*Compensation* shall mean the amount of compensation paid by the Company to an Employee after becoming a Participant in a calendar year that would be subject to tax under Section 3101(a) of the Code without application of the dollar limitation of Section 3121(a) of the Code.

Section 1.13—*Date of Employment* shall mean the first date on which an Employee completes an Hour of Service, provided that in the case of a Break in Employment an Employee's Date of Employment shall be the first date thereafter on which he completes an Hour of Service.

Section 1.14—*Employee* shall mean any person who is employed by the Company.

Section 1.15—*Entry Date* shall mean June 1 and December 1 of each year.

Section 1.16—*Fund, Trust or Trust Fund* shall mean the sum of the contributions made by the Company and held by the Trustee in a Trust created pursuant hereto increased by any profits or income thereon and decreased by any losses or reasonable expenses incurred in the administration of the Trust and any payments made therefrom under the Plan.

Section 1.17—*Hours of Service* shall have the following meanings:

(a) For an Employee paid on an hourly basis or for whom hourly records of employment are required to be maintained: Each hour for which the Employee is directly or indirectly paid or entitled to payment.

(b) For an Employee paid on a non-hourly basis or for whom hourly records of employment are not required to be maintained: Each week for which the Member is directly or indirectly paid or entitled to payment shall be equal to 45 Hours of Service.

(c) An Employee shall receive an Hour of Service for each hour for which back pay has been awarded or agreed to by the Employer, provided that each such hour shall be credited to the Plan Year or applicable computation period to which it pertains, rather than the Plan Year or application computation period in which the award or agreement is made, and further provided that no such award or agreement shall have the effect of crediting an Hour of Service for any hour for which the Employee previously received credit under (a) or (b) above.

Section 1.18—*Normal Retirement Date* shall mean the latter of (1) the first day of the month in which a Participant attains age 65; or (2) the first day of the month following the month in which a Participant completes 15 years of service with the Company.

Section 1.19—*Participant* shall mean every Employee on June 1, 1976, who was a Participant in the Plan on May 31, 1976, or who would have been eligible to become a Participant in the Plan on June 1, 1976, had the provisions of the Plan continued unchanged after May 31, 1976. Also, the term shall include every Employee on the Entry Date coincident with or next following the date on which he completes one (1) Year of Service, provided, however, that no Employee shall be admitted to participation in this Plan if he or she has attained 60 years of age or if he or she is no longer an Employee on the Entry Date as of which admission to participation would otherwise have been effective.

Section 1.20—*Plan* shall mean "Jones Stationery Supply Company Pension Plan," as set forth herein or in any amendment hereof.

Section 1.21—*Plan Year* shall mean the fiscal year commencing each June 1 and ending on each May 31.

Section 1.22—*Trustee* shall mean the one or more persons appointed by the Board to hold and manage the Fund.

Section 1.23—*Year of Service* shall mean a period of 12 consecutive months beginning on the Date of Employment or any anniversary thereof during which an Employee has completed at least 1,000 Hours of Service. All of an Employee's Years of Service, computed to completed years, shall be counted, subject to the following qualifications and exceptions:

(A) Years of Service performed prior to a Break in Employment shall not count unless:

(1) If such service were performed before January 1, 1976, it would have constituted Continuous Service under the Plan as in effect prior to such date.

(2) If such service were performed after May 31, 1976, it meets the following conditions:

(a) The Employee completed a Year of Service after such Break in Employment, and

(b) The Employee had a vested interest at the time of his Break in Service and his Break in Service or a series of consecutive Breaks in Service were not equal to or greater than his prior years of Service.

(B) Years of Service as of June 1, 1976, shall include the Continuous Service any Employee would have had on June 1, 1976, under the rules of the Plan in effect on May 31, 1976.

ARTICLE 2
Contributions

Section 2.01—*Contributions by the Company*. The contributions required to fund the cost of pension and other benefits provided by the Plan shall be made solely by the Company. The Company shall contribute to the Trustee of the Trust Fund from time to time such sums as are required, in accordance with actuarial practices acceptable to the Internal Revenue Service, to fund the total cost of benefits provided by the Plan, whether by premium payments on insurance and annuity policies or by other investment or a combination thereof.

Section 2.02—*Voluntary Contributions*. Any Participant in this Plan may make voluntary contributions in each Plan Year to the Trustee of the Trust Fund, not in excess of 10% of the Employee's Compensation. Voluntary Contributions may be made only on January 1, and July 1 of each year unless the Committee, upon application, permits such contributions at other times.

Section 2.03—*Voluntary Contributions Accounts and Vesting*. The Trustee shall open and maintain for each Participant who makes voluntary contributions to the Plan, a Voluntary Contribution Account in which all such contributions shall be recorded and which shall, at all times, together with any earning on such funds, be fully vested in the Participant.

Section 2.04—*Voluntary Contribution Investments and Use.* Voluntary contributions may be invested in such investments as may be directed by the Participant or, if the Participant fails to so direct, in the same investments as are available to the Trustee with respect to Company contributions.

Section 2.05—*Voluntary Contribution Account Credits.* Income and gains or losses shall be credited or charged to the Voluntary Contribution Account of a Participant.

Section 2.06—*Voluntary Contribution Account Withdrawals.* A Participant may, upon 10 days notice to the Trustee, withdraw the amount credited to his Voluntary Contribution Account, provided it has not been invested in an investment which requires a longer period to liquidate, in which event, such longer period shall apply.

Section 2.07—*Rollover Contributions.* The Trustee is authorized to accept rollover contributions from Participants as described in Sections 402(a)(5), 403(a)(4), 408(d)(3) and 409(d)(3) of the Code and shall invest them in accordance with the directions of the Participant.

ARTICLE 3
Normal Retirement Pension and Deferred Retirement Pension

Section 3.01—*Eligibility for Normal Retirement Pension.* Every Participant in the Plan who retires on his Normal Retirement Date shall be eligible to receive a normal retirement pension.

Section 3.02—*Amount of Normal Retirement Pension.* Subject to Articles 7 and 8, the normal retirement pension of each Participant shall be.

(a) 14.926% of his Average Annual Compensation plus

(b) 33.333% of his Average Annual Compensation in excess of his integration level, as determined by the table set forth in Section 3.03 below.

Section 3.03—*Integration Level.* The integration level of each Participant shall be determined by reference to the following table:

YEAR OF BIRTH	INTEGRATION LEVEL
1906	5,520
1907	5,652
1908	5,856
1909	6,024
1910	6,180
1911	6,324
1912	6,456

YEAR OF BIRTH	INTEGRATION LEVEL
1913	6,564
1914	6,672
1915	6,768
1916	6,864
1917	6,936
1918	7,020
1919	7,092
1920	7,152
1921	7,212
1922	7,272
1923	7,320
1924	7,380
1925	7,428
1926	7,464
1927	7,512
1928	7,548
1929	7,584
1930	7,716
1931	7,836
1932	7,968
1933	8,076
1934	8,184
1935	8,304
1936	8,412
1937	8,520
1938	8,628
1939	8,736
1940	8,808
1941	8,868
1942	8,904
1943	8,928
1944	8,964
After 1945	9,000

Section 3.04—*Payment of Normal Retirement Pension.* Subject to Articles 7 and 8, a Participant's retirement pension shall be paid in the form of a single life annuity in monthly amounts equal to 1/12th of the annual normal retirement pension, shall commence on the Normal Retirement Date of the Participant, and shall continue until the first day of the month in which the Participant dies.

Section 3.05—*Deferred Retirement Pension.* A Participant may, with the consent of the Company, remain in its employ after his Normal

Retirement Date; provided, however, that no further pension benefits shall accrue to his benefit. In such event, subject to Articles 7 and 8, payment shall be in the form of a single life deferred annuity payable monthly which shall be the actuarial equivalent of the normal retirement pension.

ARTICLE 4
Early Retirement Pension

Section 4.01—*Eligibility for Early Retirement Pension.* A Participant who is 55 years of age or older but who has not attained Normal Retirement Date and who has completed 10 or more Years of Service with the Company, may elect to retire prior to Normal Retirement Date and to receive an early retirement pension based on his Accrued Benefit as of the early retirement date and, at the election of the Participant, commencing on the first day of any month after the actual retirement of the Participant and prior to his Normal Retirement Date.

Section 4.02—*Amount of Early Retirement Pension.* A Participant who is eligible for early retirement pursuant to Section 4.01, subject to Articles 7 and 8, shall be entitled to a pension equal to the normal retirement pension to which he would have been entitled had he continued to serve the Company until his Normal Retirement Date without change in his compensation, reduced by 1/12th for each of the first 5 Years of Service and 1/24th for each of the next five Years of Service by which such Participant's early retirement precedes his Normal Retirement Date.

Section 4.03—*Payment of Early Retirement Pension.* Subject to Articles 7 and 8, a Participant's early retirement pension shall be paid in the form of a single life annuity in monthly amounts equal to 1/12th of the early retirement pension payable as provided in this Article 4 which shall commence on the date of his early retirement and shall continue until the first day of the month in which the Participant dies.

ARTICLE 5
Disability Pension

Section 5.01—*Eligibility for Disability Pension.* If the Pension Committee determines that a Participant is unable to engage in any substantial gainful activity by reason of any medically determinable physical or mental impairment which can be expected to result in death or has lasted or can be expected to last for a continuous period of not less than 12 months and which condition has existed for a period of at least 3 months, such member shall be eligible to receive a disability pension.

Section 5.02—*Amount of Disability Pension.* The amount of a disability pension shall be computed in the same manner as the early retirement pension pursuant to Section 4.02.

Section 5.03—*Payment of Disability Pension.* A Participant's disability pension shall, subject to Articles 7 and 8, be payable in monthly amounts equal to 1/12th of the disability pension computed as provided in Section 5.02 which shall commence at the time of the disability retirement and shall continue until the first day of the month in which the Participant dies.

ARTICLE 6
Vested Deferred Pension

Section 6.01—*Amount of Vested Interest.* In the event that a Participant incurs a Break in Service other than by death or retirement, he shall be entitled to a vested interest in his Accrued Benefit pursuant to the following table and the balance shall be forfeited:

Participant's Years of Service at time of Break in Service	Vested Percentage
Prior to six years	None
Six years or more	100%

Section 6.02—*Vested Deferred Pension.* Subject to Section 6.03, a Participant who incurs a Break in Service after acquiring a vested interest in his Accrued Benefit in accordance with Section 6.01 shall be entitled to a pension commencing at Normal Retirement Date equal to his vested interest in his Accrued Benefit; provided, however, that if such Participant has completed 10 Years of Service, he shall have a right to commencement and payment of a pension in accordance with Article 4 except that the benefit shall be payable when he attains age 55 and it shall be actuarially reduced.

Section 6.03—*Cash-Out of Vested Benefits.* If lump-sum actuarial equivalent of the vested interest of a Participant described in Sections 6.01 and 6.02 is $1,750 or less, or if it exceeds $1,750 and such Participant consents, the Committee may direct the Trustee to pay to the Participant such sum at any time.

Section 6.04—*Early Commencement Option.* Notwithstanding anything above to the contrary, a Participant who has served the Company for 10 years, may elect in a writing filed with the Committee, to receive his vested deferred pension as of his 55th birthday. If such election is made, the vested deferred pension as computed in Section 6.02 shall be reduced by 1/12th for each of the first 5 years and 1/24th for each of the next 5 years that the commencement date preceeds the normal retirement date.

ARTICLE 7
Spouse's Optional Pre-retirement Death Benefit

Section 7.01—*Elective Spouse's Benefit.* A Participant may elect, in the manner prescribed in Section 7.02, a survivor annuity payable to his spouse upon his death in an amount equal to 50% of the reduced pension to which he would have been entitled under Section 8.01 if he were retired and his pension had commenced on the day preceding his death. Such election shall be effective if, at the time of the Participant's death, he has completed 10 years of service, has attained at least 55 years of age but has not yet reached his normal retirement age, and on the date of his death, his spouse is living and he and such spouse have been married for one-year period immediately preceding such date.

Section 7.02—*Manner of Election.* An election or revocation of an election of a spouse's benefit as described in Section 7.01 shall be made on a form prescribed by the Committee and may be made at any time during the period beginning 90 days prior to a Participant's reaching age 55 and ending on the earlier of his normal retirement age or the date his pension is scheduled to commence. Before the commencement of the election period, the Committee will furnish to each Participant who may become eligible for the spouse's benefit election described in Section 7.01 a written explanation in nontechnical language of the availability of the election and of the terms and condition of such benefit and the financial effect upon the Participant's pension (in terms of dollars per pension payment) of an election or revocation of an election of a spouse's benefit. An election may be revoked during the election period and a new election may thereafter be made. An election shall be effective on the later of the date it is filed with the Committee or the date the Participant completes 10 Years of Service and reaches age 55. A revocation of an election shall be effective as of the date filed with the Committee.

ARTICLE 8
Married Participants and Optional Forms of Benefit Payment

Section 8.01—*Form of Benefit—Married Participants.* Unless he elects in the manner prescribed in Section 8.03 not to take the joint and survivor annuity as provided in this Section 8.01, the pension of a Participant who is married on the date his pension is scheduled to commence shall be paid in the form of a joint and survivor annuity which is the Actuarial Equivalent of his pension and which provides for 50% of the reduced pension payable to the Participant during his lifetime to continue after his death to his spouse. In addition, if a Participant dies after Normal Retirement Age while an Employee of the Company and before his pension has commenced, and if he has been married for at least the one-year period immediately preceding the date of his death, his spouse (if living on the date of his death) shall be entitled to a survivor annuity, commencing upon the death of the Participant, in an amount equal to 50% of the reduced pension to which the Participant would have been entitled if he were retired and his pension had commenced on the day preceding his death.

Section 8.02—*Optional Forms of Benefit Payment.*

a. *Joint and Survivor Annuity.* A participant who is eligible for a pension other than a disability pension under this Plan may elect in accordance with Section 8.03, to receive his pension in the form of a joint and survivor benefit which is the Actuarial Equivalent of his pension and which will provide a pension payable to and during the lifetime of the Participant, with the provision that after his death such pension or 75% or 50% thereof, as chosen by the Participant, shall continue to and during the life of his designated joint pensioner; provided that, if the joint pensioner is someone other than the Participant's spouse, the arrangement must be sure that it is contemplated that more than one-half of the value of the benefit would be paid to the Participant during his lifetime.

b. *Other Optional Forms.* A Participant who has elected against the joint and survivor annuity form of benefit provided by Section 8.01 or who has made no election for optional benefits provided by Section 7.01 or 8.02a may elect in accordance with Section 8.03 to receive any of the following actuarially equivalent forms of benefits in lieu of the normal form of benefits:

(1) Single life annuity for five (5) years certain and then for life;

(2) Single life annuity for ten (10) years certain and then for life;

(3) Single life annuity for fifteen (15) years certain and then for life;

(4) Single life annuity for twenty (20) years certain and then for life;

(5) A Period Certain Annuity, with payments guaranteed for a period of five, ten, or fifteen years.

(6) Payments in installments as nearly equal as possible over a period of five, ten or fifteen years, but in no event over a period exceeding the Participant's life expectancy or the joint life expectancy of the Participant and his spouse, as of his benefit commencement date;

(7) Lump-sum distribution.

Section 8.03—*Manner of Elections.* Elections provided under Sections 8.01 and 8.02 shall be made on a form prescribed by the Committee. The Committee will furnish to each Participant who is eligible for the joint and survivor annuity provided by Section 8.01 a written explanation in non-technical language of the terms and conditions of such joint and survivor annuity and the financial effect upon the Participant's pension (in terms of dollars per pension payment) of making an election not to take the joint and survivor annuity. An election not to take the joint and survivor annuity provided by Section 8.01 may be made at any time during the 90 day period preceding the date the Participant's pension is scheduled to commence, or, if later, during the 90 day period following the date on which the information specified in the preceding sentence is given to the Participant. Notwithstanding the preceding sentence, if a Participant notifies the Committee less than 90 days before his pension is scheduled to commence of his intent to terminate employment, an election not to take the joint and survivor annuity provided by Section 8.01 may be made at any time during the latest to end of the following periods:

(a) The date the Participant's pension is scheduled to commence;

(b) The 14 day period following the date such notice is given; or

(c) The 14 day period following the date on which the information specified in the second preceding sentence is given to the Member.

An election under Section 8.02 may be made at any time during the 90 day period preceding the date the Participant's pension is scheduled to commence. An election provided under Section 8.01 or 8.02 may be revoked on a form prescribed by the Committee during the applicable election period and a new election may be made thereafter if it otherwise complies with this Section. Elections provided under Sections 8.01 and 8.02, if timely made, shall be effective on the date the Participant's pension is scheduled to commence. Revocations of elections provided under Sections 8.01 and 8.02 shall be effective when the designated form is completed and filed with the Committee.

ARTICLE 9
Payment of Benefits

Section 9.01—*In general.* Pensions shall in general be payable by the Trustee directly to the Participant entitled thereto. However, the Committee, in lieu of instructing the Trustee to pay the pension to which a Participant of this Plan is entitled directly from the funds of the Pension Trust, may instruct the Trustee to purchase from an insurance company selected by the Committee a nontransferrable annuity contract which will provide pension and other benefits in an amount identical to that to which the Participant is entitled under this Plan. In the event that an annuity contract is purchased for the benefit of a Participant from an insurance company, the contract may either be assigned to the Participant or held by the Trustee for the benefit of such Participant pursuant to instructions from the Committee.

Section 9.02—*Small Amounts.* In the event that the pension provided for any Participant in the Plan shall amount to less than $50 per month, the Committee may, but shall not be required to, cause such benefit to be satisfied by the payment to the Participant entitled thereto of an Actuarial Equivalent pension payable in quarterly, semi-annual or annual installments or in lieu thereof a lump sum which the Committee determines to be of Equivalent Actuarial Value to said pension.

Section 9.03—*Whole Dollars.* If the pension computed is not in whole dollars, it shall be increased to the next whole dollar.

Section 9.04—*Nonduplication of Benefits.* In the event any part or all of a Participant's Accrued Benefit is distributed to him and such Participant at any time thereafter again becomes a Participant, the Accrued Benefit of such Participant based on all Years of Participation shall be offset by the Accrued Benefit attributable to such distribution.

Section 9.05—*Beneficiary Designation.* The beneficiary of a Participant shall be the person(s), entity or entities designated by the Participant on forms supplied by the Committee, except that Participants receiving annuity benefits shall be governed by the provisions of any contracts providing such benefits. In the absence of an effective beneficiary designation or controlling annuity contract provisions, benefits shall be paid in equal amounts to the member(s) of the first class listed below in which there are qualified recipients, to the exclusion of all subsequently listed classes:

(1) Surviving spouse;

(2) Natural and adopted children, per stirpes;

(3) Surviving parent or parents;

(4) Brothers and sisters, per stirpes;

(5) The Participant's estate.

A Participant may change beneficiary designations at any time by filing with the Committee a written change on a form provided by the Committee. Changes shall become effective only upon receipt of the form by the Committee, but upon such receipt the change shall relate back to and take effect as of the date the Participant signed the request (which shall be presumed to be the date appearing on such form) whether or not the Participant is living at the time of such receipt. Neither the Committee (nor its appointed delegate) nor the Trustee shall be liable by reason of any payment of the Participant's death benefit made before the receipt of any form designating or changing the designation of a beneficiary.

The rights of beneficiary designation hereunder shall be superseded by the provisions of any annuity contract providing benefits for the Participant or serving as a funding vehicle for such if those provisions conflict with the rights granted hereunder.

Any change of beneficiary designation filed in proper form with the Committee by a Participant shall revoke all prior beneficiary designations.

ARTICLE 10
Other Provisions Affecting Benefits

Section 10.01—*Benefits Not Assignable.* No benefit under this Plan shall in any manner or to any extent be assignable or transferable to any Participant or beneficiary under the Plan or subject to attachment, garnishment or other legal processes. No attempted assignment or transfer of any benefit under the Plan shall be recognized.

Section 10.02—*Limitation on Benefits in the Event of the Early Termination of the Plan or Upon Failure to Meet the Current Costs of the Plan.* In the event that the Plan is terminated or the full current costs attributable to the additional benefits, as hereinafter defined, have not been met at any time before the expiration date, as hereinafter defined, the following rules shall apply:

(A) Upon the occurrence of any of the above conditions, the additional benefits which may be provided from contributions by the Company for any of its 25 highest-paid Employees, as hereinafter defined, shall not be greater than the amount of benefits which can be provided by the larger of the following amounts:

(1) $20,000 or

(2) An amount equal to 20 percent of the first $50,000 of the employee's average annual Compensation for the preceding 5 years multiplied by the number of years since the revision date, as hereinafter defined. If on or before the expiration date the full current costs attributable to the additional benefits are not met, the restrictions will continue to apply until the current costs are funded for the first time.

(B) The provisions of subsection (A) shall not restrict the current payment of full retirement benefits called for by the Plan for any retired Employee while the Plan is in full effect and its full current costs have been met. In the event that any funds are realized by operation of the restrictions set forth in subsection (A), they shall be used to reduce subsequent contributions by the Company or if the Company has ceased its contributions, they shall be used for the benefit of Employees other than those restricted by subsection (A) on a basis which shall not result in substantial discrimination in favor of the more highly-compensated Employees.

(C) For purposes of this section, the following definitions shall apply:

(1) "additional benefits" shall mean the benefits provided by the Plan which are over and above those which would have been provided by the provisions of the Plan in effect prior to the applicable revision date had the Plan been continued without changes.

(2) "twenty-five highest paid Employees" shall mean the twenty-five highest paid Employees of the Company as of the applicable revision date, exluding, however, any Employee whose anticipated annual benefits are not expected to exceed $1,500.

(3) "revision date" shall mean the effective date of adoption of the Plan by the Company or the effective date of any amendment to the Plan which increases the benefits;

(4) "expiration date" shall mean the tenth anniversary of any revision date.

Section 10.03—*Forfeitures.* Forfeitures, if any, shall not be applied to increase the benefits any Participant would otherwise receive under the Plan.

Section 10.04—*Annual Benefit Limit.* In no event shall the projected annual benefit of a Participant at any time within the limitation year exceed the lesser of $75,000 or 100 percent of his average annual compensation. Annual benefit for this purpose shall mean the normal retirement pension as computed in accordance with Section 3.02, before any adjustment for any optional forms of payment. The $75,000 maximum annual benefit shall be adjusted according to procedures outlined in regulations prescribed by the Secretary of the Treasury or his delegates under the Code. The limitation year for purposes of this Section shall be the Plan Year.

Section 10.05— *Merger of Plans.* In the case of any merger or consolidation of this Plan alone or together with the Pension Fund with or the transfer of the assets or liabilities of the Plan or the Pension Fund to, any other plan, the terms of such merger, consolidation or transfer shall be such that each Participant shall receive (in the event of termination of this Plan or its successor immediately thereafter) a benefit which is equal to or greater than the benefit he would have received in the event of termination of this Plan immediately before such merger, consolidation or transfer.

ARTICLE 11
Relating to Life Insurance and Annuity Contracts
and Death Benefits

Section 11.01—*Application and Purchase of Policies.* Subject to Section 11.02, on or before the Entry Date of a Participant, the Committee shall deliver to the Trustee sufficient information to permit him to promptly apply for a life insurance policy on the life of such Participant. Upon delivery of the necessary information, the life insurance policy shall be applied for by the Trustee from a legal reserve life insurance company as may be approved by the Committee. The policy shall designate the Trustee as the owner thereof, subject, however, to the right of the Trustee to deliver such policies to payees. All dividends paid on such policies, while in the possession of the Trustee shall be considered investment earnings of the Trust Fund and shall be applied to reduce the Company's obligation to contribute to the Plan. The policy shall provide a death benefit not to exceed the Participant's normal monthly retirement pension multiplied by 100.

Section 11.02—*Duties of Employee with Respect to Life Insurance.* Upon being notified that he is or is about to become a Participant in the Plan, an Employee shall provide the Committee with such information as it requires to permit the Trustee to apply for the life insurance policy or policies provided for pursuant to Section 11.01 and he shall also execute such forms and submit to such physical examinations as may be required for that purpose.

Section 11.03—*Death Benefits.* Upon the death of a Participant, unless at the time of his death he or his beneficiary was entitled to a joint and survivor or survivor annuity pursuant to Articles 7 or 8 of this Plan, his beneficiary or beneficiaries shall be entitled to receive a death benefit equal to his normal monthly retirement pension multiplied by 100; provided, however, that such death benefit shall be reduced to the extent that the normal amount of insurance is reduced or eliminated pursuant to Sections 11.04 and 11.05. The death benefit shall be composed of the proceeds of all life insurance policies owned by the Trustee on the life of the Participant plus an additional sum which, when added to the life insurance proceeds, is equal to the death benefit.

Section 11.04—*Insurability at Substandard Rates.* If the Participant to be insured pursuant to Section 11.01 is not insurable at standard rates, the Trustee shall apply for and purchase such insurance policy or policies as are available at substandard rates which provide benefits as close as possible to those provided pursuant to Section 11.03; provided that the premium charge does not exceed the amount which would have been required had the Participant been insurable at standard rates. Notwithstanding the preceeding sentence, however, upon written request of the Participant to the Trustee and his agreement to pay annually the additional premium resulting from his substandard rating, the Trustee shall apply for a policy or policies providing the benefits described in Section 11.03.

Section 11.05—*Noninsurability.* If the Participant to be insured is not insurable at standard or substandard rates, the Trustee shall apply for and purchase an annual premium deferred annuity in such amount as may be purchased with the premium which would have been charged had the Participant been insurable at standard rates.

Section 11.06—*Insurance Companies.* No insurance company dealing with the Trustee shall be deemed a party to the Trust created pursuant to this Plan, nor shall such insurance company have any obligation to determine that any person with respect to when the Trustee makes an application for a policy or annuity is, in fact, eligible for benefits or participation under this Plan. The insurance company shall have no obligation to determine any fact, the determination of which is necessary or desirable for the proper issuance of such policy or annuity, and shall be fully protected in acting upon any advice, representation, or other instrument executed by the Trustee. In no event shall the insurance company be responsible for any lack or failure of proper authority in the establishment of the Plan or Trust, or for any acts of any person or of the Employer in the establishment or maintenance thereof.

Section 11.07—*Right of Insurance Company to Rely Upon Certification of Trustee.* A certification in writing to the insurance company by the Trustee as to the occurrence of any event contemplated by the Trust or the Plan shall constitute conclusive evidence of such occurrence, and the insurance company shall be fully protected in accepting and relying upon such certification and shall incur no liability or responsibility for so doing.

Section 11.08—*Responsibility of Insurance Company.* The insurance company shall not be responsible to see that any action taken by the Trustee with respect to any insurance policy or annuity is authorized by the terms of the Trust or the Plan. Any change made or action taken by the insurance company under any insurance policy or annuity upon the written direction of the Trustee shall fully discharge such insurance company from all liability with respect thereto, and the insurance company shall not be obligated to see to the distribution or further application of any moneys paid by it to the Trustee or in accordance with the written direction of the Trustee.

Section 11.09—*Form of Payment of Death Benefit.* A death benefit payable to the beneficiary of a Participant pursuant to Section 11.03 shall be payable in a lump-sum or in installments as nearly equal as possible over a period not to exceed five (5) years, as determined by the Committee. Such benefit shall commence as promptly as practicable after the death of the Participant.

ARTICLE 12
Administration of the Plan

Section 12.01—*Appointment of the Committee.* The administration of the Plan, as provided herein, including the payment of all benefits to Participants or their beneficiaries, shall be vested in and shall be responsibility of the Administrative Committee, which is the administrator and named fiduciary of the Plan. The committee shall consist of three individuals who shall be appointed from time to time by the Board of Directors and shall serve at its pleasure, without compensation, unless otherwise determined by the Board.

Section 12.02—*Conduct of Committee Business.* The Committee shall elect a Chairman who shall be a member of the Committee, and a Secretary who may or may not be a member of the Committee and shall appoint such subcommittees as it shall deem necessary and appropriate. The Committee shall conduct its business according to the provisions of this Article and shall hold regular meetings in any convenient location not less often than annually. A majority of all of the members of the Committee shall have power to act, and the concurrence or dissent of any member may be by telephone, wire, cablegram or letter. In the administration of the Plan the Committee may, subject always to the requirements of Section 12.07:

(a) Employ agents to carry out non-fiduciary responsibilities;

(b) Employ agents to carry out fiduciary responsibilities (other than trustee responsibilities as defined in Section 405(c)(3) of ERISA);

(c) Consult with counsel, who may be of counsel to the Company;

(d) Appoint an investment manager or managers (as defined by Section 3(38) of ERISA) to manage (including the power to acquire and dispose of) all or any part of the assets of the Plan;

(e) Provide for the allocation of fiduciary responsibilities other than trusts responsibilities (as defined in Section 405(c)(3) of ERISA) among its members;

(f) Direct the Trustee to invest or reinvest part of all of the Trust Fund in policies or contracts issued by insurance companies and to exercise all rights, privileges, options and elections contained therein.

Section 12.03—*Procedure for the Allocation or Delegation of Fiduciary Duties.* Any action described in subsections (b), (d), (e), or (f) of Section 12.02 may be taken by the Committee only in accordance with the following procedure:

(a) Such action be approved by a majority of the Committee in a resolution signed by a majority of the Committee;

(b) The vote cast by each member of the Committee for or against the adoption of such resolution shall be recorded and made a part of the written record of the Committee's proceedings;

(c) Any delegation of fiduciary responsibilities or any allocation of fiduciary responsibilities among members of the Committee may be modified or rescinded by the Committee according to the procedure set forth in subsections (a) and (b) of this Section.

Section 12.04—*Investment Responsibilities.* Except as provided in Section 12.02(f), the Committee shall have no authority over or responsibility for the management and investment of the assets of the Plan, which function shall be the sole responsibility of the Trustee; provided, however, that if according to the provisions of Sections 12.02 and 12.03 the Committee appoints an investment manager or managers to manage (including the power to acquire and dispose of) any assets of the Plan, authority over and responsibility for the management of the assets so designated shall be the sole responsibility of the investment manager or managers.

Section 12.05—*Expenses of the Plan.* The expenses of administering the Plan and the compensation of all employees, agents or counsel of the Committee, including the Trustee's fees, shall be paid by the Company.

Section 12.06—*Records and Reports of the Committee.* In addition to whatever records may be required by Section 12.03, the Committees shall keep written minutes of all its proceedings, which shall be open to inspection by the Board of Directors. In the case of any decision by the Committee which affects the rights of any Participant or beneficiary who has made a claim for benefits under the Plan, the Committee shall include in its minutes a brief explanation of the grounds upon which such decision was based and the vote cast by each member of the Committee regarding such decision. The Committee shall prepare and submit to the Board of Directors an annual report which shall include a statement of the fiscal transactions of the Plan for the preceding Plan Year; a balance sheet showing the financial condition of the Plan; an evaluation of the performance of the Trustee and, if applicable, the investment manager or managers; recommendations regarding the retention or replacement of the Trustee and, if applicable, the investment manager or managers; an evaluation of the success of the current policy for investing the assets of the Plan in fulfilling the defined goals of the Plan and Section 404(a)(10) of ERISA; any revised investment goals and proposals to achieve them; and such other information as the Committee deems necessary or advisable.

Section 12.07—*Duties of the Committee.* The Committee shall administer the Plan and adopt such rules and regulations as in the opinion of the Committee are necessary or advisable to implement and administer the Plan and to transact its business. The Committee shall establish a funding policy and method and shall review at least annually such funding policy and method. All actions taken with respect to such funding policy and method and the reasons therefor shall be reflected in the written records of the Committee. In performing their duties, the members of the Committee shall act solely in the interest of the Participants of the Plan and their beneficiaries and:

(a) For the exclusive purpose of providing benefits to the Participants and their beneficiaries;

(b) With a care, skill, prudence and diligence under the circumstances then prevailing that a prudent man acting in like capacity and familiar with such matters would use in the conduct of an enterprise of a like character and with like aims; and

(c) In accordance with the documents and instruments governing the Plan insofar as such documents and instruments are consistent with the provisions of Title I of the Act. In addition to any other duties the Committee may have, the Committee shall periodically review the performance of the Trustee and the performance of all other persons to whom fiduciary duties have been delegated or allocated pursuant to the provisions of Sections 12.02 and 12.03.

Section 12.08—*Indemnification.* The Company agrees to indemnify and reimburse the members of the Committee and the Trustee against any and all claims, loss, damages, expense and liability arising from their responsibilities in connection with this Plan, unless the Board of Directors determines that they are due to gross negligence or willful misconduct.

Section 12.09—*Claims Procedures*. Pursuant to procedures established by the Committee, adequate notice in writing shall be provided to any Participant or beneficiary whose claim for benefits under the Plan has been denied. Such notice shall set forth the specific reason for such denial, shall be written in a manner calculated to be understood by the claimant, and provided review is requested within 60 days after receipt by the claimant of written notification of denial of his claim shall afford a reasonable opportunity to any claimant whose claim for benefits has been denied to a full and fair review by the Committee of the decision denying the claim.

ARTICLE 13
Amendment and Termination

Section 13.01—*Right to Amend or Terminate the Plan*. It is the intention of the Company to continue the Plan indefinitely and to make contributions as herein provided. The Company expressly reserves the right, however, to terminate the Plan at any time of the Board of Directors of the Company shall determine that business, financial, or other good causes make it necessary or desirable to do so or to amend the Plan at any time and in any particular, provided that any such amendment shall be made in accordance with the Act.

Section 13.02—*Termination*. Upon termination of the Plan, the rights of all Employees to benefits accrued to the date of such termination to the extent then funded, or the amounts credited to the Employees' accounts, shall be nonforfeitable, and upon the occurrence of such event, the assets of the Fund shall be allocated among the Participants and their beneficiaries in accordance with Section 4044(a) of the Act and administered and distributed at such time or times as is determined by the Committee. In the event of a partial termination of the Plan, this section shall be considered as applying, at such time, only to those Participants with respect to whom the Plan has been terminated. All other Participants shall be unaffected by such partial termination.

ARTICLE 14
Agreement of Trust

Section 14.01—*Trustees to be Selected by the Company*. In order to implement the Plan, the Company has entered into a Trust Agreement to the end that such funds as may be irrevocably contributed from time to time for the payment of all or any part of the benefits under the Plan shall be segregated from the Company's own assets and held in trust by the Trustee for the exclusive benefit of the Participants or their beneficiaries under the Plan who may, in accordance with the terms of the Plan and such Trust Agreement be entitled to participation thereunder.

Section 14.02—*Trust Funds are for Exclusive Benefit of Participants of the Plan and Their Beneficiaries.* It shall be impossible under any circumstances at any time prior to the satisfaction of all liabilities with respect to Participants and their beneficiaries for any part of the corpus or income of the Trust Fund to be used for or diverted to purposes other than the exclusive benefit of the Participant of the Plan and their beneficiaries except under the circumstances described in Section 7.04 of the Jones Stationery Supply Company Pension Trust which are incorporated herein by reference.

ARTICLE 15
Miscellaneous

Section 15.01—*Titles are for Reference Only.* The titles are for reference only. In the event of a conflict between a title and the content of a Section, the content of the Section shall control.

Section 15.02—*Construction.* Except to the extent preempted by federal law, the provisions of the Plan shall be interpreted in accordance with the laws of the Commonwealth of Pennsylvania.

Section 15.03—*Gender and Number.* The masculine pronoun whenever used shall include the feminine pronoun and the singular number shall include the plural number unless the context of the Plan requires otherwise.

Section 15.04—*Legal Effect.* The terms and conditions of the Plan as restated herein shall amend and supersede as of June 1, 1976, the terms and conditions of the Jones Stationery Supply Company Pension Plan, as amended; provided, however, that the provisions of such prior Plan shall continue to govern the rights of all Employees who retired or otherwise ceased to work for Jones Stationery Supply Company prior to June 1, 1976, except as otherwise expressly stated herein.

Approved this 15 day of April, 1977.

JONES STATIONERY SUPPLY COMPANY

By: _____
                                        President

(CORPORATE SEAL)

Attest: _____
                                        Secretary

JONES STATIONERY SUPPLY COMPANY
PENSION TRUST AGREEMENT

Gilbert M. Cantor, Esquire
Sixth Floor
1700 Sansom Street
Philadelphia, Pennsylvania 19103

JONES STATIONERY SUPPLY COMPANY
PENSION TRUST AGREEMENT

Table of Contents

JONES STATIONERY SUPPLY COMPANY
PENSION TRUST AGREEMENT
(Amended and Restated as of June 1, 1976)

This amended Trust Agreement is made and executed this 15th day of April, 1977, by and among Jones Stationery Supply Company, a corporation organized under the laws of the Commonwealth of Pennsylvania, referred to herein as the "Company," and John Jones and Janet Brown, Trustees, referred to herein individually and collectively as the "Trustees."

PREAMBLE

WHEREAS, the Jones Stationery Supply Company Pension Trust was established effective May 27, 1972 for the benefit of the employees of Jones Stationery Supply Company; and

WHEREAS, by Item Twelve of the Trust Agreement, the Company reserved the right to amend the Trust Agreement at any time; and

WHEREAS, the Company and the Trustee have agreed to amend the Trust Agreement in order to bring it into conformity with the requirements of the Employee Retirement Income Security Act of 1974 (ERISA); and

WHEREAS, this amended Trust Agreement is intended to qualify under the provisions of Sections 401(a) and 501(a) of the Internal Revenue Code of 1954, as amended;

NOW, THEREFORE, the Company and the Trustee do hereby agree, each with the other, as follows:

ARTICLE 1
Name, Effective Date, and Administration

Section 1.01—*Name.* The name of this Trust shall be "Jones Stationery Supply Company Pension Trust."

Section 1.02—*Effective Date.* The effective date of this Amended Trust shall be June 1, 1976.

Section 1.03—*Accounting Year.* The accounting year of this Trust shall end May 31 of each year.

Section 1.04—*Definitions.* Definitions in the Jones Stationery Supply Company Pension Plan shall have the same meaning wherein used in this Trust, unless the context clearly indicates otherwise.

Section 1.05—*Committee.* The Committee as appointed under the terms of the Plan shall be named fiduciary and administrator of the Plan and Trust. The Committee shall provide the Trustee with a certified copy of the Plan and with copies of all amendments promptly upon their adoption. From time to time the Committee shall communicate to the Trustee in writing the liquidity needs that have been established to carry out the objectives of the Plan and the Trustee shall keep such portions of the funds in cash or cash balances as may be specified from time to time by the Committee shall, upon the request of the Trustee, furnish the Trustee with such reasonable information as is necessary for the Trustee to carry out its fiduciary responsibilities under ERISA.

ARTICLE 2
Investment and Administrative Powers of the Trustee

Section 2.01—*Investment Powers of the Trustee.* With respect to any and all sums received by the Trustee from the Company, the Trustee is authorized and empowered, in its sound judgment:

(A) To hold uninvested from time to time, without liability for interest thereon, such sum of money as is necessary for the cash requirements of the Plan; and to keep such portion of the fund in cash or cash balances as the Trustee may from time to time deem to be in the best interests of the Trust Fund.

(B) To invest and reinvest the principal and income of the trust fund, without distinction between principal and income, in such securities (except that in the event that the Trustee at a future time is a corporate Trustee, then securities of such corporate Trustee shall not be authorized investments) as, but not limited to, common stocks, preferred stocks, bonds, bills, notes, commercial papers, debentures, mortgages, equipment trust certificates, investment trust certificates, and also in other investments, whether real, personal or mixed property, including investments in federally insured bank or similar deposits which bear a reasonable rate of interest provided that no more than 10 percent of the assets of the trust fund shall be invested in securities and real estate which qualify as qualifying employer securities and qualifying employer real estate under ERISA.

(C) To invest and reinvest all or any specified portion of the Trust Fund collectively with funds of other pension and profit-sharing trusts exempt from the tax under Section 501(a) of the Internal Revenue Code of 1954 by reason of qualifying under Section 401(a) of said Code (as such Sections may be renumbered, amended or reenacted) by investment collectively with such other funds through the medium of a common, collective or commingled trust fund which has been or may hereafter be established and maintained by a duly empowered bank or trust company, the instrument or instruments establishing such trust fund or funds, as amended from time to time, being made part of this Agreement so long as any portion of the Trust Fund shall be invested through the medium thereof.

Section 2.02—*Administrative Powers of the Trustee.* The Trustee shall be authorized and empowered, in its discretion (except as provided in Section 2.03), to exercise any and all of the following rights, powers, and privileges with respect to any cash, securities or other properties held by the Trustee in Trust hereunder:

(A) To sell any such property at such time and upon such terms and conditions as the Trustee deems appropriate. Such sales may be public or private, for cash or credit, or partly for cash and partly for credit, and may be made without notice or advertisement of any kind.

(B) To exchange, mortgage, or lease any such property and to convey, transfer, or dispose of any such property on such terms and conditions as the Trustee deems appropriate.

(C) To grant options for the sale, transfer, exchange, or disposal of any such property.

(D) To exercise all voting rights pertaining to any securities; and to consent to or request any action on the part of the issuer of any such securities; and to give general or special proxies or powers of attorney with or without power of substitution.

(E) To consent to or participate in amalgamations, reorganizations, recapitalizations, consolidations, mergers, liquidations, or similar transactions with respect to any securities, and to accept and to hold any other securities issued in connection therewith.

(F) To exercise any subscription rights or conversion privileges with respect to any securities held in the Trust Fund.

(G) To collect and receive any and all money and other property of whatsoever kind or nature due or owing or belonging to the Trust Fund and to give full discharge and acquittance therefor; and to extend the time of payment of any obligation at any time owing to the Trust Fund, as long as such extention is for a reasonable period, and continues reasonable interest.

(H) To cause any securities or other property to be registered in, or transferred to, the individual name of the Trustee or in the name of one or more of its nominees, or one or more nominees of any system for the centralized handling of securities, or it may retain them unregistered and in form permitting transferability by delivery, but the books and records of the Trust shall at all times show that all such investments are a part of the Trust Fund.

(I) To organize under the laws of any State a corporation for the purpose of acquiring and holding title to any property which it is authorized to acquire under this Agreement and to exercise with respect thereto any or all of the powers set forth in this Agreement;

(J) To manage, operate, repair, improve, develop, preserve, mortgage, or lease for any period any real property or any oil, mineral, or gas properties, royalties, interest, or rights held by it directly or through any corporation, either alone or by joining with others, using other Trust assets for any of such purposes; to modify, extend, renew, waive, or otherwise adjust any or all of the provisions of any such mortgage or lease; and to make provision for amortization of the investment or depreciation of the value of such property;

(K) To settle, compromise, or submit to arbitration any claims, debts, or damages due or owing to or from the Trust; to commence or defend suits or legal proceedings whenever, in its judgment, any interest of the Trust requires it; and to represent the Trust in all suits or legal proceedings in any court of law or equity or before any other body or tribunal, insofar as such suits or proceedings relate to any property forming part of the Trust Fund or to the administration of the Trust Fund.

(L) To borrow money from others for the purposes of the Trust, but the Trustee shall not be authorized to borrow any money from the Company or any subsidiary company.

(M) Generally to do all acts, whether or not expressly authorized, which the Trustee deems necessary or desirable, but acting at all times according to the principles of prudence herein expressed in Section 3.01(b).

Section 2.03—*Investment Manager.* The Company shall possess the authority to appoint an investment manager or managers to manage (including the power to acquire and dispose of) all or any of the assets of the Trust. In the event of any such appointment, the Company shall establish the portion of the assets of the Trust which shall be subject to the management of the investment manager and shall so notify the Trustee in writing. With respect to such assets over which an investment manager has investment responsibility, the investment manager shall possess all of the investment and administrative powers and responsibilities granted to the Trustee hereunder, and the Trustee shall have no investment responsibility with the respect to the assets subject to the investment responsibility of an investment manager, and shall have no duty to inquire into the direction of such investment manager, to solicit such directions nor to review and follow the investments made pursuant to any such direction, other than to the extent provided by law.

ARTICLE 3
Duties of the Trustee

Section 3.01—*General Duties of Trustee.*

(A) The Trustee shall hold all property received by it hereunder, which, together with the income and gains therefrom and additions thereto, shall constitute the Trust Fund. The Trustee shall manage, invest, and reinvest the Trust Fund, collect the income thereof, and make payments therefrom, all as hereinafter provided. The Trustee shall be responsible only for the property actually received by it hereunder. It shall have no duty or authority to compute any amount to be paid to it by the Company or to bring any action or proceeding to enforce the collection from the Company of any contribution to the Trust Fund.

(B) The Trustee shall discharge its duties solely in the interest of the Plan Participants and beneficiaries and—

(1) for the exclusive purpose of providing benefits to Participants and their beneficiaries and defraying reasonable expenses of administering the Plan;

(2) with the care, skill, prudence, and diligence under the circumstances then prevailing that a prudent man acting in a like capacity and familiar with such matters would use in the conduct of an enterprise of a like character and with like aims;

(3) by diversifying the investments of the Trust so as to minimize the risk of large losses, unless under the circumstances it is clearly prudent not to do so; and

(4) in accordance with the documents and instruments governing the Trust insofar as such documents and instruments are consistent with the provisions of ERISA.

Section 3.02—*Reports.* The Trustee shall:

(A) Keep and maintain such accounts and records as it shall deem necessary and proper to record its transactions with respect to its administration of the Trust and such other accounts upon, and permit inspection of such accounts, records, and assets of the Trust by any duly authorized representative of the Company at any time during usual business hours.

(B) Within three months following the close of each accounting year, and at such other intervals as are requested by the Committee, the Trustee shall file with the Committee a written report containing such information as is requested by the Committee with respect to the transactions effected by the Trustee during such accounting year or other period.

(C) Make such periodic reports to the Committee as the Trustee shall deem necessary and proper and such other reports as the Committee may reasonably request, including a valuation of the assets of the Trust as of any date requested by the Committee.

(D) Prepare and file such tax returns and other reports, together with supporting data and schedules, as may be required by law, with any taxing authority or any other government authority, whether local, state, or federal.

(E) Pay out of the Trust Fund all real and personal property taxes, income taxes, and other taxes of any and all kinds levied or assessed under existing or future laws upon or with respect to the Trust Fund or any money, property or securities forming a part thereof, but the Trustee may contest any such tax.

ARTICLE 4
Compensation and Immunities of Trustee

Section 4.01—*Compensation and Expenses.* The Trustee shall receive each year as compensation for its services hereunder, such amount as it and the Committee agree to be reasonable. In addition, the Trustee shall be entitled to reimbursement for all reasonable expenses incurred by it in the performance of its duties hereunder, including reasonable fees for legal services rendered to the Trustee (whether in connection with any litigation or otherwise) and all other proper charges and disbursements. Such compensation and expenses shall be a charge upon the Trust and shall be withdrawn from the Trust, unless the amount of any such compensation and expenses shall be separately paid by the Company at the option of the Committee.

Section 4.02—*Immunities.* The Trustee shall have the following privileges and immunities:

(A) A written direction, statement or certificate to the Trustee, signed by any officer or employee of the Company designated by its Board of Directors, or otherwise empowered to give directions, statements, or certificates to the Trustee, or by all the members of the Committee then in office, or by any member of the Committee authorized by a resolution adopted by the Committee to execute instruments in its behalf, shall be deemed to be the direction, statement, or certificate of the Company, or of the Committee, as the case may be, and the Trustee may rely upon such directions, statements, or certificates to the extent permitted by law. The Company shall furnish the Trustee from time to time with instruments signed as aforesaid evidencing the appointment and termination of office of members of the Committee, and of successors of such members, and the Committee shall furnish the Trustee with a copy, signed by all of its members, of any resolution adopted by it authorizing one of its members to execute instructions, notices, and directions on its behalf of the Trustee; the Trustee shall be entitled to rely upon such instruments as evidence of the identity and authority of the members of the Committee and shall not be charged with notice of any change with respect thereto until the Company, or the Committee, as the case may be, shall have furnished the Trustee with instruments relative to such change.

(B) In the event that any dispute shall arise as to the persons to whom payment of any funds or delivery of any assets shall be made by the Trustee, the Trustee may withhold such payment or delivery until such dispute shall have been determined by a court of competent jurisdiction or shall have been settled by the parties concerned.

(C) The Trustee may from time to time consult with counsel, who may be counsel to the Company, and shall be protected to the extent the law permits in acting upon such advice of coun el as respects legal questions. The Trustee may also from time to time employ agents and expert assistants and delegate to them such ministerial duties as it sees fit, provided that such delegation is permitted by the Board of Directors of the Company. In the event that the Trustee does delegate such ministerial duties, it shall periodically review the performance of the person(s) to whom these duties have been delegated.

ARTICLE 5
Resignation, Removal and Substitution of Trustee

Section 5.01—*Resignation and Removal.* The Trustee may be removed by the Board of Directors of the Company at any time by delivery of written notice of such action to the Trustee. The trustee may resign at any time upon 60 days' notice in writing to the Company. Within 60 days after such removal or resignation of the Trustee, the Trustee shall file with the Company a written account, to the date of such removal or resignation, in form similar to, and containing information similar to that required to be set forth in, the annual report provided for heretofore in Section 3.3(b).

Section 5.02—*Successor Trustee.* Upon removal or resignation of the Trustee, the Board of Directors of the Company shall designate a successor trustee to act hereunder, which shall have the same powers and duties as those conferred upon the Trustee. Upon such designation, and upon the written acceptance of the successor trustee, the Trustee shall assign, transfer and pay over to such successor trustee the assets then constituting the Trust Fund, provided, however, that the Trustee is authorized to reserve such sum of money (and for that purpose to liquidate such property as may be necessary to produce such sum) as may seem advisable for payment of all property charges against the

Trust Fund including expenses in connection with such resignation or removal, and any balance of such reserve remaining after the payment of such charges shall be paid over to the successor trustee.

ARTICLE 6
Right to Amend and Terminate

Section 6.01—*Amendment.* The Company may at any time by resolution of its Board of Directors amend, in whole or in part, any or all of the provisions of this Trust Agreement, provided that no such amendment may affect the rights duties, or responsibilities of the Trustee without its consent and, provided, further, that no such amendment may permit any part of the corpus or income of the Fund to be used for or diverted to purposes other than for the exclusive benefit of the Participants under the Plan and their beneficiaries at any time prior to the satisfaction of all liabilities under the Plan with respect to such persons. Any such amendment shall become effective when received by the Trustee.

Section 6.02—*Termination.* This Trust shall continue for such time as may be necessary to accomplish the purpose for which it was created but may be terminated at any time by the Company by action of its Board of Directors. Notice of such termination shall be given to the Trustee by an instrument in writing executed by the Company and acknowledged in the same form as this Agreement, together wtih a certified copy of the resolution of the Board of Directors of the Company authorizing such termination. The Company shall send a copy of such notice to each member of the Committee. Upon termination of the Trust, provided that the Trustee has not received instructions to the contrary from the Committee, the Trustee shall liquidate the Trust, and, after paying the reasonable expenses of the Trust, including expenses involved in the termination, distribute the balance thereof according to written directions from the Committee.

ARTICLE 7
Miscellaneous

Section 7.01—*Headings.* The headings are for reference only. In the event of a conflict between a heading and the content of a Section, the content of the Section shall control.

Section 7.02—*Construction.* This Trust shall be deemed to be a Pennsylvania Trust and shall in all respects be construed and regulated by the laws of the Commonwealth of Pennsylvania, except where such laws are superseded by the Internal Revenue Code of 1954 or by ERISA.

Section 7.03—*Successors.* This Agreement shall be binding upon, and the powers herein granted to the Company and the Trustee, respectively, shall be exercisable by the respective successors and assigns of the Company and the Trustee. Any corporation which shall, by merger, consolidation, purchase or otherwise, succeed to substantially all the trust business of the Trustee, upon such succession and without any appointment or other action by any person, shall be and become successor trustee hereunder.

Section 7.04—*Irrevocability of Trust.* All contributions made by the Company shall be irrevocable, and no part of the corpus of the Trust Fund nor any income therefrom shall revert to the Company or be used for or diverted to purposes other than for the exclusive benefit of the Participants or former Participants and their beneficiaries except that in the event that this Trust and the related Plan are not initially qualified under Section 401(a) and determined to be tax-exempt under Section 501(a) of the Code or if a contribution to the Trust is disallowed as a deduction by the Company or if a contribution to the Trust was made under a mistake of fact, in such event the sum contributed shall be returned to the Company within one year of such denial of qualification and determination of disallowance or mistake of fact.

IN WITNESS WHEREOF, the parties have caused this Trust Agreement to be executed by their duly authorized officer, and the corporate seal to be hereunto affixed, in each case on the 15th day of April, 1977.

JONES STATIONERY SUPPLY COMPANY

By:_____

(CORPORATE SEAL)   President

Attest:_____

                                                               Secretary

_____

John Jones, Trustee

_____

Janet Brown, Trustee

COMMONWEALTH OF PENNSYLVANIA   :
                                      : SS.
COUNTY OF PHILADELPHIA   :

On this 15th day of April, 1977, personally appeared before me, a Notary Public of the Commonwealth of Pennsylvania, John Jones and Janet Brown, who acknowledged themselves to be the Trustees mentioned in the foregoing instrument and contents thereof, and that they signed, sealed and delivered the same as their voluntary act and deed for the uses and purposes therein expressed.

IN WITNESS WHEREOF, I have hereunto set my hand and notarial seal.

_____
Notary Public

COMMONWEALTH OF PENNSYLVANIA   :
                                                                : SS.
COUNTY OF PHILADLEPHIA   :

On this 15th day of April, 1977, personally appeared before me, a Notary Public of the Commonwealth of Pennsylvania, John Jones, who acknowledged himself to be the President of Jones Stationery Supply Company, Inc. and that he, as such President, being authorized to do so, executed the foregoing instrument on behalf of such Corporation for the purposes therein contained, and caused the same to be attested by the Corporation and the Corporation's seal affixed.

IN WITNESS WHEREOF, I have hereunto set my hand and notarial seal.

_____
Notary Public

July 28, 1977

Internal Revenue Service
11601 Roosevelt Boulevard
Philadelphia, PA 19155

Attention: Employee Plans

Re: Jones Stationery Supply Company
     Pension Plan and related
     Trust Agreement

Dear Sir:

Your determination is requested that the Amended and Restated Jones Stationery Company Pension Plan and the related Trust Agreement complies with the Employee Retirement Income Security Act of 1974 and qualify under Code Section 401(a) and 501(a). In support of this request the following completed forms are submitted in duplicate together with the Amended and Restated Plan and Trust.

    1. Form 5300
    2. Form 5302
    3. Form 2848
    4. Corporate resolution adopting the Amended and Restated Plan and Trust.
    5. Certification

If further information is required or if you have any questions, please call the undersigned.

In the event that an adverse determination is contemplated, a conference is requested.

                        Sincerely yours,

                        Gilbert M. Cantor

GMC/hw
Enclosures
Certified Mail
Return Receipt Requested

Form **5300** (Rev. June 1976) Department of the Treasury Internal Revenue Service	Application for **Determination for Defined Benefit Plan** For Pension Plans Other Than Money Purchase Plans (Under sections 401(a), 414(j) and 501(a) of the Internal Revenue Code) **This Form is Open to Public Inspection**	**File in Duplicate** **For IRS Use Only** Case number ▶ Issue date ▶ EPMF status code ▶ File folder number ▶

▶ **Church and Governmental Plans.**—All items need not be completed. See instruction "B. What to File." N/A

▶ **Please complete every applicable item on this form. If an item does not apply, enter N/A.**

1 (a) Name, address and ZIP code of employer Jones Stationery Supply Company c/o Cantor/Franklin/Grodinsky Suite 1200, 2000 Market St. Phila., PA. 19103 Telephone number ▶ (215) L03-6060	2 Employer's identification number 23-1668119
(b) Name, address and ZIP code of plan administrator, if other than employer same as 1(a)	3 Business code number
	4 Date incorporated or business commenced 4-14-66
	5 Employer's taxable year ends May 31
(c) Administrator's identification number ▶ same as 2 Telephone number ▶ (215) L03-6060	

6 Determination requested for:
- (a) (i) ☐ Initial qualification—date plan adopted ▶ .... (ii) ☒ Amendment—date adopted ▶ 4/15/77
- (iii) If (ii) is checked, enter file folder number ▶
- (b) Were employees who are interested parties given the required notification of the filing of this application? . ☐ Yes ☐ No
- (c) If this application involves a merger or consolidation with another plan, enter the employer identification number(s) and the plan number(s) of such other plan(s) ▶

7 Type of entity: (a) ☒ Corporation   (b) ☐ Subchapter S corporation   (c) ☐ Sole proprietor   (d) ☐ Partnership
(e) ☐ Tax exempt organization   (f) ☐ Church   (g) ☐ Governmental organization
(h) ☐ Other (specify) ▶

8 (a) Name of Plan Jones Stationery Supply Company Pension Plan	(b) Plan number ▶ 001 (c) Plan year ends ▶ May 31, 19 97 (d) Is this a Keogh (H.R. 10) plan? . . . . ☐ Yes ☐ No (e) If "Yes," is an owner-employee in the plan? ☐ Yes ☐ No

9 (a) If this is an adoption of a master or prototype plan (other than Keogh) or a district approved pattern plan, enter name of such plan ▶ N/A	(b) Letter serial number or notification letter number N/A

10 (a) Type of plan: (i) ☒ Fixed benefit (ii) ☐ Unit benefit (iii) ☐ Flat benefit (iv) ☐ Other (specify) ▶	(b) Does plan provide for variable benefits? ☐ Yes ☒ No If "Yes," check appropriate box to indicate type. (i) ☐ Cost of living (ii) ☐ Asset fluctuation (iii) ☐ Other (specify) ▶

11 Effective date of plan ▶ Effective date of amendment May 27, 1972 June 1, 1976	13 Date plan was communicated to employees ▶ July 25, 19 How communicated ▶ Letter and Notice

14 (a) Indicate the general eligibility requirements for participation under the plan and indicate the section and page number of plan or trust where each provision is contained:	Section and page number *	GOVERNMENT USE ONLY
(i) ☒ All employees (v) Length of service (number of years) ▶ 1 year	1.19;p.6	
(ii) ☐ Hourly rate employee only (vi) Minimum age (specify) ▶ N/A		
(iii) ☐ Salaried employee only (vii) Maximum age (specify) ▶ N/A		
(iv) ☐ Other job class (specify) ▶ (viii) Minimum pay (specify) ▶ N/A		
(b) Are the eligibility requirements the same for future employees? . . . ☒ Yes ☐ No If "No," explain ▶	1.19;p.6	
(c) Does the plan recognize service only with this employer? . . . . . . ☒ Yes ☐ No If "No," explain ▶	1.14;p.4	

15 Coverage of plan at (give date) ▶ 6/1/76 Enter here the number of self-employed individuals ▶ N/A	Number	
(a) Total employed (if a Keogh plan, include all self-employed individuals)	N/A	
(b) Exclusions under plan (do not count an employee more than once):		
(i) Minimum age or years of service required (specify) ▶	0	
(ii) Employees included in collective bargaining	0	
(iii) Nonresident aliens who receive no earned income from United States sources . . .	0	

* of plan or trust or other document constituting the plan.

Under penalties of perjury, I declare that I have examined this application, including accompanying statements, and to the best of my knowledge and belief it is true, correct and complete.

Signature ▶   Title ▶   Date ▶ 7/22/77

c70—575-279-1

Form 5300 (6-76)   Page 2

(Section references are to the Internal Revenue Code)	Number	GOVERNMENT USE ONLY

15 Coverage (continued):

  (c) Total exclusions, sum of (b)(i) through (iii)   0

  (d) Employees not excluded under the statute, (a) less (c)   6

  (e) Ineligible under plan on account of (do not count an employee included in (b)):

    (i)   Minimum pay   0

    (ii) Hourly-paid   0

    (iii) Maximum age   0

    (iv) Other (specify) ▶...   0

  (f) Employees ineligible, sum of (e)(i) through (iv)   0

  (g) Employees eligible to participate, line (d) less line (f)   6

  (h) Number of employees participating in plan   6

  (i) Percent of nonexcluded employees who are participating, (h) divided by (d) . .   100 %

    Complete (j) only if (i) is less than 70% and complete (k) only if (i) is 70% or more.

  (j) Percent of nonexcluded employees who are eligible to participate, (g) divided by (d) . . . .   N/A %

  (k) Percent of eligible employees who are participating, (h) divided by (g) .   N/A %

    If (i) and (j) are less than 70% or (k) is less than 80%, see instructions.

  (l) Total number of participants, include certain retired and terminated employees, see instructions   6   *Section and page number*

	Yes	No	
16 Employee contributions:			
(a) Are mandatory contributions limited to 6%, or less, of compensation?	N/A		
(b) Are voluntary contributions limited to 10%, or less, of compensation for all qualified plans?	x		2.02;p.8
(c) Are benefits unaffected by forfeitures?	x		10.03;p.29
17 Employer contributions:			
(a) ☒ Full amount			2.01;p.8
(b) ☐ Balance necessary			
(c) Are employer contributions reduced by forfeitures?	x		10.03;p.29
18 Integration:			
Is this plan integrated with Social Security or Railroad Retirement?	x		3.0103.02; p.10
If "Yes," see instructions.			

19 Vesting—Check the appropriate box to indicate the vesting provisions of the plan:

  (a) ☐ Full and immediate

  (b) ☒ Full vesting after 10 years of service   6.01;p.16

  (c) ☐ 5- to 15-year vesting i.e., 25% after 5 years of service, 5% additional for each of the next 5 years, then 10% additional for each of the next 5 years

  (d) ☐ Rule of 45 (see section 411(a)(2)(C))

  (e) ☐ For each year of employment, commencing with the 4th such year, vesting not less than 40% after 4 years of service, 5% additional for each of the next 2 years, and 10% additional for each of the next 5 years

  (f) ☐ Other (specify and see instructions) ▶

20 Administration:

  (a) Type of funding entity:

    (i)   ☐ Trust

    (ii) ☐ Custodial account

    (iii) ☐ Non-trusteed

    (iv) ☒ Trust with insurance contracts   11.01;p.31

    If you checked (i) or (ii), enter date executed ▶...........................

  (b) Enter name of trustee or custodian, if any ▶ John Jones

	Yes	No	
(c) Does trust agreement prohibit reversion of funds to the employer?	x		7.04;p.19 of Trust
(d) If borrowing on insurance contracts is permitted, is it on a pro-rata basis? . .	N/A		
(e) If Puerto Rican trust, does it qualify for tax exemption under the laws of Puerto Rico?	N/A		

* of plan or trust or other document constituting the plan.   c70—575-279-1

Forms to Carry Out the Estate Plan

Form 5300 (1-76)

		Yes	No	Section and page number*	GOVERNMENT USE ONLY
21	Benefits and requirements for benefits.				
(a)	Normal retirement age is ▶ 65. State years of service required ▶ 15			1.18;p.5	
(b)	Early retirement age is ▶ 55. State years of service required ▶ 10			4.01;p.13	
(c)	If employer's consent is required for early retirement, are benefits limited to vested interest?		x		
(d) (i)	Does the plan provide that the payment of benefits, unless the employee elects otherwise, will commence not later than the 60th day after the latest of (1) the close of the plan year in which the participant attains the earlier of age 65 or the normal retirement age specified under the plan, (2) the close of the plan year in which occurs the 10th anniversary of the year in which participant commenced participation or (3) the close of the plan year in which the participant terminates his service with the employer?	x		3.04;p.11 4.03;p.13 5.03;p.15 6.02;p.16	12 14
(ii)	Does plan provide for payment of benefits if claim is not filed?	x		No provision	
(e)	Benefit at normal retirement age is ▶ 14.926% of Av. Annual Comp. plus 33.333% of Av. Annual Comp. in excess of integration level			3.02;p.10	
(f)	Benefit at early retirement age is ▶ normal retirement pension reduced by 1/12 and 1/24			4.02;p.13	
(g)	Normal form of retirement benefits is ▶ Annuity or Qualified Joint and Survivor Annuity			8.01;p.20	
(h)	If plan provides for payment of annuity benefits, does the plan provide a joint and survivor benefit unless participant elects otherwise?	x		8.01;p.20	
(i)	If benefits are measured by years of service —				
(i)	Are the years of service for eligibility purposes included in credited service?	N/A			
(ii)	Is only service as a common law employee recognized?	N/A			
(j)	Are benefits computed on the basis of total compensation? If "No," see instructions.	x		1.06;p.2	
(k)	Does the plan provide for determining an employee's accrued benefit?	x		1.01;p.1	
(l)	If participants may withdraw their contributions or earnings, may such withdrawal be made without forfeiting vested benefits based on employer contributions?	x		2.06;p.9	
(m)	If the plan defers compensation generated increases until compensation increases sufficiently, does plan provide for increases of benefits of at least $10 per month?	N/A			
(n)	Is duplication of benefits upon re-entry into the plan prohibited?	x		9.04;p.25	
(o)	Is there a disability benefit under the plan?	x		5.01;p.15	
(p)	Does the plan provide for a death benefit, other than survivor annuity, before retirement?	x		11.03;p.32	
	If "Yes," indicate whether such benefits are limited to—				
(i)	[X] 100 times the monthly pension or the reserve, if larger.				
(ii)	[ ] The actuarial equivalent of the benefits accrued to the date of death.				
(iii)	[ ] Other explain ▶			11.03;p.32	
(q)	Does plan provide for maximum limitation under section 415?	x		10.04;p.29	
(r)	In the case of a merger or consolidation with another plan or transfer of assets or liabilities to another plan, will each participant be entitled to the same or greater benefits as if the plan had terminated?	x		10.05;p.29	
(s)	Does the plan prohibit the assignment or alienation of benefits?	x		10.01;p.27	
(t)	Does the plan preclude divestment for cause?	x		No provision	
(u)	Does plan prohibit distribution of benefits except for retirement, disability or termination of employment or, in case of owner-employees, after age 59½?	x		same as (d)	
22	Termination of plan or trust:				
(a)	Is there a provision in the plan for terminating the plan and/or trust?	x		13.01;p.42	
(b)	Are the participants' rights to benefits under the plan nonforfeitable upon termination or partial termination of the plan?	x		13.02;p.42	
(c)	Has the early termination rule been included in the plan (see section 1.401-4 (c)(1) and (2) of the Income Tax Regulations)?	x		10.02;p.27	
(d)	Have the plan benefits been increased since the plan's inception?		x		

* of plan or trust or other document constituting the plan.

c70—575-279-1

Form 5300 (6–76)   Page 4

	Yes	No	GOVERNMENT USE ONLY

23 Miscellaneous:

(a) Has power of attorney been submitted with the application (or previously submitted)? . . . | x | |

(b) Have you completed and attached Form 5302? . . . . | x | |

(c) Is the adopting employer a member of a controlled group of corporations or under commonly
controlled trades or businesses? . . . . | | x |
If "Yes," see instructions.

(d) Is any issue relating to this plan or trust currently pending before the Internal Revenue
Service, the Department of Labor, the Pension Benefit Guaranty Corporation or any Court? . . | | x |
If "Yes," attach explanation.

(e) Other qualified plans—Enter for each other qualified plan you maintain (do not include plans that were
established under union-negotiated agreements that involved other employers):

   (i)   Name of plan ▶...

   (ii) Type of plan ▶...

   (iii) Rate of employer contribution, if fixed ▶...

   (iv) Benefit formula or monthly benefit ▶...

   (v) Number of participants ▶

	Yes	No	

24 In the case of a request on an initial qualification, have the following documents been included:

(a) Copies of all instruments constituting the plan or joinder agreement? . . . .

(b) Copies of trust indentures or group annuity contracts? . . . .

(c) Evidence that retirement benefits for employees in 15(b)(i) were the subject of good faith
bargaining between employee representatives and employers—where that has occurred
and is the basis for excluding certain employees, see section 410(b)(2)(A)? . . . . . .

(d) A detailed description of all methods, factors and assumptions used in determining costs or
actual experience under the plan (including any loading, contingency reserves, or special factors, and the basis of any insured costs or liabilities involved therein) explaining their source
and application in detail to permit ready analysis and verification? . . . .

25 In the case of a request involving an amendment, after initial qualification, have the following documents been included:

(a) A copy of the amendment(s)? . . . . | | x |

(b) A description of the amendment covering the items changed and an explanation of the pro-
visions before and after the amendment? . . . . | | x |

(c) A completely restated plan? . . . . | x | |

(d) A working copy of the plan in which there has been incorporated all of the previous amend-
ments representing the provisions of the plan as currently in effect? † . . . . | | x |

(e) Copies of all amendments adopted since the date of the last determination letter for which no
determination letter has been issued by the Internal Revenue Service? † . . . . | | x |

† If plan is being amended for the first time to conform to the participation and vesting standards of the Employee
Retirement Income Security Act of 1974, or if the plan has been amended at least three times since the last
restated plan was submitted, one of the documents specified under (c) or (d) must be attached.

If any item in 24 or 25 is answered "No," please explain. Completely Restated Plan is submitted.

If more space is needed for any item, attach additional sheets of the same size.

U.S. GOVERNMENT PRINTING OFFICE   c70--575 279   c70—575-279—1

Form **5302**

(Rev. June 1976)
Department of the Treasury
Internal Revenue Service

Employee Census

▶ Attach to application for determination—defined benefit and defined contribution plans.

Schedule of 25 highest paid participating employees for 12-month period ended ▶ 6/1/76

(Round off to nearest dollar)

This Form is NOT Open to Public Inspection

Name of employer Jores Stationery Supply Company

Employer identification number 23-1668119

Line no.	Employee's last name and initials (List in order of compensation) (a)	Check Officer or shareholder (b)	Percent of voting stock owned (c)	Age (d)	No. of yrs. (e)	Annual Nondeferred Compensation			Employee contributions under the plan (e)	Amount allocated under each other qualified plan of deferred compensation (f)	Defined Benefit Annual benefit expected (a)	Defined Contribution		
						Total in compensation for benefits/contribution (f)	Excluded (g)	Total (h)				Employer contribution allocated (l)	Number of units, if any (m)	Forfeitures allocated in the year (n)
1	J. Jones	O/S	100	50	10	180,796	N/A	180,796	None	N/A	37,545	N/A	N/A	N/A
2	J. Smith			50	10	18,095		18,095			5,836			
3	D. White			32	10	16,261		16,261			4,382			
4	E. Snyder			34	7	13,837		13,235			3,620			
5	J. Brown			39	10	13,235		13,235			2,861			
6	R. Wright			41	10	12,730		12,730			3,124			
7														
8														
9														
10														
11														
12														
13														
14														
15														
16														
17														
18														
19														
20														
21														
22														
23														
24														
25														
	Totals for above					254,954	N/A	254,954	None	N/A		N/A	N/A	N/A
	Totals for all others (Specify number ▶ None)					0	N/A	0	None	N/A		N/A	N/A	N/A
	Totals for all participants					254,954	N/A	254,954	None	N/A		N/A	N/A	N/A

SPECIMEN FORM

Form **2848**
(Rev. Jan. 1970)
Department of the Treasury
Internal Revenue Service

Power of Attorney

(See Separate Instructions)

Name, address including ZIP code, and identifying number of taxpayer(s)

Jones Stationery Supply Company
c/o Cantor/Franklin/Grodinsky
Suite 1200,   2000 Market Street   Philadelphia, PA   19103

I.D. No. 23-1668119

hereby appoints (name, address including ZIP code, and telephone number of appointee(s))

All matters pertaining to qualification of the Jones Stationery Supply Company
Pension Plan.

as attorney(s)-in-fact to represent the taxpayer(s) before any office of the Internal Revenue Service with respect to (specify
Internal Revenue tax matters and years or periods):

Said attorney(s)-in-fact (or either of them) shall, subject to revocation, have authority to receive confidential information and
full power to perform on behalf of the taxpayer(s) the following acts with respect to the above tax matters:
(Strike through any of the following which are not granted.)
   To receive, but not to endorse and collect, checks in payment of any refund of Internal Revenue taxes, penalties, or
   interest.
   To execute waivers (including offers of waivers) of restrictions on assessment or collection of deficiencies in tax and
   waivers of notice of disallowance of a claim for credit or refund.
   To execute consents extending the statutory period for assessment or collection of taxes.
   To execute closing agreements under section 7121 of the Internal Revenue Code.
   To delegate authority or to substitute another representative.
   Other acts (specify) .... None ....

Copies of notices and other written communications addressed to the taxpayer(s) in proceedings involving the above matters
should be sent to (Name, address including ZIP code, and telephone number):
         Robert L. Franklin, Esquire
and   Suite 1200,   2000 Market Street
         Philadelphia, PA   19103
         S.S.# 161-28-3810   (215) LO-3-6060

This power of attorney revokes all prior powers of attorney and tax information authorizations on file with the same Internal
Revenue office with respect to the same matters and years or periods covered by this instrument, except the following:

.... No other powers or authorizations are on file with respect to this matter. ....
         (Specify to whom granted, date, and address including ZIP code, or refer to attached copies of prior powers and authorizations)

Signature of or for taxpayer(s)

If signed by a corporate officer, partner, or fiduciary on behalf of the taxpayer, I certify that I have the authority to execute
this power of attorney on behalf of the taxpayer.

....	President	7-22-77
(Signature)	(Title, if applicable)	(Date)
....	....	....
(Signature)	(Title, if applicable)	(Date)

Form **2848** (Rev. 1–70)

If the power of attorney is granted to an attorney, certified public accountant, or enrolled agent, this declaration must be completed.

I declare that I am not currently under suspension or disbarment from practice before the Internal Revenue Service, and that:

I am a member in good standing of the bar of the highest court of the jurisdiction indicated below; or
I am duly qualified to practice as a certified public accountant in the jurisdiction indicated below; or
I am enrolled as an agent pursuant to the requirements of Treasury Department Circular No. 230.

Designation (Attorney, C.P.A., or Agent)	Jurisdiction (State, etc.) or Enrollment Card Number	Signature	Date
Attorney	PA.	Robert L. Franklin _R. L. J. Franklin_	August 23, 1976

If the power of attorney is granted to a person other than an attorney, certified public accountant, or enrolled agent, it must be witnessed or notarized below.

The person(s) signing as or for the taxpayer(s): (Check and complete one.)

☐ is/are known to and signed in the presence of the two disinterested witnesses whose signatures appear here:

_____
(Signature of Witness)   (Date)

_____
(Signature of Witness)   (Date)

☐ appeared this day before a notary public and acknowledged this power of attorney as his/her/their voluntary act and deed.

_____
(Signature of Notary)   (Date)

NOTARIAL SEAL
(If required)

SPECIMEN FORM

CERTIFICATION

I, John Jones, President of Jones Stationery Supply Company hereby certify that the attached copies of corporate resolutions are correct copies of the originals filed with the corporate records.

_____

John Jones
President

CERTIFICATE

I, John Jones, President of Jones Stationery Supply Company hereby certify that the enclosed Jones Stationery Supply Company Pension Plan and the Jones Stationery Supply Company Pension Trust Agreement are correct copies of the originals on file at the corporate office.

_____

John Jones

JONES STATIONERY SUPPLY COMPANY
UNANIMOUS CONSENT IN WRITING

The undersigned being all of the directors of Jones Stationery Supply Company hereby unanimously consent in writing to the following resolutions:

> RESOLVED, that the Jones Stationery Supply Company Pension Plan, as amended and restated effective June 1, 1976, be and it hereby is adopted on behalf of the corporation; and

> FURTHER RESOLVED, that the Jones Stationery Supply Company Pension Trust Agreement, as amended and restated effective June 1, 1976, be and it hereby is adopted on behalf of the corporation; and

> FURTHER RESOLVED, that the President and the Secretary be, and they hereby are, authorized and directed to execute said plan and trust on behalf of the corporation and to take such further action as is required to obtain a determination that the plan is qualified and the trust is tax exempt under provisions of the Internal Revenue Code.

_____
John Jones

_____
Sally Jones

_____
Betty Jones

Dated: April 15, 1977

JONES STATIONERY SUPPLY COMPANY

To Our Employees:

We are pleased to announce that effective June 1, 1976, our Board of Directors has amended the Jones Stationery Supply Company Pension Plan and the related Trust previously adopted for the benefit of our employees. The amendments were adopted to bring the plans into compliance with the Employee Retirement Income Security Act of 1974.

An application for a determination that the amended Plan will remain tax-qualified will shortly be submitted to the Internal Revenue Service. Further amendments to the Plan may be necessary in order to assure its continued tax-qualification.

The Amended Plan is available for your inspection at the Company office.

Sincerely yours,

July 22, 1977

_____

John Jones
President

NOTICE TO
EMPLOYEES OF JONES STATIONERY SUPPLY COMPANY

An application is to be made to the Internal Revenue Service for an advance determination on the qualification of the following employee retirement plan.

Name of Plan: Jones Stationery Supply Company Pension Plan
Name of Applicant: Jones Stationery Supply Company
Name of Plan Administrator: John Jones
Taxpayer I.D. No. of Applicant: 23-1668119

The Application will be submitted to the District Director of the Internal Revenue at Philadelphia, Pennsylvania for an advance determination as to whether or not the Plan qualified under section 401(a) of the Internal Revenue Code, with respect to tax qualification of the Plan Amendment.

All employees of the Company are eligible to participate in the Plan if they have completed 1 year of service.

The Internal Revenue Service has previously issued a determination letter with respect to the qualification of this Plan.

Each person to whom this notice is addressed is entitled to submit, or request the Department of Labor to submit, to the District Director described above a comment on the question of whether the plans meet the requirement for qualification under part 1 of Subchapter D of Chapter 1 of the Internal Revenue Code of 1954. Two or more such persons may join in a single comment or request. If such a person or persons request the Department of Labor to submit a comment and that department declines to do so in respect of one or more matters raised in the request, the person or persons so requested may submit a comment to the District Director in respect of the matters on which the Department of Labor declines to comment.

A comment submitted to the District Director must be received by him on or before September 8, 1977. However, if it is being submitted on a matter on which the Department of Labor was first requested, but declined to comment, the comment must be received by the District Director on or before the later of September 8, 1977 or the 15th day after the day on which the Department of Labor notifies such person or persons that it declined to comment, but in no event later than September 23, 1977.

A request of the Department of Labor to submit a Comment must be received by that department on or before August 19, 1977 or, if the person or persons making the request wish to preserve their right to submit a comment to the District Director in the event the Department of Labor declines to comment, on or before August 9, 1977.

Additional informational material regarding the plan and the procedures to be followed in submitting, or requesting the Department of Labor to submit, a comment, may be obtained at 236 Market Street, Philadelphia, Pennsylvania 19128.

To: All Employees:

A copy of Summary Description of the Jones Stationery Supply Company Pension Plan is attached. This is to give you general information about the coverage, benefits and other workings of the Plan. It is not the Plan itself, which is a much longer and more complicated document, and which defines and regulates all rights, benefits and duties under the plan of the Company and the Participants. If you have specific questions, please ask (personnel department) (supervisor) (etc.).

The regulations provide that the Summary Plan Description be distributed by November 16, 1977, or within 60 days thereafter if the Plan Administrator determines that there is good cause for an extension. The Administrator has determined that the volume of work of the persons preparing the Summary Plan Description was too great to meet the normal distribution date, and has extended the time for distribution accordingly.

_____
(for the) Plan Administrator

**SUMMARY PLAN DESCRIPTION
JONES STATIONERY SUPPLY COMPANY
PENSION PLAN**

Gilbert M. Cantor, Esquire
Sixth Floor
1700 Sansom Street
Philadelphia, Pennsylvania 19103

SUMMARY PLAN DESCRIPTION
JONES STATIONERY SUPPLY COMPANY
PENSION PLAN

Table of Contents

SUMMARY PLAN DESCRIPTION
JONES STATIONERY SUPPLY COMPANY
PENSION PLAN

November 1977

1. *HIGHLIGHTS*

—All employees of Jones Stationery Supply Company (in this booklet called the "Company") who are not covered by a collective bargaining agreement are eligible to participate in the Company's Pension Plan.

—The Plan costs you nothing—the Company makes all contributions to the Plan.

—The Plan provides benefits upon:

> Retirement
> Disability
> Death
> Termination of employment

—The benefits from the plan are in addition to your Social Security benefits.

—The Plan allows you to save money by contributing to the Plan.

—The Plan is a "Defined Benefit Plan." The amount that will be required in order to pay benefits determines how much is contributed each year to the Plan by the Company.

2. *BECOMING A PARTICIPANT*

You will become a Participant in the Plan if you are an employee of the Company on the June 1st or December 1 after you complete One Year of Service, provided that you are not over 60 years old.

If you were an employee on June 1, 1976, and were a participant

May 31, 1976, or would have been a Participant on June 1, 1976, under the Plan as it was then, you are a Participant in the Plan.

3. *CONTRIBUTIONS*

a. *Company Contributions*

Each year the Company will contribute amounts actuarially necessary to pay for the benefits to be paid by the Plan.

b. *Your Contributions*

On January 1 and July 1 of each year, you may make voluntary contributions to the Plan Trust, but in any one year not more than 10 percent of your annual earnings.

If you save through contributing to the Plan, you will have a Voluntary Contribution Account to which will be credited: (1) all deposits to the Trust Fund made by you and (2) any earnings or losses on those deposits. You may direct how your contribution is to be invested.

You may elect to withdraw the amount in your Voluntary Contribution Account on ten days notice, but if it takes longer to turn your investment into cash, that longer period will control.

4. *THE TRUST FUND*

All contributions by you and the Company are put into a Trust Fund to be held and invested by the Trustees, John Jones and Janet Brown. Their address is c/o the company at 236 Market Street, Philadelphia, Pennsylvania 19128. No part of the Trust Fund, including its earnings or income, is taxable until the money is taken from the Trust—this means that you are not taxed on your share of the Trust Fund until you actually receive it. The Trust is for the exclusive benefit of the Participants and their beneficiaries and can not be used for any other purpose.

5. *DEFINITIONS*

a. *Plan Year*

The Plan Year is the twelve months beginning each June 1 and ending the next May 31.

b. *Normal Retirement Date*

Your Normal Retirement Date is the later of (1) the first day of the month in which your 65th birthday occurs, or (2) the first day of the month following the month in which you complete 15 Years of Service with the Company. You may continue working after Normal Retirement Date with the Company's consent, but, if you do, you will not continue to accrue benefits for years before your actual retirement.

The earliest date at which you can retire is age 55 if you have also completed 10 or more Years of Service.

c. *Year of Service*

A Year of Service is a period of 12 consecutive months from the anniversary of your date of employment, and during which you complete at least 1,000 hours of service (125 normal days of work).

All of an Employee's Years of Service, computed to completed years, shall be counted, subject to the following qualifications and exceptions:

(A) Years of Service performed prior to a Break in Service shall not count unless:

(1) If such service were performed before June 1, 1976, it would have constituted Continuous Service under the Plan as in effect prior to such date.

(2) If such service were performed after May 31, 1976, it meets the following conditions:

(a) The Employee completed a Year of Service after such Break in Employment, and

(b) The Employee has a Vested Interest at the time of his Break in Service and his Break in Service or a series of consecutive Breaks in Service were not equal to or greater than his prior Years of Service.

(B) Years of Service as of June 1, 1976, shall include the Continuous Service any Employee would have had on June 1, 1976, under the rules of the Plan in effect on May 31, 1976.

d. *Break in Service*

A Break in Service shall mean any Plan Year during which you have not completed more than five hundred (500) Hours of Service. Any Break in Service shall be deemed to have occurred on the first day of the Plan Year in which such Break occurs. A "Break in Service" shall not be deemed to have occurred during the first twelve (12) months of an Employee's employment merely because of the failure to complete five hundred (500) Hours of Service during any one Plan Year occurring in part during such twelve-month period if the Employee completes one Thousand (1,000) Hours of Service during such twelve-month period. A Break in Employment shall not be deemed to have occurred during any period of Excused Absence unless the Employee fails to return to employment at the expiration of his Excused Absence nor shall it be deemed to occur because an Employee fails to complete more than five hundred (500) Hours of Service during a Plan Year solely because of his or her retirement, disability or death during such Plan Year.

e. *Accrued Benefit*

Your Accrued Benefit is the annual retirement pension that you have earned up to, and which will be payable at the Normal Retirement Date. This is computed as described later in Section 6a(1) and (2), and is based on the assumption that you would continue to earn at the same rate, and the amount so extended to the Normal Retirement Date is multiplied by

$$\frac{\text{years of service}}{\text{years of service to normal retirement date.}}$$

f. *Average Annual Compensation.*

Your Average Annual Compensation is 1/3 of the total compensation received from the Company during your most highly paid three consecutive calendar Years of Service during which you were a Participant in the Plan.

6. *BENEFITS*

a. *Normal Retirement Pension*

You will receive the Normal Retirement Pension if you retire on or after the Normal Retirement Date.

The amount of your pension (subject to actuarial adjustment if other than a single life annuity) will be:

(a) 14.926% of your Average Annual Compensation plus

(b) 33.333% of your Average Annual Compensation in excess of your integration level, as determined by the following table:

YEAR OF BIRTH	INTEGRATION LEVEL
1906	5,520
1907	5,652
1908	5,856
1909	6,024
1910	6,180
1911	6,324
1912	6,456
1913	6,564
1914	6,672
1915	6,768
1916	6,864
1917	6,936
1918	7,020
1919	7,092
1920	7,152
1921	7,212
1922	7,272
1923	7,320
1924	7,380
1925	7,428
1926	7,464
1927	7,512
1928	7,548
1929	7,584
1930	7,716
1931	7,836

1932	7,968
1933	8,076
1934	8,184
1935	8,304
1936	8,412
1937	8,520
1938	8,628
1939	8,736
1940	8,808
1941	8,868
1942	8,904
1943	8,928
1944	8,964
After 1945	9,000

b. *Early Retirement Pension*

If you are 55 years old or over and have completed ten or more Years of Service, you may elect to retire before the Normal Retirement Date. You will receive a Normal Retirement Pension *reduced by* 1/12 for each of the first five years and 1/24 for each of the next five years that the beginning of your Early Retirement Pension precedes the Normal Retirement Date.

c. *Disability Pension*

If the Pension Committee determines that you are unable to engage in any substantial gainful activity by reason of any medically determinable physical or mental impairment which can be expected to result in death or has lasted or can be expected to last for a continuous period of not less than 12 months and which condition has existed for a period of at least 3 months, shall be eligible to receive a Disability Pension equal to an Early Retirement Pension.

d. *Vested Deferred Pension*

If you incur a Break in Service other than by death or retirement, you will be entitled, as of your Normal Retirement Date, to a deferred pension based on the actuarial equivalent of the Vested Interest of your Accrued Benefit. The vested interest in your Accrued Benefit will be:

Years of Service at Time of Break in Service	*Vested Percentage*
Less than 6 years	None
Six years or more	100%

The portion, if any, not Vested, is forfeited and goes to reduce the amount of contribution necessary.

If or after you have 10 Years of Service, you may elect to receive a Vested Deferred Pension payable when you reach 55. If you do, it will be reduced and actuarially reduced to reflect the earlier payment.

If the lump-sum actuarial equivalent of your Vested interest is $1750 or less, or if it exceeds $1750 and you consent, the Committee may direct payment to you in full. This is called a "cash-out."

e. *Death Benefit*

(1) You may elect to have a survivor annuity paid to your spouse upon your death, provided that at the time of your death you had (1) reached age 55 but were less than 65, (2) completed 10 Years of Service, (3) were survived by a spouse to whom you had been married one or more years.

The amount of this benefit 50% of the amount of a joint-and-50% survivor annuity to which you would have been entitled had you retired on the date of death.

(2) If you die while you are a Participant (and not receiving a joint-and-survivor or survivor annuity under the plan), your beneficiary will receive a Death Benefit equal to your Normal monthly Retirement payment mutliplied by 100. This amount is subject to reduction if you are not insurable at standard rates. If you are insurable at sub-standard rates, you may bring the benefit up to the regular amount by paying the Trustee the difference between the standard premium and the sub-standard premium. If you are not insureable at all, the Trustee will use an amount equal to the standard rate insurance premium to buy a deferred annuity for your coverage.

7. *METHODS OF PAYMENT*

a. *Retirement and Disability*

The usual method of payment of your Pension at retirement is a straight-life annuity if you are unmarried, or an actuarially equivalent Joint-and-50%-Survivor Annuity if you are married. By making an election in writing, you may choose your type of pension from among:

(1) joint-and-50% survivor annuity with your spouse

(2) joint-and-survivor annuity with a dependent (not available for Disability Pensions)

(3) single life annuity

(4) single life annuity with guaranteed payments for 5, 10 or 15 years

(5) a lump sum

You should check with the Administrative Committee for the procedures required to elect other than the usual method of payment, or to exercise other allowed elections.

b. *Vested Interest*

A Vested Deferred Pension is payable in the same form as Retirement Pension, beginning on your Normal Retirement Date.

8. *AMENDMENT AND TERMINATION*

The Company intends to continue the plan indefinitely; however, it does reserve the right to amend or even terminate the Plan if it becomes necessary, provided that amendment or termination is in accordance with ERISA. If the Plan is terminated all funded Accrued Benefits become Vested and distributable in accordance with ERISA.

9. *GOVERNMENT INSURANCE OF THE PLAN*

a. Benefits under this plan are insured by the Pension Benefit Guaranty Corporation (PBGC) if the plan terminates. Generally, the PBGC guarantees most vested normal age retirement benefits, early retirement benefits, and certain disability and survivor's pensions. However, PBGC does not guarantee all types of benefits under covered plans, and the amount of benefit protection is subject to certain limitations.

The PBGC guarantees vested benefits at the level in effect on the date of plan termination. However, if a plan has been in effect less than five years before it terminates, or if benefits have been increased within the five years before plan termination, the whole amount of the plan's vested benefits or the benefit increase may not be guaranteed. In addition, there is a ceiling on the amount of monthly benefit that PBGC guarantees, which is adjusted periodically.

For more information on the PBGC insurance protection and its limitations, ask your Plan Administrator or the PBGC. Inquiries to the PBGC should be addressed to the Office of Communications, PBGC, 2020 K Street N.W., Washington, D.C. 20006. The PBGC Office of Communications may also be reached by calling 202-254-4817.

10. *OTHER THINGS YOU SHOULD KNOW*

a. *The Administrative Committee*

The Committee is composed of up to three people who may be Participants in the Plan. The members are appointed by the Board of Directors of the Company, and serve without pay. The present member of the Committee is:

John Jones

The Committee has the responsibility of making the rules under which the plan is run, and seeing to it that the Plan is administered in a fair way to all Participants. The Chairman of the Committee is the agent to receive service of legal process. The Committee's address and that of its members is the same as the Company's address, and its business telephone number is (215) 238-7892.

b. *Making Elections*

Any elections or choices you may make under the plan (for example, choosing your beneficiary) should be made in writing on the forms provided by the Committee.

c. *Claims Procedure*

If you (or in the event of your death, your beneficiary) feel you are not receiving benefits which are due you, you should file a written claim for the benefits with the committee. If your claim is denied, you will receive a written notice stating why your claim was denied, giving the plan provisions on which the decision was based. The notice will also tell you what, if anything, you can do in order to have your claim approved. You will be given an opportunity to request, in writing within 60 days after you receive notice that your claim has been denied, a review of your denied claim, and you or your representative will be permitted to review plan documents which relate to your claim. Within 30 days of the receipt of your appeal, the committee will set a date for a hearing, before a "Named Appeals Fiduciary," who is the person designated to hear and decide appeals, at which you or your representative may be present. You will receive written notice of the final decision of the Named Appeals Fiduciary which is binding on all parties.

d. *Plan Records and Number*

The Company's Employer Identification Number is 23-1668119, and the Plan number for Internal Revenue Service purposes is 001.

11. *PLAN PROVISION CONTROL*

THIS BOOKLET IS ONLY A SUMMARY OF THE PLAN; IN CASE THE CONTENT OF THIS BOOKLET AND THE CONTENT OF THE PLAN DO NOT AGREE, THE TERMS OF THE PLAN WILL CONTROL. If you have any questions about the Plan after reading this booklet, see your supervisor, who should be able to help you.

12. *STATEMENT OF RIGHTS UNDER ERISA*

Federal law and regulations require that, in addition to this summary of the plan, each participant receive a specific Statement of Rights of Participants under the Employee Retirement Income Act of 1974 (ERISA). The required text is attached.

JONES STATIONERY SUPPLY COMPANY
PENSION PLAN
Statement of Rights Under ERISA

As required by § 104(c) of Employee Retirement
Income Security Act of 1974 (ERISA), and by
29 Code of Federal Regulations § 2520.102-3(t).

"As a Participant in the Jones Stationery Supply Company Pension Plan you are entitled to certain rights and protections under the Employee Retirement Income Security Act of 1974 (ERISA). ERISA requires the following statement, which provides that all Plan Participants shall be entitled to:

"—Examine, without charge, at the Plan Administrator's office all Plan documents, including insurance contracts, and copies of all documents filed by the Plan with the U.S. Department of Labor, such as detailed annual reports and Plan descriptions.

"—Obtain copies of all Plan documents and other Plan information upon written request to the Plan Administrator. The Administrator may make a reasonable charge for the copies.

"—Receive a summary of the Plan's annual financial report. The Plan Administrator is required by law to furnish each Participant with a copy of this summary annual report.

"In addition to creating rights for Plan Participants, ERISA imposes duties upon the people who are responsible for the operation of the Plan. The people who operate your Plan, called 'Fiduciaries' of the Plan, have a duty to do so prudently and in the interest of you and other Plan Participants and beneficiaries. No one, including your employer, or any other person, may fire you or otherwise discriminate against you in any way to prevent you from obtaining a benefit or exercising your rights under ERISA. If your claim for a benefit is denied in whole or in part you must receive a written explanation of the reason for the denial. You have the right to have the Plan review and reconsider your claim. Under ERISA, there are steps you can take to enforce the above rights. For instance, if you request materials from the Plan and do not receive them within 30 days, you may file suit in a federal court. In such a case, the court may require the Plan Administrator to provide the materials and pay you up to $100 a day until you receive the materials, unless the materials were not sent because of reasons beyond the control of the Administrator. If you have a claim for benefits which is denied or ignored, in whole or in part, you may file suit in a state or federal court. If it should happen that Plan Fiduciaries misuse the Plan's money, or if you are discriminated against for asserting your rights, you may seek assistance from the U.S. Department of Labor, or you may file suit in a federal court. The court will decide who should pay court costs and legal fees. If you are successful the court may order the person you have sued to pay these costs and fees. If you lose, the court may order you to pay these costs and fees, for example, if it finds your claim is frivolous. If you have any questions about your Plan, you should contact the Plan Administrator. If you have any questions about this statement or about your rights under ERISA, you should contact the nearest Area Office of the U.S. Labor-Management Services Administration, Department of Labor."

DESIGNATION OF BENEFICIARY

TO: Jones Stationery Supply Company Plan Administrator

Gentlemen:

The undersigned hereby designates _____ , whose address is_____ , as beneficiary of any and all payments which may be made under the Jones Stationery Supply Company Pension Plan after my death. In the event that the said beneficiary does not survive me or dies prior to receiving all payments to be made under the Plan, payments shall be made to _____ , whose address is _____ _____. This designation supersedes any and all prior designations and shall be effective under such time as it should be succeeded by a subsequent designation or revoked.

DATED: _____ , 197___.

_____
Employee

Form C-16

Chapter 9, ¶902 deals with stock purchase agreements. Form C-16 is a stock redemption agreement, of the mandatory type. For a cross purchase agreement, option type, see Form C-17.

WARRINGTON DEMOLITION COMPANY
STOCK REDEMPTION AGREEMENT

This Agreement is made this 21 day of February, 1978, by and among WARRINGTON DEMOLITION COMPANY, a Pennsylvania corporation ("the Corporation"), and MORTIMER A. BLACK, RONALD B. BLACK and EDWARD C. BLACK ("Shareholders").

PREAMBLE

The Corporation has issued and outstanding shares of its capital stock, owned as follows:

Name of Shareholder	*Number of Shares*
Mortimer A. Black	33
Ronald B. Black	33
Edward C. Black	33

The parties to this Agreement desire to provide for continuity of management and to promote the interests of the Corporation and the Shareholders by imposing certain restrictions on the Corporation, the Shareholders, and the shares of stock of the Corporation, and by providing for purchase of such shares.

NOW, THEREFORE, in consideration of the mutual promises herein contained, and intending to be legally bound hereby, the parties agree to the following:

CONTRACTUAL PROVISIONS

1. *Purchase of Stock on Death.* Upon the death of a Shareholder, the Corporation agrees to purchase all the shares of stock of the Corporation owned by such Shareholder at the time of his death and such shares as have been transferred to or for the benefit of the Shareholder, his wife, or other members of his immediate family pursuant to paragraph 4 B(2) below. Each Shareholder agrees that all shares of such stock owned by him at the time of his death and such shares as he may transfer to or for the benefit of himself, his wife, or other members of his immediate family pursuant to paragraph 4 B(2) below, shall be sold and transferred by his personal representatives to the Corporation.

2. *Purchase of Stock on Disability.* If a Shareholder should be adjudicated incompetent or should suffer a disability (physical, mental or emotional) which renders him unable to devote his full time and attention to the business of the Corporation and such disability can be expected to result in death or to be of long continued and indefinite duration, the Corporation agrees to purchase all the shares of stock of the Corporation owned by such Shareholder at the time of such adjudication or determination of disability. Each Shareholder agrees that all such shares of stock then owned by him shall be sold and transferred by him or his legal representative to the Corporation. Unless there is an adjudication of incompetency, the existence of a Shareholder's disability as above defined shall be determined by the Corporation on the basis of either (a) the actual inability of the Shareholder to devote his full time and attention to the business of the Corporation for a period of one year, or (b) the written opinion of at least two of three licensed physicians selected for that purpose by the attorney then representing the Corporation, which physicians may but need not include the Shareholder's family

physician. The selection of physicians by the Corporation's attorney shall be in his sole discretion. Each Shareholder agrees to submit himself at any time or times for examination by such physicians at the request of the Corporation's attorney.

3. *Purchase of Stock on Retirement.* If a Shareholder is employed by the Corporation on the date he reaches the age of sixty years, and if there is no provision to the contrary in any employment or similar agreement then in effect, the Shareholder may retire from such employment as of the first day of the month following the month in which his sixtieth birthday occurs or at any time thereafter, as the Shareholder may elect, provided, however, that the Shareholder shall be required to retire not later than his sixty-fifth birthday. In the event of such retirement, the Corporation agrees to purchase all the shares of stock of the Corporation owned by such Shareholder at the time of his retirement, and such Shareholder agrees that all shares of such stock then owned by him shall be sold and transferred by him to the Corporation.

4. *Restriction on Voluntary Disposition.*

A. *General Rule.* No Shareholder shall sell, assign, encumber or otherwise dispose of his stock of the Corporation, either in whole or in part, during his lifetime except by making a written offer on the terms set forth below to sell all of his shares to the Corporation.

B. *Exceptions.* (1). Notwithstanding paragraph 4A above, a Shareholder may sell or donate his shares to a buyer or donee other than the Corporation upon the written approval of the holders of two-thirds of the common stock then outstanding, provided, that such buyer or donee agrees in writing to be bound by the terms of this Agreement.

(2). Notwithstanding paragraph 4A above, a Shareholder may donate all or part of his shares of stock of the Corporation to or for the benefit of himself, his wife, or other members of his immediate family, provided, however, that in such event the shares so transferred shall nevertheless be subject to mandatory redemption pursuant to paragraph 1, above, upon the death of the Shareholder who transferred the shares.

5. *Involuntary Transfers.* In the event of voluntary proceedings by, or involuntary proceedings against, any Shareholder under any provision of any federal or State statute relating to bankruptcy or insolvency, or in the event of attachment of a Shareholder's stock of the Corporation, or in the event that any judgment is obtained in any legal or equitable proceeding against any Shareholder and the sale of his stock is contemplated or threatened under legal process as a result of such judgment, or in the event that any execution process is issued against any Shareholder or his stock, or in the event of any other form of legal proceeding or process by which the stock of any Shareholder may be sold voluntarily or involuntarily, then all of the stock of such Sharehold-

er shall be deemed to have been offered for sale to the Corporation and
the other Shareholders as of the time of such proceeding, process, or
contemplation or threat of sale, as the case may be, on the same terms as
to acceptance and payment as if the offer had been made under the
provisions of paragraph 4A.

6. *Purchase Price for Stock.*

A. The purchase price per share for all stock which may be sold to
the Corporation or any person or persons under the provisions of
paragraphs 1, 2, 3, 4, or 5 of this Agreement shall be equal to the total
value (as defined in the ensuing subparagraph B) of all the shares issued
and outstanding as of the last day of the month preceding the date of the
event necessitating such purchase under paragraphs 1, 2 or 3, the date
of the initial actual offer under paragraph 4, or the date of the initial
constructive offer under paragraph 5, whichever shall apply, divided by
the total number of shares then issued and outstanding.

B. The total value of all the shares issued and outstanding as of the
valuation date specified in the preceding subparagraph A shall be the
value entered in the Valuation Schedule attached hereto. The value as of
the date of this Agreement is the amount first entered on the Valuation
Schedule. Within ninety days after the end of each fiscal year of the
Corporation, the Shareholders shall by mutual agreement redetermine
such value as of the end of such fiscal year, and the redetermined value
shall be entered in the Valuation Schedule. If the Shareholders should
fail in any year to redetermine the value, the value last entered in the
Valuation Schedule shall apply.

7. *Payment of Purchase Price.*

A. *Purchase Price on Death.* Upon the death of a Shareholder, the
Corporation shall collect the proceeds of any policies of insurance owned
by it on the Shareholder's life. When such proceeds have been received
by the Corporation and the purchase price of the deceased Shareholder's stock has been determined, the Corporation shall pay to the personal
representatives of the deceased Shareholder, in cash or by certified
check, so much of the insurance proceeds as does not exceed the purchase price. If the purchase price exceeds the insurance proceeds, the
amount of such excess shall be paid within three years from the date of
the Shareholder's death, in three equal annual installments, the first to
be due one year from the date of death.

B. *Purchase Price on Lifetime Disposition.* If a Shareholder's stock is
purchased, in whole or in part, by the Corporation or any other person
or persons under the provisions of paragraphs 2, 3, 4 or 5, the purchase
price shall be paid within five years from the applicable valuation date, in
five equal annual installments, the first to be due one year from the
valuation date.

C. *Notes for Unpaid Balance.* The obligation of the Corporation or of a Shareholder or Shareholders, as the case may be, for payments to be made in installments as provided in subparagraph A or B, above, shall be evidenced by their respective promissory notes, which shall bear interest at the local prime rate established by the Solid National Bank of Philadelphia Pennsylvania, and which may be prepaid at any time in whole or in part without penalty. The notes of each purchaser shall provide for acceleration of the entire balance due by it or him upon thirty days' default in the payment of any note given by it or him, provided, however, that if time shall be required in order to reduce the capital of the Corporation so as to render the payment of any note permissible under applicable law, the time reasonably required for that purpose shall not be taken into account in computing the thirty day default period.

D. *Security for Unpaid Balance.* The Escrow Agent appointed pursuant to paragraph 12 of this Agreement shall hold the certificates of stock representing all the shares being purchased for which notes are given for the Shareholder or his legal or personal representatives, as the case may be, as security for the payment of such notes until the entire amount due by the purchaser has been paid in full. However, so long as no default shall exist in the payment of any of such notes, the purchaser shall be entitled to vote the shares purchased. After payment of the purchase price is completed, the security interest of the Shareholder or his legal or personal representative in the shares purchased shall cease and he shall promptly deliver to the Escrow Agent such documents as are required for transfer of title to the stock.

8. *Right to Purchase Insurance.* If a Shareholder sells his shares of stock of the Corporation during his lifetime, voluntarily or involuntarily, the Shareholder shall have the right, subject to approval of the holders of two-thirds of the common stock, to purchase the policy or policies of insurance on his life owned by the Corporation. The purchase price shall be an amount equal to the cash surrender value, if any, of such policy or policies as of the effective date of sale of the Shareholder's stock. Such right of purchase shall be exercised, if at all, within thirty days following the effective date of sale of the Shareholder's stock. Upon exercise of such right the Shareholder shall deliver the purchase price of the policy or policies to the Corporation and the Corporation shall thereupon deliver to the Shareholder the policy or policies together with all the documents which are required in order to transfer ownership of the policy or policies to the Shareholder or to such other transferee as he may designate. If the right of purchase is not exercised within the time prescribed by this paragraph, the Corporation may make whatever disposition of the policy or policies it may deem proper. For the purposes of this

paragraph 8, the "effective date of sale of the Shareholder's stock" shall mean the date of determination of his disability if the sale takes place pursuant to paragraph 2, the date of his retirement if the sales takes place pursuant to paragraph 3, or the date of acceptance of the offer to sell (whether voluntary or involuntary) if the sale takes place pursuant to paragraph 4 or 5.

9. *Issuance of Additional Shares and Sale of Treasury Shares.* The Corporation agrees that it shall not issue additional shares of stock or sell, transfer, or assign treasury shares without the written approval of the holders of two-thirds of the common stock and that recipients of such shares as are issued shall, as a condition of their ownership, agree in writing to the terms of this Agreement. Further, Corporation agrees that all shares issued subsequent to the date of this Agreement shall bear the legend described in paragraph 11 hereof.

10. *Termination of Agreement.* This Agreement shall terminate upon the occurrence of any of the following events:

A. Bankruptcy, receivership or dissolution of the Corporation; or

B. Voluntary agreement of all the parties hereto.

Upon termination of this Agreement the Escrow Agent shall deliver the certificates for all the shares of stock to the Secretary of the Corporation, who is authorized and directed in that event to delete the legend endorsed thereon pursuant to paragraph 11.

11. *Endorsement of Stock Certificates.* All certificates of stock held by Shareholders who are parties to this Agreement or their transferees shall be endorsed as follows:

"The shares represented by this certificate are subject to the terms of a Stock Redemption Agreement dated the 21st day of February, 1978, a copy of which is on file with the Secretary of the Corporation."

12. *Escrow Agent.* After endorsement of the certificates of stock pursuant to paragraph 11, the certificates and all documents necessary for effective transfer of the stock shall be deposited with the Solid National Bank of Philadelphia, Pennsylvania, which is designated as Escrow Agent, and the stock certificates shall be held by the Escrow Agent pursuant to the provisions of this Agreement. Except as otherwise expressly provided in this Agreement, all rights growing out of ownership of such stock shall remain in the owner thereof, including, but not limited to, the right to vote the stock and to collect dividends payable thereon. The Escrow Agent may resign at any time by giving written notice of such resignation to the Corporation, in which event the Corporation by its Board of Directors shall designate in writing another Escrow Agent to whom the stock certificates and other papers shall be promptly delivered by the Escrow Agent who has resigned. The Corporation may, at any

time, substitute a new Escrow Agent, who or which shall be designated in writing by the Board of Directors, and the stock certificates and other papers shall be promptly delivered to the new Escrow Agent by the Escrow Agent which he or it has replaced. Upon the delivery of such stock certificates and other papers held by it to a new Escrow Agent designated under the foregoing provisions, the former Escrow Agent shall have no further responsibility or liability to any party. All shares redeemed pursuant to paragraphs 1, 2, 3, 4 and 5 of this Agreement shall be retained by the Escrow Agent until it is satisfied that the consideration has been paid in full, or the selling Shareholder, the deceased Shareholder's personal representative, the donee of the Shareholder, or the personal representative of the donee of the Shareholder, as the case may be, consents in writing to the Escrow Agent's relinquishment of possession off such stock.

13. *Notices.* All notices, offers, acceptances, requests and other communications which are permitted or required to be given hereunder shall be in writing and shall be deemed duly given only if mailed by certified or registered mail, return receipt requested, and, unless and until a party gives due notice of a different address, shall be addressed as follows:

If sent to the Corporation:

    Warrington Demolition Company
    236 S. Front Street
    Philadelphia, Pa. 19129

If sent to Mortimer A. Black:

    Mr. Mortimer A. Black
    18 Johnson Street
    Philadelphia, Pa. 19137

If sent to Ronald B. Black:

    Mr. Ronald B. Black
    3258 N. Pretty Plaza
    Philadelphia, Pa. 19101

If sent to Edward C. Black:

    Mr. Edward C. Black
    #1 Rose Court
    Philadelphia, Pa. 19102

and, in each case, a copy shall be sent in like manner to Gilber M. Cantor, Esquire, Sixth Floor, 1700 Sansom Street, Philadelphia, Pennsylvania 19103.

14. *Miscellaneous.* All prior agreements between the parties to this Agreement relating to the redemption or transfer of the stock of the

Corporation are hereby revoked. The terms of this Agreement shall be binding upon and enure to the benefit of the parties hereto and their respective heirs, next of kin, executors, administrators, successors and assigns. If any provision of this Agreement should be held invalid or unenforceable, the validity of the remaining provisions shall not be affected thereby. Wherever appropriate in this Agreement, the singular shall be taken to include the plural, and vice versa; and the masculine shall be taken to include the feminine, and each of them to include the neuter, and vice versa.

    IN WITNESS WHEREOF, the parties have executed this Agreement the day and year first above written.

SIGNED, SEALED AND DELIVERED
  in the presence of:

_____   _____ (SEAL)
                     MORTIMER A. BLACK

_____   _____(SEAL)
                     RONALD B. BLACK

_____   _____ (SEAL)
                     EDWARD C. BLACK

                     WARRINGTON DEMOLITION COMPANY

                     By:_____
                                           President

                     Attest:_____
                                           Secretary

WARRINGTON DEMOLITION COMPANY

VALUATION SCHEDULE

Year	*Value*
1978	
1979	
1980	
1981	
1982	

FORM C-17

Cross Purchase Agreement

Chapter 9, ¶902, deals with stock purchase agreements. Form C-16 is a stock redemption agreement, of the mandatory type, whereas Form C-17 is a cross purchase agreement, of the option type.

STOCK PURCHASE AGREEMENT

This Agreement is made this   day of 1978, by and among ALGERNON WHITE, of Dresher, Pennsylvania, MORRIS WHITE, of Philadelphia, Pennsylvania, and WILLIAM WHITE, of Philadelphia, Pennsylvania, hereinafter collectively called the "Shareholders."

PREAMBLE

WHITE PEST CONTROL SERVICE, INC. (Corporation) has issued and outstanding shares of its capital stock, owned as follows:

Name of Shareholder	Number of Shares
Algernon White	34
Morris White	10
William White	34
Minority Shareholders	22
TOTAL	100

The parties to this Agreement desire to provide for continuity of management and to promote the interests of the Corporation and the Shareholders, by imposing certain restrictions on the transfer of shares owned by Shareholders.

NOW, THEREFORE, in consideration of the mutual promises herein contained, intending to be legally bound hereby, and intending to supersede any and all prior agreements with respect to the subject matter of this Agreement, the parties agree to the following:

1. *Actual Offers to Sell and Other Dispositions of Stock.*

(a) No Shareholder shall assign, encumber or otherwise dispose of his shares during his lifetime, except that he may sell his shares by making a written offer on the terms set forth below.

(b) In the event that a Shareholder desires to sell his shares, he shall first make a written offer to sell all such shares to the other Shareholders, who shall have fifteen (15) days in which to accept the offer. He shall offer each of the other Shareholders that number of shares which is computed by applying the allocation fraction described in subparagraph (c) to the total number of shares offered; provided, however, that if either offeree fails to accept the offer made to him, then the offeror shall offer the unsold shares to the other offeree who shall have a further period of fifteen (15) days in which to accept such offer. Any shares of the offeror which are not sold in accordance with the foregoing procedure may be disposed of without regard to this Agreement during the fifteen (15) day period commencing at the termination of the most recent offer; but shares not so disposed of shall again become subject to this Agreement.

(c) *Allocation Fraction* shall be a fraction the numerator of which is the number of shares owned by the offeree and the denominator of which is the total number of shares owned by all offerees.

2. *Constructive Offers to Sell Stock.*

(a) *Creditors' Proceedings.* In the event of voluntary proceedings by, or involuntary proceedings against any Shareholder under any provision of any federal or state statute relating to bankruptcy or insolvency, or in the event of attachment of a Shareholder's stock of the Corporation, or in the event that any judgment is obtained in any legal or equitable proceeding against any Shareholder and the sale of his stock is contemplated or threatened under legal process as a result of such judgment, or in the event that any execution process is issued against any Shareholder or his stock, or in the event of any other form of legal proceeding or process by which the stock of any Shareholder may be sold voluntarily or involuntarily, then all of the stock of such Shareholder shall be deemed to have been offered for sale to the other Shareholders as of the time of such proceeding, process, or contemplation or threat of sale, as the case may be, on the same terms as to acceptance and payment as if the offer had been made under the provisions of paragraph 1(b).

(b) *Disability.* If a Shareholder should be adjudicated incompetent or should suffer a disability (physical, mental or emotional) which renders him unable to devote his full time and attention to the business of the Corporation and such disability can be expected to result in death or to be of long-continued and indefinite duration, then all of the stock of such Shareholder shall be deemed to have been offered for sale to the other Shareholders pursuant to an allocation established by applying the allocation fraction of subparagraph 1(c) to the shares held by the disabled Shareholder, and each of the other Shareholders agrees to accept such offer and to purchase all the shares offered. Unless there is an adjudication of incompetency, the existence of a Shareholder's disability as above defined shall be determined by the attorney then representing the Corporation on the basis of either (a) the actual inability of the Shareholder to devote his full time and attention to the business of the Corporation for a period of one year; or (b) the written opinion of at least two of three licensed physicians selected for that purpose by the attorney, which physicians may, but need not, include the Shareholder's family physician. The selection of physicans by the Corporation's attorney shall be in his sole discretion. Each Shareholder agrees to submit himself at any time or times for examination by such physicians at the request of the Corporation's attorney.

(c) *Termination of Employment.* If a Shareholder's employment with the Corporation is terminated for any reason, then all of the stock of such Shareholder shall be deemed to have been offered for sale to the other Shareholders pursuant to an allocation established by applying the allocation fraction provided in subparagraph 1(c) to the shares held by the retiring Shareholder, and each of the other Shareholders agrees to accept such offer and to purchase all the shares offered.

(d) *Purchase of Stock on Death.* Upon the death of a Shareholder, all of the stock of such Shareholder shall be deemed to have been offered for sale to the other Shareholders pursuant to an allocation established by applying the allocation fraction provided in subparagraph 1(c) to the shares held by the deceased Shareholder and each of the other Shareholders agrees to accept such offer and to purchase all the shares offered.

3. *Purchase Price for Stock.*

(a) *Per Share Value.* The purchase price per share for all stock which may be purchased by a Shareholder under the provisions of paragraphs 1 and 2 of this Agreement shall be equal to the total value (as defined in the following subparagraph (b)) of all shares issued and outstanding as of the last day of the month preceeding the date of the actual offer pursuant to paragraph 1 or the constructive offer pursuant to paragraph 2, whichever shall apply, divided by the total number of shares then issued and outstanding.

(b) *Total Value.* This total value of all the shares issued and outstanding as of the valuation date specified in the preceding subparagraph (a) shall be the value entered in the Valuation Schedule attached hereto. The value as of the date of this Agreement is the amount first entered on the Valuation Schedule. Within ninety days after the end of each fiscal year of the Corporation, the Shareholders shall, by unanimous agreement, redetermine such value as of the end of such fiscal year, and the redetermined value shall be entered in the Valuation Schedule. If the Shareholders should fail in any year to redetermine the value, the value last entered in the Valuation Schedule shall apply.

(c) *Adjustment.* In order to take into account the interest of a Shareholder or his estate in the life insurance policies on the lives of the other Shareholders, there shall be added to the purchase price a sum equal to the share of the Shareholder or his estate in the interpolated terminal value of the policies on the lives of the surviving Shareholders, as of the date of the actual or constructive offer, computed by applying the premium allocation percentages set forth in Subsection 4(a)(1) to the interpolated terminal values of said policies. The sum payable under this subsection shall be allocated between the accepting Shareholders in accordance with the allocation formula of subsection 1(c).

4. *Life Insurance—Trustee.*

(a) *Premium Payments by Shareholders.* In order to provide the funds necessary for the purchase of the shares owned by a Shareholder at the time of his death, Gilbert M. Cantor, Esquire, is appointed Trustee pursuant to this Agreement and the Shareholders agree to pay to the Trustee upon execution of this Agreement sufficient funds, allocated among them pursuant to subparagraph 4(a)(1), to pay the premiums on the following amounts of life insurance on the lives of the Shareholders.

Shareholder	Face Amount of Policy
Algernon White	$
Morris White	$
William White	$

The Trustee shall then apply for the amount of life insurance on the life of each Shareholder as provided above.

(1) Algernon White shall pay 80% of the premium on the life of William White.

Algernon White shall pay 50% of the premium on the life of Morris White.

Morris White shall pay 20% of the premium on the life of Algernon White.

Morris White shall pay 20% of the premium on the life of William White.

William White shall pay 80% of the premium on the life of Algernon White.

William White shall pay 50% of the premium on the life of Morris White.

(b) *Application for Policies and Premium Payment to Insurer.* The Trustee agrees to apply for life insurance policies referred to in subparagraph 7(a), to receive funds on account of premium payments and to pay the premiums when due. The trustee shall be designated the owner and beneficiary of the policies and he shall hold them pursuant to this Agreement.

(c) *Purchase of Policy by Selling Shareholder.* Upon the sale of a Shareholder's stock pursuant to subparagraphs 1(b), 2(a), 2(b), or 2(c), he or his legal representative shall have the right to purchase the policy on his life at its interpolated terminal value from the Trustee during the sixty day period commencing with the date of the sale. Each of the other Shareholders shall be entitled to a credit against future payments pursuant subparagraph 4(a) equal to the sum derived by applying his percentage of the premium for the policy on the life of the selling Shareholder (pursuant to subparagraph 4(a)(1)) to the interpolated terminal value of such policy. Should the selling Shareholder fail to purchase the policy on his life, the Trustee shall distribute such policy to the other Shareholders as tenants in common, each Shareholder being credited with the same interest in such policy as the percentage of the premium which he pays on it pursuant to subparagraph 4(a)(1).

(d) *Collection and Application of Proceeds.* Upon being notified of the death of a Shareholder, the Trustee shall proceed to collect the proceeds of the life insurance policy on the life of the deceased Shareholder and to make payment on behalf of the other Shareholders pursuant to subparagraph 2(d).

(e) *Other Duties.* The Trustee shall be under no obligation or duty whatsoever as to the stock covered by this Agreement or the insurance policies except the duties described above and the duty, if necessary in the opinion of Counsel, to bring suit for the proceeds and to compromise, adjust, settle or submit to arbitration any claim hereunder; provided, however, that the Trustee shall be under no duty to bring suit or take any other action unless his expenses, including counsel fees and costs, shall have been advanced or guaranteed in an amount and in a manner satisfactory to him.

(f) *Compensation.* The Trustee shall not be compensated for his services hereunder unless the Shareholders and Trustee shall agree in writing as to the amount and its allocation among the Shareholders.

(g) *Indemnification.* The Shareholders, jointly and severally, shall hold the Trustee harmless from and protect him against any and all loss, damage, or liability which might be incurred by him in connection with this Agreement excepting any such loss, damage or liability incurred by him by reason of his willful misconduct or gross negligence.

(h) *Resignation and Substitution.* The Trustee may resign at any time by giving notice to the other Shareholders. Upon such resignation, a successor Trustee shall be appointed by the Shareholders and the insurance policies and any proceeds thereof shall be turned over to the successor Trustee upon the Trustee's being furnished with evidence satisfactory to him as to the appointment of such successor trustee. The Shareholders shall have the right at any time to substitute a new Trustee for the present Trustee by delivering a written designation signed by the Shareholders. In the event of any substitution of a new Trustee, the Trustee at the time acting hereunder shall turn over to the new Trustee the insurance policies and any proceeds thereof upon his being furnished with evidence satisfactory to him as to the appointment of the new Trustee.

5. *Payment of Purchase Price.*

(a) *Purchase Price on Death.* Upon the death of a Shareholder, and as soon thereafter as is practicable, the Trustee shall pay to the estate of the deceased Shareholder the proceeds of the life insurance policy on his life, to the extent of the purchase price. Any excess over purchase price shall be allocated to each of the other Shareholders by applying his percentage of the premium for the policy on the life of the deceased Shareholder (pursuant to subparagraph 4(a)(1)) to such excess. The Trustee shall then hold, invest, and expend such allocated sums for payment of future insurance premiums. In the event the purchase price exceeds the life insurance proceeds, the balance shall be paid by the surviving Shareholders, allocated between them by applying the allocation fraction of subsection 1(c), within five (5) years from the date of the Shareholder's death, in five equal annual installments, the first to be due on the 90th day after the date of death.

(b) *Purchase Price on Lifetime Disposition.* If a Shareholder's stock is purchased, in whole or in part, by the other Shareholders under the provisions of paragraph 1(b), 2(a), 2(b) and 2(c), the purchase price shall be paid within five years from the date of the acceptance of the actual or constructive offer, in five equal annual installments, the first is to be due on the date of the acceptance.

(c) *Notes for Unpaid Balance.* The obligation of the Shareholder or Shareholders, as the case may be, for payments to be made in installments as provided in subparagraph (a) or (b) above, shall be evidenced by their respective promissory notes, which shall bear interest at the rate of six (6) percent per annum. The promissory notes may be prepaid at any time, in whole or in part, without penalty, with interest accrued to the date of payment. Such promissory notes shall provide for acceleration of all the principal and interest in the event of a default of the obligor not secured within thirty (30) days after written notice given to him.

(d) *Security for Unpaid Balance.* The Escrow Agent appointed pursuant to paragraph 9 below shall hold the certificates of stock representing all the shares being purchased for which notes are given, for the selling Shareholder or his legal or personal representative, as the case may be, as security for the payment of such notes until the entire amount due has been paid. However, so long as no default shall exist in the payment of such notes, the shares so purchased may be registered in the purchaser's name and he shall be entitled to vote them. After receipt by the Escrow Agent of satisfactory proof of full payment of the purchase price, the security interest of the selling Shareholder or his legal or personal representative shall cease and the Escrow Agent shall thereafter hold the certificates on behalf of the purchasing shareholder.

6. *Termination of Agreement.* This Agreement shall terminate upon the bankruptcy, receivership or dissolution of the Corporation.

Upon termination of this Agreement the Shareholders shall delete the legend endorsed on the shares of stock pursuant to paragraph 8. Upon termination of this Agreement, the Trustee shall distribute the policies to the Shareholders as tenants in common, each Shareholder being credited with the same interest in each policy as the percentage of the premium on said policy which he pays pursuant to subparagraph 4(a)(1).

7. *Arbitration.* Any controversy or claim arising out of or relating to

this contract, or the breach thereof shall be settled by arbitration in accordance with the Rules of the American Arbitration Association. Judgment rendered upon an Award of the arbitrator(s) may be entered in any court having jurisdiction thereof.

8. *Endorsement of Stock Certificates.* All certificates of stock held by the Shareholders shall be endorsed as follows:

> "The shares represented by this certificate are subject to the terms of a Stock Purchase Agreement dated   , 1978, a copy of which is on file with the Secretary of the Corporation."

9. *Escrow Agent.* After endorsement of the certificates of stock pursuant to paragraph 11, the certificates and all documents necessary for effective transfer thereof shall be deposited with Gilbert M. Cantor Associates, which is designated as Escrow Agent, which shall hold said certificates and documents pursuant to the provisions of this Agreement. Except as otherwise expressly provided in this Agreement, all rights growing out of ownership of such stock shall remain in the owner thereof, including, but not limited to, the right to vote the stock and to collect dividends payable thereon. The Escrow Agent may resign at any time by giving written notice of such resignation to the Shareholders, in which event the parties shall designate in writing another Escrow Agent to whom the stock certificates and other papers shall be promptly delivered by the Escrow Agent who has resigned. The parties may, at any time, substitute a new Escrow Agent, who or which shall be designated in writing by the parties, and the stock certificates and other documents shall be promptly delivered to the new Escrow Agent by the Escrow Agent which he or it has replaced. Upon the delivery of such stock certificates and other papers held by it to a new Escrow Agent designated under the foregoing provisions, the Escrow Agent shall have no further responsibility or liability to any party. All shares sold pursuant to paragraphs 1 and 2 of this Agreement shall be retained by the Escrow Agent during the continuation of this Agreement.

10. *Notices.* All notices, offers, acceptances, requests and other communications which are permitted or required to be given hereunder shall be in writing and shall be deemed duly given only if mailed by certified or registered mail, return receipt requested, and, unless and until a party gives due notice of a different address, shall be addressed as follows:

> TO Algernon White
> 28 Fox Place
> Dresher, Pa. 19023

> TO Morris White
> 3228 Easton Street
> Philadelphia, Pa. 19135

TO William White
     1927 Henry Street
     Philadelphia, Pa. 19126

and, in each case, a copy shall be sent in like manner to Gilbert M. Cantor, Esquire, Sixth Floor, 1700 Sansom Street, Philadelphia, Pennsylvania 19103.

11. *Miscellaneous.* The terms of this Agreement shall be binding upon and enure to the benefit of the parties hereto and their respective heirs, next of kin, executors, administrators, successors and assigns. If any provision of this Agreement should be held invalid or unenforceable, the validity of the remaining provisions shall not be affected thereby. Wherever appropriate in this Agreement, the singular shall be taken to include the plural, and vice versa; and the masculine shall be taken to include the feminine, and each of them to include the neuter, and vice versa.

IN WITNESS WHEREOF, the parties have executed this Agreement the day and year first above written.

_____ (SEAL)
Algernon White

_____ (SEAL)
Morris White

_____ (SEAL)
William White

CONSENT OF TRUSTEE

I, Gilbert M. Cantor, hereby consent to serve as Trustee in accordance with the foregoing Stock Purchase Agreement.

_____
Trustee

VALUATION SCHEDULE

Year   *Value*
1978

Index

All numerical references are to paragraph [¶] numbers.